International Commercial Agreements

D1286341

International Commercial Agreements

A Primer on Drafting, Negotiating and Resolving Disputes

SECOND EDITION

William F. Fox, Jr.
Professor of Law
The Catholic University of America
Washington, DC

Kluwer Law International
The Hague • Boston • London

K
1005.4
F49
1992
c.7)

Published by Kluwer Law International
POBox 85889   Tel. +31 70 308 1560
2508 CN Den Haag   Fax. +31 70 308 1515
The Netherlands

Distribution in the USA and Canada
Kluwer Law International
675 Massachusetts Avenue   Tel. 617 354 0140
Cambridge, MA 02139   Fax. 617 354 8595
USA

Library of Congress Cataloging-in-Publication Data

Fox, William F.
       International commercial agreements: a primer on drafting,
negotiating, and resolving disputes / William F. Fox, Jr. — 2nd ed.
       p.   cm.
       Includes bibliographical references (p.   ) and index.
       ISBN 9065445870
       1. Export sales contracts   2. Arbitration and award,
International.   I. Title.
       K1030.4.F69   1992
       341.7'54 — dc20   92-20546
                                                      CIP

ISBN 90-6544-587-0

© 1992.
Kluwer Law International
Den Haag, The Netherlands
All rights reserved.

ICC No. 447, ICC RULES OF CONCILIATION AND ARBITRATION.
Copyright ® 1987 by the International Chamber of Commerce, Paris, France.
All rights reserved. Reprinted with permission.

Kluwer Law International incorporates the publishing programs of Graham and Trotman Ltd.,
Kluwer Law and Taxation Publishers, and Martinus Nijhoff Publishers.

No part of this publication may be reproduced, stored in a retrieval system, or
transmitted in any form or by any means — electronic, mechanical, photocopying,
recording or otherwise — without the prior written permission of the publisher.

For my parents, William F. and Mary S. Fox,
who did a pretty good job setting me on the road to literacy.

Contents

Contents

Ten: International Commercial Arbitration:
Special Regional Considerations

Eleven: Future Trends in International Commercial Agreements and Dispute Resolution

Appendices   *327*

Preface

S everal years ago I participated in a number of international business transactions. Some concerned the drafting and negotiating of international commercial agreements. Some had to do with disputes that arose between the contracting parties after the contract was signed. One case required commencing a proceeding in federal court in the United States to confirm a Swiss arbitral award rendered on behalf of a Greek company against a middle-eastern petroleum company that was a wholly-owned subsidiary of a U.S. corporation. These cases taught me about the incredible complexity of the typical international commercial transaction and how different an international transaction is from a domestic transaction. As I tried to educate myself on all the issues that arise in either creating or disputing an international contract, I found that the bulk of the literature in this area was either concentrated in nearly impenetrable multi-volume treatises or scattered among law journal articles. Most of this literature is written by experts for experts. Legal jargon in a domestic setting is troublesome, but the assumptions of expertise and the jargon used in the literature of international commercial transactions can overwhelm and intimidate the newcomer. These experiences revealed a need for a one-volume text that less-experienced lawyers could turn to for fundamental information and analysis.

Although U.S. lawyers are almost always heavily involved in commercial transactions from start to finish, elsewhere in the world lawyers are usually brought in late in the process, if at all, and often are consulted only when something goes wrong with the agreement. My research told me that there was a need for a book on the fundamentals of international commercial transactions that could be read and understood by *both* lawyers and business executives. As international trade expands, more people need basic, precise information on setting up and performing these transactions.

Accordingly, this book addresses the needs of the increasing numbers of persons who are not lawyers but who deal with some of the legal aspects of international business transactions on a regular basis and who can profit from straightforward explanations of the law. If the book accomplishes that goal it will also be helpful to lawyers who may be experienced in narrow issues of international trade but require basic information in other areas.

I hope that persons who have in the past found the various aspects of transnational contracts impenetrable will use this book as a guide and introduction to an increasingly important area of business enterprise. I hope those who are not lawyers will join me in my belief that law is too important to be left exclusively to the lawyers.

◆

The manuscript was written at my permanent academic home, the Columbus School of Law, Catholic University of America, Washington, D.C., an institution that may be the best unsung law school in the United States. My good friend and colleague, Professor Rett Ludwikowski, gave me a number of suggestions on the organization of the book. My other friends on the faculty were, as usual, incredibly supportive. The Director of the Catholic University Law Library, Professor John Valeri and the library's associate director, Pat Petit, were tremendously helpful in obtaining copies of the multi-volume treatises. My two research assistants, Scott Squillace and Andrew Palmieri, showed great diligence in gathering the more obscure journal articles. Research on many of the dispute resolution chapters was conducted while on sabbatical leave in 1983-84 as a Senior Associate Member at St Antony's College, Oxford University. While at Oxford I was generously given study and research space at the Bodleian Law Library. That same year I enjoyed an appointment as a Visiting Scholar in the Law Department, London School of Economics and Political Science. The LSE library and the superb library at the Institute for Advanced Legal Studies in London provided me with additional research support.

Preface to the Second Edition

There are few things more gratifying to an author than having the first edition of a book sell out completely. This second edition is an expanded version of the original book, including a substantial amount of material on the European Community, the Canada-United States Free Trade Agreement and other proposed regional trading agreements, some suggestions on "doing business" in various regions of the world and updated statutory and case law dealing with arbitration and other forms of dispute resolution.

My research assistant for the second edition was Erin Sullivan, a December, 1991 graduate of the Catholic University School of Law, who proved to be absolutely superb at gathering information and ferreting out obscure information from the Library of Congress and elsewhere. I don't think my other research assistants will be hurt when I describe Erin as one of the best ever. The several hundred students at Catholic University who sat through my course in International Business Transactions have given me more ideas and citations than they probably realize. Their encouragement and enthusiasm for the first edition sparked my efforts on the second edition. I am happy to repeat everything I said in the first edition about the Catholic University Law School faculty and library staff. Steven Margeton, our new library director, has been tremendously supportive of my work on this manuscript as well as the law school's Program in Comparative and International Law. The staff at the Swiss Institute of Comparative Law in Lausanne provided me with a research office in which I prepared some of the new materials on Europe. Dr. Hans Kruck of the European Court of Justice in Luxembourg and Dr. Otmar Phillip of the European Parliament in Strasbourg spoke with me about the work of the European Community government. John Berger, the North American representative of Kluwer, is simply the most diligent and enjoyable publisher I have ever worked with. John deserves a great deal of credit for pushing both the first and second edition through to fruition. ◆

Part I: Forming International Commercial Agreements

— 1 —
Introduction

§ 1.1 International Trade and This Book

International trade has long been accepted as a fundamental requirement for survival in an economically interdependent world. While trade between different countries and regions has often waxed and waned depending on economic and political conditions, overall figures show that trade between nations is now worth hundreds of billions of dollars a year and will continue to increase as world population continues to grow. This does not mean that international trade is completely unfettered. The idea of completely free world trade is a notion whose time has not yet come. Barriers set up through tariffs and through so-called non-tariff trade barriers continue to inhibit world trade. Moreover, no country has ever been completely consistent on matters of trade. Most countries have shifted back and forth over the years from the extreme of protectionism to the uninhibited exchange of goods and services depending on how the internal political climate of that country meshes with the world-wide economic climate. At the same time, every country has at least some exports and imports; thus no country in the world is completely cut off from international trade.

There has always be a substantial amount of government intervention in trade matters even though the vast majority of transactions take place between two private entities or between a private entity and a national government (or component of government). Because these transactions involve firms in two or more different countries and often directly effect the economy of both the exporting and importing nation, it is generally impossible for national governments *not* to get involved. Every national government imposes some controls on the export and import of goods and services—controls that are usually implemented by requiring firms to secure government permission in the form of a license to export or import the good or service in question. Some of the controls are imposed to protect domestic businesses

11

(establishing the so-called *level playing field*) by regulating the importation of goods carrying prices below market costs through administrative procedures that control antidumping practices and assess countervailing duties. Some countries attempt to extend certain of their domestic commercial principles, such as antitrust regulations, to international transactions. A few countries have even attempted to impose standards of fair and ethical dealing, normally restricted to purely domestic business transactions, to their companies' business practices abroad. For example, through a still controversial statute called the Foreign Corrupt Practices Act, the United States has been particularly aggressive in policing acts of bribery of foreign public officials on the part of U.S. companies who seek to do business in foreign countries. The United States may be unique in its treatment of foreign corrupt practices, but many countries have other forms of government regulation of international trade that often must be addressed in forming a valid international commercial agreement. Unfortunately, the only effective way to deal with government regulation is on a case-by-case, country-by-country basis.

Regional and international trade agreements are becoming increasingly important in international trade. To this end, governments have cooperated on both a regional (for example, the European Community and the United States-Canada Free Trade Agreement) and a world-wide basis (the General Agreement on Tariff and Trade) to promote free trade. Many countries have negotiated and ratified bilateral treaties of friendship, commerce and navigation (FCN) whose primary purpose is to state the rights of the nationals of each country to trade, invest, or establish and operate businesses in the other country. Virtually all of the major trading countries have entered into FCN treaties with each other. The United States, for example, has ratified no fewer than 130 such treaties. Most if not all of the major trading nations recognize the concept of *most favored nation*, a term of art in international trade that attempts to promote non-discrimination in trade by giving the same trade benefits to any country that the host country extends to any other country.

Nonetheless, the day-to-day business of international trade remains primarily a private matter: i.e., an undertaking between two private businesses based on a contract drafted and negotiated between the two contracting parties to be performed by them with the occasional assistance of third parties such as financial institutions and freight carriers. This book concentrates on the private dimensions of international trade, and more precisely on the contractual aspects of that trade. On occasion, the book will touch on other matters, such as the need to secure government permission to export or import goods or services, but will do so only insofar as those peripheral matters are important to drafting and performing a valid contract.

Most private international transactions involve contracts for the sale of tangible objects or *goods*. For that reason, a significant part of the text concentrates on issues relating to the sale of goods. The book does not ignore the wide variety of other international commercial transactions such as contracts for services (for example, engineering or telecommunications services), licenses for the transfer of patents and technology, joint ventures, and franchise agreements. There are many instances when there are desirable reasons to contract for a business enterprise—such as a franchise or manufacturing joint venture—rather than merely to arrange to ship goods themselves. Subsequent chapters discuss drafting contracts to cover a wide variety of business relationships, not merely purchase and sale transactions.

§ 1.2 An Overview of International Commercial Transactions

A business executive entering into an international commercial transaction is interested in drafting a private agreement that will satisfy both parties and will be performed as drafted. This is the first principle of contract drafting. People in business rarely enter into a business transaction assuming that the contract will never be performed or that one or more of the parties will violate some aspect of the agreement. For the most part, business transactions, both domestic and international, are fully and quietly performed by the parties. This first principle also reflects a basic consideration in contract negotiation: parties sign contracts because they want to do business, not because they want to have at each other in court after one or the other breaches the contract. Nonetheless, the *possibility* of breach or non-performance must always be taken into account when parties negotiate and draft the original agreement. As distasteful as it may seem to happy parties who are just concluding what appears to be a brilliant agreement, dispute resolution must be addressed at the outset.

In drafting successful agreements, the parties must understand how contracts are formed, an understanding that includes at least a basic knowledge of the "law" of contracts and a sophisticated understanding of the technical aspects of the specific transaction entered into. For example if a contract is for the sale of telecommunications equipment, the contract itself, or documents appended to the contract will contain technical specifications for the equipment. Persons drafting and negotiating the contract should have a good idea of the equipment's technical capabilities (or be able to call on experts who have the technical answers) because these details often figure importantly in both the negotiation and drafting stages of the agreement.

Contract drafters need to be sensitive to the differences between international contracts and contracts that are to be performed domestically. It is a mistake to assume that there are no differences between the two.

Numerous considerations enter into the drafting and execution of an international agreement that are not pertinent to contracts between domestic companies. For example, in the United States oral contracts for more than modest sums of money are virtually unheard of because of a U.S. principle of contract law (the *statute of frauds*) that requires all but the smallest contracts to be evidenced by some kind of writing. By contrast, many other countries make oral contracts just as enforceable as written contracts; and cultural assumptions in those countries frequently favor oral dealings. The element of trust (the idea that a person's word is his bond) is often carried into the country's law of contract. Nonetheless, most international commercial agreements are evidenced by some kind of writing, ranging from the exchange of simple telexes and facsimile transmissions to multi-page, fully negotiated documents. In contrast to purely domestic transactions, the language differences between the parties to international contracts often demand that the parties agree to a single, official language for the contract, even if the document is translated into other languages for the convenience of the parties.

Most international contracts involve substantial amounts of money. These sums normally justify a separately negotiated agreement tailored to the specific deal, rather than the use of standard forms. Still, standard form contracts or contracts formed by the exchange of purchase and sale orders (frequently leading to what American law professors call "the battle of the forms") are not prohibited internationally.

International contracts tend to be longer and more comprehensive to fully ensure that each party's rights are protected, although proposed contracts that are too lengthy can kill the deal in its inception. U.S. lawyers seem particularly prone to writing what lawyers from other countries consider excessively long contracts. In more than a few instances, I have seen deals poisoned by the submission of a hundred page draft agreement where the non-U.S. party was expecting twelve pages. Business executives outside the United States sometimes regard lengthy documents with great suspicion.

There are other considerations in international transactions that promote length over brevity. Business practices differ from country to country so many of the assumptions and understandings (what we frequently refer to as a *course of dealing*) that might not necessarily be written into a domestic agreement need to be fully spelled out in an international contract. The parties often have never done business together so they have not developed the degree of trust present in many domestic settings. The parties' geographical separation can cause problems, although the advent of the facsimile machine and the improvement in worldwide telecommunications makes mere distance less of a factor now than it might have been in the past. Particularly when the elements of prior acquaintance or personal trust are missing, the dispute resolution clause of the contract becomes a matter of major importance. All of these matters must be addressed in some fashion if the contract is to have a solid foundation.

Negotiation is intimately related to the drafting process. The timing of the negotiation can differ from transaction to transaction. Parties occasionally sit down with a blank piece of paper and hammer out the entire agreement on a face-to-face basis. Some contracts are consummated over the telephone or telex, followed by the exchange of rudimentary confirming memoranda.

Most transactions begin with one side proffering a letter of intent or a draft contract for the other side's consideration. The parties then negotiate only those provisions in the draft over which there is genuine disagreement. This is normally the most efficient process, but it also can have the effect of giving the negotiation momentum to the party who writes the draft, in the same way that the outcome of a meeting can often be dictated by the person who writes the agenda for that meeting. Parties sometimes spar with each other to see who gets to go first.

Lawyers and business executives can also think through the process of negotiation in order to achieve the best possible result. There are certain techniques of negotiation and certain guidelines for preparing for negotiation that can be taken into account prior to doing the actual negotiation. Thinking about negotiation generally and planning the negotiation at hand, sometimes even to the point of rehearsing a negotiation session, often pays off in better results. One of the premises of this book is that many negotiation techniques can be reviewed and analyzed, even though many traditionalists view negotiation as purely a matter of personal experience. Although most experienced negotiators contend that prescribing elaborate and rigid doctrinal rules for negotiation—and especially for cross-cultural negotiation—is a formula for disaster, as much thought as possible should be given to the negotiation process before the negotiation itself begins.

The end result of the negotiation is normally the drafting and execution of the final agreement. That agreement is often performed without incident. However, some transactions unravel; and when they unravel, the matter of dispute resolution becomes of paramount importance. In business agreements, there is no limit to the possible reasons for a party's failure to perform. Typically, these include shifts in the financial circumstances of a party, changes in overall economic conditions, loss of sources of supply or of customers, the repeal of necessary government permissions, and wholly unanticipated acts of God. Long-term contracts are especially vulnerable to changes in the conditions necessary for performance and require provisions that will permit the contract to adapt to these changes without the need for either renegotiation or some other type of dispute resolution. Properly drafted adaptation clauses, such as flexible price and supply terms and force majeure clauses, can permit the contract to flex with those underlying changes without destroying the contractual relationship itself. If the adaptation clauses prove unequal to the task, and if the parties wish to continue the relationship, one of the best devices to preserve the contract is simple renegotiation—i.e., the parties get together again and craft new additions to the contract that allow the transaction to go forward.

Sometimes the breach is so immense and injurious to one of the parties that neither adaptation nor renegotiation suffice. When this occurs, the dispute resolution mechanisms built into the agreement (or agreed to later or imposed by law) come into play. Most written international commercial agreements specify the precise dispute resolution technique to be used. For a number of different reasons, including ease of enforcement, arbitration is the device of choice for most parties to international contracts. If the contracting parties choose to include an arbitration clause, attention must be devoted to the procedures to be followed in the arbitration (including normally a selection of one or another of the major arbitral rules systems), to the physical location of the arbitration, and to the applicable law to be applied to the dispute. The arbitration will be conducted under procedural rules set out in the contract itself (so-called *ad hoc* arbitration, a fairly rare practice) or conducted under the supervision of and under rules promulgated by domestic entities such as the Japan Chamber of Commerce or the American Arbitration Association or an international body such as the International Chamber of Commerce.

Most arbitrations are final in the sense that the losing party pays up and goes away. But there are instances in which choosing arbitration does not guarantee that the dispute will not reach the courts. For example, when a dispute arises one of the parties may refuse to abide by the arbitration clause and thereby force the other side to seek the assistance of a court to compel arbitration. If the arbitration goes forward and an arbitration hearing is held, the parties present their cases and the arbitrator (or arbitration panel) renders a decision in the form of an arbitral award. If the losing party does not comply voluntarily with the terms of the award, the award must be enforced by some court, normally a court having jurisdiction over the losing party.

When the dispute resolution clause does not specify arbitration, the injured party may seek to litigate the dispute in an appropriate court. There are no international courts that deal with private commercial matters so any court selected is, by definition, a domestic court within one country. International commercial litigation is difficult and complicated because the jurisdiction of domestic courts does not normally extend to parties physically outside that country who do not own property in that country. Nonetheless, if the difficulties can be worked out, litigation has certain advantages of process, certainty and finality not enjoyed by other forms of dispute resolution.

Many dispute resolution experts who are committed to the idea of international commercial arbitration view litigation as evidence that the parties' dispute resolution planning process has failed. However, it need not be regarded as such. Disputes can occur under the most competently drafted contracts. When disputes occur, litigation in domestic courts has a significant number of advantages over arbitration along with a substantial number of pitfalls, defects, and disadvantages. Unplanned litigation may indeed be attributable to a failure to plan; but a conscious decision to resolve a dispute by litigation can frequently be cost-effective in the long run. As one might expect, it is also a favorite dispute resolution mechanism of lawyers.

Litigation and arbitration are not the only choices. Parties who wish to preserve a continuing business relationship may profit from the effective use of the less adversarial devices such as mediation/conciliation or mini-trial. Indeed, members of some cultures react so negatively to the rigid, adversarial, never-give-an-inch posture of U.S.-style litigation that even the threat of litigation can destroy an on-going relationship. These milder dispute resolution devices are often ignored because they have only recently become part of the international dispute resolution vocabulary. In many cases, these techniques are far less expensive, stressful and time-consuming and frequently promote a more satisfactory solution.

Sadly, the use of the less confrontational settings of mediation and conciliation are presently underutilized in international trade, even though more and more dispute resolution agencies such as the International Chamber of Commerce, the United Nations Commission on International Trade Law (UNCITRAL) and the American Arbitration Association have promulgated rules for various processes that are neither litigation nor arbitration. While each of these techniques has its own advantages and disadvantages, the less-drastic alternatives are rarely considered because lawyers advising on international business transactions often take a very traditional view of dispute resolution, frequently accepting commercial arbitration or litigation in domestic courts because those are the only two devices they have experience with. The most thoughtful and creative parties to international commercial agreements are those who are aware of all the dispute resolution possibilities.

§ 1.3 How to Use This Book

As the subtitle points out, this book is to be read and used as a functional or transactional guide to international commercial agreements. The author has not assumed that the typical reader will read the book from preface to final chapter but instead has assumed that most readers are interested in obtaining guidance and information relating to a specific transaction or problem.

This book can help a lawyer or business executive plan and carry out various types of international commercial transactions. Readers requiring more depth on a topic will be guided by the footnotes to appropriate additional sources: treaties, rules, statutes and other primary sources of the law, the multi-volume treatises that deal with these topics, and numerous journal articles that provide additional depth and clarification. Most of these materials are English language materials, although materials from and citations to appropriate literature in languages other than English have also been included. Business executives who are not lawyers will find that the book gives them the understanding and perspective necessary to work effectively with the legal experts.

This book organizes commercial agreements according to the three stages of an agreement: entering into, performing, and disputing a contract. For example, the book begins with the premise that virtually all international commercial transactions start not with a dispute but rather with the negotiating and drafting of a contract by two parties that wish to do business together. That business may involve the sale of goods, the establishment of an agency relationship, the transfer of intellectual property such as patents and copyrights through a license, or the providing of engineering or construction services. Contracts may run from one-time purchase and sale agreements involving small amounts of money to long-term arrangements worth millions of dollars.

Because international contracts are legal instruments, anyone seeking to understand the basis for an agreement must know a little about the various legal systems in the world and something of the general law of commercial transactions. Persons lacking this knowledge should turn first to Chapters 2 and 3. Immediate guidance on drafting commercial agreements and suggestions for specific contractual language can be found in Chapter 4. With this background, readers unfamiliar with some of the new thinking on negotiation would do well to read Chapter 5 before walking into a negotiation session. That chapter discusses many negotiation techniques, rules of thumb, and pointers that can help a session go much more smoothly. The chapter assumes that good negotiation is more than simply a matter of personal experience.

Some contracts do not stand the test of time and thus must be taken through a dispute resolution process. Chapters 6 through 10 discuss a large number of issues and concepts relating to dispute resolution. Contracts that have been breached and are about to become the subject of arbitration are covered in Chapters 8 and 9. Readers with specific interests in dispute resolution in a particular area of the world, such as a commercial transaction involving the Peoples Republic of China, the former Soviet Union or a Latin American country, may obtain additional guidance in Chapter 10 on the dis-

tinctions among various regions. Arbitration in Latin America is vastly different from arbitration in London. Commercial dispute resolution in the Peoples
Republic of China, a country newly emerging as a major trading nation, is
proving to be a unique experience for many companies. People in business
who fail to appreciate and allow for these regional differences may face unanticipated trouble.

If a reader is only concerned with a contract that is about to be litigated
in the domestic courts of some country, a quick review of Chapter 7 may be
helpful; although the reader should be warned that the immense differences
in procedure in various countries makes large-scale generalizations very
deceptive. Litigation is such a specialized undertaking that only lawyers
skilled in the process of a particular country are equipped to deal with it.
The book's concluding chapter, Chapter 11, attempts to predict some future
trends in international commercial arrangements.   ◆

— 2 —
Sources of the Law of International Commercial Agreements

§ 2.1 Introduction

Where does one find the rules of the game? The sources of the applicable law are numerous, but not infinite. Some of the law is to be found in the contracts themselves in the form of principles negotiated between the parties and stated expressly as provisions in the contract. This process of party-to-party formation of legal principles, often referred to as *private ordering*, is developed mainly through the process of negotiation and is discussed below. But everyone should understand that under the traditional contract doctrines of party autonomy and pacta sunt servanda such provisions are just as compelling as any other command in the law so long as these provisions do not contradict legal principles imposed by the domestic law of a country or by treaty. Because contracts do not exist in a legal vacuum, they almost always must reflect certain considerations imposed by external forces. These limiting provisions have several sources: the domestic law of a country that bears some relationship to the contract, or in certain instances principles of international commercial conduct.

It is difficult to generalize accurately about domestic law (occasionally referred to as *municipal* law) of various countries even though it is the domestic law that prescribes most of the legal principles governing commercial arrangements. To establish some predictability, most parties to international commercial agreements provide that their contracts are to be governed by the law of a particular country to insure that the applicable principles will be readily ascertainable. Most of the major trading nations have extensive and detailed systems of commercial law that are remarkably similar despite having domestic legal systems that sharply differ in origin.

It is sometimes possible to frame a few general observations about the applicable law from an analysis of the placement of a country's legal system in one or another of the broad categories or "families" of law in the world. When faced with a choice as to whether to incorporate a particular country's law into a contract—or perhaps even the more basic decision whether to do business in a particular country—lawyers can sometimes gain insights from an inquiry into where that legal system fits when compared with other legal systems.

§ 2.2 Promulgation and Enforcement of Principles of Commercial Law

There are four basic instruments for developing and promulgating principles of commercial law external to the contract itself: (1) treaties, (2) statutes, (3) court decisions (and occasionally decisions by arbitral bodies) and (4) government regulations. Most international scholars also believe that legal principles can emerge from pronouncements of international organizations such as the United Nations and through the growth of international custom; but in most instances, these latter sources have less to do with actual day-to-day commercial arrangements then the four basic sources first enumerated.

Treaties. Treaties are documents that control relationships between nations. They may be negotiated and executed between two countries (bilateral treaties) or among a number of countries (multilateral treaties). Conceptually, they are devices by which each country voluntarily surrenders some sovereignty in order to enter into the agreement. In other words, there is no power currently in existence (other than perhaps victory in war) that can compel a country to enter into a treaty, but once a country enters into the treaty, it generally becomes bound to the terms of that treaty. There are, of course, occasional problems of enforcement of treaty obligations. The International Court of Justice at the Hague (sometimes referred to as the *World Court*) is viewed as an appropriate body to adjudicate disagreements under a treaty, but some countries, including on occasion the United States, consider themselves free to ignore the court's jurisdiction in certain circumstances.

There are three steps in implementing a treaty. First, the terms of the treaty are negotiated and the participating countries prepare a final draft. Second, the final version is signed by the participating countries as a signal that they approve the final version of the negotiated document. This does not mean, however, that the treaty becomes immediately enforceable. Third, the treaty is ratified by each country's government. The process of ratification differs from country to country. Some countries permit ratification decisions to be made by the executive authority. In other countries, such as the United

States a legislative body (such as the U.S. Senate) must give its approval before the ratification process is complete. Fourth, treaties *enter into force* when a sufficient number of countries (a number generally spelled out in the treaty itself) ratify the agreement. A country may *acceed* to a treaty, thus considering itself bound by the treaty's terms without formal ratification.

There are many different types of treaties that affect commercial relationships. One of the most common is the bilateral treaty known as "Treaties of Friendship, Cooperation and Navigation." Such treaties spell out many of the details of one country's commercial relationship with another. Multilateral treaties are having an increasing impact on commercial relations among countries. For example, one of the most important treaties governing the enforceability of international commercial arbitral awards is the New York Convention on the Recognition and Enforcement of Arbitral Awards of 1958, discussed at length in Chapter Eight. Another multilateral treaty, discussed at the end of this chapter, is the Vienna Convention on the International Sale of Goods ("CISG").

Statutes. As the term is used in this section, *statutes* refers to the promulgation of principles of law by the governments of individual countries that govern commercial transactions as a whole. In some countries, these principles are stated as part of the civil code. In the United States, private commercial dealings are governed mainly by statutes enacted by the legislatures in the individual states, rather than by the national government. All states except Louisiana have enacted a comprehensive set of commercial statutes called the Uniform Commercial Code, which controls, among other things, the sale of goods, commerce in negotiable instruments, and the creation of secured transactions.

Court decisions. In virtually all countries, a great deal of commercial law is developed by courts' deciding individual cases brought by parties who claim to have suffered some legal injury in the context of a specific commercial undertaking. Many disputes arising out of international commercial agreements are first decided in the context of an arbitration proceeding, after which the winning party takes the arbitral award to some court for enforcement. In a common law system, the cumulation of individual court decisions leads to the development of legal principles (so-called "judge-made" law) that are just as valid as anything enacted by the country's legislature. Even in countries outside the common law system, the resolution of individual cases in court often helps fill in the gaps in that country's civil and commercial code.

Government regulations. In many countries with a centralized system of government, there is really no difference between government regulations and statutes since virtually all authority flows directly from the central government. By contrast, in countries such as the United States, there is often a sharp distinction drawn between statutes (which in the United States are enacted by the legislative branch of government (i.e., the state legislatures or the Congress) and regulations promulgated by government agencies within the executive branch of government such as the Department of the Treasury or the Bureau of Customs. In many countries, such as the United States, the basic principles of commercial law are normally developed through statutes and court decisions, while the peripheral aspects of commercial undertakings such as the imposition of taxes and export and import controls are implemented by government agencies.

For the most part, this book deals with private arrangements between individuals as set out in their negotiated written agreements. These agreements are generally tailored to the specific problems and issues faced by the parties; and in many countries, the parties are relatively free to work out their own deals. However, there is virtually no private deal that is totally exempt from external controls. Lawyers and business executives who seek to draft enforceable contracts must have an understanding both of what they and the other side hope to accomplish privately and what will be permitted by the various governments involved.

§ 2.3 The World's Major Legal Systems

Virtually all international commercial agreements choose some body of law to govern the contract. Knowing something about the different national legal systems makes it a little easier to understand why so may contracting parties affirmately choose law rather than leave the decision on governing legal principles to a court or arbitrator. An understanding of the legal system of another country may also help negotiators better appreciate the context in which the other side is functioning. At the same time, this is one of the areas of law in which too much generalization can be dangerous. This section is not intended to be an exhaustive inquiry into this fascinating area of comparative law, but rather is a relatively brief overview that demonstrates how each system accommodates commercial undertakings.[1]

Most comparative law scholars agree that there are at least four broad classifications (occasionally referred to as *families*) of law: the civil law, the common law, socialist law and Islamic law. Viewed even more deeply, one can discern subcategories such as Latin American law, generally derived from a mixture of the various versions of European civil law; hybrids such as Japanese law—a mixture of indigenous rules and customes, the German

---

1. Readers wishing additional depth in these topics should consult: INTERNATIONAL ENCY-CLOPEDIA OF COMPARATIVE LAW; R. DAVID & J. BRIERLEY, MAJOR LEGAL SYSTEMS IN THE WORLD TODAY (3d ed. 1985).

civil code and United States law; and aboriginal systems such as African tribal law.

The common law systems have their roots in the British law and include virtually all present and former members of the British empire plus the largest trading nation, the United States. The United States has developed separately from Britain for the last two hundred years and now has an internal system of commercial law known as the Uniform Commercial Code. The UCC, as it is generally referred to in the United States, has become a national system of commercial law by virtue of its enactment by all the states except the state of Louisiana.

The civil code countries are primarily the countries of the European continent and those countries, such as most of Latin America whose legal systems derive either from the French or German systems. Socialist legal systems (a set of legal principles derived from the tenets of Marxism) appear to be a dying breed in the last decade of the twentieth century. Formerly, the major socialist legal systems comprised the Soviet Union, China and those countries of Eastern Europe and Asia that found themselves under Soviet domination. However, as China modernizes its external legal principles; as the Soviet Union fragments into the Commonwealth of Independent States and as the countries of eastern Europe begin to look west for their new economic and political systems, the concept of a socialist legal system has become nearly an anachronism. The Islamic systems, principally but not exclusively located in the Middle East, obtain their commercial doctrines from the teachings of the Koran and other Islamic religious teachings.

In recent years, there has been some movement toward development of commercial law principles on a regional basis. For example, the European Community (*Common Market*) has begun to promulgate certain commercial and antitrust principles applicable to all the countries of the E.C. The countries in Latin America's Andean Group and the ASEAN nations of the Far East have also started discussing regional economic and commercial practices. There is an increasing tendency to form regional trade groupings such as the potential North America Free Trade Agreement—within which certain commercial principles will be applicable to all participating countries.

These movements toward unification are definitely healthy and would go a long way toward eliminating the significant uncertainty one encounters in putting together an international business transaction; but they remain the exception rather than the rule. As noted earlier, the vast bulk of applicable commercial law is to be found in the domestic law of various countries. A nation's domestic commercial law is best understood with reference to the comparative law family within which it exists.

In a book such as this, it is impossible to illustrate every conceivable nuance of commercial law within each of the four families of law. Some examples, however, are instructive to indicate how each system deals with certain fundamental issues of commercial practice. As a result, the discussion of each of the families of law set out below will address, among other things, how legal systems within that family deal with three important commercial concepts: (1) impossibility or frustration of performance, (2) the requirement of good faith in commercial dealing, and (3) the application of trade usage or course of dealing to the interpretation of contracts.

Impossibility of performance in a contractual arrangement is encountered when events occur that impede performance of the contract or make performance flatly impossible. For example, fire or shipwreck may destroy the goods themselves or government action may occur that makes the contract a crime (such as the United States' imposing criminal penalties on anyone buying or selling alcoholic beverages in the 1920s).

Good faith is difficult to define with any precision but is probably the fundamental assumption in commercial dealing. If merchants cannot presume good faith on the part of the other contracting party, they probably would not enter the transaction initially. But even if good faith is somewhat elusive and theoretical, it is important in allocating blame and risk when a dispute arises under the contract.

Trade usage is also a somewhat elusive concept, but is often of vital importance. Even the best-drafted contracts contain ambiguities. Contracts that are to be performed over a long period of time may develop ambiguities even if the original language is clear. When ambiguities have to be addressed, it is often helpful to see how other members of the same industry or business conduct their activities. However, not all systems of law permit reference to an industry's usage of trade or course of dealing as a tool for determining normal practices within an industry. To the extent that a legal system does not comprehend reference to terms outside the contract it may not have the necessary flexibility to be a good system for dealing with commercial matters.

§ 2.4 The Civil Law System

The civil law system traces its origins to Roman law and, more specifically, to probably the most distinguished contemporaneous compilation of Roman law, the sixth century Corpus Juris Civilis of Justinian (the *Justinian Code*). This compilation of law was revived for both study and application as the Western European countries began to develop mature, modern legal systems. The Justinian Code set the stage for many of the concepts of the present civil law system, and has many of the attributes of a modern legal system.[2] For

---

2. See, e.g., Wieacker, *The Importance of Roman Law for Western Civilization and Western Legal Thought*, 4 B.C. Int'l & Comp. L.Rev. 257 (1981).

example, it was intended to be a complete and exhaustive statement of the law, a concept that led directly to the modern idea of a civil code as an exhaustive and fully integrated body of law.

Certain concepts of canon law also affected the development of Roman law; but these principles, while generally accepted in most of Europe for a number of centuries, proved not especially suitable for commercial transactions. Because some of the early legal principles did not lend themselves easily to commercial practices, merchants began creating informal modes of dealing with each other that eventually hardened into legal principles accepted by the domestic courts of the various countries.

As the European nation-states proliferated in the eighteenth and nineteenth centuries, national legal systems emerged through the process known as *codification*, a movement that began in the Scandinavian countries and later found its way into the remainder of Europe. The codification movement culminated in the two most prominent codes in existence today, both of which provide the basis for today's civil law tradition. The *Code civil des français* (often referred to as the *Code Napoléon*) was promulgated in 1804 and was followed nearly a century later by the German Civil Code of 1896.

The French Code has been adopted by or has significantly influenced a large number of domestic legal systems, including the legal systems of Belgium and Luxembourg, the Netherlands Civil Code of 1838, the Portugese Civil Code of 1867 (now replaced with a new code promulgated in 1967), the Spanish Civil Code of 1888, some of the Eastern European countries including Poland and virtually all of France's colonial possessions. The German code, drafted almost 100 years later, was created in a different political atmosphere and under a far different tradition of legal scholarship. While the French code was viewed as a kind of everyman's law—written in general terms so that it could be read and understood by the average citizen—the German Code *(Burgerliches Gesetzbuch)* grew out of so-called scientific legal scholarship and resulted in a highly detailed set of provisions drafted with specific reference solely to Germany. The German Code is a distinguished work of legal scholarship by any standard but it one that, as one set of commentators stated, "was not built to travel."[3] Nevertheless, the German code has had a substantial influence on a number of countries including Greece, Switzerland, Brazil and, perhaps most importantly, Japan.

Codification in these countries was only the first step, however. As the nations developed more sophisticated forms of government, and as the work of government became more complicated, the judiciary began to affect the law contained in the codes by deciding individual cases. This led inexorably to a body of judge-made law that exerts a strong influence on the legal system,

---

3. M. GLENDON, M. GORDON & C. OSAKWE, COMPARATIVE LEGAL TRADITIONS (1985).

even though, in theory, in civil law systems courts are not permitted to modify the code by judicial decision-making. One comparative law scholar, Professor Ferdinand Stone has identified four basic goals of a code system: (1) that the law be written essentially in the form of statutes, rather than in the form of court opinions; (2) that the provisions of the code be drafted and arranged systematically (for example, organizing contract principles beginning with the formation of the contract and perhaps concluding with remedies for breach of contract); (3) that the code be dealt with by courts and subsequent legislatures in a unified fashion (a "seamless web" as it were); and (4) that the code be constructed by experts rather than lay persons.[4] Have all these goals been achieved? Not exactly. Is a code system the perfect system of law? Probably not. Most codes have as many disadvantages as advantages.

Generally, the civil code systems try to separate the law into *public* law and *private* law, but with little success in preventing a great deal of overlap. In addition, although a civil code governs a large number of issues of private law it is not necessarily an exhaustive treatment of all possible questions. For example, France adopted a separate commercial code, the *Code de Commerce*, in 1807 shortly after adopting the *Code Napoléon* because the *Code Napoléon* simply did not address all the issues that a modern commercial system requires. German courts have historically recognized certain principles of *Handelsrecht* (commercial law) standing separate and apart from the main codification. Today, the most important aspects of civil and commercial law are merged in most civil code countries. Professor Rene David notes "[t]he Civil law has been commercialised to such a degree in all economically developed nations that there are hardly any rules left in which commercial obligations are treated differently from civil obligations."[5]

Because the civil law codes grew up in nations with strong traditions of business and contract, the codes are generally sympathetic to the formation and performance of contracts. For example, both the French and German codes recognize both bilateral (promises made by both contracting parties) and unilateral (a promise made by one party yet enforcible by the other party) contracts. Article 1101 of the French Code defines *contract* as "an agreement through which one or more persons obligate themselves to one or more other persons to give, or to do or not to do, something. Article 1102 provides: "A contract is synallagmatic or bilateral when the contracting parties mutually obligate themselves each toward the other." Article 320 of the German Civil Code elaborates on the duties of persons who are parties to bilateral contracts: "A person who is bound by a mutual contract may refuse to perform his part until the other party has performed his part, unless the former is bound to perform his part first."

---

4. Stone, *A Primer on Codification*, 29 Tul.L.Rev. 303 (1955).
5. David & Brierley, supra note 1, at 90.

Both systems explicitly recognize impossibility of performance (the excuse of performance when it becomes impossible for one or the other party to live up to his obligations), require good faith and recognize common business practices (course of dealing or usage) in commercial arrangements. Note, for example, the following extracts from both the French and German Codes:

1. *Impossibility and frustration of performance.* Under the French Code, most courts and commentators have viewed the general article on contracts, Article 1134 (providing that contracts "cannot be revoked except by mutual consent or on grounds allowed by law") as a firm, virtually inflexible command of performance irrespective of unanticipated changes in circumstances. There are, of course, additional provisions in the Code such as Article 1147: "An obligor shall be ordered to pay damages [for non-performance] ... whenever he does not establish that the non-performance is due to a foreign cause that cannot be imputed to him ... ." But these provisions have never been used as a basis to override Article 1134's fundamental duty of performance. The German Code also contains a number of provisions suggesting that performance under a contract might be forgiven or adjusted due to unforeseen circumstances. For example, Article 275 states: "The obligor becomes free of the duty to perform to the extent that the performance becomes impossible after the obligation arose as a result of a circumstance for which he is not responsible." The German Code goes on to provide that a contract for an impossible performance is void [Art. 306] [but] the impossibility of performance does not prevent the validity of the contract if the impossibility can be removed and if the contract is intended to be binding only when the performance becomes possible." (Art. 308)

While the language of each of these articles is reasonably clear, even in civil code jurisdictions courts can determine the application of code provisions to specific facts. In both the French and German systems forgiveness of performance has generally been allowed only if the event that impedes performance was not reasonably foreseeable and when the performance is humanly impossible. Moreover, the event that makes the contract nonperformable must not be attributable to any action by one of the contracting parties.[6]

2.*Good Faith and Custom and Usage*: The French Code states that "[Contracts] must be performed in good faith" (Art. 1134) and "ambiguous

---

6. See e.g., Durlach v. Grandgerard, Cour de cassation, Chambre des requetes, 3 July 1918 (a lease would not be vacated simply because the city of Nancy was under enemy bombardment since the plaintiff did not show that the premises themselves were uninhabitable). German courts may on occasion revise the contract if the parties were agreeable to a revision. W. v. K., Deutsches Reich, Reichsgericht, Fifth Civil Senate, 6 January 1923, 106 ERG (Z) 7. See also, Dawson, *Judicial Revision of Frustrated Contracts: Germany*, 63 B.U.L.Rev. 1039 (1983).

provisions are to be interpreted in accordance with the usage of the region in which the contract is concluded." (Art. 1159). The German Code states that "Contracts shall be interpreted according to the requirements of good faith, ordinary usage being taken into consideration." (Art. 157)

These extracts make clear that a great deal of the two codes were written to promote commercial dealings by providing both stability and predictability for contracting parties. Stability and predictability largely flow from the establishment of clear and easily understood rules that allow people in business to draft and negotiate their own agreements without heavy handed interference by either legislature or courts. As such, the French and German civil codes enhance rather than impede the formation of contracts and the honoring of business obligations.

Impossibility of performance, good faith, and custom and usage are not the only legal concepts encountered when dealing with companies in civil code countries. While the influence of the codes is great, of equal importance for modern commercial practice is the overlay of regulatory provisions, such as licensing, antitrust, intellectual property and consumer protection measures, that now affect large numbers of commercial transactions in virtually every country in the world.

§ 2.5 The British Common Law System

Although the common law and civil law systems share roots in Roman law, the evolution of the common law system has been much different than that of the civil law. Most scholars begin an analysis of the common law systems with the Norman conquest of England in 1066 and the subsequent work of the royal courts of justice. The general principles of the common law grow not out of codification, but rather out of the deciding of specific cases by individual judges over a long period of time.

Through the doctrine of *stare decisis* these decisions, properly read and categorized, eventually result in discernible, generally applicable principles on which future decisions must be based. *Stare decisis* itself requires at least three assumptions: (1) that a court will render a principled and properly articulated decision—that is, that a court will give sound reasons for its decision; (2) that decisions will be published in some fashion so that other courts dealing with similar cases will know how earlier cases came out; and, (3) that the judicial system will be set up as a hierarchy, with the lower courts required to abide by the decisions of the higher courts.

By definition, the common law system concentrates enormous power in the courts and gives primary influence within the system to lawyers (the system's legal specialists) because lawyers are the only professionals properly schooled in the methods of the common law. At the same time, decisions were not rendered blindly or without regard for history and tradition. The early common law judges searching for a reasoned basis for substantive legal rules often consulted Roman sources. For example, the sanctity of contract doctrine (*pacta sunt servanda*) that was developed to its highest degree in England is historically a principle of Roman law. English commercial law has other roots in the conventional practices of business people, just as in the civil law systems. In 1666, an English court noted, "the law of merchants is the law of the land, and the custome is good enough generally for any man, without naming him merchant."[7] thus recognizing judicially what had probably been the case for centuries—that the basis for the development of a comprehensive, judge-made body of commercial law lies largely in those common trade practices and usages known as *lex mercatoria* or *the law merchant.*

For those not familiar with the common law tradition, it is sometimes difficult to understand the immense influence of the courts on commercial practices in the common law countries. A short example may be helpful. In England prior to the mid-1800s it was not entirely clear whether lost profits could be awarded to a company that was injured by another company's breach of a contract. Certainly, the British Parliament could have passed a statute establishing some rule on point. However, because it did not do so at that time—and rarely legislates on commercial topics in any event—the development of an applicable principle of law was left to the British courts.

In the classic case in point, *Hadley v. Baxendale,*[8] a crankshaft in a mill broke and the mill owners had to send off to the manufacturer for a new shaft. The owners contracted with a transportation company to carry the new shaft from the manufacturer to the mill. The shipment was delayed and as a result the mill did not operate for several days. The mill owners sued the transportation company not only for the price of the shipment (a sum of 2 pounds, four shillings) but also for the lost profits over those days when the mill did not operate, a far greater sum of money.

The case eventually made its way the the Exchequer Court that determined and announced in a written opinion, after litigation between the parties: "Where two parties have made a contract which one of them has broken [here the contract for the transportation of the mill shaft], the damages which the other party ought to receive ... should be such as may fairly and reasonably be considered either arising naturally, i.e., according to the usual course of things, from such breach of contract itself, or such as may reasonably be supposed to have been made in the contemplation of both parties, at the time they made the contract." The court went on to determine that the lost profits had not been contemplated by the parties, because there had been no discussion of profits—or of the consequences of a delay in the

---

7. Woodward v. Rowe, 2 K.B. 132, 84 Eng.Rep.84 (1666).
8. 9 Exch. 341 (1854).

shaft's shipment—when the transportation contract was entered into. Consequently, profits were not "reasonable" damages and thus not awarded to the mill owners.

Once this decision was announced, the principle of *stare decisis* required that other courts follow the rule of *Hadley v. Baxendale* in all similar cases. The vast majority of British commercial law principles, even those applicable today, were constructed in this fashion. Eventually, over a long period of time, an entire body of commercial law was developed that is probably as good as any other in the world. The doctrines of impossibility of performance, good faith and the use of commercial custom and usage so easily spotted in the French and German civil codes are firmly established in British law by way of case decisions rather than statutes. So, for example, impossibility in British law is a nearly absolute concept, forgiving a party's performance of a contract only when matters become either physically impossible (for example, when the entire supply of goods is destroyed in a fire) or legally impossible (a legislature makes it a crime to sell alcoholic beverages), not when matters become merely impracticable (such as a mere rise in price).[9]

Even so, the common law method for creating commercial rules is viewed by many continental legal scholars as inefficient and somewhat haphazard since it depends on the decision of only those cases that parties chose to litigate. It is also exceptionally time-consuming. The length of the court's opinion in the *Hadley* case is as long as dozens of French or German code provisions put together. Moreover, readers of court opinion sometimes find it difficult to separate grain from chaff and even more difficult to determine whether a court might apply an earlier case in a new situation in which the facts are just slightly different. This means that most of the system is in the hands of lawyers. Laypeople cannot normally perform these feats of analysis on their own.

Codes—in theory but often not in practice—are intended to remove many of these difficulties. At the end of the Nineteenth century, the British parliament entered the arena of commercial law by enacting two detailed statutes, the Bills of Exchange Act (1882) and the Sales of Goods Act (1893). These two statutes began as reform movements but ended as attempts to merely reproduce in statutory form, the existing judge-made principles of commercial law.[10] Since then, Parliament has occasionally legislated in specific areas of commercial transaction such as import and export matters, but has left most of British commercial law in the hands of the courts. Fortunately, the case law is well parsed and most fundamental principles of contract so well

---

9. See, e.g., Ford & Sons, Ltd. v. Henry Leetham & Sons, Ltd., 21 Comm. Cas. 55 (K.B. 1915)(m

10. R. Chalmers, *Sale of Goods Act* (14th ed. 1963).

established that British merchants have virtually the same sense of stability and predictability as enjoyed by their counterparts in the code countries. Today, British contract and commercial law is highly developed and exceptionally sophisticated, as one might expect of one of the world's major trading nations.

§ 2.6 Commercial Law in the United States of America

U.S. commercial law is derived from the British common law but has lately moved in the direction of codification and national uniformity. To a large extent, the individual states in the United States have sufficient sovereignty to develop their own commercial law principles. This means that there is not absolute uniformity within U.S. commercial law. However, the state-by-state differences tend to be relatively small and insubstantial. Over the past thirty years, a great deal of uniformity has been created by the state-by-state adoption of the Uniform Commercial Code (UCC). The UCC is now the law in 49 states and the District of Columbia. The one state that has not adopted the UCC is Louisiana, a state that entered the Union as a former French colony and that derives some of its commercial principles from the Code Napoléon. However, there are so few trade barriers within the United States that this discrepancy creates very few problems in commercial dealings involving businesses in Louisiana.

It is uncertain whether the UCC was intended to develop as a true code in the French and German sense. Many U.S. legal scholars disagree on this issue. Karl Llewellyn, sometimes regarded as the father of the UCC, saw the UCC as a kind of hybrid "case-law Code" that would set a firm—and uniform—basis for commercial rules, but that would permit the courts to fill in any gaps in the UCC by case law. Other scholars disagree with the Llewellyn view while still of the opinion that the promulgation of the UCC has been a one of the most important developments in U.S. commercial law.[11]

The UCC is separated into nine articles, dealing variously with sales of goods (Article Two), commercial paper and bank deposits and collections (Articles Three and Four), letters of credit (Article Five), bulk transfers (Article 6), documents of title (Article 7), investment securities (Article 8), and secured transactions (Article 9). A number of provisions in Article Two on sales of goods addresses the same matters examined under French, German and British law.

---

11. Gilmore, *In Memoriam: Karl Llewellyn*,71 Yale L.J. 813 (1962). See also, Hawkland, *Uniform Commercial "Code" Methodology*, 1962 U.Ill.L.F. 291 (UCC is a true code) and Kripke, *The Principles Underlying the Drafting of the Uniform Commercial Code*, 1962 U.Ill.L.F. 321 (UCC is merely a proper restatement of common law principles).

Under the UCC, impossibility of performance has been transmuted into a concept of "impracticability of performance" (§ 2-615) by providing: "Delay in delivery ... by a seller ... is not a breach of his duty under a contract for sale if performance as agreed has been made impracticable by the occurrence of a contingency the non-occurrence of which was a basic assumption on which the contract was made or by compliance in good faith with any applicable foreign or domestic governmental regulation." The official comments to the UCC make clear that the use of the term *impracticable* is intended to include circumstances that are less onerous than absolute impossibility of performance, although there is a serious question whether section 2-615 excuses performance of a contract merely because of increases in prices.[12]

Similarly, section 1-203 establishes a fundamental obligation of good faith for all transactions governed by the Code by providing: "Every contract or duty within this Act imposes an obligation of good faith in its performance or enforcement." Section 2-208 permits a contract to be construed in terms of the merchants' course of performance and the general usages of trade unless the contract provides otherwise.

The UCC is not the sum total of U.S. commercial law, however. Even though the UCC is the primary source of commercial law in the United States, and even though it has had an impact far beyond the boundaries of the United States because it is so often incorporated as the law applicable to international commercial agreements, there is a great deal of American commercial practice that is not covered by the Code. For example, the UCC does not cover leases or contracts for services. It has virtually nothing to do with the purchase and sale of real estate. For the law governing these matters, American lawyers look to the common law of each state and statutes in the various states apart from the UCC that may affect the subject matter of the transaction.

§ 2.7 Socialist Legal Systems

In the last decade of the Twentieth century, this section is something of an anachronism. Nonetheless, because a few socialist state remain—and because no firm predictions may be made about the fate of the former Soviet Union—socialist legal systems may be encountered. The 1917 revolution in Russia set the stage for a parallel revolution in the legal system of that country that, in turn, has affected a number of other countries in the world that adopted socialism as their form of government. While ideally the govern-

---

12. See generally, J. EDDY & P. WINSHIP, COMMERCIAL TRANSACTIONS: TEXT, CASES & PROBLEMS (1985) 543-52 (1985) and Speidel, *Excusable Non-Performance in Sales Contracts: Some Thoughts About Risk Management*, 32 S.Car.L.Rev. 241 (1980).

ment—and by implication, the law—was eventually to whither away under communism, in the interim all socialist countries have developed highly sophisticated systems of legal controls that affect not only the conduct of individuals within those societies, but also the nature and course of commercial practices in those countries.

In theory, the concept of a private contract is antithetical to a socialist system. Under socialism, the state has three tasks: (1) to provide for national security, (2) to enhance economic development so that each person receives goods and services according to his need, and (3) to eliminate the acquisitive tendencies of human beings that are characteristic of capitalist societies and that are according to socialist doctrine so detrimental to the building of a truly fair and just society. None of these goals comprehends commercial contractual relationships between private persons. To the extent that the state must engage in international trade either with other collective systems or with private companies outside the socialist country, those contracts are executed and performed by the government, not by individuals.

Of course, theory gives way to reality in most systems of government. In virtually all socialist systems, the law springs primarily from the central government in the form of legislation and proclamations. The following is an illustration, based on practices in the former Soviet Union, that typify a socialist legal systems development of commercial legal principles.

As a byproduct of the central government's economic activities, many countries, including the former Soviet Union, established a concept of internal contracting that was based on various economic plans written by the government. Within the strictures of the economic plan, each affected economic enterprise is required to enter into a plan contract with another related enterprise for the supply of the raw materials needed for it to meet its production plan. Thus, for example, an enterprise that produces automobiles will be required to contract with an enterprise that produces tires.[13]

Disputes that arise under these plan contracts are typically handled through a system of economic courts that function in much the same way as a Western arbitration system. They review disputes in terms of state economic goals rather than in terms of narrow principles of contract law and are frequently dissociated from the regular courts of the country.[14]

These arbitral bodies are generally limited to internal disputes between governmental entities. Contracts between the national government and foreign private companies are negotiated and performed between the private companies and a governmental body referred to as a foreign trading organization or foreign trading commission. The foreign trading commission functions much

---

13. Glendon, supra note 3, at 766-67. For an excellent general work on Soviet law see J. HAZARD, W. BUTLER & P. MAGGS, THE SOVIET LEGAL SYSTEM (3d ed. 1977).

14. Id.

like a private party in that it negotiates and signs contracts and participates in various types of dispute resolution.[15] In the former Soviet Union, such contracts were often standard form contracts of adhesion. If the western participant chose to enter the deal, it either accepted the standard clauses proferred by the foreign trading commission or did not do the deal.

§ 2.7.1 The Commonwealth of Independent States

The more difficult, yet fascinating question is what happens when a country throws off its socialist legal system. In Eastern Europe and in many of the republics of the former Soviet Union (now referred to as the Commonwealth of Independent States), the governments are rushing, with Western assistance, to develop modern systems of commercial practice and regulation. Within Russia, there is a body of law that might form the basis for a new system of contract law. There are many useful provisions to be found in the basic civil code for the Russian Republic, a code with heavy Germanic influences that might outlive socialism. For example, the Article 130 of the Russian civil code prescribes that a contract must contain the following elements to be valid: "the subject matter of the contract, the price, the time, as well as all other particulars with respect to which, according to the preliminary declaration of either party, agreement was to be reached." The civil code contains a flavor of impossibility and frustration in Article 144 that provides, in part: "If performance of a bilateral contract by one of the parties becomes impossible owing to circumstances for which neither party is liable, then, unless the law or contract provides otherwise, such party shall have no right to claim any benefits under the contract from the other party." Article 235 provides: "An obligation is terminated by impossibility of performance, if the impossibility is caused by a circumstance for which the obligor is not responsible ..."

It is impossible to predict the final dimensions of the political system of either the republics of the Commonwealth of Independent States or of the Eastern European countries that were under Soviet domination. Russia, Ukraine, Belarus, and other republics west of the Urals seem intent on adopting western european legal regimes as to countries such as Poland, Czechosolvakia and Hungary. Indeed, the latter three countries are under consideration for associate membership in the European Community. To the extent that these trends continue, Western European models may provide the best predictions of future systems. To the extent that countries such as

---

15. The best work on trade with the former U.S.S.R., now dated, is T. HOYA, EAST-WEST TRADE: COMECON LAW, AMERICAN-SOVIET TRADE (1984). Mr. Hoya is also the author of several law review articles on the same subject that are now incorporated in his book. See, e.g., Hoya & Stern, *Drafting Contracts in U.S.-Soviet Trade*, 7 L. & Pol'y in Int'l Bus. 1057 (1975). See also, Berman & Bustin, *The Soviet System of Foreign Trade*, 7 L. & Pol'y in Int'l Bus. 987 (1975).

Cuba and North Korea persist in maintaining a socialist legal system, they may be even further removed from the community of trading nations.

§ 2.7.2 The Peoples Republic of China

China is just now emerging as an important trading nation. The current Chinese government appears quite enthusiastic about expanding its trade opportunities and has set about to develop modern legal regimes to govern contracts with private companies outside China. Indeed, many regions of China, particulary the province of Guandzhou, are now functioning almost independently of the central government and have instituted market mechanism economic principles—and related legal principles—that have greatly enhanced economic growth in those regions. China has accepted the Vienna Convention on the International Sales of Goods, the Berne Copyright treaty and a number of other important international agreements that are intended to promote and harmonize world trade. It has sought membership in the General Agreement on Tariff and Trade, although its membership has not yet been accepted.

However, in many instances, the Chinese follow the basic Soviet approach of insisting that all contracts be with a state contracting entity. In addition, the terms and conditions of the contract are set, in part, through a series of Chinese government pronouncement that resemble administrative agency regulations in the United States. So, for example, the 1979 joint venture law promulgated by the government of the People's Republic contains only 15 articles that cover such matters as registration of the joint venture, taxation of the venture, marketing and distribution arrangements, and a kind of "buy-Chinese" provision that obligates the joint venture to seek raw materials in the first instance from Chinese sources. This very rudimentar enactment, primitive by Western legal standards, was hailed as a breakthrough in Chinese attitudes toward the West and toward entreprenurial activities in 1979. It was followed by a number of increasingly sophisticated legal instruments—for example, the Foreign Economic Contract Law—that confirm China's desire to become a major trading nation.

§ 2.8 Islamic Legal Systems

Most Islamic legal systems are a mixture of civil codes (the Code Napoleon has had particular influence in the Middle East) and the principles of law that grow out of the fundamental tenets of the Islamic religion. To the extent that a predominantly Islamic country conducts its commercial business by civil code devices, it will not differ too much from the basic guidelines discussed in § 2.3 above. However, to the extent that a particular country has returned to a theocratic base for its legal system, an understanding of some basic principles of Islam is necessary even if one's only interest is in the commercial area.

The Islamic legal system is normally referred to as the Shari'ah (a literal translation of which is "way to follow"). The Shari'ah prescribes detailed codes of conduct for Muslims in all areas of their life, both personal and commercial. As a consequence there are few of the sharp distinctions between private matters, such as, say, domestic relations, and commercial law that are common in Western societies. The Shari'ah flows from four sources. The Koran is the cornerstone of Islam—a recitation of the words spoken by God to Mohammed. The Sunna is what might be regarded as the pronouncements of Mohammed himself and includes descriptions of his activities while he was alive and his statements on various human activities. The Ijma is the work of Islamic scholars who attempted to fill gaps in the principles set out in the Koran and the Sunna; and the Qiyas is another work of scholarship by which various principles are derived by analogy from the pronouncements in the Koran and the Sunna.

It is not inappropriate to refer to these writings as a sort of codification of legal principles. However, the application of the principles themselves is almost always on a case-by-case basis with few individual decisions committed to writing. To analogize, perhaps too broadly, to American law, the Shari'ah is something like a system based on the Uniform Commercial Code without reported court decisions construing the UCC's individual provisions.

Westerners sometimes blanch at the use of a theologically-based system of law in a commercial setting while forgetting that more than a little Western law (for example, certain prohibitions on usury and the enforcement of certain unilateral promises in some civil code countries) has definite religious underpinnings. In many countries, the Shari'ah has evolved to the point where it has some utility in controlling mercantile behavior.[16]

However, it does take some getting used to under the best of circumstances. For example, certain precepts in the Shari'ah prohibiting certain forms of interest as usurious, have inhibited the negotiation and execution of a number of commercial transactions. By contrast, a number of principles to be found in the Koran and the Sunna admonish Moslems to abide by their promises and obligations and extend the protections of the Shari'ah to both Moslems and non-Moslems. This suggests that an elaborate document freely consented to by the parties will go a long way toward preserving an agreement.

The tenets of the Shari'ah tend to preserve an obligation of good faith, but also insist upon a literalist approach to the contract which often forbids

---

16. See generally, N. COULSON, COMMERCIAL LAW IN THE GULF STATES: THE ISLAMIC LEGAL TRADITION (1984).

cancellation or revision on the basis of impossibility or frustration. To this extent, it is a more inflexible system than, say, the American UCC. However, the incorporation of the Shari'ah is often insisted upon by government entities in Islamic countries and as a consequence cannot always be avoided.

Impossibility and frustration are generally recognized through the doctrine of "Riba" which seeks to protect against risk and uncertainty, but which is normally fleshed out in the context of individual cases in the Islamic courts. It appears to be a much more relaxed doctrine than the doctrine of impossibility in Western courts (which, as noted above, usually forgives performance only in instances of absolute inability to perform, rather than mere inconvenience or impracticability) and in the views of some commentators may have impeded commercial development by making it too easy for a contracting party to avoid his obligations under the contract.[17] One recent development of concern to Western business executives is the use of some of the pronouncements in the Shari'a on the collection of interest on a loan (generally forbidden by the Shari'a) as grounds for avoiding loan contracts whose interest rates are deemed excessive by courts in Islamic countries. Some Saudi Arabian courts have suggested that interest bearing loan agreements would not be enforceable in Saudi courts.[18]

This observation is not, of course, intended to cast aspersions on the legitimacy of the Islamic system of law. As noted earlier, most Western systems also have a historical basis in religion and religious practices. It is rather to illustrate some of the often unanticipated difficulties which arise when a contract is grounded in a system of law with which one of the parties may be unfamiliar.

§ 2.9 The Impact of International Principles of Commercial Law

§ 2.9.1 International law generally

International law is also beginning to contribute significant principles for the execution and performance of international commercial agreements. These principles have been developed on the international level through two separate sources. The first is the body of law known as public international law. As Wolfgang Friedmann recognized over twenty years ago, "private corporations are now active participants in the evolution of public international law. This is mainly the result of the manifold international economic activities of

---

17. See Grant, Book Review of COMMERCIAL LAW IN THE GULF STATES, 20 Int'l Law. 442, 447 (1986).

18. See, e.g., 8 International Lawyers' Newsletter 1 (Kluwer, May/June, 1986).

private corporations coupled with the emergence of a large number of economically underdeveloped countries claiming [sovereignty] over their natural resources but needing foreign financial, technical and managerial assistance" in the development of those resources.[19]

Within public international law there are a number of sources of doctrine. These sources are now recognized in codified form in Article 38(1) of the Statute of the International Court of Justice and include:

1. international conventions (treaties), whether general or particular, establishing rules expressly recognized by the contesting states;
2. international custom, as evidence of a general practice accepted by law;
3. the general principles of law recognized by civilized nations; and, in certain circumstances,
4. judicial decisions and the teachings of the most highly qualified publicists of the various nations.

Most commentators regard the statute as an exclusive statement of the sources of international law. Even though the sources are not expressly stated to be heirarchical, most scholars regard sources 1 and 2 as the most important.[20] Within the last three categories lies the genesis of a special system of international commercial law which some scholars refer to as *lex mercatoria* (the law merchant)—a synthesis of generally held and generally-accepted commercial principles that may be expected to be applied to contracts among the major trading nations.

The substantive general principles that have emerged are essentially threefold: (1) a merchant must deal in good faith, (2) an agreement between merchants is binding on them—a principle derived from the old Roman doctrine known as *pacta sunt servanda*, and (3) if a dispute arises, a merchant is obligated to abide by the decision of a merchants' court (an early form of arbitration) or face commercial ostracism.[21] Whether the lex mercatoria really exists, however, is not fully certain. At least one commentator suggests that it is simply a reflection "of the increasing uniformity of commercial laws in the major jurisdictions and of a judicial tendency to uphold international contracts."[22] Some commentators see a new lex mercatoria arising from the decisions of arbitrators in international commercial arbitrations.[23]

---

19. W.G. FRIEDMANN, THE CHANGING STRUCTURE OF INTERNATIONAL LAW 375 (1964).

20. I.A. BROWNLIE, PRINCIPLES OF PUBLIC INTERNATIONAL LAW 3 (3d ed. 1979).

21. See, e.g., Trakman, *The Evolution of the Law Merchant: Our Commercial Heritage*, 12 J.Mar.L. & Com. 1, 153 (1980); Berman & Kaufman, *The Law of International Commercial Transactions (Lex Mercatoria)*, 19 Harv. Int'l L.J. 221 (1978); von Caemmerer, *The Influence of the Law of International Trade on the Development and Character of the Commercial Law in the Civil Law Countries*, in THE SOURCES OF THE LAW OF INTERNATIONAL TRADE 88 (C. Schmitthoff, ed. 1964).

22. P. WOOD, LAW AND PRACTICE OF INTERNATIONAL FINANCE (1984).

23. Cremades & Plehn, *The New Lex Mercatoria and the Harmonization of the Laws of International Commercial Transactions*, 2 Boston U. Int'l L.J. 317 (1984).

In recent years the United Nations has taken the lead in developing more uniformity in international commercial law through various conventions and agreements primarily encouraged through the actions of the United Nations Commission on International Trade Law (UNCITRAL). The U.N.'s work in developing the Vienna Convention on the Sale of Goods, its work in developing the UNCITRAL Model Law of International Commercial Arbitration and other ventures have begun to unify much of the law and practice of international trade.[24]

It is clear that one might compose a fairly lengthy list of commercial principles on which most nations would agree. But such a list does not necessarily constitute an articulable or enforceable body of law. In all likelihood most lawyers and business people knowledgeable in this area would agree with the comment that "transnational law" is something of a misnomer, or at least a "phrase without meaning" and a recognition that the existing bodies of law are not quite up to coping with international commercial dealings in the latter part of the Twentieth Century.[25] There is, however, one relatively recent development that cannot be ignored and which may ultimately provide a true, enforceable set of commercial law principles to govern international contracts—the Vienna Convention on the International Sale of Goods.

§ 2.9.2 The 1980 Vienna Convention on Contracts for the International Sale of Goods

The 1980 Convention on Contracts for the International Sale of Goods (sometimes referred to as the Vienna Convention or by a portion of its initials "CISG") is best understood in reference to its historical context and in terms of its specific provisions. Between World War One and World War Two the League of Nations established the International Institute for the Unification of Private Law (sometimes called UNIDROIT), one of whose primary missions was to develop a uniform set of legal principles governing international sales of goods. World War Two interrupted the work of UNIDROIT and the demise of the League of Nations deprived the Institute of its momentum.

Only in 1951, at the instigation of the Dutch government, did a group of countries convene at the Hague to draft a Uniform Law on the International Sale of Goods and a Uniform Law on the Formation of Contracts for the Sale of Goods. While a few countries adopted these laws, so few of the major trading nations acceded to them that they remained primarily of academic interest through the mid-1960s. In 1966, the United Nations formed the U.N. Commission on International Trade Law (UNCITRAL) with a far larger membership and work began anew on a unified international sales law. In

---

24. See, e.g., Cigoj, *International Sales: Formation of Contracts*, 23 Netherlands Int'l L. Rev. 257 (1976); L. LAZAR, TRANSNATIONAL ECONOMIC AND MONETARY LAW (1981).

25. Lazar, supra note 24, at 103.

1980, the final convention was prepared and by September, 1981 twenty one countries had signed the agreement (signing a convention is a step leading toward ratification but which does not constitute ratification itself). The United States ratified CISG on January 1, 1987. CISG formally entered into force on January 1, 1988. By the early 1990s over thirty countries, including most of the major trading nations, had ratified CISG.[26]

As a consequence of U.S. ratification and the treaty's entering into force, CISG may ultimately become the unifying thread that so many international legal scholars and practitioners have been waiting for. As such it bears close attention by persons who may draft or negotiate international sales contracts in the near future.[27] It is reproduced as Appendix A of this book and is probably best understood by working through some of its major provisions.

a. *Scope*:

The Convention is not intended to be a comprehensive statement of commercial principles. It applies on its terms only to the sale of certain goods. In this respect is analogous, but not identical to Article Two of the Uniform Commercial Code. Among other things, it does not apply to sales of ships or aircraft, sales of stock or negotiable instruments, or sales of goods purchased for personal or household use (Article 2). This suggests that it is to be a device applicable only between merchants and is not to be regarded as some kind of international consumer protection statute.

The Convention becomes the applicable law only when the buyer and the seller both reside in countries which have adopted the Convention (Article 1). So, for example, if the United States and West Germany have ratified the Convention, it will govern a transaction for the sale of widgets between XYZ, Inc. (an American corporation) and MMM AG of Germany. However, if only one of the countries has ratified, the Convention would not apply, and the parties would have to resort to other legal principles to identify the law applicable to the contract if the contract does not specify a choice of law.

---

26. As of late 1991 the countries are Argentina, Austria, Bulgaria, Belarus, Chile, China, Czechoslovakia, Denmark, Egypt, Finland, France, Germany, Ghana, Guinea, Hungary, Iraq, Italy, Lesotho, Mexico, The Netherlands, Norway, Poland, Singapore, spain, Sweden, Switzerland, Syria, Ukraine, Russia (as the successor to the Soviet Union), United States, Venezuela, Yugoslavia and Zambia. The United Nations staffs a direct telephone line that can provide callers with additional signatories. The number is (in the U.S.A.), (212) 963-5467. UNCITRAL is also commissioning a compendium of interpretations and court decisions construing CISG.

27. A sizeable amount of literature has been generated on the 1980 Convention. See, e.g., J. HONNOLD, UNIFORM LAW FOR INTERNATIONAL SALES UNDER THE 1980 UNITED NATIONS CONVENTION (Kluwer, 1982); Symposium, International Sales of Goods Convention, 18 Int'l Law. 3 (1984). This symposium contains an extensive bibliography on the Convention collected by Professor Peter Winship. An updated bibliography also by Professor Winship appears in 21 INTL LAW. 585 (1987).

An interesting question not yet fully resolved by international legal scholars is whether contracting parties could "choose" the 1980 Convention as the applicable law even if it would not be applicable on its own terms. (A longer analysis of choice of law is set out in § 4.4.2 in Chapter 4.) The converse—whether contracting parties may *exclude* provisions of the 1980 Convention by specific language—is covered in Article 6: "The parties may exclude the application of this Convention or, subject to Article 12 (the requirement of a writing), derogate from or vary the effect of any of its provisions." As a consequence of this last provision, the United States Department of State recommends the following language to be inserted into any contract that the parties do not wish governed by CISG:

"The rights and obligations of the parties under this agreement shall not be governed by the provisions of the 1980 U.N. Convention on Contracts for the International Sale of Goods; rather these rights and obligations shall be governed by the law of _____." There are other possibilities. If the parties wish to use the CISG as the primary law governing the document but to resort to, say, the UCC as a gap-filling device, the State Department recommends: "This agreement shall be governed by the CISG. However, any ambiguities or items not covered by the CISG shall be governed by the Uniform Commercial Code of the State of New York." Most persons who have compared the CISG and the UCC find the UCC more detailed on matters such as fraud, mistake and the like.

   b. *Individual Provisions:*

The Convention contains 101 individual articles which might best be analyzed in terms of five general categories: (1) application of the Convention, (2) interpretation of the Convention, (3) contract formation, (4) provisions relating the obligations of seller and buyer, breach and risk of loss, and (5) provisions relating to adoption, reservations and ratification. Viewed generally, the Convention makes it relatively easy to form contracts, is relatively well-balanced between the rights of the seller and the rights of the buyer, and contains those crucial seeds of flexibility and predictability so necessary to the doing of business on an international basis.

   In analyzing CISG, a good starting point is to recognize that CISG does not prohibit oral contracts. To use the U.S. term it does not contain a "statute of frauds" and thus purely oral undertakings can be enforced under CISG. Article 11 provides expressly: "A contract of sale need not be concluded in or evidenced by writing and is not subject to any other requirement as to form. It may be proved by any means including witnesses." Beyond that, course of dealing or usage may be relevant to a contract. Article 9 provides: "The parties are bound by any usage to which they hve agreed and by any practices which they have established between themselves." Article 9(2) amplifies this: "[The parties are bound by] a usage of which the parties knew or ought to have known and which in international trade is widely known to, and regularly observed by, parties to contracts."

Contract formation is somewhat different from conventional practice. Article 14 defines *offer* as any proposal that is "sufficiently definite and indicates the intention of the offeror to be bound in case of acceptance." The same article defines *sufficiently definite* as a proposal that "indicates the goods and expressly or implicitly fixes or makes provision for determining the quantity and the price." An offer become effective when it reaches the offeree (article 15); but silence may not be construed as an acceptance. An acceptance, like an offer, is effective only when it reaches the offeror (article 18). The acceptance of the offer must be the "mirror image" of the offer (article 19): "A reply to an offer which purports to be an acceptance but contains additions, limitations or other modifications is a rejection of the offer and constitutes a counter-offer."

Warranties under the CISG may prove troublesome. The CISG warranty provisions are not as nearly detailed as the UCC. The basic seller's warranty is merely (article 35): "The seller must deliver goods which are of the quantity, quality and description required by the contract ... The goods do not conform with the contract unless they (a) are fit for the purposes for which goods of the same description would ordinarily be used [or] are fit for any particular purpose expressly or impliedly made known to the seller at the time ... of the contract." By contrast, the buyer has an obligation to inspect the goods (article 37) and (article 39) "loses the right to rely on a lack of conformity of the goods if he does not give notice ... within a reasonable time after he has discovered [the non-conformity] or ought to have discovered it." Both the seller and buyer have various remedies available to them including the remedy of strict performance (article 46: "the buyer may require performance by the seller ... unless the buyer has resorted to a remedy which is inconsistent with this requirement." article 62 is the parallel remedy for the seller). Compensatory damages permit the recovery of profit in certain circumstances (article 74): "Damages for breach of contract ... consist of a sum equal to the loss, including loss of profit ... [but] such damages may not exceed the loss which the party in breach foresaw or ought to have foreseen ... as a possible consequence of the breach." The non-breaching party, as in virtually all legal systems, has the obligation to mitigate damages (article 77): "A party who relies on a breach of contract must take such measures as are reasonable in the circumstances to mitigate the loss, including loss of profit, resulting from the breach."

The CISG is not a perfect code. No such perfect sales code has ever existed. Nonetheless, it serves some very important purposes and deserves all the attention international lawyers and business executives choose to give it. First, it is sufficiently comprehensive and balanced that parties electing its provisions should feel comfortable with its terms. Second, it is a creation of the United Nations, so even contracting parties in developing countries should feel free to use its provisions without the worry that this is an unbalanced, made-in-the-west body of law imposed on them by patronizing major trading nations. Third, it is consistent with traditional principles of sales, and in that sense, may be regarded as a codification of the lex mercatoria. The drafters of this convention may justifiably take pride in their work. Conversations between the author and numerous international lawyers suggest that more and more contracts are either affirmatively choosing CISG or at least not opting out of it. In the next few years, it should prove its value to the international business community.   ◆

— 3 —
Planning International Commercial Agreements

§ 3.1 Introduction

By definition, international commercial agreements transcend national boundaries. This feature creates a number of problems for the lawyers and business executives who plan and draft the agreement because it introduces complications and uncertainties that typically do not exist in domestic commercial arrangements. For example, it is often uncertain which country's commercial law governs the transaction. In many cases, modes of payment for goods and services that are taken for granted in a domestic context are often too insecure and untimely for deals that involve businesses in more than one country. If a dispute arises under the agreement, access to a favorable court system is never a sure thing.

This section lays a foundation for some of the more sophisticated issues discussed in later sections in this chapter. Readers not fully acquainted with basic principles of contract law should look closely at section 3.2 before moving to subsequent sections in this chapter and to Chapter 4. Readers who contemplate entering into one of the more complex undertakings such as a franchise agreement or a joint venture should spend some time considering the issues discussed in section 3.3 before venturing further.

For the purposes of this book, an international commercial agreement or transaction is defined as some kind of business arrangement reflected in a contract, either written or oral:

1. Between a company or individual in one country and a company or individual in another country, or

2. In certain circumstances, between a private company or individual and a foreign government or some component of a government such as a state-owned trading company.

This definition is deliberately broad, but it excludes, with a few exceptions, those intergovernmental transactions between sovereign entities that legal scholars often refer to as *international relations* and whose rules are set by the body of law normally referred to as *public international law*. The transactions analyzed in this chapter are essentially private commercial transactions. For the most part, these transactions are presumed to be transactions between people in business (or, as some of the commercial codes put it "between merchants") and thus do not require an extensive inquiry into consumer protection laws.

The final general assumption made throughout the remainder of this book is that the commercial agreement, whatever its nature, will be evidenced by some kind of writing. Oral agreements in international commercial transactions are not totally unheard of, but they are so unusual as to be relatively insignificant in terms of total dollar value. Many systems of national law such as the United States' Uniform Commercial Code normally require a writing for a contract to be enforceable — a doctrine known in Anglo/American law as the *Statute of Frauds*. By contrast, Article 11 of the relatively new Convention on the International Sale of Goods (frequently referred to as the *Vienna Convention* or by its acronym, *CISG*) does not require a writing for a contract to be valid and enforceable, permitting the existence of an agreement to "be proved by any means, including witnesses." As the CISG takes hold, it is possible that the world will see more oral contracts. But in all likelihood, the bulk of international commercial agreements will continue to be evidenced primarily by a writing.

In international trade, parties to an agreement almost always execute a writing of some sort to establish a contract enforceable at law, to remove uncertainty and to reduce risk. As Professor Andreas Lowenfeld points out, there are risks inherent in all commercial dealings, but there are special risks in international trade, including war, the dangers of carriage on the high seas, expropriation, currency fluctuations, boycotts, and changes in governmental controls such as tariffs and export and import regulations.[1] Parties that have never dealt with each other may feel insecure about payment or about delivery of the goods or services. A written agreement goes a long way toward removing much of this uncertainty.

Any number of different types of commercial arrangements may be negotiated between businesses, including the sale or lease of goods, the sale of services, the licensing of patents, copyrights or trademarks, the selling of franchises, or the creation of joint ventures. Because we presume that each of these arrangements is sparked by a profit motive, each agreement also involves money or something else of value changing hands—which, in turn,

---

1. A. LOWENFELD, INTERNATIONAL PRIVATE TRADE 2-3 (2d ed. 1981).

requires some analysis of the proper method of payment for the transaction. The payment component of an agreement may add another party to the transaction (typically a bank), a whole new set of legal principles (generally those principles governing negotiable instruments or other payment devices), and the creation of financing documents (such as bank checks, money orders, negotiable bills of lading, and one of the mainstays for payment of international transactions—the irrevocable letter of credit).

Contracts that involve the sale of goods, and occasionally contracts that provide for the delivery of certain types of services, also involve a transportation component, which introduces yet another player—the transportation company or *carrier*—and another piece of paper, such as a bill of lading or warehouse receipt that is in effect a separate contract between the seller or buyer and the carrier.

In certain circumstances, government agencies will underwrite all or part of the transaction. In the United States, the Export-Import Bank is established to help fund certain types of transactions. The Overseas Private Investment Corporation (OPIC) provides insurance for United States businesses against certain types of overseas losses for selected transactions. A new component of the World Bank, the Multi-lateral Investment Guarantee Agency (MIGA) has been established to perform functions parallel to OPIC under the World Bank's umbrella.

Finally, because international commercial agreements are often of considerable interest to the governments of both the seller and the buyer's countries, both seller and buyer will normally have to obtain import and export permissions from government agencies and will often have to cope with other facets of government regulation such as taxes, the imposition of antitrust laws, dumping and countervailing duty principles and, on occasion, the enforcement of various public health and safety measures such as consumer safety and employee protection standards. These issues are discussed below.

§ 3.2 Some Fundamental Principles of Contract Law

It is virtually impossible to begin a discussion of planning and drafting an international contract without some idea of what the contract must contain in order to be valid and enforceable. However, the validity and enforceability of a commercial agreement normally turns on the commercial principles developed within the country whose law is to be applied to the agreement. This issue sometimes causes a chicken and egg dilemma: the parties cannot draft a contract whose validity they have faith in without understanding the principles of law applicable to that particular agreement. And yet, in some instances, the applicable law is determined long after the contract is drafted when some dispute arises that forces a court or an arbitrator to investigate and resolve the issue of applicable law.

This issue, normally referred to as the *choice of law* problem, is discussed extensively in Chapter 4. This section will concentrate on some fundamental concepts of contract law that are common to or at least not incompatible with most legal systems. However, once again the reader should understand that the resolution of some of these issues may differ significantly depending on the law applicable to the specific contract under examination.

The classic definition of *contract* in Anglo-American jurisprudence is "a promise, or set of promises, for breach of which the law gives a remedy, or the performance of which the law in some way recognizes as a duty."[2] In most systems of law, this basic definition gives rise to two other propositions that are fundamental. First, unless other laws make a contract or any portion of a contract unlawful (such as the selling of alcoholic beverages in countries that forbid such sales), the parties are free to make whatever agreement they wish. This concept, normally referred to as *party autonomy* or *freedom of contract* suggests that a contract can say nearly anything; and, if it is otherwise valid, the parties will be held to the terms of their agreement. Second, once a contract is formed, the parties must perform the bargain as agreed. This proposition, sometimes referred to in civil law systems by its Latin name, *pacta sunt servanda* (sanctity of contract), means that, absent extraordinary circumstances, the parties must perform as agreed even if performance becomes uncomfortable or inconvenient.

Flowing from these basic propositions, an international contract normally includes provisions (either in the language of the contract itself or provided by way of external legal principles that fill in gaps not covered by the contract), covering the following five issues: a. formation and subject matter b. performance c. breach d. remedy e. dispute resolution. Each of these components is discussed separately below. A number of more specific contract principles and some sample clauses are set out in Chapter 4.

§ 3.2.1 Formation and subject matter

Although not all legal systems use the same terminology, a contract is normally formed through the acts of *offer* and *acceptance*. Put simply, a seller writes to a potential buyer: "I will sell you 15 telescopes for $150.00 per telescope." The buyer writes back saying: "I accept. I will buy your 15 telescopes for $150.00 each." In the Anglo-American legal system and in most civil code systems, once this exchange of writings has taken place, a contract has been formed and becomes a legally-enforceable obligation for both parties because there has been an offer and an acceptance and the subject matter of the con-

---

2. 1 WILLISTON ON CONTRACTS § 1 (3d ed. 1957).

tract is not unlawful. The mutual promises ("I promise to sell" and "I promise to buy") also satisfy the requirement of *consideration*— the third vital ingredient of a contract in the Anglo-American system.

Problems arise in a number of ways. Occasionally, persons who purport to enter into a contract do not have the proper *capacity* to agree. In all systems, contracts with children or mentally ill persons are generally not enforceable. On the international level, the problem of capacity is a little different. When business executives are dealing across international boundaries with entities that they do not know personally, it is sometimes difficult to ascertain precisely which person in a company has the necessary authority to sign a contract that binds the company. It is difficult to create any generalizations about this dimension of capacity because businesses around the world have varying organizational structures. However, as a general rule, the higher the rank of the officer signing the contract the more likely it is that the officer has the necessary power to sign enforceable contracts.

There are other areas of potential trouble. Consider, for example, what might happen if the offer is made by the seller's sending a pre-printed form to the buyer. The form contains a price for the goods that is effective only if the *buyer* pays the transportation charges from seller's factory to buyer's place of business. The buyer then tries to accept, not by signing or endorsing the seller's form, but by sending the buyer's own pre-printed form. The buyer's form says: "I accept at seller's price if the *seller* pays for the transportation of the goods to my place of business."

In traditional contract law, for example, under Article 19 of the Convention on the International Sale of Goods (CISG)—and in many Continental legal systems—to be effective an acceptance must be the *mirror image* of the offer. That is, the buyer cannot append any conditions to the acceptance that were not part of the original offer. If the buyer attempts to do so, the buyer's form is construed not as an acceptance but rather as a *counter-offer*, which the *seller* must then affirmatively accept before a valid contract is formed.[3]

In the United States, the Uniform Commercial Code (UCC) (set out in Appendix B) handles this problem in a slightly different fashion. In section 2-207 (the famous "battle of the forms" section), the UCC provides that an acceptance that varies from the precise terms of the offer may still operate as an acceptance unless the offer expressly states that the acceptance must exactly conform to the offer or unless the terms of the acceptance "materially alter" the offer. If the offer does not expressly require conformity, or if the

---

3. See, e.g., Winship, *Formation of International Sales Contracts Under the 1980 Vienna Convention*, 17 Int'l Law. 1 (1983); Note, *The United Nations Convention on Contracts for the International Sale of Goods: Contract Formation and the Battle of the Forms*, 21 Colum.J.Transnat'l L. 529 (1983).

new conditions in the acceptance do not materially alter the deal, the new conditions become proposals by the buyer for additions to the contract. In our hypothetical, the shift in the obligation to pay for transportation charges has an substantial impact on the total price of the contract and thereby would, in all likelihood, be considered a *material* alteration. If the acceptance is considered a material alteration, the acceptance (as under traditional contract law) operates as a counter-offer that is not effective unless the seller accepts the new terms.

By contrast, assume that the buyer's form simply adds: "All disagreements under this sale shall be resolved by arbitration." The UCC is not itself clear as to what types of alteration constitute a *material* alteration and United States courts disagree on whether merely adding an arbitration clause constitutes a material alteration.[4] Many U.S. legal scholars believe that the mere addition of a dispute resolution clause does not materially alter the basic agreement—the purpose of which is to buy and sell goods. Interestingly, under the CISG, the result would be about the same, but the analytical process is somewhat different. Under CISG Article 19(2), non-material changes contained in the acceptance become part of the contract unless the offeror objects to these changes either orally or in writing in a timely fashion. However, the CISG deems an arbitration clause to be a *material* addition to the contract. Since the CISG requires an acceptance that is the mirror image of the offer, an acceptance that contains an arbitration clause when the offer is silent on arbitration would be construed only as a counter-offer.

Consider another common problem in contract formation. The seller's letter says: "I offer to sell you 15 telescopes for $150.00 per telescope. This offer is open until July 29, 1993." The buyer writes back: "I accept your offer" and mails her letter on July 29. However, the buyer's letter is not received by the seller until July 31, 1993. On July 30 the seller sold the telescopes to another company. In most domestic systems of contract law and under the CISG, an acceptance is not effective until it is *received* by the seller.[5]

However, under British contract law as delineated in the case of *Adams v. Lindsell*[6] and under the contract law of a few states in the U.S., an acceptance may be effective when the letter of acceptance is mailed (that is, put into the hands of the postal authorities).[7] This is the so-called *mail box* rule. The rule was initially based on the supposition that once a letter is placed in

---

4. See, e.g., E. A. FARNSWORTH, CONTRACTS 157-66 (1982). For a discussion of the battle of the forms under the Vienna Convention see Vergne, *The "Battle of the Forms" under the 1980 United Nations Convention on Contracts for the International Sale of Goods*, 33 Am.J.Comp.L. 233 (1985).

5. See Winship, supra note 3.

6. 1 B. & Ald. 681, 106 Eng. Rep. 250 (K.B. 1818).

7. Farnsworth, supra note 4, at 166-70.

the post, the sender of the letter loses control over the letter. In our case, courts applying the mail box rule would likely determine that the seller bound herself to the agreement when she put the letter into the mail box. While the basic supposition is not necessarily true today (many postal systems permit a sender to retrieve correspondence), it has nonetheless remained a provision in the contract law of many jurisdictions.

The UCC is somewhat more ambiguous on this point. Under the UCC an offer may demand a particular type of acceptance (i.e., a statement in the offer to the effect that "acceptance of this offer is effective only when received by offeror"). Conversely, if the offer does not make such a statement, an offer will be construed "as inviting acceptance in any manner and by any medium reasonable in the circumstances."[8]

Many other problems can arise when contracts are being formed. The illustrations of offer and counteroffer and the problem of acceptance set out above are merely two examples of problems that can occur when sellers and buyers are operating at some distance from each other. Note that all of the possible solutions have both advantages and disadvantages. None of them is necessarily commanded by reference to some higher principle of ethics or morality. They are simply a practical, realistic way to deal with common business problems. In most business transactions, we have learned that the most important thing is simply to tell the business executives what the rules are—or, in certain cases, to inform them that there are no external rules and that they are free to agree among themselves. Once people in business understand the rules, they normally can accommodate their behavior or their contracts to the terms of the rules.

There is a message here for persons about to begin a contract drafting exercise. The contract itself may be drafted to overcome many of these problems. So, for example, an offer may state: "Buyer may not alter the terms of this offer in any way." This language requires a mirror-image response for a valid contract to be formed. Similarly, an offer can state: "Your acceptance is effective only when it is actually received by us." This inserts an *actual* receipt provision in the contract that supplants the mailbox rule in British and certain U.S. jurisdictions. It also makes clear what would otherwise be an ambiguity under the UCC.

These two exercises further illustrate another major point that will be constantly reiterated through the remainder of this book. Contracting parties may either work out and draft provisions of their choosing (remember the doctrine of freedom of contract) or may let the contract law of a particular jurisdiction fill in those matters not specifically addressed in the contract. If a seller is in a business situation in which he absolutely must receive notice

---

8. UCC § 2-206(1)(a).

of acceptance, it would be silly and possibly dangerous not to insist on an "acceptance effective only when received" clause in the contract. By contrast, if the seller has a large and fast manufacturing capacity for his products and can sell those products to many buyers at any given time, he may be happy with mailbox rule. A manufacturer in this position would operate on the assumption that he can always make more products if he has already sold, to another buyer, the quantity promised to a buyer whose acceptance was received later than he expects.

The subject matter of a contract sometimes poses problems in drafting international commercial agreements. Among the major trading nations, contracts for the sale of most goods are almost always valid, unless the sale of the product in question (for example, alcohol, firearms, explosives and other dangerous commodities) is prohibited under other laws of either the seller or the buyer's country. For example, a contract between a Nepalese company and an American furrier to purchase the pelts of the Himalayan snow leopard is unenforceable in the United States because the U.S. government has placed the snow leopard on its list of endangered species and thus made the importation of snow leopard pelts illegal.

Problems with the subject matter of a contract occasionally arise when contracting parties wish to enter into some of the other forms of business arrangement such as a franchise, licensing or joint venture agreement. Many countries do not permit certain types of services contracts. For example, for-profit employment services occasionally run into prohibitions that make it a crime to accept a fee for finding employment for workers.

A number of developing countries are less-than-enthusiastic about externally-owned manufacturing operations and prefer licensing agreements, technology transfer arrangements, or carefully structured joint ventures that keep the business itself—and most of the proceeds generated by the business—in the hands of the country's own citizens. In many cases, business arrangements may not be concluded unless a national of the host country is involved as a major actor in the business operation. Other countries, such as India, do not forbid foreign entities from entering the country per se, but provide special benefits and concessions for those businesses in which Indian nationals participate.

The Anglo-American doctrine of *consideration* is a special inquiry into a contract's subject matter. Unilateral promises under British and American law are almost never valid. That is, merely saying to another "I will make you a telescope" is not normally construed as an enforceable agreement. The Anglo-American system instead contemplates some sort of mutuality of obligation such as "I will make you a telescope if you pay me $150" to which the offeree replies, "Okay." Consideration in this instance is evidenced by the mutual promises of offeror and offeree: Seller promises to make the telescope and buyer promises to pay $150. In the British and U.S. legal systems, the notion of consideration is normally indispensable to a valid contract.

At the same time, Anglo-American courts rarely inquire into the amount (sometimes referred to as the *adequacy* of consideration. So, for example, even if an automobile's fair market value is $10,000, a court will still enforce a contract for the sale of that automobile for $100, if that is what the parties fairly agreed to. This explains why, on occasion, people will enter into a contract based on an express payment of $1. Such a contract is valid, all other things being equal, because the adequacy of the consideration for the contract is normally not something that a court will examine. Remember the underlying principle of party autonomy. People may make whatever bargains they please so long as those bargains do not involve an unlawful subject matter and so long as one is not committing fraud on the other.

Another problem that can arise regarding subject matter is the issue of *mistake*. Mistakes occur every now and then in domestic contracts and perhaps even more often in international contracts where differences in language and culture sometimes interfere with a proper understanding of the matter under negotiation.

Mistakes involving linguistic differences are easy to imagine; but serious mistakes can occur just as easily when the only difference between the parties is a matter of culture and normal business practices. Consider a contract between a U.S. paper manufacturer and an English stationer that calls for the sale of "1000 reams of bond business stationery" without mentioning the precise size of the paper. Conventional business stationery in the United States is 8 and 1/2 inches wide and 11 inches long. Conventional business stationery in Great Britain is the "A4" paper, which is approximately 8 and one-quarter inches by 11 and three-quarter inches. The actual difference is relatively small, but the consequences of a mistake are enormous. Photocopiers and typewriters must be readjusted. Business envelopes don't fit. Files must often be reorganized. In short, even small differences in paper size can create considerable inconvenience and discomfort for the average business. For these reasons, stationery cut to American dimensions is not a very attractive commodity in Britain.

Most legal systems recognize two different types of mistake in contracts. The first is a mistake on the part of only one of the contracting parties, referred to as *unilateral mistake*; and the second is a mistake shared by the parties known as *bilateral mistake*. An 1864 British court addressed the question of bilateral mistake in a case called *Raffles v. Wichelhaus*,[9] in which a contract called for shipment of goods to the United States on the ship *Peerless*. It turned out that there were two ships named *Peerless*. Unfortunately, the U.S. buyer expected the goods to be shipped on the *Peerless* scheduled

---

9. 2 H. & C. 906, 159 Eng.Rep. 375 (1864).

to arrive in October, while the seller shipped the goods on the *Peerless* that arrived in New York in December. A law suit for breach of contract ensued in England. The British court held that the contract was ambiguous and that the mistake was essentially bilateral because it was a jointly held misunderstanding. It therefore concluded that no contract had been formed.

In the case of the mis-sized paper, if both the American paper manufacturer and the English stationer were simply unaware that each country had a different size of paper for business stationery, the result might well be the same as in the *Raffles* case. No contract would have been formed and the parties would simply go their own way.

The result is often different, however, when only one party makes the mistake or if only one party is aware of the ambiguity and could have taken steps to resolve the ambiguity. In these instances, courts deal with the issue in a number of different ways. Traditionally, courts have imposed the doctrine of *caveat emptor* against buyers of goods or services. In other words, a buyer has the obligation to investigate the deal before he agrees to buy and any misunderstanding on his part will be assessed against him. On occasion, the same doctrine is levied against a seller who is not aware of the true worth of the thing she is selling—as for example, the person who inadvertently sells an original Rembrandt painting for $10 after finding the painting in the attic of her grandmother's house and after mistakenly concluding that the painting is nearly worthless when it is actually worth millions of dollars. Under traditional legal concepts, the seller would have had to live up to her bargain, however much money she lost in the transaction.

Recently, courts have been taking a harder and more sophisticated look at unilateral mistake; and on occasion reasoning as follows: (1) contracts imply a duty of good faith on the part of both parties, (2) there are instances in which one party was aware of the ambiguity and failed to disclose it to the other party or failed to take steps to reduce the harm that ensues because of the mistake, (3) accordingly, the burden should be levied against the party with the superior knowledge who could have corrected the mistake but did not. In the case of the mis-sized paper, a traditionally-minded court might simply invoke the doctrine of *caveat emptor* against the British buyer and enforce the contract as written. Thus, the buyer would have to pay for the paper and take on the additional burden of getting rid of the unwanted paper. The court's reasoning would be something to this effect: The buyer could have inquired or investigated further as to the size of the paper but did not. Therefore, he must live with his failure to inquire. By contrast, under some of the newer theories of unilateral mistake, if the British stationer had never before done business with a U.S. manufacturer and the manufacturer had frequently sold to British businesses, it might be established that the manufacturer knew full well of the crucial difference in paper size but failed to mention it to the buyer. In this case, the ambiguity might well be assessed against the manufacturer and the contract would be held not enforceable.

The doctrine of mistake illustrates the vital necessity of getting *all* the important facts straight before signing an agreement. It is particularly important when parties are dealing with each other over long distances and when differences in language or culture are likely to impede a full understanding on both sides. Perhaps more than any other concept under discussion, it shows the vital need for proper pre-contract planning.

§ 3.2.2 Performance

Performance is the centerpiece of any contract. By definition, it is the reason why the parties entered into the agreement in the first instance. In most international contracts of any size, performance is spelled out in considerable detail in the contract itself or in related documents. For example, a contract between an American manufacturer of communications devices and a Brazilian purchaser for the sale of cellular telephones will state the quantity, the price, the shipment dates, the quality of the goods (usually by way of spelling out the precise engineering and performance specifications for the telephones), any warranties that the seller is providing the buyer, the duration of the contract, and any special conditions that might attach to the bargain—as, for example, "this sale is contingent on buyer's obtaining permission to import the goods from the Brazilian government" or "this agreement will continue in effect so long as the Brazilian government permits the importation of U.S.-manufactured cellular telephones."

A large body of law, both judge-made and statutory, has helped develop the doctrine of performance and the related concept of *conditions* in virtually all major trading nations. It is difficult to generalize further on these points because performance in the context of a contract for the sale of goods is vastly different from performance in the context for the sale of a franchise, which in turn is different from the type of performance that one might expect in the context of a manufacturing joint venture.

Nonetheless, it may be helpful at this point to distinguish between *promises* and *conditions* and to introduce the concept of standard contract clauses, sometimes referred to as "conditions," that are imposed or recommended in a number of international transactions, such as international construction contracts. In the past, contracts written with the countries that made up the former Soviet bloc were almost always drafted on the basis of standard conditions. It is helpful to attempt some preliminary definitions. A *promise* in a contract is the obligation to which one or the other parties commits himself. For example, in a transaction involving the sale of a computer, the buyer will likely say: "I promise to pay you $100,000 for your Model 2001-A computer." The seller will state: "I promise to sell you my Model 2001-A computer for $100,000." These two promises are regarded by legal scholars as unconditional—that is, they are dependent on nothing other than themselves.

But it is rare for sophisticated commercial dealings to be this simple. Most business dealings are made contingent on a number of occurrences that must take place before the deal is finally consummated. For example, our computer buyer, being a typically cautious business executive, might say: "I promise to pay you $100,000 for your Model 2001-A computer if the computer passes a government-imposed quality test." The additional occurrence—that the device pass the test—is regarded as a condition to the agreement.[10] Stated a bit differently, the buyer's promise is now conditional rather than unconditional.

The possibilities for conditions may well be nearly infinite. The condition stated above presumably requires an affirmative act on the part of the seller: the Model 2001-A computer must be submitted to the appropriate government authority for testing, and the computer must pass that test. Of course, the buyer could probably protect his interest just as easily by stating the condition in negative: "I will pay you $100,000 for the Model 2001-A computer unless the computer fails the appropriate government inspection." The consequence of either type of condition is just about the same. If the computer does not pass muster with the government, the buyer has no obligation to purchase. In the parlance of contracts, her performance is thereby excused.

There is another way to look at conditions that fascinate professors of contract law. A condition may be stated so that it must occur before a party's obligation under the contract is triggered—a happening referred to as a condition *precedent*. The condition of the government inspection in our computer contract is a condition precedent. The buyer has no obligation to purchase until and unless the computer passes. By contrast, performance on a contract can be required *until* some event occurs. This is the idea of a condition *subsequent*. If the computer contract contained a provision that buyer would buy one computer each month for five years "unless the government withdraws its approval of the Model 2001-A computer" the contract would be viewed as containing a condition subsequent. The buyer's performance obligation continues until the government fails to approve the computer.

Reams of commentary have been written on these issues. It is usually only the smallest and briefest international contracts that do not contain both conditions precedent and conditions subsequent. For example, a contract's government approval clause is normally stated either as a condition

---

10. The discussion of basic concepts of conditions in Farnsworth, supra note 4, at 538-74 is especially lucid.

precedent ("I will buy if you get your government's permission to export the material.") or a condition subsequent ("I will continue to buy so long as your government grants export permission.") A government permission clause can be stated as both a condition precedent and a condition subsequent: "This contract goes into effect when the Kenyan government gives permission to import the goods and will continue in effect so long as the Kenyan government approves the import of the goods."

Because of the singular dangers involved in bicultural, bilingual international commercial transactions, a number of international bodies have developed standard provisions for contracts that are often referred to as "conditions" even though not every one of these standardized provisions would be regarded as a true condition by legal scholars. Many of these standardized terms and conditions are discussed further in Chapter Four; but for the purposes of this discussion a few illustrations will suffice. For example, the International Chamber of Commerce has developed a set of standardized provisions, known as *Incoterms,* that cover the terms and conditions of transportation of goods across international boundaries. These terms provide standardized definitions for such things as *FAS* (free along side ship) and *FOB* (free on board) and may be inserted into international contracts at the election of the parties.[11] The Federation Internationale des Ingenieurs-Conseils (FIDIC), an international body of construction engineers, has developed standard conditions for international construction contracts that contain standard definitions of such crucial terms as *employer* and *contractor.* The FIDIC has standard clauses on virtually all other matters of interest to contracting parties such as site inspection, insurance, payment and settlement of claims.[12]

Some governments and groups of governments have also developed sets of standard clauses and standard form contracts. The Economic Commission for Europe has published standard form contracts to try to more equitably balance the relative bargaining power of contracting parties.[13] In the former Soviet bloc, the now-defunct Council for Mutual Economic Assistance (referred to as CMEA or CEMA in most of Europe and more often as COMECON in the United States) promulgated mandatory standard conditions for incorporation into commercial contracts with the foreign trade organizations of any of these countries. Because a few socialist states remain in the world, international contract negotiators may continue to encounter the COMECON standard forms even if the organization itself no longer exists.[14]

---

11. Publication No. 350, International Chamber of Commerce (1990 edition).

12. FIDIC, Conditions of Contract (International) for Works of Civil Engineering Construction (3d ed. 1977).

13. See, e.g., G. DELAUME, TRANSNATIONAL CONTRACTS, part 5 (Booklet 2) at 4-5 (1983).

14. See generally, T. HOYA, EAST-WEST TRADE: COMECON LAW AND AMERICAN-SOVIET TRADE (1984). As the second edition of this book goes to press, North Korea and Cuba retain their

Whether parties use standard clauses or draft tailor-made provisions for their contract, the terms and conditions of performance will be set out in the various documents underlying the agreement and the vast majority of transactions are fully performed without incident. Many contracts are written with sufficient clarity and foresight that no problems of performance ever arise. The difficult cases are those in which one party seeks to be excused from performance for various reasons or in which one party simply refuses to perform. These problems are best discussed under the next heading, breach of contract and excuse.

§ 3.2.3 Breach of contract and excused performance

Breach and excused performance are directly related to the normal expectation of full performance that underlies every contract. These two components of our analysis are evaluated in terms of the express language of the contract and the law that governs the contract. Obviously, if full performance has occurred there is usually no further issue that can arise under the contract. So, for example, if a contract calls for the purchase of 100 facsimile machines at $300 per unit, the contract is concluded when the machines are delivered, determined to be satisfactory under the terms of the contract, and final payment is made. Any further dealings between the parties will normally spring from a new contract. Similarly, if a contract calls for the sale of "100 compact disc players per month so long as the buyer's government permits the sale of compact disc players, or for five years, whichever period is longer" the contact is concluded when the buyer's government makes the prohibition effective or at the end of the fifth year of the contract. If either of these acts occurs (denial of government permission or the expiration of the five year period) the contract is concluded without any breach. Put another way, the manner in which performance is described in the contract frequently is used as the primary factor determining whether breach has occurred.

However, when a party does not perform all the terms of the contract, that party will probably be deemed to be in *breach* of the contract. If the parties cannot work out their differences on their own through renegotiation or some form of mediation, they will probably take the dispute before a court or arbitrator. In those instances, the party allegedly in breach may respond by disclaiming any breach or by arguing that his performance is excused for some reason. Much less frequently, one party to a contract who seeks to be excused from performance will go before a court or arbitrator for what amounts to a declaration that further performance is not required. In either case, some decisional authority must determine whether the contract should

---

(Note 14 continued) socialist systems, so COMECON-style conditions are likely to be utilized by those countries when they attempt to contract with non-socialist entities.

be performed as written, whether the contract should in some fashion be modified (the civil code term for certain types of modification is *revision*), or whether performance should be excused entirely.

The difficult issues arise when one of the parties performs almost all of the agreement but for some reason refuses to or cannot perform the remainder of the agreement; or when performance is prevented or diminished because of some external event such as a strike or a war. On these points, it is important not to forget the doctrine of party autonomy. Most of the time, the parties can spell out the consequences of these occurrences in the contract itself, and that language will normally be honored by a court or arbitrator. If the contract is not clear on these occurrences, quite often the applicable law will provide some answers.

Assume, for example, that a contract calls for the shipment of 1200 telescopes over a one-year period with 100 telescopes shipped each month. The seller ships 1100 telescopes in the first eleven months of the contract, ships 50 telescopes in the twelfth month and refuses or is somehow unable to ship any more. Assume further that the contract calls for payment in full at the end of the twelfth month, rather than for installment payments. Would it be possible for the buyer to keep the 1150 telescopes and refuse to pay for any of the telescopes because of the seller's breach—that is, because the seller refused to deliver the last 50 telescopes?

In most legal systems, the answer is "no." As a matter of common sense, the law recognizes what the Anglo-American system calls *substantial performance* and would probably require at least payment for the goods actually received unless it was absolutely clear from the circumstances that the goods were totally useless unless all 1200 were shipped and received and that both parties understood this at the inception of the contract. Even then the court might order the telescopes returned to the seller, even if the buyer's obligation to pay is forgiven and even if the buyer might be compensated for the consequences of the seller's breach. The reason for this is that virtually all systems of contract law forbid unjust enrichment on the part of one or the other parties. The buyer's keeping the 1150 telescopes and paying nothing whatsoever is clearly an instance of unjust enrichment.

Under U.S. contract law, the doctrine of substantial performance is not simply a matter of mechanics. Courts almost never establish a specific fixed level of performance, say, 60 percent, that is always deemed to be substantial performance. Each case is examined on its facts and a determination of substantial performance is measured in terms of many factors—such as the hardship on the parties, the willfulness or negligence involved in the failure to perform, and the benefit that accrues to the injured party from the performance actually accomplished.[15] But once again, this is a situation in which

---

15. Restatement Contracts § 275.

the parties can take care of any problem by contract language. If the buyer absolutely insists on all 1200 telescopes, the contract can be written to include language such as: "payment under this contract is due if and only if the seller delivers all 1200 telescopes in good condition within the twelve month period." Of course, even with this kind of provision, if a court or arbitrator were to determine that the 1150 telescopes in the hands of the buyer had some intrinsic worth, it is doubtful that the buyer would be permitted to keep them while still paying nothing. At the very least, the buyer would probably be instructed to ship the telescopes back to the seller at the seller's expense. Most courts and arbitrators try to do justice to both parties in this kind of situation.

Parties frequently seek to be excused from all or part of their performance when performance becomes difficult or impossible. More often than not, the idea of impossibility of performance or frustration of the contract's purposes is addressed in the contract through specific clauses (such as "Seller will ship the computers so long as the Nigerian government approves the shipments") or through a general *force majeure* clause that excuses performance on the part of either of the parties because of, for example, acts of God, war, insurrection and other unforeseen events. While some courts and legal scholars have sought to distinguish sharply between impossibility and frustration, for the purposes of this discussion, they will be regarded as synonyms. Moreover, although many legal systems have different names for excused performance, the concepts themselves are viewed similarly, if not identically, by virtually all systems. For purposes of convenience and efficiency, the following discussion will consider excuse in terms of U.S. contract law.[16]

The United States legal system recognizes a number of instances in which contract performance will be forgiven. For example, the UCC permits a buyer to reject goods that on inspection after delivery do not conform to the specifications in the contract.[17] When a contract calls for the sale of specific, non-fungible goods and those goods are destroyed through no fault of the buyer or seller before the risk of loss passes to the buyer, the buyer's performance will be forgiven.[18] Contract law in the United States also excuses all or

---

16. For a discussion of excuse in other systems see, e.g., Rapsomanikis, *Frustration of Contract in International Trade Law and Comparative Law*, 18 Duq.L.Rev. 551 (1980) and Smit, *Frustration of Contract: A Comparative Attempt at Consolidation*, 58 Colum.L.Rev. 287 (1958); Note, *Some Aspects of Frustrated Performance of Contracts Under Middle Eastern Law*, 33 Int'l & Comp. L.Q. 1046 (1984). For comments on the CISG see Nicholas, *Force Majeure and Frustration*, 27 Am.J.Comp.L. 231 (1979). For a comparative note, see Marcantonio, *Unifying the Law of Impossibility*, 8 Hastings Int'l & Comp. L.Rev. 41 (1984). For an excellent article containing a very sophisticated discussion of many of these issues see Puelinckx, *Frustration, Hardship, Force Majeure, Imprévision, Wegfall der Geschäftsgrundlage, Unmöglichkeit, Changed Circumstances: A Comparative Study in English, French, German and Japanese Law*, 1 J.Int'l Arb. 47 (1986).

17. UCC § 2-601.

18. UCC § 2-613.

part of the performance when the contract is *impossible* to perform or when the purposes of the contract become *frustrated* even when a force majeure clause is not in the contract.

To evaluate an argument that the contract has become impossible to perform, American courts generally apply what is referred to as the *objective* standard of review. In other words, the court must determine not merely that the party to the contract could not perform, but that *no* person, faced with the same problems, could have performed the agreement.

There are two types of impossibility, impossibility because of supervening illegality and impossibility because the subject matter of the contract has been destroyed. A supervening illegality is a change in the law that makes performance unlawful. For example, assume that a U.S. furrier and an African seller enter into a ten year contract for the sale of the hides of the white rhinoceros at a time when it is perfectly legal to ship those hides into the United States. Eight years after the contract is signed, the U.S. government puts the white rhinoceros on its list of endangered species (thus making it illegal to import the hides into the U.S.). The hide contract will be deemed impossible to perform because of a *supervening illegality*. Any further obligation to perform on the part of the African shipper will be forgiven, and the parties will simply go their own way.

If a British construction firm promises to build a hotel on an island in the Pacific Ocean and the entire island is destroyed or rendered totally and permanently uninhabitable by a typhoon, the *subject matter* of the contract has been destroyed and performance made impossible. In this instance, both U.S. and British courts would excuse performance.

Except in the context of the sale of goods under the UCC (which forgives performance in certain instances of mere *impracticability*, rather than impossibility), U.S. and British courts generally require two things to be present before performance will be excused: (1) the event must be unforeseeable, and (2) performance must be physically or legally impossible in an absolute sense. Moreover, if performance is only temporarily inhibited (e.g., the island could be restored to human habitation or hides that are in transit will be permitted to enter the U.S.) the parties must generally perform to the extent that they are capable of performing.

By comparison, commercial impracticability under § 2-615 of the UCC, while not contemplating mere inconvenience, may forgive performance even for certain substantial increases in the costs of performance when "the rise in cost is due to some unforeseen contingency which alters the essential nature of the performance."[19] But readers should not interpret this provision

---

19. Official Comment Number 4 to UCC § 2-615. For further reading on commercial impracticability under the UCC see Speidel, *Excusable Non-Performance in Sales Contracts: Some Thoughts About Risk Management*, 32 S.C.L.Rev. 241 (1980).

too expansively. The official comments to § 2-615 make clear that the section is to be applied only to cases in which the inhibiting event could not reasonably be foreseen at the time of contracting; and most importantly, the UCC provides that the contracting parties can bind themselves to a different standard of behavior by express language in the contract.[20]

There are other interpretative questions associated with the doctrine of excuse of performance. The specific language of the force majeure clause may cause problems. For example, some courts have had trouble excusing performance because of, say, labor strife if the contract's force majeure clause contains only those events that are naturally occurring—flood, typhoon, earthquake, and so forth. By contrast, as is discussed in Chapter 2, German courts between World War One and World War Two occasionally forgave performance because of the rampant inflation that occurred under the Weimar Republic. The courts determined that inflation of such drastic proportions was unforeseeable by the parties. For these reasons, parties who may have some worries about their ability to perform may try to negotiate very lengthy force majeure clauses containing all sorts of excuses for performance. Of course, the other side will likely insist on the narrowest possible force majeure for the same reasons. Contract drafters should always keep in mind the basic rule: a contract requires performance; excuses are rarely accepted.

§ 3.2.4 Remedy

What happens when a party is in breach of contract and the breach is not forgiven? All legal systems have developed rules for compensating the person who suffers because of the breach. In the Anglo-American system, the basic rule of compensation, frequently referred to as the principle of *compensatory* damages, is that the injured party should be placed in the same position he would have been in had the contract been fully performed.[21] Normally, this means that the injured party will be given monetary compensation.

In most instances, money damages will include the additional expenses the injured party incurred to restore his position, known as *incidental* and *consequential* damages, to the extent that those expenses are reasonable and foreseeable.[22] To illustrate, the buyer who received 1150 of 1200 telescopes

---

20. Official Comment Number 8 to § 2-615.

21. See, e.g., Farnsworth, supra note 4, at 811-16. For a discussion of remedies under the CISG see Herber, *The Rules of the Convention Relating to the Buyer's Remedies in Cases of Breach of Contract*, 7 Digest of Commercial Laws 104 (1980).

22. Readers of this book who reside outside the United States may find some of the new U.S. thinking on the economic consequences of contract damage awards fascinating. One of the principal words is the fourth chapter of Professor (now Judge) Richard Posner's ECONOMIC ANALYSIS OF THE LAW (2d ed. 1977). See also Barton, *The Economic Basis of Damages for Breach of Contract*, 1 J.Legal Stud. 277 (1972); Birmingham, *Breach of Contract, Damage Measures, and Economic Efficiency*, 24 Rutgers L. Rev. 273 (1970).

would be permitted to pay for only 1150 telescopes. In certain circumstances, the seller would have to compensate the buyer for his expenses in seeking out and purchasing the remaining 50 telescopes from some other manufacturer.

But at the same time, the law seeks to give both parties the benefit of their bargain. In the 1150 telescope case, a court or arbitrator would likely not find the 50 telescope shortage a substantial breach of the contract, absent unusual circumstances, and thus would require the buyer to compensate the seller for the value to him of the 1150 telescopes received. When evaluating damage claims courts are always concerned about avoiding situations that result in unjust enrichment for one party or the other.

Moreover, courts normally require a party who is injured to take reasonable steps to reduce his injury. This doctrine, normally referred to as the requirement of *mitigation*, prohibits a court from awarding damages to a party if he simply sat back and did nothing while the injury continued to accrue. In this regard, consider a slight change in the facts of the 1150 telescope case. Assume that the 1200 telescopes obtained from the seller will be used by the buyer to complete a separate contract that the buyer formed with the AAA School for Astronomers. The second contract is to be completed by July 1, 1992 or buyer is liable for a penalty of $1000 per day for each day after July 1 that the contract is unfulfilled. Further assume that buyer could readily obtain the additional 50 telescopes from another company with only two days lost time on the second contract. Instead, buyer sits around for 10 additional days doing nothing to purchase the last 50 telescopes, thus performing the second contract 12 days late. Under the contract between buyer and AAA School of Astronomy, buyer will be assessed a $12,000 penalty. Assume finally that seller was notified and fully aware of the existence of the second contract and the importance of the 1200 telescopes to the second contract. This knowledge on the part of the original seller arguably makes the penalty suffered by buyer a matter of incidental or consequential damages.

However, the doctrine of mitigation applies here. If buyer were to seek to recover the full $12,000 from seller because of seller's failure to ship all 1200 telescopes, his claim would almost surely be denied. Under the principle of mitigation a court or arbitrator is very unlikely to give B any more than two days lost time compensation ($2000) since she delayed ordering the replacement widgets for ten days for no good reason. By contrast, the two day delay was directly attributable to the fault of the seller and the seller knew about the related School of Astronomy contract and the penalties, in that contract, that would be incurred for late performance. The two day penalty would probably be held to be foreseeable by the seller and to the extent that the $1000 per day penalty clause was seen as reasonable, the court or arbitrator would likely award $2000 to the buyer as part of her incidental and consequential damages.

Occasionally, parties will be seriously injured through some type of willful and malicious conduct on the part of the other party and will ask a court for *punitive* or *exemplary* damages. While not totally unheard of in cases of breach of contract, this type of damage award is rare, particularly in the context of an international commercial agreement. Indeed, the CISG does not mention exemplary damages, although it is arguable that the Convention's silence does not exclude them. Moreover, there are instances in the United States in which punitive damages have been awarded even by arbitrators for particularly egregious breaches of contract.[23]

Many contracts are silent on the issue of damages. But some contracts try to anticipate the consequences of a breach by providing a specific formula for computing damages or by establishing a specific figure (known as a *liquidated damages* clause) that both parties agree at the outset is proper compensation for breach. Most courts and arbitrators in both common law and civil systems will honor a formula for a liquidated damages clause so long as the amount is not excessive or seen to be a penalty and so long as it bears some reasonable relation to the injuries actually suffered.[24]

There are occasions when the subject matter of a contract is so unique that mere monetary damages are not sufficient to compensate the injured party. For example, in the case of real estate transactions, a contract to purchase a particular plot of land on which the buyer expects to erect a hotel can not normally satisfied by giving the buyer money. A buyer who needs and contracts for unique goods that can be manufactured only by one company can not be properly compensated except by receiving these unique goods. Injured parties involved in agreements involving this kind of product often seek the remedy known as *specific performance* by which a court orders the other party to perform the contract as written, no matter what the inconvenience or expense might be to the party in breach.

§ 3.2.5 Dispute resolution

Virtually all international commercial agreements contain some type of dispute resolution clause. The clause can call for arbitration, for litigation in a particular country's judicial system, or for some less-drastic resolution procedure such as mandatory renegotiation or mediation. The pros and cons of each of these procedures is discussed at length in section 3.4. For the purposes of this section, it is sufficient to understand that the parties will gener-

---

23. See, e.g., Jones, *Punitive Damages in Arbitration in the USA*, 14 Int'l Bus. Law. 188 (June, 1986); Sullivan, *Punitive Damages in the Law of Contract: The Reality and the Illusion of Legal Change*, 61 Minn.L.Rev. 207 (1977).
24. See, e.g., Farnsworth, supra note 4 at 895-904; UCC § 2-718(1).

ally be expected to adhere to the dispute resolution device or devices specifically set out in the contract. In many instances, the parties may be compelled to engage in the selected procedure even if one party has changed its
mind since the contract was drafted.

§ 3.3 The Different Forms of International Commercial Agreement

The contract principles and concepts discussed in section 3.2 are generally
applicable to virtually any type of commercial agreement even though most
of the examples used were drawn from agreements involving the sale of
goods—still the most prevalent form of international commercial transaction.
But the sale of goods is not the only form of agreement that exists at the
international level. Particularly over the past few years, many private parties
and government agencies have executed contracts for franchises, for joint
ventures, for the transfer of technology in the form of licensing agreements,
and for the sale of services.

Each of these forms of agreement is designed to accomplish a specific
goal and each has its own complications and intricacies. In understanding
the general nature of each form the reader will go a long way towards understanding the entire gamut of international commercial agreements. The different forms will be addressed in the following order: contract for the sale of
goods or services, agency and distributorship, franchise, licensing, and joint
venture.

§ 3.3.1 Sales of goods or services

[a] The sale of goods generally

The sale of goods is one of the most common international commercial
transactions and has been extensively discussed in previous portions of this
chapter. By definition, it is the sale of some tangible object for a specified
price. Most principles of law that address the definition of a good tend to
define it as a residual concept. For example, the CISG defines the sale of
goods as being sales of something other than, among other things: ships,
aircraft and hovercraft, goods bought for family or personal use, or goods
bought at auction.[25] The UCC defines goods as "all things ... which are movable at the time of identification to the contract ... "[26] Problems related to
payment for the sale of goods and peripheral issues such as dumping and
countervailing duty problems and antitrust issues are discussed below.

---

25. CISG, Article 2.
26. UCC § 2-105(1).

[b] Barter and countertrade

There are other commercial transactions, generally referred to as *barter* and *countertrade* that are becoming more frequent and that resemble the sale of goods in that the primary goal of each transaction is to obtain a particular good. The exchange of another good is simply used as a payment substitute—that is, another good is provided by the buyer in lieu of a monetary payment. While the international trading community has not completely resolved these terms as words of art some attempt at defining each term is helpful. As used by many lawyers and business executives *countertrade* is a set of at least two separate buy and sell agreements negotiated between the same two parties, both of which agreements must be performed to satisfy the entire obligation.[27] Put a little more colloquially, it is a situation in which A says to B (both companies in the hospital supply business, "I will buy your test tubes if you agree simultaneously to buy my surgical gloves." While each contract theoretically can stand on its own two feet, both parties enter into the agreement only on the expectation that *both* agreements will be fully performed.

Barter is a concept related to countertrade and is often defined in its traditional sense as an exchange of one thing for another, with each thing serving as payment for the other. In other words, "I will give you 10,000 test tubes if you give me 20,000 surgical gloves." Or, as Boeing agreed recently: "We will give you X number of airplanes if you, Saudi Arabia, will give us X barrels of oil." Barter serves virtually the same purposes as countertrade by preserving scarce hard currency and enhancing export volumes and market penetration. Much like countertrade, it is really just a substitute for the payment of money. The bartered goods, by definition, constitute payment for each other.

The United Nations Commission on International Trade Law (UNCITRAL) has proffered a somewhat more cumbersome definition: "A countertrade transaction ... is an economic transaction in which one party supplies, or procures the supply of, goods or other economic value to the second party and in return, the first party agrees to purchase or procures to be purchased from the second party, or from a party designated by the second party, goods or other economic value, so as to achieve an agreed ratio between the reciprocal performances."[28] Under the UNCITRAL definition, barter (described below) is a subset of countertrade. Under the UNCITRAL definition, parties

---

27. See, e.g., Lochner, *Countertrade and International Barter*, 19 Int'l Law. 725 (1985); Schmitthoff, *Countertrade*, J.Bus.L. 115 (Mar.1985) and McVey, *Countertrade: Commercial Practices, Legal Issues and Policy Dilemmas*, 16 Law & Policy Int'l Bus. 1 (1984). Two good book-length works on countertrade are P. VERZARIU, COUNTERTRADE, BARTER & OFFSETS (1985) and L.G.B. WELT, TRADE WITHOUT MONEY: BARTER & COUNTERTRADE (1984). Sometime in late 1992 or 1993 UNCITRAL intends to promulgate standard clauses for countertrade agreements.

28. UNCITRAL, Preliminary Study of Legal Issues in International Countertrade (1988).

can engage in either a bilateral arrangement (A ships computers to B B ships telescopes to A) or the transaction can be multi-legged: A ships computers to B, B ships telescopes to C, C ships running shoes to A. It is at least theoretically possible for the transaction to have even more than three components; but as the following discussion shows, each new actor in the transaction simply compounds the difficulty of putting together a fully-satisfactory agreement. Recall that the economic rational of barter and countertrade is that each of the goods constitutes payment for the other.

Barter and countertrade transactions are popular in countries that have limited hard currency resources because an exchange of goods dispenses with the need to expend hard currency to obtain those products. These transactions are also viewed as devices to assist fledgling businesses in one country to penetrate the markets of more developed countries without huge expenditures of funds for such things as agents and advertising. While barter and countertrade are innovative — and frequently beneficial devices to do business — they do not really affect or require the alteration of basic principles of contract law. The exchange transaction is in reality merely a substitute for the payment of money for goods.

There are a number of pitfalls that business executives may encounter in setting up barter or countertrade transactions. First, a proper comparative valuation of both products is vitally important to the deal. In other words, the parties must each have a solid understanding of how many pairs of surgical gloves equal how many test tubes in the example set out above. If either party makes an inappropriate valuation of either her product or the product offered by the other side, the economic value of the deal is placed in jeopardy. Second, most barter and countertrade transactions need to be performed almost simultaneously, otherwise the party who receives the goods late winds up giving what amounts to an interest-free loan to the other side. Consider the following example, X agrees to ship Y 100 computers in exchange for 300 telescopes. The standard assumption in a barter transaction is that X need not be paid in cash because he can sell the telescopes in his own market for an amount of money that results in a profit from his shipping the computers to Y. If X ships the computers on day 1 and Y receives them on day 10, Y can put the computers immediately to use or re-sell them. If Y delays the shipment of the telescopes, X will not have the use of the telescopes or be able to re-sell them, but having shipped the computers is obligated to pay for those computers. Over the time that X has shipped the computers but has not received the telescopes, he is in essence subsidizing the transaction in favor of Y. A barter contract can incorporate language that alleviates this problem. It could, for example, contain a clause that assesses some kind of penalty against Y (or against X if he is the delaying party) for every day that one shipment of goods is delayed after the other side receives its goods. However, because of the inherent nature of barter, many barter agreements are oral undertakings conducted over the telephone with perhaps a few documents transmitted by telex or facsimile machine. Getting both sets of goods shipped at about the same time is usually a primary consideration in barter and countertrade.

A third factor to consider is the issue of quality control. Recall that the essence of a barter arrangement is the notion that a certain number of computers is equal to a certain number of telescopes. That valuation presumes that both the computers and the telescopes are manufactured and perform up to certain standards. If, upon receipt, one of the sets of products proves to be defective, the receiving party is stuck with either suing his counterpart for breach of contract or having to take steps—frequently costly steps—to bring those products up to a appropriate quality standard for resale. For all of these reasons, the reader should be aware that barter and countertrade have their own special problems and pitfalls. Many lawyers and business executives avoid such transactions completely. They are not normally preferred transactions for persons new to international commercial agreements.[29]

[c] The sale of services

The sale of services across national borders is becoming increasingly common. The traditional service contract was a contract for engineering and construction services, or in many instances, a mixed service and goods construction contract that constitutes a "turnkey" arrangement (by which an entire facility such as an electric power plant is built and placed in operation by a foreign company and the key to the project turned over to the host government or the purchasing company).[30] These days contracts for the sale of services can run the gamut from financial and data processing services to employment services to expert consulting services. Countries that participate in the General Agreement on Tariffs and Trade (GATT) are now beginning to negotiate free-trade provisions governing the sale of services.[31] The United States-Canada Free Trade Agreement contains some innovative provisions on the sale of services between those two countries.[32]

---

29. For a much longer discussion of all these issues see the three articles: Montague, *An Introduction to Countertrade*; van Dort, *Some Conceptual Problems of Countertrade*; and del Campo Wilson, *Advantage and Disadvantage of Countertrade: The Argentine View, as an Importing Country*, at 17 Int'l Bus. Law. 360-72 (Sep.1989). See also, Guyot, *Countertrade Contracts in International Business*, 20 Int'l Law. 921 (1986).

30. For a good commentary on some of the issues involved in turnkey projects see Frilet, *Price and Terms of Payment in Large International Turnkey Contracts*, 18 Int'l.Bus.Law. 362 (Sep.1990).

31. See, e.g., Lazar, *Services and the GATT: US Motives and a Blueprint for Negotiations*, 22 J.World.Trade L. 135 (1989); Kakbadse, *Trade in Services and the Uruguay Round*, 19 Ga. J.Int'l & Comp.L. 384 (1989).

32. See, e.g., Tuomi, *The Canada-U.S. Free Trade Agreement: implications for the Bilateral Trade Balance*, 13 Maryland J. Int'l L. & Trade 105 (1988).

Construction and engineering services contracts are so common around the world that they frequently incorporate standard provisions and clauses (discussed more extensively in Chapter 4) developed by the International Federation of Consulting Engineers and by the European Development Fund. More recently, the United Nations has promulgated a comprehensive set of construction contract provisions, entitled *Legal Guide on Drawing Up International Contracts for the Construction of Industrial Works*.[33] While focusing on the construction of factories and other similar construction projects, many lawyers who have read through the Legal Guide believe it is helpful for virtually any kind of construction project. The Legal Guide identifies a number of elements that are normally contained in a construction contract: description of the work, guarantees, technology transfer, pricing, payment, scheduling, role of the consulting engineer,[34] subcontracting, inspection, completion, acceptance, risk of loss, security (including guarantees of performance by the contractor and guarantees of payment by the purchaser), delays, damages (including liquidated damages), excusability, changes, suspensions, terminations, post-construction obligations (such as the provision on training programs and spare parts), choice of law and dispute resolution. Large-scale construction contracts are usually massive documents with exceptionally detailed contract provisions. They are not matters that are usually put into the hands of beginners.

One type of service contract increasingly popular in developing countries is the management contract—an agreement by which a host country can take advantage of foreign expertise without giving over valuable natural resources, as it might have to in the context of a conventional concession agreement.[35] A company involved in the purchase of a management contract is in essence buying expertise which is to be applied to some activity in the purchaser's operation. A management contract can be, for example, an agreement to operate a country's data processing services or to operate a system of cellular telephones.

It is not uncommon for a management contract to be coupled with a long-term licensing agreement. The management contract insures that the process subject to the license will be performed properly from the beginning by persons who know what they are doing while permitting nationals in the host country to be trained to eventually perform the operation themselves.

---

33. UNCITRAL, Legal Guide on Drawing Up International Contracts for the Construction of Industrial Works (1988).

34. For additional commentary on the crucial functions performed by the engineer see Hochuli, *Role of the Engineer Under FIDIC Standard Contracts*, 19 Int'l Bus. Law. 542 (Dec.1991).

35. See, e.g., N. BEREDJICK & T. WALDE (eds.), PETROLEUM INVESTMENT POLICIES IN DEVELOPING COUNTRIES (1988); Westring, *Construction and Management Contracts* in THE TRANSNATIONAL LAW OF INTERNATIONAL COMMERCIAL TRANSACTIONS at 184-90 (N.Horn & C.M. Schmitthoff eds. 1982).

Since a portion of the funds flowing from a management contract will be expended in the host country for the support and well-being of the management personnel in the form of salaries and living expenses, the host country gets to keep more of its money in-country than might otherwise be the case.

§ 3.3.2 Agency and Distributorship Agreements

These arrangements are common on the international level and are usually associated with contracts for the sale of goods or services. Companies that wish to sell goods abroad have a number of ways to get the goods into the hands of the ultimate purchasers. The company may establish a branch office or a foreign subsidiary under the rules and regulations pertaining to the organization and registration of subsidiaries in the target country. The company's goods may then be marketed through the subsidiary. This is often a risky operation since the capital investment and the expenses associated with starting up and maintaining the business can be considerable without any guarantee that the product will catch on among the target country's consumers. Moreover, many countries establish significant regulatory barriers to this type of undertaking.

A company that wishes to explore the possibilities of marketing a good or service in a foreign country without the need to commit huge amounts of money to the undertaking may decide to appoint an agent in that country or to contract with a company in the host nation to serve as a distributorship for the company's products. A distributorship is distinguished from an agency agreement mainly by the method of compensation for the distributor or agent.

An *agent* brings the product of the seller to the attention of potential purchasers by contacting potential customers, showing and demonstrating samples of the products and soliciting orders. However, the actual sales contract is executed directly between the seller and the purchaser. An agent is normally compensated for his efforts on a percentage commission for products actually sold. Often, the agent does not even see the product change hands and works on the basis of samples, models and printed specifications. The actual goods are shipped by the seller directly to the purchaser.

A distributorship, by contrast, is a commercial arrangement by which the *distributor* undertakes to sell the foreign company's product in the target country and takes as remuneration a profit on the goods sold, bearing virtually all the risks for obtaining products, selling those products and receiving payment from the ultimate purchasers. In this instance, the sales contract is between the distributor and the purchaser.

In virtually every country there are principles of law specially developed for the agent-principal relationship. For example, in the Anglo-American system, agents are regarded as fiduciaries of their principals, owing them duties such as the duty of loyalty (an agent may not work for a competitor under most circumstances) and the duty of full disclosure (an agent is not supposed to keep secrets from his principal). Because there is a perception in many countries that in-country agents have not been treated properly by their foreign principles, many countries have enacted laws that give certain protections to in-country agents from arbitrary or unreasonable termination by foreign principles.[36] Distributorships, by contrast, are more of an arms-length transaction that are normally dealt with by the application of conventional rules of contract law.

Agency and distributorship agreements are generally entered into as risk-avoidance devices because the distributor buys the product from the manufacturer and bears the risk of selling the product in the host country. In many countries, such as the United States, foreign distributorships are an attractive way of doing business because of favorable tax treatment of the relationship afforded by one or another of the countries involved.

Distributorship arrangements are not totally free of risks and problems. These arrangements sometimes trigger antitrust problems at home and abroad. Some countries have established regulations on the arbitrary termination of distributorship contracts.[37] Virtually every country in which agents and distributorships are permissible also have tight controls on registration of the arrangement and require detailed and continuous reporting of the activities of the undertaking.[38] Still, even with all the pitfalls and strictures on formation and operation, agency and distributorship agreements remain a popular form of transnational business relationship.

§ 3.3.3 Franchises

In scope and concept, a franchise agreement falls somewhere between a distributorship and a licensing agreement.[39] It is a comparatively new and quintessentially U.S. form of doing international business. The relationship itself

---

36. See, e.g., Sperling, *Termination Under Dutch Law of Agency Agreements*, 18 Int'l Bus.Law. 462 (Nov.1990); Dobson & Gaudenzi, *Agency and Distributorship Laws in Italy*, 20 Int'l Law. 997 (1986).

37. See, e.g., Korah, *Group Exemptions for Exclusive Distribution and Purchasing in the EEC*, 21 Common Market L.Rev. 53 (1984); Jones, *Practical Aspects of Commercial Agency and Distribution Agreements in the European Community*, 6 Int'l Law. 107 (1972).

38. King, *Legal Aspects of Appointment and Termination of Foreign Distributors and Representatives*, 17 Case W.Res. J. Int'l L. 91 (1985). For a continental viewpoint see Toepke, *EEC Law of Competition: Distribution Agreements and Their Notification*, 19 Int'l Law. 117 (1985); Burkard, *Termination Compensation to Distributors Under German Law*, 7 Int'l Law. 185 (1973).

39. For an excellent and thorough discussion of many franchising issues see A. KONIGS-BERG, INTERNATIONAL FRANCHISING (1991).

is fairly simple and is best described in terms of a hypothetical. Assume that XYZ Corporation has designed a new fast food hamburger that has entranced the U.S. public. After massive advertising and exceptionally successful market penetration, consumers in the United States now flock to buy XYZ Burgers. Successes such as these make XYZ want to expand its operation as quickly as possible. The corporation has essentially two options in expanding its hamburger market. It can finance, build and operate retail outlets wherever it chooses to do business; or it can sell franchises.

Within the United States, creating company-owned facilities in different states is not a difficult undertaking. The U.S. Constitution permits businesses to cross state lines to establish new enterprises. There are relatively few legal impediments to starting a business in New York and eventually opening company-owned outlets in California and Florida. However, the business considerations and the financial consequences may not make sense. Huge numbers of company-owned outlets will require a large capital outlay, possibly greater than the corporation's ability to raise capital funds. The current tax climate may militate against large numbers of company-owned outlets; or the corporation's business strategy may warrant trying to displace some of the risk of starting up large numbers of company-owned outlets in untested markets.

XYZ (the *franchisor*) may prefer to sell franchises by which a private individual (the *franchisee*) obtains permission to use the XYZ trade name and its proprietary processes so long as these individuals hold themselves out as XYZ Burger outlets, follow company-dictated procedures and practices, and pay the company a percentage royalty for the right to use the XYZ logo. The franchisee usually contributes a substantial sum of money as part of his personal investment and is often required to spend time at the XYZ headquarters receiving training in XYZ methods of business. In the United States, one of the premier hamburger franchises, McDonald's, requires that new franchisees attend "hamburger college" before operating a new franchise.

Benefits to both franchisor and franchisee are considerable. The franchisor expands its operations faster and wider with far less capital investment and with far less risk than would be the case if it set up wholly-owned outlets. The franchisee derives enormous marketing benefits from the nationwide or worldwide reputation and advertising efforts of the franchisor. The royalties paid by the franchisee pays for the use of the franchisor's name and good will. Royalties are sometimes stated as a percentage of gross revenues rather than profits. Thus, the franchisor gets paid whether or not the franchisee makes a profit.

Franchises have become an enormously popular method of doing business in the United States, particularly in the services industries. The most

popular franchises in the United States, such as McDonald's, are now exceptionally difficult to obtain, but once obtained are usually gold mines for both
parties.

As might be expected, there have been abuses associated with the franchise process. Government agencies in the United States have noticed that
there is a considerable disparity in the bargaining power between franchisee
and franchisor. The franchisor almost always dictates the precise extent and
nature of the agreement, normally proffering a standard form contract that
the franchisee must sign. These standardized agreements are weighed heavily in favor of the franchisor, especially in the areas of amount of royalties,
strictures on operating arrangements and grounds for termination. In a
number of countries, including the United States, this imbalance has led to
government-imposed constraints on the entire franchising process.[40] Other
locations, such as Hong Kong, are relatively free-wheeling and non-inhibitory
when franchises are concerned so long as royalty outflow is not excessive.[41]

The European Community now appears to be interested in strong, yet
realistic regulation of franchise relationships.[42] In 1986, the European Court
of Justice issued an opinion, now generally referred to as the *Pronuptia*
case,[43] that held squarely that franchise relationships were subject to the
European Community's competition laws. Prompted by the Pronuptia decision, the European Commission in Brussels issued E.C. Guidelines on franchises to conform franchise regulation with the E.C.'s competition policies.
These guidelines are too lengthy to restate here, but briefly summarized,
they permit a franchisor to safeguard know how and other trade secrets in
the franchise relationship, permit termination of the franchise relationship
on a number of grounds yet prohibit price-fixing and certain types of market
sharing arrangements.[44]

As popular as they are in the United States, franchise agreements are
not uniformly admired elsewhere in the world. Some countries faced with
what appears to be an increasingly Americanized retail business sector

---

40. The United States Congress investigated the franchise practices of major American oil
companies and decided to impose severe restrictions on the ability of an oil company to terminate
a retail gasoline franchise through the Petroleum Marketing Practices Act, 15 U.S.C. §§ 2801-14
(PMPA). The United States Federal Trade Commission has developed regulations which attempt to
equalize imbalances in bargaining power in franchises outside the oil industry. See, e.g., 16 C.F.R.
Part 436. For a discussion of the PMPA see W.FOX, FEDERAL REGULATION OF ENERGY at 364-
84 (1983 w/annual supplement).

41. See, e.g., Woods, *Franchising in Hong Kong*, 1985 Int'l Bus. Law. 440.

42. van Empel, *Franchising and Strict Liability in the EEC*, 18 Int'l Bus.Law. 169 (Apr.1990).
Symposium, *Franchising in Europe, 1987*, 16 Int'l Bus.Law. 117 (Mar.1988); Goebel, *The Uneasy
Fate of Franchising Under EEC Antitrust Laws*, 10 Eur.L.Rev. 87 (1985).

43. Pronuptia de Paris GmbH v. Pronuptia de Paris Irmgard Schillgallis, reported in 1
Common Market L.Rev. 414 (1986).

44. See, e.g., Schmitz & Van Hamme, *Franchising in Europe—The First Practical EEC
Guidelines*, 22 Int'l Law. 717 (1988).

object to franchises on cultural and social grounds as well as on economic grounds.

Franchises create additional concerns for developing countries because the payment of royalties causes a hard currency outflow. As a consequence, franchising on an international level has developed much more slowly than it has in the United States, although it appears to be of growing interest in virtually every area of the world.

There are any number of ways that an international franchise may be established and administered. It can be a joint venture between the foreign franchisor and a host-country business entity. The franchise may be administered at long-distance from the parent company's location in another country; or the franchisor may establish an administrative office in the host country to manage all the franchises within that country. The parent company may establish operations on a regional basis which in turn have the authority to establish franchises in an established territory.

Depending on the host country selected for the franchising operation, there can be many or few constraints on the business operation.[45] Stated briefly, the primary issues of concern in foreign franchising operations are: protection of intellectual property including both patents, trademarks and know-how (see § 3.3.4 below); specific regulations on termination of franchises established by the host country; any special matters of taxation applicable to franchises; and any special controls on utilization of personnel in the franchise operation.

§ 3.3.4 Licensing and technology transfer

Licensing is a process by which the holder of some form of intellectual property (*licensor*) such as a patent, copyright, or trademark—each of which is a form of intellectual property that requires formal registration with an appropriate government body—or unpatented trade secrets and commercial processes (sometimes referred to as "know how") gives permission to another person (the *licensee*) to make use of the property. The license is normally stated for a term of years or, in certain instances, for the life-span of the underlying intellectual property. In return, the licensee uses the intellectual property and pays the licensor royalties for that use.

There are a large number of reasons for selecting the license agreement as a device for expanding business operations into foreign countries.[46] The country of origin may have established trade or tax barriers that make the

45. The European Community, for example, has initiated some comprehensive rules on the creation and operation of franchises within the E.C. See Regulation No. 4087/88, Application of the Treaty to Categories of Franchise Agreements (November 30, 1988).

46. For some excellent and lengthy readings on all these topics see, e.g., ANTITRUST, TECHNOLOGY TRANSFER AND JOINT VENTURES IN INTERNATIONAL TRADE (B. Hawk ed. 1983); L. ECKSTROM, LICENSING IN FOREIGN AND DOMESTIC OPERATIONS (1983). There is a vast

export of the finished product cost prohibitive. The holder of the license may not have the financial wherewithal to establish an elaborate manufacturing operation in the country of destination. The government of the country of destination may have established barriers of its own to foreign-owned manufacturing ventures. At the same time, that country may want access to new devices and new technology so long as the manufacture and marketing of those devices are carefully constrained by the government—and, for the most part, in the hands of that country's nationals.

Of course, there can be considerable risks in a licensing agreement. Patents and trade secrets are valuable because of their uniqueness and are normally given a great deal of protection within the country of origin by conferring exclusive control over the patent or secret on the person who developed it. Western nations and particularly the United States have stringent controls on patent infringement. Because these protections are not always available in the country to which the patent is to be exported, secrecy clauses are a prime ingredient of licensing contracts. Even so, loose and casual policing of intellectual property and trade secrets rights by government agencies and courts in the host country can lead to the leaking of the secret to persons who are not licensees.

There are other pitfalls, as well. The country within which the license originated may not want the license exported if it believes that the technology represented by the license is a matter of national security. The United States, for example, through the Export Administration Act, has in the past placed stringent limitations on export of certain types of technology as an outgrowth of the government's national security concerns, although many of these controls are being lifted.[47]

Even though a license is regarded as an exception to antitrust constraints, an attempt on the part of the licensor to control the activities of the licensee too tightly, or to insist on the licensee's purchasing (tie-ins) or refraining from purchasing (tie-outs) goods or processes other than the license can trigger antitrust problems. Countries with hard currency problems quite often object to large royalty payments flowing out of the country and thereby make it extremely difficult to obtain government approval for the importation of the license without the imposition of stringent controls on royalty amount and royalty collection.

(Note 46 continued) amount of information on licensing to be found in legal periodicals. Some representative articles are: *Symposium on the Transfer of Technology in the International Marketplace*, 7 B.C. Int'l & Comp. L. Rev. 235 (1984); Byington, *Planning and Drafting of International Licensing Agreements*, 6 N.C.J. Int'l L. & Com. Reg. 193 (1984). Brunsvold, *Negotiating Techniques for Warranty and Enforcement Clauses in International Licensing Agreements*, Vand.J.Transnat'l L. 281 (1981); Unkovic, *Negotiating and Preparing an International Licensing Agreement*, 25 Prac.Law. 77 (1979). For a comparative view see THE KNOW HOW CONTRACT IN GERMANY, JAPAN AND THE UNITED STATES (Kluwer 1984).

47. 50 U.S.C. app.

These problems have led to a surprising number of regional and country-by-country initiatives to control licensing and technology transfer. The European Community has paid close attention to licensing within the EC, especially insofar as licensing affects EC antitrust policy.[48] A number of Latin American countries have begun to develop tight controls on licensing. The countries that are now part of the Andean Group (Bolivia, Columbia, Ecuador and Peru) have developed joint, uniform licensing rules in an attempt to protect host countries and individuals in the host countries and to prevent internecine bidding wars between Andean members.[49] Some of the abuses associated with the licensing process that have had a particularly detrimental effect on developing countries prompted the United Nations Conference and Trade and Development (UNCTAD) to draw up a code of conduct (discussed in Chapter Five) attempting to regulate technology transfer between developed and developing countries by placing constraints on the negotiating process.

Licensing agreements tend to have a number of common characteristics.[50] First, they are normally for a long period of time. Indeed, the more complex technology requires a longer start-up time. This means that royalties and other forms of remuneration do not begin to flow back to the licensor for months and even years. Moreover, licensees and host countries normally do not wish to enter into short-term agreements because setting up licensed projects often consume a vast amount of time and effort on the part of both private parties and the government itself.

Second, the secrecy clause is the heart of the licensing agreement. Licensors normally insist on strict confidentiality and on elaborate mechanisms for policing confidentiality. This need for secrecy also has a palpable effect on any assignment of the license or on sublicensing agreements. Frequently, a licensing agreement will flatly prohibit either assignment or sublicensing entirely.

Third, a licensor's business reputation is often at stake because people know that the licensor is behind the product ultimately manufactured. To that extent, licensors look as carefully at quality control provisions in a contract as they do at the secrecy clause.

Beyond these matters, the amount and timeliness of the royalty payments is of great concern to both parties as are the termination provisions in the contract. Host governments do not take lightly to licensors withdrawing a license on spurious or arbitrary grounds after large investments have been

---

48. See, e.g., Dessemontet, *Transfer of Technology Under UNCTAD and EEC Draft Codifications*, 12 J.Int'l L.& Econ. 1 (1979); Noonan, *Technology Licensing: Common Market Competition Implications*, 19 N.C.J. Int'l L. & Com'l Reg. 439 (1984).

49. See, e.g., C. FURTADO, ECONOMIC DEVELOPMENT OF LATIN AMERICA (1976); Lacey, *Technology and Industrial Property Licensing in Latin America*, 6 Int'l Law. 388 (1972).

50. These points are covered in different form in Byington, supra note 46, at 196-200.

made. At the same time, licensors have a legitimate interest in being able to extricate themselves from a deal gone sour since their world-wide reputation and good will may be at stake.

§ 3.3.5 Joint ventures

As more and more countries require at least some control over business operations within their boundaries, the older forms of doing business such as the take-over of foreign companies, the establishment of foreign subsidiaries and the execution of concession agreements are giving way to joint ventures. Viewed in its simplest form, a joint venture is a contract that creates a partnership for the purpose of performing some kind of business operation—e.g., the sale of goods or the construction of a power plant.

One fundamental characteristic of joint ventures is that they are almost always substantial undertakings. In one instance, an American lawyer was asked whether it would be feasible for an American company with less than $1 million in assets even to consider a joint venture given the incredible complexity of the regulatory structure, the time and effort necessary to prepare and execute the agreement itself and the direct start-up investment. He replied: "I would have a very difficult time imagining how [such a company] could get involved in a joint venture outside the United States ... [Such a business] should do so first with a commissioned agent ... . [B]usinesses go by stages in international transactions and if you try to get ahead of the stage, you'll go wrong every time."[51]

There are any number of ways to begin an analysis of joint ventures. Professor Detlev Vagts, among others, has developed a framework for categorizing these undertakings.[52] In the first instance, he distinguishes between a joint venture that is merely a partnership (including a partnership between two corporations or between an individual and a corporation) and a joint venture in which the joint venturers, whoever they may be, form a separate corporation to conduct the business of the joint venture.

In addition, a joint venture may comprise: (1) two or more firms from the same country engaging in a joint venture in a second country; (2) a party from country A and another from country B engaging in a joint venture in country C; (3) a joint venture between a party from country A and a party in the country in which the venture takes place; (4) a joint venture between a foreign private party and a government in the host country; and (5) a joint venture established as a free standing business created by investors from abroad and investors in the host country.

---

51. Hushon, *Joint Ventures Between Multinationals: Government Regulatory Aspects*, 9 N.C.J.Int'l L. & Com.Reg. 207 (1984).
52. D. VAGTS, TRANSNATIONAL BUSINESS PROBLEMS 421 (1986).

These categories suggest some of the problems that may occur in setting up a joint venture. They range from possible antitrust violations, to host country employment regulations, to those special problems a company faces when the other party to the venture is a government rather than a private entity. Moreover, in terms of current popularity, many developing countries no longer view types 1 and 2 as attractive arrangements since the host country obviously derives far fewer benefits from the venture than might be the case with the latter three types.

There are other ways to categorize joint ventures. The Andean nations define a joint venture as "foreign" if less than 51 percent of the venture is in the hands of host country nationals or the host country government, as "mixed" if the venture is controlled between 51 and 80 percent by host nationals and "national" if at least 80 percent of the venture is in the hands of nationals.

These categorizations provide both ways to review joint venture plans and a definitional structure for regulation of the venture by the host government. For our purposes, it is sufficient to note that a joint venture is mainly a matter of who controls the operation and how the profits and risks are to be allocated, rather than a concept which affects the subject matter of the business. Thus, a joint venture may be formed to sell goods or services, to launch and administer a franchise operation or to establish a licensing scheme.

To the extent that a joint venture is affected by legal principles outside the context of specific government regulation (either by the country of origin or the host country), the law to be applied will be the law of partnerships and corporations. Persons planning joint ventures are typically concerned with provisions on duration of the venture, financing, termination, control of the venture, the distribution of profits and the allocation of risks (normally allocated on the basis of percentage participation in the joint venture), day-to-day management of the venture, destruction of the subject matter of the undertaking and addition, deletion and substitution of parties to the venture.[53]

Transnational joint ventures are increasingly popular. One of the more remarkable breakthroughs in doing business in the People's Republic of China occurred in 1979 when the government of the People's Republic authorized joint ventures between itself and foreign companies.[54] Other developing countries appear to be watching the Chinese experiments to see whether the Chinese experience may be drawn upon for their own joint ventures.

---

53. See, e.g., Hushon, supra note 51, at 233.

54. See, e.g., Surrey, Fishburne & Chaudhri, *Joint Ventures in China: The First Water Stop*, 21 Tex.J.Int'l L. 221 (1986); Brace, *Joint Ventures in the People's Republic of China (Non-Corporate Form)*, 1985 Int'l Bus. Law. 434; Jaslow, *Practical Considerations in Drafting a Joint Venture Agreement with China*, 31 J.Am.Comp.L. 209 (1983). See generally, J. DOBKIN, INTERNATIONAL TECHNOLOGY JOINT VENTURES IN THE COUNTRIES OF THE PACIFIC RIM (1988).

§ 3.3.6 Other forms of agreement

There are a number of other forms of agreement that have been used over time. One of the more important is the natural resource concession agreement—a form of international transaction pioneered by major Western oil companies in the Middle East early in the Twentieth Century to move oil from the sands of the Middle East to western consumers. The use of concession agreements was later expanded to other regions of the world where developing countries had control of large amounts of unexploited natural resources. A concession agreement (now sometimes referred to as a development agreement) is an agreement that permits a foreign entity to enter the country in which the resources are located and, generally for royalty payments and other remuneration to the host government, permits the company to remove the resources and sell them elsewhere.

The earliest concession agreements are now viewed with considerable disfavor because of the nearly unconscionable terms negotiated between the Western developers and the host countries.[55] Typical provisions gave the foreign company exclusive and long term exploration and development rights, covered huge amounts of the country's territory, called for the payment of royalties that bore virtually no relationship to the injury to the land and the depletion of non-replaceable natural resources, and gave the host government virtually no say in the concession's operation.[56]

These days, development agreements tend to be far better balanced and tend to relinquish far less control to the foreign entity while still preserving the developing country's access to both investment funds for development and major markets for sale of the resources. But considerations such as these are mainly matters of public policy and negotiation. The legal principles governing development agreements—which these days often take the form of joint ventures—normally do not differ from those principles applicable to the forms of business discussed above.[57]

§ 3.4 Planning for Dispute Resolution

Many persons entering into international agreements for the first time have a difficult time thinking about the possibility of something going wrong with the agreement. People enter these transactions with the expectation that they will be fully performed. Frequently, when a negotiation session is going

55. See, e.g., D. SMITH & B. WELLS, NEGOTIATING THIRD WORLD MINERALS AGREE-MENTS (1975); Vock, *The Evolution of the Legal Relationship Between International Petroleum Mining Companies and Host Countries*, 1983 Int'l Bus. Law. 244.

56. See the excellent history of Middle East oil development in J. BLAIR, THE CONTROL OF OIL (1976).

57. See Beredjick & Walde, *supra* note 35.

well and after some decent personal relationships have been formed, it is almost impossible to look across the table and conceive of the other person reneging on the deal. But it is in the planning and drafting process that a party *must* anticipate problems and *must* consider how disagreements might be managed if they do arise.

Dispute resolution is the management of disagreement over a broad spectrum of different possibilities. It is something that cannot be ducked in international commercial transactions because the parties will be at great distances from each other after the agreement is consummated. Those persons responsible for drafting and negotiating the agreement are rarely those who have the day-to-day responsibility for performance. Even if the parties have the greatest sense of well-being and security at the time of signing the contract, external conditions can still disrupt the agreement no matter how much personal regard and trust the negotiating parties have for each other.

For this reason, virtually all properly drafted international contracts contain some kind of dispute resolution clause. For those contracts fully performed without incident, the clause is superfluous. However, for those deals that fall apart, the clause can be crucial. A few minutes of inattention to dispute resolution at the planning and drafting stage of an agreement can cost millions of dollars later on when a dispute has to be resolved.

Many dispute resolution clauses are drafted haphazardly and put in as an afterthought and without the consideration that they really deserve. Many less-than-acceptable clauses simply incorporate some boilerplate from a book of forms with very little inquiry into how the clause might actually work if a dispute occurs. Worse, garden variety dispute resolution clauses often incorporate the more rigid techniques of dispute resolution such as arbitration and litigation before obligating the parties to try to work things out between themselves in a milder, less-threatening arena such as renegotiation or mediation.

A lot of these mistakes are made because many of the people who draft and plan contracts know little about dispute resolution. The following discussion is an introduction to the various forms of dispute resolution for contract drafters and planners. Chapter 4 sets out some useful dispute resolution clauses, and Part Two of this book contains an extensive discussion of each of these different devices as they are employed in practice.

There is no uniform world view of dispute resolution. Lawyers in the United States have a favorite saying: "One person's delay is another person's due process." Developing proper dispute resolution procedures in domestic controversies now occupies a great deal of the time of many U.S. legal scholars. In international transactions many additional factors, such as cultural and language differences, often affect the dispute resolution process. For example, the antagonism and ferocity of U.S. litigation is taken for granted in the United States, but is regarded as totally unproductive—perhaps even despicable—by societies in the Far East and elsewhere in the world. Understanding the apprehensions that these cultural differences create might persuade the parties negotiating a contract to opt for some less-drastic dispute resolution mechanism—such as mediation—to be attempted before a more adversarial process such as arbitration or litigation is utilized.

Yet those processes which are less adversarial such as mediation and arbitration are often much less final and certain; and finality of result (that is, the understanding that a dispute has been conclusively resolved and that the final decision is enforceable against the losing party) is very important in most commercial transactions. Agreeing to engage in a process of dispute resolution that cannot lead, in and of itself, to a final decision may have the effect of lengthening the overall dispute resolution phase of an agreement and multiplying the costs of obtaining a permanent resolution of the dispute.

There are a number of devices regularly used to resolve international commercial matters. They include the device of *adaptation* by which the contract itself is drafted in a sufficiently flexible fashion to accommodate unanticipated occurrences such as supply shortages, strikes or sharp price increases or decreases. Similarly, since international contracts are normally the product of negotiation, by definition they are always subject to *re-negotiation*. Frequently, adaptation and renegotiation go hand in hand. The twin concepts of *mediation* and *conciliation* are essentially processes by which negotiation between the parties takes place in the presence and with the assistance of a third party who is sometimes referred to as a facilitator. The more structured forms of commercial dispute resolution, *arbitration* and *litigation*, are probably the best known among the public at large and easily the most frequently utilized devices on the international level. But each of these can still be rigid, costly, time-consuming, totally under the control of specialists, and so adversarial that the parties' relationship is permanently damaged.

§ 3.4.1 Adaptation

Contract provisions such as *force majeure* clauses and flexible pricing terms that turn, say, on the increase or decrease of a published cost of living index are provisions that allow a contract to change with new circumstances without provoking a breach or forcing the parties into some kind of formal dispute resolution. Long term contracts almost always contain a number of adaptation provisions. Frequently, even when the contract does not contain such clauses, the law underlying the contract will supply certain adaptation and gap filling terms. For example, under the UCC a contract for the sale of goods does not even have to specify a price. If the contract is silent as to price, UCC § 2-305 provides that the price is "a reasonable price at the time of delivery [of the goods.]" The legal doctrines of impossibility and frustration may excuse performance in whole or in part or for a certain period of time even if the contract does not contain a *force majeure* clause or even if the *force majeure* clause does not expressly cover the incident that has caused the problems.

§ 3.4.2 Renegotiation

If the contract cannot itself adapt to changing circumstances, the parties may always renegotiate. Some parties place an express obligation of renegotiation in the contract with the expectation that the parties will not resort to a more formal method of dispute resolution without first trying to talk to each other. Some companies that have a large stake in preserving existing contracts, such as the U.S. airplane manufacturer, Boeing Corporation, insert renegotiation clauses in their contracts that specify that the renegotiation must take place between two high-level corporate officials. In multi-billion dollar contracts to be performed over a period of many years, renegotiation can be a matter of life and death for the contracting parties. Like the initial negotiation, renegotiation is simply a dialogue or discussion between the disputing parties that has as its goal the resolution of the dispute by mutual agreement. Normally, it is cheap, quick and has the advantages of a solution that is neither coerced nor imposed by external entities. One of its best features is that it can be undertaken while the contract continues to be performed. To the extent that a negotiated solution is possible, it is almost always the most advantageous and cost-beneficial device.

§ 3.4.3 Mediation/Conciliation

The twin devices of mediation and conciliation are, as noted above, negotiation in the presence of or with the help of a third party. In some settings, mediation can be nothing more than a friendly conversation. In other settings, particularly when conducted under formal commercial mediation rules it can rival the formality of commercial arbitration. To a certain extent, mediation has many of the advantages of a negotiated settlement in that it is relatively uncoerced, fast and confidential; but in complex matters it may take a great deal more time. The addition of the third party mediator is an additional expense and the educating of that person on the facts of the dispute can lengthen the proceeding. However, to the extent that the parties believe they have worked out the final solution themselves, they may find the end result highly satisfactory.

§ 3.3.4 Arbitration

Most international commercial agreements call for arbitration of any disputes that may arise under the contract by incorporating standard form arbitration clauses. These clauses, in turn, usually incorporate the procedural rules of one or another of the major international arbitral bodies such as the International Chamber of Commerce (ICC) or the United Nations Commission on International Trade Law (UNCITRAL). Some clauses incorporation the rules of a national arbitral body such as the American Arbitration Association (AAA) or the Japan or Stockholm Chamber of Commerce.

Under modern procedural systems, arbitration is essentially the litigation of a dispute before an arbitrator rather than a judge. The procedure is adversarial and almost always handled by lawyer-specialists. However, there are many arbitrations in which non-lawyers sit as arbitrators and there is usually no requirement that either the representatives of the parties or the arbitrator be a lawyer. It is just that arbitration is such a complicated undertaking and is so close in concept to litigation that most parties put themselves in the hands of their lawyers if they have to arbitrate. Often, the arbitration clause will require that the arbitrator be expert in the underlying subject matter. For example, an arbitration clause in, say, a construction contract might call for an arbitrator with at least ten years experience in the construction industry.

Parties who are worried about the ability or integrity of a single arbitrator, irrespective of whom that person may be, often provide for a three-person arbitration panel with each side choosing one of the arbitrators. The two party-appointed arbitrators then pick the third member of the panel, who normally chairs the panel and presides over the arbitration. Contrary to the beliefs of many lay persons, arbitration is often costly, time-consuming, and far from satisfactory. Especially antagonistic opponents frequently go into court both before, during, and after the arbitration to test the ultimate validity of the process. As a result, arbitration is not always a complete substitute for litigation. The administrative fees that must be paid at the outset merely to commence the arbitration under the supervision of organizations such as the ICC or the AAA are substantial.

There is very little so-called non-binding arbitration in international commercial arbitration. To the extent that this concept exists, it is probably only a species of mediation and is used mainly in the labor relations sector. Thus, the decision of the arbitrator is—at least in theory—final and conclusive. However, in certain instances when the losing party balks at the decision of the arbitrator, a pronouncement known as the *arbitral award*, it must be taken into some domestic court system for confirmation and enforcement against the losing party. Sometimes a party will refuse to commence arbitration. Then the party seeking to arbitrate must resort to domestic courts for an order compelling the other party to arbitrate.

Even with these inherent disadvantages, arbitration is generally favored by most commentators and appears to be the dispute resolution device of choice in most international commercial agreements. One of the major reasons for this pride-of-place is that an international treaty, the New York Convention on the Recognition and Enforcement of Foreign Arbitral Awards—permits the enforcement of arbitral awards rendered in one country to be enforced in another country. Except within the European Community, there is no parallel treaty for the enforcement of court judgments. As a result, if one is worried about where enforcement might take place, arbitration is often superior to litigation.

§ 3.4.5 Litigation

Litigation is a formal proceeding conducted in an appropriate court in the country of the buyer or the country of the seller, or in some instances in a country perceived to be neutral by the parties. There is really no such thing as international litigation or an international court for parties to private agreements. The International Court of Justice at the Hague is restricted to disputes between countries, although recently it has served as the site for arbitration of commercial disputes between the United States and Iran under the Algerian Accords of 1981. As litigation's detractors constantly note, the process is expensive, costly and often protracted. It can be handled only by lawyer-specialists. Indeed, in most countries no one other than a lawyer may litigate a case.

In many circumstances, litigation can cause additional hostility and antagonisms between the parties. Unlike arbitration or mediation, parties usually do not resort to litigation until and unless the entire agreement has fallen completely apart. By contrast, arbitration and mediation can often be utilized to resolve a dispute that arises within the overall commercial undertaking without the necessity of terminating the agreement itself. Litigation has some advantages. It is generally final when concluded—that is, there is no other forum and no other recourse for the losing party except to honor the judgment of the court. A failure to comply with a court's judgment in most countries creates contempt of court problems for the recalcitrant party. Litigation is sometimes the mechanism of choice even in international commercial contracts, because a number of lawyers—particularly in the United States—are cynical about the other forms of dispute resolution and conclude that they might as well go into court in the first instance because in all likelihood that's where the parties will wind up in any event. However, there are some special difficulties in using litigation in domestic courts to resolve international commercial disputes. Domestic courts frequently lack jurisdiction over parties in other countries. They also have a great deal of difficulty in enforcing their judgments abroad. To a certain extent, domestic courts can evidence prejudice against foreign parties who come into those courts.

Some contracting parties try to eliminate the problem of local prejudice by providing for litigation in the courts of a third country. To the extent that the third country agrees to hear the case, this maneuver is always a possibility. For example, in one important case eventually decided by the United States Supreme Court, *The Bremen v. Zapata Off-Shore Oil Company*,[58] a dispute arising between a German shipping company and an American oil company, the contract provided for dispute resolution in the High Court of Justice in London. Great Britain had nothing to do with the contract or the two parties. The United States Supreme Court honored that choice of forum even when one of the parties tried to litigate the dispute in a federal court in the United States. Within the European Community choice of forum clauses, including clauses that call for litigation in a neutral forum, are generally honored so long as one of the parties is deemed to be domiciled within the jurisdiction of a signatory state.[59]

§ 3.4.6 Other forms of dispute resolution

There are other forms of dispute resolution worthy of attention that may have increasing utility for commercial disputes even though they are not now widely used by the international business community. For example, businesses in the United States have experimented with a commendable device known as the "mini-trial," a procedure in which lawyers for the contending parties present a summary of each parties' case to an important corporate official, such as a corporation vice-president, for each of the parties. That official must attend the proceeding with express authority to settle the case. The executives listen to a shortened presentation by the parties' attorneys and are frequently assisted by a third-person referee, often a retired judge. After the abbreviated presentations are concluded—and normally they last only a day or so—the executives and the referee consider the presentations and attempt to negotiate a final agreement.

Some jurisdictions in the United States, notably the State of California, now permit parties to seek out and hire their own judge in a program formally referred to as the California Reference Procedure, but colloquially labeled "rent-a-judge." No party can be forced into this procedure, but if both parties

---

58. 407 U.S. 1 (1972).

59. Article 17, EEC Convention on Jurisdiction and Enforcement of Judgments in Civil and Commercial Matters, *done*, September 27, 1968, *reprinted in* 8 Int'l Legal Materials 229 (1969). Choices will not be enforced if a particular court has exclusive jurisdiction or if undue influence or a contract of adhesion (a printed form agreement) is involved.

agree to its use, it is helpful in moving quickly to a resolution of the case because it avoids the congestion of the regular system of state courts (many civil cases in the United States take three to four years to reach a final decision). Moreover, the decision rendered by the judge is binding on the parties just as if it had been rendered in a regular court. There is no evidence that the rent-a-judge procedure has caught on elsewhere in the world, however.

Having set out these elaborate descriptions of the various forms of dispute resolution, it may be helpful to see some of the same ideas presented in pictorial form. The following chart depicts the alternatives in terms of various factors. On the left side of the chart are the factors of time, cost, and finality. Those factors *increase* as one moves down the chart. For example, the mechanisms become more time consuming (in terms of how long from start to finish it normally takes to complete the procedure) and more expensive. By definition, litigation—because it is procedurally far more complex and because it is heavily dependent on court-imposed timetables and court-created congestion—is more expensive than mediation. The final factor on the left side of the chart, finality, simply reflects whether the parties may move to another form of dispute resolution if they do not like the result in the mechanism in question. Put another way, if mediation fails or if an arbitral award is not complied with voluntarily by the losing party, the parties must normally go into court to resolve the dispute. By contrast, there is no subsequent dispute resolution forum after litigation. There the parties receive a final judgment rendered by a court that must be complied with, so long as the court has jurisdiction over both parties. All the mechanisms other than litigation require consent by both parties. Litigation is the only process that one party may utilize without the consent of the other side. (Of course, even this requires a small disclaimer. If the parties have already signed an agreement to arbitrate, they will be held to that agreement even if one party now wishes to litigate.)

The factors on the right side of the chart, party autonomy and confidentiality, *decrease* as one moves down the list. Party autonomy is the matter of party control. Obviously, the parties have less control over an arbitration or a court proceeding (those devices are much more in the hands and under the control of arbitrators or judges) than over renegotiation. As one moves down the list, the dispute is placed in the hands of neutral, third parties over whom the disputing parties have very little control. The factor of confidentiality is frequently an important one in commercial dispute resolution, particularly for those disputes that involve important commercial or trade secrets. To the extent that one moves down the chart, more and more people become aware of and have knowledge of the parties' dispute.

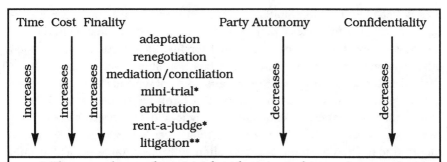

Time	Cost	Finality		Party Autonomy	Confidentiality
increases	increases	increases	adaptation renegotiation mediation/conciliation mini-trial* arbitration rent-a-judge* litigation**	decreases	decreases

* The procedures of mini-trial and rent-a-judge are too new to make accurate estimates of time and cost
** Litigation is a non-consensual device; all other devices require the consent of both parties before they may be utilized.

None of these procedures is perfect. No perfect procedure is likely to be discovered. For persons engaged in planning and drafting international commercial agreements, one thing is clear. To the extent that the parties do not choose a method of dispute resolution on their own, one will be imposed on them whenever a dispute arises under the contract.

§ 3.5 Financing and Paying for International Commercial Agreements

Securing funds for international commercial agreements is often more difficult than creating the agreements themselves. Since commercial transactions are not charitable undertakings, the efficient securing and transmitting of money is indispensable to the success of the deal. Sales of goods and services require payment for those goods and services. The other forms of agreement normally require investment money flowing from one country to another to get the venture started and, once begun, call for royalty payments that flow back to the country of origin. International businesses and financial institutions have worked out a large number of alternatives for financing and payment.

§ 3.5.1 Direct payment

Virtually any method of payment that is used for the payment of obligations under domestic contracts may be used for the payment of obligations in international dealings, including such things as cash, checks, promissory notes, and negotiable bills of lading. But on closer examination, many of these payment devices have serious deficiencies for international transactions. Cash is normally too dangerous a commodity to ship abroad, although it has been used on occasion. Some countries, particularly those in the former Soviet bloc, have prohibitions against the export of their national currency. Bank checks are less subject to theft than cash but just as in domestic transactions they can be dishonored for insufficient funds and various other reasons. This sort of uncertainty has a stifling effect on transactions that take place over long distances because buyers typically want their goods quickly while sellers prefer to wait until a bank check clears the buyer's bank—an event that can take an enormously long time between banks in different countries. Promissory notes, generally regarded as negotiable instruments under United States law and often fully acceptable on a domestic basis in many other countries, create many of the same problems as checks.

The sporadic nature of many international transactions, the distances involved and the lack of previous business dealings between the parties normally prompt the seller to look to sources other than the buyer to guarantee payment. There are many ways to protect the seller's interests. The seller can seek government assurances of payment, or at least private or government-sponsored insurance to protect against certain risks. Or, the seller can insist on one or another of the traditional forms of international payment, such as a letter of credit.

§ 3.5.2 Payment devices

Two methods of payment on contracts—*cash in advance* and *payment on account*—are frequently used in domestic transactions but are far less common in international transactions. They are essentially mirror images of each other. Cash in advance (the payment of the contract price in full by the buyer prior to any performance whatsoever by the seller) gives the seller total security and places all the risks of non-performance on the buyer. A cash in advance term in a contract indicates that the seller's negotiating strength is nearly overwhelming and that the buyer for whatever reason is almost completely at the mercy of the seller but desires the goods or services so desperately that he will agree to this kind of payment term.

Payment on account switches these risks almost completely. Here, the seller ships the goods or provides the services and the buyer pays either periodically or in a lump sum into an account established by the seller. This type of device places the seller almost completely at the mercy of the buyer and again may indicate significantly disparate bargaining power between the parties. Another form of payment that tilts heavily in favor of the buyer is known as a *clean draft collection*. In this instance, the seller ships the goods, sends the papers relevant to the transaction directly to the buyer and merely presents a draft for payment to the buyer's bank in the same fashion that the buyer's check would ultimately be presented to the buyer's bank for collection. While a little more elaborate in terms of the total number of documents involved, the procedure for a clean draft collection is not much different from that of payment by check.

Given the risks associated with cash in advance and payment on account and the possibility that more equally balanced parties would never agree to them in the first place, international businesses and international banks have worked out two other devices of payment that are much more common. The first is *payment on collection*. In this case, the seller gathers the relevant documents of the transaction such as bills of lading, invoices, and insurance certificates and sends them to the buyer's bank along with a draft for money payable by the buyer's bank.

The draft can be either a *sight draft* (a negotiable instrument payable as soon as the buyer's bank "sees" it) or a *time draft* (an instrument payable on a particular date). In the case of a sight draft, the buyer's bank will not release the other documents of the transaction (bill of lading, etc) until the buyer pays the draft. In the case of a time draft, the buyer's payment is due on some fixed date after the other documents are released to the buyer. It is easy to spot the allocation of risks here—sight drafts give solid protection to the seller; time drafts make it easier for the buyer to inspect the goods or services before payment is due.

There are still some problems with this mode of payment. It is more secure than cash in advance or payment on account, but it remains a transaction solely between seller and buyer. If the buyer's financial status is shaky, or if the parties have never done business with each other, a seller might not accept even the relatively secure device of payment on collection as the payment mechanism. Even if this device gives the seller essentially two claims—seller can sue on the underlying contract for breach of contract or separately on the dishonored draft—the seller still has to track the buyer down and move against the buyer directly.

To strengthen the seller's sense of security, international businesses and banks have established a much more secure form of payment that has become one of the most common forms of payment for international commercial agreements, the *irrevocable letter of credit.*

Legal scholars like to distinguish between *revocable* and irrevocable letters of credit, and most legal systems recognize both types of instrument. A revocable letter of credit may be changed or canceled by the issuing bank at any time with no notice to the beneficiary. This makes the letter of credit almost worthless as a protective device and as a consequence revocable letters of credit are virtually unheard of in international commercial agreements. At the same time, the term *irrevocable* does not mean immutable. Irrevocable letters of credit may be changed or canceled but only after all parties to the letter give their consent to the modification or cancellation.

The actual mechanics of a letter of credit are not terribly different from payment on collection. The transaction has several steps:

1. The buyer (normally referred to as the *applicant*) applies to a bank for a letter of credit. This bank, known as the *issuing* bank, analyzes the application and if it approves, draws up the letter of credit and sends the letter of credit to a second bank known as the *advising* bank.

2. The advising bank gets in touch with the seller (usually referred to as the *beneficiary*) and delivers the letter of credit to the seller. This is one of the crucial steps because at this point, the seller knows that a letter of credit has been issued and *most importantly* knows that the issuing bank guarantees payment so long as the goods are shipped and the seller's papers are in order. In other words, the seller may proceed against the bank itself if the letter of credit is dishonored and need not track down the buyer. Since banks are traditionally stable and credit-worthy, this pledge of the issuing bank's guarantee provides the seller with vastly more security than he would have if he had only the buyer's assurances that payment would be made.

3. Upon delivery of the letter of credit, the seller ships the goods and simultaneously gathers all the other documents relevant to the letter of credit, including the sight or time draft, appropriate invoices, export and import permissions (if applicable), documents of insurance and bills of lading, and presents these documents to the advising bank which normally pays the draft and then forwards the documents to the issuing bank for final collection.

Under the legal principles applicable to letters of credit, if the documents presented are in order, the issuing bank must pay the draft, irrespective of any change of mind on the buyer's part. The banks will examine the relevant papers in minute detail for their validity and consistency but will not serve as a quality control mechanism with regard to the goods themselves. In other words, even if the buyer discovers that the goods are defective, he cannot renege on the letter of credit.[60] A letter of credit is not cheap. Banks spend a great deal of time and attention on them both as issuing bank and advising bank. The fee for a typical letter of credit is a percentage of the dollar amount of the letter of credit itself. The fee is increased as the

---

60. See, e.g., Article 5, UCC for principles of law applicable to American letters of credit. For an excellent discussion of letters of credit (again from the American perspective) see J. WHITE & R. SUMMERS, UNIFORM COMMERCIAL CODE 601-639 (1972). For an international perspective see A. LOWENFELD, INTERNATIONAL PRIVATE TRADE 125-83 (1981). For some comparative insights see Armstrong, *Letters of Credit in East-West Trade: Soviet Reception of Capitalist Custom*, 18 Vand.J.Transnat'l L. 329 (1984).

individual letter of credit transaction increases in complexity. For parties seeking to save money on letter of credit transactions, the basic message is: keep it simple.

Letter of credit transactions are subject to both legal constraints and customary banking practices. In the United States, Article 5 of the UCC provides many of the controlling legal principles. For international letters of credit, many of the governing legal principles are provided by a set of rules drafted by the International Chamber of Commerce called the Uniform Customs and Practice for Documentary Credits (UCP). When reviewing the UCP, the reader should keep in mind that these are rules that favor the banks. Banks are always skittish about substituting their creditworthiness for that of their customers, and they've written the UCP so that their obligations for handling letters of credit are both clearly spelled out and limited in scope. For example, Article 15 provides that the bank's only obligation is to examine the relevant documents on their face. Article 17 specifies that banks do not "assume any liability or responsibility for the description, quantity, weight, quality, condition, packing, delivery, value or existence of the goods represented by any documents." Article 5 of the UCC contains similar but not identical provisions. The UCP and the UCC should be closely consulted by any lawyer working with letters of credit.

The letter of credit transaction described above is a conventional letter of credit. Some international commercial relationships involve transactions in which the parties require some security but for various reasons choose not to use the letter of credit as the payment device itself. In these cases, the parties may negotiate a *standby* letter of credit which follows the same format as the conventional letter of credit but which is activated only if one of the parties does not live up to his contractual obligations. A standby letter of credit may be triggered only when one of the parties certifies that the other party did not perform their part the bargain. When triggered, however, the issuing bank guarantees payment as it does under a conventional letter of credit. For these reasons, the standby letter of credit operates more like a performance bond than an irrevocable letter of credit. For transactions to be performed in installments over a long period of time such as an international construction contract, the parties may agree to a *revolving* letter of credit by which the seller draws from the letter of credit account periodically and the purchaser replenishes the account whenever the account falls below a certain level.

The letter of credit device obviously gives the seller tremendous security and the resulting security explains better than anything else why letters of credit are so frequently used. But recall that letters of credit are expensive transactions. Banks charge substantial fees for all the work they do and for the exposure they take on if the deal somehow falls through. Further, because the issuing bank's credit is pledged to the transaction, they put applications under a very high powered microscope even to the point of requiring that the entire amount of the payment term be deposited in an account with the issuing bank before the letter of credit application is approved. Many foreign buyers cannot meet the banks terms. Some foreign buyers in especially strong negotiating positions vis-a-vis the seller will simply not agree to a letter of credit.

Just as importantly, if the parties have not done business with each other and if both parties feel somewhat insecure a buyer might not agree to a letter of credit because the exposure is too great. One of the legal principles underlying letters of credit stipulates that even if the goods or services are completely faulty, the letter of credit must be honored. That leaves the buyer with only a claim against the seller for breach of contract and forces the buyer to track the seller down to bring an action for breach wherever the seller can be found. Over all that time the seller has the enjoyment of the money. Much like virtually every other contract term and condition, the insertion of letter of credit provisions in a contract depend heavily on the respective bargaining power of the parties.

§ 3.5.3 Insuring against risks

There are other devices that parties may use to insure against various risks such as the risk of non-performance or risks external to the deal itself such as the risk of expropriation. To guarantee performance, parties often negotiate the execution of various types of bonds such as surety bonds. These are issued by private entities such as banks and insurance companies and guarantee performance of the contract (or stated a bit more accurately guarantee that the injured party will be compensated in case of failure of performance).[61]

Some government entities may serve as guarantors of certain types of international commercial agreements. For example, the three components making up the World Bank group, the International Bank for Reconstruction and Development (IBRD), the International Development Association (IDA) and the International Finance Corporation (IFC) engage in various activities that can serve as a form of loan guarantee. The IBRD loans money to developing countries for specific development projects, such as construction of large hydroelectric facilities and major transportation projects. The IFC works with private entities to work out underwriting and technical assistance arrangements.

---

61. See, e.g., Horn, *Securing International Commercial Transactions: Standby Letters of Credit, Bonds, Guarantees and Similar Sureties*, in INTERNATIONAL COMMERCIAL TRANSACTIONS, supra note 35, at 275-303.

In 1988, the Convention Establishing the Multilateral Investment Guarantee Agency (MIGA) entered into force, creating MIGA as a component of the World Bank. MIGA insures various investments made under World Bank auspices in terms of: (1) currency inconvertibility, (2) expropriation, (3) war, revolution, and civil disturbance, (4) certain types of breach of contract that cannot be resolved through arbitration proceedings.[62] There are a number of regional development banks such as the African Development Bank, the Asian Development Bank and the Inter-American Development Bank which provide both loans and loan guarantees for projects within their respective regions.[63]

In the United States, the Export-Import Bank (sometimes called the *Ex-Im Bank*) makes loans to certain foreign importers who could not otherwise qualify for financing to purchase American products and services. A government corporation, the Overseas Private Investment Corporation, provides various types of guarantees against expropriation and other unforeseen circumstances in certain developing countries. Both of these entities produce masses of information on many aspects of U.S. export activity in addition to engaging in the execution of guarantees and contracts of insurance.[64] A consortium of private insurance companies organized as the Foreign Credit Insurance Association writes policies for protection against short-term risks that foreign buyers will not pay for goods or services.

§ 3.6 Other Considerations in Planning Commercial Agreements

The planning and drafting of private commercial agreements does not take place in a vacuum. There are a large number of other matters that must be taken into account before a company can be assured that the agreement is sound, lawful and enforceable. An in-depth analysis of the following topics is beyond the scope of this book but some awareness of each of these issues is necessary to have a well-rounded grasp of all the ingredients of an international commercial agreement.

---

62. See, e.g., L. Weisenfeld, *Specialized Sources of Financing and Political Risk Insurance for Trade and Investment Abroad* in GOING INTERNATIONAL: INTERNATIONAL TRADE FOR THE NON-SPECIALIST (ALI-ABA, 1992); *Multilateral Investment Guarantee Agency General Conditions of Guarantee for Equity Investments* (dated January 25, 1989), 4 For.Investment L.J. 112 (1989).

63. See generally, P. WOOD, LAW AND PRACTICE OF INTERNATIONAL FINANCE (1980); Symposium, *Restructuring of Sovereign Debt*, 23 Colum.J.Transnat'l L. 1 (1984); Semkow, *Syndicating and Rescheduling International Financial Transactions*, 18 Int'l Law. 869 (1984).

64. The Ex-Im Bank is located at 811 Vermont Ave., N.W., Washington, D.C. 20571; OPIC is located at 1129 20th Street, N.W., Washington, D.C. 20527.

§ 3.6.1 Tax matters

There is no easy way to generalize about matters of taxation. Indeed, generalizations in this area can be dangerous because there is virtually no area of the law that changes with such rapidity and little notice as do the taxation laws of any country. Some brief observations may prove useful, however. Virtually all countries impose taxes of one sort or another on both individuals and businesses. These taxes run the gamut from *sales taxes* (often referred to as value added taxes outside the United States), *property taxes* for the use of real estate in a particular country, taxes in the nature of various types of *license fees*, and perhaps most importantly in the United States, *income taxes* (imposed on both individuals and corporations).[65]

The United States tax system is incredibly complicated and is frequently subject to revision. Some generalizations will probably hold true for the near future, however. The basic scheme of U.S. income taxation requires the identification of taxpayers (either individuals, corporations or partnerships), requires those entities to report their income (generally all money earned from their activities) and then permits taxpayers to reduce their taxable income by an extraordinarily complicated set of exemptions, exclusions and deductions. For example, the United States tax system permits American corporations to deduct certain taxes paid to foreign governments against the tax they owe to the United States and further permits American citizens living abroad to exclude a certain amount of foreign earnings from U.S. taxation. U.S. law permits business entities to establish Domestic International Sales Corporations and Foreign Export Sales corporations that qualify for special tax treatment because of their export activities.[66]

The U.S. also has a number of tax treaties with foreign governments that affect the manner in which U.S. citizens are dealt with under foreign tax schemes.[67] Recently, there has been increasing attention paid to the impact of taxation on business activities in developing countries.[68] When a company plans a transaction with a specific country, a quick and generally accurate

---

65. Three excellent guides to international taxation written from an American perspective are: J. ISENBERGH, INTERNATIONAL TAXATION: U.S. TAXATION OF FOREIGN TAXPAYERS AND FOREIGN INCOME (1990); P. POSTLEWAITE & M. COLLINS, INTERNATIONAL INDIVIDUAL TAXATION (1982 w/annual supplement); P. POSTLEWAITE, INTERNATIONAL CORPORATE TAXATION (1980 w/ annual supplement). See also, Mulroney, *Foreign Transactions and Persons: United States Income Taxation, A Primer* in GOING INTERNATIONAL: INTERNATIONAL TRADE FOR THE NONSPECIALIST (ALI-ABA, 1990); J.E. Bischel, FUNDAMENTALS OF INTERNATIONAL TAXATION (in 2 volumes, 1985).

66. See, e.g., Bretz, *Current Developments on DISCs*, 19 N.C.J.Int'l L. & Com'l Reg. 385 (1984).

67. See, e.g., IRS, Tax Treaties and Rates (IRS Pub. No. 901, 1985); Rosenbloom, *Tax Treaty Abuse Policies and Issues*, 15 L. & Pol'y in Int'l Bus. 763 (1983).

68. See, e.g., Goldberg, *Considerations for the Elimination of International Double Taxation: Toward a Developing Country Model*, 15 L. & Pol'y in Int'l Bus. 833 (1983).

summary of that country's taxation laws may be found in *World Tax Series*.

In the final analysis, advice and information on tax matters both foreign and domestic must be left in the hands of the experts. There is no other area of the law that is trickier and so fraught with hazards for the uninitiated. Nonetheless, tax considerations always have a major impact on an international commercial undertaking.

§ 3.6.2 Antitrust issues

Most international transactions create no antitrust problems, but those that do tend to create enormous problems. Like taxation, antitrust is a legal topic on which generalizations are dangerous; but some basic concepts may be helpful.[69] The entire concept of antitrust, both in the United States and abroad, is grounded in a belief that competition among businesses is generally a good thing. As a consequence, most antitrust law seeks to promote competition and prohibits various practices which inhibit or restrain competition. The principal U.S. antitrust law, the Sherman Antitrust Act,[70] prohibits, among many other things, "every contract, combination ... or conspiracy, in restraint of trade or commerce among the several States, or with foreign nations ... " The U.S. courts have framed some basic principles that flesh out this statute. For example, two companies that get together to fix prices automatically violate the act. Getting together to divide up sales territories is also what is known as a *per se* violation of the Sherman Act. For most other situations, the courts apply what is termed a *rule of reason* to determine whether a company's conduct has violated the antitrust statutes.

The United States government has always taken these principles very serious for purely domestic business enterprises. The problems become far more difficult, however, when they involve companies doing business abroad. First, there is a serious question, not yet resolved, as to whether the United States has the jurisdiction to enforce its antitrust principles abroad in any event. Attempts to do so have greatly offended a number of countries. Second, the U.S. antitrust principles are not identical to those applicable in other countries. If country X is happy to permit American company A to do business on its territory, why should the United States government be permitted to interfere through an extra-territorial application of its domestic antitrust laws. Third, the fundamental purpose of the antitrust laws—to promote competition within the United States—may have little consequence when U.S. companies are attempting to increase foreign sales.

---

69. Probably the best single book-length source on these issues is J. ATWOOD & K. BREWSTER, ANTITRUST AND AMERICAN BUSINESS ABROAD (2d ed., 1981 w/annual supplement).
    70. 15 U.S.C. § 1.

The United States Congress recognized this last factor in an early statute, the Webb-Pomerene Act,[71] which provides a partial exception to the Sherman Act for activities abroad. More recently, Congress has enacted the Export Trading Company Act of 1982,[72] a statute that permits American manufacturers, exporters and banking institutions to form export trading companies as a joint activity without having to worry about antitrust violations for these practices.

The U.S. Justice Department has attempted to clarify some of the basic principles as they apply to activities abroad by promulgating guidelines for companies doing business abroad. These principles, referred to as the Antitrust Enforcement Guidelines for International Operations[73] caused significant controversy when initially issued in 1977, but are much more realistic in their 1988 configuration. In essence, the Justice Department now takes the position that it is not interested in violation of U.S. antitrust principles abroad unless that conduct has a direct impact on U.S. consumers. Justice Department spokesmen strive mightily to confirm that these guidelines are solidly based in an understanding of the U.S. competitive position abroad and in the concept of the rule of reason. However, they are not without their detractors. A former high-ranking Justice Department officer described them as statements that "read more like a preacher's sermon than a counselor's guide."[74] That judgment may be a little harsh. What the Guidelines attempt to do is state a number of hypothetical transactions and to suggest the position that the Justice Department might take in each of those cases. The analysis is somewhat tentative, and perhaps that gives little comfort to business executives and lawyers who are trying to work out a specific compliance posture. There are signals that the Department is becoming more aggressive about extra-territorial application of the U.S. anti-trust laws, so anyone setting up a transaction with some connection to the United States should pay attention to the Guidelines.

However, even if companies avoid domestic antitrust problems flowing out of their foreign activities, they may still run into problems under the antitrust laws of the host country. The European Community, for example, has some highly developed antitrust principles that it enforces with a great deal of aggressiveness.[75] The Community has become particularly concerned

---

71. 15 U.S.C. § 12.

72. 15 U.S.C. § 62

73. The guidelines were initially issued by the Justice Department in 1977, but substantially revised in 1988.

74. Baker & Rushkoff, *The 1988 Justice Department International Guidelines: Searching for Legal Standards and Reassurance*, 23 Cornell Int'l L.J. 405 (1990). See also, Fugate, *The New Justice Department Antitrust Enforcement Guidelines for International Operations—A Reflection of Reagan and, Perhaps, Bush Administration Antitrust Policy*, 29 Va.J.Int'l L. 295 (1989).

75. Articles 85, 86 & 87 of the Treaty of Rome (establishing the European Community) provide the basic foundation. See, e.g., P. Raoul-Duval, *The EEC Merger Control Regulation* in GOING INTERNATIONAL: INTERNATIONAL TRADE FOR THE NON-SPECIALIST (ALI-ABA, 1992); Brown,

about business merger activity in recent years.[76]

§ 3.6.3 Anti-dumping and countervailing duty issues

Most countries impose customs duties on products imported into the country. Many countries also do not wish to see foreign goods enter the country with prices that undercut domestic companies, especially if those prices are set lower than domestic prices for the same product in the country of origin (the idea of *dumping*) or if those prices are somehow subsidized by the country of origin in order to give its companies unfair leverage for market penetration in the country of destination (the basis for the imposition of *countervailing* duties).[77]

The process by which these duties are computed and the administrative procedures by which they are finally adjudicated (in the United States by the International Trade Commission) are too complicated to go into here. Suffice it to say that the pricing of products in a fair and competitive manner is highly important for all contracts for the sale of goods. Artificially low or subsidized prices will likely give rise to protests from competing companies in the country of destination. Those protests could result in the imposition of additional duties which raise the seller's prices. Worse, dumping and subsidization can lead to additional monetary penalties which can make the price of doing business abroad very expensive indeed.

§ 3.6.4 Export and import controls

Virtually every country has strict controls on those things that can be brought into the country and those things that can be taken out. The rationale for these controls may range from an interest in the conservation of natural resources to a desire to protect national security. In the United States, the control of exports is governed mainly by the Export Administration Act of 1979,[78] a statute that requires potential exporters to secure export permission in the form of a validated license (for certain high-technology items and for certain items going to certain countries) or a general license (for other products). The U.S. export controls have been greatly eased as East-West

---

(Note 75 continued) *The Impact of European Community Antitrust Law on United States Companies*, 13 Hastings Int'l & Comp. L.Rev. 383 (1990); Van Bael, *A Practitioner's Guide to Due Process in EEC Antitrust and Antidumping Proceedings*, 18 Int'l Law. 841 (1984).

76. See, e.g., Huie & Hogan, *The New European Community Merger Control Regulation and the Short-Term Horizon of United States Firms*, 6 Am.U.J.Int'l L. & Pol'y 325 (1991).

77. See generally, P. Erenhaft, Remedies Against "Unfair" International Trade Practices in GOING INTERNATIONAL: INTERNATIONAL TRADE FOR THE NON-SPECIALIST (ALI-ABA, 1992); H. KAYE, P. PLAIA, M. HERTZBERG, INTERNATIONAL TRADE PRACTICE (1981 w/annual supplement); Horlick, *A Manual of United States Trade Laws*, Int'l Bus. L. 249 (1985).

78. 50 U.S.C. app. §§ 2401-2420.

tensions have diminished. In 1989 and with subsequent adjustments, the U.S. sharply reduced the number of items that require a validated license and removed most of the countries of Eastern Europe from the list of countries singled out for special export control treatment.[79] Another multilateral organization, the Coordinating Committee for Multilateral Exports (COCOM)—a cold war organization consisting of the U.S. and many of the nations of Western Europe—may shortly disintegrate, thus removing many of the COCOM prohibitions on exports of high-technology equipment to former Soviet-bloc countries.[80]

Import controls are imposed by the country of destination of the product or service in question. There is no feasible way to generalize about these controls. In private international commercial transactions, both import and export controls are normally dealt with by requiring the buyer to obtain all necessary government permissions for the importation of the product, by requiring the seller to obtain the parallel export permissions and making a failure to obtain or to continue these permissions grounds for excuse of performance.

§ 3.6.5 Ethical considerations

In the late 1970s the United States Congress became concerned over a number of documented cases in which U.S. corporations had paid bribes to foreign officials in order to do business in other countries. The outcome of this concern was the Foreign Corrupt Practices Act of 1977 (FCPA),[81] a statute that makes it a crime for any U.S. company to give anything of value to any foreign official or foreign political party to induce or assist in "obtaining or retaining business." In 1988, the FCPA was amended to exclude from its scope a payment for "facilitating or expediting" what the amended Act refers to as the "performance of a routine governmental action." In addition, parties accused of violations of the FCPA may base their defense on either of two other assertions: (1) that the payment is lawful under the written laws and regulations of the foreign country; or (2) that the payment is a reasonable and bona fide expenditure directly related to promotion of products or services or the performance of a contract with a foreign government or agency."[82] These exceptions should not be read too broadly, however. The remainder of the Act and its legislative history state clearly that the FCPA still covers any payments to influence "any decision by a foreign official

---

79. See, e.g., Griffin et al, *U.S. Department of Commerce Takes Further Steps to Ease Export License Requirements*, 18 Int'l Bus.Law. 42 (Jan.1990).

80. See, e.g., Cinelli, *The Impact of 1992 on United States Export Control Laws*, 13 Hastings Int'l & Comp.L.Rev. 395 (1990).

81. 15 U.S.C. § 78dd-2.

82. 15 U.S.C. § 78dd-2(c).

whether, or on what terms, to award new business to or to continue business with a particular party."[83]

Since the statute contains criminal penalties (businesses may be fined up to $2 million and individuals may be fined up $100,000 and imprisoned for up to 5 years), U.S. businesses must pay close attention to compliance matters. Moreover, the FCPA cannot be circumvented by employing a foreign agent or representative to do things which American business people could not themselves get away with.

There have been many assertions that the FCPA (especially before it was amended in 1988) harms the international competitiveness of U.S. businesses since the U.S. is probably the only country in the world with an FCPA. As of 1979 the U.S. Department of Justice estimated that the Act had cost around $1 billion in lost business opportunities. That study has not been updated. The Justice Department appears to prosecute only the most egregious examples of bribery of foreign officials. The Department's lukewarm attitude toward the statute was signaled once again in 1990. The 1988 Amendments to the FCPA suggested that the Justice Department might wish to promulgate guidelines for FCPA compliance. In July, 1990 the Department announced its conclusion that compliance with the FCPA would not be enhanced by such guidelines. The final story on the FCPA has not yet been written.

Of course, the United States is not the only entity with an interest in ethical business conduct in the context of international transactions. The United Nations Conference on Trade and Development is developing codes of conduct for transfer of technology and multinational corporations that attempt to place certain limitations on a company's negotiation posture and techniques and to effectuate a proper and equitable dispute resolution mechanism between MNCs and developing countries.[84]

Among many other things, the UNCTAD Codes of Conduct (1) require that foreign corporations respect the sovereignty of the host government; (2) respect the right of the host government to control its natural wealth and resources; (3) abstain from interference in the internal political affairs of the host country; (4) remain sensitive to the political, economic and social environment of the host country.[85]

---

83. 15 U.S.C. § 78dd-1(f)(3)(B), 78dd-2(h)(4)(B).

84. See, e.g., drafts of the codes at 17 Int'l Legal Materials 453 (1978). For a book length work on MNCs and the codes of conduct see EMERGING STANDARDS OF INTERNATIONAL TRADE AND INVESTMENT: MULTINATIONAL CODES AND CORPORATE CONDUCT (S. Rubin & G. Hufbauer, eds. 1984); LEGAL PROBLEMS OF CODES OF CONDUCT FOR MULTINATIONAL ENTERPRISES (Horn ed., Kluwer, 1980); Roffe, *Transfer of Technology: UNCTAD's Draft International Code of Conduct*, 19 Int'l Law. 689 (1985).

85. For a lengthy discussion of the Codes of Conduct see Asante, *The Concept of the Good Corporate Citizen in International Business*, 4 ICSID Review/Foreign Investment L.J. 1 (1989).

In the United States there have been sporadic and as-yet unsuccessful attempts to force the foreign subsidiaries of American companies to comply with health and safety standards abroad that would be imposed on the company if it were operating in the United States.[86] As this chapter goes to press, the United States Supreme Court is considering whether the U.S. Endangered Species Act has extra-territorial application. The Court recently ruled that the job discrimination statutes of the United States (the U.S. equal employment opportunity laws) do not apply outside the country.[87]

§ 3.7 Special Regional Considerations in Planning International Commercial Agreements

As the second edition of this book goes to press, world trade is in more ferment than perhaps any other time in the twentieth century. The Soviet bloc has disintegrated. Countries such as Poland, Hungary and Czechoslovakia are developing democratic political systems and clamoring to join the European Community.[88] The former Soviet Union has become the loose, unwieldy Commonwealth of Independent States many of whose republics, particularly Russia and Ukraine, are moving in the same directions as the central European countries. Perhaps the smoothest integration has been the unification of East and West Germany after the fall of the Berlin Wall in 1989 — and even that integration has not proved to be trouble-free.

Much of the rest of the world appears to be coalescing into regional trade groupings. The United States and Canada ratified the U.S. - Canada Free Trade Agreement in 1988. That agreement is likely to merge with a comprehensive North American Free Trade Agreement when negotiations among Mexico, Canada and the United States are concluded in 1992. There is now talk of a Western Hemisphere free trade group that would include virtually all the countries of North, Central and South America. Regional trade groupings are appearing among the countries of the Pacific Rim, prompted in part by the phenomenal post-war economic achievements of Japan—a country that now constitutes a primary economic force in and of itself. Perhaps the singular achievement of the final decade of the twentieth century is the planned conomic integration of the European Community at the end of 1992.[89]

---

86. See, e.g., Street, *U.S._Exports Banned for Domestic Use, but Exported to Third World Countries*, 6 Int'l Trade L.J. 95 (1981).

87. EEOC v. Aramco, 111 S.CT. 1227 (1991).

88. See, e.g., Note, *Return to Europe: Integrating Eastern European Economies into the European Market Through Alliance with the European Community*, 31 Harv.Int'l L.J. 660 (1990).

89. For a comprehensive listing of sources on this topic see *Selected Bibliography on Europe 1992*, 11 Mich.J.Int'l L. 526 (1990).

§ 3.7.1 Trade with the European Community

Dreamers such as Jean Monnet talked of a politically and economically unified Europe well before World War Two; but it took the destruction and chaos of that war to stimulate realistic plans for integration. In 1951 a number of European nations signed the Treaty of Paris creating the European Coal and Steel Community to help the countries cope with substantial shortages of both commodities caused by the devastation of the war. The ECSC worked so well that by 1957 six nations (Belgium, The Netherlands, Luxembourg, West Germany, Italy and France) signed the two Treaties of Rome, establishing the European Economic Community and the European Atomic Energy Community.[90] Since 1957 the European Community has broadened its membership to twelve (the original six plus Denmark, Ireland, the United Kingdom, Greece, Portugal and Spain) and is considering the admission, at least as associate members, of several countries of central Europe (primarily Czechoslovakia, Hungary and Poland).

In 1986, the EC members came together once again to sign the Single European Act—a statute that merges the three original treaties, sets out certain objectives of the EC and provides, most strikingly, for the economic and monetary integration of the entire Community by the end of 1992.[91] (The singular *community* will be used in reflection of the single market concept even though as a technical matter the proper term remains the plural *communities*.) When accomplished, the economic integration of Europe will result in the creation of a single $4 trillion market consisting of at least 320 million consumers. If the countries of Central Europe are added to the EC the total population will jump to around 400 million. If some of the former Soviet republics are added to the EC, say, Russia and Ukraine, the total population of the EC will be nearly 600 million people. Within that market, the Community hopes to achieve virtually barrier-free movement of goods, services, people, and capital.

At the same time, integration will not be a seamless process. In 1990, the European Commission identified a sizable number of impediments to full integration (particularly on the matter of a common agricultural policy and the movement of services and professionals across national boundaries).[92] The Federal Republic of Germany has encountered some difficulties in integrating the eastern portion of Germany. If the countries of central Europe and any of the former Soviet republics are added to the equation, the difficulties of integration—both political and economic—will be immense. It is whol-

---

90. The EEC Treaty is 298 U.N.T.S. 11 (Mar. 25, 1957).

91. See the Single European Act, Feb. 28, 1986, 30 Official Journal European Community (No. L 169) 1 (1987).

92. See, e.g., EC Commission, Fifth Report Concerning the Completion of the Internal Market (March, 1990).

ly unlikely that all the work will be completed by the target date, January 1, 1993.[93]

The EC consists of three governing bodies, the European Parliament that holds its plenary sessions in Strasbourg, France, the European Commission (located in Brussels) the body that functions as the executive branch of the EC and the European Court of Justice, the high court of the Community.[94] In addition the EC's Council of Ministers meets periodically in order to develop policy for the EC at the highest level of the Community.

[a] *The Council of Ministers*

The Council of Ministers is comprised of the Heads of State or Heads of Government of each of the member states. The Council meets at least three times each year either in Brussels or in the capital of the member state that holds the Council's presidency (the presidency is a six month term that is rotated among member states). The Council is the highest political body within the EC. Its power is reflected in the fact that its pronouncements do not have to be ratified by the parliaments of the member states. It is charged with the task of establishing what might be called the highest law of the Community. Voting on various pronouncements by the Council is taken on the basis of a *simple majority*, a *qualified majority* (a complicated methodology for counting votes set out in the Treaty of Rome)[95] and *unanimity*. Most of the truly monumental pronouncements by the Council have been taken on the basis of unanimous votes. In the past, that has frequently led to a kind of legislative paralysis. However, the Single European Act extends majority voting to certain decisions in the areas of (i) the completion of the single market, (ii) research and technology, (iii) regional policy formation, and (iv) improvement of the working environment.[96]

The legislation of the Community is set out in a hierarchy of pronouncements as established by Article 189 of the Treaty of Rome.[97] These include:

---

93. Indeed, the full integration of the two most recent additions to the EC, Spain and Portugal, is not scheduled for completion until January 1, 1996. See, e.g., Spanish-Portuguese Accession Treaty, June 12, 1985, 28 O.J. EUR. COMM. (No. L 302) 9 (1985). See also, Meessen, *Europe en Route to 1992: The Completion of the Internal Market and Its Impact on Non-Europeans,* 23 Int'l Law. 359 (1989); Symposium, *1992: Doing Business in the European Internal Market,* 9 Northwestern J.Int'l L.& Bus. 463 (1989)

94. A single commission and a single council were established by what is referred to as the Merger Treaty signed in Brussels in 1965 with an effective date of July 1, 1967. [1967] O.J.EUR.COMM. L-152/2.

95. For a qualified majority, 54 votes out of 76 are required. Germany, France, Italy and the United Kingdom have 10 votes each; Spain has 8 votes; Belgium, Greece, the Netherlands and Portugal have 5 votes each; Denmark and Ireland have 3 votes each; and Luxembourg has 2 votes. EC, THE INSTITUTIONS OF THE EUROPEAN COMMUNITY 7 (1990).

96. *Id.*

97. A similar discussion is set out in Broderick & Calmann, *Introduction to a New Europe: A Primer for 1992,* 20 Int'l Bus.Law. 9 (Jan.1992).

1. *Regulations*: these are directly applicable and binding on member states without the need for enactment of any implementing legislation at the national level by the member states;

2. *Directives*: these are binding on the members states in terms of the *result* commanded by the directive, but each member state is free to work out its own method of compliance;

3. *Decisions*: these are pronouncement that can be issued directly to companies and individuals as well as to member states. They are normally derived from the subject matter of regulations and directives.

4. *Recommendations and Opinions*: These are, as the terms connote, not binding but rather are exhortations or admonitions that are intended to promote certain practices and activities within the EC without having the force and effect of law.

[b] *The European Parliament*

The Parliament is comprised of members (currently 518) elected by direct suffrage from within each member state on the basis of a specific country-by-country apportionment. For example, France, Germany, Italy and the United Kingdom have 81 members each while Ireland has 15 and Luxembourg 6. The members of the Parliament sit within the Parliament on the basis of political affiliation rather than national identity. Their loyalty is expected to be to their constituency, rather than to the government of the country from which they come. Because of the structure of the remainder of the EC, the Parliament sits in what is regarded as an essentially consultative role—providing advice on legislation and the EC's budget. The true power of the EC emanates from the Council and filters through the Commission.

[c] *The Commission*

The European Commission has its headquarters in Brussels and currently consists of 17 members appointed for 4 year terms. The Commission is essentially the executive secretariat for the EC. Its members are not permitted to take instruction from their national governments. It performs essentially two tasks: (1) it may propose initiatives to the Council; and (2) it carries out the various promulgations of the Council. It can bring cases in the Court of Justice in the name of the Community, if it believes that any pronouncements have not been complied with. More specifically, under Article 155 of the EEC Treaty it has the following responsibilities:

1. to monitor and insure compliance with the application of the various treaty provisions and Council initiatives

2. to provide recommendations or opinions on matters within the cognizance of the various treaties;

3. to participate in the preparation of the acts of the Council of Ministers and the European Parliament; and

4. to implement the pronouncements of the Council.

To use a U.S. analogy, the Commission is the executive branch of the EC and exercises most of the day-to-day functions of the Community.

[d] *The Court of Justice*

The European Court of Justice at this writing consists of 13 judges and 6 advocates-general. Both the judges and advocates-general are appointed for 6 year terms with the consent of the member states. Under various articles of the Treaty of Rome, the Court is empowered to quash, at the request of any EC institution, national government or individual, any measure issued by either the Council, Commission or any national government that is incompatible with the various treaties. In addition, in certain circumstances, the Court is empowered to issue interpretations and preliminary rulings on various points of Community law at the request of a national court.[98]

The Single European Act also created a Court of First Instance that functions as a lower echelon of the Court of Justice. The Court of First Instance took its first cases in October, 1989. Persons who come before the Court of First Instance have a right of appeal as to the law to the Court of Justice. Its primary subject matter jurisdiction concerns the Community's competition rules and certain claims for damage brought by private parties under the treaties.[99]

Everyone interested in world trade eagerly awaits the development of the single market. Perhaps of primary concern to persons outside the Community is the question of whether the single market will produce what has been referred to as a "Fortress Europe." Most insiders debunk that particular fear. For example, an EC Commission vice-president has stated: "The achievement of the Internal Market will be of economic benefit not only to Community citizens, but also to the world economy as a whole ... Both Community producers and foreign exporters will benefit directly from operating in an Internal Market with a generally uniform set of regulations, standards, testing, and certification procedures. They will no longer have to face twelve divergent sets of requirements, nor intra-Community border controls."[100]

---

98. See EC Institutions, supra note 94. For a much more comprehensive statement of the European Court see T. HARTLEY, THE FOUNDATIONS OF EUROPEAN COMMUNITY LAW (2d ed. 1988).

99. See, e.g., Millett, *The New European Court of First Instance*, 38 Int'l & Comp.L.Q. 811 (1989).

100. Bangemann, *Fortress Europe: The Myth*, 9 Northwestern J. Int'l L. & Bus. 480 (1989)

§ 3.7.2 The Canada-United States Free Trade Agreement

On March 17, 1985, Saint Patrick's Day, two national leaders of Irish descent, President Brian Mulroney of Canada and President Ronald Reagan shook hands on one of the most important free trade agreements in the history of international trade, the Canada-United States Free Trade Agreement (FTA or Agreement).[101] Reporters then began referring to the accord as the "Shamrock Agreement." Its importance, however, goes much farther than mere lip service to Irish traditions. It is in many respects the most ambitious bilateral trade agreement ever completed. When completely implemented, it will produce a common market between two of the richest nations on earth. The innovative dispute resolution mechanisms set out in the FTA may serve as models for trade disputes throughout the world. The FTA's impact has been so profound in the Western Hemisphere that Mexico, Canada and the United States are now in the process of negotiating an even larger North American Free Trade Agreement that will be closely patterned on the FTA; and the nations of Central and South America now seem willing to discuss a comprehensive Hemispheric Free Trade Agreement, eliminating most trade barriers throughout the hemisphere. Most of these developments are salutary; some are clearly a reaction to the perceived creation of a Fortress Europe and the slightly more palpable fears of a Fortress Japan.

The FTA has been fully ratified by Canada and the United States and had an effective date of January 1, 1989 although many of its provisions phase in over a nearly ten year period from 1989 to 1998.

The FTA is set out in 20 separate chapters with annexes that comprise another 1500 pages of tariff schedules. Its stated objectives are straightforward:

— to eliminate barriers to trade in goods and services
— to facilitate conditions of fair competition
— to liberalize conditions for investment
— to establish effective procedures for resolving disputes
— to lay a foundation for further cooperation[102]

On occasion, this rather flowery language obscures a proper understanding of the FTA. In speaking of the Agreement, this author frequently describes the treaty as: "wine and architects; but not beer or lawyers." What this little homily captures are a product (wine) and a professional service (architectural services)

---

101. The treaty is set out at 27 I.L.M. 281 (1988). Implementing legislation in the United States is contained in Pub. L. No. 100-449, 102 Stat. 1851 (1988). Most of this section is taken from Fox, *The Canada-United States Free Trade Agreement: Implications for Latin America*, a paper delivered to the 27th Conference of the Inter-American Bar Association, Cartagena, Colombia (May 8, 1989). See also, J. JOHNSON & J. SCHACHTER, THE FREE TRADE AGREEMENT: A COMPREHENSIVE GUIDE (1988); Kazanjian & Craig, The Canada-United States Free Trade Agreement, 16 Int'l Bus.Law. 112 (March, 1988).

102. FTA, Article 102.

that are within the FTA and which are supposed to move freely between the two countries, and a product (beer) and a professional service (legal services) that are totally excluded from the FTA—and, one would expect, will encounter traditional barriers between the two nations. The reader should understand that for all its innovations and benefits, the FTA is neither perfect, nor totally comprehensive. If it has a possible negative outcome, its ratification (and the interest in adopting similar initiatives elsewhere in the world on a bilateral basis) may signal the end of the General Agreement on Tariffs and Trade (GATT). Even though the FTA is expressly in harmony with GATT—that is, the FTA is not to be implemented in any manner that violates one of the provisions of GATT—its very existence may kill GATT. For countries lucky enough to participate in regional or bilateral trade arrangements, this may not be a bad development. For those countries of the world that remain on the outside looking in, the consequences could be devastating.

The FTA is most easily understood in terms of its major components: (1) the elimination of tariffs on goods, (2) the rules of national origin, (3) the diminishing of barriers to trade in various services and professional activities; and (4) a number of special dispute resolution mechanisms.

[a] *Elimination of tariffs on goods*
Roughly 80 percent of exports from Canada to the United States and around 65 percent of exports from the U.S. to Canada carried no duties whatsoever even before the FTA went into effect. While much of this trade was in automobiles and automobile parts, it is clear that a lot of trade was already flowing between the two countries without trade barriers of any kind. However, on the remaining items, Canada imposed duties averaging 9 to 10 percent, a figure that was roughly double the average U.S. duty (4 - 5 percent) on imports from Canada.

Under the Agreement, virtually all tariffs between the two countries will be phased out between 1989 and 1998 with nearly 10 percent already eliminated (i.e., as of 1989) and about 30 - 40 percent of the tariffs removed over the first five years of the FTA. Typical goods in the first category (i.e., elimination of tariffs as of 1989) include automatic data processing equipment, leather, fur and fur garments, whiskey and rum, telephones, and motorcycles. In the five-year elimination period are such products as: furniture, most machinery, petroleum, chemicals (other than drugs and cosmetics), explosives, subway cars, and paper and paper products. In the final category (tariffs to be eliminated by 1998) are: steel, rubber, tires, textiles and wearing apparel, plastics, wood products, appliances and railcars.[103]

---

103. FTA, Annex § 401.2.

[b] *The rules of origin*

One of the primary concerns of the negotiators of the FTA was to insure that only goods actually produced in either the U.S. or Canada receive the special protections of the agreement. As a consequence, the agreement's rules of origin are crucial to a proper application of the FTA and are somewhat different from the rules of origin in the GATT. Under the FTA, goods that are produced exclusively in either country, including the products of mines and agriculture, are fully covered. If a good is partially the product of some other country, a complicated formula involving customs classifications and the notion of *value added* is applied to determine the origin of the goods. For example, for goods assembled in the U.S. or Canada, at least 50 percent of the total processing costs and value of the original materials of the goods in question must have originated in either country.[104] At the same time, the FTA makes clear that merely repackaging the materials, or adding something to a good (such as water) that does not "materially alter" the good, or doing something to a good simply to try to circumvent the rules of national origin does not suffice.[105]

[c] *Trade in services*

Perhaps the most important innovation of the FTA is the mechanism for freeing trade in services. While complicated in actual operation, the FTA attempts to liberalize trade in services by insisting that most services receive *national treatment* by each country.[106] National treatment provides, in essence, that each country will impose no greater restrictions or limitations on the providers of services from the other country than it imposes on its own service providers. Initial estimates by the United States Department of Commerce were that these provisions would benefit over 150 separate service industries in the United States including tourism, engineering services, architectural services, accounting services, the sale of insurance, management consulting services and many others. However, as noted above, this portion of the FTA is not comprehensive. Through the negotiation process a wide range of services was completely exempted from the FTA, including: lawyers, doctors, dentists and certain transportation and telecommunications services. Even for the services covered by the agreement, the FTA makes clear that service providers must reside in either Canada or the United States.

---

104. FTA, Article 301.
105 FTA, Article 301.2, 301.3.
106. FTA, Chapter 14.

[d] *The dispute resolution mechanisms*

Another contribution of the FTA to improving international trade is the institution of new dispute resolution mechanisms. Here, the FTA distinguishes between two different events that might affect the provisions of the agreement: changes in domestic laws or regulations (referred to in the FTA as *legislative changes*) and actions that implicate antidumping or countervailing duty issues.

If any disagreement between the two countries arises under the FTA or when a new legal principle emerges in either country that might have an impact on the agreement, the two countries are first obliged to give notice of the possible impediment and then to engage in consultation. If, within 30 days of notification, the device of consultation is not productive, either country may request a convening of the FTA Commission—a body that is composed of representatives from both countries with the principal representative being the U.S. Trade Representative and the Canadian Minister of Trade.[107] The Commission is empowered to establish its own procedures and to decided matters by consensus.

If the Commission cannot resolve the problem (including resolution with the possible assistance of a mediator), the Commission is authorized the submit the dispute to arbitration or, in certain cases, to special panels of experts. Arbitration is to be conducted by arbitration panels consisting of two arbitrators appointed by each side who then pick a fifth member. The arbitral award is binding on both parties. If a matter is not submitted to arbitration, it may be submitted to a panel of experts that essentially makes a recommendation to the Commission. It is expected that such recommendations will be accepted by the Commission. For those matters that are not, the FTA contains special sanctions that may be imposed if the dispute is not resolved, such as suspending the application of equivalent benefits under the FTA to the non-complying party.[108]

The FTA anticipated that between 1989 and 1998 there may be disputes under the remaining tariff schedules that implicate antidumping and countervailing duty issues. The FTA replaces the normal in-country devices for resolving these issues with a bi-national panel whose procedures are not substantially different from those set out for the legislative review panels discussed in the preceding paragraph. The agreement provides that these panels are the final arbiters of such cases—the panel's decisions may not be questioned in the domestic courts of either country.

---

107. FTA, Chapter 18. There is some lingering question of the constitutionality of these procedures under either the U.S. or Canadian constitution. However, most observers believe that the procedures are fully consistent with either document. See, e.g., Christenson & Gambrel, *Constitutionality of Binational Panel Review in Canada-U.S. Free Trade Agreement*, 23 Int'l Law 401 (1989).

108. FTA, Article 1807.9

[e] *Other Aspects of the Agreement*

There are many other matters in the FTA that can only be covered briefly. For example, the two countries commit to the gradual elimination of virtually all agricultural subsidies over the term of the agreement.[109] Trade in energy, especially oil, natural gas and hydroelectric power is eventually supposed to move without barriers or encumbrances.[110] Additional provisions in the FTA urge uniformity of treatment in matters of government procurement.

There is no question that the agreement is a monumental one. It may prove to be a model for other agreements, not just in the Western Hemisphere but around the world. The joint U.S.-Canada entity is going to be quite powerful in world markets and if these two countries join with Mexico a multi-trillion dollar common market will have been formed—easily the economic equivalent of the European Community.   ◆

---

109. FTA, Chapter 9.
110. FTA, Chapter 7.

— 4 —
Drafting International Commercial Agreements

§ 4.1. Introduction

Most lawyers talk in terms of "negotiating and drafting" of contracts, suggesting that negotiation always precedes the actual drafting of contract language. That is not necessarily a realistic way to view this process, although in most cases negotiation and drafting go hand in hand. Many agreements are based on standard form contracts that one or the other party has drafted long in advance of the actual transaction. In other cases, negotiation of the agreement's provisions takes place after one party submits a draft agreement to the other party for consideration. There are still other cases in which a letter of intent—a document that has many of the attributes of a contract without necessarily being a binding instrument—is the first meaningful communication between the parties. There are many instances in which an exchange of documents precedes face-to-face negotiation. Submitting a preliminary document such as a draft contract or letter of intent may itself be a powerful negotiating tactic in the same sense that power accrues to the person who sets the agenda for a meeting. As a consequence, it is frequently more logical to think about what you would like *your* version of the contract to say, and then to see what occurs during the negotiating sessions.

Often the party who proffers the first draft will carry the day on many of the points of the transaction simply by having been first to suggest written language. Even if the contract is substantially redrafted during the negotiation process, the party who has thought about the wording of various provisions and who has at least tried to put some words on paper before the meeting frequently develops a great deal of negotiation leverage when alternative provisions are discussed and drafted.

For all these reasons, this chapter discusses contract drafting and Chapter Five takes up negotiating techniques and strategy. There is nothing wrong, however, with a reader beginning with Chapter Five if he or she does not agree with this analysis. Contract drafting and contract negotiation go together—to use a favorite American expression—like ham and eggs.

§ 4.2. Some Threshold Considerations

There are probably as many theories on how to draft contracts as there are drafters of contracts. Anyone who has tried to write anything from a personal letter to a short story to a legal document has a store of pet language, a list of "do's" and "don'ts" and various rules of thumb for everything from the length of sentences to the alignment of paragraphs. If there is any principle that cuts through all these individualized techniques and idiosyncrasies, it is simply this: *language is communication*, or put a bit more realistically, the use of language is an attempt by two or more persons to communicate with each other.[1] At bottom, any drafting exercise is simply a matter of taking what is in one person's mind and putting that information on paper in a sufficiently precise form to convey that same information into the mind of the other party. As everyone recognizes, this is easier said than done.

Is writing something that most people do naturally? Is it something that can only be left to the specialists? Are lawyers necessarily the best judge of contract language? The answer to all three of these questions is either "no" or, since lawyers always hedge their bets, "probably not." Is it possible even to discuss contract drafting generally? This author's firm belief is that it can be discussed and that the best contracts are drafted by people who take some time to review basic concepts of drafting before committing themselves to paper.

If the normal goal of writing is to communicate, the specific goal of a contract is to express the agreement between the parties as clearly and as fully as possible so that there is little need to go beyond the document if later

---

1. There is no way for an American law professor writing about legal drafting to ignore the contributions of probably the foremost scholar in the area, Professor F. Reed Dickerson; see, e.g., his newest work, F.R. DICKERSON, MATERIALS ON LEGAL DRAFTING (1981) and his classic treatise on the subject, F.R. DICKERSON, THE FUNDAMENTALS OF LEGAL DRAFTING (1965). One of the best statements of a growing development in U.S. legal circles known as the Plain English movement is C. FELSENFELD AND A. SIEGEL, WRITING CONTRACTS IN PLAIN ENGLISH (1981). There are many law journal articles devoted to specific categories of international contracts. Some representative articles include: Grabow, *Negotiating and Drafting Contracts in International Barter and Countertrade Transactions*, 9 N.C.J. Int'l L. & Com. Reg. 255 (1984); Jaslow, *Practical Considerations in Drafting a Joint Venture Agreement with China*, 31 Amer.J.Comp.L. 209 (1983); Byington, *Planning & Drafting of International Licensing Agreements*, 6 N.C.J.Int'l L. & Com. Reg. 193 (1982); Hoya & Stein, *Drafting Contracts in U.S.-Soviet Trade*, 7 L & Pol'y in Int'l Bus. 1057 (1975). George Delaume's multivolume treatise on international contracts contains scattered drafting hints. See G. DELAUME, TRANSNATIONAL CONTRACTS (1983) *passim.*

misunderstandings arise between the parties. Recall the twin principles of basic contract law: the parties are generally free to frame whatever agreement they choose (party autonomy) and once having agreed, they will be held to the terms of that agreement (*pacta sunt servanda*).

One of the basic dilemmas of contract drafting is that all forms of human communication are subject to misunderstandings and misinterpretation. It is virtually impossible to put anything on paper that is totally free of ambiguity. Even so, a writer can strive for clarity and precision even if no document drafted by mere mortals is going to be perfect.

§ 4.2.1 Identifying goals and objectives

The first step toward clarity and precision is understanding what the contracting party desires. This means that the first obligation of a business executive is to communicate effectively with those persons in the company who are responsible for the transaction. The first obligation of a lawyer is to communicate effectively with the client to ascertain the client's wishes. Establishing a common denominator of understanding between people on the same side of a business deal usually enhances pre-contract communication. This is not easily accomplished. A lawyer working with new clients is well advised to spend a substantial amount of time in discussions with that client to make absolutely certain that there is a meeting of the minds between lawyer and client. This is one reason why even experienced lawyers often resort to contract drafting outlines and checklists when working with a client. Lists of important elements may seem a tool only for beginners, but they can help insure that even the most experienced lawyers cover most of the important components in the transaction.

Most people in business have a good idea of what they want to accomplish from a business standpoint. Understanding the fundamental nature of the transaction in question is the first place to start. A contract's aim may be to sell 20,000 brass fittings on a one-time basis to an Argentine retailer, or to commence a multi-million dollar turn key construction project in Pakistan. If the drafter is a business executive drafting her own contract, it is likely that she will have a fairly good grasp of the contract's basic goals. Some business executives will stop at that point and simply turn the remainder of the transaction over to the lawyers for implementation. A favorite client of the author's probably expressed this attitude best when he said: "I don't want you to tell me *no*; I want you to tell me *how*."

Most clients remain involved far longer than the initial consultation with the lawyer and, in any event, American lawyers have an ethical obligation to zealously represent their clients within the bounds of the law.[2] This

---

2. See, e.g., Canon 7, Model Code of Professional Responsibility.

means that a lawyer engaged in drafting a contract for a client cannot be satisfied with merely learning the client's basic short-term goals. The client may have objectives beyond the specific business deal at hand that will affect the manner in which the contract is drafted and the negotiation carried out. For example, the sale of the 20,000 brass fittings may be viewed by the your client, the seller, as a pilot project with the additional goal of establishing a long-term business relationship with the buyer. This single fact might prompt the drafter of the contract to include more evenly-balanced and conciliatory terms in the document—and to negotiate more gently—than might be the case if the transaction is merely incidental to the seller's domestic business and one in which the seller does not have any long term interests. In the latter case, a contract drafter representing the seller might emphasize speed and security of payment and might write language that makes it very difficult for the buyer to terminate the contract once it is executed. If the seller regards the sale as merely a sideline and one in which the seller does not want to incur any great expense, the seller's lawyer may decide to rely more heavily on pre-printed forms or clauses copied out of form books rather than create a completely new document. Whether lawyers admit it or not, this type of informal cost-benefit analysis (i.e., how much professional time and attention does this deal deserve?) always takes place in the mind of the lawyer, if not in conversations with the client.

Moreover, communication cannot be one-way. The client can articulate both short-term and long-term goals; but it is normally up to the lawyer to identify both problems and opportunities. Some people in business do not realize the importance of the parole evidence rule—a legal requirement that severely limits the amount of external evidence a court will consider in construing a contract. In the Anglo-American legal systems, the document is supposed to stand or fall on its own terms and normally cannot be altered by oral understandings or extraneous documents. Other legal systems are more accepting of evidence outside the contract itself, but most contract drafters seek to describe the entire agreement in the contract, even if certain matters such as specifications for equipment, are left to annexes or subsequent agreement. Contract language can also have consequences beyond the agreement itself. The way in which a contract is drafted could trigger serious tax or antitrust consequences for either buyer or seller. Business executives are not normally experts in these matters. Developing a sensitivity to all the consequences of a contract is more often the lawyer's role.

A business deal can sometimes become far more complicated than the business executive may suspect when first setting up the transaction. The executive new to international transactions may not know, for example, that it may be nearly impossible to deal with Argentine retailers without the use of an agent in Argentina. The government of Pakistan may insist on the foreign company's forming a joint venture with Pakistani citizens for construction projects of any magnitude in Pakistan. There is a great need for a proper flow of information back and forth from client to lawyer. It is embarrassing and often professionally dangerous to learn something new about the deal, the client's wishes, or the state of the law only when sitting across from the other side in the final negotiating session. Proper planning and client counseling at the pre-drafting stage will substantially reduce the number of subsequent problems and surprises.

§ 4.2.2 Research as a planning and drafting tool

Chapter Five will constantly remind the reader that in business negotiations knowledge is power. It is axiomatic that the more knowledge negotiators have, the more leverage they will accrue in negotiating a deal. Obviously, the more research that can be performed before negotiation, the better. In most instances, the problem is not so much where to start but rather where to stop.

Business executives often perform a great deal of relevant research long before the transaction is begun. Trade fairs and business publications convey a great deal of information on the business climate in particular countries. Credit reporting services can quickly obtain information on the financial status and the creditworthiness of individual companies in many countries. In the United States, as in other countries, various government agencies such as the Department of State, the Department of Commerce, the Export-Import Bank and the Overseas Private Investment Corporation (a government corporation rather than agency) regularly collect and publish an enormous amount of information on international transactions and on targeted countries. Prior to entering into a contract, businesses frequently exchange information on themselves, especially if they do not have an existing relationship. All of this information can enhance both the drafting and negotiating phases of international transactions.

Proper interviewing and counseling of the client is vitally important. An understanding of the legal issues is indispensable. But how far should a lawyer go? Is the question just a matter of economics? In other words, does the lawyer research only as much as the client is willing to pay for. For American attorneys, the problem is not simple. Lawyers have special responsibilities and special difficulties in this area because ethically they are not permitted to handle cases in which they are not competent and they are generally not permitted to educate themselves at the expense of their clients.[3]

There is no easy way to resolve the problem of where to halt one's research or investigation. Obviously, lawyers should not attempt transac-

---

3. Disciplinary Rule 6-101, Model Code of Professional Responsibility; Rule 1.1, Model Rules of Professional Conduct.

tions on which they are not at least minimally informed and competent; but even experienced lawyers must grapple with many of these questions. Consider, for example, an issue that is discussed extensively in section 4.4 below—choosing the law applicable to the contract, previously discussed, for the sale of 20,000 brass fittings by an American manufacturer to an Argentine company. Most international contracts take a very cavalier approach to this problem. Almost as an after-thought the contract drafter will state that the governing law is "the law of the State of New York" if the seller is located in New York. If the buyer does not have enough negotiation leverage to insist on a choice of Argentine law (assuming that is his preference), this clause will likely find itself in the final contract.

In practice, choice of law can be more complicated than one might assume. Given that New York has adopted the Uniform Commercial Code (UCC), given that Article Two of the UCC expressly covers the sale of goods, and given that almost all U.S. lawyers specializing in commercial transactions have extensive education and training in the UCC, there should be no major problems arising from the choice of law issue from the seller's standpoint. The Argentine buyer might be agreeable, particularly if the buyer is represented in the transaction by New York lawyers. If both sides feel comfortable with the body of law chosen, the transaction should proceed smoothly.

But assume the contrary. The U.S. seller is so desperate to get rid of those brass fittings that he will agree to nearly anything in terms of a choice of law clause. He may, in fact, have instructed his lawyer not to argue over peripheral matters in the contract. The Argentine buyer may insist on Argentine law governing the contract. How deeply does the seller's lawyer have research Argentine law to protect the seller's interests and the lawyer's own professional interest in not committing malpractice. If money and time is no object, the New York attorney might perform substantial research on Argentine sales law and possibly even hire a consultant on Argentine commercial law to help advise the client. If the fittings contract is to be the first of many such agreements, both seller and the seller's lawyer have a long-term stake in knowing more about Argentina's legal system so a greater initial investment in legal research may be justified.

But if the fittings contract is for a modest amount of money and if it is viewed as a one-time transaction, the research problem becomes stickier. There are a number of options over a wide spectrum. In the first place, a contract's choice of law becomes relevant only if the contract is subject to some kind of dispute and if the person (judge or arbitrator) deciding the dispute has to refer to legal principles outside the document to reach a decision. The seller's lawyer could simply do nothing and hope for the best, estimating that the possible range of disputes under the contract would not turn out differently even if the law of Argentina is applied. At the other end of the spectrum, the lawyer could simply turn the transaction over to an attorney knowledgeable in Argentine law and shift the burden onto an attorney trained in the underlying legal system. That, of course, might require sharing the fee, or giving up the fee entirely. Not many lawyers are willing to go that far.

There is a middle ground. The seller's lawyer could try to personally research Argentine law using resources available in New York. The lawyer could commission a qualified lawyer to perform research in Argentine law only on a limited number of legal issues that the lawyer anticipates might arise and use that research as a comfort factor. The lawyer could hire an Argentine practitioner solely to review the final contract, rather than to draft the initial document so that any unseen pitfalls would be spotted before the contract is signed.

There are no hard, fast answers here. Pre-drafting and pre-negotiation research is not just a matter of business wisdom. For lawyers involved in international contracts, it can become a difficult question of professional responsibility. In any event, it should be given close attention by both lawyers and clients.

§ 4.2.3 Beginning the drafting process

The blank page syndrome that all authors face is equally common in contract drafting. How does a writer begin to fill up the paper? One method used by a large number of contract drafters is to begin from some kind of checklist or standard outline for commercial contracts. Using a typical contract for the sale of goods as an example, most contracts address the substantive matters of the contracts in something like the following order:

1. Date and place of the agreement
2. Description including full names and addresses of the parties
3. Definitions, if any
4. Description of the subject matter of the contract
5. Recitation of offer and acceptance
6. Price term
7. Payment term
8. Security interest, if any
9. Delivery term
10. Title, risk of loss and insurance
11. Specifications and warranties, if any
12. Taxes
13. Authorizations, permits and licenses
14. Breach, termination and liquidated damages, if any
15. Notices

16. Cancellation and rescission
17. Applicable law
18. Official language
19. Dispute resolution
20. Force majeure
21. Assignment of contract
22. Alterations (including a prohibition on oral modifications, if desired)
23. Annexes, if any
24. Signatures and counterpart provision (if necessary)

Most of these clauses are self-explanatory or are discussed more elaborately later in this chapter.

A counterpart provision is a clause in or near the signature lines that provides that each party may sign a copy of the contract in his or her location. Each of these signed copies will be merged into a final single contract, but the date of execution is the date on which all of the parties put their signatures to the document, rather than the date of final merger. A counterpart provision is particularly helpful if the parties are a long distance from each other and if they don't want to spend the time and expense to travel to a central location for a signing ceremony. Counterpart provisions are also helpful if a contract must be executed as of a particular date when the parties cannot all come together for signing on that date. As more and more drafting and negotiation takes place via facsimile machine and modem, counterpart provisions may become more common. The reader should check the law of the applicable jurisdiction to make sure that counterpart clauses are valid.

Contracts for the sale of goods are the most common form of international commercial agreement, but there are many other types of contracts. For example, in the context of international licensing agreements, a contract normally includes clauses on the following:

1. Transfer of the license from licensor to licensee
2. Royalty rate
3. Place and manner of payment of royalties
4. Determination of rates of exchange [a currency fluctuation clause
5. Allocation of tax burdens between the parties
6. Government approvals
7. Registration and recordation of the license
8. Compliance with export laws in country of origin

Contracts for multi-million dollar turnkey construction projects can be even longer and more extensive. The following is an example of an international construction contract for the construction of off-shore oil drilling platforms.

CHAPTER SEVEN: DELIVERY AND PAYMENT

Article 27: Delivery and Completion of the Work

Article 28: Payment, Invoices and Audit

Article 29: Invoice Retention/Bank Guarantee

Article 30: Title and Liens

Article 31: Guarantee and Final Acceptance Certificate

CHAPTER EIGHT: BREACH OF CONTRACT

Article 32: Contractor's Delay

Article 33: Contractor's Liability for Breach of Guarantee

Article 34: Termination Because of Contractor's Default

Article 35: Company's Breach of Contract

CHAPTER NINE: RISK, LIABILITY, INDEMNIFICATION AND INSURANCE

Article 36: Passing of Risk for Contract Object and Company Provided Items

Article 37: Liability and Indemnification

Article 38: Insurance

CHAPTER TEN: PROPRIETARY RIGHTS

Article 39: Ownership of Drawings, Plans and Specifications

Article 40: Patents and Inventions

Article 41: Confidential Information

Article 42: General Competence

CHAPTER ELEVEN: MISCELLANEOUS CLAUSES

Article 43: Subcontracting and Assignment

Article 44: Non-Waiver of Default

Article 45: Force Majeure

Article 46: Governing Law and Dispute Resolution

Article 47: Notices

Article 48: Alteration of Contract

Article 49: Signatures

ANNEXES AND ATTACHMENTS

Note that the construction contract outline is far longer and far more detailed than a typical contract for the sale of goods. There are any number of reasons for this. One is that the dollar amount of a large-scale construction contract justifies far greater detail in the document. A second reason is the fact that construction contracts typically extend over a period of years in a setting where changed conditions and fresh thinking on the part of the contracting parties is likely to require changes in the original understanding. A third is that the risks on all sides are far greater in a contract of this dimension. The parties typically do not want to have a great deal of uncertainty or ambiguity in the transaction.

The construction contract also illustrates another common technique in drafting lengthy contracts. There are plenty of occasions when the parties will want to set out specifications for the goods or services in question in separate annexes or attachments to the basic contract. Simply because the dimensions of a few bolts in the oil platform must be changed is no reason to revisit and redraft the underlying contract. It is far easier to change an annex of specifications. It may also be procedurally dangerous to revisit the basic contract. If one party's mind has changed substantially over time, that party might use the excuse of a change in bolt specifications as an excuse to re-do the entire agreement. For expensive, long-duration contracts, annexes and attachments play an important role.

A contract drafter can find sample outlines and checklists in various form books. A drafter can create an original contract outline by simply considering all the elements that he or she would like to see in the contract. Even though that list is likely to be modified during conversations with the client and with the other side, an outline is a good place to begin and a good way to work around the blank page trauma. Once a drafter has set out most if not all of the ingredients in the contract, she can begin to order these items into an outline and to think about how to fill in the blanks with precise, substantive contract language.

Drafting actual contract language is something that many lawyers find highly intimidating. Traditional contract language is so abstruse and complex that it bears little relation to the way in which people normally communicate with each other. One recourse for the neophyte contract drafter is to borrow from form books. Contract drafting is one form of human activity where the concept of plagiarism simply does not apply. Lawyers in particular borrow constantly from documents that have gone before. One reason for this is simply the innate conservatism of the legal profession. Lawyers hesitate trying anything new if they can adopt something that has gone before. Another reason is that the doctrine of *stare decisis*—a litigation concept that requires courts to abide by previous court decisions—is carried over, often inappropriately, to transactional work. If a lawyer finds a document that seems to have passed muster sometime previously, he is happy to use it for his own transaction. Sometimes that makes sense; other times it is the height of stupidity.

Because lawyers tend to be such large-scale borrowers most law libraries stock numerous form books containing sample contract clauses, checklists for the content of contracts, and often complete contracts. For the easily intimidated lawyer, these may simply be copied with appropriate changes in the parties' names and other specific details and presented to the client as a newly created legal document.

There are better ways to think about contract drafting. Form books ought to be a drafter's starting point, not her finishing point. When using pre-existing language or when creating language of one's own, there are some generic considerations that ought to be applied. If there is a cardinal rule in contract drafting it is that you rely on other people's work at your peril. Section 4.5 discusses the use of standardized clauses and form agreements in more depth. Most contracts for any substantial amount of money are tailored to the parties' specific situation.

How then does one go about this process of refinement? A contract drafter, whether lawyer or non-lawyer, should not forget everything he has already been taught about the use of language and what constitutes good writing.[4] While there is no single approach to writing of any sort, there is no question that well written contracts go a long way toward avoiding problems. To be even a little more patronizing, contracts ought to be properly punctuated, verb tenses ought to agree and language ought to be used accurately and with precision.

In working with form books and other pre-existing language, or in drafting original contracts, a drafter should consider three generic problems that occur in contract drafting: the use of *superfluous* language, the use of *ambiguity* and the use of legal or industrial *terms of art*. The modern trend in legal drafting is to eliminate excessive legalisms in contracts while avoiding colloquialisms. Modern contracts do not need terms such as *witnesseth*, *heretofore*, the frequently used *whereas*, or the particularly disgusting *said* as in "This contract is for the sale of fittings. *Said* fittings ... . " When these words are strung together in a single clause in a contract they become hilarious. One clause of similar import from an actual contract reads: "NOW, THEREFORE, in consideration of the premises and of the mutual covenants of the parties hereto to be faithfully performed as hereinafter specified, the parties hereto hereby covenant and agree as follows." What the parties are trying to say is that they have come together to make a contract and the terms of the agreement follow that clause. Is all this language necessary to a valid agreement? Absolutely not.

Terms such as these are archaic; their origins are obscure. If they ever had a special meaning or purpose, such things have been lost in history.

---

4. Felsenfeld and Siegel, supra note 1, is a particularly good source of material on these issues.

They contribute nothing but word count to the contract. Tragically, too many lawyers and not a few clients do not realize this and insist—wholly without justification—that contracts must contain such language to be valid agreements. When the author drafted a contract for a client several years ago, the client rejected the document saying: "It just doesn't look like a contract." When asked why, the client said: "Because it doesn't have any "wittnesseths" in it, like my other lawyer's contracts." After a long-distance hassle as to what a real contract looked like, the client concluded the discussion by saying: "If you don't put those words back in, I'm not going to pay you." The words were put back in. This is the second lesson on superfluous language. Even if it does not contribute anything to a contract, it probably does not destroy the legal integrity of the document either.

Superfluous language has a first cousin: verbosity. Lawyers often try to accomplish too much and wind up saying nothing of consequence. Verbosity and complexity in contract language often *causes* rather than cures problems. For example, a sales contract might say something such as: "Seller agrees to sell and Buyer agrees to buy 1000 fittings at $1.00 per fitting." There are plenty of other simple variations on this language that are perfectly permissible and that accurately convey the intent of the parties. What is not needed is something such as: "Seller agrees to sell, convey, transfer, assign and otherwise relinquish claim to and otherwise commit into the permanent possession and ownership of buyer 1000 fittings."

Language such as this occurs in contracts for two different reasons, one somewhat commendable and understandable; the other far less so. The less commendable reason simply reflects the drafting process in so many law firms. Each lawyer cannot feel that he or she has made a contribution to the document unless something is added to the contract. Even a few extra words will suffice, but the contract cannot escape the average lawyers desk without having something else grafted on to it.

The second reason at least has a legitimate purpose behind it even if the purpose is rarely accomplished. In writing clauses such as this, lawyers are trying to cover all bases, to prepare for all possible contingencies. There may have been actual litigated cases long in the past where the absence of one or another synonym caused a court to declare the agreement invalid. Even without close examination of the facts of those early cases, we can now say with certainty that this sort of verbosity is not necessary today. Worse, unlike purely superfluous language, many of the verbs in the quoted price term do not mean the same thing: for example, assignments in the U.S. legal system are somewhat different from pure sales transactions, so to *assign* is not necessarily to *sell.* To the extent that the verbs are completely synonymous, they are superfluous—akin to saying, "Seller seller seller agrees agrees agrees to buy to buy to buy."

Contract drafters should appreciate that all human communication is imprecise and that additional detail does not necessarily constitute additional precision. Business executives are almost always far more realistic. When one executive says "buy" the other knows pretty much what is meant. Lawyers ought to be secure enough to accept and utilize this sort of simplicity.

Many contract drafters agonize over the meaning of words. For the most part that is a good trait. In most instances contract drafters should avoid ambiguity and imprecision. For example, a contract that states: "The price of each fitting *may* be $5.00 per fitting" is simply bad usage. A price term is usually expected to be clear and definite. The use of the verb *may* creates ambiguity where none should exist. In the English language, the mandatory verb is *shall*. By contrast, there are times when contract drafters may want to use what is called *deliberate* or *purposeful* ambiguity. For example, a contract could specify the actual shipping vessel (SS Hermes, say) on which the fittings are to be shipped. This is the height of precision, but it is probably uncalled for. In all likelihood, other problems may occur if the Hermes is not available. In the alternative, using the device of deliberate ambiguity, the contract might simply state: "Seller agrees to transport the fittings using a mutually acceptable form of surface transportation." Or, "seller agrees to transport the fittings by rail." Underlying legal systems occasionally invoke deliberate ambiguity. The Uniform Commercial Code in the United States provides that when a contract does not specify price, the price shall be a price that is *reasonable* at the time of shipment of the goods. Deliberate ambiguity can accomplish two things: it can leave open a contract term on which the parties cannot agree while permitting them to achieve agreement on everything else; and it can leave peripheral matters to the discretion of one or another of the parties without triggering a breach of contract simply because the other party might have done something differently.

The use of *terms of art* can also shorten the length of contracts or lead to substantial conflict. On this point, there are a few good rules of thumb. Most courts and most people who work with contracts define words by applying the ordinary, dictionary meaning of those terms. So a contract that calls for the sale of 120 "eggs" would generally not be construed as calling for the sale of 120 Scotch eggs (the British pub food). There are, however, some departures from the plain meaning rule. Within specific industries, and among merchants in those industries, it may be permissible to use terms in other than their ordinary meanings on the plausible assumption that "everybody" knows what the contract talking about. So a contract for the sale of 120 Scotch eggs between two British pub owners might conceivably use only the term "egg" to describe the commodity. Petroleum refineries use a device called a *reformer* to manufactured lead-free gasoline. A contract for the construction of an oil refinery that calls for the installation of a reformer, without further definition, would probably not cause problems. None of the parties would define that term as "a person who seeks to change things by making them better."

There is another way to deal with terms in a contract. Certain terms may be defined specifically in a separate definition section of the contract. A definitional section has the advantage of explaining the term in the contract itself and thus not leaving a definition to the vagaries of judges or arbitrators. Lawyers know that even so-called everyday definitions can vary from time to time and place to place. A definitional section has the additional advantage of making the body of a contract shorter. For example, two merchants can agree to buy and sell 100 wooden boxes. The definitional section (or conceivably a separate addendum on specifications) can prescribe that each box shall be of top grade walnut and of certain dimensions. Once having set out this definition, the contract may then simply refer to "box" or "boxes" whenever it is necessary to mention the commodity in question without reiterating the boxes' specifications.

These are just a few of the things that contract drafters should consider before setting words down on paper. There are no categorical rules in this regard except perhaps the homily that well-written contracts cause fewer problems than poorly written contracts. The remainder of this chapter considers more specific contract drafting issues.

§ 4.3 The Use and Effect of a Letter of Intent

In complicated undertakings, the parties often need a document that signals that they have "agreed to agree." The drafting of a *letter of intent* or a *memorandum of understanding* is often necessary when matters central to the final agreement such as financing and government approval are not yet a certainty. A letter of intent may occasionally be taken to a government official or bank officer in order to get the permissions or funding necessary for the agreement. On other occasions, a letter of intent has the effect of resolving certain preliminary matters while a long-term negotiation hammers out the remaining components of the deal.

The difficulty, of course, is that a letter of intent itself has to be drafted and negotiated. While this is usually not terribly difficult, persons engaged in contract drafting who also draft letters of intent should be aware that these documents can sometimes take on a life of their own, particularly in jurisdictions where the requirement of a writing allows a contract to be formed by something less than a comprehensive, fully executed agreement.

In most legal systems, letters of intent and memoranda of agreement are viewed as merely preliminary and have virtually no force and effect. In international contracts for the sale of goods that incorporate U.S. law as the contract's choice of law there are particular dangers. Under the U.S. legal doctrine known as the *statute of frauds*, a preliminary letter or memorandum signed "by the party to be charged" (i.e., the person accused of breaching the agreement) may be sufficient proof of the existence of a contract, and any violation of that document and whatever else is deemed to constitute the agreement, may lead to court imposed sanctions for breach of contract. A writing that satisfies the statute of frauds can be terribly vague and incomplete. The U.S. Uniform Commercial Code merely points out that

> The required writing need not contain all the material terms of the contract and such material terms as are stated need not be precisely stated. All that is required is that the writing afford a basis for believing that the offered oral evidence rests on a real transaction. It may be written in lead pencil on a scratch pad. It need not indicate which party is the buyer and which the seller. The only term which must appear is the quantity term which need not be accurately stated but recovery is limited to the amount stated. The price, time and place of payment or delivery, the general quality of the goods, or any particular warranties may all be omitted."[5]

Coping with this problem is often easier said than done. George DeLaume suggests that the letter of intent or memorandum include express language that the document is merely evidence of the parties' "willingness to negotiate and nothing more." He suggests that language be put into the letter of intent such as: "This memorandum is not intended to constitute a binding contract" or this letter refers to "the *possible* formation of a joint venture."[6] Such disclaimers may very well work if the only goal is to eliminate problems with an U.S.-style statute of frauds. But what happens when a government official who is being asked to give permission to export or import the commodities in question or a bank officer who is being asked to approve a multi-million dollar loan reads the letter of intent. The very disclaimers that may keep the document from being construed by a court or arbitrator as a binding agreement may persuade the government or bank that the parties are still so far apart that they should not take the action requested. This often puts contracting parties between the "rock and a hard place" often described by President Abraham Lincoln when the choices he was offered gave him no meaningful way out.

There is another way to view letters of intent and preliminary memoranda—i.e., as *potentially* enforceable documents. In other words, the parties may proceed on the basis that the terms and conditions spelled out in the

---

5. UCC § 2-201, comment 1.
6. DeLaume, supra note 1, (Booklet 5, p.28)

letter of intent could at some subsequent time be considered enforceable. However, the letter of intent may still include express language making for- mation of the actual contract expressly conditional on the happening of later events (in American contract parlance the occurrence of a *condition subse- quent*). This might cause the parties to write into the letter of intent language such as: "This letter may not be viewed as a final contract unless Govern- ment X gives final export approval [or unless Bank Y gives final approval to the financing agreement.]"

There are, of course, dangers associated with this action. If those sub- sequent conditions fall into place, the parties may have an agreement even if one or another is not quite ready to put a signature to the final document. This possibility shows up the dilemma of a letter of intent. If it is too loose, persons external to the agreement may not want to act on the basis of the letter. If it is too detailed and not sufficiently disclamatory, the letter of intent itself could be construed as a binding contract. There is probably a moral here, if not a complete answer in the law. Parties should be wary of putting their signatures to *any* document, however preliminary and no matter what the document's language, if they are not sure they want to enter into the agreement.

§ 4.4 Choosing the Language and the Law of the Agreement

§ 4.4.1 Choosing the contract's language

International lawyers to warn of the pitfalls and dangers of negotiating and drafting contracts that cut across cultural and linguistic lines. In even the most innocuous settings language differences can cause severe problems of interpretation. Consider a partial list of terms from Professor George DeLaume's book on transnational contracts to show the enormous contrasts between French and English legal expression:

English	*French*
compromise	transaction
agreement to arbitrate	compromis
execution	signature
performance	execution[7]

These are striking differences and point up the problems that occur even in cultural systems and languages that are somewhat similar and that have common roots. Contemplate what could happen when there are vast differ- ences in culture, legal system and language.

---

7. *Id.*.

If a contract is between two parties who speak different languages, it is generally conceded that an international commercial contract should have an "official" language as well as be translated into the languages of the various contracting parties. For example, a contract drafted for an English seller and a French buyer might state that while the contract has been translated into both English and French "the English language text is to be regarded as the definitive and official text of the agreement." There are occasions when the parties simply cannot agree on language. In that instance, the contract can simply remain silent on official language, letting a judge or arbitrator fill in the blank.

For the most part, contracting parties should view a choice of language clause as simply another matter to be expressly addressed in the document. Generally, the choice is negotiable; and even when, for various reasons, one party insists on using his native language as the official language, the other party has a simple means of insuring that the choice does not hamper further negotiations or actual performance under the contract. If you are not comfortable with a contract's language, hire a translator—preferably one who is also something of a legal specialist. Courts and arbitrators will not disturb a choice of official language so long as no fraud or undue influence was exercised by one party against the other in making the choice.

The actual wording of a choice of language clause need not be complicated. The traditional samples are excessively cumbersome: "Notwithstanding subsequent translations of this agreement, whether or not said translations are made contemporaneously with the negotiation and execution of said agreement, the English language version of said agreement shall exclusively control." The following wording should suffice: "This contract may be translated into languages other than English. The English language version of this contract is the official version and shall be controlling in any dispute arising under this contract."

§ 4.4.2 Choosing the contract's applicable law

The discussion in this chapter and in Chapter 2 should give the reader a good understanding why a choice of law clause in a contract is often crucial. As will be seen in section 4.6, choosing a system of law applicable to the contract could have the effect of inserting clauses or terms in the contract without the express consent of the parties. In other words, the underlying legal system can provide a *gap-filling* function for the agreement. This is not necessarily a bad thing. Gap-filling can free the parties from drafting clauses on many peripheral matters. It does, however, require that the parties be alert to how gap-filling may occur.

But even though risks are involved in choosing a body of law applicable to the contract, there are far more dangers associated with executing a document that is silent on choice of law.[8] Silence on applicable law can come back to haunt the parties if any dispute arises under the contract. Moreover, it is difficult to negotiate and draft a contract when the parties have no idea which legal system or body of law will govern the undertaking because the constraints of the chosen system will govern many of the provisions in the contract. For these reasons, this subsection will first discuss why most parties go about affirmatively choosing the law of the contract.

a. *Affirmatively choosing the law.*

There are essentially two ways to choose law affirmatively. First, the parties may try to avoid all choice of law problems by spelling out, in intricate detail in the contract itself, all the interpretative and substantive rules necessary to resolve any dispute under the contract. For small transactions in the hands of lawyers and business executives who are both brilliant and psychic, it is conceivable that such a contract could be drafted. However, excessive detail in the written document could lead to the breakdown of negotiations. Companies rarely have an infinite amount of time to spend on any individual agreement; and even assuming all this detail could be plausibly reduced to contract language, the contract itself would be gargantuan. Excessive detail sometimes also hampers efficient dispute resolution. If arbitrators have to plow through hundreds of pages, they may miss the central issues in the dispute.

There is a far more workable alternative. The parties can draft all the clauses that they believe are necessary to a proper agreement and then can choose law that fills in the remaining details. In the past, parties have normally chosen the law of a single country, usually that of either the seller or the buyer or, in some cases, the law of a respected, neutral third country. Swiss law, for example, is frequently chosen by parties who cannot agree on the law of either the seller's or the buyer's country. Since the entering into force of the Convention on the International Sale of Goods (CISG), parties involved in sale of goods transactions may choose the CISG as the applicable law. One attorney of the author's acquaintance sometimes dispenses with choosing the law of a specific country. When his clients cannot agree on choice of law, he incorporates a clause in the contract requiring arbitrators to apply "generally accepted principles of international trade and commercial practice" (or similar language) to resolve the dispute. Another version of this

---

8. See generally, Baxter, *International Conflict of Laws and International Business*, 34 Int'l & Comp. L.Q. 538 (1985); Zaphiriou, *Choice of Forum and Choice of Law Clauses in International Commercial Agreements*, 3 Int'l Trade L.J. 311 (1978).

alternative permits the parties to declare an arbitrator as an *amiable compositeur*, a device that permits the arbitrator to apply fundamental principles of equity, fairness and common sense to settle the dispute without the necessity of referring to and applying a body of specific municipal law. The selection of an international code of commercial law or the amiable compositeur alternative could be particularly attractive to negotiating parties who are unwilling to adopt each other's domestic commercial legal system as the choice of law. Under the twin doctrines of party autonomy and *pacta sunt servanda*, there appears to be no reason why such choices would not be honored.[9]

There is some debate as to whether the contracting parties' choice is completely unfettered, however. Classic choice of law doctrine in most of the major trading nations has generally required some connection between the legal system chosen and the contract itself. Under the U.S. Uniform Commercial Code's (UCC) rules for contracts involving the sale of goods, the choice of law must bear some *reasonable relation* to the contract and the contracting parties.[10] In other contracts in the U.S. and under British law, the parties' choice of law is honored so long as there is some reasonable basis for the choice.[11] For example, in an important choice of law case in the United Kingdom, *Vita Food Products v. Unus Shipping Co.*[12] the contract for a shipment of goods from Newfoundland, Canada to New York was to be governed by English commercial law. The British court enforced the choice and determined that if contracting parties voluntarily choose a body of law, that choice will be honored irrespective of whether the law chosen has any special connection with the contract. The United States Supreme Court in the important case, *Scherk v. Alberto-Culver Co.*,[13] concluded that choice of law clauses in contracts promote "the orderliness and predictability essential to any international business transaction" and thus suggested that U.S. courts would honor virtually any reasonable choice. Similarly, the recently promulgated European Communities Convention on the Law Applicable to Contractual Obligations[14] appears to follow the United States Supreme Court

---

9. See §4.9 of this Chapter and the discussion in Chapter Nine.

10. UCC § 1-105 states: "when a transaction bears a reasonable relation to this state and also to another state or nation the parties may agree that the law either of this state or of such other state or nation shall govern their rights and duties." This appears to limit a contract's choice of law solely to the country of the seller or the country of the buyer. However, judicial construction of this term has generally permitted the parties to choose the law of a neutral third country.

11. Restatement (Second) of Conflict of Laws §187(2)(a). Readers not familiar with the American system of Restatements of the Law should simply consider that these documents are attempts by groups of law professors, practitioners and judges to gather into a single source, as a kind of private codification, legal principles derived and announced by courts throughout the United States. Principles of law set out in the Restatements are frequently cited by U.S. courts on an advisory basis but they have no controlling effect on the outcome of cases.

12. [1939] A.C. 277.

13. 417 U.S. 506 (1974).

14. 23 O.J. Eur. Comm. (No. L-266) (1980).

in promoting party autonomy and honoring the parties' choice.[15] In a number of other countries whose legal systems are based on civil law doctrine, the courts usually require some fairly close connection between the transaction, the parties and the system of law chosen. In a few countries, contract drafters must cope with legal principles that provide that contracts that are to be performed within the country are to be governed by that country's law, irrespective of whether the parties might have made another choice.[16] For example, petroleum agreements with the Kingdom of Saudi Arabia, for example, are to be governed solely by Saudi law.[17]

Making a choice can eliminate a great deal of uncertainty, although parties must be careful in their choice. If a third country is chosen, it should be a country with an easily researched, well-defined body of commercial law. Far out choices—for example choosing the law of Tanzania in a contract between a seller in Iceland and a buyer in Taiwan—would raise eyebrows among arbitrators and reviewing courts. Such a choice is so bizarre and so totally unrelated to the transaction, that a court or arbitrator might feel free to disregard it. Choosing, as a neutral country, the law of one of the major trading nations is the better alternative.

There is a secondary problem in choice of law that bears discussion. When courts or arbitrators apply choice of law, they generally apply those legal principles that are in effect in the chosen country at the time of the arbitration or litigation, rather than those principles that might have existed when the contract was drafted. Usually this is not a major problem. The commercial principles of most countries evolve so slowly that drastic changes are not likely to occur in the life of the average contract. The parties could try to stipulate that the choice of law is the set of legal principles in effect at the time the contract was executed, but it is uncertain whether a court or arbitrator would be bound by such a stipulation.

Once the choice itself is made, there is no trouble drafting the clause itself. The parties may simply state: "This contract shall be governed by and construed in accordance with the laws of _____." The Japanese External Trade Organization (JETRO) suggests that contracts contain a provision stating: "Governing law: This contract shall be governed in all respects by the laws of Japan." More cumbersome clauses sometimes attempt to show the relation between the choice of law and the contract in the clause itself. The following is an example: "This contract shall be subject to and shall be construed and enforced pursuant to the laws of _____ (country),

---

15. See, e.g., Weintraub, *How to Choose the Law and How Not To: The EEC Convention*, 17 Tex. Int'l L.J. 155 (1982).

16. Chile is an example. See the Chilean Codigo de Comercio, art. 113.

17. See, e.g., Smith & Dzienkowski, *A Fifty Year Perspective on World Petroleum Arrangements*, 24 Tex. Int'l L. J. 13 (1989).

which is the location of the headquarters of the Seller [or Buyer]." Lawyers and business executives outside the United States must understand that if U.S. commercial law is chosen, the choice of law clause must specify a particular state in the United States. There is no body of national commercial law that can be chosen for a contract between private parties. The U.S. Uniform Commercial Code comes into being only through the sovereignty of the various states. It is national only in the sense that each state's version of the UCC is essentially the same as any other state. It is also possible, although terribly cumbersome, to choose different systems of law for different portions of the contract. This can lead to a lot of confusion when disputes arise, but even here the parties' choices will generally be honored.

b. *Choosing the law when the contract is silent*

The question here is why any contracting party would let such an important matter as choice of law be decided at some later date by a decision-maker who may not be fully under the control of the parties. The short answer is that many negotiating parties cannot come to an agreement on choice of law. Rather than forego the deal itself, the parties simply leave that matter for later resolution by a third party such as a court or arbitrator. To a certain extent, silence reflects a hope that no dispute will ever arise under the contract; or, in the alternative, that if a dispute arises, the arbitrators or judge will make an intelligent choice, hoping, obviously, that no dispute will ever arise. As noted earlier, some contracts try to avoid problems by providing that the governing law will be "principles of law common to 'civilized nations,'" or that the parties undertake the contract in "mutual good will and good faith" without applying a specific country's legal system. But there is no readily accepted or generally available reference source for these common principles. The practical effect of such clauses is to simply turn over the dispute to the good sense of the judge or arbitrator.

Some of these issues have been the subject of litigation. In an oil concession agreement entered into between a British oil company and the country of Abu Dhabi, the parties recognized that they could not agree as to a specific body of law and inserted a clause providing merely: "[The parties] declare that they base their work in this Agreement on good will and sincerity of belief and on the interpretation of this Agreement in a fashion consistent with reason." In 1951 a dispute arose under the concession and was submitted to arbitration. Lord Asquith, sitting as one of the arbitrators, asked:

> What is the "Proper Law" applicable in construing this contract? This is a contract made between Abu Dhabi and wholly to be performed in that country. If any municipal system of law were applica-

ble, it would prima facie be that of Abu Dhabi. But no such law can reasonably be said to exist. The Sheikh administers a purely discretionary justice with the assistance of the Koran; and it would be fanciful to suggest that in this very primitive region there is any settled body of legal principles applicable to the construction of modern commercial instruments. Nor can I see any basis on which the municipal law of England could apply.[18]

Thus, the question faced by the Asquith was: Is it possible to construe or interpret a commercial contract without reference to an identifiable system of municipal law? Lord Asquith hit on a Solomonic solution: he invoked certain principles of British commercial law that he deemed "of ecumenical validity" but chose to disregard other rules of British commercial practice that he characterized as excessively "rigid." This was probably not a bad solution for Lord Asquith as arbitrator; he had to come to *some* decision under the contract. But there is considerable danger in this approach. There is no assurance that every judge or arbitrator will have the stature and brilliance of Lord Asquith. A different arbitrator might well have applied Abu Dhabi law or the whole of British commercial law, however inappropriate, or some melange of commercial principles that did violence to the underlying agreement. When a contract is silent on choice of law many unpredictable things can happen.

There are, of course, certain legal concepts derived from that body of law known as conflict of laws that assist courts and arbitrators in determining which body of municipal law to apply in the absence of an express choice by the parties. A compilation of legal principles in the United States entitled the *Restatement (Second) Conflict of Laws* suggests that the law to be applied is the law of the country having the "most significant relationship to the transaction and the parties" taking into consideration the place of contracting, the place where the contract was negotiated, the place where the contract is to be performed, the location of the subject matter of the contract and the domicil, residence, nationality, place of incorporation and place of business of the parties.[19] The Uniform Commercial Code (now effective in all states except Louisiana) provides that the when the parties have not chosen law, the applicable law is the law of the state bearing the most "appropriate relation" to the commercial agreement. In other countries the rules vary. In some instances the domestic commercial law provides that the applicable law will be the law of the place where the contract was made. In other

---

18. Petroleum Development Ltd. v. Sheikh of Abu Dhabi, September 1951, [1951] Int.L.Rep. 144.

19. The reader should understand that while the Restatement is prestigious, it is essentially a compilation of legal principles by law professors and, accordingly, is not regarded as controlling law in any jurisdiction in the United States.

instances it is the law of the place where the contract is to be performed; and in yet other countries it is the national law of the contracting parties if they are of common nationality or the law of the country where the contract was made or where it is to be performed if the parties are not of common nationality.[20] But, again, the ultimate choice is not certain and will be made by someone other than a party to the contract.

§ 4.5. Using Standardized Clauses and Forms

There are both benefits and dangers in using standard forms in contracts. Chapter Three, section 3.4, has warned about certain problems that parties involved in contracts for the sale of goods will encounter if the buyer and seller merely exchange forms. But standard forms save money and for low-cost contracts they may be virtually the only way that the companies can do business.

On the international level, contracts tend to be for larger amounts of money and are often performed over longer periods of time. Accordingly, those contracts' provisions tend to be more detailed and intricate. As a result, many international contracts are separately negotiated between the parties and the resulting contract is tailored to the deal at hand. But even these contracts are likely to contain a large amount of standardized language. There is absolutely nothing wrong with this. Using certain standardized clauses promotes efficiency and economy in contract drafting. There is no need, normally, to draft each and every word in a contract from scratch. On occasion, use of standard language will promote agreement and may enhance any dispute resolution since arbitrators and judges are likely to have encountered this standard language previously.

There are any number of sources for standard clauses. Most law libraries contain form books that recite language from earlier contracts. There are a number of useful compendiums of sample contracts covering different types of agreements. One such work, *International Business Transactions* (edited by Dennis Campbell and Reinhard Proksch and published by Kluwer) contains computer software that permits a contract drafter to insert phrases and clauses from those sample contracts directly into his or her own contract without retyping. A number of international bodies now provide

---

20. For a lengthy and complex discussion of all these issues see G. DELAUME, TRANSNATIONAL CONTRACTS, supra note 1, Booklet 2 (1982). See also, Baxter, *International Conflict of Laws and International Business.*, 34 Int'l & Comp.L.Q. 538 (1985) Lowe, *Choice of Law Clauses in International Contracts: A Practical Approach*, 12 Harv. Int'l L.J. 1 (1971); For a discussion of some of the civil law doctrines on choice of law see, e.g., C. REITHMANN, INTERNATIONALES VERTRAGSRECHT 2-17 (2d ed. 1972). For a distinguished but perhaps now some what dated statement that civil law requires a reasonable relationship between parties, performance and choice of law (and that discusses the "excesses" of party autonomy) see NIBOYET, 5 TRAITE DE DROIT INTERNATIONAL PRIVE FRANCAIS 51-60 (1948).

stock contract language. For example, the United Nations Commission on International Trade Law (UNCITRAL) has recently released a compilation of contract terms applicable to large-scale international construction contracts entitled *Legal Guide on Drawing Up International Contracts for Construction of Industrial Works.*

Many contracts for the sale of goods include stock language known as *trade terms*, such as F.O.B., C.I.F., or F.A.S. Trade terms are often familiar to laypersons, but from a legal standpoint they actually fulfill three separate functions in a contract. They function as part of the price term (determining who pays for what portion of the transportation of the goods); they help allocate risk of loss, and they affect the transportation requirements for the goods. Domestic legal systems such as the U.S. Uniform Commercial Code contain specific definitions for these terms that would apply if a contract chose the UCC as the applicable law. For international sales of goods contracts that do not utilize the UCC, the International Chamber of Commerce has promulgated a similar set of trade terms, updated in 1990, called *Incoterms*. Incoterms include definitions of ten major trade terms as those terms are believed to be understood in 18 major trading nations. However, there can be subtle differences when compared with parallel definitions in, say, the UCC. For example, Incoterms define "FOB" ("Free on Board") as: "The goods are placed on board a ship by the seller at a port of shipment named in the sales contract. The risk of loss or damage to the goods is transferred from the seller to the buyer when the goods pass the ship's rail."[21] The UCC definition is slightly different: "when the term is FOB the place of shipment, the seller must at that place ship the goods in the manner provided [in this article] and bear the expense and risk of putting them into the possession of the carrier ... the seller must in addition at his own expense and risk load the goods on board...."[22] Incoterms defines "C & F" as: "The seller must pay the costs and freight necessary to bring the goods to the named destination but the risk of loss of or damage to the goods, as well as of any cost increases, is transferred from the seller to the buyer when the goods pass the ship's rail in the port of shipment."[23] The UCC defines CIF somewhat differently: "The term CIF means that the price includes in a lump sum the cost of the goods and the insurance and freight to the named destination."[24]

The actions of the I.C.C. in promulgating Incoterms was certainly a good faith effort; but even with these ostensibly uniform definitions, there is little true uniformity. Some countries such as Japan simply do not abide by uniform rules.[25] In England sellers and buyers only infrequently make use of

---

21. Incoterms 1990, International Chamber of Commerce Brochure No. 350 (1990).
22. UCC, § 2-319.
23. *Id.*
24. UCC § 2-320.
25. See Tanikawa, *Risk of Loss in Japanese Sales Transactions*, 42 Wash.L.Rev. 463 (1967).

Incoterms.[26] In the United States those domestic contracts that are controlled by the Uniform Commercial Code use the U.C.C. definitions rather
than the Incoterms.[27] While the definitions in all these systems are similar,
there are just enough linguistic differences to provide interpretative problems. Most drafters of international commercial contracts now simply define
the terms in the document or refer to a specific country's system of commercial terms. If a contract uses Incoterms or any other set of privately-commis-
sioned uniform definitions, it should identify those terms in the contract to
avoid later confusion. For example, a contract stating a price of fittings to be
"$5.00 per fitting, FOB New York" should, if the drafters are using Incoterms,
additionally provide: $5.00 per fitting, FOB (Incoterms 1990) New York." In
the alternative, the definition section of the contract could specify that when
trade terms are used the definitions are those provided by Incoterms [or the
UCC] or some other definitional source.

§ 4.6. Sample Clauses in International Commercial Agreements—Formation and Performance

However an agreement is reached, the final document will almost always
contain, at a minimum, language covering the matters discussed below.
While an omission of any particular term (except, possibly, the quantity
term) is not necessarily fatal to the formation of a valid and enforceable
agreement, careful drafters of contracts do not normally write contracts that
are silent on these matters. A provision may be deliberately flexible—as, for
example, a price term that turns on the rise or fall of a specified cost of living
index—but the term will still be mentioned in the contract. Many contracts
begin with a recitation of the purposes of the agreement and contain boilerplate establishing the promises made by each party to the other. The sample
clause set out on page 124, supra, is a short example of some of these recitations. In traditional contracts, the recitations are frequently preceded by the
term *whereas*: "Whereas the two parties to this agreement wishing to commence a commercial relationship for the purchase and sale of brass fittings
do hereby solemnly and mutually promise and agree to the following ... ." As
discussed in section 4.2 this is great lawyerese, and conceivably may be
indispensable language under the law of some country, but really counts for
nothing in the typical commercial agreement. The best agreements are specific and to the point, including clauses that set out the parties' agreement
on all the important aspects of the relationship. Senior partners in law firms

---

26. See Note, *Incoterms and the British Export Trade*, 1965 J.Bus.L. 114.
27. Some U.S. based international contracts have used a different set of uniform terms, the
Revised American Foreign Trade Definitions ("AFTD"), but these terms are not generally favored.

for reasons of tradition rather than rationality also get caught up in these hackneyed expressions and can't be persuaded that a document that does not contain these recitations can be valid. If the contract drafter is not the person who has to sign the document, he or she may have to knuckle under to traditions which fly in the face of wisdom and efficiency. Nonetheless, all other things being equal, a good contract generally begins with a plain statement describing the parties and the subject matter of the agreement: "This is a contract between Buyer [including full name and address] and Seller [full name and address] for the purchase and sale of brass fittings." The contract then normally sets out definitions, if the drafters have decided to insert a separate definition section.

Following these preliminary items, the contract then moves to those provisions that insure the proper formation of a contract. Subsequent sections will deal with other parts of the contract.

§ 4.6.1 The quantity term

In contracts for the sale of goods a quantity term is indispensable. It can be either a fixed quantity (100 arm chairs) or a flexible term stated in terms of the seller's output or the buyer's requirements in any given period of time, e.g., "Buyer shall purchase all Windsor chairs manufactured by Seller between January 1 and June 30, 1992." (an output contract) or "Buyer shall purchase from Seller a quantity of Windsor chairs equal to the total requirements for Windsor chairs incurred by Buyer during the period January 1 through June 30, 1992." (a requirements contract). Other possible arrangements include an exclusive dealing agreement by which a seller agrees to sell only to a single buyer over a specified period of time.

§ 4.6.2 The price term

Specifying price in a contract has always been tricky, particularly in periods of sharp inflationary or deflationary movements.[28] A contract may specify a fixed price, ("$100 per chair"), or may provide a price reference that becomes effective at the time of shipment or the time of receipt of the goods. Petroleum contracts, for example, are rarely fixed price contracts because of the volatility of the price of crude oil. To compensate for this volatility, a typical contract will state the price of the contract with reference to the spot market price for a barrel of crude oil on one of the internationally-recognized markets in, say, New York or Rotterdam effective on the day of receipt by the buyer of the actual commodity. In theory, a price term for the sale of any good could be

---

28. See, e.g., Hurst, *Drafting Contracts in an Inflationary Era*, 28 U.Fla.L.Rev. 884 (1976).

pegged to the price of, for example, a barrel of crude oil. This is a rare practice except in the context of barter and countertrade agreements.

When a contract drafter is writing a flexible price term, the important consideration is to make sure all parties fully understand the reference point for the price. For example, many contracts for the sale of goods that are to be performed over a long period of time contain a price escalation clause tied to a cost of living index. The difficulty is that there are a number of cost of living indexes published in the United States. A precise cost of living index will (1) specify the particular cost of living index—e.g., the "Consumer Price Index published monthly by the United States Department of Commerce"; and (2) will specify the specific point in time on which the index is to reset prices— e.g., "prices under this contract shall increase by the percentage increase of the Consumer Price Index annually on the anniversary date of this contract." Some long-term contracts for both goods and services set fixed prices that increase over time on a particular schedule. The price-increase schedule is sometimes included in the basic price term; more often it is included in an annex to the agreement and the contract's price term simply incorporates the annex by reference. There are any number of variations for all these alternatives that will pass muster with courts and arbitrators.

Buyers typically favor fixed price contracts so that they can predict their future costs of doing business while sellers often prefer flexibility. There are times when both parties want to contract with each other but simply cannot settle on a specific price for the goods. There are other times, particularly in transactions involving the exchange of forms rather than carefully drafted contracts, where the price cannot be ascertained from the documents. In these circumstances some legal systems, for example the U.S.'s Uniform Commercial Code, the underlying law will fill in a "reasonable" price term if price is not specified in the contract.[29] More specifically, the Code provides for a reasonable price established by the parties in good faith at the time for delivery if:

a. nothing is said as to price; or

b. the price is left to be agreed upon by the parties and they have not agreed; or

c. the price is to be fixed in terms of some agreed market or other standard.

Other well known variants in international commercial contracts include cost-plus contracts, often used in contracting with governments (the price is the seller's cost of producing the good plus a fixed percentage increment added to that cost) and gold clauses (the price is a specified number of

---

29. See Uniform Commercial Code §2-305.

ounces of gold, even though the ultimate price will fluctuate depending on the sales price of gold).

Price terms in some contracts such as licensing agreements are normally stated in terms of a percentage royalty, rather than a price per unit shipped. Licensing agreements also frequently contain minimum royalty payment requirements that are stated in fixed dollar terms. A typical percentage royalty term is: "Licensee shall pay to Licensor, annually from the date of execution of this agreement, a royalty of four percent (4%) of licensee's ex-factory price on each gross of brass fittings manufactured under the license granted in this contract."

However price is stated in the contract, the drafter should not lose sight of the fact that this is one of the central provisions of any transaction. People make commercial agreements to earn a profit; proper pricing is essential to a profit.

§ 4.6.3 The payment term

In most domestic contracts, payment is simply made at a time specified (e.g., "within 30 days following delivery") with an understanding that payment will be made in the legal tender of that country or by way of a recognized negotiable instrument (such as a check). In the United States the bank collection system and sources of financial information are quite efficient. Most businesses in the U.S. have standard courses of dealing with regard to payment that rarely have to be stated in elaborate form.

Such is not the case, however, in international commercial contracts. For international transactions, the payment term is crucial. Many contracts provide expressly for both a time of payment and the currency in which payment is to be made. Some contracts provide for payment in any one of several currencies at the option of one of the parties. Some contracts contain payment terms with currency fluctuation clauses to accommodate drastic changes in the valuation of the specified currency. One way to circumvent most problems associated with currency fluctuation is to call for payment in a highly stable currency—Swiss francs are an international favorite—rather than drafting a complicated fluctuation clause.

If payment is not made in cash, the contract will likely contain a detailed clause calling for the issuance of a letter of credit. Occasionally payment will be made in the form of barter—as, for example, when Boeing exchanges jet aircraft for Saudi Arabian oil. Much like other clauses in the contract, payment terms range from the simple to the highly complicated. The following is an example of a payment term involving a letter of credit: "Payments under this contract shall be made in Swiss francs by the means of an irrevocable and confirmed documentary credit at the date of order issued by a bank acceptable to seller." In construction contracts, progress payments are usually made without the requirement of a letter of credit. A term of payment for a construction contract might state: "Contractor shall, upon reaching of each payment milestone as described in Annex B, submit to Company an invoice covering such payment milestone, with relevant documentation to verify the appropriateness of the invoice. Company shall, within 30 days from receipt of the invoice, pay to a bank account designated by Contractor all undisputed portions of the invoice. Company shall advise contractor promptly of any amount in dispute. Any invoice which is not paid within the period stipulated in this clause shall be subject to interest at the rate set out in Annex B."

§ 4.6.4 Provisions allocating risk of loss during shipment.

Virtually no contract fails to include some provision for allocating the risk of loss during shipment. Some contracts simply specify which party shall bear the loss at any given time during the transit of goods; other contracts also provide expressly for the passing of title to the goods from seller to buyer. In most contracts, the point in time at which title passes is also the time at which risk of loss shifts from seller to buyer. Like so many other clauses in the typical contract, risk of loss and passing of title provisions are of no consequence. The contract is fully performed and everyone goes away happily. If something goes wrong, however, it's a different story. These clauses become crucial to the transaction when the shipment is destroyed. They are also one of the contract provisions that are typically borrowed from external sources such as the International Chamber of Commerce's Incoterms. In contracts where the goods are highly perishable—a contract for gasoline, for example— the parties might want to draft a lengthy risk of loss clause that reflects industry practice in shipping gasoline from seller to buyer.

    In many contracts, a number of the clauses discussed above are merged into a single paragraph in the contract. The clause—"Buyer shall purchase 100 fittings at a unit price of $5.00 per fitting, FOB (Incoterms) Seattle, payment by check on receipt of goods."—is simultaneously a quantity term, a price term, a payment term and a risk of loss term. By Incoterm definition, risk of loss passes when the goods pass the ship's rail.

§ 4.6.5. Performance clauses and express and implied warranties

Most international contracts contain some type of performance or warranty requirement. These clauses can include express promises that the goods or the services will be of adequate quality. Express performance or warranty provisions are more important in international contracts because there is no uniformity as to express or implied warranties under the domestic law of most countries. Particularly in construction contracts, performance is central to the agreement and performance obligations should be spelled out in the document.

If warranties are not spelled out in the contract itself they may not necessarily be filled in by operation of law. While the commercial law of most countries contains some requirement that goods be delivered free of defects the scope and effect of those warranties diverges greatly.[30] The United States Uniform Commercial Code, for example, contains some sophisticated warranty provisions that may be disclaimed by sellers only with difficulty.[31] The warranty provisions in the Convention for International Sales of Goods (CISG) differ from those in the UCC. Warranty law in many other countries is not nearly so highly developed, however. Consequently, if parties to international contracts want the special protections that warranties afford, the wisest course of action is to spell out those warranties in the document itself, or to very carefully select a system of underlying law that provides those warranties desired by the parties.

§ 4.7 Sample Clauses—Breach, Remedies and Miscellaneous

Some contracts actually spell out some of the acts of either party that will constitute breach of the contract. For example, a contract for the sale of goods under an installment payment agreement might specify: "Buyer's failure to pay any single payment within 15 days of the date payment is due constitutes breach of this agreement." Another clause might specify that "Any dishonor of buyer's letters of credit constitutes breach of this agreement." There may be occasions when such language is called for, but by and large, such clauses are superfluous. In virtually all legal systems, a contract is breached when one of the parties fails to live up to the terms of the agreement. Put another way, the act of breaching the contract is usually obvious to both parties. Even when breach is more subtly evidenced, it is rare that the contract itself will have anticipated subtle breaches.

There are, of course, numerous cases inquiring into whether the breach is *material* or whether the party deemed in breach *substantially per-*

---

30. See, e.g., Wortley, *Mercantile Usage and Custom, in* 24 RABELS ZEITSCHRIFT FUR AUS-LANDISCHES UND INTERNATIONALES PIRVATRECH 259 (1959); Jacobson, *International Sales of Goods,* 3 Int'l & Comp. L.Q. 659 (1954)

31. The U.C.C. recognizes express warranties (i.e., those inserted specifically in the contract) and two different forms of implied warranty: (1) a warranty of merchantibility (that the goods are fit for the ordinary purposes for which such goods are used and are of fair average quality) and (2) a warranty of fitness for a particular purpose (which is in effect if the seller knows that the buyer has a particular purpose for the goods and is relying on the seller's skill or judgment to select appropriate goods. U.C.C. §§ 2-313, 2-314, 2-315.

formed even if it did not fully perform; but there is little that a contract drafter can do to cover such situations. As a consequence, many contracts forego such language and concentrate on drafting provisions such as *force majeure* clauses to identify those circumstances in which performance may be forgiven.

§ 4.7.1 Force majeure clauses

When Professor Andreas Lowenfeld enumerated the special risks of international trade he specifically mentioned "the risk of international turmoil, tension and change."[32] These risks include war, riots, insurrection, invasion and other matters that may not be totally foreseeable but may certainly be anticipated by appropriate contract language. The inability of human beings to foresee everything that might go wrong in a transaction is a principal reason for *force majeure* clauses. These clauses typically contemplate natural disasters, although most clauses also extend to political disruptions. Many of the traditional clauses recite a list of different occurrences such as war, fire, flood, embargo, explosion, import or export prohibitions, strikes or other labor troubles, and supply interruptions due to similar causes. In effect, a *force majeure* clause suspends performance without penalty for the party affected by the disruption. The forgiveness is normally only for the period of the disruption.

Some *force majeure* clauses have included "inflation beyond the expected rate" as a possible ground for invoking *force majeure*. One legal system, the U.S. Uniform Commercial Code, forgives performance that has been made *commercially impracticable*.[33] Other systems recognize certain changes in government policy as a proper basis for forgiving or suspending performance. Under the fundamental doctrine of party autonomy, parties should be able to include virtually any event of their choosing in the *force majeure* clause. However, traditional force majeure clauses normally are restricted to events unforeseen at the time of the execution of the contract and typically confined to a physical inability to perform, so-called acts of God.

There are many variations of *force majeure* clauses. Recall that the central purpose of such clauses is to forgive performance when events occur to dispute performance that were outside the contemplation of the parties when they first signed the agreement. As a result, force majeure clauses may simply state: "A party shall not be considered to be in default in the performance of its obligations to the extent that it proves that such performance has been prevented by *force majeure*." In the definitional section of the contract, *force majeure* is defined as: "An occurrence beyond the control of the party affect-

---

32. A. LOWENFELD, INTERNATIONAL PRIVATE TRADE 3 (1981).
33. UCC § 2-615.

ed, provided that such party could not reasonably have foreseen such occurrence at the time of entering into the contract or could not reasonably have avoided or overcome its consequences." This clause may be viewed as a modern form of *force majeure* clause. The more traditional clauses tend to be far more verbose, without adding that much more to the parties' understanding of *force majeure*: "The parties hereto shall not be responsible for failure to perform this contract due to force majeure. Force majeure includes but is not limited to: fires, floods, riots, strikes, labor strife, transportation disruptions, interruptions in the supply of raw materials, Acts of God or other causes that are beyond the reasonable control of the affected party." *Force majeure* clauses in contracts using the U.S. Uniform Commercial Code as the applicable law that do not wish to incorporate the UCC's more flexible concept of *commercial impracticability* should include an express disclaimer: e.g., "Force majeure is limited to a party's physical inability to perform the contract. It does not include disruptions that make the contract's performance merely commercially impracticable."

2. *Government Approval Clauses*

Some private international transactions, particularly those involving transfer of technology, require the approval of one or more governments. The specific approval mechanism may be a registration requirement, the obtaining of export or import permission, or formal approval for a joint venture. If approvals are necessary most contracts simply provide that the contract is not fully effective until the necessary approvals have been obtained. In other words, government approvals are usually treated as a condition precedent to the *formation* of the contract, rather than a failure that leads to breach of the contract.

In addition, most contracts place the obligation to obtain the permission from the party in the country that must issue the permission. Buyer usually obtains any necessary import permissions; seller obtains permission to export the goods. This is a rational approach to something that can occasionally prove troublesome in practice. The burden of obtaining permission should fall on the person with the best access to the government in question. A typical government permissions clause for a sale of goods contract might read: "Seller shall obtain all necessary permits, licenses or permissions to export the goods. Buyer shall obtain all necessary permits, licenses or permissions necessary to import the goods. This contract is not fully executed and enforceable until all such permissions have been received."

§ 4.7.2 Penalty and Liquidated Damages Clauses

Contracting parties often wish to have some special protection against the possibility of non-performance by the other party, particularly in agreements such as construction contracts in which time is of the essence. It is not unusual for an international contract to contain some type of *penalty* or *liquidated damages* clause that provides for the payment of a penalty (e.g., "Builder shall pay Purchaser $5000.00 per day for each day the project remains uncompleted after January 1, 1984.") or for liquidated damages (e.g., "The parties agree that in the event of a breach of this contract by either party the breaching party shall pay the amount of $15,000.00 in damages.").

In some legal systems liquidated damages provisions will be honored while provisions deemed *penalty* clauses will not, even though there is a very thin line between clauses that might constitute penalties and those that appear to be liquidated damages clauses. As a consequence, contract drafters should be aware that not all penalty or liquidated damages clauses will be honored by courts or by arbitrators.[34]

The foregoing discussion was intended to be only an illustrative list of possible contract provisions. Contracts for specific purposes other than the sale of goods such as distributorship and licensing agreements or complex financing contracts require many other provisions to be fully satisfactory. There are numerous sources of information on appropriate clauses for these contracts.[35]

§ 4.8 Drafting the Dispute Resolution and Choice of Forum Clauses

Most international contracts contain some kind of dispute resolution clause. The typical dispute resolution clause provides for arbitration under the rules of some domestic or international arbitration association. Indeed, many of these associations, notably the American Arbitration Association and the International Chamber of Commerce, furnish model arbitration clauses that may be inserted into contracts.

Most of these prototype arbitration clauses also provide for a choice of forum (i.e.," Disputes under this contract shall be subject to the rules of American Arbitration Association and any arbitration under this clause shall take place in Washington, D.C.") Some commercial contracts provide for dispute resolution by litigation in the domestic courts of one party or the other or for litigation in the domestic courts of a country regarded as neutral by the contracting parties. For the most part, the parties' choices on these

---

34. See e.g., Benjamin, *Penalties, Liquidated Damage and Penal Clauses*, 9 Int'l & Comp. L.Q. 600 (1960); Thilmany, *Fonctions et Revisibilite des Clauses Penale en Droit Compare*, 1980 Revue Internationale de Droit Compare 17.

35. See, e.g., H. MAYERS & B BRUNSVOLD, DRAFTING PATENT LICENSE AGREEMENTS (2d ed. 1984); P. WOOD, LAW AND PRACTICE OF INTERNATIONAL FINANCE (1984); T. JOHNSON, INTERNATIONAL DISTRIBUTOR AND AGENCY AGREEMENTS (1967).

issues will be honored. In one important case eventually decided by the United States Supreme Court, a dispute arose between a German shipping company and an American oil company under a contract that provided for the resolution of any disputes by litigation in the High Court of Justice in London. The United States Supreme Court honored that agreement, commenting that international commercial transactions are usually carefully negotiated bargains between sophisticated parties and the agreement of the parties, including their agreement as to choice of forum must be honored to preserve the stability and integrity of international agreements.[36] Within the European Community choice of forum clauses are generally honored so long as one of the parties is deemed to be domiciled within the jurisdiction of a signatory state.[37]

It is possible, of course, for the contract to be silent on dispute resolution. For contracts that lack express dispute resolution clauses, the parties may simply negotiate differences that arise during the performance of the contract. They may agree to negotiate in the presence of a third-party mediator or conduct some other type of dispute resolution process without having made special provision for these events in the original document.[38] Alternatively, the parties may execute a subsequent written agreement to arbitrate any grievances that have arisen under the contract; or the parties may simply choose to litigate their differences in some appropriate court.

Those drafters who prefer to include a dispute resolution clause in their contracts—and most international commercial agreements contain such clauses—should remember that the vast majority of international agreements choose arbitration, even though the author of this book would urge all drafters to at least consider incorporation of some language urging re-negotiation, mediation or a mini-trial *before* the parties go to arbitration, because of the expense and procedural complexity now associated with commercial arbitration. Many international contracts simply use a domestic form of arbitration, such as: "All disputes under this agreement shall be settled through arbitration under the commercial arbitration rules of the Stockholm Chamber of Commerce." If the parties are predisposed to sign a simple arbitration clause, the contract drafter should be prepared to brief the client on some of the components of arbitration under that system, including typical fees assessed, the manner of selecting the arbitrator, the rules governing the arbitration hearing, and the mechanisms for either compelling or enforcing

---

36. The Bremen v. Zapata Off-Shore Company, 407 U.S. 1 (1972).

37. Article 17, EEC Convention on Jurisdiction and Enforcement of Judgments in Civil and Commercial Matters, *done*, September 27, 1968, *reprinted in* 8 Int'l Legal Materials 229 (1969). Choices will not be enforced if a particular court has exclusive jurisdiction or if undue influence or a contract of adhesion (a printed form agreement) is involved.

38. See generally, ADAPTATION AND RENEGOTIATION OF CONTRACTS IN INTERNATIONAL TRADE AND FINANCE (N. Horn, ed.1985).

arbitration that exist in the host country's domestic courts. One good reference for this type of information is the *International Handbook on Commercial Arbitration.*[39] In certain circumstances, the parties may have very little choice. For example, in the past in negotiating contracts with the former Soviet Union, the Soviet negotiators normally insisted on arbitration before a domestic U.S.S.R. tribunal, the Foreign Trade Arbitration Commission. However, if a foreign party objected, the Soviet negotiators usually had no problem agreeing to arbitration in Sweden, with a Stockholm arbitration site using the arbitration rules of the Stockholm Chamber of Commerce.[40] It remains to be seen whether the republics constituting the Commonwealth of Independent States will retain these rigid attitudes toward dispute resolution. The likelihood is that they will not. Given that the republics are so hungry for foreign commerce, they are likelier to adopt modern and far more flexible arbitration techniques than those applied by the Soviet Union. Nonetheless, there are countries, China for example, that are still in existence whose attitude toward dispute resolution is equally rigid. In dealing with those countries, contracting parties may simply have to decide whether they want to do the deal (and thereby concede the matter of dispute resolution) or contract with parties in countries that are more flexible.

In most international commercial negotiations, the choices are broader. The parties may simply elect the arbitration system of either the seller or the buyer's country or choose arbitration under the domestic arbitration laws of a third country. Recall that in most countries, including the United States, when the parties select arbitration they will be held to that choice even if, at some later point in time, they conclude that litigation would be preferable.[41] If the contracting parties believe that all domestic arbitration systems are inappropriate they may choose arbitration under the rules and supervision of one of the international arbitration bodies. A few agreements provide for *ad hoc* arbitration, by which the parties concoct (or borrow) their own rules, select the arbitrators and administer the arbitration proceeding completely on their own. While permissible, and while there are some cost savings associated with ad hoc arbitration, it should be elected only by experienced companies accompanied by experienced counsel. Most disputing parties need the assistance of a recognized arbitral institution. As a result, most dispute resolution clauses in international commercial agreements choose among the major arbitration institutions such as the International Chamber of Com-

---

39. INTERNATIONAL HANDBOOK ON COMMERCIAL ARBITRATION (P. Sanders, ed.)(Kluwer, 1984 w/ supplements).

40. Hoya & Stein, *Drafting Contracts in U.S.-Soviet Trade,* 7 L. & Pol'y in Int'l Bus. 1057 (1975) (With the demise of the Soviet Union and the fragmentation of the former Soviet republics, Mr. Hoya's work may now be of purely historical interest.)

41. See the discussion of the United States Supreme Court's decision in *Mitsubishi v. Soler,* Chapter 8, § 8.2.

merce or among highly experienced national systems of arbitration such as the London Court of Arbitration or the American Arbitration Association.

Once these preliminary choices have been made, drafting the dispute resolution clause is relatively simple: most contracts adopt the sample clause suggested by the supervising institution and then modify that clause to suit their particular needs and desires. The much harder part of the equation is knowing which body's rules to select. The discussion in Chapter Eight of the different procedural systems for international commercial arbitration should be consulted to determine the advantages and disadvantages of each of the major procedural schemes.

The major arbitration bodies such as the AAA and ICC have drafted standard form arbitration clauses that they believe will suffice as a contract's dispute resolution clause. The AAA suggests: "Any controversy or claim arising out of or relating to this contract, or any breach thereof, shall be settled by arbitration in accordance with the Rules of the American Arbitration Association, and judgment upon award rendered by the arbitrator(s) may be entered in any court having jurisdiction thereof." The London Court of International Arbitration recommends: "Any dispute arising out of or in connection with this contract, including any question regarding its existence, validity or termination, shall be referred to and finally resolved by arbitration under the Rules of the London Court of International Arbitration, which Rules are deemed to be incorporated by reference into this clause." The sample clause drafted by UNCITRAL states: "Any dispute, controversy or claim arising out of or relating to this contract, or the breach, termination or invalidity thereof, shall be settled by arbitration in accordance with the UNCITRAL Arbitration Rules as are present in force." The ICC suggests: "All disputes arising in connection with the present contract shall be finally settled under the Rules of Conciliation and Arbitration of the International Chamber of Commerce by one or more arbitrators appointed in accordance with the Rules."

If a contract drafter needs a quick arbitration clause, any of these will suffice because the institution's underlying rules will supply the missing details. However, most experienced international lawyers find those clauses too simplistic, and recommend that the contract set out more of the details of dispute resolution even when the parties agreed to use a supervising institution and that institution's rules.

As a *minimum*, the dispute resolution clause in a contract electing institutional arbitration (i.e, a proceeding supervised by one of the recognized arbitration institutions) should specify the following:

1. *The type of dispute resolution to be employed.* If two different devices are to be utilized, such as mediation and arbitration, the

clause should make clear that mediation is to take place before arbitration.

2. *The rules system for the arbitration.* (ICC, AAA, UNCITRAL, etc.) Note that many of the institutions will agree to supervise an arbitration using UNCITRAL rules, rather than the institution's rules. Under normal circumstances, it is advisable to use the rules promulgated by the institution that will be supervising the arbitration.

3. *The language of the arbitration proceeding and the arbitral award.* The language of the arbitration in most cases will be the same as the official language of the contract. However, there may be instances when the parties want to utilize another language—for example, the language of the country that is the site of the arbitration—to make it easier for any arbitrators who are selected from that country to follow the proceedings.

4. *The site of arbitration.* There many choices available here. Typical choices include the country of the buyer or the country of the seller. If a neutral site is selected, most parties choose a site such as London, Cairo or Stockholm that has solid experience with arbitrations and an ample supply of arbitrators. The arbitrators may be imported for the hearing, of course, but that greatly increases the expense of the arbitration. Most parties choose a site in a country that has signed the New York Convention for the Recognition and Enforcement of Arbitral Awards.[42] Recall that an arbitral award rendered in a country that has signed the New York Convention is enforceable under the terms of the Convention even if one or more of the parties is from a country that has not signed. A final consideration for selecting the arbitration site is the court structure of the host country. Because parties sometimes have to refer pre-arbitration issues to a court and because the winning party sometimes has to seek enforcement of the arbitral award in court, the host country's court system could figure importantly in the arbitration.

5. *The number of arbitrators.* In most international commercial arbitration systems, the rules provide for the appointment of a panel of three arbitrators (one selected by each of the two parties with the third selected by the two party-appointed arbitrators; this third arbitrator normally presides over the arbitration as chairman). If the parties want to reduce expenses associated with any arbitration, they must expressly provide for a single arbitrator. Some arbitration clauses also set out the credentials of the arbitrators (for example, "each arbitrator shall have at least ten years experience in commercial real estate matters"). If there are special reasons for specifying

---

42. See the discussion of the New York Convention in Chapter 9, § 9.3.

credentials, these choices will normally be honored by the supervising institution. Most arbitration clauses do not go this far.

If institutional arbitration is selected, the parties may still go ahead and specify the nationalities of the arbitrators, specific procedures for the arbitration (including, for example, whether pre-hearing discovery is permitted and under what circumstances) and other details. This is probably drafting over-kill. It adds enormous detail to the contract itself when the rules of the supervising institution can fill in most of the details. Obviously, if the parties disagree with the procedures set out in the institution's rules, they need to set out the different procedures either in the contract itself or in a subsequent arbitration agreement.

If the parties want to go ahead on their own without the assistance of a supervising institution, choosing what is know as *ad hoc* arbitration, the contract—or a subsequent agreement—needs to contain far more detail. Harry Arkin, a U.S. lawyer who is an experienced international arbitrator suggests the following components for a proper *ad hoc* arbitration clause:[43]

1. Scope of the arbitration
2. Jurisdiction of the arbitrators
2. Demand for arbitration and response time
3. Representation by counsel
4. Selection of arbitrators (including credentials, a party's failure to select, removal and replacement)
5. Site of arbitration
6. Language of arbitration
7. Applicable law
8. Procedural rules (including hearing procedures, taking of evidence, discovery, provisional remedies)
9. Issuance of the award (including appeal or vacating the award, modification or correction of the award)
10. Enforcement of the award
11. Allocation of costs of arbitration

It is possible to make both too much and too little of a dispute resolution clause. The author has experienced contract negotiations where the negotiators have resolved the price term in thirty seconds and spent three days on the arbitration clause. There have been other negotiations where the contract drafters casually toss a standard form arbitration clause into the agreement without thirty seconds of thought. Neither approach makes a great deal of sense. No one enters an agreement expecting the contract to be breached, but when breach occurs, dispute resolution becomes a vital component of the transaction.

---

43. Arkin, *International Ad Hoc Arbitration: A Practical Alternative*, Int'l Bus. Law. 5 (Jan. 1987).

§ 4.9 Some Concluding Comments

The drafting of a contract deserves all the time and attention that the parties can afford to devote to it. Care in the planning, negotiation, and drafting stages will prevent disturbances during the life of the agreement. In the final analysis, drafting a contract is no more—or less—than the parties saying what they mean in a way that conveys the same meaning to both persons. If all contracts could accomplish this, there would be far less need for the dispute resolution mechanisms discussed in the second half of this book. But before we move to a comprehensive analysis of dispute resolution, some hints on how to negotiate the initial agreement should prove helpful.   ◆

— 5 —
Negotiating International Commercial Agreements

§ 5.1 Introduction

Some lawyers and business executives may scoff at the title of this chapter. Until recently, the common understanding within these two professions was that negotiation—although always important and frequently crucial to the proper consummation of a commercial agreement—could not be taught, discussed, or even written about in any fashion other than the merely anecdotal. In the past, to the extent that negotiation was discussed as a separate topic, it was generally couched in the form of a simple admonition to the negotiator to know the subject matter (both the commercial and legal aspects) of the deal thoroughly. A few less-than-satisfactory writings on negotiation deal with the topic in terms of psychological intimidation or under-the-table manipulation. Thus, the prevailing view has long been that negotiation is purely a matter of experience. People learn to negotiate simply by doing negotiations. It was often suggested that every negotiation is so unique that no systematic evaluation of negotiating is possible. At best, certain hints on negotiation technique can be related in case history or "war story" form but nothing more could be said.

There is something to this viewpoint. All things being equal, an experienced negotiator who knows the subject matter thoroughly will probably prevail over an ignorant neophyte. But that is not all there is to consider about negotiation, whether it is negotiation between two spouses trying to agree on tonight's restaurant or between two business executives trying to reach agreement on the sale of $100 million worth of telecommunications equipment.

Fortunately, a number of academics and practitioners have begun to write on and analyze negotiation in ways that can be conveyed in print and that are helpful to persons just entering the field. Best of all, many of these recent attempts to analyze negotiation have made it possible to systematically evaluate actual negotiations and thus to provide a framework by which even experienced negotiators can evaluate their behavior. This chapter describes and analyzes some of these newer approaches to negotiation. The chapter begins with some basic considerations on negotiating generally and then moves to a comprehensive discussion of cross-cultural negotiation, a matter vital to international business agreements. The chapter concludes with a little-discussed topic—the ethics of negotiation—too frequently ignored by professionals in many fields, but one that can have pragmatic as well as moral repercussions.

§ 5.2 Establishing a Basic Framework for Negotiation: a short excursus in negotiation theory

The best place to begin a discussion of negotiation theory and practice is with the proposition that there are many different negotiation settings and countless different styles and techniques of negotiating. Moreover, things that work in one setting might be terribly inefficient or downright counter-productive in another. For example, the negotiation between husband and wife about where to have dinner is going to be far different in tone and content from a multilateral negotiation to resolve problems of cross-boundary air pollution. A multilateral environmental negotiation is, in turn, going to differ substantially from negotiations between two lawyers in a divorce proceeding. Although certain factors are common to all negotiations, this chapter concentrates on negotiating commercial agreements between businesses in two or more countries.

This assumption—that we are dealing with a commercial arrangement—provides a solid foundation for analyzing some of the more sophisticated issues in negotiation. Thus, for the most part, this chapter will assume a two-party negotiation between business people who *want* to reach an agreement and who also may want to use the current negotiation as a precursor for future business dealings. This makes the discussion in this chapter more efficient, but does not necessarily make the actual negotiations any easier. Virtually all negotiations are characterized by uncertainty; and, in many instances, the two parties are not compelled to do business with each other—i.e., each can find willing buyers and sellers elsewhere if an agreement cannot be reached. All persons approaching negotiation should keep in mind a few fundamentals.

§ 5.2.1 Diagramming a negotiation

The first principle to keep in mind is that all negotiations are characterized by a negotiating range developed in confidence by each of the parties prior to the actual negotiation. In other words, in a contract for the sale of goods, the parties normally establish in their own minds prices below which they will refuse to sell or above which they will refuse to buy. Thus, the price becomes not a fixed point, but rather a range of potential prices that each party may find acceptable. These ranges are usually established through business decisions based on costs of materials or services, labor, shipping, risk of loss and the like. In most business negotiations, the price of the contract is usually the most important component of the agreement, while in non-commercial negotiations such as multi-lateral treaty negotiations, price is often not an issue or serves a secondary role to such considerations as national honor and domestic politics. Although the psychological dynamic is present in all negotiations, it is usually less intrusive in commercial negotiations than it might be in, say, a domestic relations negotiations. Recall the fundamental precept of this chapter, in normal business negotiations the parties want to agree. Such is not the case in many divorces.

To understand how price ranges affect a commercial contract, assume that Parties A (seller) and B (buyer) come together to try to work out an arrangement for the buying and selling of 100 telescopes. Both A and B want to do business, but being good executives, A does not want to sell at a loss nor does B want to buy at such a high price that he cannot resell the product for some profit. Assume further that A and B are knowledgeable generally about pricing conditions in their industry, but have no idea how the telescopes will sell in the country of destination.

Pre-negotiation preparation by each party leads to the following preliminary conclusion by each. A would like to sell the telescopes for $100 per unit (resulting in a fairly large profit) but can make a five percent profit if the telescopes are sold for $50 each. He will break even at $40 per unit. Assume, however, that B is so uncertain about the demand for telescopes in his country that he is willing to risk no more than $35 per widget and had hoped to pay as low as $10 per unit. Further assume that these prices represent what Americans like to call the *bottom line*—i.e., no other factors, however nicely stated, will budge the parties away from these numbers.

The parties' pre-negotiation posture results is illustrated by the following diagram:

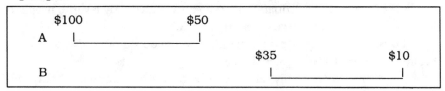

Unless B is willing to take more of a risk, or unless A is willing to sell at a loss, no agreement is possible no matter how skilled the negotiators or how much time they spend negotiating.

By contrast, consider the potential result if A's range is $100 to $25 and B's range is $75 to $15:

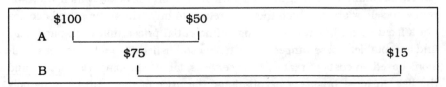

In this case, even the most inept negotiators are probably going to be able to conclude an agreement satisfactory to both sides because the overlap of prices is substantial. This analysis suggests that while studying the theory and technique of negotiation is important, most commercial agreements stand or fall on the congruence of the pricing determinations made by each party.

There are other cases in which there is not nearly so much overlap. Consider, for example, the following:

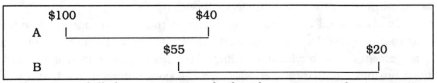

In this case, skilled negotiation on both sides may save the transaction, while ineptness may result in both parties not only walking away from the deal but walking away with such distaste that they never again seek to do business with each other. For these reasons, it makes sense to examine the theory of negotiation in greater depth.

The literature of negotiation runs from highly quantitative studies by social scientists to rudimentary rules-of-thumb proffered by lawyers who are self-styled expert negotiators. The social science literature tends to be nearly impenetrable for lay persons and so esoteric that even when it can be understood, the information conveyed has virtually no practical value. On the other hand, much of the literature generated by people in the legal and business communities tends to be so purely anecdotal (a sort of "great-negotiations-in-which-I-have-prevailed" approach) and so personalized that it provides no useful framework for others. If the reader is searching this chapter only for a single useful rule-of-thumb for negotiators, consider the wisdom of a lawyer of the author's acquaintance who once stated: "My favorite negotiating position is my foot on the other guy's neck."

Fortunately, there is now something of a middle ground. Negotiation is beginning to be studied systematically with good results. Indeed, the literature is growing exponentially, although it is also becoming somewhat repetitive and overlapping.[1] With the profusion of literature, we may have come full circle. There may be a limit to what one can say about negotiation in an analytical context, perhaps thereby confirming what those older negotiators would have use believe—that good negotiation is still mainly a matter of experience and not a matter of theory.

Nonetheless, to understand theory, there are some good starting points. One place to begin to search for a theory of negotiation is in the rather arcane mathematical field, the theory of games, an area of inquiry derived from probability theory. Games theory is at bottom a set of concepts that mathematicians developed to try to explain the behavior of persons involved in conflict.[2] It is based on the following postulates:

a. the participation of two (or more) persons or entities in the transaction;

b. the availability of more than one course of action available to each party (sometimes referred to as *strategies*);

c. the existence of one or more points of congruence between or among the various strategies (i.e., there must exist at least one point at which the participants can agree);

d. the existence of some set of conditions that form boundaries for each party's behavior (i.e., the parties' behavior cannot be simply random; it must be limited by, for example, commercial legal principles, the laws of physics (as might govern, say, the operation of ballistic missiles), or existing world economic conditions.[3]

There are in essence two types of matrices that can be drawn on this basis. The first, commonly referred to as a *win/lose* situation, is one in which one party must lose if another wins. Examples include a criminal trial where either the prosecutor or the defendant wins—an outcome that automatically means that the other loses. Trading in stock options is another illustration, albeit outside the context of negotiation. In normal options trading, a deal is struck because one person believes that the underlying stock is going to go down while the other believes that the stock is going to go up. Obviously, both cannot be right; thus, one wins and the other must lose. This type of game, sometimes referred to as *distributional bargaining* is diagrammed very simply as:

---

1. Any list of solid negotiation literature would likely include: R. FISHER & W. URY, GETTING TO YES: NEGOTIATING AGREEMENT WITHOUT GIVING IN (1981); H. RAIFFA, THE ART AND SCIENCE OF NEGOTIATION (1982); P. SPERBER, ATTORNEY'S PRACTICE GUIDE TO NEGOTIATIONS (1985); H. EDWARDS & J. WHITE, THE LAWYER AS NEGOTIATOr (1977); G. WILLIAMS, LEGAL NEGOTIATION AND SETTLEMENT (1983); G. BELLOW & B. MOULTON, NEGOTIATION (1979); R. NIERENBERG, FUNDAMENTALS OF NEGOTIATING (1973); Menkel-Meadow, *Toward Another View of Legal Negotiation: The Structure of Problem-Solving*, 31 U.C.L.A. L.Rev. 754 (1984) [cited as "Problem Solving Structure"]; Menkel-Meadow, *Legal Negotiation: A Study of Strategies in Search of a Theory*, 1983 Am.Bar.Fdn.Res. J. 905 [cited as "Study of Strategies"].

2. See, e.g., E. GOFFMAN, STRATEGIC INTERACTION (1969).

3. Bellow & Moulton, supra note 1, at 40.

A	win	lose
B	lose	win

In a criminal prosecution, the defendant is found either guilty or not guilty. In a divorce in which the wife wants the divorce and the husband does not, the divorce is either granted or not granted—thus, one of the two must lose. Fortunately, there are few international commercial relationships which are characterized as win/lose situations. Most commercial dealings permit both parties to consummate a transaction satisfactory to both, but in which it is highly unlikely that either will be able to prevail totally (the expression in the United States is "getting taken to the cleaners."). These types of transactions, frequently referred to in the literature as "win/win" negotiations, require the assessment of probabilities.

In a commercial context, calculating probabilities is almost never as complicated as it might be in, say, a multilateral negotiation on air pollution or even bilateral arms reduction negotiations. It involves mainly the assignment of probabilities based on some kind of estimate as to how the other party will behave. Assigning probabilities is largely a matter of experience, judgment, and research. Consider a very simply example. Assume that an U.S. seller wishes to sell stainless steel fittings for a particular manufacturing operation. A potential buyer, a French company, has purchased only aluminum fittings in the past.

Research on the French buyer's previous behavior may reveal that the buyer has never paid more than $10 per unit for aluminum fittings. However, the seller may conclude, as a matter of business judgment and experience in domestic sales, that stainless steel fittings are far superior in quality to aluminum, but not so superior that any previous buyer has been willing to double the price. In addition, the engineering information available indicates that while stainless steel is superior, it is not indispensable to the French manufacturing operation. Thus, it is clear that the French company will not be compelled to do business with the seller, although it is obvious that there will be some interest in replacing aluminum with stainless steel.

This analysis suggests that there is a virtual certainty that buyer will not be willing to pay $20 per fitting. So in analyzing the prospective negotiation along games theory lines, Seller might assign a probability of close to 95 per cent against the buyer being willing to buy at $19. At the same time, the buyer should be willing to pay more that $10 for an item clearly superior in quality to the aluminum fittings it currently purchases. The seller might then assess the probability of the French purchaser insisting on a sale price of $12 or below to be less than 5 percent. All of this suggests that there is a substantial probability, perhaps around 90 per cent, that the final contract price will be between $12.50 per unit and $18.50 per unit.

This example is of course very simplistic. When buyers and sellers crank in imponderables such as risk of loss, risk of expropriation, possible cancellation of export or import permissions and other uncertainties that are frequently encountered in an international transaction, the combinations and permutations of agreement increase drastically. So, for example, consider a situation in which a buyer might be willing to buy at a higher unit price if seller did not insist on a letter of credit, or a 'negotiation in which seller could accept a far lower unit price if buyer was willing to sign a requirements contract (one in which the buyer purchases all of his required parts from the same seller).

Are there any advantages to this type of analysis even if a negotiator is not a mathematician? Two prominent American writers on negotiation, Professors Gary Bellow and Bea Moulton, suggest that at the very least it forces negotiators to think about the structure of the negotiation and further helps negotiators to think through the possible range of choices and the manner in which each party might influence the final agreement. Put another way: "For many inexperienced negotiators, the major problem in framing bargaining strategy seems to be in their inability to envision the bargaining situation as a complex of intersecting choices and perceptions; for some, games theory may provide a useful way to begin to think systematically about the relationships involved."[4]

Readers who recoil from overly quantified approaches to a topic may be put off by games theory. Unfortunately, the only other help available in the literature is derived from social science data on the behavior of individuals and of groups. Indeed, some negotiation scholars believe that most current writing on negotiation by legal and business writers is characterized by an inability to develop a comprehensive theory of negotiation that fits both adversarial negotiation (prosecutor versus defense attorney, for example) and the win/win negotiation that typifies much of commercial negotiations. In other words, most of the literature focuses on "competitive gain" when "[w]ork on the purpose and evaluation of goals and outcomes much precede any consideration of strategy and tactics."[5]

Notwithstanding the lack of a unifying theory, virtually all of the literature recognizes essentially three points: (1) negotiation is a function of leverage (leverage is the allocation of power or control between the two sides), (2) negotiation can often turn as much on the personalities and behavior of the negotiators as on the relative merits of the parties' positions; and (3) in a commercial setting, as well as many other settings, legal principles frequently shape the outcome, irrespective of the desires of the individual parties. Consider these propositions in a little more depth. First, all bargaining is a

---

4. Id. at 44-45.
5. Study of Strategies, supra note 1, at 922.

function of leverage. People come together to bargain because they want something (in either the affirmative or negative sense of the term). Merchants want to buy and sell telescopes, not for the mere doing of the transaction, but to make either short-run or long term profits. Divorcing spouses frequently want not only a monetary benefit from the dissolution of the marriage, but also possibly some kind of psychological vindication, or even some type of retribution. Leverage is simply the ingredient that forces people to bargain. Anyone who is completely lacking in leverage is totally at the mercy of the other side. Such parties have no reason to negotiate.

Leverage is almost always present in commercial dealings because commercial relationships are normally characterized by (1) parties who wish to do business together; (2) a range of possible outcomes that will be generally satisfactory to both parties (note the diagrams set out above) and (3) a fairly dispassionate approach to the deal making itself. While high emotion occasionally intrudes into commercial decision making and while vindication and retribution are not totally foreign to the behavior of business people, these ingredients are not commonplace. Leverage in business dealings is derived mainly from information and knowledge, whether openly held or secretly acquired, on the type and quality of the goods or services offered for sale, on the status of foreign markets, the trends in national currencies, anticipated consumer interests and behavior, and the like.

To establish a non-quantitative analytical framework for negotiation, many dispute resolution professionals now use Roger Fisher's and William Ury's *Getting to Yes* as a starting point. *Getting to Yes* is probably the single most popular book ever written on negotiation and has attracted both praise and criticism from an entire spectrum of readers. It has been followed by a somewhat less popular and less helpful sequel, *Getting Together*. Fisher and Urey believe that there is virtually no conflict that cannot be negotiated if the parties engage in what they refer to as *principled negotiation.* Principled negotiation begins when both parties appreciate and began to accommodate the fact that each has both conflicting and compatible interests. By building on the identification of compatible interests it becomes far easier for the parties to reach some kind of reconciliation on the conflicting issues. Indeed, even when interests directly collide and seem totally irreconcilable, there may be—at the very least—a shared interest in preserving the negotiation as a dispute resolution device rather than resorting to more costly and cumbersome forms of conflict resolution.

From these basic premises, *Getting to Yes* moves to a series of what look suspiciously like anecdotal rules of thumb for negotiators but which are, arguably, general principles applicable to virtually any negotiation.[6]

---

6. See, e.g., the debate between Professor James White, a University of Michigan law professor who likes to be regarded as a hard nosed traditional negotiator and Roger Fisher in an acade-

Since these guidelines have a great deal of applicability to the relatively harmonious, non-belligerent discussions of people in business, they bear close analysis by persons interested in succeeding in international commercial negotiations. The guidelines are:

    a. Separate the people from the problem

    b. Focus on interests, not positions

    c. Invent options for mutual gain

    d. Insist on objective criteria

    e. Know your "best alternative to a negotiated agreement" (BATNA)[7]

§ 5.2.2. Separating the people from the problem.

When initially set out, these guidelines sound intriguing, but they are not easily understood without putting them into a more practical setting. Assume that two people in business, a seller in the United States and a buyer in Japan, wish to negotiate a contract for the sale of telecommunications equipment. While thinking through the negotiation beforehand, a negotiator (or the parties themselves as is often the case) may wish to begin by understanding that there is a great difference between the problem (executing an equipment contract) and the people who are going to be negotiating that contract (the lawyers, for example) or the people (buyer and seller themselves) who are standing behind that contract. A negotiator can over generalize by simply deciding that profit is the single motivating force in the transaction and may try to hammer through a deal on that basis. However, a more careful, more sophisticated negotiator will recognize that business executives, like all other human beings, are an amalgam of personal needs and professional goals.

For example, an U.S. negotiator may be put off by the personal desire of the Japanese to begin the project with some social amenities or by the inclination of Japanese to bow rather than shake hands. The U.S. party may, conceivably, harbor some residual dislike of Japanese for that country's role in World War Two. But those things are not the *problem*; they are the *people*. The problem is mainly to consummate a purchase and sale agreement within the instructions given the negotiator by the client, not to refight World War Two or muse over the relative wisdom of shaking hands or bowing as a greeting.

(note 6 continued) mic law journal. Professor White believes that Getting to Yes is excessively soft, concentrating on win/win negotiation to the almost total exclusion of win/lose negotiation—a setting that is far more difficult to deal with. Compare White, "The Pros and Cons of Getting to Yes", 34 J.Leg.Educ. 115-16 (1984) with Fisher, Comment [in response to White], 34 J.Leg.Educ. 120 (1984)(Professor Fisher believes that even win/lose bargaining can profit from a Getting to Yes-type analysis).

7. Fisher & Ury, supra note 1, at 10.

This may seem like such a commonplace that it is not worth mentioning; but when one considers some of the horror stories set out below in section 5.5 on cross-cultural negotiation, it is obvious that this is one of the first lessons forgotten by negotiators. Merely recognizing this does not necessarily tell a negotiator what to do in a specific situation. This guideline and those that follow provide assistance in developing a *structure* for analyzing the negotiation. The next section of this chapter contains some practical hints on handling specific negotiation problems.

§ 5.2.3. Focus on interests, not positions.

This is another concept that frequently gets lost in the negotiation process. Inexperienced negotiators may hear a statement from the other side to the effect that "I will not agree to a letter of credit" and automatically turn on the heat, deciding that this is obviously a time to get tough. The positions then become hardened and a shouting match ensues that frequently leads to a total breakdown in the negotiation. There is another way to view such a statement, however.

In an international commercial setting, a buyer may enter a negotiation with the announced *position* that he will simply not execute a letter of credit. It could be that he was hurt in an earlier unrelated transaction in which a seller shipped non-conforming goods—a defect that may have taken years to resolve—yet the seller received instant payment in full under the letter of credit. Even if the seller ultimately has to reimburse the buyer for the non-conforming goods, it frequently happens in international transactions that the reimbursement is made with inflated funds, so the buyer is never made fully whole. A seller may take the position that she absolutely demands a letter of credit because she shipped goods to another buyer and was years collecting on the invoice. However the buyer may hear the demand for a letter of credit as an accusation that his credit is no good.

Note that the *position* of the buyer is flatly: "No letter of credit." Yet his *interest* is much different: he really wants protection against the risk of having to receive and contend with non-conforming goods while the seller walks away with all the money due under the contract. Simply recognizing this difference may make all the difference between a successful and unsuccessful negotiation because recognition will permit the parties to work with the third Fisher/Ury guideline.

§ 5.2.4. Create options for mutual gain.

This factor is nearly self-explanatory. But as Fisher and Ury explain, it is not so easily factored into an on-going negotiation. They recognize that there is more than a little tension and pressure associated with even the smoothest and friendliest negotiations: "Trying to decide in the presence of an adversary narrows your vision. Having a lot at stake inhibits creativity. So does searching for the one right solution."[a] This is, nonetheless, a factor that marks a good negotiation. Take the letter of credit imbroglio. Buyer and seller could simply butt heads forever on this and eventually walk away from what could be a very lucrative deal simply because of mutual stubbornness. A wise negotiator will take a step back and ask: "Is there any reasonable alternative to the letter of credit?" It could be that some other payment device would sufficiently protect the seller's interest. Not every international commercial agreement is accompanied by a letter of credit. If seller suspects the buyer's creditworthiness, some kind of credit check such as a Dun & Bradstreet report might provide the assurances she needs to let the deal go forward on an open account basis. She might be willing to accept a partial payment on the goods before shipment in lieu of a letter of credit. Granting that none of these forms of payment provide the absolute security of a letter of credit, the seller might be persuaded to accept a less-secure form of payment in order to consummate the transaction. On the buyer's part, his *interest* in obtaining conforming goods (the underlying reason for his reluctance to execute the letter of credit) may be satisfied by having some right to inspect the goods prior to payment; for example, the letter of credit might be made payable only after he has had an opportunity to inspect. In the alternative, the buyer could appoint a third party inspector who inspects the goods at the seller's factory immediately prior to shipment, releasing for shipment only those goods which are truly conforming. In commercial transactions, there are usually a myriad of options available for any situation. Creativity, rather than intransigence, ought to be the hallmark of commercial negotiators.

§ 5.2.5. Insist on objective criteria.

This factor ties in with the previous factor. It recommends that crucial evaluations be measured by devices that are outside the control of either party. The public international law prototype is the use of United Nations military peacekeeping forces composed of personnel from wholly uninvolved nations to monitor and keep separate belligerent forces. Consider again the problem with the letter of credit. Assume that the seller will agree to on-site inspection of goods prior to shipment. Seller may say something such as: "We'll inspect the goods before we crate them up and make sure they're okay." Buyer may like the idea of inspection before shipment as one part of a quality control protocol, but will likely object to the seller's employees performing that crucial inspection. At the same time, buyer may not have the financial

---

8. Id. at 12.

wherewithal to station an employee at the seller's factory; and even if she could afford it, seller may worry that an employee of the buyer's would object to the tiniest discrepancy, however insignificant. One way to incorporate objective criteria into this agreement is to have that final pre-shipment inspection performed by a third party who is trusted by both seller and buyer. The presence and reputation of this third person will frequently provide all the objectivity required by the contracting parties.

§ 5.2.6. Know your "best alternative to a negotiated agreement (BATNA)"

This guideline urges negotiators to understand what may take place if the negotiations prove unsuccessful. For lawyers negotiating settlement agreements in on-going litigation, the alternative is usually a return to litigation. Thus, the parties give over their dispute to a judge or jury for resolution. A parallel alternative in international commercial dispute resolution is to hand the matter over to an arbitrator. As a result, parties engaged in renegotiation or mediation following some breach of contract should always consider how an arbitrator might dispose of the issues as part of their evaluation of BATNA. However, in pre-contractual international negotiation BATNA has only limited applicability. A breakdown in negotiations in a commercial setting means simply that the parties do no business with each other. As a result, pre-contractual BATNA means either that a party does no deal or that a party does the deal with someone else. An Indonesian entrepreneur whose negotiation to purchase and operate a McDonald's hamburger franchise in Jakarta falls through may have to consider a deal with Burger King or may look for some other business opportunity. In initial contract negotiations a BATNA is sometimes useful as leverage ("If you don't sign, I'll take my business to IBM") but is rarely as important a factor as it is in negotiations prior to litigation.

To some readers, the Fisher/Ury guidelines may seem not much more than simplistic rules of thumb that may or may not work in any particular setting. They are really much more than that. For example, they can serve as an analytical framework that may be applied either before the fact or after the fact to virtually any negotiation. This permits observers and participants to evaluate a number of different negotiations from the same perspective. To that extent, the criteria constitute an attempt to develop a unified theory of negotiation. They represent a quantum leap beyond the merely anecdotal approach to negotiation. Moreover, they are not merely suggestions of specific negotiation techniques. The following two sections show how the Fisher/Ury criteria differ from negotiation strategy and tactics.

§ 5.3 The Stages of Commercial Negotiation

Every negotiation goes through several stages. Understanding the different stages and thinking though the stages of your particular negotiation is one secret of success. One striking study of legal negotiation performed by Professor Gerald Williams and discussed in his book, *Legal Negotiation and Settlement*, identifies four stages:

    A. Orientation and Positioning

    B. Argumentation

    C. Emergence and Crisis

    D. Agreement or Final Breakdown[9]

Much like the Fisher/Ury criteria, this framework appears simplistic and commonsensical at first glance but when analyzed and applied it becomes, as Professor Williams puts it, "a surprisingly powerful tool for the practicing lawyer. Inexperienced attorneys often misperceive which stage of the process the case is in and use tactics that are unnecessary or even harmful to the dynamics of the negotiation."[10] While Professor Williams based most of his conclusions on negotiations in other than an international commercial context, the stages prove quite useful in that setting as well.

§ 5.3.1. Orientation and positioning

At this point, the parties first come into contact with each other. In international commercial transactions, these first points of contact may be by mail, telex or telephone; but however they are made they become crucial to everything that follows. In contracts for the purchase and sale of goods, the initial contact may be made by the seller searching for new markets for his goods. The seller will typically identify potential buyers and then, either directly or indirectly, initiate contact with those persons. Those first contacts are likely to comprise a description of the seller's company, an explanation of the goods offered by the seller and a suggestion for further discussions that may lead to a sale. Buyers may initiate the contact by seeking a provider of the goods or services that they seek. Whether the seller or the buyer initiates the contact, this first approach may include a statement of the price of the goods. The statement of price may be direct or may be set out in a catalog of products or a separate price list. In more complicated international transactions, there may be an elaborate dance of protocol even before the first face-to-face meeting. In certain cultures, a direct approach is not favored and the initial contact may take place quietly through the actions of intermediaries. Outside the United States the use of agents or brokers as a conduit for busi-

---

9. Williams, supra note 1, at 70-72.
10. Id. at 72.

ness information is quite common. In Williams' parlance, these activities comprise the *orientation* stage. Orientation provides those crucial first impressions by which the tone and process of the entire negotiation is often set.

Positioning begins only when one or both of the parties sets out an opening position. In commercial transactions, it is frequently the first offering of a quantity of goods at a particular price, or the initial letter inviting the other side to bargain with specificity. Williams speculates that there are essentially three categories of positions: First, many negotiators attempt what he calls the *maximilist* position—by which a party states almost an outrageous position from which she secretly realizes she will have to retreat. Recall the earlier hypothetical involving the sale of stainless steel fittings. A seller might ask $30 per unit knowing full well that no buyer has ever paid more than $20 and fully expecting that the price will inevitably come down from $30 to, say, $20 per unit. But $20 represents an extremely high price for the fittings—indeed, it is the highest price others have paid. If the buyer and seller agree on $20, the seller will be very happy. Even so, the maximalist position can have palpable disadvantages. What happens if the buyer has done *his* research and knows that the highest price ever paid is $20? A well-informed buyer may react with outrage to a $30 price and walk away from the deal. At the very least, the seller may severely damage her credibility at a crucial point in the negotiation.

Professor Williams has identified a second tactic. His research shows that many negotiators stake out what he calls an *equitable* position—one that is intended at the outset to be fair and equitable for both sides. Note that this has advantages, particularly in international commercial negotiations between sophisticated sellers and buyers. For example, the seller sends an early letter to the buyer detailing the specifications of the fittings, the labor costs, and the other components of the final price. She then asks for $18 per unit. The buyer, being familiar with these products, recognizes instantly that this is a fair price, although clearly one at the high end of what we might call the zone of reasonableness. Taking an equitable position may result in a quickly consummated transaction; but, at the same time, it eliminates the possibility of the seller's realizing a price of $20 per unit.

A third possible position is developed by Professor Williams by taking a page out of the Fisher/Ury book. Williams describes the matter of *integrative positioning*—initial bargaining characterized by one or the other party's setting forth a number of possible options to be considered by the other side. For example, the seller of fittings might offer a unit price of $22 with freight and insurance prepaid to buyer's place of business or, in the alternative, a unit price of $17 on an FOB basis. There are other possibilities: the seller might reduce the price by $1 per unit if the buyer pays cash prior to delivery.

In his empirical study of students who take part in simulated negotiations, Williams observed that integrative positioning was frequently adopted by those student negotiators who were ultimately rated as "effective" by the observers of the negotiations. But like the other positioning techniques, it has its drawbacks. If the seller sets out a number of pricing possibilities at the outset of the negotiation, the buyer may require a much longer time to evaluate and compare all the alternatives. The statement of multiple possibilities by one side may trigger multiple counteroffers by the other side, increasing the complexity of the negotiation itself. If the parties begin jumping around among the various options during the negotiations, their discussions are likely to take a long time and increase the frustration level for the negotiators to the point that one party walks away.

Williams' evaluation of the various positions shows that there is no single permissible approach to the orientation and positioning stage. Whatever the techniques used, orientation and positioning is likely to encompass more time than all the other stages of negotiation put together.[11]

§ 5.3.2. Argumentation

This stage is characterized by a defining of issues—attempts by the parties to discover the true positions of the other side and a stage in which at least a few concessions are made by each side. Put a little more colloquially, this is the "back and forth" part of negotiation. For example, a buyer might agree to a letter of credit but ask for a $1 per unit discount because of the letter of credit. The seller might counter with a price reduction of $ .50 per unit if the buyer agrees to use a particular bank for the letter of credit. The parties can go around and around at this stage, but at some point they will move to stage number three.

§ 5.3.3. Emergence and crisis

However long the argumentation takes, at some point the parties will begin to see the final shape of the bargain or to identify those points on which agreement is simply not possible. Professor Williams refers to this stage as *emergence and crisis*. This is the point at which Fisher/Ury's suggestions for the development of options often come into play. As Williams sees the negotiation process, a crisis can occur when each side believes it has conceded all it can and is still without an agreement, or when a psychological sense of being exploited begins to form in the minds of one or another of the negotiators. If there is a rigid chronological deadline for the negotiations, or if a deadline is imposed by rapidly changing business conditions, this step in the

---

11. Id. at 78.

negotiation process can take on an almost frantic quality. For example, in negotiations for the sale of oil drilling equipment, fluctuations in the price of crude oil may have a substantial effect on the buyer's willingness to purchase the equipment. If the bottom appears to be dropping out of the market, the negotiations may be terminated long before the contract is drafted and signed.

§ 5.3.4. Agreement or breakdown

Here the parties either reach an agreement or postpone or completely break off negotiations. This is not to say that every last detail needs to be worked out at this stage. The actual agreement can be stated in general terms, leaving the details to be fleshed out later. By contrast, some parties may need a comprehensive agreement before they leave the table. In some circumstances, the negotiations may be concluded with a handshake and the final contract will be drafted at a later date. In others, the parties may not leave until all the contract language has been agreed upon and the document signed. There are many models for completing a transaction. Professor Williams' contribution to an understanding of this stage is an important one. Note that he uses the term agreement *or* final breakdown. Parties must understand that many negotiations fail, even when the parties come to the table wanting to do business with each other. A breakdown can occur simply by the passage of time when the parties cannot reach an agreement within the deadline. It can occur because of an outright failure to agree—for example, when a seller will take no less than $15 per unit and a buyer is willing to offer no more than $13. The harder question is whether breakdown should be regarded as a failure. This analysis may turn on the precise issue under negotiation. The breakdown of settlement negotiations in litigation mean that the parties simply let the judge or jury decide who wins. In some fashion, the dispute will be resolved whether or not the parties do it themselves. Breakdown in a pre-contractual negotiation may simply mean that the parties do business with someone else. If A cannot buy shoes from B, he can still deal with C. It is possible, of course, for inept negotiators to poison a negotiation that would have been successful but for their ineptness. That might properly be classified as failure. In another sense, true failure probably occurs only when a negotiator fails to carry out the wishes and instructions of the client. That is the final evaluation of any negotiation.

§ 5.4 Negotiating Styles, Strategy, and Tactics

Many books on negotiation begin with a discussion of these issues and never provide any unified framework for analyzing negotiations. Many negotiators never get beyond the rule-of-thumb approach to negotiations and frequently establish inflexible principles when perhaps the hallmark of successful negotiation is flexibility. For example, a lawyer of the author's acquaintance absolutely refuses to negotiate in the offices of opposing counsel, no matter how much inefficiency, ill-will and consternation he creates by such a refusal. It seems that he was told in law school, that one should never negotiate on the turf of the opposition. Another lawyer counsels new associates that one should *never* be the first to mention a price in a commercial negotiation. She believes that stating price is regarded as a sign of weakness. While there may be a grain of truth in each homily, each can quickly become counterproductive. What happens in a commercial negotiation if no party ever mentions price? People do not have endless amounts of time to dance around the central issues at hand. Is it possible that agreeing to meet in the other party's office could trigger some beneficial concession on the part of the person in whose office the parties are meeting? While Fisher and Ury are quick to remind us that being nice is not the answer, most successful negotiations are characterized by civility, if not cordiality. In reality, if there is any kind of axiom for successful negotiation, it might well be: "Don't artificially hamper yourself as a negotiator by establishing inflexible axioms of negotiation."

Still, so many people believe that tactics and strategy are the stuff of negotiation that no discussion of negotiation can ignore them completely. Fisher and Ury, for example, have a chart of "hard/soft" negotiation styles. An example of a soft negotiator is one who changes her position easily; a hard negotiator sticks to his position. "Soft" is characterized by an attempt to be "friends" with the other party; "hard" negotiating posits that the parties are adversaries and must treat each other as such.[12]

There are lots of other examples. Virtually everyone recognizes the classic technique sometimes referred to as the "Mutt and Jeff" or "good cop/bad cop" tactic in which one negotiator in a team of negotiators constantly takes hard positions while another member of the team takes ostensibly soft positions seeming to protect the other side from the "bad" guy on his own team. Another negotiating tactic, *Boulwarism*, is now named after Lemuel Boulware, a corporate vice president in charge of labor relations who pioneered it. Mr. Boulware had a standard tactic: he simply announced the corporation's position in detail to the newspapers, stated that the company's position was a "take-it-or-leave it" offer and then refused to participate in any further discussions at the bargaining table. Ultimately, the United States National Labor Relations Board denounced this tactic as an unfair labor practice because it effectively destroyed any meaningful collective bargaining. Tactics such as this may work at one point or another in some negotiations.

---

12. Fisher & Ury, supra note 1, at 9.

Unfortunately, because Boulwarism is seen by so many as a tough negotiation tactic (and who in his or her right mind ever wants to be perceived as a "weak" negotiator) it has gotten much more attention than it deserves. Properly analyzed, Boulwarism is most often stupid rather than tough.

There are other detrimental side effects in approaching negotiation in this manner. Experienced negotiators almost always have a tactic or strategy worked out to counter any ploy by the other side. A seller who engages in a lot of Boulwarism may soon find himself without customers. Most commercial negotiations are characterized by calm, rational bargaining, rather than by stunts and shams—contrary to the convictions of novice negotiators who insist that negotiation is nothing more than a matter of ploy and counter ploy. If there is a central theme to this chapter, it is this: For the most part, people in business are neither fools, children nor charlatans. They should not be dealt with as such.

Moreover, most of these cracker-barrel homilies and ill-considered stunts are detrimental to effective negotiation. Business negotiations are characterized by people who normally want to do business with each other and who may want to preserve the elements of a long-lasting relationship. These elements dictate a lot of a negotiator's style and behavior. Think of how much damage is done to a business relationship by an overly aggressive negotiator who saws off the legs of his counterpart's chair so that he can appear taller or more in control? How long will an executive want to continue a relationship when she finds out that your Mutt and Jeff act was all gamesmanship? What happens if a third company inquires of a negotiator (whom you have just devastated and ridiculed) as to the prospects of doing business with your company? These are important points to ponder.

Is there a place for consideration of tactics and strategy? There is, but only if a negotiator fits individual tactics and strategic moves into an overall framework. The nice thing to remember is that most good negotiation tactics are simply a matter of common sense. The best first move is almost too obvious for comment. *Prepare* for the negotiation. Preparation can run the gamut from investigating the business behavior of the other party, to market and price surveys, to developing an understanding of the character and personality of the person who will be sitting on the other side of the table, to understanding human behavior in general, to actual rehearsals of the negotiations before entering into the negotiation itself. Remember that knowledge is power and power is leverage. Knowledge should include a thorough grasp of one's product and company, of the other company and its negotiators and of oneself.

In commercial negotiations where the negotiator is someone different from the principal, the first order of business is to have an absolutely clear understanding of the instructions and positions of the client. For lawyer/negotiators, this understanding is crucial because, as the discussion in § 5.7 shows, a failure to accommodate a client's instructions may lead to ethical abuses and issues of professional liability. Even after the most elaborate briefings, conditions in the negotiation change so drastically that the client must be consulted further. Good preparation requires that the parties allow ample private time for consultation with the respective clients when this occurs. One of the worst possible mistakes in negotiating on behalf of others is to blunder through to an unsatisfactory agreement when a quick telephone call or a fax could have alleviated a misunderstanding. For these same reasons, careful negotiators instruct clients to stand by during negotiations for these consultations. Many negotiations break down when clients cannot be reached for further instructions.

How much time should be spent on matters peripheral to negotiation and how important are these matters? No one knows for sure. The negotiators of the Paris Peace Accords, by which the Vietnam War was ended, devoted a substantial percentage of the entire negotiating process to the shape of the table. Some experienced negotiators refuse to sit, as a matter of principle, at a square table—insisting that only a round table can create the psychological climate necessary to reach an agreement. In recent discussions between Israel and other countries in the Middle East, the geographical setting of the negotiations is of primary importance to many of the parties. Peripheral matters may be merely minor impediments on the road to a final agreement or may become as important as any other issue under discussion. These questions are best analyzed in terms of relative costs and benefits. If the negotiation is extremely important and if your client agrees to spare no expense to reach an agreement—and if time is not a factor—resolving the shape of the table might be productive in the long-run because it contributes to the sense of comfort felt by all the parties throughout the negotiations. By contrast, arguing over the shape of the table simply to show yourself as a strong, aggressive negotiator when that behavior is viewed as ridiculous and childish by the other side is highly counterproductive.

Most negotiation is verbal. The negotiators talk to each other throughout the negotiation. At the same time, a sophisticated negotiator may want to inquire thoroughly into so-called body language—a concept that suggests that a great deal of human communication is non-verbal (surely an unassailable proposition). Negotiators should be observant and sensitive to such things as physical stiffness on the other side of the table and facial expressions of discomfort or disbelief. But much like the negotiation ploys discussed earlier, some proponents of body language carry their theories to the extreme by listing all sorts of physical behavior and by trying to correlate precise aspects of that behavior with a person's mental state or with what it might reveal about a party's secret negotiation positions.

Professionals who know a lot about human behavior caution about generalizing too much on this topic. One book on negotiating written by a lawyer who ought to know better insists that a person who puts his hands together in the form of a church steeple (both hands touching with the fingers pointed up) is signaling that he feels "confident" and that the opposing party should quickly calculate whether too much is being conceded.[13] Maybe it does, and maybe it does not. Individual physical movements are too idiosyncratic to be used as a basis for generalized comments on human behavior.

There are other negotiation ploys that go well beyond even an artificial analysis of body language. One lawyer describes at length how an office ought to be set up to facilitate a negotiation—and to enhance the influence of the office holder. He talks about the color of the carpeting, whether one uses fluorescent lights or table lamps, the tone set by various wall colorings and the like. His basic point is unassailable: the physical setting of a negotiation can often have an effect on the substantive outcome. But he carries this much too far. What happens when one party goes to such great lengths to arrange an office setting and then discovers that he is up against one of those negotiators who refuses to negotiate on the other side's turf? In international commercial negotiations, the parties often have very little choice in terms of physical location, and it's rare that one side or the other can artificially manipulate the setting. These days lots of international negotiation takes place through the telephone and the facsimile machine. Many companies use agents rather than negotiating directly. A lot of face-to-face negotiation takes place in sterile hotel suites and borrowed offices. No competent negotiator should put much stock ploys and trickery, particularly if the planning of tricks and ploys takes away preparation time on the truly important issues. The best negotiators spend time investigating far more productive matters such as the nature of his client's product and the reasons why another company might want to purchase it.

Other commentators on negotiation like to talk about "power" negotiating techniques such as threats, ridicule, intransigence and the like. Some work on these topics is productive mainly because a negotiator should always be aware that the other side may try to manipulate him. After all, no one goes into a negotiation wanting to lose; and these tactics may be frequently encountered in win/lose bargaining. But, commercial transactions are rarely win/lose propositions and most people in business prefer to build rather than destroy relationships.

Consequently, much of this discussion is out of place in a book devoted to successfully managing international commercial transactions. Even if

---

13. I hope my readers will forgive me if I do not cite to the actual work. All that needs to be said is that far too many books on negotiation follow this approach. Heaven only knows what violence they are doing to rational bargaining and to the proper study of negotiation.

these platitudes are accurate, they are designed for negotiation within the American culture and are totally inapplicable and may have a devastating impact when negotiating on a cross-cultural basis. Even the use of humor can have a negative impact on cross-cultural negotiations. One of the author's frequent guest lecturers, a career state department employee with ambassadorial status who has managed a number of important multilateral negotiations frequently tells the students to avoid making jokes in multilateral discussions because there is no joke, however well-written that can survive translation into five or six languages. Commercial negotiators should keep his admonition in mind and consider one thing more. Persons new to negotiation should remember one thing: *games are for children; games are not for negotiators.*

§ 5.5 Cross-Cultural Negotiation

Successful cross-cultural negotiation begins by keeping in mind the fact that different people have different backgrounds, attitudes and beliefs. Most commercial negotiators normally take into account their counterpart's gender, racial and ethnic background whether they're negotiating a domestic or international transaction. This is usually done not out of any ulterior motive but simply out of a recognition that we do not all spring from the same roots. In domestic commercial negotiation, many of these things are taken for granted and if adjustments are made, they are generally only slight, almost imperceptible shifts in behavior or tactics.

It is more complicated when a transaction cuts across national boundaries.[14] Differences in language, behavior and attitude are instantly apparent and successful negotiators must normally accommodate those differences. This is not to say that all of one's personal beliefs and attitudes must be sacrificed for the sake of negotiation. It is quite difficult for businesses in the United States to cater to parties who categorically refuse to deal with blacks or women. Indeed, U.S. companies could get themselves into serious trouble under the domestic civil rights laws if they did cater to these attitudes. And no one should forget that commercial negotiation is always a two-way street. In other words, both sides presumably want to reach an agreement and will normally be willing to curb many personal idiosyncrasies for the sake of the agreement.

Many companies try to minimize any problems that might arise due to differences in cultural background by conducting the negotiation through

---

14. One excellent treatise on general aspects of cross-cultural business dealings, examining these matters from a historical perspective is P. Curtin, CROSS-CULTURAL TRADE IN WORLD HISTORY (1984).

agents who have a common background. It is not unusual for Third World countries to employ an American agent in the United States to conduct their commercial negotiation with domestic U.S. companies. Companies in the United States seeking to do business abroad often deal through agents and employees who are nationals of the target country rather than sending in a U.S.-based negotiation team. Each approach has advantages and disadvantages. A company that deals exclusively through agents loses a great deal of control over the outcome of the transaction. Conversely, many negotiations that might otherwise succeed have been destroyed by the ineptness and lack of sensitivity of a poorly briefed and badly prepared foreign negotiator.

It is also possible to overemphasize cultural differences in a commercial setting. Normally the party that is most anxious to consummate the transaction will also be the party most likely to submerge any sense of injury over perceived slights or offenses. A lawyer of the author's acquaintance dealt with a Latin American counterpart on a daily basis for well over a year. Nearly fourteen months after first meeting the Latin American representative, the U.S. lawyer could not properly pronounce his counterpart's last name. The lawyer got away with this lapse because his counterpart desperately needed the lawyer's assistance. Most business executives are not quite so desperate.

There is an acceptable middle ground. Even if a company prefers to use national agents for on-site negotiations and even if a company perceives itself as being the stronger of the two parties, all persons involved in the deal should make some attempt to come to terms with cultural differences because those differences are likely to penetrate to the marrow of the agreement. Personal slights that may not have an effect on a one-time transaction may destroy the possibility of establishing a long-term business relationship.

There are additional considerations to keep in mind. No one should assume that cultural differences are superficial or that cultural differences can be accommodated by doing only trite things. For example, one of the suggestions often found in U.S. business literature dealing with negotiation with Japanese companies urges U.S. business executives to have their business cards printed in Japanese. Elsewhere in the literature can be found hints on bowing rather than shaking hands, comments on the need to put up with a large-scale social event before getting down to business, and developing a taste for raw fish.

There is nothing intrinsically wrong with these admonitions. Japanese-language business cards can be very helpful. Japanese executives frequently prefer a social gathering before negotiations begin. But suggestions such as this can be taken too far and may lead to serious problems because they fool people into thinking that a person's culture can be understood as a series of platitudes, clichés or generalities. For example, one of the typical generalities made for Latin American business people is that they have less of a sense of time and urgency than do North American executives. One book on business negotiation recommends that North American negotiators not expect their Latin counterparts to be on time for appointments or to scrupulously follow a chronological agenda. This homily may have come from someone's actual experience. It is conceivable that some Latin American business person involved in some deal was perpetually tardy for appointments. It's also entirely possible that this generality is derived from nothing more than the ugliest sort of ethnic stereotype; and any negotiator who bases his conduct on such things—who, for example, indicates that his counterpart is not likely to be on time for any future activities—is likely to find himself dealing with an exceptionally hostile counterpart.

The best place to start is not with the platitudes and homilies but with serious research into the backgrounds of the people who are going to be involved in the negotiation. Here again, cost-benefit analysis is likely to play a major role. A company entering into a $10,000 transaction may not do very much in terms of exploring the culture of the opposite party; the dollar amount of the contract—particularly if the contract is seen as a one-time deal—simply does not justify the expense and effort of a full-blown cultural analysis. By contrast, companies negotiating multi-million dollar contracts may wish to conduct a thorough investigation into the host country's culture

Obtaining solid information on other cultures is often difficult. For the most part, the information is not to be found in the literature on negotiation although a few reasonably well written books exist.[15] Fortunately, there are some readily available sources of information in the United States which can provide good information. The U.S. State Department publishes one-volume area manuals on different regions and on individual countries that provide a quick grasp of a country's history, society and economy. These are cheap and normally accurate; but on occasion they do not track the most recent developments in the target country. Even when they are a little out of date,

---

15. See, e.g., J. W. SALACUSE, MAKING GLOBAL DEALS: NEGOTIATING IN THE INTERNATIONAL MARKETPLACE (1991) (This book emerged from several columns on international business negotiation written by Mr. Salacuse for the Harvard Negotiation Journal. It is written mainly for U.S. business executives; readers from outside the United States may have problems with Mr. Salacuse's frequent use of U.S. colloquialisms.); P. CASSE & S. DEOL, MANAGING INTERCULTURAL NEGOTIATIONS: GUIDELINES FOR TRAINERS AND NEGOTIATORS (1985) (this book is more a syllabus for a negotiations training program than a book on theory); INTERNATIONAL NEGOTIATION: ART & SCIENCE (D. Bendahmane & J. McDonald eds., 1983)(This is a collection of papers delivered at a conference on negotiation sponsored by the U.S. Foreign Service Institute. While it's focus is on country-to-country negotiation, many of the individual papers provide good insight into private international negotiation); A. KAPOOR, PLANNING FOR INTERNATIONAL BUSINESS NEGOTIATION (1985) (Professor Kapoor's book is based on a series of case histories. He does, however, try to derive some general insights from those case histories which can be beneficial particularly for those who have to deal both with a host government and with a private company).

they can provide a basis for understanding current events. For example, the area manual on Iran goes into some detail on the Shah's accession to power, pointing out that the Shah, while claiming an historic lineage, in fact derived his title from his father who acquired it just after World War Two. That fact provides some understanding of the rise of Islamic fundamentalism in Iran even when that edition of the handbook on Iran made no mention of the Ayatollah Khomeni. The historical discussion in the area manual on the Philippines gives much insight into the fall of Ferdinand Marcos and the rise of Corazón Acquino even though it was written before Mrs. Acquino attained the presidency.

There are other sources of information. In one of the few readable, yet scholarly treatments of private, cross-cultural negotiation, Professor Ashok Kapoor of New York University School of Business describes four case histories of transnational negotiations and has developed some criteria for analyzing such negotiations.[16] His central principle should not be forgotten. Major cross-cultural business negotiations normally involve heavy negotiation not only with a company in the host country, but also with the host government. This intrusion by the government is a factor that businesses in the United States do not always have to contend with. As Professor Kapoor points out, the success with which a negotiator deals with the host government is likely to determine the success of the business negotiation.

Professor Kapoor has identified four typical defects—what he calls *failures*—in coping with commercial negotiations that provide a good framework for analysis of any agreement. Failure One is a lack of empathy with the people and government of the host country. This goes much deeper than merely having one's business cards printed in the host country's language. It extends to a lack of knowledge and appreciation for the totality of that country's existence, including—when dealing with former colonies—an understanding of their recently acquired independence. Negotiators must take into consideration the entire fabric of the host country.

Failures Two and Three are characterized by a lack of appreciation for and understanding of a country's governmental system and the manner in which decisions are made. Overcoming these failures requires knowing which people at what level of government are likely to make decisions. In the case of Japan it would include some sensitivity for the unique relationship between Japanese corporations, the Ministry of International Trade and Industry (MITI) and other government agencies, and the University of Tokyo—the educational institution from which virtually all the important Japanese actors graduate. Failure Four is the absence of planning and organization when entering into these negotiations. This lapse may include an inability to make decisions on the spot due to a negotiator's constantly hav-

---

16. Kapoor, supra note 15.

ing to communicate with headquarters; an inability to adjust to crucial, on-the-spot-shifts in the negotiation; and poor communication and training among the negotiators themselves.

Professor Kapoor's failures should not be taken as a panacea. They do not answer all questions; but they can be used profitably as a checklist when planning for cross-cultural negotiation. At bottom, of course, is the central theme of this entire chapter: knowledge is power.

§ 5.6 Negotiation When Disputes Arise Under an Existing Agreement

This aspect of negotiation is treated more extensively in Chapter 6 under the heading *renegotiation*. It is both a process of reaching an agreement and an identifiable form of dispute resolution. Contracts in China, by statute, require disputing parties to first engage in "friendly discussions" and only later to engage in the more adversarial forms of dispute resolution. In certain contacts executed by the Boeing Corporation, renegotiation by specific corporate officers in the two contracting companies is required under the contract's dispute resolution clause.

When the parties are trying to adjust a contract to unanticipated circumstances in a friendly, non-confrontational manner, renegotiation does not differ materially from the initial negotiation. However, when renegotiation is conducted under the threat of litigation or arbitration because one side believes the other breached the contract, it takes on many of the characteristics of win/lose (*distributional*) negotiation. In that setting the negotiators are usually attorneys who are negotiating in the shadow of the court. While actual negotiating behavior would not necessarily change, the atmosphere of the re-negotiation may be far more adversarial than that of the initial discussions. As a consequence, persons engaged in renegotiation should be prepared to deal with a great deal more hostility.

§ 5.7 The Ethics of Negotiation

§5.7.1 Ethics generally

There are three ethical dimensions in negotiation. The first is simply the normal duty one human being owes to another human being. In this context, the term *ethics* is used in its dictionary sense of morality: as the Oxford English Dictionary puts it—a set of principles that "direct men's actions to the production of the greatest possible quantity of happiness." All negotiators are subject to certain constraints on their behavior as human beings wholly apart from the subject matter of the negotiation. While cultures differ greatly in their approach to and definition of morality, some minimal ethical conditions apply to virtually all negotiations. Consider, for example, the issue of lying in negotiation.[17] While defining "lie" is never easy, most people will probably concede that telling an outright misrepresentation on which the other side is expected to rely is a lie. In the negotiation hypothetical involving stainless steel fittings that was discussed extensively in preceding sections of this chapter, a seller-negotiator who describes his fittings as being able to bear a stress of 100 pounds per square inch when he knows for a fact that they will bear only 50 pounds is clearly lying. The lie is compounded if the negotiator knows for certain that stress-bearing capacity is an important factor in the buyer's purchasing decision and further knows that the buyer is not likely to have instrumentation capable of measuring stress-bearing capacity. Virtually no culture or legal system excuses this kind of affirmative misrepresentation.

The harder question is whether simply remaining silent in negotiation is also a lie. For example, if the buyer acts as if he believes that the fittings can bear a stress of 100 foot pounds and the seller says nothing to disabuse him of that notion, is the seller's inaction a lie? Would the definition turn on the specific context of the non-disclosure; as, for example, when the seller knows that the buyer's processes will never expose the fitting to a stress greater than 10 pounds. Would non-disclosure constitute a lie if the seller knows that the fittings are to be a part of, say, an aircraft wing exposed to varying stresses?

Ethicists may debate these questions at length. A number of legal systems have attempted to deal with such issues. The Anglo-American legal system centuries ago established the doctrine of *caveat emptor* (let the *buyer* beware). This doctrine places virtually all risks on the buyer and imposes virtually no duties of disclosure on the seller. But it is an exceptionally harsh doctrine, particularly when it is imposed in a setting where most of the knowledge and information is in the hands of the seller. In the United States, the harsher aspects of *caveat emptor*—particularly in consumer transactions—have been modified by legislation. Most countries now have legal principles that place some burden of disclosure on the party who is in the best position to know of defects or limitations in a product.

At the same time, there is a thin line between the sort of misrepresentation or non-disclosure discussed above and the more innocuous statements that takes place in most negotiations. Is it ethically impermissible for the seller to tell buyer: "our fittings are the best in the world"? Probably not.

---

17. It is something of an indictment of the American legal profession that the best general book on the lie written in the United States has been written by a non-lawyer, albeit a person married to the former dean of the Harvard Law School. See generally S. BOK, LYING (1979).

This type of behavior, commonly referred to as *puffing*, is age-old business conduct and has almost never led to either official or unofficial sanctions. Most people, whether they are consumers or business executives automatically discount such comments as soon as they are offered.

A purely philosophical discussion of these issues may make many business executives uncomfortable. In the United States it is a commonplace that morality bears very little relation to business practices. For readers who find the philosophical dimension unproductive, it is entirely possible to address these questions from a pragmatic standpoint. Setting philosophy aside, a negotiator should simply ask the question: "what may happen if the other side finds out I'm lying?" This analysis forces a negotiator to consider the risks of lying (whether affirmative misrepresentation or non-disclosure) in a practical context. There could be legal ramifications involved in a negotiator's misleading the other side on the stress-bearing capacity of fittings used in an airplane wing. If the aircraft crashes, a product liability lawsuit may implicate the seller as well as the buyer. But even in a non-life-threatening context, truth-telling has a lot of advantages. For example, assume a negotiator who comes into the room with instructions from her client to do two things: make the best deal possible on the transaction at hand *and* do everything you can to build toward a long-term business relationship. A negotiator armed with these instructions would normally not only not commit an affirmative misrepresentation, but would probably go out of her way to make full disclosure even where she might not be faced with a specific request for information. Buyers who are lied to are unlikely to want to continue the business enterprise. Can there be any doubt, for example, that a stainless steel fitting negotiator armed with these instructions would have an obligation to disclose stress capacity even if the buyer forgot to ask the question? When the risk of lying is the possible destruction of the long-term business relationship, the negotiator has very little alternative but to tell the truth.

There are other issues that a good negotiator should consider. In the examples discussed above, the misrepresentation or non-disclosure involved the capability of the good to be sold—what the lawyers would call the heart of the bargain. Now assume a situation in which a fitting negotiator needs some time to think during the actual negotiation and obtains this thinking time by implying that he cannot set the price when in fact his price-setting authority runs from $0 to $45 per unit (i.e., encompasses virtually the entire range of possible price outcomes). Is it a lie for the negotiator to leave the room pretending to make a telephone call to the client when he already has all possible authority to agree? While there may be a misrepresentation here, the misrepresentation does not relate to the quality of the goods. A price for the fittings is eventually going to be established if the parties are to have a contract at all. The actions of the negotiator here are more in the nature of a delaying ploy, rather than a lie that goes to the heart of the bargain. Second, the risk of some adverse reaction by the other side if the buyer finds out that the negotiator did have price-setting authority is likely to be minimal. Many negotiators use such techniques, and it is virtually certain that the other negotiator is engaged in similar activities. The end product of lying on one's price setting authority may make the other side a little more skeptical in later negotiations but is not likely to drive them away from the bargaining table. It is doubtful that such a ploy would damage long-term relationships or in any way affect the health or safety of the ultimate users of the product.

The issue might be resolved differently, however, if the negotiator gets a direct question from the other side: "Do you have independent authority to set the price of this contract?" A negative response to such a direct question would be, by definition, be an affirmative misrepresentation, and might lead to future hostility between the parties. In this instance, a negotiator might permissibly choose either not to answer the question or to give an evasive response if she believes that concealing her price-setting authority is important to the negotiation. It is highly unlikely that concealment in this setting will poison the business relationship.

Many commentators on negotiation go even further. If negotiation is viewed as a game then it is axiomatic that good gamesmanship will pay results. It is something of a conundrum, at least as seen by Professor James White, who has written:

> On the one hand the negotiator must be fair and truthful; on the other he must mislead his opponent. Like the poker player, a negotiator hopes that his opponent will overestimate the value of his hand. Like the poker player, in a variety of ways he must facilitate his opponent's inaccurate assessment. The critical difference between those who are successful negotiators, and those who are not, lies in this capacity both to mislead and not to be misled.[18]

Readers should not be mislead. Professor White is mainly concerned with win/lose bargaining where winner takes all, while most business negotiation is a matter of win/win bargaining, permitting both sides to gain advantages from the deal.

There are no easy answers here. Cynical readers of this book can point to large numbers of ethical abuses on the part of negotiators who seem to be highly successful. But at least in win/win negotiation, ethical issues can best be handled by application of the famous golden rule: "Do unto others as you would have them do unto you."

---

18. White, *Machiavelli and the Bar: Ethical Limitations on Lying in Negotiation*, 1980 Am.B.Fdn.Res.J. 926, 927.

§ 5.7.2 Ethical constraints on U.S. lawyer-negotiators

Lawyers in the United States and in many other countries are subject not only to general constraints on their behavior but also to express principles governing their professional behavior. Violations of the lawyers code of ethics can lead to disciplinary action against the lawyer irrespective of whatever effect the ethical abuses have on the client. One U.S. code of ethics, the *Model Code of Professional Responsibility*, addresses dishonesty (including the matter of lying to others) mainly in generalities. The Code admonishes a lawyer to "represent his client zealously within the bounds of the law."[19] In so doing, however, a lawyer is not to "engage in conduct involving dishonesty, fraud, deceit, or misrepresentation."[20] The Code contains some other restrictions on lying, but those restrictions essentially prohibit lying to a court—as contrasted to lying to another lawyer or to a third person. A new statement of ethical behavior, the *Model Rules of Professional Conduct*, has been adopted by a majority of the states in the U.S. and, for the first time, contains some specific admonitions on lying in a negotiation context. Rule 4.1 requires that a lawyer "shall not knowingly: (a) make a false statement of material fact or law to a third person; or (b) fail to disclose a material fact to a third person when disclosure is necessary to avoid assisting a criminal or fraudulent act by a client [unless, however, the matter is covered by attorney-client privilege]." This principle is limited by a comment to the rule that states: "whether a particular statement should be regarded as one of fact can depend on the circumstances. Under generally accepted conventions in negotiation, certain types of statements ordinarily are not taken as statements of material fact. Estimates of price or value placed on the subject of a transaction and a party's intentions as to an acceptable settlement of a claim are in this category."[21]

These express constraints may not be terribly helpful in raising the level of the typical lawyer/negotiator's conduct. There are virtually no reported instances involving sanctions imposed on a U.S. lawyer for violating Rule 4.1, for example. Nonetheless, Rule 4.1 is one of the first instances of a lawyer-drafted code of conduct that specifically refer to conduct in a negotiation and that attempt to establish at least some principle of minimally acceptable behavior. If effective enforcement of Rule 4.1 is not forthcoming, its requirements will remain largely a platitude.

---

19. Canon 7, Model Code of Professional Responsibility ("MCPR")
20. Disciplinary Rule 1-102(A)(4), MCPR.
21. MRPC, Comment to Rule 4.1.

§ 5.7.3 Statutory controls on negotiator conduct

There are other restrictions on the negotiating behavior of both lawyers and non-lawyer negotiators imposed by U.S. law. Article One of the U.S. Uniform Commercial Code provides expressly that: "Every contract or duty within this Act imposes an obligation of good faith in its performance or enforcement."[22] But it remains unclear whether this provision governs pre-contract negotiations. In the United States the controversial Foreign Corrupt Practices Act (FCPA),[23] places severe constraints on the giving of certain gratuities to foreign agents in order to obtain business. While there are no constraints in the act specifically devoted to the negotiation process, the FCPA may constrain negotiating behavior that in the past has been regarded as normal and permissible. Even so, the FCPA, discussed at length in Chapter 3, § 3.6.5, is mainly a constraint on the paying of bribes to foreign government officials, rather than a specific constraint on international business negotiations.   ◆

---

22. UCC § 1-203.
23. 15 U.S.C. § 78a note.

— 6 —
The Less-Drastic Forms of Commercial Dispute Resolution

§ 6.1 Introduction

Lawyers and business executives occasionally lose sight of the fact that inserting terms in a contract that promote flexibility, or drafting a clause that calls for renegotiation when the deal becomes unstuck can solve a lot of problems that otherwise would have to be dealt with through the vastly more expensive processes of arbitration or litigation. Flexibility, particularly in long-term contracts, should be a matter of concern both when a contract is initially drafted and when disputes arise during the life of a contract.

The language of the contract can alleviate many problems. Express provisions that work to resolve disputes can be inserted in many contracts. Even when the contract is silent on some of these matters, many legal systems have created rules of law that permit contracts to be adjusted *without breach* (1) over the life of the contract either automatically (for example, a contract whose price term increases a fixed percentage each year) or at the insistence of one or another of the parties (for example, when one party is allowed to adjust quantity or quality requirements unilaterally) or (2) on the occurrence of certain specific events, such as war, strikes or currency devaluations. Most transnational contracts contain some of these provisions as a matter of course;[1] but even if a contract is totally inflexible when it is initially drafted, renegotiation of the entire contract or portions of the contract is always a possibility.[2] Occasionally, renegotiation takes place in the presence of a third party mediator/conciliator who attempts to assist the parties in

---

1. See the discussion of typical contract provisions in Chapter 4, supra.

2. The first portion of this chapter owes a great debt to two of the principle works on contract adaptation and renegotiation: ADAPTATION AND RENEGOTIATION OF CONTRACTS IN INTERNATIONAL TRADE AND FINANCE (N. Horn, ed., Kluwer, 1985) (hereafter cited as Contract Adaptation) and M. BARTELS, CONTRACTUAL ADAPTATION AND CONFLICT RESOLUTION (Kluwer, 1985).

reaching a satisfactory solution. Finally, there is a new device on the horizon, the minitrial, not yet fully accepted by international business executives but which shows great promise as an alternative to formal arbitration or litigation. Each of these options is discussed in depth below, but one thing should be kept firmly in mind: all of these options are far less disruptive to the underlying business relationship and far less costly than either litigation or arbitration. In some cultures, notably many of the Pacific Rim countries, these devices are preferred over the more traditional methods of arbitration or litigation. While none of these techniques is the perfect dispute resolution device, they may be profitably explored before a party commences a lawsuit or triggers the contract's arbitration clause.

§ 6.2 Contract Adaptation

The term *contract adaptation* generally refers to the incorporation of certain terms and conditions in a contract that promote flexibility and that permit the contract to conform to certain changes in conditions without automatic termination or without the need for renegotiation. Adaptation is most important in those contracts that are expected to be of long duration. Contracts calling for a one-time sale of goods transaction or a single service activity to be performed over a short period of time immediately after signing normally do not require adaptation provisions. Similarly, contracts executed by parties who have no expectation of ever seeing each other again or ever doing business again usually have little or no interest in adaptation provisions.

Short-term contracts can be safely drafted with a view toward only the conditions existing at the time of the transaction or at the anticipated time of performance. By contrast, contracts of longer duration require more thought and planning and generally include a number of clauses that are specifically designed to promote flexibility over the life of the contract. Even contracts involving single sales transactions in which the parties want to continue to do business in the future will often contain clauses promoting flexibility because both parties wish not to antagonize each other. An easy way to antagonize someone is to accuse him of breach of contract.

The longer the duration of the contract the more interest the parties are going to have in proper adaptation clauses because the parties are rarely able to to predict internal or external conditions over the long run. On the international scene, at least in the twentieth century, *change* in circumstances rather than stability has been the rule. In exceptionally long contracts such as petroleum and other natural resource production agreements—which often have a duration of thirty years—the drafters of the original contract will of necessity include a sizeable number of adaptation provisions.

There are a number of ways to categorize adaptation provisions. Professor Norbert Horn, for example, has developed a classification that makes a great deal of sense: "[Adaptation] clauses are designed either to specify details of contractual obligations (gap filling) or to slightly modify the contents of these obligations (adjustment, adaptation)"[3] Clauses such as *force majeure* clauses are normally referred to as automatic adaptation clauses. In other words, the happening of certain events external to the contract—such as strikes, political insurrection, or war— automatically suspends or, in certain cases, alters one or both parties' performance obligations.

Sometimes, adaptation can be triggered unilaterally by one of the parties. For example, a contract may contain a "most favored" clause that requires a contract to receive the same treatment as a contract subsequently negotiated with another party, even though the first party may have absolutely nothing to do with the later agreement.[4] The concept is akin to the idea of most favored nation: when one country is extended certain trade benefits, all other countries with most favored nation status must be given the same treatment. In other circumstances a contract may provide that a party may unilaterally assign all rights under the contract or may terminate the contract on the occurrence or non-occurrence of certain conditions. So, for example, if a contract calls for the buyer to purchase all his requirements from a seller and the contract contains a provision that provides for a minimum amount of requirements that never materialize, the contract might permit the buyer to terminate, irrespective of the wishes of the seller, because the buyer's actual requirements never reach the amounts specified in the contract.

In many cases, conditions may change to the point where both parties see the need for adaptation. Occasionally, bilateral adaptation may occur simply by minor adjustments in the manner of performance by one or both parties that do not trigger an objection by the other side. For example, a contract may call for payment in a the currency of a specific currency, say, Swiss francs. If that currency for some reason cannot be utilized, the buyer may simply proffer payment in a substitute currency, say U.S. dollars, that the seller then accepts without protest. Usually, however, bilateral adaptation follows some intense renegotiation between the parties. Many long-term contracts provide an express mechanism for bringing the parties together to work out appropriate adaptation clauses.

There are a number of other ways to categorize adaptation provisions. Professor Horn has developed four different classifications. In his view, con-

---

3. Horn, *Standard Clauses on Contract Adaptation in International Commerce, in* Contract Adaptation, supra note 2, at 112.
4. Mr. Bartels notes that "most favored" clauses are not very common. Bartels, supra note 2, at 35.

tracts may be grouped into "open" contracts such as turnkey construction projects or complex technology transfer projects in which the parties concede that all the details cannot be anticipated and written into the basic document; "flexible" contracts in which certain of the details underlying the basic agreement such as the price of a vital natural resource is expected to change over time and thus cannot be specified in the original document; "special risks" which the parties did not specifically anticipate but for which they incorporated a special risk clause; and *force majeure* provisions.

The first two categories are self-explanatory. With regard to the latter two categories, there is not a great deal of difference between a special risk clause and a force majeure clause in actual operation. The effect of both is to forgive or suspend performance, or, in certain instances, to alter performance requirements. A special risk clause is usually inserted in a contract when the parties believe a certain event might happen—such as a change of government that might lead to nationalization of a certain industry. The special risk clause will make specific adjustments in the contract to accommodate that occurrence. A force majeure clause, by contrast, is inserted in virtually every commercial contract, whether or not of transnational scope, and provides for relief from the occurrence of unanticipated events of a more general nature such as earthquakes, floods and war.

Another way to look at adaptation issues is with regard to the ultimate effect of the change in circumstances. Some changes can be so drastic that they totally prevent further performance under the contract. Other changes can have a somewhat milder effect in that they merely make the contract more difficult or more burdensome to perform. For example, British commercial law recognizes the doctrine of "frustration" and may occasionally apply the doctrine to forgive performance, but the British courts have almost always applied the doctrine narrowly to mean that performance has become technically impossible, not merely difficult.[5] For example, a change in a government regulation may make performance of the contract unlawful. A contract between a Scottish distillery and a United States liquor dealer to sell single malt whisky in the United States would have been deemed "frustrated" and performance thereby forgiven when the United States government made the sale of liquor illegal in 1919.

The United States' Uniform Commercial Code is considerably more flexible on this point. The U.C.C. recognizes through its doctrine of "commercial impracticability," that excessively burdened performance may require forgiveness. While the burden of increased costs is usually never a proper excuse (as the Code points out: "that is exactly the type of business risk which business contracts made at fixed prices are intended to cover"), such

---

5. See, e.g., Ford & Sons, Ltd. v. Henry Leetham & Sons, Ltd., 21 Com. Cas. 55 (1915, K.B.D.).

matters as severe shortages of raw materials or unforeseen shutdowns of major sources of supply may excuse performance or at least permit delayed performance. Other countries deal with these issues of difficult or impossible performance on a case-by-case basis by construing the *force majeure* clause in individual contracts.

In drafting contracts, there are essentially two ways in which parties can cope with changed conditions: they can let the contract remain silent on these matters with the expectation that the law underlying the contract will fill in the necessary gaps; or they can address them specifically in the contract by drafting clauses which provide the necessary flexibility to accommodate the changes.

§ 6.2.1 Gap filling mechanisms in the underlying law

To understand this topic, it is important to have some understanding as to the manner in which the law underlying the contract is ascertained. As discussed in Chapter 2, the applicable law may be expressly stated in the contract by way of a choice-of- law clause. If the contract contains no express choice of law clause, virtually all mature legal systems provide rules and mechanisms by which a court may determine which law to apply.[6] These court- or arbitrator-imposed rules can be complex; but for the purposes of the following discussion it is enough to realize that if the the parties become engaged in a dispute under the contract the entity charged with resolving the dispute will choose a body of law to apply to that contract if the parties have not made their own choice of law.

Frequently, a choice made by a judge or arbitrator satisfies neither party. That is, a court or an arbitrator choosing a body of law may not make the same choice the parties might have made had they chosen the law when the contract was drafted. Nonetheless, when a body of law is chosen, that law will frequently impose certain gap filling mechanisms on the parties through the operation of its own legal principles. These principles will apply in addition to whatever is said in the contract.

Leaving the choice of law to others is dangerous. It greatly lessens both predictability and stability under the contract. It can have consequences never intended by the parties; and, if the contract becomes the subject of an intense dispute culminating in arbitration or litigation, the lack of an express

---

6. An intense discussion of choice of law rules in various jurisdictions is beyond the scope of this chapter. For additional information on this topic see Baxter, *International Conflict of Laws and International Business*, 34 Int'l and Comp. L.Q. 538 (1985); Weintraub,. *How to Choose Law for Contracts, and How Not To: The EEC Convention*, 17 Tex. Int'l L.J. 155 (1982); Delaume,. *The European Convention on the Law Applicable to Contractual Obligations: Why a Convention?*, 22 Va.J.Int'l L. 107 (1981); and Zaphiriou, *Choice of Forum and Choice of Law Clauses in International Commercial Agreements*, 3 Int'l Trade L.J. 311 (1978).

choice of law provision in the contract often prolongs the dispute because parties then have to fight over which law to apply as well as fighting over the substantive parts of the contract. Most transnational contracts contain a carefully considered choice of law provision even if the remainder of the contract is less detailed. When the negotiators cannot agree on a choice of law, some contract drafters invoke "commonly accepted principles of commercial behavior" as a kind of choice of law that avoids tying the contract to any particular country's system of contract law.

By and large, the parties' choice of law will be honored by courts and arbitrators. In a few instances, the choice will not be honored for reasons of public policy. The court or arbitrator is then empowered to impose a choice of its own. This is a rare occurrence, of course, and to avoid it, contract drafters should simply insure that there is a reasonable relation between the law chosen for the contract, the identity of the parties and the place of performance. A contract between a Swiss seller and a Mexican buyer that chooses either Swiss or Mexican law will virtually never have its choice of law disturbed. By contrast, a contract between an United States seller and a Ghanian buyer that chooses Icelandic law will be automatically suspect and possibly not honored. When parties, for whatever reason, make a rather exotic choice of law, they should probably explain their reasons for doing so in the contract itself or in some contemporaneous sidebar document. Even an exotic choice of law properly explained by the contracting parties will normally be accepted by the court or arbitrator when a dispute occurs.

Some legal systems are better equipped to fill gaps than others. Under the United States' Uniform Commercial Code (UCC), many details of a contract may permissibly be left open with the expectation that the general legal principles applicable under the UCC will fill in many of the gaps. For example, in the United States, a contract for the sale of goods governed by Article 2 of the UCC can be silent on a number of important matters and still remain enforceable. Under the UCC, an offer that does not specify a time during which it may be accepted is deemed to remain open "a reasonable time, but in no event [in excess of] three months."[7] A contract that leaves the price term open will require the payment of "a reasonable price at the time of delivery."[8] In other circumstances, as discussed above, the UCC forgives performance in cases in which performance becomes "commercially impracticable" due to unforeseen supervening circumstances not within the contemplation of the parties at the time of contracting.[9]

Accordingly, a transnational commercial contract that incorporates the UCC as its substantive legal framework could in theory dispense with a sub-

---

7. UCC §2-205.
8. UCC §2-305.
9. UCC §2-615.

stantial amount of detail, could leave out a large number of specific terms, and might still be an enforceable document. But even a contract that chooses the UCC that leaves too many things out exposes the parties to some risks. Most of the gap filling of the UCC turns on the concept of "reasonableness"—a term that may be readily understood by two parties in the United States who are used to functioning in the same commercial atmosphere, but that may be very difficult to ascertain by business executives from other cultures whose concepts of acceptable commercial behavior (what is frequently called the "course of dealing" or "course of performance") may be radically different from practices in the United States. Moreover, even U.S. contract drafters find themselves extremely uncomfortable leaving open all the terms permissibly left open under the UCC. In transnational contracts, especially between two parties who have not had prior dealings and who come from different cultural and legal backgrounds, leaving open such crucial items such as price and delivery is almost never done.

Virtually no other legal system provides for the breadth of gap filling permitted under the UCC. Under French law, the basic concept of *force majeure* excuses performance only when an event occurs that is totally beyond the control of one of the parties. In limited circumstances involving contractual dealings between private parties and the state, the doctrine of *imprevision* permits a court to forgive performance when conditions change such that performance becomes extremely burdensome for one of the parties. However, Professor Horn notes that those French courts that have recognized the principle of imprevision have also required, apparently as a condition precedent, that the parties attempt to renegotiate the terms before seeking forgiveness of performance in court.[10]

Under German law the doctrine of impossibility of performance may be used to excuse performance when the non-performing party is not negligent and when the event which inhibits performance is found to be beyond that party's control. Under British common law, performance under a contract is virtually never excused unless the non-performing party can show "frustration" of performance—i.e., that performance was *absolutely* impossible due to an event beyond that party's control.

A number of recent commentators have suggested that to the extent there exists a transnational law of contract—and most observers seem to have concluded that in practice there is really no such thing because virtually all contracts which cross national boundaries remain tied in some fashion to *some* nation's domestic substantive law—it may be possible to ascertain gap filling provisions in these principles of international law. For example, Professor Horn points to Article 62 of the Vienna Convention on the Law of

---

10. Horn, Changes in Circumstances and the Revision of Contracts in Some European Laws and in International Law, in Contract Adaptation, supra note 2, at 18.

Treaties[11] and its language on fundamental change of circumstances as an instance of international recognition of the doctrine of impossibility or frustration. Similarly, Article 79 of the United Nations Convention on Contracts for the International Sale of Goods (CISG) contains a forgiveness provision that operates essentially as a force majeure clause: "A party is not liable for a failure to perform any of his obligations if he proved that the failure was due to an impediment beyond his control and that he could not reasonably be expected to have taken the impediment into account at the time of the conclusion of the contract or to have avoided or overcome it or its consequences." As more and more countries accept the CISG, and as more and more parties choose the CISG as the law applicable to their contract, article 79 may be used more frequently as a gap-filling device.

§ 6.2.2. Coping with uncertainty through express contractual provisions—some typical adaptation clauses

Most contracting parties will probably not wish to leave important details in the contract to the mercy of gap-filling mechanisms derived from the underlying substantive legal system. Instead, they will likely wish to deal with as many uncertainties and create as much flexibility as possible through express provisions in the contract itself. Although express contractual language will not totally eliminate risk—there is virtually nothing that can accomplish this—it does give a great deal of control over most of the important matters to the parties themselves; because in virtually all instances, whether the contract is simply performed, whether it is litigated or whether it goes to arbitration, the contract language will be honored and enforced in the dispute resolution process.[12]

There are essentially two ways that contracting parties can incorporate adaptation clauses in the contract. On the one hand, the parties may simply search the literature for standard form clauses and write those clauses into the document with perhaps slight changes. A number of organizations provide such clauses. For example, for international construction contracts, two organizations, the Federation Internationale des Ingenieurs-Consiels (FIDIC) and the United Nations International Development Organization (UNIDO) have developed standard form clauses covering a variety of matters including alterations, delays, cost overruns, special risks and other issues.

---

11. This is the so-called "treaty on treaties" and is reprinted in 8 Int'l Legal Materials 679 (1969).

12. The reader should be aware that there are instances in which courts have refused to honor contractual provisions which somehow violate a nation's "public policy" or which are so unfair or biased as to be deemed "unconscionable"; but such rulings are relatively rare. Most courts and arbitrators insist that the parties live with language that they have previously agreed to.

The FIDIC clauses have been frequently used even though many of the clauses have internal defects and are are not universally appropriate. As Professor Horn puts it: the clauses "do not display much consistency with regard to [their] terminology or scope ... and, as an offspring of British contractual practice, are hardly compatible with [the legal systems] of civil law countries."[13] The UNIDO clauses are often useful for only very narrow specific purposes, because they have been drafted in the context of specific model construction contracts, such as turnkey fertilizer plant construction projects. Many domestic commercial organizations such as trade associations and chambers of commerce also provide model contracts or standard form clauses.

Models and standard forms are cheap and quick; but they contain a number of pitfalls and hazards. First, they may not fit precisely the commercial dealing in question, just as clothing off the rack rarely fits as well as custom-made clothing. Second, it is virtually impossible to draft a single model contract or standard clause that meets the legal requirements of all the world's legal systems. It is always possible, of course, to alter a standard form to meet the requirements of a specific transaction; but it is sometimes more difficult and time-consuming to change a standard clause than it is simply to draft an original clause that satisfies the desires of the parties.

At the same time, striving for complete originality is rarely called for or even possible in most circumstances. Given that so many contracts are drafted by or with the assistance of lawyers, and that lawyers in all countries tend to be inordinately conservative when it comes to breaking new linguistic ground, most contracts are based on pre-existing, traditional language. Also, standard form clauses and model contracts may contain a great deal of language that is suitable for the transaction in question; and, at the very least, may provide a checklist of issues and phrases that the parties should consider for incorporation in their document.

If the parties choose to draft their own language, they are well advised to consider—as gap filling or adaptation provisions—the following checklist of possible clauses:[14]

1. *Variation and change clauses.* These clauses, often incorporated in construction contracts, permit the parties to alter materials specifications, techniques of construction and the like so that excessive

---

13. Horn, Standard Clauses on Contract Adaptation in International Commerce *in* Contract Adaptation, supra note 2, at 113-14.

14. Space limitations do not permit a comprehensive discussion of all these clauses. Readers who wish specific illustrative language for these clauses should consult two of the preeminent multivolume treatises in the area. THE TRANSNATIONAL LAW OF INTERNATIONAL COMMERCIAL TRANSACTIONS (N.Horn and C.Schmitthoff eds. 1983) and G. DELAUME, TRANSNATIONAL CONTRACTS (1982).

rigidity in the original contract does not prevent the completion of the project.

2. *Price escalation clauses*. These clauses cope with price uncertainty and permit the seller to maintain his profit margins even if costs begin to escalate. As one might expect, there are virtually no fixed price contracts in, for example, the international petroleum industry. Almost all natural resource contracts provide for some type of automatic price escalation (or in certain cases, price reduction) based on the prices set at the source.

3. *Stabilization and Tax clauses*. These clauses help protect against changes in government and government policy. They typically excuse performance when government policy changes to the extent that contract performance is impaired. Tax clauses address expressly the prospect of changes in a nation's tax policy that may impair the economic worth of the contract.

4. *Review clauses*. Review clauses are essentially renegotiation clauses and obligate the parties to discuss unanticipated changes in circumstances with a view toward amending the contract language to cope with those changes. However, as noted in the next section, renegotiation may take place without a specific contractual provision obligating the parties to do so.

§ 6.3 Renegotiation

To a certain extent, this section restates the obvious. In most instances when a contract begins to cause trouble, the parties voluntarily get together to see what can be done to preserve the business relationship. People in business, pragmatists that they are, rarely jump immediately into court merely because something troublesome occurs.

The obligation to renegotiate can also be built into the contract and conceivably enforced as any other provision in the document. Renegotiation clauses are not a panacea, of course. On occasion, uncooperative parties who are forced to renegotiate simply because a contract clause demands that they renegotiate will probably make sure that the negotiation fails and that the contract is put through some more formal—and adversarial—type of dispute resolution mechanism. Readers about to enter a renegotiation session should refresh their recollection of the basic negotiation principles set out in Chapter 5. Renegotiation is distinct from initial contract negotiation in only one sense: it is negotiation as Professor Horn puts it, "in the shadow of the court." When an initial negotiation fails, the parties simply do not execute the contract; when a renegotiation fails, the parties generally resort to some more structured type of dispute resolution mechanism such as arbitration or litigation. But even at this point parties should seriously consider the two other mechanisms discussed in this chapter—mediation/conciliation and the minitrial before resorting to either arbitration or litigation.

§ 6.4 Mediation and Conciliation

§ 6.4.1 Mediation and conciliation generally

Mediation as a commercial dispute resolution process has been with us probably as long as there have been people doing business. Conceptually, it is not much more than negotiation in the presence of, and facilitated by, a third person or persons. It can be informal, as for example, when two disputing shop owners ask a third shop owner to help resolve their conflict, or it can be relatively structured with the application of rules of procedures, the exchange of written memoranda prior to the mediation, the formal appointment of a mediator, a final written agreement and the like. There is even a lack of consensus on the basic terminology. A number of writers on the topic, particularly some of the European commentators, appear to distinguish sharply between mediation and conciliation, viewing *mediation* as the use of a third party facilitator who, both literally and figuratively, sits between the contesting parties and helps them come to terms and *conciliation* as a process by which each party designates a conciliator for his or her side who then, on their own, meet to hammer out some kind of resolution that is then presented to the actual parties for their confirmation.

This distinction is probably not necessary in most circumstances since there are any number of successful models for mediation/conciliation that have been worked out over the years. Accordingly, for the purposes of this section, the term *mediation* will be used as the generic term for this type of dispute resolution.

§ 6.4.2 A general theory of mediation

Mediation is a device for resolving disputes that attempts to defuse a great deal of hostility and anguish between the parties by using a third party as a go-between.[15] And while it places enormous (sometimes excessive) impor-

---

15. Unfortunately the mediation literature, while growing, is still relatively sparse. For some basic works see, e.g., J. FOLBERG & A. TAYLOR, MEDIATION (1984) (hereafter cited as Folberg); R. FISHER & W. URY, INTERNATIONAL MEDIATION: A WORKING GUIDE (1978) (emphasizing diplomatic mediation rather than private commercial mediation); the classic jurisprudential work by Professor Fuller, *Mediation—Its Forms and Functions*, 44 S.Calif.L.Rev. 305 (1971); Stulberg, *The Theory and Practice of Mediation: A Reply to Professor Susskind*, 6 Vt.L.Rev. 85 (1981); and Perlman & Nelson, *New Approaches to the Resolution of International Commercial Disputes*, 17 Int'l Law. 215 (1983).

tance on the role of the mediator has a number of characteristics that commend it for commercial disputes. For example, mediation is relatively inexpensive and compared with some of the more adversarial forms of dispute resolution, not very time consuming. It is normally confidential—thus sparing the parties the prospect of a fight in open court—and it is normally not burdened by such things as rigid rules of procedure and evidence. Best of all, it is a superior device for preserving the underlying business relationship while permitting the parties to resolve the dispute at hand because it is not nearly as confrontational as litigation. A skillful mediator can sometimes preserve a spirit of good feeling between the parties even as they work through the specific problem at hand.

In theory, mediation is not that different from negotiation, so many of the concepts and issues discussed in Chapter 5 are relevant here. The insertion of the third party mediator, however, lends a slightly different atmosphere to mediation. For this reason, much of the theory of mediation revolves around the behavior of the mediator. Professors Jay Folberg and Allison Taylor in their book, *Mediation: A Comprehensive Guide to Resolving Conflicts Without Litigation*, postulate seven stages for mediation that now serve as a model for much mediation research. The Folberg-Taylor stages are almost self-explanatory and bear a distinct and understandable relation to the Fisher and Urey stages of negotiation. They are:

1. Introduction—creating trust and structure
2. Fact finding and isolation of issues
3. Creation of options and alternatives
4. Negotiation and decision making
5. Clarification and writing of a plan
6. Legal review and processing
7. Implementation, review and revision

Set in an international commercial context, the stages might work in the following manner. In the beginning, the mediator works with the parties to defuse whatever hostility and distrust has arisen from the dispute so far. This may be merely a matter of getting the parties to talk quietly with each other in some neutral setting such as a hotel suite. If tempers are too hot for this, a mediator might begin the mediation by some kind of shuttle diplomacy, by which the mediator keeps the parties in their respective rooms and moves back and forth between the two sides, conveying information, clarifying positions and discussing issues. There are additional complications of linguistic and cultural differences in international contracts. A mediator who is sensitive to these nuances can make all the difference in the world between success and breakdown.

Stages 2 and 3 in an international commercial setting are frequently crucial to a successful outcome. Often the parties come together knowing only their side of the story because so much of the business transaction has been conducted over long distances. A mere appreciation of the difficulties faced by the other party is sometimes enough to provoke an amicable resolution. Mediators can play a crucial role in developing creative options. The two parties frequently become what the psychologists call *field dependent* and can see only their own point of view filtered through all their own prejudices. They lose sight of other possibilities that are not within their limited field of vision. A mediator who knows something about international transactions can suggest possibilities that would never occur to the two disputants.

Stages 4 and 5 are inevitable in any mediation or negotiation. A decision that is acceptable to both parties must be reached to have a successful conclusion. In a commercial setting that decision is almost always committed to paper. The paper may be a wholly new contract or a mere addendum to the existing contract. Occasionally, it is signed on the spot by the parties' representatives, if they have been given that power, or it is drafted, initialed and returned to corporate headquarters for ratification.

Folberg and Taylor's Stage 6 (legal review and processing) is a stage more important to disputes in the area of domestic relations or community grievances and is rarely a factor in international commercial disputes unless those disputes are already in some form of litigation and the mediation is used in an attempt to settle the litigation. By contrast, Stage 7 (implementation and review) is highly important and sometimes ignored. It is vital that two parties dealing at long distance develop some process by which the mediated agreement can be properly monitored.

The monitoring can be by third parties or by a requirement of periodic reporting between the parties; but it must occur in some fashion if only to avoid the re-occurrence of the problems that lead to the initial dispute. One common deficiency in renegotiated or mediated agreements is a lack of some kind of policing mechanism to insure that the new agreement is being fully performed. Another common defect is falling into the trap of thinking that renegotiation or mediation need occur only once, thus failing to establish some mechanism by which the parties can reconvene if any problems arise. The mechanism need not be elaborate. It can be something as simple as a letter notification process by which one party notifies the other that a problem has occurred and that invites the other party to participate in a mediation.

There are inherent problems with mediation, of course. No one should consider it a panacea for all commercial disputes. One of the problems with the rush toward mediation in the United States is that its proponents emphasize its positive attributes but are generally blind to its defects. Mediation is often unsuccessful when there is disproportionate power or

leverage on one side or another. In contrast, the formal procedures of litigation can go a long way toward equalizing leverage. Like negotiation, mediation is normally useless when one party insists on acting in a confrontational, take-it-or-leave it manner. While the mediation itself is usually fairly
quick—speed is one of its distinct advantages—a mediation failure means
that the parties must resort to some more formal mechanism such as arbitration or litigation when they could have begun with that process. So it can
waste a lot of time and expense for the parties and leave them no better off
than they were at the beginning.

Even the benefit of confidentiality can sometimes be a two-edged
sword. Parties who first try to mediate may be forced to reveal a great deal
of their case in a forum that cannot finally resolve the dispute and thus
find all their arguments in court fully anticipated and countered by their
opponent.

Perhaps the most glaring defect of mediation is that its result is not
truly enforceable in the same way that a court decision or arbitral award is
enforceable. Obviously, a mediation that results in a new written agreement
signed by the parties has created a new contract that can be enforced in the
same fashion as any other contract, through arbitration or litigation. But
note that this merely moves the dispute back into a forum that, presumably,
the mediating parties were seeking to avoid.

Moreover, it is unclear whether a provision in the original contract by
which the parties agree to mediate is enforceable. This is in sharp contrast to
numerous decisions holding *arbitration* clauses in contracts fully enforcible.[16]
But, here again, compulsory *mediation* is both superfluous and probably a
contradition in terms. A party who does not want to mediate will simply poison the mediation at the first possible opportunity and go on to the more
adversarial forms of dispute resolution.

§ 6.4.3 Procedures for international commercial mediation

If rules making activity is any indication, it appears that international com-
mercial mediation is a dispute resolution technique whose time is coming.
The International Chamber of Commerce (ICC), the United Nations
Commission on International Trade Law (UNCITRAL) and the American
Arbitration Association (AAA) as well as many other national arbitration
institutions have promulgated specific procedures for mediation.

Each of these procedural systems is characterized by brevity and simplicity. For example, the UNCITRAL procedures (referred to as *conciliation*

---

16. See, e.g., a United States Supreme Court decision, Mitsubishi v. Soler, 473 U.S. 614
(1985) in which the Court demanded that parties abide by an agreement to arbitrate even when
many of the issues involved antitrust claims—an issue in the United States that normally is taken
directly into the court system.

rules) comprise only 20 separate rules. Under the UNCITRAL system, the following steps are mandated:

1. The party initiating mediation sends a notice to the other party describing the matter in dispute and inviting mediation under the UNCITRAL rules. If the other party objects, that is where the process stops. There is simply no mediation.[17]

2. The parties may agree on a single mediator, or if they wish to have a three-person mediation panel, they may each appoint one mediator and those two mediators choose the third.[18]

3. The mediator has the parties write up their statement of the claim and of the issues involved for submission to the mediator and to the other party.[19]

4. Once these papers are exchanged and examined, the mediator convenes a mediation session "in such a manner as he considers appropriate" and is expected to "be guided by principles of objectivity, fairness and justice, giving consideration to, among other things, the rights and obligations of the parties, the usages of the trade concerned and the circumstances surrounding the dispute, including any previous business practices between the parties."[20]

5. The proceedings are terminated by either the signing of a written agreement between the parties or by a declaration by one or both of the parties that further proceedings would be futile.[21]

Note that the rules are deliberately relaxed and somewhat ambiguous, vesting enormous discretion in the mediator as to the conduct of the proceedings. The parties themselves also carry a substantial burden. They may propose possible points of settlement; they may take the lead in drafting the final agreement; and they may terminate the process unilaterally. This does not, of course, do great violence to the process. When the UNCITRAL procedures were initially drafted, they were intended to be voluntary, non-binding and simple.[22]

The procedures for the ICC are similar, although they use a different vocabulary. The ICC process is actually two separate procedures: the ICC Rules for Optional Conciliation and the 1978 Rules for the Regulation of Contractual Relations. The Optional Conciliation Rules establish a process by which, separate from arbitration, the parties submit the dispute to a conciliation committee (generally composed of three persons) appointed by the

directly into the court system.
17. UNCITRAL Conciliation Rules, Art. 2.
18. Id., Art. 4.
19. Id., Art. 5.
20. Id., Art. 7.
21. Id., Art. 15.
22. Dore, *Peaceful Settlement of International Trade Disputes: Analysis of the Scope of*

ICC who listen to the parties, examine the record and submit proposed terms of settlement to the parties. The parties are free, of course, to accept, modify, or reject the terms.

By contrast, the Rules for the Regulation of Contractual Relations establish mediation rules closer in form and substance to the UNCITRAL conciliation rules. In this instance, the parties apply to the ICC for the appointment of a "third person" (which can become a panel of three persons) who examines the evidence and conducts a hearing—apparently in somewhat of an adversarial context—and submits a decision adapting the contract to the changed circumstances.[23] However, in sharp contrast to the UNCITRAL rules, the ICC's rules provide expressly: "When the third person [mediator] takes a decision, that decision is *binding* on the parties to the same extent as the contract in which it is deemed to be incorporated. The parties agree to give effect to such a decision as if it were the expression of their own will."[24] This last requirement may explain why there have apparently been very few disputes submitted under this part of the ICC's rules.

§ 6.4.4 Mediation in the future

The fact that mediation has not yet caught on in the international commercial community is something of a disappointment. Mediation, even when it is used, is rarely reported in the legal or business literature. For persons as conservative as lawyers and business executives, this lack of a track record for mediation severely inhibits its use. Few lawyers want to be attacked by their clients or to get a reputation among other lawyers for engaging in costly, futile actions. This fear of failure probably stifles a lot of innovative dispute resolution techniques. But while the process has both advantages and disadvantages, it is a process that bears more attention and consideration than it is now getting. Some disputes—especially those involving certain Pacific Rim cultures who abhor the adversarial nature of arbitration and litigation—simply cry out for mediation. It would be a shame if the innate conservatism of international commercial lawyers were the only thing standing in the way of increased use of these techniques.

§ 6.5 The Minitrial

§ 6.5.1 The minitrial generally

Although mediation has been with us practically since time immemorial, the minitrial device is newly developed and just beginning to be appreciated. No

---

23. ICC Rules for the Regulation of Contracts, Arts. 9 & 11.
24. Id., Art. 11(3).

one knows precisely when or where the idea was first developed. One of the first articles describing a minitrial was written in 1978 by Professor Eric Green who may remain the device's strongest and most articulate proponent.[25] Recently, the Canton of Zurich promulgated minitrial rules that may catch on in Europe and elsewhere. The American Arbitration Association has now gotten into the act with minitrial rules and it appears as if a number of other arbitral bodies may follow suit.

The process is relatively simple. The disputing parties convene for a short period of time, usually for not more than two days. The lawyers for each side make summary presentations of the cases to a senior executive from each of the companies involved. Under normal ground rules, that executive attends on condition that he or she have full settlement authority in the dispute. In other words, the executives present must be capable of coming to an agreement on the spot when the minitrial concludes. Frequently, the executives will enlist the help of some third party such as a retired judge who is commonly referred to as a "neutral advisor," to help them understand and evaluate the factual presentations and the legal issues involved. The proceeding is conducted in a private setting (i.e., confidentiality is enforced), without a record, under informal rules of procedure and without rules of evidence, and is nonbinding. Once the presentations are concluded, the executives sit down together either by themselves or in the presence of the neutral advisor and negotiate a settlement of the dispute.

Note the advantages to this procedure. The delay factor caused by court congestion is eliminated. The parties work out their own schedule. The expense and agony of a lengthy trial is eliminated by three components of the minitrial procedure: the summary presentations, the lack of an excessive number of formal rules of procedure, and the absence of rules of evidence. To the extent that the executives have to be educated on the legal issues of the case, they are educated by the neutral adviser, presumably a person with some degree of expertise and prestige. Confidentiality is usually assured, and if things blow up in the parties' faces, they may move into binding arbitration or litigation without having made any damaging formal and public concessions on any of the issues. Most importantly, the presentations are made to, and the ultimate decision made by, two persons with the requisite authority to commit their companies to the settlement. In other words, a draft agreement does not have to be cleared through successive echelons of a corporate structure long after the minitrial has been completed.

---

25. Green, *Settling Large Case Litigation: An Alternative Approach*, 11 Loyola of Los Angeles L.Rev. 493 (1978).

§ 6.5.2 Specific minitrial rules

For persons interested in utilizing the minitrial, a short description of two typical rules systems may be helpful. One of the first sets of minitrial rules was promulgated by the Zurich, Switzerland Chamber of Commerce in October, 1984. Described by the Chamber as an "attractive fourth route," the rules were compared with arbitration which was explained as being perhaps too "cumbersome and expensive," were seen as preferable to mere negotiations by senior executives who may be insufficiently briefed when they enter a conventional negotiation, and as an improvement over mediation which the Chamber of Commerce drafters believed is too "unstructured and unpredictable."

A Zurich minitrial is commenced in much the same way as an UNCITRAL mediation. One of the parties to a dispute files a petition with the Zurich Chamber of Commerce and sends a copy of the petition to the opposing party.[26] Once the opposing party is notified and has consented to the procedure, the two parties designate "a member of their senior management" as associate members of the minitrial panel. The two associate members either agree on the appointment of one "neutral person" as an umpire for the proceeding or the Zurich Chamber of Commerce will appoint an umpire.[27] After the minitrial panel is fully constituted the umpire directs the parties (who may be represented by lawyers, although lawyers are not obligatory) to file written statements of their claims in a document not to exceed 25 typewritten pages. These statements are exchanged and one reply document for each party is permitted in response to the statement of claims.[28]

Once the paperwork is exchanged, usually under a 30 day deadline, the panel convenes and essentially works out its own rules of procedure. As Rule 11 states: "[The panel] may invite the parties to plead orally, to attend meetings or to clarify the facts further in writing. It may also request information from knowledgeable third parties. Then the panel discusses the dispute with the parties orally at what the rule describes as "meetings," which may take more than one day.

After these presentations, the panel may simply assist the parties in drafting a settlement agreement or may recommend the terms of an agreement if the panel is unanimous. If the panel is not unanimous, the umpire is permitted to draft and recommend an agreement. The rules further provide that all information is to be confidential and most importantly, "[f]or the duration of the Minitrial the parties shall be deemed to have waived their rights to submit the ... dispute to the ordinary courts or to an arbitral

---

26. Zurich Mini-Trial Rules, Rule 3.
27. Id., Rule 5.
28. Id., Rule 9.

tribunal or to continue judicial or arbitral proceedings ... unless, in their opinion, the taking of such action is critical in order to avoid applicable limitation statutes or in order to preserve rights which would otherwise be endangered."[29]

The AAA rules are patterned closely on the Zurich rules with only slight shifts in vocabulary. For example, the presiding officer is called the "neutral advisor" rather than the umpire and rules of evidence are expressly prohibited. If the senior executives on the panel cannot agree, the neutral advisor is required to "render an advisory opinion as to the likely outcome of the case if it were litigated in a court of law. The neutral advisor's opinion shall identify the issues of law and fact which are critical to the disposition of the case and give the reasons for the opinion is offered."[30]

§ 6.5.3 Minitrials in the future

The proponents of minitrials view the process as one that is particularly suited for breaking a negotiation impasse. Note that the presence of the senior executives is crucial to a successful outcome. At least some cost savings are realized through the element of speed and the relaxation of rules of judicial procedure and evidence. Among other things, a minitrial directs the panel's attention to crucial issues of law and fact that lie at the heart of the dispute rather than spending endless amounts of time arguing about and briefing issues on the periphery of the problem.

At the same time, not all commercial disputes are suitable for a minitrial. Some recent experience in the United States suggests that a minitrial might be most efficient after litigation has commenced—that is, after the parties have developed a fair amount of the factual basis for the case and after the legal issues have been carefully identified. This, of course, makes the minitrial a kind of court-annexed dispute resolution process, a development that does not appear to have been envisioned by the drafters of the Zurich and AAA rules. Further, minitrials are not necessarily cheap. While none of the rules systems require the presence of lawyers it is clear, at least in the United States, that lawyers will drive the system even if the executives make the final decision. If a minitrial is used mainly as an intermediate step in litigation, parties will not be able to avoid many of the costs associated with such things as discovery and pre-trial motions. Finally, much like all the other less-drastic dispute resolution devices if a minitrial breaks down, the parties must still resort to some other forum, thus duplicating a fair amount of time and effort.

---

29. Id., Rule 13.
30. AAA Mini-Trial Rules, Rule 12.

At the same time, the device has a distinct appeal for commercial disputes. In the words of Professor Green, the minitrial process [reconverts] into a business problem what has often been transformed by the litigation process into a technical, lawyers' fight."[31] Most importantly, the dispute is in the hands of executives who are experienced at cutting through chaff, at making difficult decisions and "who often are better able than the legal representatives to assess the strategic risks and overall importance of the case to the client."[32] All of these characteristics make it an exceptionally inviting form of dispute resolution, but one whose future is not yet certain.   ◆

---

31. Green, *The CPR Mini-Trial Handbook*, in Corporate Dispute Management (1982).
32. Id.

— 7 —
Litigation

§ 7.1 Introduction

Litigation is probably the single most costly dispute resolution technique available to resolve international commercial disputes. Most lawyers in the United States instinctively think about litigation whenever their clients get into any kind of trouble. That kind of reaction is understandable given the system of law and the structure of legal education in the United States. There is great emphasis (some might argue overemphasis) on litigation throughout the system. Litigation is normally the bench mark under which we test other forms of dispute resolution. The *alternative* dispute resolution movement in the United States measures all other forms against of litigation. Without question, litigation, both inside and outside the United States, has both advantages and disadvantages. It is such an important dispute resolution process that it is discussed before this book's lengthy discussion of arbitration—the dispute resolution of choice in most international commercial disputes. Moreover, it is helpful to have a solid understanding of litigation before thinking about arbitration since arbitration is probably best understood as an *alternative* to litigation.

Litigating a dispute means going to court.[1] Because there is no true international court system available for private international commercial disputes, litigation means going to court in the domestic courts of some country. While the International Court of Justice (ICJ) at the Hague occasionally deals with commercial problems, only national governments may invoke the ICJ's jurisdiction, and the Court spends the bulk of its time on questions of

---

1. For some good general reading on many of the topics covered in this chapter see Symposium, *A Guide to International Civil Practice*, 17 Vand.J.Transnat'l L. 1 (1984); Symposium, *Transnational Litigation*, 18 Int'l Law. 522 (1984); von Mehren, *Transnational Litigation in American Courts: An Overview of Problems and Issues*, 3 Dick.J.Int'l L. 43 (1984).

public international law. Since this book concentrates on private contractual relationships between private parties, the term *litigation* is defined as the resolving of commercial disputes through the processes of the domestic court system of an appropriate country.

Although court procedures differ markedly from country to country, litigation has certain general characteristics irrespective of where it actually takes place. Almost everywhere, litigation is slow, cumbersome, costly and usually administered through a monopoly of lawyers. With the exception of the European Community, many domestic court decisions are unenforceable outside the country in which the litigation took place. By contrast, litigation's singular advantage is that it is normally final and enforceable within that country. The twin characteristics of finality and enforceability often warrant the litigation of many commercial disputes even when alternatives are available. Lawyers often favor litigation simply because they are comfortable with the process. Clients often lack the sophistication necessary to steer their lawyers to other less costly and less time-consuming techniques. Moreover, as discussed in Chapter Six and Chapter Nine, the other forms of dispute resolution frequently require parties to go into court even after they have mediated or arbitrated the dispute because the party losing the mediation or arbitration does not voluntarily concede. In many cases, going directly to court may be the most cost-beneficial solution for all concerned.

§ 7.2. Litigation — generally

It is difficult to generalize about litigation because domestic court systems around the world differ significantly. A judicial proceeding in Zaire is different from one in Singapore and both are substantially different from a trial in the United States. However, similarities and common concepts do exist; so it is possible to discuss litigation in general terms irrespective of the country in which it occurs. Litigation is a proceeding in a properly constituted domestic court before a judge or magistrate with the parties normally represented by their own counsel. The court conducts either an investigation or an adversarial hearing, witnesses frequently testify, relevant documents are examined, and some type of formal decision is rendered by the presiding officer. In most countries this decision normally may be appealed to a higher authority, and once the appeals are exhausted, the parties have a final judicial decision, enforceable at least within that country.[2]

In order to properly litigate a dispute a court must have jurisdiction over the *subject matter* of the dispute. In other words, the court must be

---

2. For practitioners facing international litigation problems in U.S. courts one of the best and most comprehensive references is G. BORN & D. WESTIN, INTERNATIONAL CIVIL LITIGATION IN UNITED STATES COURTS (Kluwer 1988).

authorized to hear cases of this type. Some courts have limitations based on the monetary amount of the controversy presented (so-called small claims courts are an example of a monetary limitation). After the court assures itself that it has subject matter jurisdiction, it will also determine whether both parties are subject to the power of the court (the concept of *personal jurisdiction*). Once these two threshold considerations are satisfied, the controversy evolves under the court's procedural framework. In virtually all judicial systems there is some mechanism enabling either the court or the parties themselves to find out the relevant facts and to gather evidence that can be used at trial. This type of pre-trial fact gathering is referred to in many systems as the process of *discovery*. In United States practice, the party bringing the lawsuit is normally referred to as the *plaintiff* and the person responding to the lawsuit is the *defendant*. The remainder of this chapter will use that terminology solely as a matter of convenience for the reader.

Many of these concepts prove difficult to work with when parties to a commercial agreement have a dispute that cuts across national boundaries. Moreover, much more so than any other type of dispute resolution technique discussed in this book, litigation is a matter that must be left in the hands of the *experts*. No matter where the case is brought, it requires handling by someone sophisticated not just in the broad-brush aspects of litigation, but thoroughly schooled in the local courts. In most countries, only lawyers licensed to practice in a particular court are permitted to appear in those courts on behalf of clients. Thus, in considering litigation as a possibility for resolving a dispute, contracting parties should take into account, among other things, the following:

1. Does the intended court have jurisdiction over both the subject matter of the dispute and the parties;
2. Is any resulting judgment fully enforceable in the country of issue;
3. Might the judgment be enforceable in other countries;
4. Will the procedures used by the court lead to a fair result;
5. Are foreign parties treated fairly in that particular court;
6. Are properly trained and instructed counsel available;
7. How long will it take to get a final decision and what will everything cost?[3]

The sections that follow will assist the reader in answering most of these questions.

---

3. These questions were suggested by a similar checklist in D. VAGTS, TRANSNATIONAL BUSINESS PROBLEMS 158-59 (1986)

§ 7.3. Subject Matter Jurisdiction

Subject matter jurisdiction is a question of whether a particular court has the power to adjudicate the issues presented in the case. It is a concept that looks simply to the nature of the issues (or subject matter) in controversy rather than to the parties who are involved in the action. In many other systems, these same doctrines are discussed in terms of a court's *competence* (to hear the dispute) rather than a court's jurisdiction. For example, in the United States, and certain other jurisdictions, small claims courts may hear disputes involving claims of, say, less than $5000. A small claims court by definition will not have subject matter jurisdiction over a breach of contract claim in which $1 million in damages is sought. In countries with bifurcated court systems—those, for example, that divide their courts into *law* or *equity* courts—claims of breach of contract are often heard in one court while cases seeking relief against a government agency are heard in a wholly separate court.

As a consequence, it is usually crucial to have the case filed in the proper court. In some legal systems, a party that files in the wrong court will not be permitted to refile the action in the proper court. In the United States' system of federal courts, limitations imposed by the U.S. Constitution permit the raising of subject matter defects even when the case is on appeal. For most breach of contract actions, the U.S. Federal courts require that the amount in controversy be over $50,000 and that the plaintiff and defendant be citizens of different states, or that the suit be one between a citizen of some U.S. state and a citizen of a foreign country.[4] However, state courts in the United States are normally courts of *general* jurisdiction; these courts have the power to dispose of virtually any case. In England most important commercial disputes are tried in the High Court of Justice. Commercial disputes in France may be heard initially in the Tribunaux de premiere instance, or in certain cases in courts staffed by merchants, the tribunaux de commerce. In Germany, a lawsuit will likely begin in one of the Landgericht or, if the parties choose, in a commercial chamber (Handelssachen) annexed to the Landgericht.[5] In China, commercial disputes are normally heard in the Economic Division of an appropriate level of the Peoples' Courts.[6] In Japan, many international commercial disputes are filed in the Tokyo District Court, a development that reflects Tokyo's prominence among Japanese cities, but there seems to be no special reason why international matters could not be heard elsewhere in Japan.[7]

---

4. 28 U.S.C. § 1332.
5. A.T. VON MEHREN, THE CIVIL LAW SYSTEM at 82, 86 (1958).
6. Haney, *The Trial of A Contract Dispute in China*, 22 Int'l Law. 475 (1988).
7. See, Matsuo, *Jurisdiction in Transnational Cases in Japan*, 23 Int'l Law. 6 (1989).

In virtually every country some court will be available for the lawsuit. The task is simply to identify the proper court and then to commence the litigation. Once again, an experienced litigator will be able to provide the proper guidance.

§ 7.4 Foreign Sovereign Immunity and the Act of State Doctrine

§ 7.4.1 Sovereign immunity

A number of issues frequently arise in international commerce that affect a court's ability to take up the dispute. These barriers to litigation are probably best discussed under the concept of subject matter jurisdiction because the underlying legal doctrines affect all such cases. In other words, principles of sovereign immunity and the act of state doctrine may block a lawsuit categorically, no matter what the particular merits of the dispute may be.

In commercial contracts between two private parties, sovereign immunity (commonly referred to as *state immunity* outside the United States) is rarely a factor. However, when one of the parties to a contract is a private person and the other is a government — or some entity such as a state trading company closely associated with a national government —, a serious question arises as to whether the governmental entity may be sued because the doctrine of sovereign immunity holds squarely that a sovereign cannot be sued unless it consents to be sued.[8] The doctrine derives from the concept, nicely put by Justice Oliver Wendell Holmes, that: "there can be no legal right as against the authority that makes the law on which the right depends."[9]

There are now two conflicting schools of thought on the topic of sovereign immunity in international matters. The so-called classical or *absolute* theory concludes simply that a sovereign cannot, without its consent, be forced to be a defendant in the court of another sovereign.[10] The other school of thought, generally referred to as the *restrictive* theory, contends that a sovereign may be immune when it comes to public acts of state (*jure imperii*) but is not immune when it engages in essentially private acts (*jure gestionis*) such as entering into commercial contracts, committing personal injury and

---

8. One good discussion of sovereign immunity is: Lalive, *L'immunite de juridiction des Etats et des Organizations Internationales*, 3 Recueil des Cours 285 (Hague Academy of Int'l Law, 1953). See also, Delaume, *The State Immunity Act of the United Kingdom*, 73 Am.J.Int'l L. 185 (1979).

9. Kawananakow v. Polybank, 205 U.S. 349 (1907).

10. This sentence is a paraphrase from the famous "Tate Letter" written by a member of the United States Department of State commenting on foreign sovereign immunity. 26 Dep't State Bull. 984 (1952). See also, Marasinghe, *A Reassessment of Sovereign Immunity*, 9 Ottowa L. Rev. 474 (1977).

the like. In these latter instances, there is less interest in protecting the juridical integrity of the state. Thus, a state may be amenable to suit when it functions like a private person.

As might be expected, many countries particularly those of Eastern Europe and the Soviet Union follow the absolute school while the restrictive school has gained a number of adherents in Western Europe. Moreover, a number of countries have voluntarily relaxed the doctrine by treaties such as the Brussels Convention of 1926 in which a large number of signatories waive sovereign immunity in the case of vessels owned by the government.

Many of the problems in this area are definitional. How does one distinguish between *jure imperii* and *jure gestionis*. Occasionally, courts conclude that *jure imperii* involve only acts that an individual simply cannot do, such as declare war, establish national boundaries, or conduct diplomatic relations. However, these distinctions break down when a national government contracts to purchase armaments from a private manufacturer for the purpose of waging war, when state-run industries send air pollution over international boundaries or when a country contracts to purchase an office in a foreign country to be used as its consulate.

Some countries have attempted to deal with these problems by statute. For example, in 1976 the United States enacted the Foreign Sovereign Immunities Act,[11] (FSIA) an statute that establishes as a general rule the proposition that "a foreign state shall be immune from the jurisdiction of the courts of the United States and the States." The FSIA has a few narrowly-drawn exceptions such as when a nation gives its express consent to be sued and when a treat requires the waiving of immunity. The FSIA also attempts to create a commercial activity exception and defines *commercial activity* as: "either a regular course of commercial conduct or a particular commercial transaction or act. The commercial character of an activity shall be determined by reference to the nature of the course of conduct ... rather than by reference to its purpose."

What this definition tries to do is relax sovereign immunity in those cases, among others, in which a country buys an airplane from an American manufacturer that it intends to use in its air force. The *purpose* of the transaction may be to assist the country's warmaking, but the *nature* of the transaction is the mere purchase and sale of a piece of merchandise. Of course, even this attempt at a definition has not pleased everyone; the courts still struggle with it.[12]

---

11. 28 U.S.C. §§ 1602-11.

12. See, e.g., McCormack, *The Commercial Activity Exception to Foreign Sovereign Immunity*, 16 Law & Pol'y Int'l Bus. 477 (1984); Carl, *Suing Foreign Governments in American Courts: The United States Foreign Sovereign Immunities Act in Practice*, 33 Southwestern L J 1009 (1979).

The United Kingdom has enacted a similar statute, the State Immunity Act of 1978, which defines commercial transaction more specifically as:

a. any contract for the supply of goods or services;
b. any loan or other transaction for the provision of finance and any guarantee or indemnity in respect of [the loan or guarantee]; and
c. any other transaction or activity (whether of a commercial, industrial, financial, professional or other similar character) into which a State enters or in which it engages otherwise than in the exercise of sovereign authority.

A number of other countries such as Canada, Australia, Singapore and Pakistan have addressed the issue by enacting statutes delineating their understanding of sovereign immunity.[13] Of these, perhaps the most important is the promulgation of the Council of Europe: The European Convention on State Immunity and Additional Protocol. The European Convention is essentially a restrictive doctrine formulation. It carries special weight emanating as it does from the Council of Europe.[14]

These concepts set the stage, but it is never easy to work with sovereign immunity concepts in a practical setting. Governments do not like to be sued; and they particularly do not like to be hampered in their conduct of foreign affairs. Many international commercial transactions are closely connected with diplomacy. Sovereign immunity issues generally arise anytime one does business with either the state itself or with a state-owned or state-run entity. There is no sharp, bright line that permits us to distinguish between commercial activity and "other than commercial activity;" so it is obvious that a large part of these conflicts are going to be resolved either in court on a case-by-case basis or by diplomatic means.

§ 7.4.2 The Act of State doctrine

A concept closely related to sovereign immunity is the Act of State doctrine, a legal principle that typically affects individual issues in a case rather than, necessarily, the case as a whole. It most commonly occurs in cases involving expropriation of private property by a national government. While sovereign immunity comes into play only when a private party is attempting to sue a state or a state-owned enterprise, the Act of State doctrine can affect even lawsuits purely between private parties.[15]

---

13. See, e.g., Molot & Jewett, *The State Immunity Act of Canada*, 20 Can. Y.B. Int'l L. 79 (1982).

14. See, e.g., Sinclair, *The European Convention on State Immunity*, 22 Int'l & Comp. L.Q. 254 (1973).

15. For some general reading on the Act of State doctrine, see: Conant, *The Act of State Doctrine and Its Exceptions*, 12 Vand. J. Transnat'l L. 259 (1979); Jones, *Act of State in English Law*, 22 Va. J. Int'l L. 433 (1982).

In essence, the doctrine prevents a court from setting aside a decision made by a foreign sovereign dealing with property in that country. Once the decision—for example, a decision to expropriate property—is made, the decision may not be questioned in court.[16] As explained in a German case in which Chilean expropriation of its copper mines was at issue:

"an expropriation which has been effected abroad must in principle be recognized as being formally valid, since in accordance with the internationally recognized principle of territoriality, measures of expropriation cover without limitation the property which was subject to the [country's] sovereignty ... This means that an expropriation effected in the course of nationalization or socialization measures remains an internal matter of the foreign state as long as it does not cover property located outside of its boundaries ... ."[17]

In the United States, the Act of State doctrine was best enunciated by the Supreme Court in *Banco Nacional de Cuba v. Sabbatino*,[18] a case involving Cuban nationalization of the sugar industry. The private company argued that the government's taking of the property without any kind of indemnification was contrary to public policy and thus the actions of the Cuban government were not exempt from review under the Act of State doctrine. The Supreme Court restated the doctrine: "Every sovereign state is bound to respect the independence of every other sovereign state, and the courts of one country will not sit in judgment on the acts of the government another, done within its own territory"; and thus confirmed that the action could not be challenged in an American court. As the Court put it: "However offensive to the public policy of this country ... an expropriation of this kind may be, we conclude that both the national interest and progress toward the goal of establishing the rule of law among nations are best served by maintaining intact the act of state doctrine in this realm of its application."[19]

Somewhat alarmed at the *Sabbatino* rationale, Congress has tried to modify the result somewhat by stating in the FSIA that disputes over "rights in property taken in violation of international law" are not subject to sovereign immunity and thus may be litigated in U.S. courts. There are other statutory provisions attempting to narrow *Sabbatino* elsewhere in the U.S. statutes; but the basic principle appears to remain intact. Sovereign acts

---

16. That peculiar phenomenon of U.S. law, the American Law Institute's Restatement (Third) Foreign Relations Law of the United States at sec. 443 defines act of state as:

In the absence of a treaty or other unambiguous agreement regarding controlling legal principles, courts in the United States will generally refrain from examining the validity of a taking by a foreign state of property within its own territory, or from sitting in judgment on other acts of a governmental character done by a foreign state within its own territory and applicable there.

17. Decision in Hamburg District Court in re: Kennecott Copper, 12 Int'l Leg. Mat. 251 (1973).

18. 376 U.S. 398 (1964).

19. Id.

taken by a state on its own territory may not be questioned in the courts of another country.

These days, the international debt crisis is provoking some new case law on the act of state doctrine. For example, just a few years ago, Costa Rica attempted unilaterally to restructure its international financial obligations in a manner which caused a number of Costa Rican banks to default on their obligations to a number of banks in the United States. One of the arguments mustered in the ensuing litigation by the defaulting Costa Rican banks was that the decision of the Costa Rican government to restructure the country's debt constituted a non-reviewable act of state.

In *Allied Bank International v. Banco Credito Agricola*,[20] a U.S. court of appeals dealt with this argument by examining not only the debt restructuring, but also International Monetary Fund policy (which generally enforces obligations to pay the debts while permitting certain restructuring) and the nature of the particular indebtedness at issue in the case. The court concluded that the obligations to pay were in the nature of private contracts, that those private contractual obligations had been incurred in New York and not in Costa Rica and that, "while Costa Rica has a legitimate concern in overseeing the debt situation of state-owned banks ... its interest in the contracts at issue is essentially limited to the extent to which it can unilaterally alter the payment terms. Costa Rica's potential jurisdiction over the debt is not sufficient to locate the debt there for the purposes of the act of state doctrine ... The act of state doctrine is, therefore, inapplicable."[21]

It is difficult to tell from some of these new cases whether the doctrine is in true ferment or whether it is simply being narrowly confined to traditional settings of expropriation. Only time will tell. Fortunately, for most private contracts, the doctrine has limited applicability.

§ 7.5 Personal Jurisdiction over Private Parties

Sovereign immunity and act of state problems rarely surface in litigation between private parties. The much more difficult problem posed in litigating private international commercial agreements is the matter of whether a court has jurisdiction—judicial power—over all of the parties. Indeed, this is the Achilles heel of litigation because most parties live at great distances from one another and are normally not to be found in the same country.

Consider the following hypothetical. A, a small shoe manufacturer resident in Singapore, contracts to sell 100,000 industrial safety shoes to B, a

---

20. 757 F.2d 516 (2d Cir. 1985).
21. Id.

wholesaler in the United States. B has a contract with several manufacturing companies for the shoes which are of unique grade and quality. The shoes are shipped to the United States and after inspection are found to be defective. The shoes were designed to very narrow specifications and while they could eventually be replaced, there is no way that B can order replacements within the time she is expected to perform on *her* contract.

Assume further that B has lost a $500,000 contract because of A's breach. All of B's attempts at negotiation fail miserably. A will not even respond to B's telexes or telephone calls so B is probably justified in concluding that the less-drastic dispute resolution techniques simply will not work. There is no arbitration clause in the contract.

On these facts, B and her lawyers may conclude that the only meaningful option is to litigate. The question then becomes: "litigate where?" One clear-cut solution to any question of personal jurisdiction is simply to track down the party in breach (the *defendant* in U.S. practice) and sue him where you find him. Under normal circumstances, a domestic court has power over its own nationals within that country's boundaries. Within the United States this is often the preferred solution because courts throughout the country are similar in terms of procedure, power and outlook. It is more complicated, however, when one moves across national boundaries because domestic courts in a particular country may be hostile to foreigners suing its own nationals, may follow only the most rudimentary procedures, may have a reputation for arbitrariness, and, at bottom, may simply be unpleasant sites for litigation.

Of course, Singapore's legal system is essentially British, has highly trained and very sophisticated judges and lawyers, and is quite capable and experienced in dealing with complex commercial matters. There is probably no reason on these facts to avoid Singapore as a reasonable forum for the law suit. And, at the very least, suing in a Singapore court will totally alleviate any personal jurisdiction problems since that jurisdiction is where the defendant is to be found. There is virtually no question that Singapore courts have jurisdiction over a business executive found within Singapore's boundaries.

Assume, however, that B strongly prefers to bring the lawsuit in the United States. Such a decision is not totally implausible. All of the defective shoes are there. They may be useful as evidence. Presumably, B will call a number of experts to testify as to the precise defects in the shoes. These experts may well be located in the United States. Transporting evidence and experts to Singapore is expensive. There may be some evidence of fraud in the case. In many U.S. jurisdictions, an act of fraud that induces someone to enter into a business relationship (so-called *fraud in the inducement*) may be a ground for recovering *exemplary* damages, sometimes referred to as *punitive* damages. Consider the plaintiff's choice of forum if we assume that the

Singapore courts have no power to award exemplary damages in this type of breach of contract suit, or that proof of fraud is much more difficult under Singapore law.

Is it possible for a United States court to obtain personal jurisdiction over the Singapore manufacturer, who is, in personal jurisdiction parlance, a *non-resident* defendant? Under U.S. law, there are some possibilities for doing so, although under the facts we hypothesized, it will be difficult. Questions of personal jurisdiction in the United States in garden-variety commercial matters turn on the power of the state courts, rather than the power of the federal courts, since in these cases, the federal courts normally have no greater powers over non-resident defendants than do the state courts.[22]

As a consequence, plaintiffs in the United States who wish to sue a non-resident defendant must examine two different issues. First, each state has what is called a *long-arm* statute which authorizes its courts to exert personal jurisdiction over defendants who are not physically present in the state if those persons have committed various acts within the state such as causing personal injury or engaging in a commercial transaction within the state. In the shoe case, let us assume for the sake of simplicity that B's state has an appropriate long arm statute.

Unfortunately, the question is not resolved at that point. The United States Constitution requires that all persons, including non-resident defendants, be afforded due process by courts, so the United States Supreme Court has required that every case be examined to determine whether the non-resident defendant has the necessary *minimum contacts* with the state before permitting a plaintiff to sue a non-resident defendant.[23] While the nuances of the minimum contacts doctrine are sometimes difficult to parse, the U.S. Supreme Court has just decided a case which, albeit somewhat muddled and confused, may resolve many of these issues. Indeed, the case may tell us a great deal about how American courts will deal with questions of personal jurisdiction involving foreign defendants in the future.

In *Asahi Metal Industry Co v. Superior Court of California*,[24] Asahi, a Japanese company, manufactured tire valve assemblies that were sold to Cheng Shin Rubber Industrial Company, a Taiwanese tire manufacturing company. The tires were then sold around the world including the United

---

22. For persons wishing more depth on personal jurisdiction issues in the United States, see, e.g., J. FRIEDENTHAL, M. KANE & A. MILLER, CIVIL PROCEDURE at 95-161 (1985); Note, *Federalism, Due Process and Minimum Contacts*, 80 Colum.L.Rev. 1341 (1980).

23. The minimum contact doctrine was first articulated in a 1945 decision, International Shoe Co. v. State of Washington, 326 U.S. 310 (1945). For two good articles on the minimum contacts doctrine in international transactions see Born, *Reflections on Judicial Jurisdiction in International Cases*, 17 Ga.J.Int'l & Comp.L. 1 (1987); Lilly, *Jurisdiction Over Domestic and Alien Defendants*, 69 Va.L.Rev. 85 (1983).

24. 107 S.Ct.1026 (1987).

States. Approximately 20 percent of the Taiwanese company's American sales took place in the state of California. In September, 1978 a California resident and his wife were riding on a motorcycle that collided with a farm tractor. The husband was severely injured and the wife was killed. The husband filed a lawsuit making various claims and allegations, including a claim that the tire was defectively manufactured. Consequently, the husband's lawyer sued Cheng Shin and Cheng Shin, in turn, filed a claim against Asahi, alleging that if the tire was defective, the defect lay in the valve manufactured by Asahi.

In affidavits filed in the lawsuit, Asahi executives admitted that they knew that the valve assemblies were placed in tires that were later sold in the United States, but indicated that they never expected that their activities would subject them to product liability lawsuits in various American state courts. Nonetheless, the California state courts ruled that Asahi knew that tire sales took place in California, that Asahi intentionally put the valves "in the stream of commerce," and that Asahi earned substantial revenues from Cheng Shin's California sales.

After review by the U.S. Supreme Court, Asahi was let off the hook. The Court determined that mere awareness of the fact that goods manufactured by another which contain goods manufactured by Asahi are sold in the United States does not provide the requisite minimum contacts between Asahi and the state of California. Unfortunately, the Court's opinion is considerably blurred by a series of separate opinions in the case.

While the Court was unanimous in concluding that Asahi was not amenable to suit in California, there was no unanimity on the rationale for the case. For example, Justice O'Connor, who authored the lead opinion in the case, concluded that a company's merely placing goods into the stream of commerce was not sufficient. In this case, Asahi had no direct sales in California, maintained no offices or agents there, did not solicit tire valve business in the state and had no control over the tire distribution system which brought Cheng Shin's tires into California. Four other justices, however, rejected Justice O'Connor's use of the stream of commerce approach and were willing to conclude only that hauling Asahi into a California court in these circumstances would offend "traditional notions of fair play and justice."

With regard to U.S. court jurisdiction over foreign defendants, the Court was unanimous on the following point:

> [U.S. courts should] consider the procedural and substantive policies of other *nations* whose interests are affected by the assertion of jurisdiction by the California court. The procedural and substantive interests of other nations in a state court's assertion of jurisdiction

over an alien defendant will differ from case to case. In every case, however, those interests, as well as the Federal [national] interest in its foreign relations policies, will be best served by a careful inquiry into the reasonableness of the assertion of jurisdiction in the particular case, and an unwillingness to find the serious burdens on an alien defendant outweighed by minimal interests on the part of the plaintiff or the forum state. *Great care and reserve should be exercised when extending our notions of personal jurisdiction into the international field.*[25]

Asahi suggests that our company in Singapore might not be amenable to suit in a U.S. court; but one should not be too sanguine on this point. Note the essential differences. Asahi was one step removed from the actual U.S. sales and apparently conducted no other direct activities in the U.S. By contrast our hypothetical Singapore company dealt individually and directly with the U.S. buyer and shipped the goods directly to the United States. The amount in controversy in our case, something in excess of one-half million dollars, is not an insignificant transaction. So it might be possible for a U.S. court to conclude that A is amenable to suit even given the Supreme Court's admonition to the contrary.

Not too many years ago it was sufficient to find some property in the United States, such as a bank account, some real estate or perhaps even an account receivable that could be seized. That property then could be used to obtain personal jurisdiction over the non-resident defendant; and if he failed to appear and defend the lawsuit, the plaintiff could at least take the property seized in partial fulfillment of the obligation (occasionally referred to as *quasi in rem* jurisdiction). However, the Supreme Court in *Shaffer v. Heitner*,[26] decided that even in those instances, a court must apply a minimum contacts analysis. So merely finding out that A has a $5000 bank account in a New York bank may not be sufficient to make him amenable to suit in the U.S., particularly if the $5000 has nothing to do with the transaction sued upon.

But what about other countries? Are they quite as expansive as the United States in determining that their courts can exert personal jurisdiction over non-resident defendants? English courts are generally reluctant to entertain suits over persons not served with process within the United Kingdom, but Order 11 of the Rules of the Supreme Court of Judicature[27] allows a plaintiff, *after* getting a court's permission, to sue a non-resident in certain actions for breach of contract. Article 14 of the French Civil Code provides

---

25. Id., at 1036 (first emphasis in the original, second emphasis added, quotation marks and citations deleted).

26. 433 U.S. 186 (1977).

27. 3 Stat.Instr. 2529 (No. 2145) (1962).

that an "alien, even one not residing in France, may be summoned before the French courts for the fulfillment of obligations contracted by him in France with a French person [or] may be brought before the French courts for obligations contracted by him in a foreign country towards French persons."

By contrast, the German legal system appears to have a fairly broad notion of quasi-in-rem jurisdiction, articulated in Section 23 of the German civil procedure code (Zivilprozessordnung): "For complaints asserting pecuniary claims against a person who has no domicile within the country, the court of the district within which this person has property, or within which is found the object claimed by the complaint, has jurisdiction ..." Sometimes the smallest piece of property—an abandoned undershirt in one case—has been used as the basis for asserting jurisdiction over an absent defendant.

However, it is important to recognize that these traditional notions of personal jurisdiction in Europe have been modified within the European Community by the 1968 Brussels Convention (Jurisdiction of Courts and the Enforcement of Judgments in Civil and Commercial Matters).[28] Under the Brussels Convention, a person's domicile is normally the controlling element in establishing personal jurisdiction—i.e., a person may be sue where he is domiciled. In this instance, domicile in essence means where that person has his permanent place of residence. However, in something of a bow to the newer American long arm statutes, the Convention also permits personal jurisdiction to be found in the place of performance of a contract or where a defendant has committed certain types of personal injury. The Convention also forbids French and German courts to invoke either Article 14 (French Code) or Article 23 (German Code) as a basis for jurisdiction when a lawsuit involves a citizen of another Common Market country.[29]

Issues of personal jurisdiction are not easily resolved, particularly when the law suit crosses national boundaries. Since there are rarely any conclusive answers and since personal jurisdiction is crucial to going forward with the lawsuit, many litigators simply take the path of least resistance and sue the defendant where the defendant can be found.

§ 7.6 Service of Process

Service of process is sometimes confused with personal jurisdiction because courts occasionally use the term *service of process* when they are actually worried about personal jurisdiction—that is, a court's power over a non-resident person. In reality, service of process is a mechanical step by which the

---

28. See, e.g., 18 Int'l Leg. Mat. 8 (1979).

29. Id. The Brussels Convention is further discussed in § 7.10. For a general discussion of the Convention see Kohler, *Practical Experience of the Brussels Jurisdiction and Judgments Convention in the Six Original Contracting States*, 34 Int'l & Comp. L.Q. 563 (1985).

court notifies a person that she is being sued. In its simplest terms, service of process means getting papers relating to the lawsuit into the hands of the defendant. In certain circumstances, a plaintiff may also attempt to seize property belonging to the defendant when the suit is begun to guarantee satisfaction of any judgment that may be obtained. This is not to say that this step is unimportant. Virtually all courts have detailed service of process rules and a person is not subject to a court's jurisdiction until he is properly served.

In the United States, plaintiffs filing suits filed in federal court follow the requirements of Rule 4 of the Federal Rules of Civil Procedure. Basically, this rule requires that the plaintiff serve the defendant with a copy of the complaint and a summons which tells the defendant something of what the lawsuit is about and warns the defendant not to ignore his obligations to respond. In many instances, these papers may be served by registered mail or by a special process server. Usually, a defendant is properly served when the documents are placed in his hands either through the mails or by the process server.[30]

Service of process across national borders is always a little more difficult than domestic service of process; but most legal systems recognize that it is a necessary step in a lawsuit and provide special rules for transnational service. Between countries, even registered mail is sometimes faulty and using a process server can be enormously expensive and frequently not justified—particularly when, for example, the defendant's whereabouts are known and when he is not likely to flee to avoid process.

The United States Congress has greatly assisted international service of process by providing that federal courts may assist foreign courts and tribunals in making service of process on persons in the United States even when there is no prior judgment that the foreign entity is seeking to enforce.[31] Service of process by federal courts in the United States on persons in foreign countries is permitted under Rule 4 of the Federal Rules of Civil Procedure which allow service by mail, with some kind of return receipt, under any method allowed by the courts in that country including the device of a letter rogatory[32] and by special process server.

---

30. For some of the hazards of service of process generally see Mullinex, *The New Federal Express: Mail Service of Process Under Amended Rule 4*, 4 Review of Litigation 299 (1985).

31. 28 U.S.C. § 1696. According to this section: "The order [of service of process] may be made pursuant to a letter rogatory issued, or request made, by a foreign or international tribunal or upon application of any interested person." Moreover, "[t]his section does not preclude service of such a document without an order of court." Id.

32. A letter rogatory used in this context means a written document "whereby one country, acting through its own courts and by methods of court procedure ... to assist the administration of justice in the former country." BLACK'S LAW DICTIONARY (Rev. 4th ed. 1968). See also, Horlick, *A Practical Guide to Service of United States Process Abroad*, 14 Int'l Law. 637 (1980).

There is an important international convention governing service abroad—The 1965 Hague Convention on the Service Abroad of Judicial Documents in Civil or Commercial Matters (Service Convention).[33] The Hague Service Convention, now ratified by approximately 22 countries including the United States and most of the Western European countries, requires each signatory country to designate a central authority to manage matters of service of process from abroad. Generally, this service will be accomplished in the same manner that its own courts serve process, although there are some grounds such as public policy on which the country may object to making the service. The Service Convention also sets out special rules for what might be done if a party who is served abroad fails to appear for the litigation. In this instance in the United States a default judgment is generally entered almost automatically. Under the Service Convention, however, the signatory countries commit themselves to examining closely the precise manner in which process was served and whether it was actually served before granting the default.

None of these procedures is inherently difficult. The practical problems in international service of process stem largely from (1) the inability to locate the proper party and (2) occasional mechanical breakdowns in transmitting the necessary papers. These are not problems of the law, but rather are problems inherent in all types of conflict resolution. There are relatively few legal barriers to proper service abroad, especially in the context of international commercial agreements between established companies. While it is faintly possible that our Singapore seller might flee the jurisdiction just to avoid a lawsuit brought in Singapore by the American buyer, it is highly unlikely. Corporate entities rarely resist service of process. They fight fiercely on all the other grounds.

§ 7.7 Choice of Forum, Venue and Forum Non Conveniens

As we have seen, many considerations dictate the place where the litigation takes place. Frequently, the parties simply have no choice as to the location of the lawsuit. A defendant who chooses to be uncooperative may require litigation in his home country to the exclusion of all other possibilities because his country's courts are the only legal system that has personal jurisdiction over him. In other instances, the location of the evidence may dictate litigation in that jurisdiction. In smaller cases, costs may severely limit the choic-

---

33. 20 U.S.T., 361 T.I.A.S 6638 (1965). American readers will find the Convention reprinted in 28 U.S.C., Rule 4, note. See also, Parmalee, *International Service of Process: A Guide to Serving Process Abroad under the Hague Convention*, 39 Okla.L.Rev. 287 (1986).

es among locations.[34] However, when choice of forum is possible, the parties might well refer to the contract's choice of law clause for guidance. It makes a great deal of sense to try a case in the country whose substantive law is going to be applied to the dispute to avoid the complications inherent in attempting to prove another country's law in the forum court.[35] Having to "prove" foreign law normally requires bringing experts into the litigation to testify as to the foreign law and performing an elaborate review of applicable treatises. A court dealing with foreign law never feels perfectly comfortable and, on occasion, may make baffling mistakes of construction and interpretation simply because it is unfamiliar with the applicable law.

All other things being equal, the parties might also consider the judicial procedure to be applied to the case by various courts. Litigating in a court with acceptable trial procedures is a benefit.

Chapter Four explored the issue of whether it is possible for litigating parties to choose the forum for litigation when they draft the contract. Those choices are generally honored even when the forum is in a neutral country. In *The Bremen v. Zapata Off-Shore Oil Co.*,[36] the United States Supreme Court honored a forum selection clause in an international commercial agreement between an American and a German company that identified the High Court of Justice in London as the proper forum for any litigation, even though—in theory at least—the American courts could have exercised jurisdiction over the case. Clearly, the Supreme Court believes in forcing parties to live with the contract language that they drafted and is especially sensitive to the special considerations at issue in international commercial agreements. The Court noted that the choice of London was a rational one:

> Not surprisingly foreign businessmen prefer, as do we, to have disputes resolved in their own courts, but if that choice is not available, then in a neutral forum with expertise in the subject matter. Plainly the courts of England meet the standards of neutrality and long experience in admiralty litigation. The choice of that forum was made in an arm's-length negotiation by experienced and sophisticated businessmen and absent some compelling and countervailing reason it should be honored by the parties and enforced by the courts.[37]

At least in the United States, the touchstone for judging the validity of a contractual choice of forum is one of reasonableness. A prominent collection of what American law professors frequently refer to as black letter law,

---

34. For a good general exposition of some of these issues see Cowen & Da Costa, *The Contractual Forum: A Comparative Study*, 43 Can.B.Rev. 453 (1965).

35. von Mehren, supra note 5, at 47.

36. 407 U.S. 1 (1972).

37. Id.

the newest Restatement on conflict of laws admonishes courts to give effect to such agreements unless the parties choice is "unfair or unreasonable."[38] Courts in other countries may not be quite so amenable to such clauses, however. A number of decisions appear to worry about clauses that purport to oust local courts of jurisdiction or that bear no reasonable relation to the contract itself.[39]

But what of those instances in which the contract does not choose a forum, or where the choice strikes a court as improper? In these cases, a court will determine a forum after the plaintiff attempts to litigate it somewhere. Occasionally, a case may be tried in a number of different places and it will be left to some court to determine the proper place for the litigation. This concept, usually referred to as *venue*, is closely related to the issue of *forum non conveniens*. While few scholars, practitioners or judges discuss or distinguish these two doctrines with clarity, for the purposes of this chapter, venue will be defined as a site for the litigation that is permissible under the law.

In many domestic cases, there is only one place where venue is proper. However, in international commercial agreements, there are almost always at least two places where a case might be litigated: the country of the buyer or the country of the seller. Forum non conveniens—the issue of the "best" or optimum place to bring a lawsuit—is a concept that comes into play when there are two or more locations in which it is legally permissible to bring the case.

Venue is normally dictated either by the rules of the court or by an underlying statute. For example, suits involving breach of contract in the U.S. federal courts may be brought, theoretically, in three places in the United States: the judicial district (1) where any defendant resides, (2) where the defendants are subject to personal jurisdiction, or (3) where a substantial part of the events or omissions giving rise to the law suit have occurred.[40] These three sites are only theoretical possibilities. Issues of service of process and other factors may cancel out one or more of the sites for other reasons.

Most other countries have narrower venue rules. Foreign venue provisions, unlike American venue, tends to be more defendant-oriented. Note, for example, that Article 23 of the German civil procedure code limits certain suits to the district in which the defendant has property. Certain foreign jurisdictions are so small geographically that venue is not really a factor. In our shoe manufacturing hypothetical, if B wants to sue A where he lives, she

---

38. RESTATEMENT (Second) CONFLICT OF LAWS, § 80. This provision is nearly identical to a provision in the RESTATEMENT OF THE FOREIGN RELATIONS LAW OF THE UNITED STATES (Revised) § 421(2)(g).

39. See the cases collected in Gruson, *Forum Selection Clauses in International and Interstate Commercial Agreements*, 1982 U.Ill.L.Rev. 133.

40. 28 U.S.C. § 1391(a).

will sue in the city of Singapore. By contrast, if her company has operations in, say, New York, Connecticut and California and she attempted suit in the U.S., she may be able to bring it in the courts of any of those states (again, so long as one of those states somehow can exert personal jurisdiction over the defendant; venue always takes a back seat to personal jurisdiction).

When there are options as to the site of the lawsuit, the question becomes slightly different. What is the most *convenient* place to try the case. In this instance, the choices are frequently left to the courts, rather than to the statutory law. The United States Supreme Court has identified a number of factors that it requires lower federal courts to apply and that constitute almost a codification of the American law of forum non conveniens. In the 1981 case of *Piper Aircraft Co v. Reyno*,[41] a wrongful death action was brought in a California state court and later removed to a federal court in California. The litigation stemmed from the fatal crash, in Scotland, of an aircraft manufactured by Piper. Only Scottish citizens were killed, but the American law of wills and trusts permitted the lawyer for the Scottish decedents to appoint his secretary, a Ms. Reyno, as an administrator of their estates for the purposes of pursuing the wrongful death action where *she* lived in California.

Subsequently, the case was transferred to central Pennsylvania where the Piper Company at that time manufactured its aircraft. At that point, the defendants, Piper and Hartzell Propeller Company (the American company that manufactured the plane's propellers) asked the court to dismiss the action entirely because a trial of this case in the United States would be inconvenient to the defendants and because an adequate forum existed, namely Scotland. Reyno resisted this request, arguing that Scottish law could not provide all the remedies that might be available under U.S. law.

On review in the United States Supreme Court, the Court held that the lawsuit should have been dismissed on forum non conveniens grounds. The Court stated expressly that "the possibility of an unfavorable change in law should not, by itself, bar dismissal.[42] The case is truly remarkable for a number of reasons. First, this is one of the first instances in which the Supreme Court has suggested that plaintiffs who are properly in a U.S. court can be kicked out of that court and forced to try the case outside the United States. Second, it was one of the few times that the Court fully articulated a number of grounds for assessing the issue of forum non conveniens.[43] Briefly stated, there are what the Court calls *private* factors and others it refers to as *public* factors. Private factors which a court should consider include: access to

---

41. 102 S.Ct. 252 (1981).
42. Id.
43. The factors were originally elucidated in slightly different form in Gulf Oil Co. v. Gilbert, 330 U.S. 501 (1947).

sources of proof; availability of procedures for compelling the attendance of unwilling witnesses; possibility of view of the premises; "and all other practical problems that make trial of a case easy, expeditious and inexpensive." Public factors include: court congestion; the local interest in having local controversies decided at home; a forum that is at home with the law governing the action; and the avoidance of unnecessary problems in conflicts of law, or in the application of foreign law.[44]

What does this mean in practical terms? It is difficult to give the question a precise answer because the Supreme Court also made clear that trial courts in the United States have a great deal of discretion in deciding questions of forum non conveniens. In other words, if the trial court had considered the factors enumerated in *Piper v. Reyno* and concluded that the case should be heard in an American court, the Supreme Court would probably not disturb that decision. The Supreme Court was mainly troubled by the fact that the trial court's refusal to dismiss the American case and to send the case to a Scottish court was based on solely on the court's judgment that Scottish law was too pro-defendant, and that the U.S. plaintiff could not obtain all the remedies in Scotland that she had at her disposal in the United States. The mere fact that a plaintiff would be treated differently under the law of another country is not a proper basis for determining forum non conveniens.

How might *Piper* affect our shoe case, assuming other questions such as personal jurisdiction do not forestall the possibility of a U.S. forum? It's a tough question. On the one hand, the goods are now in the United States. They may be tested there and examined by American experts. Presumably, the specifications for the shoes are set out in the contractual documents; that is, it may not be necessary for a judge or jury to travel to Singapore merely to see what was said in the contract. By contrast, the Singapore defendant may have his own experts who might testify to the fact that the buyer's specifications were inaccurate or impossible to obtain—or, as often happens, merely that the plaintiff's experts are wrong and the defendant's experts are right. At bottom, a judge would simply have to balance all the interests and make a decision. In U.S. law, the plaintiff's choice of forum counts for a lot; but after *Piper* it is obviously not a controlling factor.

Professor Delaume reports that English courts react much more mechanically to forum non conveniens problems than do American courts; and courts in civil law countries have failed entirely to develop a concept of forum non conveniens in part because civil system courts "do not enjoy the same discretion as those in common law countries and have little choice but to adjudicate a case on the basis of existing jurisdictional rules."[45]

---

44. Id. at 265 n.6.
45. G. DELAUME, TRANSNATIONAL CONTRACTS (Booklet 11) at 68-70.

§ 7.8 Choice of Law

The law applied to a commercial dispute is frequently dispositive of the case. As a consequence, it is no wonder that so many lawyers, judges and legal scholars spend a great deal of time on these issues. In the context of international commercial agreements, there are two ways in which law can be "chosen" for the dispute. First, the parties may insert a choice of law provision in the contract. Generally, if that choice is reasonable, a court will honor it. Reasonableness here is a matter of showing some kind of relationship between the body of law chosen and the contract. Chapter 4 contains a lengthy discussion of these issues.

But assuming that a contract does not specify the applicable law—or that a court refuses to honor the law chosen—what principles will a court apply to establish the applicable law? This issue is difficult to discuss in the abstract, so it may be helpful to reconsider our hypothetical dispute over the shoes manufactured in Singapore and sold to a U.S. buyer. The U.S. company intends to sell the shoes to industrial customers in the United States. The shoes traveled directly from Singapore to the United States and were not altered en route. To make the hypothetical a little easier to apply, assume that the shoe manufacturer came to the United States and signed the contract in New York.

Under these circumstances, it should be clear that if the contractual documents expressly choose, say, the Uniform Commercial Code of some state in the United States or Singapore's law pertaining to sales of goods, choice of law should not pose further problems. A court or an arbitrator in all likelihood will simply honor that choice and apply the chosen law to the dispute. However,if the parties chose Soviet law (a concededly implausible situation inserted here purely for illustrative purposes), a court or arbitrator would probably feel free to disregard this choice. It bears no meaningful relation to the parties or their contract. At the same time, parties sometime choose the law of a country that is neither the country of origin or the country of destination. For example, in a major U.S. case between a Japanese car manufacturer and a car dealership in Puerto Rico, the contract chose Swiss law—a choice that all reviewing courts seemed to accept without question. It would seem that if two contracting parties choose the law of a major trading nation, even if it is not the law of their respective countries, the choice will remain undisturbed by either arbitrator or courts.

When a contract is silent on choice of law, the court typically is forced to make the choice. When a court chooses law, it deals with an arcane but frequently crucial topic known as conflict of laws. Both courts and legislatures have worked out governing principles that are generally applied on a case-by-case basis. In the United States, codified principles of choice of law may be found in the Uniform Commercial Code (indicating simply that the applicable law is the law of a state that "bears an appropriate relation to the transaction"[46]) and the Restatements (both First and Second), Conflict of Laws. The Restatements must be discussed in tandem because some American states follow one document and some states abide by the other.

The First Restatement is concededly a mechanical approach to determining applicable law, but its mechanical nature also makes it a relatively simple system to apply. Under the First Restatement, the law applicable to a contract dispute is the place where the contract is to made so long as the dispute concerns issues such as the *capacity* of the parties to make a contract, whether the contract contained all the proper *formalities* and the like. Put a little differently these are all the issues that tell us whether a contract was formed in the first instance.[47] That place is the place where "the principal event necessary to make a contract occurs";[48] and for a formal contract, the principal event is the act of delivery.[49]

However, if the dispute involves issues of performance such as delivery of defective goods or a failure to abide by manufacturing specifications, another section of the Restatement provides that the applicable law will be the "law of the place of performance."[50] Thus, if we use Restatement First to solve the shoe manufacturing problem, the applicable law would almost surely have to be the law of some U.S. state since both delivery and performance (if one regards actually using the shoes or the act of reselling the shoes as the "performance" under the contract) occur in the United States.

Most mechanical rules in law eventually lead to trouble; and the First Restatement was no exception. The Second Restatement was deliberately made much fuzzier and more ambiguous to avoid some of the problems of the overly-mechanical earlier version. Under Restatement Second, the choice of law depends on the type of contract and the issue in dispute, but at bottom, the law chosen is to be the jurisdiction that bears the "most significant relationship" with the contract,[51] a concept evaluated in terms of (a) the place of contracting, (b) the place of negotiation, (c) the place of performance, (d) the location of the contract's subject matter and (e) the domicile, residence, nationality, place of incorporation and place of business of the parties.[52]

Applying this analysis to the shoe problem, the law chosen would again probably be the law of an appropriate U.S. state. While it is difficult to deter-

---

46. UCC § 1-105.
47. Restatement (First) Conflict of Laws, § 332.
48. Id., § 311.
49. Id., § 312.
50. Id., § 358.
51. Restatement (Second) Conflict of Laws, § 188.
52. Id.

mine which state, it is unlikely that any court in the United States charged with choosing law for this dispute would consider itself bound to apply the law of Singapore.

Choice of law outside the United States appears to be moving away from purely mechanical principals to one of interest analysis and party autonomy. For example, the E.C. Convention on the Law Applicable to Contractual Assessments permits a court to infer a choice of law by the parties from such things as use of language that is unique to a particular legal system or by a choice of forum clause.[53] The Convention on the International Sale of Goods (CISG) adopts essentially the "substantial relation" approach of the UCC.[54]

Within the European Community, the Rome Convention on the Choice of Law for Contracts provides a number of rules for choosing law that are applied by many of the European nations. While too complex for a lengthy discussion here, the Rome Convention sets out a number of detailed rules based on the subject matter of the litigation, for example, contract, personal injury, and the like.

§ 7.9 Discovery and Gathering Information and Evidence Abroad

Once the important threshold matters such as choice of forum and choice of law are made, the adversaries can get down to the business of actually litigating the dispute. Frequently, a contract dispute turns on questions involving facts that are not always readily apparent at the outset of the litigation. Many legal systems also require that information presented at trial be gathered and preserved in some specific form—i.e., the originals of documents—or that oral evidence be taken under oath or in the presence of a magistrate. Finding, collating and evaluating the materials and information necessary to try a case is one of the most cumbersome and time-consuming aspects of litigation.

In the United States, pretrial gathering of evidence and information, referred to as *discovery*, is almost as important as the trial. U.S.-style discovery has become increasingly expensive and protracted. This has led to a great deal of criticism of the U.S. procedures abroad. In many other countries, the trial process tends to be more inquisitorial. Information gathering and analysis tends to be put into the hands of court officials and thus less under the immediate control of the parties or their attorneys. An in-depth analysis of the relative merits of the U.S. versus continental systems of litiga-

---

53. § 3(1). For an excellent, but more general discussion, see Syposium, *The Influence of Modern American Conflicts Theories on European Law*, 30 Am.J.Comp.L. 1 (1982).

54. See the discussion of the CISG, supra, § 2.9.2.

tion is not within the scope of this book. What is important, however, is to understand how both systems work.

Discovery in the United States is based on three premises.[55] First, the U.S. system of litigation is adversarial in nature. That leads to the assumption that a determination of the *truth* of any matter is best and most efficiently reached when adversaries hammer at each other in court. Second, the adversarial process is best served by eliminating surprise, unfairness, or games playing at trial. That can be done by creating rules of procedure that tend, insofar as possible, to let the parties develop as much information as possible on the dispute before trial in order to eliminate surprise at trial. Third, as the adversaries come to know more and more about the case, they may choose to settle the matter rather than proceed to trial. Thus, comprehensive pre-trial discovery may actually enhance the efficiency of the judicial system by promoting settlement and thereby eliminating the need for an actual trial.

While procedures differ in some states, the discovery rules used by the federal courts are a good example of a modern American system at work. The rules permit a party to inquire into virtually any kind of information pertaining to the litigation so long as the information is *relevant* to the case and is not *privileged* (this term is used in the sense of doctor/patient or attorney/client privilege—concepts drawn from the law of evidence).[56] The rules then establish several devices for the gathering or preserving of information and evidence:

1. the deposition,
2. written interrogatories,
3. requests for the production of documents or physical inspections,
4. requests for mental or physical examinations of persons, or
5. requests to the other party that something simply be admitted so that proof on the point does not have to be adduced at trial.[57]

Some of these devices are used far more often than others. Perhaps the most frequently used discovery tools are depositions and interrogatories. In a deposition, a lawyer for one of the parties is permitted to question another person under oath in the presence of a court stenographer who takes down a verbatim transcript of the questions and answers. Interrogatories, as that term is used in the federal courts, are written questions proffered by one party to the other party to which that party responds in writing. Without

---

55. For elaborate commentary on discovery in federal courts, most lawyers refer to two multi-volume treatises: C. WRIGHT & A. MILLER, FEDERAL PRACTICE AND PROCEDURE and W. Moore, FEDERAL PRACTICE. For two good commentaries on the system, see Miller, *The Adversary System: Dinosaur or Phoenix*, 69 Minn.L.Rev. 1 (1984); Frankel, *The Search for Truth: An Umpireal View*, 123 U.Pa.L.Rev. 1031 (1975).

56. Rule 26(a), Federal Rules of Civil Procedure

57. Id. Rules 27-37.

going further into the nuances of federal discovery, the reader should be able to see how time consuming and expensive this process can become. Its benefit, of course, is that both sides come to learn a great deal about the case long before they have to appear before a judge.

Legal systems outside the United States rarely give this much control and freedom of inquiry to the adversaries themselves. In most systems, a great deal of the elucidation of facts is done outside the context of the judicial proceeding (e.g., by private investigator) or under closely controlled orders issued by the court.[58] The court officials themselves are frequently the primary investigators. Of course, one reason why this is not ineffective is that the so-called trial in civil law countries extends over a number of sessions; it is usually not a single event; and, accordingly, the cases of each side may be developed as the proceeding moves along.[59] In these systems, the parties are far more passive. Discovery, as that term is used in the United States, is virtually unheard of.

Fact gathering for litigation within a particular country obviously requires the parties to use whatever procedures are allowed within that country by that country's judicial system. It is much more complicated to obtain information and take evidence outside the forum country.[60] Consider the problems faced by a lawyer in the United States who anticipates trying the case in the U.S., but who now wants to obtain information abroad. The rules applicable in the U.S. federal courts are a good starting place to illustrate U.S. practice. Federal Rule of Civil Procedure 28 now addresses these problems by providing for the taking of depositions in foreign countries either under procedures authorized by the law of the host country or by U.S. civil procedure rules. The request to that country for permission to take the deposition may be made either by commission or by letter rogatory; and the information discovered or the testimony taken abroad is not excludable in the U.S. court merely because it was not given under oath or because a verbatim transcript was not taken.

Some definition may be necessary here since even experienced American lawyers sometimes have a difficult time distinguishing between *commissions* and *letters rogatory*. First, readers should realize that the U.S. State Department cooperates in the taking of evidence abroad. When evidence is taken by commission, the commissioner is normally an employee of

---

58. For two principal articles on point, see, Osakwe, *The Public Interest and the Role of the Prosecutor in Soviet Civil Litigation*, 18 Tex.Int'l L.J. 37 (1983); Kaplan, von Mehren & Schaefer, *Phases of German Civil Procedure*, 71 Harv.L.Rev. 1193 (1958).

59. Merryman, *The Civil Law Tradition*, in, J. MERRYMAN & D. CLARK, COMPARATIVE LAW: WESTERN EUROPEAN AND LATIN AMERICAN SYSTEMS at 652-3 (1978).

60. See generally the fine discussion on these issues in INTERNATIONAL CIVIL LITIGATION IN UNITED STATES COURTS, supra, note 2, at 261-334. See also, Lowenfeld, *Some Reflections on Transnational Discovery*, 8 J.Comp.Bus. & Cap.Mkt. L. 419 (1986).

the State Department who is authorized to administer oaths. On occasion, he may also be a lawyer. Commissions come in two forms: *open* or *closed.* An open commission permits the commissioner to inquire of the witness on a particular matter without the structure of prepared questions. A closed commission requires the commissioner to submit written questions to the witness whose responses are recorded, normally in a verbatim transcript.

A letter rogatory, by contrast, is a formal request from one court to another to have the second court take evidence. The examining magistrate in the second country normally summarizes the testimony. At least one experienced international litigator has described letters rogatory as "useless" for obtaining evidence abroad because of the difficulties of working through another legal system and because of the time delays in the State Department's forwarding the letter rogatory to the appropriate foreign court.[61]

The United States is now a signatory to the Hague Convention on the Taking of Evidence Abroad in Civil and Commercial Matters (Evidence Convention).[62] The Evidence Convention permits a lawyer in one country to request permission through the host country's courts to take evidence on essentially the same terms as would be permitted in his home country without doing violence to the host country's legal system. As some commentary on the Evidence Convention indicates, the purpose of the Convention is to permits easier taking of discovery in ways that are "tolerable to the authorities of the State where [the discovery] is taken and at the same time utilizable in the forum where the action will be tried."[63]

One of the difficulties with the Convention is that Article 23 gives the country receiving the request a great deal of discretion in refusing to honor the request; and the Convention is still so underutilized that its precise boundaries remain unsettled.[64] It probably comes as no surprise to the reader that the U.S. was one of the moving forces behind the Evidence Convention. Few countries outside Western Europe have ratified it.

In 1987, the United States Supreme Court added to the legitimacy of the Hague Evidence Convention when it decided the case of *Societe Nationale Industrielle Aerospatiale v. United States District Court.*[65] In *Aerospatiale*, the Court addressed the question of whether parties must use the procedures set out in the Convention when seeking answers to interrogatories, the pro-

---

61. O'Kane, *Obtaining Evidence Abroad*, 17 Vand.J.Transnat'l L. 69 (1984). Mr. O'Kane's article contains a parallel discussion of commissions and letters rogatory. See also, Baade, *International Civil and Commercial Litigation: A Tentative Checklist*, 1973 Tex.Int'l L.J. 5.

62. 23 U.S.T. 2555, T.I.A.S. 7444 (Mar. 18, 1970).

63. Report of the United States Delegation to the Hague Conference, 8 Int'l Legal Materials 785, 806 (1969).

64. von Mehren, supra note 5, at 53-54.

65. 107 S.Ct. 2542 (1987)

duction of documents or admissions when the party from whom the information is sought is a French company over which a U.S. federal court has personal jurisdiction. The U.S. litigant argued that in this situation, it was free simply to use the discovery rules in the federal rules of civil procedure, rather than following the dictates of the Convention. In a lengthy, troubled, and far from unanimous opinion, the Supreme Court refused to adopt a rule that would have required the litigants to first resort to the Convention. Rather, the Court enunciated a test requiring the lower court to consider and balance various interests such as particular facts of the case, interest of the sovereign governments, the likely effectiveness of the Evidence Convention devices and other matters in order to decide which mechanism (either the Convention or the U.S. federal discovery rules) are to be used. The dissenting justices spoke sharply to the point that the Court's refusal to require a first resort to Convention discovery techniques effectively abrogated the United State's obligations under the treaty.

It is difficult to predict accurately where the *Aerospatiale* decision will lead. On the one hand, the Court acknowledged the fundamental legitimacy of the treaty. But on the other hand, the opinion seems almost to suggest that Convention discovery procedures are merely optional in many cases. Two highly regarded international lawyers in the United States have recently concluded:

> The majority opinion in *Aerospatiale* creates an undesirable and unworkable framework in which lower courts must make determinations about the appropriate use of the [Hague Evidence Convention]. Lower courts, inexperienced in transnational litigation and unfamiliar with [the Convention] have given little weight to concerns of international comity or to the legitimate interests of foreign states in their laws and sovereignty, and they have applied the [Supreme Court] majority's ad hoc test unevenly."[66]

It is hard to fault this conclusion. Fortunately for the international interests of the United States, some amendments to the federal rules of civil procedure intended to bring those rules closer to Convention practices are working their way through the system.[67]

---

66. Griffin & Bravin, *Beyond Aerospatiale: A Commentary on Foreign Discovery Provisions*, 25 Int'l Law. 331, 349 (1991).

67. The proposed amendments to rules 26 and 28 would, in general, require parties to resort to the Convention's procedures if a party can take effective discovery under the treaty. Id. at 343-345.

§ 7.10 Trial Procedure

Some of the sharpest differences between American practice and litigation elsewhere in the world are to be seen in the actual trial of a case. Indeed, the word *inquiry*, rather than *trial*, might be a better word to describe courtroom procedure in civil code countries. In those countries, as noted above, the process is a protracted series of hearings over time in which the presiding officer plays an important role in developing facts, questioning witnesses and generally shaping the outcome of the proceeding. The parties and their attorneys are in essence assistants to the magistrate for this purpose.

The trial process in the United States normally follows a prescribed format:

a. Plaintiff's opening statement

b. Defendant's opening statement (which the defendant may delay until the close of plaintiff's case)

c. Plaintiff's presentation of evidence (the so-called direct case)

d. Defendant's presentation of evidence

e. Plaintiff's rebuttal evidence

f. Defendant's rebuttal evidence

g. Plaintiff's opening final argument

h. Defendant's final argument

i. Plaintiff's closing final argument

j. Decision on the case by either judge or, if one has been empaneled, by the jury, who take the case after listening to instructions by the judge.

k. Appeal, if any, to a higher court

Because the trial process in civil code countries is organized much more around the activities of the presiding officer, the party's lawyers have far less maneuvering room. Nonetheless, the comparative legal scholar, Professor John Merryman, among others, warns that there may be too much emphasis put on the role of the judge in civil code litigation. As he describes it: "[In actual practice in civil code countries] the determination of what issues to raise, what evidence to introduce, and what arguments to make is left almost entirely to the parties. Judges in both traditions have some power to undertake inquiries on their own, but civil law judges seldom exercise this power."[68]

In Merryman's view, the sharpest distinguishing factor between the two legal systems is not the role of the judge. In fact it is the considerable emphasis on putting matters in writing in civil code countries as contrasted with the emphasis on oral presentations in common law countries. But even

---

68. Merryman, supra note 59, at 655.

this comment may be a bit overbroad. In the United States the trial of complicated commercial matters relies heavily on documentary evidence, in contrast to oral testimony because so much modern business is conducted in writing, so even in U.S. trials the court must review a lot of paperwork. Nonetheless, writings in American trial practice are generally introduced and confirmed by live human witnesses. They do not normally stand on their own merits. This practice stands in sharp contrast to other legal systems in which the documents frequently speak for themselves.

This emphasis on what U.S. legal scholars frequently call *orality* comes into play in international commercial litigation even in areas involving the applicable law. As discussed in section 7.4, a dispute involving an international commercial agreement may require the application of law different from the law of the jurisdiction in which the case is being tried. The problem of how to prove foreign law is common to all systems. In the United States, federal courts generally prove foreign law through the testimony of expert witnesses, rather than by relying on treatises or written documents. Treaties, by contrast, are frequently interpreted with the help of the U.S. State Department and, on occasion, by statements provided by other signatory countries.

U.S. trials are heavily dependent on rules of evidence, in large part because the system has devised certain principles for presenting matters to a jury composed of lay people. These rules are intended—at least in theory—to permit the jury to come to a rational, focused, unemotional decision. Rules of evidence are somewhat relaxed in American practice when the party's agree to a bench trial (trial before the judge sitting alone) and are virtually non-existent in civil code countries.

Once a trial is completed, parties in the United States invariably have the opportunity to appeal to a higher court, although not all cases are appealed. Appeals, while even less common in other countries, are frequently permitted. This step has its own rules and procedures, protracts the dispute even further, and increases expenses. However, once both the trial and any appeals are concluded, the case is normally resolved once and for all. Rarely can a party reopen a judgment or bring another action challenging the first action.

§ 7.11 Enforcement of Judgments at Home and Abroad

Once a final judgment has been rendered, the losing party must comply with the dictates of the court. Many parties comply voluntarily by paying damages or by obeying other orders of the court. When a losing party fails to comply, it is usually necessary to go back into either the same court or another court for an order compelling the losing party to abide by the judgment. This final step involves the issue of *enforcement* of the judgment. Enforcement is never easy even within a court's jurisdiction. It becomes even more difficult when a court judgment issued in one jurisdiction must be taken into another jurisdiction for enforcement. This issue—when and under what circumstances a court's judgment will be enforced elsewhere—is the last matter encountered in litigation.

In the United States, an important provision in the U.S. Constitution requires any state to fully abide by a final court judgment in any other state. Through the *full faith and credit* clause in the Constitution, each state is required to treat sister state judgments just as if they had been rendered in the state's own courts. The framers of the Constitution realized that such a provision was vitally necessary to break down the economic barriers which then existed among the former colonies. Now, in the United States, this point is taken for granted; and while lawyers can always argue about what constitutes a *final* judgment, the basic proposition—that states must enforce each other's judgments—is no longer subject to question.

The issue is not so clearly resolved on the international level. To put this discussion in perspective, consider once again the sale of those special shoes manufactured in Singapore and sold to the U.S. buyer. Let us assume that B, the buyer, has obtained a judgment in a Singapore court against A for $500,000 damages. Presumably, Singapore will enforce the judgments of its courts against a resident of Singapore, so in this case, enforcement should be no problem. But what might happen if, under a choice of forum clause, a U.S. court has rendered the same judgment—for $500,000 damages—but the Singapore manufacturer leaves the U.S. without paying the bill? In this case, B's lawyers will probably search for countries in which A has property and seek to enforce the U.S. judgment in those places. The question then becomes: do those countries' courts have to abide by the decision of the U.S. court?

To begin with, we are actually dealing here with two separate concepts: enforcement and recognition. A court *enforces* a foreign judgment when it orders the losing party to comply with the original judgments terms with no further proceedings. A court gives *recognition* to a foreign judgment when it gives only partial effect to the judgment, permitting the parties to relitigate certain issues in the case that had already been litigated abroad.

Tragically, there is no comprehensive international convention governing either recognition or enforcement of judicial decisions, although as will be seen in Chapters Eight and Nine there is such a convention for foreign arbitral awards. The existence of the arbitral award convention is one of the primary reasons why arbitration is the dispute resolution mechanism of choice in international commercial transactions. Since there is no worldwide treaty, courts sometimes enforce decrees and sometimes refuse enforcement based on much looser, more ambiguous doctrines.

To deal with these problems, most courts invoke the doctrine of *comity* when they are confronted with a foreign judgment. While comity is a somewhat elusive concept in actual practice, it is fairly easily stated: comity is the natural respect that one court should have for the judgments of another court irrespective of where those courts are located. A famous U.S. Supreme Court decision, *Hilton v. Guyot*,[69] expressed the doctrine in the following manner when the Court was asked to give effect to a French judgment:

> [The rule of comity—and thus recognition and enforcement—will be applied] where there has been an opportunity for a full and fair trial abroad before a court of competent jurisdiction, conducting the trial upon regular proceedings, after due citation or voluntary appearance of the defendant, and under a system of jurisprudence likely to secure an impartial administration of justice between the citizens of its own country and those of other countries, and there is nothing to show either prejudice ... or fraud.

The Court examined all these criteria and determined that there was nothing wrong with the French judgment. However, it then moved to another level of analysis—whether the French courts would similarly enforce the judgments of a U.S. court—and concluded that there was no real reciprocity between the courts of the two countries. It therefore refused to give conclusive effect to the French decree.

The *Hilton* decision was not especially pleasing to many people in the United States. Many courts have chosen to disregard it as inappropriate. While the U.S. cases are sometimes difficult to harmonize, it appears that courts now consider four questions in deciding how to treat a foreign judgment: (1) did the foreign court have jurisdiction over both the subject matter and the parties; (2) was the defendant given proper notice; (3) was there any evidence of fraud or trickery in the earlier case; (4) will enforcement or recognition of the decision somehow violate U.S. public policy?[70]

Reciprocity, while discussed by some courts, appears not to be the sole determinant. In a recent case, a wealthy U.S. oil man, Nelson Bunker Hunt, became embroiled in a controversy with British Petroleum over oil assets that had been nationalized by Libya. BP brought suit in the English High Court of Justice claiming that the company had provided a number of oil field services for Hunt prior to expropriation from which he benefited and for which he should compensate the company. The court awarded BP roughly $20 million, but when BP came to the United States seeking the money,

---

69. 159 U.S. 113 (1895).
70. On this topic see, e.g., von Mehren, *Recognition and Enforcement of Foreign Judgments*, 167 Recueil des Cours 13 (1980).

Hunt refused to pay and instead went to court in Texas arguing that U.S. courts should neither recognize nor enforce the British judgment.[71]

The U.S. court took a close look at the judgment itself, at the *Hilton* case and a number of other factors and concluded: "There is little justification for judicial imposition of a reciprocity requirement [because, among other things, it penalizes individuals who have obtained foreign judgments in good faith]... . [E]ven if reciprocity can be used to bring foreign pressure on foreign countries to recognize American judgments, such [actions] would probably be more effective and appropriate as part of executive or legislative action ..."[72] The U.S. court found Hunt's claim that the British courts did not afford him an adequate hearing by pointing out: "[T]he rendering forum's system of jurisprudence has been a model for other countries in the free world, and whose judges are of unquestioned integrity ... ."[73]

This seems to be a remarkably healthy decision in the highest traditions of comity. It also signals the strong movement among U.S. courts toward more generous recognition and enforcement of foreign court judgments. Within the United States, the various state legislatures have moved in the same direction. Over 12 states have enacted the Uniform Foreign Money-Judgments Recognition Act. This act provides generally that foreign money judgments are to be recognized and enforced on the same terms as a "sister state." Grounds for refusing recognition include a lack of personal or subject matter jurisdiction, inadequate notice to the defendant, fraud, a judgment that is contrary to U.S. public policy, or the fact that the foreign court "was a seriously inconvenient forum for the trial of the action."[74] It appears from the legislative history of the uniform act that these exceptions are to be construed narrowly. In other words, it is expected that recognition and enforcement will be enhanced by the statute.

But is this same inclination toward greater enforcement and recognition typical of other countries? On a regional basis the most serious attempts to provide uniform treatment for another nation's court judgments has emerged from the work of the European Community. The EC took serious steps to promote recognition and enforcement among its member nations when it devised the Convention on Jurisdiction and the Enforcement of Judgments in Civil and Commercial Matters (the *Brussels Convention*).[75] The Brussels Convention forbids each country from adopting special procedures for recognizing and enforcing judgments from other member countries and from making any substantive revisions (so-called *revision Au fond*) in

---

71. Hunt v. BP Exploration Co. (Libya) Ltd., 492 F.Supp.885 (N.D.Tex.1980).

72. Id. at 893.

73. Id. at 890.

74. 13 Uniform Laws Anno. 417

75. See, e.g., Herzog, *The Common Market Convention—An Interim Update*, 17 Va.J.Int'l L. 417 (1977).

those judgments. There are four exclusive grounds on which a court may refuse enforcement:

1. that the judgment violates the public policy of the enforcing country;
2. that there was lack of adequate notice of the litigation to the defendant, preventing the defendant from mounting an adequate defense;
3. that the enforcing country has adjudicated the matter prior to the judgment that it is being asked to enforce; or
4. in limited instances, that the courts in the originating country failed to properly apply conflict of law principles.

Within Western Europe there was another major development in September, 1988 when the Lugano Convention on Jurisdiction and the Enforcement of Judgments in Civil and Commercial Matters opened for signature. As of mid-1991 ten countries within the European Community (Belgium, Denmark, France, Germany, Greece, Italy, Luxembourg, the Netherlands, Portugal, and the United Kingdom) and five other European countries (Finland, Iceland, Norway, Sweden and Switzerland) had signed the convention, but at that time ratification had occurred in only two countries, France and the Netherlands.

Stated briefly, the Lugano Convention attempts to clarify and make simple the enforcement of judgments within signatory states in much the same fashion as the Brussels Convention accomplishes this within the EC. The Lugano Convention applies mainly to contractual matters and extends to all persons (both natural persons and corporations) domiciled in a signatory state who enters into a contract with a person domiciled in another signatory state. With regard to enforcement of judgments, the convention specifies that court judgments rendered in one signatory state are to be enforced in another signatory state without any special procedure or requirements.[76]

For non-EC judgments, most jurisdictions have mixed records on enforcement and recognition. For example, in France, a party seeking recognition and enforcement must apply for a writ of exequatur; and under the doctrine of *revision*, the French courts take the position that they may question virtually anything in the underlying judgment. Many countries place great weight on the reciprocity factor.[77] In other words, they refuse to enforce judgments if the country of origin doesn't give their judgments equal treatment. Reciprocity has become a barrier rather than an enhancement to enforcement.

---

76. Gautier & Stormann, *Lugano Convention on Jurisdiction and on the Enforcement of Judgments*, 19 Int'l Bus. Law. 410 (Sep. 1991).

77. See, e.g., H. STEINER & D. VAGTS, TRANSNATIONAL LEGAL PROBLEMS (3d ed. 1986).

What this means for our shoe purchaser, B, is not entirely clear. Singapore's legal system springs from the British common law; and courts within the Anglo-American system may well be predisposed to honor a judgment from another country within that same system. We might evaluate the prospects by simply applying the American criteria: the U.S. court had both subject matter and personal jurisdiction. A, the seller, was properly served with process and thus had adequate notice of the lawsuit. There was no fraud, and it would be difficult to argue that it is contrary to Singapore's public policy to enforce a judgment for breach of contract emanating from a U.S. court. Of course, the result might be different if the U.S. court for some reason awarded punitive damages, contrary to Singapore law, or, if the underlying contract were for some transaction prohibited in Singapore.

Even if Singapore insists on some kind of reciprocity, the *Hunt* case stands for the proposition that U.S. courts would likely recognize and enforce a similar judgment emanating from the Singapore courts. Thus, B might well prevail in a recognition and enforcement action in Singapore. Whether she would prevail in other countries where A may have property is far more problematic.

§ 7.12 Conclusion

There are both similarities and differences among the world's litigation systems. On close examination, it is difficult to argue that one system is inherently better than another in ascertaining truth and providing satisfactory resolutions of disputes. Still, the legal process in some countries is flawed not so much by such things as rules of procedure and evidence (what some law professors refer to as *law on the books*) but rather by the ineptness and chauvinism of the court personnel, outright chicanery, or even by the imposition of inappropriate constraints through the country's political system (so-called *law in action*). Nationals from one country are frequently terrified of the courts of another country, partly because of the strangeness of the surroundings and partly because the courts may not be able to expunge bias against foreigners from the system.

Litigation is not a happy event in the best of circumstances. When one fears an arbitrary outcome, litigation can be totally intimidating. One of the reasons for the establishment of our current system of international commercial arbitration is the preference, particularly among business executives, for a confidential dispute resolution mechanism that stands apart from the other party's legal system and domestic courts. For some countries, those fears are misplaced; for others they are quite well founded. Sometimes it is very difficult to determine which country fits into which category.   ◆

— 8 —
International Commercial Arbitration:
Commencing Arbitration, the Arbitration Hearing and the Arbitral Award

§ 8.1 Introduction

Arbitration is usually the dispute resolution device of choice among parties entering into international commercial agreements. Unfortunately, many contracting parties blithely drop a standard form arbitration clause into an agreement without paying much attention to its consequences and frequently without understanding fully the nature of international commercial arbitration. To begin with, arbitration is voluntary in nature; the parties must agree to arbitrate. That agreement must be found either in the original contract or in a subsequent agreement. An agreement to submit a commercial dispute to arbitration puts the resolution of the dispute into the hands of a third party, either a single arbitrator or a panel of three arbitrators. Arbitration is similar to litigation in that it contains many elements of the adversary process—particularly in the hands of lawyers from the United States—and it is, at least in theory, final and binding on the parties.[1] In this last respect, it differs materially from the less-drastic forms of dispute resolution such as mediation/conciliation, mini-trial and renegotiation.

The arbitration process has some singular advantages. Because it avoids the courts and court congestion, it can be far speedier than litigation. Arbitration is normally confidential, so two disputing companies do not have

---

1. The classic work on commercial arbitration in the United States (and often recognized as such throughout the world) deserves the first footnote in this chapter. See generally, DOMKE ON COMMERCIAL ARBITRATION: THE LAW AND PRACTICE OF COMMERCIAL ARBITRATION (Rev. ed. G. Wilner, 1984). Another outstanding work which blends elements of a text, a collection of essays and undigested case law is J.G. WETTER, THE INTERNATIONAL ARBITRAL PROCESS: PUBLIC AND PRIVATE (1979).

to worry about revealing important trade secrets in a public courtroom. The arbitrator is usually an expert in the industry or the transaction concerned, a factor that not only increases the speed of the decisional process since the arbitrator usually does not need nearly as much educating as a judge, but also promotes a technically sound decision. For international commercial transactions, an arbitration hearing held in a neutral country before unbiased arbitrators goes a long way toward alleviating the problems of prejudice and unfairness frequently encountered in local courts.

Although arbitration is not subject to the myriad technical rules of litigation, it is a rules-based decisional process. While simpler in text and direction than typical rules of litigation, arbitration rules can be cumbersome. Because arbitration can be difficult to administer, international commercial arbitrations usually are subject to the supervision of one of the major arbitration institutions such as the International Chamber of Commerce (ICC), the London Court of Arbitration, or the American Arbitration Association (AAA). Because governments recognize arbitration as a good device for resolving disputes, virtually all countries have established some form of underlying law that guides arbitration and permits the use of that country's courts to deal with certain pre-arbitral problems, to compel arbitration, or to enforce arbitral awards. Through various treaties, principally the New York Convention on the Recognition and Enforcement of Arbitral Awards (see Chapter 9) many countries have agreed to honor arbitral awards even when the arbitral award is made in another country.

Moreover, the United Nations has begun to take arbitration seriously. Not too many years ago, the United Nations Commission on International Trade Law (UNCITRAL) promulgated a first-rate set of procedural rules for arbitration. In 1985, in one of the most promising developments on the international scene, UNCITRAL adopted a Model Law on International Commercial Arbitration—which, if adopted by all or most of the members of the UN, may prove to be the one of most significant developments in the history of international commercial dispute resolution.

Arbitration is not free of defects, however. For many disputing parties, it may be far less satisfactory from a procedural standpoint (there is very little discovery permitted in arbitration, for example) and far less final than litigation (disgruntled parties to arbitration frequently try to string things out in court after the arbitration is concluded). For example, one prominent arbitration in the United States involved a complicated contract for the construction by Condec Corporation of aluminum liquefied natural gas containers for Kaiser Aluminum. The parties had signed an agreement containing what has been described as a "limited" arbitration clause that attempted to identify only a small number of issues that would be subject to arbitration. Any issues not specified in the arbitration clause were to be disposed of only in court. In theory it is permissible for parties to segregate issues into two separate categories: arbitration and court. But in practice, segregation of issues is extremely difficult. In the Condec arbitration the haggling over the issues proved to be almost endless. Condec eventually won a $25.5 million award ($12 million of which was interest). However, that victory came only after Condec spent eight years in both arbitration and court; after the record grew to more than 30,000 pages of transcript, 5,000 exhibits, 2,500 hearing days and a 600 page final opinion; and after Condec had incurred around $350,000 in arbitration costs and paid around $5 million in legal fees. Satirizing an earlier AAA announcement boosting arbitration as a speedy and economical alternative to litigation (apparently no longer the AAA's position), one writer described Condec-style arbitration as, "the slower, more expensive alternative."[2]

The absence of a lot of procedural detail in typical arbitration rules often cause problems for lawyers schooled in litigation techniques. Lawyers in the United States who are comfortable in the highly structured and highly proceduralized setting of U.S.-style litigation often find international commercial arbitration highly disconcerting. In one case involving a protracted arbitration under the much looser rules of the ICC, an American lawyer lamented:

> There was no transcript, and the arbitrators resisted any sort of transcript. There was really no record of the proceedings that had gone before, even though there had been well over one hundred hearing days. There were little blue books, like we use for [law school] exams here in the States, in which the [previous counsel, British] barristers had taken notes in a microscopic script that was indecipherable by anyone I knew of, including the barristers [themselves] .... Our predecessors had not prepared any witnesses for our case, and the first problem I was confronted with was the need to cross-examine [the opposing party's] last two witnesses for approximately 30 days each."[3]

These two horror stories are not necessarily typical of all international commercial arbitration, but they do serve to illustrate some of the disadvantages of arbitration. Arbitration is a good device for resolving disputes; but it is not a panacea, and it is definitely not free of defects.

---

2. Lyons, *Arbitration: The Slower, More Expensive Alternative?* The American Lawyer 107 (Jan./Feb. 1985).

3. Statement of Robert Wallace, Esq., in the *District Lawyer* (publication of the Washington, D.C. bar)(November/December, 1985) at 49-50. For a more academic discussion of a number of problems associated with international commercial arbitration see Rhodes & Sloan, *The Pitfalls of International Commercial Arbitration*, 17 Vand. J. Transnat'l L. 19 (1984).

This chapter concentrates on the major international commercial arbitration rules systems and on the arbitration hearing process including an examination of how arbitral awards are drafted. Chapter 9 is an intensive examination of the role of the courts in arbitration and Chapter 10 analyzes some important regional and national peculiarities of commercial arbitration for those readers whose interest focuses on, say, Latin America or the Pacific Rim. Chapter 10 should not be disregarded because in some countries a private agreement to arbitrate may not be honored. For example, Saudi Arabian contracts involving petroleum may not be arbitrated outside Saudi Arabia. When contracts involving the Peoples Republic of China mention *arbitration*, the Chinese parties frequently require some type of *mediation* because the Chinese find arbitration too adversarial in nature. Readers who are reading this chapter and Chapters 9 and 10 prior to drafting an international commercial agreement should also review Chapter 4.

For readers new to arbitration as a dispute resolution process, a brief overview and an introduction to some basic arbitration vocabulary may be helpful. Arbitration is normally triggered when parties to a commercial agreement encounter a dispute that they cannot resolve by less-drastic means. Arbitration is not permissible unless both parties have agreed to arbitrate. That agreement is set out either as an arbitration clause in the original contract or in the form of a subsequent agreement to arbitrate signed by the parties. On occasion, parties agree to arbitrate after a dispute arises and when other, less-drastic means have failed to resolve their differences.

The language of the arbitration clause establishes many of the terms and conditions of the arbitration. Although some traditional arbitration clauses are excessively wordy, there are certain minimum requirements for an acceptable clause. The simplest form of arbitration clause provides that any dispute arising under the contract will be subject to arbitration under the rules and supervision of some institution (such as the AAA or ICC) in a particular place (the forum or site of the arbitration hearing). Parties are always free to administer their own arbitration, thus avoiding the fees and administrative delays involved in dealing with one of the arbitral institutions. If the parties conduct the proceeding on their own, the process is called *ad hoc* arbitration. If the parties elect to have one of the arbitration organizations such as the AAA or the Japan Commercial Arbitration Association supervise the arbitration, the process is referred to as *institutional* arbitration. However, ad hoc arbitration is not for beginners; it should be elected only by parties who have previous experience with arbitration who feel confident of their own ability to manage a procedure that can become extraordinarily complicated. The major arbitral institutions contribute a large administrative staff, pre-printed forms, long and carefully screened lists of potential arbitrators and a lengthy institutional memory that can frequently be invoked to help the parties avoid peripheral problems.

While some contracting parties may simply insert a standard form arbitration clause and then rely on the rules of the supervising arbitral institution to flesh out the terms and conditions of the arbitration, large-scale contracts between sophisticated companies usually set out additional details in the arbitration clause such as: the number of arbitrators, the credentials of the arbitrators, the manner in which the arbitrators are to be appointed, the language of the arbitration, whether the arbitrators can use equitable decisional principles to resolve the dispute (the concept of *amiable compositeur*), the courts to which the parties will resort for either compelling arbitration or enforcing the award and other matters.

When a dispute arises, the party who wishes to arbitrate will send a notice to that effect, referred to as a *demand* for arbitration, to the other party. If the other party agrees to arbitrate, it usually files a written reply, the *answer*, and may append a *counterclaim* to the answer. As soon as this initial paperwork is exchanged, the remainder of the arbitration process can go forward. These papers are usually short and simple declarations. Many of the arbitration institutions such as the AAA provide pre-printed, fill-in-the-blank forms for both demand, answer and counterclaim. The ICC does not provide pre-printed forms for the demand, but suggests that at a minimum the demand include the full names, descriptions and addresses of the parties, the statement of the claimant's case, copies of the relevant agreements, information on the number of arbitrators and proposals for the appointment of particular arbitrators. The ICC demand must be accompanied by a payment of $2,000 as an advance on the ICC's administrative costs, otherwise the ICC will not begin processing the arbitration.[4]

If the other party resists the demand, the party seeking arbitration may be forced into an appropriate court for a court order to *compel* arbitration. Similarly, the responding party may attempt to block the on-going arbitration by filing, with an appropriate court, a request to *stay* the arbitration. The possibility of having to bring an action to compel or to respond to an action to stay is one of the Achilles heels of arbitration. Long after the parties have agreed to arbitration by signing a contract containing an arbitration clause, a resisting party may be able to delay the proceedings by forcing an action to compel or bringing an action to stay. In most jurisdictions the courts will act quickly to order the parties to arbitrate, but such an order can occasionally be taken up on appeal, delaying matters even further. Many parties who thought an arbitration clause would let them arbitrate their dispute quickly and efficiently find themselves involved in protracted litigation in court merely to determine whether the arbitration should commence.

---

4. 1 ICC, International Court of Arbitration Bulletin 7 (Dec. 1990).

If the parties have selected an institution to assist with the arbitration, many of the details of the proceeding will be taken care of by that institution including, for example, providing forms for the demand, identifying and, on occasion, selecting arbitrators, and transmitting various documents between the parties. This work is not free, of course. The arbitration institutions perform their administrative functions only after the party demanding arbitration pays the proper administrative fee.

The jurisprudence of arbitration is beyond the scope of this book. But any analysis of the underpinnings of arbitration should not ignore a remarkable book, *Applicable Law in International Commercial Arbitration*, by Julian Lew. Mr. Lew identifies four theories, or juridical bases, for arbitration that provide a good understanding of the jurisprudential roots of arbitration: (1) the jurisdictional theory (arbitration springs from the sovereignty of nations and their authority to prescribe methods of dispute resolution within their boundaries) exemplified by arbitration legislation in the various countries; (2) the contractual theory (arbitration springs from the freedom of contract established for private parties in many countries) demonstrated by the fact that arbitration is largely a matter of agreement between private parties under the umbrella of a nation's legal system; (3) the hybrid theory (arbitration really has elements of both sovereignty and contract); and (4) the autonomous theory (a relatively new idea that arbitration is really a creature unto itself and fits squarely within none of the older theories).[5]

Viewed practically, the arbitration process has five stages: (1) the exchange of the initial paperwork (demand and answer); (2) the selection of the arbitrator or arbitrators; (3) preparation for the arbitration hearing (a process that may involve the gathering of facts and documents as well as the preparation of witnesses); (4) the arbitration hearing; and (5) the issuing of the arbitrator's decision—a document called the arbitral *award*. If the losing party abides by the terms of the award, the dispute is concluded when the losing party pays the amount of the award to the winning party. However, if the award is ignored by the losing party, the winning party may be forced to enter a court of law to have the award implemented through the judicial process of *recognition and enforcement*. The enforcement of arbitral awards in some jurisdictions may involve the process of *confirmation*—a judicial procedure by which the award is effectively converted into a court judgment. If a court agrees to enforce the award, the losing party usually complies because a refusal to abide by a court judgment exposes the losing party to various types of judicial sanctions such as contempt of court.

---

5. J. LEW, THE APPLICABLE LAW IN INTERNATIONAL COMMERCIAL ARBITRATION at 51-61 (1978).

§ 8.2 A Brief History of Commercial Arbitration

Some form of the arbitration process may be found even in the earliest societies. Professor Peter Stein has noted a rudimentary form of arbitration in ancient Athens, with commercial arbitration in disputes involving large sums of money subject to institutional arbitration as early as 403 B.C.[6] The process he describes is even now instantly recognizable as what we might call a form of "mediation/arbitration" with only a limited opportunity for judicial review: "[A]ll civil cases involving substantial sums were sent first to an arbitrator. If he was unable to bring the parties to a settlement [a rudimentary form of mediation], he heard witnesses and tried the case [arbitration]. His decision could be appealed to the popular court [judicial review], but only on the basis of the arbitrator's record, and new evidence could not be admitted [on judicial review]."[7]

Some of the modern trappings of arbitration spring from an exceptionally harsh principle of Roman law that in the first instance did not recognize freedom of contract and in the second instance gave no legal force or effect to the decision of an arbitrator. However, as Professor Rene David notes, private parties in Rome were able to circumvent some these difficulties by framing a double promise (eventually known as a *com-promissum*) by which the parties mutually agreed to arbitrate and to pay a penalty if the arbitration were not honored. A reviewing court would then examine not the arbitration, but only the existence of the double promise.[8]

Those same Renaissance merchants who gave the world the substantive law that we now refer to as *lex mercatoria* (the law merchant) because their trade crossed international boundaries and required uniform principles of commercial dealing also worked out forms of arbitration because their transnational dealings could not be suitably dealt with in domestic courts. Court procedures were rudimentary; justice was frequently arbitrary; the judges were not particularly skilled in commercial disputes; and prejudice in favor of the local party was palpable. Additionally, workable principles of commercial law did not exist in many countries. For all these reasons, the merchants simply did not trust the courts to render reasonable decisions. The merchants set up their own system of arbitration as an alternative to the courts.

In addition, the merchants took an important concept of commercial arbitration, the doctrine of *amiable compositeur*, and grafted it onto the process of arbitration. When the parties have agreed to the principle of *ami-*

---

6. P. STEIN, LEGAL INSTITUTIONS: THE DEVELOPMENT OF DISPUTE SETTLEMENT 17 (1984).

7. Id. at 17-18.

8. R. DAVID, ARBITRATION IN INTERNATIONAL TRADE 84 (1985). The English version of Professor David's book is a translation of *Arbitrage dans le commerce international*.

able compositeur, the arbitrator is permitted either to render a decision within established legal principles, or—growing out of his role as a mediator (in Latin, *amicabilis compositor*)—to work out a just and equitable solution (sometimes referred to as *Solomonic justice*) and to impose that decision on the parties.[9]

In the United States, arbitration caught on quickly in the business community. Even before the turn of the century, business people in New York City developed sophisticated arbitration schemes because the courts were crowded and because arbitration institutionalized under the auspices of the New York Chamber of Commerce gave them more control over the process (and over their consumer opponents) than they might have had in court.[10]

These developments were not without their detractors, of course. English courts, in particular, exhibited a fair degree of hostility to arbitration as did certain courts in the United States. This hostility—usually exhibited as a disdain for arbitration and an inclination simply to ignore arbitral awards—was based on the idea that a court was not obligated to recognize any dispute resolution mechanism that ousted the courts of jurisdiction over that dispute. The overt hostility of the judiciary severely weakened both domestic and international arbitration. As a consequence, many legislatures began to get into the act. One of the major developments in modern international commercial arbitration has been the enactment of statutes and the ratification of treaties that make arbitration a recognized and legitimate process and that minimize interference and second-guessing on the part of the courts. For example, in the United States, all fifty states have an arbitration act and Congress has enacted the Federal Arbitration Act.[11] In the United Kingdom one of the major recent breakthroughs in arbitration was Parliament's enactment of the 1979 Arbitration Act—a statute that "drastically reduced the supervisory powers of the English courts over arbitrations."[12] In 1981, France enacted a powerful statute limiting the manner in which a French court may interfere with an international commercial arbitration award.[13] Virtually all of the major trading nations have similar provisions and in most instances arbitration is fairly well insulated from judicial intervention.

Even the courts are beginning to recognize the legitimacy of the arbitration process. In two striking decisions by the United States Supreme Court

---

9. David, supra note 8, at 87.

10. J. AUERBACH, JUSTICE WITHOUT LAW? RESOLVING DISPUTES WITHOUT LAWYERS 101-02 (1983).

11. 9 U.S.C. §§1-14.

12. Steyn, *Arbitration in England*, in INTERNATIONAL HANDBOOK ON COMMERCIAL ARBITRATION: NATIONAL REPORTS, BASIC LEGAL TEXTS (P. Sanders, ed., 1984).

13. Decree of May 12, 1981, Noveau Code de Procedure Civile; for an authoritative commentary on this statute see Delaume, *International Arbitration Under French Law: The Decree of May 12, 1981*, 37 Arb. J. 38 (1982).

issued slightly over ten years apart, the Court has moved from something of an interventionist court historically to a court that lets arbitration alone. In the first case, *Scherk v. Alberto-Culver Co.*,[14] an U.S. company bought several businesses and certain trademark rights from a German citizen. The contract, signed in Austria, contained a standard form arbitration clause providing for arbitration in Paris under the rules of the ICC. The U.S. purchaser disputed some of the trademark rights and brought an action in a United States federal court alleging that the seller had violated U.S. securities law and arguing that such securities violations were not arbitrable in the United States.

However, the Supreme Court disagreed with this proposition. The Court issued an opinion ordering the U.S. buyer to arbitrate under the terms of the arbitration clause. The Court reasoned that the sanctity of arbitration clauses must be preserved because a substantial degree of certainty and predictability in *international* contracts is important for American business. In the 1985 decision, *Mitsubishi v. Soler*,[15] the Supreme Court decided that a standard form arbitration clause encompasses even disputes under a contract involving potential violations of U.S. antitrust laws. There the parties had signed an agreement calling for arbitration in Tokyo under the rules of the Japan Commercial Arbitration Association. The Court concluded that it would not be impossible to find arbitrators in Japan who knew something about U.S. antitrust law; and, if enforcement of an award were ever sought in the United States, a U.S. court could review the award to insure that it did not do violence to U.S. antitrust doctrine.

Mitsubishi has been read by many as making the U.S. Supreme Court almost totally non-interventionist in matters subject to arbitration.[16] At the moment, probably the only large category of issues that is not subject to arbitration are certain violations of U.S. civil rights laws—a matter rarely encountered in international commercial contracts. Many other national courts take similar positions.[17] *Mitsubishi* has prompted some contract drafters to attempt drafting elaborate arbitration clauses that try to distinguish between arbitrable and non-arbitrable issues; but these maneuvers are highly dangerous and almost always lead to more problems and delays. The basic message of *Mitsubishi* is plain and should not be disregarded. When a U.S. party

---

14. 417 U.S. 506 (1974).

15. 473 U.S. 614 (1985).

16. See, e.g., Fox, *Mitsubishi v. Soler and Its Impact on International Commercial Arbitration*, 19 J.World Trade L. 579 (1985).

17. Professor Carbonneau believes that the French courts take a non-interventionist position regarding international commercial transactions while remaining somewhat interventionist when it comes to domestic arbitration. See Carbonneau, *The Elaboration of a French Court Doctrine on International Commercial Arbitration: A Study in Liberal Civilian Judicial Creativity*, 55 Tul.L.Rev. 1 (1980); see also von Mehren, *International Commercial Arbitration: The Contribution of the French Jurisprudence*, 46 La. L. Rev. 1045 (1986).

signs a contract containing a standard arbitration clause, any dispute under that contract will be subject to arbitration.

§ 8.3 The Statutory Basis for Arbitration

The difficulty of looking to courts for support and assistance in conducting arbitration is that courts move slowly and without a great deal of predictability—that is, there is no special guarantee that a particular national court system will not continue to be hostile to the idea of arbitration. Consequently, there is more wisdom and efficiency in the use of legislation to tidy up international commercial arbitration.

It is impossible in a book of this length to analyze or even discuss every piece of arbitration legislation, but there is some merit in briefly examining three different statutes, the United States' Federal Arbitration Act, the relatively new 1979 Arbitration Act in Great Britain and, one of the most important recent developments in the entire area of international commercial arbitration, the United Nations Model Law on International Commercial Arbitration.

§ 8.3.1 The Federal Arbitration Act

The Federal Arbitration Act,[18] enacted in 1924, governs interstate and maritime transactions in the United States and provides a solid statutory base that clearly establishes the legitimacy of arbitration. Indeed, the United States Supreme Court in cases such as *Mitsubishi v. Soler, supra,* invoke it frequently as a statement from the United States Congress that arbitration is a proper and respected form of dispute resolution. The act begins by making arbitration clauses in contracts generally enforceable and irrevocable "save upon such grounds as exist at law or in equity for the revocation of any contract."[19] It then permits the federal courts to stay any attempt by a party to litigate the dispute when an arbitration clause is applicable and permits the federal courts to compel arbitration in appropriate cases.[20] The *Mitsubishi* case, for example, went up to the Supreme Court as an action brought by Mitsubishi in federal court to compel Soler to arbitrate the dispute. In instances of *ad hoc* arbitration in the United States, the act permits a court to appoint an arbitrator, provides the arbitrator with subpoena power to "summon in writing any person to attend before [the arbitrator] ...as a witness and in a proper case to bring with him ...any [documents] ...which may be deemed material as evidence in the case." Any failure to abide by an arbi-

---

18. 9 U.S.C. §§ 1-14.
19. Id., § 2.
20. Id., §§ 3, 4.

trator's subpoena may be litigated in federal court and the person failing to honor the subpoena may be subject to contempt of court proceedings.[21]

The act goes on to provide for the recognition and confirmation of arbitral awards in court and to severely limit the grounds on which a reviewing court may overturn an award. The grounds for overturning an award are interpreted narrowly (that is, a court has very little authority to vacate awards) and include: (a) when the award was procured by fraud or undue influence; (b) when the arbitrator was guilty of various types of misconduct such as refusal to hear pertinent evidence; and (c) when the arbitrator exceeded his power or wrote an incomplete award.[22]

Simply reciting the act's provisions conceals many of the major contributions made by the statute to the arbitration process in general. First, note that the statute was enacted in 1924, long before the alternative dispute bandwagon began rolling. Second, it minimizes—at least in theory—the manner in which a court may interrupt or interfere with the arbitration process. In an important U.S. Supreme Court decision, *Moses H. Cone Memorial Hospital v. Mercury Construction Corp.*,[23] the Court noted that the enactment of the federal act "is a congressional declaration of a liberal federal policy favoring arbitration agreements, notwithstanding any state substantive or procedural policies to the contrary.... [Moreover, under the act] any doubts concerning the scope of arbitrable issues should be resolved in favor of arbitration, whether the problem at hand is the construction of the contract language itself or an allegation of waiver, delay or a like defense to arbitrability."[24] Thus, the act has assisted the Supreme Court in its recent moves to enhance the credibility of arbitration and to urge disputing parties to try some dispute resolution mechanism apart from litigation.[25]

§ 8.3.2 The English Arbitration Acts

As a major center of international commerce, London has had long experience with arbitration, but the history of arbitration in England appears to be a pattern of continued judicial intervention and, indeed, outright hostility to arbitral awards.[26] However, by the middle of the twentieth century,

---

21. Id., § 7.

22. Id., §§ 9, 10.

23. 460 U.S. 1 (1983).

24. Id., at 19. Since the decision in Cone, the Supreme Court has continued to reaffirm the legitimacy of arbitration as an alternative to the courts. Dean Witter Reynolds v. Byrd, 470 U.S. 213 (1985)(the Federal Arbitration Act creates a presumption in favor of arbitration); Shearson/American Express v. McMahon, 107 S.Ct. 2332 (1987)(domestic securities disputes are subject to arbitration clauses in the same fashion as the international contract at issue in Mitsubishi).

25. For additional general commentary on arbitration in the U.S. see Smit, *Elements of International Arbitration in the United States*, 1 Am. Rev. Int'l Arb. 64 (1990).

26. International Handbook, supra note 12 at 1 (England).

Parliament recognized that the arbitration process required modernization and enacted what remains the fundamental statute in England and Wales on arbitration, the Arbitration Act of 1950, a statute that codified and consolidated various legislation and that attempted to rationalize the entire process of arbitration. For example, Section 1 of the 1950 Act makes an arbitration clause irrevocable. Subsequent sections permit a court to stay litigation if arbitration has been agreed to, to appoint aribtrators if the parties cannot agree, gives the arbitrator various powers to conduct the hearing, and authorizes the arbitrator to fashion the award. In addition, the act permits the arbitrator to issue subpoenas and to frame interim awards. Merely reading the Act, one might come away with the feeling that arbitral awards are generally free from judicial scrutiny.

Unfortunately, according to most observers, the Act contained two defects that made it far too easy for British courts to interfere in arbitration proceedings and to set aside arbitral awards. Indeed, one observer of the European arbitration scene recently determined that the number of ICC arbitrations taking place in England was less than half the number sited in Switzerland and roughly one-third the number of arbitrations held in France.[27] A distinguished British jurist, Lord Hacking, was told by a lawyer from New York that New York firms believe that any lawyer who permits his client to sign a contract with an arbitration clause calling for arbitration in England was committing an act of professional malpractice.[28]

The perceived defects grow out of two practices under the 1950 Act: (i) the *special case* procedure (sometimes referred to as the *stated case*) by which arbitrators could be compelled by the High Court to submit various questions of law to the court for resolution; and (ii) the provision in the act that permitted the court to set aside an arbitral award for errors of law or fact apparent on the face of the award. The upshot of these two provisions was to give England a reputation for being an exceptionally strong interventionist state, in which courts commonly set aside arbitral awards.

To counter this reputation and to strengthen the arbitration process generally, Parliament enacted the Arbitration Act of 1979, a statute that appears to have abolished both the *stated case* procedure and the prerogative of a court to overturn an award for factual and legal errors with a simpler provision permitting an appeal to the High Court, with leave of the Court, on questions of law.[29] While the reaction to the 1979 Act remains mixed—a number of commenters are convinced that even the 1979 Act per-

---

27. Jarvin, *London as a Place for International Arbitration,* 1 J.Int'l Arb. 59 (1985).
28. Hacking, *Where We Are Now: Trends and Developments Since the Arbitration Act (1979),* 1 J.Int'l Arb. 9 (1985).
29. Samuel, *The 1979 Arbitration Act—Judicial Review of Arbitration Awards on the Merits in England,* 1 J.Int'l Arb. 53 (1985).

mits too much judicial interference—it does appear to be a move away from unfettered judicial intervention. However, the final chapter on this question has not yet been written in England.

§ 8.3.3 The UNCITRAL Model Law on International Commercial Arbitration

The difficulties created by such wide variances in the domestic arbitration law of various countries prompted UNCITRAL in the early 1970s to commence drafting a model law on arbitration that may prove to be one of the most important developments in the history of international commercial arbitration—the Model Law on International Commercial Arbitration (discussed more fully in Chapter 11). This proposal, a model act that is becoming the domestic law of many countries (and, more recently, of a number of states within the United States such as California, Florida, Connecticut and Texas, each of which may be seeking to become a major site of international commercial arbitration),[30] establishes a comprehensive framework for international commercial arbitration that preserves a substantial degree of party autonomy but with a modicum of sensitivity for a country's own institutions and legal system.

The Model Law, restricted on its terms to international commercial agreements (although there is no special reason why a country could not adopt it for its domestic arbitration law as well), attempts to preserve party autonomy, insure fairness in the arbitration process and minimize judicial intervention. Many of its provisions are similar to the UNCITRAL rules on arbitration discussed below. When adopted by individual countries, the primary contribution of the law will be uniformity and equality of treatment. If adopted around the world, it will once and for all legitimize arbitration as the premier international commercial dispute resolution mechanism. However, until nations begin enacting the Model Law, most international commercial arbitration will be processed under domestic arbitration statutes and will abide by rules of procedure promulgated and administered by domestic arbitration agencies or by the major international arbitration institutions.

§ 8.4 The Lex Loci Arbitri and "Ad hoc" versus "Institutional" Arbitration

One factor that all parties to an international commercial agreement must consider is the manner in which an arbitration will proceed and under

---

30. See the list of states and appropriate statutory citations in Garvey & Heffelfinger, *Towards Federalizing U.S. International Commercial Arbitration Law*, 25 Int'l Law. 209 (1991). For specific commentary on California's adoption of the Model Law see Wright, *California's International Commercial Arbitration Act*, 17 Int'l Bus. Law. 45 (1989).

whose body of law the arbitration will be administered. There are actually three issues here: (1) what body of substantive law will apply to the contract under dispute (this is the issue of choice of law, discussed extensively in Chapter 4), (2) which country's judicial system will supervise the arbitration and the enforcement of the arbitral award, and (3) which system of arbitration procedure will apply.

Today, issue 1, choice of law, is mainly a matter of party autonomy and is often stated expressly in the contract. But parties to a contract must also confront issues two and three. Although a debate is currently in progress as to whether an arbitral award can survive if divorced from the law of the country in which it is made, most arbitration scholars seem to concede that, to quote a friend of the author's, an arbitration needs a juridical "home." If an arbitration does not have a home, crucial questions such as which judicial system supervises the arbitration or recognizes and confirms the award may not be resolved. There are times when parties to an arbitration must turn to an appropriate court for various types of interim relief, asking for, say, an injunction when one of the parties shows signs of transferring assets subject to the arbitration. An arbitrator may have the nominal power to grant interim relief, but effective enforcement of that relief can come only through a court order. When an arbitrator's subpoena is ignored, a party must resort to a court for subpoena enforcement. On occasion, when the parties cannot agree on the identity of the arbitrators, they must seek court appointment of the arbitration panel. As Professor William Park has put it, very succinctly: "Some legal system, therefore, must legitimise the arbitrator's authority. Otherwise, the award remains an unenforceable conciliation attempt that the parties are free to treat as mere foreplay to litigation."[31] Professor Park's co-author, Jan Paulsson disagrees, arguing that an international commercial arbitral award may exist "without a specific legal system serving as its foundation."[32] The debate is fascinating and suitable for tomes on the jurisprudence of international commercial arbitration, but a safer, more conservative view is simply to concede that, generally speaking, an arbitration proceeding needs a juridical home and that home will be normally be the courts of the country in which the arbitration hearing takes place and in which the award is issued, even though the award may ultimately be enforced elsewhere.

The second major question is whether the parties are obliged to have the arbitration supervised by an arbitration institution such as the ICC or the AAA. These days, there is little question that the parties may proceed

---

31. Park, *The Lex Loci Arbitri and International Commercial Arbitration*, 32 Int'l & Comp.L.Q. 21 (1983).

32. Paulsson, *Arbitration Unbound: An Award Detached from the Law of the Country of Origin*, 30 Int'l & Comp.L.Q. 358 (1981).

entirely on their own under a form of dispute resolution known as *ad hoc* arbitration. In this instance, the parties themselves work out the entire process and administration of the arbitration without the assistance of an outside body. In ad hoc arbitration, they provide for selection of the arbitrator, location of the arbitration, the language of the arbitration, the rules applicable to the proceeding, the applicable law and the arbitrator's fees and costs. They resolve between themselves as well the administrative expenses associated with the dispute.[33] There are certain advantages to this approach to resolving disputes: the fees and costs are likely to be less; the parties retain virtually complete control over all aspects of the arbitration—permitting them to provide for things such as limited pre-arbitration discovery of information pertinent to the disputes (something not normally countenanced under traditional arbitration rules). Since no institution's bureaucracy is involved, the arbitration may well proceed in a more timely fashion.[34]

However, there are certain disadvantages, as well. If the dispute is a sizable one, the parties may be taking on an enormous task in an area in which they have very little expertise. What may have seemed to be a full and complete ad hoc arbitration agreement may be seen to be full of holes and ambiguities when the parties actually arrive at the dispute resolution stage. They may have a difficult time even identifying appropriate persons to serve as arbitrator. Or, they may disagree on the appointment of an arbitrator. To avoid many of these problems, most contracting parties provide for, or subsequently agree to, *institutional* arbitration, a process by which some institution such as the ICC or London Court of Arbitration administers and supervises the arbitration under prescribed rules.

There are a number of arbitration institutions that deal with most international commercial arbitrations, the ICC, the AAA, the London Court of Arbitration and to a lesser extent, the Zurich Chamber of Commerce, The Japan Commercial Arbitration Association and, particular in the case of East-West arbitration (at least for China and for the former Soviet Union), arbitration under the supervision of the Stockholm Chamber of Commerce. Recently, other centers of commerce, such as Brussels, Cairo, Hong Kong, and Kuala Lumpur have begun to hold themselves out as proper sites for international commercial arbitration.[35] When seeking a site for arbitration, factors such as ease of access, good telecommunications, a corps of well-educated potential arbitrators and a non-hostile judiciary are of primary importance.

---

33. See, e.g., Arkin, *International Ad Hoc Arbitration: A Practical Alternative*, 15 Int'l Bus. Law. 5 (1987).

34. Id.

35. For details on most of these centers see AAA, Survey of International Arbitration Sites (1984). For a more comprehensive treatment of virtually all possible arbitration sites see the Kluwer compilation, INTERNATIONAL HANDBOOK ON COMMERCIAL ARBITRATION (P. Sanders, ed., 1984 with updates).

Each of the major arbitration institutions has promulgated rules for commercial arbitration that control the major aspects of the arbitration process. In addition, these entities help administer individual arbitrations by transmitting documents between the parties; providing interpretations of ambiguous rules or procedures; and assisting in the selection and replacement of the arbitrator, in the proper recordation of the arbitral award, including assistance in obtaining judicial recognition if necessary. For parties new to arbitration or simply unwilling to burden themselves with all the administration of an arbitration, institutional arbitration makes a lot of sense.

§ 8.5 A Description of the Major International Arbitral Institutions Including a Brief Summary of Their Rules

Just a few years ago, parties drafting an arbitration clause in an international commercial agreement would probably call for arbitration in Paris under the rules of the International Chamber of Commerce. The ICC was then—and remains—the pre-eminent international arbitral body. Other agreements, particularly if one of the parties was from the United States might call for arbitration in New York under the rules of the AAA and other contracts might specify a London forum under the rules of the London Court of Arbitration. But these days there is a great deal of ferment in the area of institutional arbitration. The World Bank set up within the Bank a specialized arbitration body, the International Center for the Settlement of Investment Disputes (ICSID) established specifically to resolve—in an arbitral forum—investment disputes between private companies and banks in the developed countries and sovereign entities in the developing countries. More recently, UNCITRAL promulgated rules for international commercial arbitration without providing an institutional framework—thus enabling parties who choose the UNCITRAL rules to select some established arbitration institution such as the AAA to administer the arbitration under UNCITRAL procedures. Unique forms of arbitration have sometimes been created to difuse an otherwise totally hostile environment between nations. For example, an innovative arbitration process sited at The Hague was set up specifically to permit the United States and the government of Iran to resolve numerous commercial disputes that grew out of the fall of the Shah of Iran and the seizure of the American embassy.

This book does not attempt to work through each of the arbitral systems on a rule-by-rule basis. Rather, by way of illustration, this section will select three rules systems, the ICC, the AAA and UNCITRAL as examples of the process of international institutional commercial arbitration. Any reader interested in institutional arbitration under other systems should carefully review the specific procedures established for those systems. While there are many similarities under all the systems, the nuances of the arbitration process in each system are sufficiently different that over-generalization is dangerous.[36]

§ 8.5.1   The International Chamber of Commerce

The ICC administers international commercial arbitration under the auspices of its Court of Arbitration, located in Paris.[37] The Court—actually an administrative secretariat composed of a Secretary General, a General Counsel and five Counsel (who take an active role in administering each ICC arbitration)—is responsible for the promulgation of the ICC's Rules of Conciliation and Arbitration as well as responsible for administering individual arbitrations. In September, 1990 the ICC logged in the 7000th request for ICC arbitration.[38]

Under the ICC's rules, an arbitration is commenced by one party's (the *claimant*) filing a Request for Arbitration that describes the parties, states the claimant's case, appends relevant documents, including, of course, the basic contractual document, and identifies the party's choice of arbitrator. The ICC's Secretariat sends a copy of this request to the opposing party.[39] The responding party, referred to as the *defendant*, must respond in thirty days with his defense and any counterclaims and with his comments on the number and selection of the arbitrators.

Under normal circumstances, it is up to the parties to agree on the number and identity of the arbitrators. Only when the parties disagree will the Court step in and appoint a sole arbitrator, although either by contract language or in exceptional cases by decision of the Court, the Court will appoint a panel of three arbitrators, designating one as the chairman). If the Court makes the appointment, the ICC rules provide that the arbitrator is to "be chosen from a country other than those of which the parties are nationals," although in certain circumstances, and if the parties do not object, an arbitrator may come from one of the parties' countries. The Court rules on

---

36. Two good comparative articles are: Branson & Tupman, *Selecting an Arbitral Forum: A Guide to Cost-Effective International Arbitration*, 24 Va. J. Int'l L. 917 (1984); Stein & Wolman, *International Commercial Arbitration in the 1980s: A Comparison of the Major Arbitral Systems and Rules*, 38 Bus.Law. 1685 (1983).

37. The definitive work on ICC arbitration is W. CRAIG, W. PARK AND J. PAULSSON, INTERNATIONAL CHAMBER OF COMMERCE ARBITRATION (Oceana, 1984). For some additional general commentary on the ICC see Wetter, *The Present Status of the International Court of Arbitration of the ICC: An Appraisal*, 1 Am.Rev.Int'l Arb. 91 (1990) and the rejoinder by an ICC official, Bond, *A Comment on an Appraisal*, 1 Am Rev. Int'l Arb. 108 (1990).

38. 1 ICC International Court of Arbitration Bulletin 4 (Dec. 1990).

39. ICC Arbitration Rules, Article 3.

any challenges to the arbitrators and replaces arbitrators who are unable to carry on their duties.[40] The Court's internal rules require that an arbitrator "be and remain independent of the parties."[41] If the parties have not agreed to a hearing site, the Court determines an appropriate site.[42]

Once the arbitration is initiated, the Request is responded to by the defendant, and the arbitrator selected. The arbitrator then draws up the *terms of reference*, a crucial document under the ICC's rules. The terms of reference identify and describe the parties and the arbitrator, provide addresses for the giving of notice, establish the arbitration site, summarize the parties' claims and set out the issues in the dispute. One commentator has described the function of terms of reference as "bringing clarity and safety to the arbitration process ...an educational value to the parties [and] a protection of awards against attack."[43] The ICC's Rules expressly provide that the parties may choose the applicable law. The law governing the dispute will be established by the arbitrator if no choice has been made in the contract. Moreover, the arbitrator is expressly permitted to act as an *amiable compositeur* (permitting the arbitrator to apply his own concepts of fairness and equity, in addition to principles of law) if the parties so agree. The terms of reference are signed by both the parties and the arbitrator.[44]

Shortly after the terms of reference are completed and signed the arbitrator commences the arbitration hearing—a proceeding almost entirely within his control and of his own construction. The ICC's rules do not expressly provide for pre-hearing discovery, rules of evidence or a precise order of presentation in the hearing. The arbitrator may call experts on his own initiative, may hear from the parties or their representatives and may entertain additional claims or counterclaims so long as those new matters are within the terms of reference.[45]

After the hearing concludes, the arbitrator, in his discretion, may permit the parties to try to reach an award by settlement. If he decides that settlement is not a possibility or if the parties refuse his invitation or cannot reach a negotiated agreement, the arbitrator must then write the award which is then submitted in draft form to the ICC's Court of Arbitration before it becomes final. This is a time-consuming but mainly ministerial step; the Court's review is normally a matter of reviewing the award for form, rather than for substance. It is rare for the Court to tamper with the arbitrator's decision on the merits of the controversy, although the rules expressly provide that the Court "without affecting the arbitrator's liberty of decision, may

---

40. Id., Art. 2.
41. Internal Rules of the Court of Arbitration, Rule 14.
42. Art. 12.
43. Goldsmith, *How to Draft Terms of Reference*, 3 Arb. Int'l 298 (1987).
44. ICC Arbitration Rules, Article 13.
45. Id., Articles 14-16.

also draw his attention to points of substance."[46] Once the Court has performed its review, the parties are notified and the award is automatically
made final—that is, there is no appeals process within the ICC.[47] A party that
objects to the arbitral award has recourse only to an appropriate court for
corrective action.

The ICC's rules are brief in the extreme. It is just this brevity that has
triggered a number of criticisms of the rules. The traditional ICC rules contained no express provision for any kind of interim relief to be awarded by of
the arbitrator, such as conferring authority on the arbitrator to attach property to insure that the award will be honored. The parties are free, of course,
to request such pre-hearing attachment from a competent court, but such
petitions often prolong the arbitration process indefinitely.[48] Sensing this
weakness in its rules, the ICC has just recently instituted a "pre-arbitral referee procedure" that permits a neutral referee to: "order any conservatory
measures or any measures of restoration that are urgently necessary either
to prevent immediate damage or irreparable loss" and to take other interim
steps (for example, to preserve evidence) that may be necessary even before
the parties can launch a full-blown arbitration proceeding.[49]

Second, even though the ICC's fee schedule has recently been reduced
somewhat, the fees turn on the amount in controversy, not on the work
actually performed in the arbitration. However, the Court does have the
authority to reduce the arbitrator's fee and the administrative fee in exceptional circumstances.[50] In the absence of such circumstances, the fee schedule as of July 1, 1988 is:

Sum of dispute (in U.S. dollars)	Administrative expense	Arbitrator fee Min.	Max.
up to 50,000	$2,000	1,000	10%
50,001 – 100,000	3.0%	1.5%	6.0%
100,001 – 500,000	1.5%	.8%	3.0%
500,001 – 1,000,000	1.0%	.5%	2.0%
1,000,001 – 2,000,000	.5%	.3%	1.5%
2,000,001 – 5,000,000	.2%	.2%	.6%
5,000,001 – 10,000,000	.1%	.1%	.3%
10,000,001 – 50,000,000	.05%	.05%	.15%
50,000,001 – 100,000,000	$50,500	.02%	.10%
over 100,000,000	$50,500	.01%	.05%

---

46. Article 21.2
47. Id., Articles 18-24.
48. Id., Article 8(5).
49. Article 2.1, ICC Pre-ARBITRAL Referee Rules. See Paulsson, *A Better Mousetrap: 1990 ICC Rules for a Pre-arbitral Referee Procedure*, 18 Int'l Bus. Law. 214 (1990).
50. Id., Article 20(3).

When one considers that these figures do not include attorneys fees, ICC arbitration can be expensive indeed. Final costs for the arbitration including arbitrators fees and expenses, administrative expenses, expert fees and expenses and the parties' "normal legal costs" are fixed by the Court of Arbitration.[51]

§ 8.5.2 American Arbitration Association Procedures

Most attorneys in the United States who are familiar with arbitration are usually familiar with the AAA's commercial arbitration rules, a procedural setting that the AAA has adapted for international commercial arbitration by some supplemental rules designed to bring the arbitration procedures more in line with existing international practice and expectations. The AAA has also tailored special sets of rules for specific disputes involving patent and construction matters that are suitable for international disputes arising in those areas.

The AAA's rules are somewhat more detailed than those of the ICC and are closer in scope and concept to American litigation practice, although they are, of course, nowhere nearly as detailed and complex as U.S. litigation procedures. There is, for example, more of an adversary flavor to the rules and more emphasis on the arbitration hearing as the place in which things are resolved.

Under the AAA rules, an arbitration under the AAA's supervision is commenced by a party's filing notice of its intention to arbitration, usually referred to as a *demand*, accompanied by relevant papers, such as the underlying contract, with the AAA. The AAA then notifies the opposing party who has seven days to prepare and submit a response along with any counterclaim.[52] The parties may agree on an arbitrator or a panel of arbitrators; if the parties cannot agree the AAA will appoint the arbitrator or the panel.[53] The rules provide expressly that in international commercial arbitration, "the sole Arbitrator or the neutral Arbitrator [an arbitrator appointed by two arbitrators selected by each of the parties] shall, upon the request of either party, be appointed from among the nationals of a country other than that of any of the parties."[54]

Unlike the ICC's rules, the AAA provides for a pre-hearing conference at which the parties exchange information and resolve uncontested facts by stipulation. In addition, the arbitrator has the discretion to hold a preliminary hearing to organize the hearing process by identifying witnesses to be

---

51. Id., Article 20.

52. AAA Commercial Arbitration Rules, Rule 7, Articles 2 and 3, AAA Int'l Arb. Rules [hereafter IAR]. Just as this edition was going to press, the AAA modified its international rules. Those rules are set out in full text in Appendix D.

53. Id., Rules 12-14, IAR, Art. 6.

54. Id., Rule 16, IAR, Art. 6.

called, arranging for the exchange of documents and establishing the final hearing schedule.[55] To a large extent, these two conferences reflect American trial practice and as such largely substitute for the ICC's terms of reference—a procedure conducted almost entirely on paper.

In conducting the hearing, the arbitrator has a great deal of discretion in terms of hearing witnesses, ruling on issues of evidence, ordering the presentations and conducting site inspections and investigations. Again conforming somewhat to American practice, the AAA's rules tilt in favor of oral testimony and oral presentations. For example, affidavits may be submitted in lieu of oral testimony at the hearing, but the arbitrator need "give it only such weight as the Arbitrator deems it entitled to after consideration of any objections made to its admission."[56] Unlike the ICC's rules, the arbitrator is given express authority to sequester or conserve the property at issue in the dispute during the course of the arbitration "as may be deemed necessary to safeguard the property which is the subject matter of the arbitration without prejudice to the rights of the parties or to the final determination of the dispute."[57]

After the hearing is closed, the arbitrator has 30 days in which to frame and issue the award; but there is no review of any draft under AAA rules as there is under ICC rules. In some instances in purely domestic arbitration there is no obligation for an American arbitrator to produce an elaborate written award setting out the grounds and reasoning of the award. The typical domestic AAA award simply identifies the parties and the dispute and specifies the winning party and the amount of the award. Recognizing that this is usually not the case on the international level, the AAA's supplemental rules for international arbitrations provide: "Parties in international cases often expect arbitrators to provide a written opinion explaining the reasons for their award. The AAA will make arrangements for such an opinion in consultation with the parties and the arbitrators."[58]

There are at least two other distinguishing features for AAA arbitration. First, the rules contemplate an expedited process for controversies which do not involve a great deal of money. When a case in which the total claim of any party does not exceed $15,000 exclusive of interest and costs, the expedited rules apply. Those rules speed up the arbitration time frame and cut down on expenses in the following manner:

1. the various notices may be provided by telephone (although they are to be confirmed in writing);

---

55. Id., Rule 10.
56. Id., Rule 32.
57. Id., Rule 34, IAR, Art. 22.
58. IAR, Art. 28.

2. the parties are given a fixed list of five arbitrators from which the parties may strike two names on a peremptory basis; the list is returnable within 10 days to the AAA and the AAA retains the authority to make the appointment from the persons remaining on the list;

3. The time and place of the hearing is set on seven days notice with the expectation that the hearing will be conducted in one day or less;

4. The arbitrator is required to render the award within 5 business days of the close of the hearing.[59]

Second, the AAA's fee schedule is more modest than that of the ICC. As of May 1992, the AAA's fees are:

Amount of Claim	Administrative Fee
up to $25,000	$300
above $25,000 to $50,000	$500
above $50,000 to $250,000	$1,000
above $250,000 to $500,000	$2,000
above $500,000 to $5 million	$3,000
above $5 million	$4,000

When the claim exceeds $5 million the AAA charges no additional administrative fee. These administrative fees do not, of course, include the arbitrator's fee; but those fees are generally set on a per diem basis (on small domestic arbitrations, a typical fee may be $200 per day), not on the basis of the amount in controversy.

§ 8.5.3 The UNCITRAL procedures

The most recent set of comprehensive, generally applicable rules for international commercial arbitration have been promulgated by UNCITRAL in an attempt to develop some uniformity among arbitral bodies around the world. Many national and international arbitral bodies, including the AAA and the ICC, will supervise arbitrations conducted under the UNCITRAL rules. The United States - Iranian Claims Tribunal at the Hague adopted the UNCITRAL rules with only a few minor modifications.[60] The former Soviet Union was generally agreeable to the use of UNCITRAL procedures in commercial arbitration with Western firms in Stockholm; it may be expected that most if not all of the republics of the Commonwealth of Independent States will be similarly agreeable.[61]

---

59. AAA Commercial Arbitration Rules, Rules 54-58.

60. See, e.g., Selby & Stewart, *Practical Aspects of Arbitrating Claims Before the Iran-United States Claims Tribunal*, 18 Int'l Law. 211 (1984).

61. See, e.g., T. HOYA, EAST WEST TRADE: COMECON LAW, AMERICAN SOVIET TRADE 326 (1984).

The UNCITRAL rules are expressly designed to work among business from all over the world and to help alleviate the inevitable differences of culture, language and legal systems that frequently impede dispute resolution. In the words of Pieter Sanders, who had a large hand in drafting them, "[The rules] offer a well balanced and modern set of arbitration rules, prepared with the assistance of arbitration experts from all parts of the world. They may also be particularly welcomed by developing countries, who were vigorously represented in [their] drafting and ...preparation ...."[62] One international body, the Inter-American Commercial Arbitration Commission, headquartered in Rio de Janiero, Brazil has adopted the UNCITRAL rules as the Commission's rules virtually without change.[63] Adopted in 1976, the rules are frequently used in ad hoc arbitration, as well as institutional arbitration.

Briefly summarized, the UNCITRAL rules require a party commencing arbitration, the *claimant*, to provide the opposing party, the *respondent*, with a notice of arbitration.[64] Arbitrators may be appointed by the parties, but if there is no agreement, the supervising institution (if there is one) may make the appointment. Illustrating the UNCITRAL rules' adaptability, if there is no supervising institution, the parties are permitted to apply to the Secretary-General of the Permanent Court of Arbitration at the Hague to designate the appointing authority.[65] The rules contain extensive provisions on the challenge of arbitrators by one or both of the parties.[66]

While the arbitration may include an oral hearing at the request of the parties or the discretion of the arbitrator, it is obvious that a great deal of the dispute is to be handled on the basis of the paper record. In a direct parallel to the ICC's terms of reference, the claimant (and the respondent if any counterclaim is filed) is expected to state the claim, the points at issue, and the relief sought in writing. That writing is submitted to the respondent and to the arbitrators. The respondent is then, within a period of time specified by the arbitrators but generally not to exceed 45 days, to submit a statement of defenses to the claim.[67] The rules authorize the arbitrator to take interim measures "including measures for the conservation of the goods forming the subject-matter in dispute, such as ordering their deposit with a third person or the sale of perishable goods."[68]

A written award is required and the arbitrators are permitted to sit as amiable compositeurs or in ex aequo et bono only if the contract—or subse-

---

62. Sanders, *Procedures and Practices Under the UNCITRAL Rules*, 27 Am.J.Comp.L. 453 (1979).

63. Rules of Procedure of the Inter-American Commercial Arbitration Commission.

64. UNCITRAL Arbitration Rules, Article 3.

65. Id., Articles 6-8.

66. Id., Articles 9-12.

67. Id., Articles 18 & 23.

68. Id., Article 26.

quent party agreement—expressly authorizes them to do so.[69] Because the UNCITRAL rules were developed outside the context of a specific supervising institution, they are vague on fees. Costs comprise only the fees of the arbitrators, including their travel and living expenses, the costs associated with expert advice provided the arbitrators and witness costs, "the costs for legal representation and assistance of the successful party if such costs were claimed during the arbitral proceeding and only to the extent that the arbitral tribunal determines that the amount of such costs is reasonable" and any fees and expenses incurred by the appointing authority.[70] The rules contemplate that the costs of the arbitration be borne by the losing party unless the arbitrator decides to apportion all or part of the costs.[71] The arbitrator may require the parties to make a deposit against costs either before or during the arbitration.[72]

However, since there is no continuing supervising body, costs are merely to be "reasonable" and are not set expressly with reference to a fixed schedule unless a selected supervising authority has a schedule of fees. In other words, the arbitration will merely incorporate a fee schedule of, say, the ICC or the AAA, depending on which institution is the appointing authority.

Do the UNCITRAL rules work? The short answer appears to be yes. They have been accepted by virtually all the major international arbitration bodies and by a large number of developing countries. They appear to have been a large factor in keeping the U.S. - Iranian Claims Tribunal functioning smoothly over the past several years. Granted that the rules make no major breakthroughs—they are very similar in language, content and thrust to the AAA's rules—they are one of the most recent attempts to develop workable yet flexible rules of procedure, and for that reason alone they deserve considerable attention.

§ 8.6 Commencing the Arbitration

The preceding sections have provided an overview of the arbitration process and the major rules systems. But how does arbitration work in practice? For this kind of insight it makes sense to step away from most of the international literature, much of which tends to be more theoretical than practical[73] and to examine some of the advice provided by lawyers whose primary experience is domestic commercial arbitration.[74] The insights provided by some of these

---

69. Id., Articles 31-33.
70. Id., Article 38.
71. Id., Article 40(1).
72. Id., Article 41.
73. This statement should specifically *exclude* the Craig, Park, Paulsson book on ICC arbitration, *supra* note 37, which is filled with helpful, practical hints.
74. Martin Domke's classic, Commercial Arbitration, now edited by Professor Gerard Wilner remains the standard. One of the best small books, is G. GOLDBERG, A LAWYER'S GUIDE TO

experts will prove highly useful in any arbitration setting. The following sub-sections are essentially a distillation of the comments of a large number of writers.

Most arbitrations involve only two parties: the party that makes a claim and the party that responds to the claim. The reason for this is that traditionally most international commercial arbitrations grew out of bilateral contracts. Modern arbitration, especially in matters such as construction project and joint venture disputes, can become much more complex and may require even more creativity on the part of the lawyers and business executives who seek to resolve their grievances through arbitration.[75] Multi-party disputes are the Achilles Heel of dispute resolution devices such as arbitration. It is extremely difficult in normal circumstances to arbitrate between more than two parties and to entertain a multiplicity of claims. None of the arbitration systems have developed and articulated comprehensive rules for multi-party, multi-claim disputes as have most of the truly sophisticated court systems in the major trading nations.[76]

Understanding arbitration is the sort of analysis that may be further clarified by frequent reference to a hypothetical fact pattern that weaves through the discussion in the remainder of this chapter. Consider a purchase and sale transaction between a manufacturer-seller in Los Angeles, California, Tangerine Corporation, and a purchaser, Parthenon Ltd. in Athens, Greece. The contract is for 100 computers to be shipped in five installments of 20 computers each and contains all the common elements including a choice of language clause (English), a choice of law clause (the Uniform Commercial Code of the State of New York), and a conventional arbitration clause that requires the arbitration of any dispute arising under the contract to be conducted in New York City under AAA supervision using only one ("sole") arbitrator and applying the UNCITRAL arbitration rules.

Further assume that Parthenon received four of the five shipments of computers all of which were fully satisfactory. The last shipment arrived two months ago but consisted of computers that did not meet the contract specifications. The Greek buyer intends to use these computers for highly detailed accounting matters and business projections and thus the speed with which the computer processes the data is extremely important. The final shipment consisted of computers that contained a slower mechanism ("chip") than the

---

(Note 74 continued) COMMERCIAL ARBITRATION (2d ed. 1983). Also useful are: R. RODMAN, COMMERCIAL ARBITRATION WITH FORMS (1984) and C. PETERSON AND C. McCARTHY, ARBITRATION STRATEGY AND TECHNIQUE (1986).

75. For some advice on managing complex commercial disputes see *Handling the Complex Commercial Case*, 46 Arb. J. 6 (1991).

76. See, e.g., Wetter, A Multi-Party Arbitration Scheme for International Joint Ventures, 3 Arb. Int'l 2 (1987). For a discussion of the U.S. courts' views on consolidating a number of disputes into a single arbitration, see MacKellar, *To Consolidate or Not to Consolidate: A Study of Federal Court Decisions*, 44 Arb. J. 15 (Dec. 1989).

computers in the first four shipments. The defective computers are currently in a warehouse in Athens where the storage charges are $150 per day (the computers have to be kept in a temperature controlled building that also has with good security because of their value). Parthenon's staff productivity is not what it should be because the company does not have all the fast computers it needs.

Parthenon executives have corresponded with Tangerine officers, notifying them of the defect and requesting that Tangerine cure the defects or refund 20 percent of the contract price, that is, $125,000. Tangerine has not responded to any of these letters; and accordingly, Parthenon's attorney recommends that the company trigger the arbitration clause in the contract by filing a request for arbitration. The threshold question to be addressed is whether the issues presented by this dispute are arbitrable. These days, at least in the United States, the answer to that question will almost always be "yes."

§ 8.6.1 Determining the issues to be arbitrated

Since the recent U.S. Supreme Court decision in *Mitsubishi v Soler*,[77] there was some question as to whether certain issues such as violations of securities laws or antitrust complaints were subject to arbitration or whether those issues could only be resolved by a court. In *Mitsubishi* the Supreme Court wrote an exceptionally broad decision holding that even a general arbitration clause encompasses, and thus makes arbitrable, virtually all issues that might spring up under an international commercial agreement. There are precious few exceptions. For example, a party claiming that he was fraudulently induced into entering into a contract that contained an arbitration clause will probably not be permitted to take that issue directly to court. In *Prima Paint Corp. v Flood & Conklin Manufacturing Co.*,[78] the United States Supreme Court determined that such claims would be subject to arbitration unless the claim of fraud went directly to the arbitration clause itself. In other words, a party would have to arbitrate even a claim of fraud in the inducement unless he could show a court that he was specifically induced to agree to arbitration.

Thus, the lawyers' traditional dilemma—which issues are arbitrable and which are not—seems to be no longer a major question in the United States. Most of the major trading nations now also approach this question in similar fashion. As a consequence, the question faced by a party trying to decide on how to structure an arbitration is which issues to press before the arbitrator. Here, an attorney will proceed in the same fashion as he or she

---

77. 473 U.S. 614 (1985).
78. 388 U.S. 395 (1967).

would get ready for court. Obviously, both the facts and the law need to be researched to determine what is truly at issue in the case. The arbitration clause—as noted so often in the preceding chapters—is crucial to this investigation. Properly drafted, it will provide the answers to a number of questions including:

1. The law applicable to the arbitration
2. The site of the arbitration
3. The procedural rules applicable to the arbitration.

In the *Parthenon vs. Tangerine* controversy, there is nothing that suggests there was fraud in the inducement to agree to the arbitration clause, so it is beyond dispute that the issues presented in this case will be subject to arbitration. Moreover, the contract resolves forum selection, choice of law, the applicable system of procedure and gives supervisory authority to the AAA. Parthenon attorneys investigate further and, in consultation with their experts, determine that there was, in their experts' view, a breach of the contract specifications concerning the computers' processing speed.

§ 8.6.2 Drafting the demand for arbitration

Once this preliminary analysis is complete, the complaining party will prepare the demand for arbitration. This can be a crucial document and must be drafted with extraordinary care since amendments to this demand are permitted only in the discretion of the arbitrator. Attorneys used to the virtually unfettered possibilities of amending pleadings under the United States' Federal Rules of Civil Procedure need to understand that a demand for arbitration normally requires more precision. Moreover, arbitrators are not nearly as lenient in permitting changes as are U.S. federal judges.

The specific contents of the demand for arbitration are fixed by the applicable rules. For example, under the UNCITRAL rules the request for arbitration includes, at a minimum:

1. The names and addresses of the parties;
2. The demand for arbitration;
3. A reference to either the arbitration clause or any separate agreement between the parties requiring that disputes be submitted to arbitration;
4. A reference to the contract in question;
5. The general nature of the claim, including an indication of the amount of money involved;
6. The relief or remedy sought;
7. A proposal as to the number of arbitrators if the number is not contained in the arbitration clause.

Lawyers who do not want to create a document from scratch may choose to use some of the standard forms available. For example the AAA has a demand form that might be used, although the use of a pre-printed form is not necessary under UNCITRAL rules. Counsel for Parthenon may simply send a letter to Tangerine through AAA. Recall that the supervising institution normally serves as a collection point and clearing house for all documents exchanged between the parties. The use of an institution to forward documents used to be a singular disadvantage of institutional as opposed to ad hoc arbitration; but easily accessible air courier services and facsimile machines have reduced what used to be nearly intolerable delays. Moreover, there is an advantage to clearing the documents through the institution. Their expertise may help avoid a lot of beginner's mistakes for parties who are new to the arbitration process. It might be helpful, of course, to secure an agreement between the parties either in the contract or in the initial stages of the arbitration that all documents shall be sent air courier.

A common question is the amount of detail to be put into the original demand. George Goldberg suggests that the claimant simply make out a prima facie case in the demand (showing only that a contract exists, that defective goods were shipped and some kind of request for a remedy); and "[t]o the extent the claimant can avoid discussion of quality claims, laboratory tests, and the like, so much the better."[79] Other authorities on arbitration suggest that the demand be fairly detailed—at least in terms of the issues—to make sure that the claimant does not have to file an extensive amendment of claim later on, because amended arbitration claims may be denied by an arbitrator more readily than a U.S. federal judge might be able to deny permission to amend a court pleading. In court, a judge must permit amendments freely and in the interests of justice[80] while an arbitrator under the UNCITRAL rules and in most other systems, may deny amendments in his discretion if "the arbitral tribunal considers it inappropriate to allow such amendment having regard to the delay in making it or prejudice to the other party or any other circumstances."[81] The UNCITRAL arbitration rules recognize some of the difficulties a claimant faces at this point and permit the claimant to file a skeletal demand for arbitration, so long as a more comprehensive "statement of the claim" is filed prior to the hearing. Under ICC rules, the terms of reference are more important as an outline of the arbitration than is the arbitration demand; but even parties employing ICC rules should not take the drafting of the demand lightly.

Once the demand is drafted and served on the responding party, the respondent may reply with an answer and a counterclaim, or in certain sys-

---

79. Goldberg, supra note 74 at 31.
80. Federal Rule of Civil Procedure 15(a).
81. UNCITRAL Arbitration Rules, article 20.

tems may remain silent, simply waiting to see what the complaining party can prove at the arbitration hearing. Under the UNCITRAL rules, the respondent is required to file a "statement of defense" after the claimant files the statement of claim. In certain cases, if the responding party believes that the issues are not properly subject to arbitration, he or she may ignore all of these matters and simply wait for the complaining party to move into court for an order compelling arbitration or, in the alternative, might move into court for a declaration that the subject matter is not legally fit for arbitration.

As noted above, there is very little hope these days—at least in the context of international commercial agreements—that the court will agree to hear the case in lieu of the arbitration. But it is a tactic, nonetheless, that might buy a little time—understanding, of course, that interposing such a defense *solely* for the purposes of delay might create ethical problems for the attorney, both in the United States and abroad. The response is generally more detailed than the original demand, although it can be a simple categorical denial of all the assertions made by the claimant—a signal that the respondent is simply willing to wait and see what develops at the hearing. Once these preliminary papers have been exchanged, the next order of business is selection of the arbitrator, one of the most important stages in the entire process.

§ 8.6.3 Selecting the arbitrator

Once again, a wisely drafted arbitration clause may take care of much of this problem. An arbitration clause may specify, for example, the number of arbitrators and the arbitrator's credentials. At the same time, it is extremely rare for a contract's arbitration clause to specify an arbitrator by name, so the parties need to identify a specific individual who will serve as the arbitrator. There are two common models for arbitrator selection. If the contract calls for a sole arbitrator, the parties may simply agree on the arbitrator. Some contracts provide for a detailed selection process. For example, the party seeking arbitration could be required to produce a list of five acceptable arbitrators; and the responding party would be permitted to strike four of the names. When an arbitration panel is required under the contract, the parties typically appoint their own arbitrator (referred to as *party appointed* arbitrators) who then appoint a third, neutral panel member who usually presides at the hearing. On occasion, the parties will not be able to reach an agreement as to the arbitrator. Under all of the major arbitration rules systems, an appointing authority will simply choose an arbitrator if the parties are unable to agree. In ad hoc arbitration conducted under an arbitration statute, the parties may apply to the court to appoint the arbitrator if they themselves cannot agree.

Selection of the arbitrator is an important step, perhaps the most important in the entire process. The major factors to look for in selecting an arbitrator are: (1) experience in and knowledge of both the subject matter of the contract and the arbitral process itself; (2) an ability to converse and read and write in the language of the arbitration, unless the parties are agreeable to providing on-site translation services, (3) availability over the time chosen by the parties for the arbitration, and (4) for so-called *neutral* arbitrators, lack of personal connection with either of the parties.

This last point gets to the issue of bias and is sometimes difficult to penetrate. Obviously, it would be a fine thing to find an experienced arbitrator skilled in the subject matter of the dispute who had never had any contact, however slight, with any of the parties. However, this is not always possible. Arbitrators tend to specialize in a particular subject matter. Companies who arbitrate frequently may see the same arbitrator more than once. There are procedures in all the major rules systems for moving to disqualify an arbitrator but such disqualification is always easier said than done. For example, merely knowing one or another of the parties is not sufficient. Having a social relationship with one of the parties is probably not enough. The AAA has promulgated a Code of Ethics for Commercial Arbitrators which requires an arbitrator to "disclose any interest or relationship likely to affect impartiality or which might create an appearance of partiality or bias" but normally this disclosure requirement is limited to:

1. any direct or indirect financial or personal interest in the outcome of the arbitration; or

2. any existing or past financial, business, professional, family or social relationships which would affect impartiality or create an appearance of partiality or bias.[82]

The International Bar Association has promulgated a parallel set of ethical rules for international arbitrators that also deserves attention.[83] Under the IBA rules, the arbitrator has similar disclosure obligations even if he or she is party-appointed (this is in contrast to the AAA's relatively relaxed approach to party-appointed arbitrators). The IBA's rules also strictly limit unilateral contacts between the arbitrators and the parties and prohibit unilateral agreements on fees or expenses between one of the parties and the arbitrators.

Irrespective of which set of rules one refers to, most of the ethical constructs involve concededly ambiguous language. No one ever knows with certainty what circumstances will require disqualification. Pecuniary bias, a sit-

---

82. AAA, Code of Ethics for Arbitrators in Commercial Disputes, Canon II.
83. See, e.g., *Rules of Ethics for International Arbitrators*, 15 Int'l Bus. Law. 336 (Sep. 1987). Branson, *Commentary on Ethics for International Arbitrators*, 3 Arb. Int'l 72 (1987).

uation in which the arbitrator has a financial stake in the outcome of the case (as, for example, owning shares in one of the companies) is surely a disqualifying factor. Seeing a party's chief executive officer at a party is probably not sufficient to disqualify; but a long-standing personal relationship even if it is only a relationship founded in friendship may be sufficient to disqualify. Arbitration systems tend to require arbitrators to make the fullest disclosure and then to permit the parties to challenge the arbitrator if grounds for disqualification exist.[84] For lawyers involved in arbitration, perhaps the best advice is to investigate an arbitrator as thoroughly as possible, make the objection as early as possible and be sure of the grounds offered for disqualification. Probably no tactic can more quickly rebound against a party and with such devastating results as a request for disqualification that fails.

§ 8.7 Preparing for and Conducting the Hearing

Most practitioners approach an arbitration in the same way that they approach litigation. Experienced lawyers gather all the facts available, thoroughly analyze the underlying contractual documents and the various legal issues presented by the controversy, interview and prepare both lay witnesses and expert witnesses and, in general, try to insure that there are no surprises when everyone gets into the hearing. In the case of *Parthenon v. Tangerine*, counsel for each party would analyze the contract, discuss the controversy thoroughly with the client, identify and consult with experts (who may also give testimony at the hearing) and probably inspect all the goods or at least one of the defective computers.

All of this is frequently easier said than done. As this chapter has continually reiterated, arbitration is different from litigation, particularly litigation as it is practiced in the United States. There are few devices available by which an attorney may compel production of evidence; there is usually only a limited subpoena power (calling for witnesses or the production of documents at the hearing) available to parties in arbitration. There are usually few or no meetings between the parties and the arbitrator prior to the arbitration hearing itself. Finally, the hearing, because it depends so much on the discretion of the arbitrator, is not always the predictable carefully staged event that litigation often is.

But no lawyer can use any of this as an excuse for being casual about arbitration. As has been discussed and as will be seen with even greater clarity in Chapter 9, the decision of an arbitrator—i.e., the outcome of an arbitration hearing—is normally final. Thus, a client's interests are usually con-

---

84. Id.

clusively determined in the arbitration just as they would be in court. Too many lawyers seem to take arbitration less seriously than they do litigation— a tragic mistake in many instances. This section discusses some of the ways that a lawyer can turn the pre-hearing stage to his or her advantage even if all the tools available to a litigator are not present.

§ 8.7.1 Discovery

Perhaps the best place to begin an analysis of the discovery issue is to restate the normal rule—there is usually no discovery in arbitration cases. There are two primary reasons for this. First, arbitration is intended to be less formal and time consuming than litigation. Indeed, one reason why lawyers outside the United States tend to be somewhat skittish about U.S.-based arbitration is because they fear becoming entangled in endless pre-trial discovery. Massive, interminable discovery is not the rule even in American arbitration, but it is sometimes difficult to convince others of that fact. Second, one of the premises of arbitration is that most if not all of the dispute will be predicated on matters either already committed to paper or readily reduced to documentary form, and that most of the documents will be exchanged by the parties in the ordinary course. The contract is normally on paper. The demand for arbitration and the response to the demand along with any counterclaims will similarly be on paper, accompanied by other documents of relevance to the controversy. Thus, extensive pre-hearing discovery in the form of, for example, depositions (in which a witness orally answers questions put to him by the opposing counsel) are rarely necessary.

There are other ways to work around the absence of elaborate discovery rules. Discovery may be handled informally by agreement among the parties using, if necessary, the leverage that an arbitrator has to grant postponements and to admit or exclude evidence. For totally recalcitrant parties, many arbitration statutes, including for example, the United States' Federal Arbitration Act, permit the arbitrator to issue subpoenas for witnesses who are to give oral testimony (traditionally referred to as a *subpoena ad testificandum*) or for witnesses who are expected to bring documents (*subpoena duces tecum*). However, under normal circumstances, the subpoena may compel only attendance at the hearing or documents to be produced at the hearing. If the subpoenaed party refuses to comply, the arbitrator may resort to the domestic court system in which the hearing is taking place country for sanctions against the uncooperative party so long as that country's arbitration act recognizes and enforces subpoenas.[85]

---

85. See, e.g., U.S. Arbitration Act § 7. For more extensive commentary on discovery in U.S. arbitration, see Tupman, *Discovery and Evidence in U.S. Arbitration: The Prevailing Views*, 44 Arb.J. 27 (Mar.1989). For some commentary on discovery in an English and continental context see Morgan, *Discovery in Arbitration*, 3 J.Int'l Arb. 9 (1986).

In many instances, likely including the Parthenon/Tangerine case, extensive discovery is probably not needed. The basic document, the contract, is in the hands of both parties and will be appended to the statement of the claim. Documents supporting the location and storage fees for the defective computers will be submitted by the claimant. It is possible, of course, that an expert witness will have examined the computers, run tests on the computers and reduced his findings to paper, and then not be called for hearing, thus suggesting that the other party could request the arbitrator to issue a subpoena duces tecum. But there is probably no need for such action. The dispute is not that complicated and the amount in controversy is probably not sufficient to justify massive efforts to secure pre-hearing information.

§ 8.7.2 The pre-hearing conference

Although many systems of arbitration procedure do not allow for either pre-hearing conferences or preliminary hearings, in virtually every system, the arbitrator probably has the inherent discretion to order some kind of pre-hearing procedure by which the issues are narrowed, stipulations are proffered and accepted, and the hearing process clarified. Granting that international commercial arbitrations that occur over long distances may find such a procedure inefficient and counter-productive, many of these things can be taken care of through correspondence and modern telecommunications. However, there may be instances, particularly in the case of complex arbitration when there is a real need for a "hearing before the hearing" to expedite matters.

Consider how beneficial a pre-hearing conference might be even in the relatively small Parthenon/Tangerine dispute. The hearing is to take place in New York City. The defective computers are in a warehouse in Athens. Assume that the final shipment consists of 30 individual computers. It is arguable that the claimant would have to present each of the 30 computers for the inspection of Tangerine's experts and for the arbitrator. A pre-hearing conference could result in a stipulation by both parties that all 30 computers are identical, irrespective of whether they are truly defective, and a single computer could be shipped from Athens to New York for inspection during hearing as representative of all the others in that Athens warehouse. Or, even better, the parties might be able to agree to present for inspection a prototype computer from Tangerine's U.S. factory as representative of that final shipment now residing in Athens. All in all a significant saving of time and money and one of the major contributions that a pre-hearing conference can make. Again, there are a number of creative ways to deal with some of the inherent procedural limitations in arbitration.

§ 8.7.3 The hearing

The comparative absence of an elaborate scheme of pre-hearing devices makes the arbitration hearing all the more important to the parties. It is the central device for making each party's presentation, for the direct and cross-examination of witnesses and the production and examination of documents. It is frequently one of the first points of face-to-face contact between the parties and the arbitrators. It is at the hearing that the arbitrator becomes completely familiar with the evidence.

a. Order of presentation.

The arbitrator has virtually unfettered discretion to conduct the hearing. To that extent, a hearing may be highly structured or thoroughly relaxed depending on the personal preferences of the arbitrator. European hearings tend to be very relaxed, reflecting the differences in lawyer behavior and litigation style in those countries. In most instances in the United States, however, arbitration hearings tend to be highly adversarial and contentious. There is a relatively fixed order of presentation similar to the order of presentation in courts in the United States:

1. Opening statement by the claimant (the party who demanded arbitration (opening statement by respondent at this point is usually optional

2. Presentation of claimant's case and cross-examination of claimant's witnesses by respondent

3. Opening statement (if reserved) by respondent

4. Presentation of respondent's case

5. Rebuttal evidence and witnesses by claimant

6. Closing arguments

Documents are typically introduced and marked as exhibits. However, under most arbitration systems, testimony is not under oath and a verbatim transcript of the proceeding is taken only if one of the parties requests and is willing to pay for a stenographer.[86]

Most of the remainder of the proceeding is subject to the wishes of the arbitrator. A litigation format is frequently used because this type of presentation makes for a relatively orderly and rational hearing; but arbitrators always have the discretion to depart from any fixed format. Because one of the hallmarks of arbitration is its confidential nature, the arbitration hearing usually takes place behind closed doors with the parties, their representatives and

---

86. See, e.g., AAA rule 23: "Any party wishing a stenographic record shall make such arrangements directly with the stenographer and shall notify the other parties in advance of the hearing. The requesting party or parties shall pay the cost of such record."

the arbitrator the only people in continuous attendance during the hearing.[87]

b. *Rules of evidence*

One of the singular characteristics of arbitration is that there are no formal rules of evidence. But what this statement really means is that there are no *elaborate* rules of evidence applicable by rule in commercial arbitrations. This does not mean that there are no boundaries placed on evidentiary matters, however. The UNCITRAL rules, for example, provide that "Each party shall have the burden of proving the facts relied on to support his claim or defense."[88] The AAA rules are a little more explicit: "The parties may offer such evidence as is pertinent and material to the controversy ...The Arbitrator shall be the judge of the relevancy and materiality of the evidence offered."[89] So there are some limits: The evidence must be relevant and the parties share the burden of proof.

Other dimensions to rules of evidence sometimes escape persons new to the arbitration process. Consider that many rules of evidence have a logical, rational basis. In this regard three concepts of evidence need not be codified to be applied in arbitrations. First, the concept of relevance is, as Justice Oliver Wendell Holmes was frequently heard to say, "a concession to the shortness of life." Arbitration hearings should not be dragged out because one of the parties insists on presenting evidence on things that have nothing to do with the controversy at hand. In any arbitral system, the arbitrator must always have the discretion to halt presentations on irrelevant matters even if the rules systems does not contain a formal rule of relevance. Second, the evidentiary doctrine of competence is intended to insure that witnesses testify only as to matters on which they have some knowledge. If a witness in the Parthenon/Tangerine arbitration who has never even seen a computer attempts to give testimony on computer processing speed, he should not be listened to. As a corollary to this, the counsel putting that witness on the stand should have an obligation to show the witness's competence, before the witness begins his testimony on the specific issue of the Tangerine computers' speed.

Third, the notion of *foundation* has some applicability to arbitration hearings. Not only must a competent witness give relevant testimony, but also there should be some demonstration that the witness knows what he is talking about. A witness who is otherwise a qualified computer expert but who has never seen and tested the Tangerine computers that are the subject of this dispute should probably not be permitted to give testimony as to their

---

87. See, e.g., UNCITRAL Rules, article 25(4): "Hearings shall be held in camera unless the parties agree otherwise."

88. UNCITRAL Rules of Arbitration, Article 24.

89. AAA Commercial Arbitration Rules, Rule 31.

processing speed. Again, the party introducing this witness should be required to develop the basis for the expert's testimony; and it that party does not, the testimony may be properly excluded.

In many instances, the arbitrator is a lawyer and the parties' representatives are lawyers. Sometimes, all concerned are products of the same legal system. Recall that in arbitration no formal rules of evidence are mandated. But that does not mean that evidence cannot be objected to or that the arbitrator cannot rule on these objections. Sometimes too much is made of the fact that the rules do not provide for the application of principles of evidence. The better practice in an arbitration hearing is that if a party has an objection on any ground, however formal, he should make it and simply see what the arbitrator says.

Of course, some caution is required. Arbitrators do not consider themselves judges and tend to become uncomfortable in the presence of counsel who constantly object on the most tenuous of grounds. Moreover, the arbitrator is both an expert and the person who will make the decision. There is no special reason for an attorney to "put on a show" to impress a jury of lay persons. One of the theories of arbitration is that the arbitrator should receive as much information as possible and, because he is something of an expert, should use his own discretion in sorting it out. In addition, although there appear to be no reported cases on this point, it is arguable that an arbitrator who insists on applying strict rules of evidence when the parties have not previously agreed to their use may be guilty of misconduct and his award overturned on that ground.

§ 8.8 Drafting the Arbitral Award

The status and prerogatives of the arbitrator have been established by the preceding sections. The arbitrator is thoroughly in control of the process, and his basic task through the conclusion of the hearing is to see that the parties are dealt with fairly and evenhandedly and that enough information is gathered so that he can render a proper award. As the UNCITRAL rules put it: an arbitral panel "may conduct the arbitration in such manner as it considers appropriate, provided that the parties are treated with equality and that at any stage of the proceedings each party is given a full opportunity of presenting his case."[90] At the conclusion of the hearing, the arbitrator closes the record and proceeds to draft the award. The closing of the hearing is a formal event that no lawyer should disregard. It means that no further testimony will be permitted and no additional documents or argumentation introduced. If an attorney representing a party has some additional matters to be addressed, she should not permit the arbitrator to close the proceeding.

---

90. UNCITRAL Rules, article 15.

If the arbitration is heard by a sole arbitrator, that person fashions the award. When the arbitration is presided over by a panel of three arbitrators, the various rules systems generally provide that the decision will be made by a majority of the arbitrators.[91]

The actual writing of the award is sometimes a difficult task; but here again, there are rarely any formal requirements; and in some systems an arbitral award simply states which party won—that is, there is no need for the arbitrator even to state reasons for her decision. However, in international commercial practice, it is customary for the arbitrator to give reasons for the decisions unless the parties specifically agree not to request reasons; and many arbitral awards wind up looking much the same as decisions rendered by a court, complete with citations to statutes and cases, elaborate recapitulations of the facts and nearly endless explanations of the arbitrator's findings and conclusions.

A few of the rules systems provide some guidance for the arbitrator. For example, the UNCITRAL rules require the arbitrator to decide the case on the basis of the law chosen by the parties or in the absence of a choice of law to "apply the law determined by the conflict of laws rules which it considers applicable."[92] If the parties have expressly authorized the arbitrator to do so, he may apply concepts of fairness and equity (*amiable compositeur/ex aequo et bono*) to the case, in addition to the law specifically applicable, giving the arbitrator some discretion to depart from rules of law that might otherwise produce an unusually harsh result. But, as the UNCITRAL rules provide, "[i]n all cases, the arbitral tribunal shall decide in accordance with the terms of the contract and shall take into account the usages of the trade applicable to the transaction."[93]

Beyond stating some obvious points, it is very difficult to describe narratively an arbitral award. One U.S. expert on arbitration, the President of the AAA, Robert Coulson, suggests that this is a profound gap in the scholarship of arbitration. Mr. Coulson urges, among other things, that parties and arbitrators look to certain axioms of psychology and human behavior to get at the process of framing an arbitral award. One of his suggestions is that "[a]n arbitrator will tend to recall evidence that has not become stale [the concept of heuristic memory]. Advocates who request additional time to file [post-hearing] briefs may be losing the advantage of this fundamental heuristic tendency."[94]

But even suggestions such as this are essentially generalizations that no writer on the topic of arbitration should be allowed to get away with. Although there is virtually nothing in the literature on the process of decid-

---

91. Id., article 31.
92. Id., article 33(1).
93. Id., article 33(3).
94. Coulson, *The Decisionmaking Process in Arbitration*, 45 Arb.J. 37 (Sep.1990).

ing an arbitration, there are ways to try to penetrate the mind of an arbitrator without lapsing into that age-old English language joke that "arbitrator" is very close to "arbitrary."

How might an arbitrator go about fashioning an award? This question needs to be put in a specific context such as the Parthenon/Tangerine dispute. Consider that the arbitrator has conducted the hearing, read the contract and all other relevant documents, listened to each sides' experts and made his own inspection of the prototype computer submitted by Tangerine. As he or she actually begins to put words on paper, the thought of avoiding jargon is particularly attractive. The best arbitral awards tend to be written in plain language.[95]

While arbitrators are never required to write formal judicial-style decisions in which they frame specific findings of fact and conclusions of law, it is very helpful for an arbitrator to consider these two concepts as he proceeds to decide the case. Findings of fact are simply the "who," "what," "where," "when" questions that must be determined in any instance of human conflict. For example, in the Parthenon/Tangerine case an arbitrator will want to know something about the nature of the two companies, possibly something about the manner in which Tangerine manufacturers the computers, the precise technical specifications of the computers at issue, and why the computers need to be kept in such an expensive storage facility? By contrast, conclusions of law spring from the specific legal principles that are to be applied to the dispute. In this instance, an arbitrator would review those portions of the New York Uniform Commercial Code that address contract specifications such as the UCC's provisions on warranties of fitness and merchantibility.

If the contract permits the arbitrator to decide the case applying amiable compositeur principles, he might consider where and under what circumstances he is willing to depart from the UCC's specific commands to do justice in this particular case. For example, the UCC has some very strict rules on disclaimer of warranties. The arbitrator could examine these rules and might conclude that a foreign buyer, even one who has agreed to a New York UCC choice of law provision, had only an incomplete understanding of these provisions. He could then decide, using his authority as amiable compositeur, either not to apply the disclaimer rules or to apply them much more gently than the UCC calls for.

The arbitrator's ultimate conclusion of law is, of course, his determination of who wins. There is no bright line between findings of fact and conclusions of law but it is a very healthy way for a judge or arbitrator to get started in writing the award. The following example puts much of this in a specific context.

---

95. Elliott, *Writing Arbitral Awards in Plain Language*, 46 Arb.J. 53 (Dec.1991).

Assume that in the Parthenon/Tangerine case the arbitrator reviews the record and ascertains that there is simply no dispute as to:

1. the computer speed specified in the contract

2. the computer speed of the conforming goods shipped in the first four installments

3. the storage charges in the Athens warehouse for the arguably non-conforming computers.

4. the applicability of the New York UCC.

This data can be immediately incorporated into his thinking (if not into the actual written award) without further consideration.

But the arbitrator must cope with many other things in the record. Assume that Tangerine introduced documentary evidence and testimony on a computer manufactured by a subsidiary company, Pepper Computers, that Tangerine counsel claimed was exactly like the Tangerine computers shipped to Parthenon. This evidence came onto the record because the arbitrator decided to be as lenient as possible in letting the parties make their presentations—and because Parthenon's counsel did not want to be seen to be constantly objecting to Tangerine's presentation, there was no objection from the opposing counsel. Irrespective of how this evidence came in, an arbitrator would likely be justified in disregarding all of this information because it appears clearly to be irrelevant. The issue is the performance specifications of the Tangerine computers, not the performance of some computers that seemed to be similar but that were not actually shipped to Parthenon.

On a more crucial point, the arbitrator heard from Tangerine's expert witness who testified that the computer speed conformed to or exceeded the specifications set out in the contract; and he also heard from Parthenon's expert who testified that the computer speed was substantially lower than the contract specified. This "battle of the experts" is a common phenomenon in commercial litigation and arbitration, and there are a number of ways for an arbitrator to resolve the matter. On the one hand, the arbitrator can simply make a finding of credibility. In other words, he may determine that Tangerine's expert is the more believable based on the expert's previous experience with similar computers, the scientific soundness of the tests that the expert made on the prototype computer, and even the expert's educational and professional background. On the other hand, if the arbitrator finds both witnesses equally credible and if his own expertise does not prompt him to tilt in one direction or another, he can dispose of the matter on the basis of *burden of proof*, another one of those concepts of evidence that may not be expressly stated in the rules but is applied nonetheless. On that basis, he could determine that the evidence is equally balanced and that the claimant (Parthenon, the firm that is claiming that the computers' performance is faulty) did not meet its burden of proof.

Assume that the arbitrator decides that the Parthenon expert is the person to believe. Given that virtually nothing else of importance—the contract language, the applicable law, and other matters—is truly in dispute, he would be justified in deciding in favor of Parthenon. However, an arbitral award is not complete merely because the arbitrator has decided who wins. He must take the additional step of fashioning a remedy. In the Parthenon/Tangerine case, if Parthenon prevails, he might simply award Parthenon normal breach of contract damages, including as is permissible under the UCC, additional incidental and consequential damages such as Parthenon's storage expenses. It is not impossible for an arbitrator to award specific performance. So the arbitrator could conceivably order Tangerine to provide Parthenon with computers which perform up to specifications and to take the defective computers back. In some jurisdictions, it may even be possible for an arbitrator to award punitive or exemplary damage in cases in which the respondent's actions are particularly abhorrent.[96]

Once the award is drafted and signed by the arbitrator, it is given to the parties and, if necessary, filed or registered with an appropriate governmental entity, although the terms of the award remain confidential unless the parties agree to the award being released to the public. Some rules systems permit the parties to review the award and to request elaboration or clarification by the arbitrator. The UNCITRAL rules permit a party to request both an *interpretation* of the award and a *correction* (of clerical errors in) the award.[97] Each of these requests is in the nature of a motion for reconsideration, rather than an appeal of the award.

While there is normally no appeal of an arbitral award within the system of arbitration itself (although the reader should recall that under the ICC's rules the ICC as supervising authority requires that the arbitrator give a draft to the ICC's Court of Arbitration for their review), a losing party does have the right to challenge the award in court by refusing to abide by the decision. The prevailing party then must bring some kind of court action either in the country of origin or some other country asking the courts of that country to recognize and confirm the award. That action (a topic addressed in chapter 9) results in the award's becoming the functional equivalent of a court decision that will be enforced on the same terms as a judgment of a court.   ◆

---

96. Compare the following two law review articles: Jones, *Punitive Damages as an Arbitration Remedy*, 4 J. Int'l Arb. 35 (1987); Note, *An Argument Against the Availability of Punitive Damages in Commercial Arbitration*, 62 St. John's L.Rev. 270 (1988).

97. UNCITRAL Arbitration Rules, articles 35, 36.

— 9 —
International Commercial Arbitration:
Arbitration in the Courts

§ 9.1 Introduction

I n theory, courts should have very little impact on arbitration because commercial arbitration is normally viewed as an alternative rather than a predecessor to litigation. International commercial arbitration in particular ought to be more or less immune from court interference because so many contracting parties choose arbitration to avoid the domestic courts of a particular country. However, in practice, the relationship is far more complex and tangled, and likely to remain so for the foreseeable future because arbitration systems are not self-effectuating and must rely heavily on an existing judicial system to implement many of actions taken during arbitration. In other words, if a party chooses not to participate in an arbitration or refuses to honor an arbitral award, the other side has no recourse but to go to court either to *compel* the other side to engage in arbitration or to restrain (*stay*) any judicial proceedings until the arbitration is completed, or, finally, to force the losing party to honor the award by recognizing and confirming the arbitral award.

These limitations, characteristic of all arbitration systems, are partly the reason for so much of the cynical commentary on arbitration. Because courts can sometimes get involved in the arbitration process, many people contend that arbitration is nothing more than a precursor of litigation, a trial run so to speak, that merely sets the stage for the proper and far more legitimate proceeding in court. Until recently, this cynicism was probably justified; but in recent years a number of countries including the United States and England have taken steps either through statutes or court decisions to severely restrict the opportunities for courts to interfere with arbitration. In the United States, the Supreme Court has played a major role in insulating the arbitration process from court interference. In a number of major decisions between 1972 and 1990, the Court not only shored up the doctrine of party autonomy and sanctity of contract (*pacta sunt servanda*) but also instructed federal courts to let arbitral awards alone unless the court had proper grounds for stepping into the controversy—and such grounds are now very few and far between.

To be more specific, in 1972 the Court decided *The Bremen v. Zapata Off-Shore Oil Company*,[1] a case involving an international contract for towing of oil rigs in which the contract specified that the dispute resolution forum should be the High Court of Justice in London, by compelling the parties to live up to that agreement, even though the parties might otherwise have been able to litigate in federal court in the United States. Among other things, the Court noted:

> "The choice of that forum [the forum selection clause in the contract] was made in an arms-length negotiation by experienced and sophisticated businessmen, and absent some compelling and countervailing reason it should be honored by the parties and enforced by the courts... . [Moreover, the contract was an] international commercial transaction ... [and] selection of a London forum was clearly a reasonable effort to bring vital certainty to this international transaction and to provide a neutral forum experienced and capable in the resolution of admiralty jurisdiction."[2]

The Bremen set the stage for everything that followed. In a 1974 case, *Scherk v. Alberto-Culver Co.*[3] the Court honored an general arbitration clause that provided for arbitration in Paris under the rules of the International Chamber of Commerce even though the disputes in question involved violations of United States securities laws. In *Scherk*, for possibly the first but certainly not the last time, the Court noted the existence of the New York Convention on the Recognition and Enforcement of Arbitral Awards (discussed extensively in § 9.4 below) and pointed out that the parties could always come into court under the New York Convention—but only after they completed the arbitration. Approximately ten years later, in quick succession, the Court decided two cases involving purely domestic arbitration which have had an important impact on the U.S.'s view of international commercial arbitration. In *Moses H. Cone Memorial Hospital v. Mercury Construction Co.*[4] the Court read the U.S. Arbitration Act to create a statutory

---

1. 407 U.S. 1 (1972).
2. Id. at 13.
3. 407 U.S. 506 (1974).
4. 460 U.S. 1 (1983).

presumption in favor of arbitration; and in *Dean Witter Reynolds Inc. v. Byrd*[5] the Court ordered the parties to engage in arbitration even when that process would resolve only a part of the dispute. The Court reasoned that concepts of judicial efficiency and economy must give way to the federal Arbitration Act.

Finally, in the crucial 1985 decision of *Mitsubishi v. Soler*,[6] the Court held that a general arbitration clause calling for arbitration in Tokyo under the rules of the Japan Chamber of Commerce included even claims arising under the U.S. antitrust laws—laws which have traditionally been resolved in U.S. federal court. The Court, coming full circle, reiterated much of its support for the integrity of international commercial arbitration expressed in *The Bremen*, pointing out that "where the international cast of a transaction would otherwise add an element of uncertainty to dispute resolution, the prospective litigant may provide in advance for a mutually agreeable procedure whereby he would seek his antitrust recovery as well as settle other controversies... [In addition,] there is no reason to assume at the outset of a dispute that international arbitration will not provide an adequate mechanism" even for the resolution of U.S. antitrust claims. The Court, as it did in *Scherk*, went on to note the existence of the New York Convention and the fact that the Convention contains a provision permitting a reviewing court to set aside an arbitral award on public policy grounds if it determines that the arbitral tribunal did serious violence to the substance of the antitrust statutes.

Mitsubishi is a watershed case for international commercial arbitration in the United States. It has resolved conclusively the scope of general arbitration clauses in international commercial agreements (the clause encompasses virtually all issues arising under the contract) and signaled, to both courts and lawyers, the Supreme Court's special sensitivity for the integrity of the international commercial arbitration process. Since its *Mitsubishi* decision, the Supreme Court has gone on to hold that even arbitration clauses in contracts that might be viewed as contracts of adhesion bind the parties to proceed by arbitration.[7] The message is now clear—at least in the United States: when parties sign contracts containing arbitration clauses they must arbitrate.

England has taken a slightly different road. There, the courts had been regarded as strongly interventionist (and even as being hostile to arbitration)

---

5. 470 U.S. 213 (1985).

6. 473 U.S. 614 (1985). Mitsubishi has been the subject of both praise and criticism: Compare Carbonneau, *Mitsubishi: The Folly of Quixotic Internationalism*, 2 Arb. Int'l 116 (1986) with Lowenfeld, *The Mitsubishi Case: Another View*, 2 Arb. Int'l 178 (1986). See also Fox, *Mitsubishi v. Soler and Its Impact on International Commercial Arbitration*, 19 J. World Trade L. 579 (1985).

7. Rodriguez de Quijas v. Shearson/American Express, 109 S. Ct. 1917 (1989).

due to two provisions in the 1950 Arbitration Act which were used by the English courts to review and occasionally overturn arbitral awards or to interfere with on-going arbitrations. The first of these, the special (or *stated*) case procedure, required the High Court of Justice to review issues of law growing out of controversies then in arbitration. This procedure had the effect of taking a whole panoply of issues out of the arbitrators hands. Because it is frequently not difficult to convert any issue into a question of law, the stated case procedure severely undercut the integrity and continuity of the English arbitration process.

The second bone of contention in the 1950 Arbitration Act was a provision permitting the courts to set aside arbitral awards for errors of fact or law apparent on the face of the arbitral award. This provision, operating in tandem with the stated case procedure, permitted courts to review virtually any issue arising out of an arbitration—thereby destroying any finality in the arbitration process. English lawyers came to understand that arbitration was often nothing more than a rehearsal for a proceeding in court.

In 1979, the British Parliament enacted the 1979 Arbitration Act in large part to eliminate these two provisions and, presumably, to make the English courts somewhat less interventionist. While there seems to be some controversy on this point, most of the commentary on the 1979 Act supports the proposition that Parliament took this legislative action to make London a more hospitable place for international commercial dispute resolution.[8]

France appears to have created exceptional insulation from court interference in international commercial arbitrations both by case law and by statute. Professor Arthur T. von Mehren believes that French case law squarely establishes the proposition that doctrines of law which the French courts might apply to domestic arbitrations "do not apply to arbitrations which involve the interests of international commerce. The jurisprudence further intimates that certain of the rules and principles governing the regime applicable to international commercial arbitrations need not flow from rules and principles found in a national law."[9]

In addition, there has been legislative action in France that buttresses the integrity of the international arbitration process. In 1981, the French promulgated Article 1496 of Title 6, Book 4 ("L'Arbitrage") which greatly enhances party autonomy in specifying principles of law to govern the dispute irrespective of whether those principles are the applicable law in the country of the award's origin. This appears to effectively insulate international arbitral awards from any reversals in French court on substantive legal grounds.[10]

---

8. See, e.g., Jarvin, *London as a Place for International Arbitration*, 1 J.Int'l Arb. 59 (1985).

9. von Mehren, *International Commercial Arbitration: The Contribution of the French Jurisprudence*, 46 La.L.Rev. 1045 (1986).

10. Id. at 1058, citing Bellet & Mezger, *L'arbitrage international dans le nouveau code de procedure civile*, 70 Revue Critique de Droit International Prive 611 (1981) and Fouchard, *L'arbitrage en France Apres le decret du 12 Mai 1981*, 109 J.de Droit International 394 (1982).

These three examples should provide some notion of the dimensions of the relationships between courts and arbitrators. The following sections take up some of the more specific issues involving judicial action. Each of the following sections also involves the basic process of litigation—i.e., irrespective of the label of the particular proceeding (action to stay, action to compel, action to enforce) the process a court proceeding and thus is to be disposed of under traditional concepts of subject matter jurisdiction, personal jurisdiction, service of process and venue. For these reasons, it is advisable to take a close look at all the preliminary concepts discussed in Chapter Seven before working through the remaining sections in this chapter.

§ 9.2 Actions to Compel or Stay Arbitration

There are essentially four instances in which a court can become enmeshed in commercial arbitration prior to the issuance of the arbitral award:

1. Party A begins a judicial proceeding against Party B; Party B believes that an arbitration clause in the underlying contract must be honored; Party B files a request (normally in the form of a motion) to *stay the litigation* pending the outcome of the arbitration.
2. Party A commences an arbitration; Party B believes that arbitration is impermissible; Party B files a court action to *stay the arbitration.*
3. Party A sends Party B a demand for arbitration; Party B simply ignores the demand; Party A then goes to court and files a motion to *compel* arbitration.
4. A party or a witness ignores an arbitrator's subpoena; the arbitrator goes to court to *enforce* the subpoena.

Scenario number 4 was discussed in Chapter Eight. Recall that both the AAA and the UNCITRAL arbitration rules permit the arbitrator to issue subpoenas and to apply to an appropriate court for enforcement of those subpoenas if they are disregarded by the persons to whom they are addressed. Anyone who disregards the court's order is subject to a contempt of court citation.

The first three scenarios are really just different sides of the same coin. For the sake of simplicity and clarity, there will be no attempt here to analyze a large number of different arbitration statutes. Instead, we will use the United States' Federal Arbitration Act[11] as a prototype arbitration statute along with some illustrative court decisions that construe the Act.

Under the Federal Arbitration Act, a federal court has the authority either to stay judicial proceedings or to compel arbitration. The statute is not

---

11. 9 U.S.C. §§ 1-14, 201-208.

ambiguous on this point: in an action to stay judicial proceedings "the court in which such suit is pending, upon being satisfied that the issue involved in such suit or proceeding is referable to arbitration under such an agreement, shall on application of one of the parties stay the trial of the [court] action until such arbitration has been had ... ."[12] This is a good place to recall the *Mitsubishi* decision: there are now virtually no issues that are *not* comprehended under a standard form arbitration clause, so a court is now normally bound to stay the judicial action. While the language of this section suggests that a court might re-try the controversy after the arbitration is concluded, such is not the case. Once the arbitration is concluded and the award issued, the only thing a court may do is review the award under the recognition and confirmation principles discussed in § 9.3.

Similar concepts govern actions to compel arbitration. Under the Act, a party may apply for an order compelling the other party to participate in the arbitration when that party fails to respond to a demand for arbitration. After a court hearing and after the court satisfies itself that "the making of the agreement for arbitration ... is not the issue ... the court shall make an order directing the parties to proceed to arbitration in accordance with the agreement."[13] Recall again that the *Mitsubishi* case was in federal court on a motion to compel arbitration filed by the Mitsubishi Company. The Supreme Court determined that the motion to compel should have been granted.

There is another provision in the Federal Arbitration Act that can provide a party with some leverage in an international commercial dispute. In a separate section of the Act enacted to bring the United States in compliance with the New York Convention on the Recognition and Enforcement of Arbitral Awards, a federal court is authorized to issue an order compelling a party to arbitrate, under the terms of the agreement, "whether that place [for arbitration] is within or without the United States."[14]

This provision works in the following manner. Assume that seller in the United States and a buyer in Costa Rica have signed an agreement for the purchase of telecommunications equipment. The contract contains a standard form arbitration clause by which the parties agree to arbitrate their grievances in Mexico City under UNCITRAL arbitration rules. After receipt of the goods, the Costa Rican purchaser decides that some of the equipment is defective and properly serves a demand for arbitration on the seller. The seller simply ignores the demand. On investigation it appears that the seller has no presence and no assets in Mexico so it is impossible for the Mexican courts to obtain personal jurisiction over the seller. In this hypothethical there is very little if anything the *Mexican* courts can do because they lack

---

12. Id., § 3.
13. Id., § 4.
14. Id., § 206.

judicial power over either the person or the assets of the nonresponding party.

The Costa Rican buyer has essentially two choices: first, he can proceed unilaterally with the arbitration and get an award based in his favor even if the nonresponding party does not appear at the hearing. This works somewhat like a default judgment in court except that the arbitrator is required to pass on the merits of the claim even if the respondent is not present to make his presentation.

The arbitral award can then be taken to the United States where the buyer can ask a federal court to recognize and enforce the award against the American seller. This approach is a bit risky, however. An American court may be very suspicious of an award rendered in a Mexico City arbitration in which the U.S. party has not appeared and may refuse to recognize it even though both Mexico and the United States are parties to the New York Convention. U.S. courts tend not to support adversarial proceedings in which one of the adversaries has not appeared. While the award may be presumptively enforceable under the New York Convention, a U.S. court might still refuse enforcement on one ground or another. In any event, this approach has a number of disadvantages.

Fortunately, the Costa Rican buyer has another alternative which, when completed, is virtually foolproof. The buyer can travel to an appropriate U.S. federal court where the seller is located. There, the buyer may invoke § 206 of the Act to file a motion to compel arbitration. The Federal Arbitration Act empowers the court to order the seller to engage in arbitration even if the arbitration is to be held outside the United States. Given *Mitsubishi*, there is no reason why a U.S. court would not order the U.S. seller into a Mexico City arbitration, unless the buyer could show some special defect in the process or the underlying contract. On the facts of the hypothetical such a showing would be virtually impossible. If the court issues an order compelling arbitration, a failure of the seller to abide by the court's order would expose the seller to contempt of court proceedings. Disregarding a court's order compelling arbitration is a very dangerous tactic. Virtually everyone obeys such orders.

The upshot of these statutory provisions is that courts generally stay out of on-going arbitrations or issue only those orders necessary to continue the arbitration such as subpoena enforcement orders and orders compelling arbitration. The only other role for courts in the arbitration process is in enforcing the arbitral award. At the same time, the potential role of a court is sufficiently important that virtually all lawyers setting up an international arbitration try to insure that an arbitration has a juridical "home" in the sense the parties to the arbitration must always have a court to which they may refer questions and issues that cannot be resolved within the arbitration.

§ 9.3 Recognition and Enforcement of Arbitral Awards

Once an arbitral award is made final, many losing parties simply comply voluntarily with the terms of the award. There are any number of reasons for voluntary compliance. A party who loses in arbitration may want to continue the underlying business relationship, recognizing that non-compliance with the award will surely jeopardize that relationship. Some losing parties take a realistic look at what happened in the arbitration and may conclude that nothing is likely to change even if the award is taken to court since, as we shall see, the grounds on which a court may overturn an arbitral award are exceptionally narrow. In a statistical sense, arbitration is a "final" proceeding given that very few arbitral awards are ever overturned in court. Nonetheless, there is always the theoretical possibility that a court may overturn an award. For this reason, lawyers working in the arbitration setting try to make sure that the arbitration itself is as free of error as possible; but even when they have prevailed during the arbitration, they must consider the possibilities in court if the loser does not comply.

There are a number of different procedural routes available for obtaining judicial review of an arbitral award. A losing party may ask a court to *vacate* or *modify* the award. Under the Federal Arbitration Act, this must be done within three months after the award is filed or delivered and, as would be expected, the moving party must give proper notice of the court proceeding to the other side.[15] If the losing party does not voluntarily abide by the award, the arbitration winner may ask a court to *confirm* the award, an action that has the functional effect of converting the arbitral award to a court judgment, which is then enforced in the same manner as judicial decrees are enforced in the jurisdiction. Actions to confirm under the Federal Act must be brought within one year after the award is made.[16]

Under the Federal Arbitration Act, the grounds on which a court may review an arbitral award—irrespective of whether the action is to confirm, vacate or modify—are exceptionally narrow. They are:

(1) where the award was procured by corruption, fraud, or undue means;

(2) where there was evident partiality or corruption in the arbitrators, or either of them;

(3) where the arbitrators were guilty of misconduct in refusing to postpone the hearing, upon sufficient cause shown, or in refusing to hear evidence pertinent and material to the controversy; or of any other misbehavior by which the rights of any party have been prejudiced;

---

15. Id., §§ 10, 11.
16. Id., § 9.

(4) where the arbitrators exceeded their powers, or so imperfectly executed them that a mutual, final, and definite award upon the subject matter submitted was not made;

(5) where an award is vacated and the time within the agreement
required the award to be made has not expired the court may, in its
discretion, direct a rehearing by the arbitrators.[17]

The grounds for judicial review under the UNCITRAL Model Law on
International Commercial Arbitration are similar. An arbitral award may be
set aside by a court only if:

"(a)(i) a party to the arbitration agreement ... was under some incapacity; or the said agreement is not valid under the law to which
the parties have subjected it or, failing any indication thereon,
under the law of this State; or

(ii) the party [challenging the award] ... was not given proper notice
of the appointment of an arbitrator or of the arbitral proceedings
or was otherwise unable to present his case; or

(iii) the award deals with a dispute not contemplated by or not falling
within the terms of submission to arbitration, or contains decisions on matters beyond the scope of the submission to arbitration, provided that, if the decisions on matters submitted to arbitration can be separated from those not so submitted, only that
part of the award which contains decisions on the matters not
submitted ... may be set aside; or

(iv) the composition of the arbitral tribunal or the arbitral procedure
was not in accordance with the agreement of the parties, unless
such agreement was in conflict with a provision of this [the
Model] Law from which the parties cannot derogate, or, failing
such agreement, was not in accordance with this law, or

(b)(i) the subject-matter of the dispute is not capable of settlement by
arbitration under the law of this State; or

(ii) the award is in conflict with the public policy of this State."[18]

At first glance, these grounds seem to give the court extraordinarily broad
powers of review, but the language of the Federal Arbitration Act, as interpreted by the federal courts since 1925 and the legislative history of the
Model Law require that reviewing courts construe these grounds as narrowly
as possible. The American Arbitration Association believes: "Courts considering arbitral awards will resolve doubts in favor of confirming the award as
rendered. The statutory grounds for modifying or correcting an award are
exclusive; failure to plead any of the specified grounds is fatal to a request

---

17. This is verbatim language from the Federal Arbitration Act, id., § 10.
18. UNCITRAL Model Law, Chapter VII, Article 34.

for modification. In addition, judicial power to correct an award is limited to clearly discernible errors."[19]

Additionally, courts in the United States have occasionally invalidated arbitral awards on *public policy* grounds even though public policy is not an enumerated ground in the Federal Arbitration Act. This is a power that springs from a court's general common law authority to invalidate contractual arrangements after a finding that a particular contract violates a jurisdiction's public policy. To give a specific example, an arbitral award that divides the proceeds of an illegal narcotics sale between person A and person B would not have to be honored by a reviewing court even though none of the defects set out in the Act provide a ground for overturning the award.

In the past one might be able to argue that the public policy exception was on the verge of swallowing the general rule that courts should let arbitral awards alone. Fortunately, the courts have construed the term narrowly. For example, the United States Court of Appeals for the District of Columbia Circuit stated that the public policy ground is "not available for every party who manages to find some generally accepted principle which is transgressed by the award. Rather, the award must be so misconceived that it compels the violation of law or conduct contrary to accepted public policy."[20] On occasion, U.S. courts have overturned awards of punitive damages on grounds that punitive damages are not an appropriate sanction in arbitration.[21] As noted above, public policy is an express ground for review in the UNCITRAL Model Law. The public policy ground as it effects enforcement of international arbitral awards is briefly discussed in the following section.

In the United States a confirmed arbitral award is a very powerful document. In the first place, it generally precludes any new arbitration or litigation on the subject matter of the initial arbitration under those firmly established principles of preclusion known as *res judicata* and *collateral estoppel* (these concepts are now discussed in the literature under their new labels: claim preclusion and issue preclusion).[22] Stated very briefly, the principle of res judicata (or claim preclusion) prevents a party from re-litigating (or in our case re-arbitrating) a dispute that has already been litigated. Recall the lengthy hypothetical used in Chapter 8 involving the arbitration of a dispute over defective computer equipment in New York City between an American seller, Tangerine, and a Greek buyer, Parthenon. If the Greek buyer prevails on the arbitration and confirms the award in federal court in New York (or,

---

19. American Arbitration Association, INTERNATIONAL COMMERCIAL ARBITRATION IN NEW YORK at 134 (1986).

20. Revere Copper & Brass, Inc. v. Overseas Private Investment Corp., 628 F.2d 81, 83 (D.C.Cir. 1980).

21. See, e.g., DOMKE ON COMMERCIAL ARBITRATION (G. Wilner ed., 1984) at § 33.03; United States Fidelity and Guaranty Co. v. DeFluiter, 456 N.E.2d 429 (Ind., 1983)(punitive damages not available in arbitrations involving contractual relationships).

22. See, e.g., Domke, supra note 21, at § 39:04 (G.Wilner ed., 1984).

for that matter, confirms the award in New York State court), Tangerine cannot sometime thereafter ask a court to try the same dispute all over again.

Collateral estoppel is a first-cousin of res judicata and normally prevents a party from re-litigating individual issues already decided in one case in a subsequent proceeding. While collateral estoppel is a slightly more elusive concept, assume that the Greek company has a Spanish subsidiary that encounters the same problem with the Tangerine computers and initates an arbitration in New York against Tangerine. Assume that the first arbitration included a finding that Tangerine's principal place of business is Los Angeles, California. If Tangerine wants to relitigate the issue of its principal place of business in the arbitration with the Spanish subsidiary, it may be precluded from doing so under the doctrine of collateral estoppel. It had the chance to fully litigate that issue in the previous arbitration involving Parthenon and may now be barred from going over the same ground in the second arbitration. Even though the two doctrines are somewhat selectively applied, they both spring from a homily in U.S. law—that a person gets one day in court, not two.

Confirmation confers other benefits on an arbitral award. In the United States, an award confirmed in one state (including awards confirmed in federal court within that state), are given the same force and effect as a judgment in the court's of that state. Having the status of a court judgment makes the award enforceable in any other state under the U.S. Constitution's full faith and credit clause.[23] These two concepts (the process of confirmation and the doctrine of full faith and credit) make an arbitral award just as effective a pronouncement as anything handed down in court. Establishing an arbitral award's legitimacy by confirmation contributes substantially to the security and predictability of arbitral awards in general. Consider that Parthenon won the arbitral award in New York City but Tangerine does not pay up. Parthenon's lawyers would then likely search for assets belonging to Tangerine in the State of New York from which to satisfy the award. Assume further that no such assets can be found. It turns out that the siting of the arbitration in New York was simply a matter of mutual convenience for the parties. It happens, however, that Tangerine has lots of assets in California. All Parthenon has to do is take the confirmed New York award to California and ask the California courts to enforce it against Tangerine in that state. Under the full faith and credit clause, California courts must enforce the award as if it had been rendered and confirmed in California.

Furthermore, in the United States under the Full Faith and Credit clause, there is no requirement of *double exequatur*,[24] which parties some-

---

23. Id., at § 41:01.

24. For an excellent discussion of double exequatur and other issues see Craig, *Uses and Abuses of Appeal from Awards*, 4 Arb. Int'l 174 (1988).

times encounter on the international level. The concept of double exequatur asks whether an award won and confirmed in State A must be confirmed for a second time in State B. Under the U.S. Constitution the answer is no; but the proposition is best illustrated by a diagram:[25]

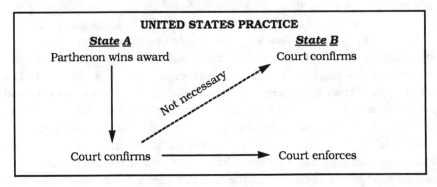

Thus, in the United States, there is no double exequatur requirement so long as the court in State A confirms. Parthenon simply presents the confirmed award from State A to the court in State B and obtains enforcement.

On the international level, however, the concept of double exequatur works in a slightly different fashion. Consider the following hypothetical under the United Nations Convention on the Recognition and Enforcement of Foreign Arbitral Awards (New York Convention) (discussed at length in the following section). Tangerine (a California company) and Parthenon (a Greek company) conduct their arbitration in London. Partnenon wins an award of $150,000 but can find no assets belonging to Tangerine in the United Kingdom (again, the forum selection was simply a matter of mutual convenience—effectively splitting the distance between Greece and California). Under the New York Convention, the holder of a valid, binding arbitral award does not need to seek *confirmation* in the country where the award was made, but may simply take the arbitral award itself to another signatory country where it will be enforced under the Convention. Under the New York Convention, the process is illustrated by the following diagram:

---

25. This diagram was provided by David Stewart, Esq., a frequent guest lecturer in the author's dispute resolution seminar.

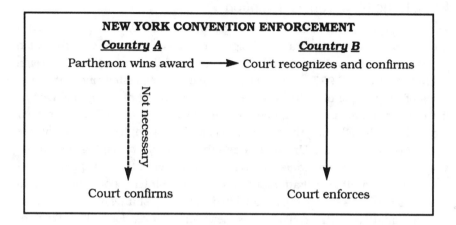

§ 9.4 International Recognition and Enforcement of Arbitral Awards

The United States Constitution makes the U.S. a single economic unit. Arbitral awards made in one state may be confirmed and enforced in another state with relative ease. That is not the case on the international level, however. International recognition and enforcement of arbitral awards present a range of different problems that typically are dealt with by treaty.

Chapter 7 points out that there is no special principle of international law that requires the courts in one nation to abide by the judgments of the courts of another nation. At the present time, the only multilateral treaty currently in effect that requires courts in one country to abide by the decisions of courts in another country governs the European Community under provisions of the Brussels Convention. Arbitration is accorded a different status, however. Since 1958, the United Nations Convention on the Recognition and Enforcement of Foreign Arbitral Awards (New York Convention) has been accepted by over 70 countries and makes recognition and enforcement of foreign arbitral awards a relatively painless and speedy process. There are other instances in which bilateral treaties contain provisions on the enforcement of arbitral awards in the two signatory countries. On occasion even when no treaty governs enforcement, a prevailing party seeking enforcement may use the domestic courts of a country as an appropriate enforcement vehicle.

§ 9.4.1 The New York Convention

The growth of international business following World War One prompted a number of countries to draft and sign the Geneva Protocol on Arbitration Clauses of 1923 and the Geneva Convention of the Execution of Foreign Arbitral Awards of 1927.[26] These two agreements, negotiated under the auspices of the League of Nations, were a good beginning but they included so many reservations and exemptions that they were not very effective on their terms. Possibly reflecting the same suspicion that prompted it not to join the League of Nations, the United States—then rapidly becoming one of the world's major trading nations—refused to sign either of the two agreements.

Another multilateral attempt to provide some international predictability in this area was initiated by the United Nations just after World War Two. The culmination of those efforts was New York Convention.[27] This time the United States participated in all of the negotiations and eventually fully ratified the treaty on February 1, 1971.[28] Fundamentally, the New York Convention is an attempt to make arbitral awards rendered in one country fully effective in any other signatory country.

While virtually all of the major trading nations have accepted the Convention, there are some notable geographical gaps in the Convention's application. Latin America is terribly underrepresented and this difficulty led a number of Latin American countries to negotiate and sign a separate treaty with much the same impact, the 1975 Panama Convention on International Commercial Arbitration(discussed in Chapter 10).[29] Unfortunately, the Panama Convention has not attracted all the countries of Latin America, although the number of its adherents is growing. Some countries—China is a prime example—have accepted the New York Convention as a signal that they wish to join the community of trading nations. In the United States, the New York Convention has been elevated to major importance by such Supreme Court decisions as *Mitsubishi v. Soler.*[30] In *Mitsubishi*, the Court cited U.S. participation in the New York Convention as a signal from Congress and the President that international commercial agreements were a special form of commercial transaction to be given special treatment.

Described briefly, the Convention applies to arbitral awards *made* in any country adopting the Convention that the prevailing party wishes to

---

26. 27 L.N.T.S. 158, adopted September 24, 1923 and 92 L.N.T.S. 301, adopted September 26, 1927, respectively.

27. 330 U.N.T.S. 38 (1959); 21 U.S.T. 2517; T.I.A.S. No. 6997 (1970).

28. See, e.g., Aksen, *American Arbitration Accession Arrives in the Age of Aquarius: United States Implements United Nations Convention on the Recognition and Enforcement of Foreign Arbitral Awards,* 3 S.W.L.Rev. 1 (1971).

29. See, e.g., Sanders, *A Twenty Years' Review of the Convention on the Recognition and Enforcement of Foreign Arbitral Awards,* 18 Int'l Law. 269 (1978).

30. 473 U.S. 614 (1985).

have recognized and enforced in any other adopting country.[31] The Convention also covers arbitral awards made in non-signatory countries when the arbitrating parties are from signatory countries. For example, the New York Convention will govern an arbitral award between an Argentine seller and a Zairean buyer (both non-signatory nations) if the award was made in London because the United Kingdom, the place where the award was made, is a signatory. Similarly, the New York Convention will apply to an arbitral award made in Argentina between a British and a U.S. party.

Basically, the Convention requires each country to recognize and enforce arbitral awards based on agreements "in writing" which "include an arbitral clause in a contract or arbitration agreement, signed by the parties or contained in an exchange of letters or telegrams."[32] There are very few instances in which a contracting state may refuse recognition and enforcement. These are:

(1) The parties to the agreement were under the law applicable to them under some incapacity, or the agreement is not valid under the law to which the parties have subjected it, or under the law of the country in which the award was made;

(2) The party against whom the award is invoked was not given proper notice of the appointment of the arbitrator or of the arbitration proceedings or was otherwise unable to present his case;

(3) the award deals with a difference not contemplated by or not falling within the terms of the submission to arbitration, or it contains decisions on matters beyond the scope of the submission to arbitration;

(4) the composition of the arbitral authority or the arbitral procedure was not in accordance with the agreement of the parties or, if there is no such agreement, with the law of the country where the arbitration took place;

(5) the award has not yet become binding on the parties or has otherwise been stayed or set aside by a court in that country;

(6) the subject matter of the award is not capable of settlement by arbitration under the law of that country; or

(7) the recognition or enforcement of the award would be contrary to the public policy of that country.[33]

Very much like the grounds for vacating or modifying an arbitral award discussed in the preceding section, these grounds are intended to be construed narrowly. Indeed, the reader will note that the grounds in the New York Convention are almost identical to the grounds for judicial review of

---

31. New York Convention, Article I.
32. Id., Articles II and III.
33. This language is a paraphrase of New York Convention Article V.

arbitral awards promulgated in UNCITRAL's Model Law of Arbitration. One of the perceived loopholes, the public policy ground, has not materialized as a major barrier to enforcement and recognition. When courts examine the public policy ground, they generally separate the issues into 2 categories: (1) questions of procedural due process and (2) questions of the arbitrability of certain issues. Due process is rarely a viable argument so long as the party objecting to recognition and enforcement has received adequate notice of the arbitration. If an arbitration has taken place under established procedural rules such as the ICC, AAA or UNCITRAL arbitration rules, there can be few complaints about the procedural aspects of the arbitration.[34]

The other component of the public policy ground—non-arbitrability of certain issues—appears to be shrinking as a basis for refusing recognition and enforcement. For example, in *Mitsubishi v. Soler*,[35] the Supreme Court of the United States held squarely that issues of competition arising under the U.S. antitrust laws were properly the subject of arbitration in Tokyo under the arbitration rules of the Japan Chamber of Commerce. The Court expressly left open the possibility of a U.S. court reviewing the outcome of the arbitration under the New York Convention and possibly holding the arbitration void as against public policy, but did not lend any great encouragement to this tactic. Essentially, the Court viewed such review as a kind of safety valve, permitting a U.S. court to refuse recognition only if the arbitration did immense violence to U.S. antitrust concepts and policies. The remainder of the Court's decision focused on determining that it was highly probably that the arbitrators would make reasonable decisions on the antitrust issues. Even as early as 1977, eight years prior to *Mitsubishi* and only six years after U.S. ratification of the Convention, at least one writer felt comfortable with this comment: "The attitude of the United States courts towards the [New York Convention's] public policy defense is not one which recognizes the defense as a 'catch-all' to protect the integrity of arbitration. Rather, the courts have considered the defense mainly as a means by which a forum might escape binding arbitration. Consequently, the courts have given the public policy defense so narrow a construction that it now must be characterized as a defense without meaningful definition."[36]

How does the Convention work in practice? One of the author's first encounters with an international commercial arbitration involved a Greek ship repair company located in Piraeus that contracted to make some repairs on an oil tanker owned by a private oil company doing business in the Middle East. The contract contained a bare-bones arbitration clause requir-

---

34. See, e.g., Barry, *Application of the Public Policy Exception to the Enforcement of Foreign Arbitral Awards Under the New York Convention: A Modest Proposal*, 51 Temple L.Q. 832 (1978).

35. 473 U.S. 614 (1985).

36. Note, *The Public Policy Defense to Recognition and Enforcement of Foreign Arbitral Awards*, 7 Calif.W.Int'l L.J. 228 (1977).

ing that any disputes be arbitrated in Switzerland under International Chamber of Commerce rules. Indeed, the arbitration clause was contained in small type text on the obverse of a pre-printed work order.

The oil company reneged on payment of the repair bill; and the matter went to arbitration in Switzerland where the Greek company prevailed, winning an award for the full amount of the repair bill plus certain costs. The loser did not pay voluntarily and when the Greek company looked for ways to satisfy the award it encountered another difficulty. The tanker itself had been secretly moved back to the Middle East (recall that obtaining pre-arbitration attachment of property is not easy, particularly outside the United States) where the ship's engine and navigational gear was removed. The hull was then turned into a floating oil storage tank anchored within the territorial waters of a country not a signatory to the New York Convention. So the losing company had no property in Greece (where the repair work was done), no property in Switzerland (where the award was made) and even if the hull could have been seized and sold to satisfy the award (a highly doubtful proposition in the judgment of counsel), its new value as a floating oil tank might not have covered the amount of the award.

The winner came to the author with a request for some suggestions on how to satisfy the award. Put more colloquially, the winner wanted to know where to find some money. Fortunately for the winner, the New York Convention governs arbitral awards *made* in contracting countries, even if one or both of the parties are not nationals of contracting countries. Switzerland is a contracting country so the award was subject to recognition and enforcement in any other contracting state where the losing party might be found or where the losing party had property. After a quick but fruitful investigation, it became apparent that the oil company, albeit using as part of its title the name of a middle eastern country, was in fact a private corporation and a wholly owned subsidiary of a major U.S. oil company with its corporate headquarters in Delaware. This revelation made the rest of the process relatively simple.

In the United States, actions for recognition and enforcement are commenced in federal court under the authority of a part of the Federal Arbitration Act specifically enacted by Congress to implement the New York Convention.[37] This meant that counsel for the party seeking enforcement had merely to go to federal court in Wilmington, Delaware, where he filed a copy of the arbitral award along with a request for recognition and enforcement. After a short courtroom proceeding, the award was recognized and thus converted into an enforcible federal court judgment. Recall again that the New York Convention does not require a double exequatur—i.e., the party seeking enforcement does not first have to seek confirmation or enforcement in the country where the

---

37. 9 U.S.C. §§ 201 - 208.

award is made, but can go immediately to a contracting country where the losing party has property. Recall further that there are virtually no viable defenses to recognition and enforcement. The U.S. court properly gave short shrift to certain arguments from opposing counsel about the procedural primitiveness of arbitration in Switzerland under the ICC's rules.

After a few hours of negotiation, the losing company gave up any pretense of a defense and shortly thereafter, the client got his check for the full amount of the award. There are few better illustrations of the powerful contributions the New York Convention has made to international commercial dispute resolution. This explains as well as anything why arbitration is usually the dispute resolution device of choice in international commercial transactions.

§ 9.4.2 Enforcing awards not subject to the New York Convention

One of the problems with the New York Convention is that it has not been accepted by every country in the world. Earlier it was noted that Latin American countries, in particular, have failed to ratify it. As of January 1, 1991 less than 80 countries have become contracting states; and while this list includes virtually all of the major trading nations of the world, there are almost an equal number of United Nations members who have not agreed to the Convention. What is to be done when an arbitral award must be enforced in a country that is not a contracting state within the New York convention?

There are two viable paths to enforcement. First, many countries have signed bilateral treaties of friendship, commerce and navigation (so-called FCN treaties) that may contain language sufficient to persuade a court in one country to recognize and enforce the arbitral awards made in the other country. FCN treaties should be thoroughly explored when a prevailing party is seeking enforcement in a non-New York Convention country.

The second route to be explored is simply the internal arbitration law of the country in question. Just because a country has not signed the New York Convention does not mean that it has a primitive legal system or that it is hostile to arbitral awards. Its internal law may be all the authority necessary to have the award enforced on its terms.[38]

The fundamental point to be kept in mind is that arbitration is becoming accepted around the world. Many countries, including many who have not joined the New York convention are modernizing their domestic arbitration laws and executing FCN treaties with each other. Merely because the New York Convention does not apply is no reason to give up on enforcement of an award. ◆

---

38. For a discussion of these points see, e.g., Domke, supra note 21, Chapters 45 and 46 and Note, *Enforcing International Commercial Arbitration Agreements and Awards Not Subject to the New York Convention*, 23 Va.J.Int'l L. 75 (1982).

— 10 —
International Commercial Arbitration:
Special Regional Considerations

§ 10.1 Introduction

The two preceding chapters discussed international commercial arbitration generally and concentrated on those instances in which two parties are generally free to write whatever agreement they choose and to agree on any of a number of dispute resolution alternatives. Faced with a great deal of choice, parties to international contracts normally agree on a conventional arbitration clause with appropriate choices of applicable law and site of arbitration. However, in some situations, the parties' choice of dispute resolution is constrained by the requirements of the particular country in which they are doing business. Many countries impose certain limitations on private dispute resolution. This chapter is a survey of some of the special considerations that apply in certain instances. It is not an exhaustive treatment of any particular country or region nor a comprehensive list of those settings in which special problems may occur. It is simply intended to be a representative sample of some of the limitations faced by business executives and lawyers in different parts of the world.

For readers wishing some instant depth on any of these topics, there are two sources that are frequently helpful: Kluwer's *International Handbook on Commercial Arbitration*, a loose-leaf publication that provides both commentary and primary legal materials on arbitration in a large number of different countries. The International Handbook is edited by one of the world's preeminent commercial arbitration scholars, Pieter Sanders. The staff of the American Arbitration Association has prepared a shorter book entitled *Survey of International Arbitration Sites* (1984) that provides capsule descriptions of various sites for arbitration. The *World Arbitration Reporter*,

edited by Professors Hans Smit aned Vratislav Pechota provides both primary material and commentary on a large number of different places for arbitration. Under Professor Smit's supervision, the Parker School of Foreign
and Comparative Law at Columbia University also publishes *The Guide to
International Arbitration and Arbitrators*, a helpful source for the various
countries' arbitration rules and for the names of potential arbitrators.

§ 10.2 The International Centre for the Settlement of Investment Disputes

One of the world's most sophisticated systems of commercial arbitration has
been developed by the World Bank's International Centre for the Settlement
of Investment Disputes (ICSID). However, the ICSID process has severe jurisdictional limitations (it is essentially limited to disputes between private parties and the governments of developing countries) that place it out of reach of
the conventional private-party-versus-private-party dispute that is the focal
point of this book. Nonetheless, the ICSID procedures warrant attention
because of their sophistication and because the readers of this book may
encounter a few commercial disputes that may be processed under the auspices of ICSID.

     Most systems of international commercial arbitration are based on pro-
cedures that are developed by essentially private (i.e., non-governmental)
organizations such as the American Arbitration Association and the
International Chamber of Commerce. Because arbitration normally must
have a juridical and geographic base, domestic legislation in the country in
which the arbitration is held provides the remaining legal framework. In
sharp contrast, ICSID was created by treaty—the Convention on the
Settlement of Investment Disputes between States and Nationals of Other
States[1]—and is administered by a component of the World Bank, an organization that is essentially a financial agency that administers loans made by
private banks in the developed countries to governments in the developing
countries. Currently, the ICSID Convention has been signed by 89 governments and ratified by 83 nations. ICSID derives its importance from the status of the World Bank in international finance, but the ICSID arbitration
process is not a numerically significant system of international commercial
arbitration. As of 1990, in its entire lifetime of nearly 20 years ICSID has
processed fewer than thirty individual cases and has put fewer than 20
cases through its full-blown arbitration process.[2]

---

1. Opened for signature March 18, 1965, 17 U.S.T. 1270, T.I.A.S. No. 6090, 575 U.N.T.S.
159.
    2. See News from ICSID (Winter, 1984); and Delaume, *ICSID Arbitration in Practice*, 2 Int'l Tax
& Business Law. 58 (1984).

Nonetheless, ICSID is a prestigious organization with a well-thought out process of arbitration that bears further examination.[3] Three basic criteria, set out in Article 25 of the ICSID Convention, are used for determining ICSID's jurisdiction: (1) whether the case is a dispute arising out of an investment agreement; (2) whether the dispute is between a contracting state (or an entity or component with authority to contract in the name of the country) and a national of another contracting state; and (3) whether the parties have consented to ICSID arbitration by way of a written agreement.[4] George DeLaume, now retired as a senior legal adviser at ICSID, agree that these jurisdictional terms are to be construed as broadly as possible, they severely limit the total number of disputes that may be brought before ICSID.[5] This is the primary reason why there have been so few arbitrations actually conducted by ICSID. However, once jurisdiction attaches, a number of other consequences flow: first, once having given its consent to ICSID jurisdiction a party cannot later withdraw that consent; second, no domestic court in a contracting country may interfere with the ICSID arbitration process; third, courts in all the contracting nations are obliged by the terms of the treaty to give "prompt and effective recognition" to any ICSID award.[6]

ICSID has developed some exceptionally sophisticated dispute resolution processes. Its procedures are viewed as models by many scholars of dispute resolution. As a threshhold matter, the parties may choose one of two dispute resolution processes—conciliation or arbitration. They initiate either process by filing a request in either of the three official ICSID languages (English, French or Spanish) for either conciliation or arbitration with the ICSID Secretary-General at World Bank Headquarters in Washington, D.C.[7] The ICSID Secretary General *registers* the request for dispute resolution "unless he finds, on the basis of the information contained in the request, that the dispute is manifestly outside the jurisdiction of the Centre."[8] The act of registration is the equivalent of a court is docketing a case; and ICSID's supervision of the dispute commences from the date of registration.

If the parties seek conciliation, the ICSID Conciliation Rules provide for either a sole conciliator or an uneven number of conciliators appointed as agreed between the parties. The ICSID Conciliation Rules, although highly detailed, are essentially an informal process by which the conciliator requests the basic documents underlying the dispute, receives written state-

---

3. ICSID Annual Report (1989).

4. Rand, Hornick & Friedland, *ICSID's Emerging Jurisprudence: The Scope of ICSID's Jurisdiction*, 19 Int'l L. & Politics 33 (1986).

5. See G. DELAUME, TRANSNATIONAL CONTRACTS, Chapter XV; and Rank, Hornick & Friedland, supra, note 4.

6. Delaume, *ICSID Arbitration: Practical Considerations*, 1 J.Int'l Arb. 101 (1984).

7. Articles 28 and 36 of the ICSID Convention.

8. Id. Article 36(3).

ments of the case and other evidence from the parties, and conducts, if necessary, a hearing attended by the parties. At that hearing, the conciliator may also hear experts or other witnesses produced by the parties.[9] The assumption under the conciliation rules is that the conciliation process will result in a settlement agreement between the parties and that the conciliator will simply prepare a report to that effect that is submitted to the parties and the ICSID Secretary General. If the conciliation process fails, a report recounting the failure is prepared for both the parties and the Secretary General and the parties may then resort to arbitration under the ICSID rules.

Arbitration under the ICSID rules may be resorted to after conciliation fails or directly without going through the conciliation process. Once a request for arbitration is filed with the Secretary General and the arbitral tribunal is appointed (generally the number and the identity of the arbitrators will be agreed on by the parties, or failing an agreement, will be determined by ICSID), the arbitral process begins under a format that the ICSID rules describe as "two distinct phases: a written procedure followed by an oral one."[10] The written procedure requires the drafting and submission of a *memorial* by the party requesting arbitration, a *counter-memorial* submitted by the responding party and, if the parties request or if the arbitrator wishes, the filing of a *reply* by the requesting party and a *rejoinder* by the responding party.[11]

The oral hearing is a conventional arbitration hearing in which much of the conduct of the proceeding and the submission and consideration of evidence is under the control of the arbitration tribunal. Following the close of the hearing the tribunal is expected to frame an award within sixty days that addresses all the important issues adduced during the proceeding and gives reasons for the tribunal's decision. The award is filed with the secretary-general and transmitted to the parties.[12] In appropriate circumstances, the tribunal may fashion interim relief to preserve the rights of the parties.[13] Arbitration hearings may be held in any location agreed upon by the parties, subject to the approval of ICSID, although ICSID apparently prefers that hearings be held in either Washington, D.C., Cairo, Kuala Lumpur, or The Hague.[14] If the parties cannot agree on a location, ICSID requires that the hearing be held at its headquarters in Washington, D.C.

A limited right of appeal, by which a party requests *annulment* of the award may be taken to the secretary-general.[15] Once the award becomes

---

9. ICSID Conciliation Rules 22-29.
10. ICSID Arbitration Rules, Rule 29.
11. Id. Rule 31.
12. Id. Rules 33 through 48.
13. Id. Rule 39.
14. ICSID Pamphlet No. 12, at page 9.
15. ICSID Convention, Article 52.

final, the winning party may seek recognition and enforcement of the award if the losing party does not voluntarily abide by the decision of the arbitrators. The ICSID Convention requires each contracting state to recognize and enforce ICSID arbitral awards "as binding and enforce the pecuniary obligations imposed by that award within its territories as if it were a final judgment of a court in that state."[16] Note that this is somewhat different from the recognition and enforcement mechanisms built into the New York Convention on the Recognition and Enforcement of Foreign Arbitral Awards. Under the New York Convention a reviewing court has authority, albeit limited, to set aside the award (See the discussion of the New York Convention in Chapter Nine), as for example when an award is contrary to that country's "public policy." Under the ICSID Convention, there seems to be no such power. An ICSID arbitral award is to be treated as a final *court* judgment in each contracting state.

The ICSID dispute resolution process has been described as "a considerable advance in the progressive development of international law."[17] While that description may include a bit of hyperbole, there is no doubt that the existence of ICSID has enhanced international trade by providing a dispute resolution process that is both intrinsically rational and acceptable to both the investing nations and the developing countries. The knowledge that any dispute arising out of the investment agreement will be handled through an effective international arbitration process provides that necessary margin of comfort that investors normally require. At the same time, the ICSID procedures, while sophisticated, are very much like the UNCITRAL arbitration and conciliation procedures. Anyone already experienced in other forms of international commercial arbitration should be able to function effectively in an ICSID proceeding.

§ 10.3 The European Community

Since so many of the members of the European Community (EC) are major trading nations, commercial arbitration is a well-known and frequently-utilized dispute resolution device. Moreover, many of the countries of Europe are beginning to experiment with the more innovative devices such as mediation/conciliation and mini-trial. The commercial arbitration systems of England and France have been used frequently throughout this book to illustrate many fundamental concepts. London and Paris have traditionally been centers for international commercial arbitration. More recently, because of a new 1985 Belgian statute that almost completely prohibits

---

16. Id., Article 54(1).
17. Sutherland, *The World Bank Convention on the Settlement of Investment Disputes*, 28 Int'l & Comp.L.Q. 367 (1979).

domestic courts from setting aside either domestic or international aribtral awards, Brussels may become what the drafter of that new statute calls, "a paradise for international commercial arbitration."[18]

Thus, the current issues in the EC are not so much a matter of promoting interest in commercial arbitration but rather are matters associated with uniformity of application among members of the Community since the EC has an express provision (Article 177 of the Treaty of Rome) which emphasizes the need for uniformity of law among the EC countries.[19] In one instance, *Nordsee v. Reederei Mond,*[20] the EC Court of Justice noted:

> "Community law must be observed in its entirety throughout the territory of all the Member States; parties to a contract are not, therefore, free to create exceptions to it. In that context attention must be drawn to the fact that if questions of Community law are raised in an arbitration resorted to by agreement the ordinary courts may be called upon to examine them [perhaps under the authority of Article 177] either in the context of their collaboration with arbitration tribunals ... or in the course of a review of an arbitration award ... ."[21]

Noting that arbitration takes place in private and is generally confidential, William Brown succinctly puts the issue: "The problem therefore arises as to whether, and if so, to what extent, the EC [judicial policy will] ensure the uniform interpretation and application of Community law by commercial arbitrators as well as by national courts."[22] Mr. Brown hints that one solution might be to permit arbitrators to refer certain questions of law to the EC Court of Justice much in the same fashion that certain questions of law have been referred to English courts by arbitrators in that country under the now significantly-altered "stated case" procedure (see the discussion on the stated or special case procedure in Chapter Nine). However, the Court of Justice has steadfastly refused to permit such reference.

The British House of Lords has decided two important cases since the 1979 Act was passed that seem to promote additional stability in arbitral awards. In *The Nema*, the Lords recommended that judicial review of arbitral awards ought to be permitted only when a review of the award on its face shows that the arbitrator "is obviously wrong."[23] The subsequent decision by the House of Lords in the *Antaios* case reiterated the concepts of finality of arbitral awards expressed in *The Nema* decision while providing for some

---

18. Storme, *Belgium: A Paradise for International Commercial Arbitration*, 1986 Int'l Law. 294.

19. Most of the discussion in this section is taken from Brown, *Commercial Arbitration and the European Economic Community*, 2 J.Int'l Arb. 21 (1985).

20. 1982 E.C.R. 1095.

21. Id.

22. Id.

23. See the discussion of the Nema case in Marriott, *Arbitrating International Commercial Disputes in the United Kingdom*, 44 Arb. J. 3 (Sep. 1989).

additional standards of review when British judges refuse to review an award. The two cases have been viewed by one British commentator as making it "clear that judicial review for errors of law by arbitrators will take place only in exceptional circumstances."[24] Decisions such as these make clear that England will become an even more hospitable site for international commercial arbitration in the future.

Thus, among the EC nations there exists the continuing possibility that country-by-country differences in substantive law may emerge from individual arbitrations even though Article 177 promotes uniformity in the substantive law with regard to domestic court decisions. Looking at the situation somewhat differently, uniformity may be a dispensable requirement—that is, a requirement that individual business executives and lawyers may be willing to forego—for the benefits speed, confidentiality and finality provided by commercial arbitration. Of course, one prominent commentator, Professor Clive Schmitthoff takes a slightly different view. He acknowledges that the EC "has done virtually nothing for the harmonization and unification of the law of arbitration of the Member States of the Community[; and] [t]his is not due to any lack of powers."[25] But this does not trouble him. He believes—and many of the actions of the European Community seem to echo his views—that uniformity in international commercial arbitration is properly a global matter rather than a regional problem. So, for example, any European Commuity pronouncement on the enforcement of foreign arbitral awards would in all likelihood simply duplicate the requirements of the New York Convention on the Recognition and Enforcement of Foreign Arbitral Awards. Moreover, if decisional uniformity is the only problem posed by commercial arbitration with the EC, the Community ought to be considered well off.

Even one of the two newest members of the EC, Spain, is beginning to develop a modern system of commercial arbitration fully compatible with those of the other EC countries and with the major trading nations.[26] All other indications suggest that commercial arbitration in concert with some of the less-drastic means of commercial dispute resolution will continue to thrive within the EC.

Within Europe but not yet part of the EC, Switzerland may be poised to regain its previous reputation as a good site for international commercial dispute resolution. The Zurich Chamber of Commerce was among the first to promulgate mini-trial rules (see Chapter 6, § 6.5). In 1989 the Swiss confed-

---

24. Id. at 8. For a much lengthier excursus on U.K arbitration see M. MUSTILL & S. BOYD, THE LAW AND PRACTICE OF COMMERCIAL ARBITRATION IN ENGLAND (2d ed., 1988).

25. Schmitthoff, *Arbitration and EEC Law*, Common Market L. Rev. 143 (1987).

26. See, e.g., Verdera y Tuells, *International Commercial Arbitration and the Spanish Court of Arbitration*, 3 J.Int'l Arb. 47 (Mar. 1986).

eration promulgated a modern law of arbitration that appears to remove much of the danger of excessive judicial interference with arbitration.[27]

§ 10.4 The Iran–United States Claims Tribunal

The Iran–United States Claims Tribunal ("Tribunal") is a unique commercial dispute resolution body that derives its entire identity and reason for being from the seizure and holding as hostage of a number of the members of the staff of the United States embassy in Teheran in 1979. With the subsequent release of the hostages under a negotiated agreement usually referred to as the Algiers Accords, the United States and Iran agreed to submit a large number of commercial claims growing out of contracts made during the regime of the deposed Shah of Iran.[28] The claims settlement aspects of the Accords are unique in that the two contending parties, the United States and Iran, still have no diplomatic relations with each other; the claims grow out of the Islamic Revolution in Iran, rather than as the result of a war between the parties; and the vast bulk of the claims are invariably arbitrated between private companies in the United States and the Government of Iran, rather than between two private parties in a traditional arbitration setting.[29]

In this last sense, the arbitration process is perhaps closer to the ICSID model (discussed above) than to the models of private arbitration discussed elsewhere in this chapter and the preceding chapters. Moreover, unlike the other models, the Tribunal is scheduled to go out of business as soon as all the claims are arbitrated, something that will probably occur before the end of the century. Nonetheless, it provides a very good example of how arbitration, properly structured and organized, can serve as a helpful bridge between two countries who otherwise find very little to agree upon.

---

27. O'Neill, *Has Switzerland Solved Its Problems as a Site for Arbitration?* 45 Arb. J. 16 (1990). Mr. O'Neill comments: "On balance, the new Swiss law on international arbitration is a very positive step forward in aiding Switzerland to solidify its place as a highly favored neutral site by Americans." *Id.* at 22.

28. The full title of the Accords is: The Declaration of the Government of the Democratic and Popular Republic of Algeria Concerning the Settlement of Claims by the Government of the United States of America and the Government of the Islamic Republic of Iran. It is reprinted in 20 Int'l Legal Mat. 230 (1981).

29. Selby & Stewart, *Practical Aspects of Arbitrating Claims Before the Iran-United States Claims Tribunal*, 18 Int'l Law. 211 (1984). Mr. Stewart has served as Assistant Legal Adviser for International Claims and Administrator for Iranian Claims in the United States Department of State. A portion of the following discussion is taken from this article and his earlier article, Stewart & Sherman, *Developments at the Iran-United States Claims Tribunal: 1981-1983*, 24 Va.J.Int'l L. 1 (1983). Other helpful and provocative articles on this topic include: Jones, *The Iran-United States Claims Tribunal: Private Rights and State Responsibility*, 24 Va.J.Int'l L. 259 (1984) (Mr. Jones, an English barrister, provides a healthy non-U.S. view of the Tribunal); and Lowenfeld, *The Iran-U.S. Claims Tribunal: An Interim Appraisal*, 38 Arb.J. 14 (1983). For the views of an American practitioner who has appeared before the Tribunal, see Belland, *The Iran-United States Claims Tribunal: Some Reflections on Trying a Claim*, 1 J.Int'l Arb. 237 (1984).

The Tribunal's jurisdiction includes a gamut of issues: claims against Iran by private companies in the United States, claims by individuals and companies in Iran against the United States, and certain claims between the two governments themselves. The claims are paid out of monies formerly held by banks, mainly in the United States, that were sequestered by the President of the United States shortly after the United States embassy was taken over and the hostages seized. Under the Accords, these deposits were placed in a Security Account, originally funded at the level of $1 billion which the Iranian government has agreed to maintain at the level of no less than $500 million. In other words, as claims are satisfied from the Security Account, the Iranian government takes steps to insure that the amount remaining never drops below $500 million.

The Tribunal, whose make-up was part of the original negotiation of the Accords, consists of nine members selected in a traditional arbitration style: Iran appoints three, the United States appoints three and those six choose the remaining three. In certain circumstances, the Tribunal sits as a nine member board, but normally the Tribunal hears individual cases in panels (the Tribunal term is *chambers*) of three arbitrators each. The procedural rules used for the individual cases are the UNCITRAL rules modified slightly to meet the conditions of the Accords.

One significant modification, imposed early on by agreement between the parties and the Tribunal was the institution of regular pre-hearing conferences for virtually all individual cases, even though the pre-hearing conference is not expressly contemplated by the UNCITRAL rules.[30] Other modifications of the UNCITRAL rules were necessary because of the sizeable number of cases with which the Tribunal must contend over its lifetime. Even though there was a short cut off date of January 19, 1982 on the submission of all claims (claims could be filed no earlier than October 20, 1981), a total of 3,835 claims were eventually filed, over 2,700 of which were designated as small claims (amounts in controversy of less than $250,000).[31] As of mid-1991, the Tribunal has adjudicated approximately three-quarters of the individual cases pending before it.

The Tribunal gets generally high marks from persons who have observed or participated in its work. Professor Andreas Lowenfeld believes the Tribunal has done "moderately well" in accomplishing its goals, even though he faults the Tribunal for not developing "full collegiality among the arbitrators, the process that makes so many proponents of international arbitration associate the process with development of the conditions for peace."[32] Of course, given the history of the Tribunal, its required member-

---

30. Selby & Stewart, supra note 29, at 222.
31. Id. at 215.
32. Lowenfeld, supra note 29, at 23.

ship and the fact that both countries are estranged if not actually hostile over ten years after the Accords were signed, a lack of collegiality is certainly understandable. Indeed, the Tribunal's work is even more impressive given the ostensible lack of collegiality.

There are other complaints. A British barrister, David Lloyd Jones, faults the Tribunal for what he sees as the failure of the Tribunal to address and properly resolve "[a] number of important questions as to the nature and function of the ... Tribunal and the standards and rules it is to apply [in individual cases]... ."[33] But his qualms seem relatively insignificant ten years later. All in all, a unique experiment appears to have worked. Although it is unlikely that the precise circumstances leading to the Algiers Accords will ever be repeated, the Iran-United States Claims Tribunal could serve as a model for resolving other large-scale monetary disputes between nations that remain hostile toward each other. Indeed, the Tribunal's greatest contribution to international commercial arbitration generally is the large body of case law developed by the Tribunal under the UNCITRAL arbitration rules. This body of law is a major reference work for all other parties who elect the UNCITRAL rules for their arbitrations.

§ 10.5 Latin America

Among the regions of the world, Latin America—and particularly the countries of South America—have been unusually hostile to the idea of international commercial arbitration generally and to the idea of recognition and enforcement of arbitral awards through multi-national treaties. Most of the countries of Latin America have refused to sign the 1958 New York Convention on the Recognition and Enforcement of Foreign Arbitral Awards and only twelve countries have ratified a substitute convention, the Inter-American Convention on International Commercial Arbitration. Even the United States, the country that spearheaded the effort to draft the Convention has been a little laggard; full U.S. implementation occurred only in September, 1990.[34]

The reasons for this hostility vary from country to country, but the region's general reluctance to engage in arbitration or enforcement of arbitral awards apparently stems from those countries' fear of foreign economic and political domination. As recently as 1984, one commentator asserted: "Arbitration is little practised, statistical information on the use of arbitration cannot be found, legal commentaries and treaties on the law of arbitration

---

33. Jones, supra note 25, at 285.

34. See Norberg, *United States Implements Inter-American Convention on Commercial Arbitration*, 45 Arb. J. 23 (1990). The text of the Convention may be found in the appendix to Title 9, United States Code.

are rarely published, and reported decisions on the enforcement of foreign arbitral awards are almost nonexistent."[35] By contrast, companies and individuals outside the region are suspicious of domestic courts in the region as a proper dispute resolution forum. One of the reactions of the Latin American countries to these fears of foreign domination has been the development of the *Calvo Doctrine* (sometimes referred to as the *Calvo Clause*) which is commonly inserted in investment contracts, particularly concession agreements, between Latin American countries and foreign companies. Basically, the doctrine requires investing companies to waive any opportunity to resolve any commercial dispute growing out of the agreement through diplomatic means and to consent to resolution of the dispute in the domestic courts of the host country. There are normally four components in any Calvo clause:

1. Submission of any disputes to an appropriate domestic court;
2. A choice of law clause that chooses the domestic law of the host country;
3. A waiver of any diplomatic protection for the foreign participant;,
4. The surrender of any rights that might be provided under international law.[36]

It is clear that the underlying rationale for the Calvo clause is protection against foreign economic domination through improperly balanced concession agreements that disfavor the host country and that force that country to engage in dispute resolution outside its own boundaries or under the supervision of some international arbitration institution. The seeds for these fears of economic domination were sown over several centuries of rapacious behavior on the part of some of the major trading nations. However, the current problem is far different. Concession agreements, while not totally unknown these days, are not regarded as an acceptable form of modern international commercial agreement. Yet the Calvo clause continues to be inserted in conventional commercial agreements between private parties. What had been a device intended to provide some protection for the host country in a concession agreement now engenders distrust on the part of the investing party, particularly in those commercial transactions that bear no relation whatsoever to a concession agreement. It is unquestioned that the existence of the Calvo doctrine has inhibited business relations between the major trading nations and the countries of Latin America.

There are ways to work around the Calvo doctrine. Virtually all Latin American countries have established conventional systems of commercial

---

35. Garro, *Enforcement of Arbitration Agreements and Jurisdiction of Arbitral Tribunals in Latin America*, 1 J. Int'l Arb. 293 (1984).

36. Wesley, *The Procedural Malaise of Foreign Investment Disputes in Latin America: From Local Tribunals to Factfinding*, 7 Law & Pol'y in Int'l Bus. 813, 818 (1975).

arbitration within their boundaries with normal limitations on judicial review of arbitral awards.[37] There is some evidence that domestic commercial arbitration is seen as an increasingly attractive dispute resolution mechanism in Latin America,[38] although a number of countries appear to remain hostile to any kind of arbitration, domestic or international. The prevailing view in those countries is that the only acceptable form of dispute resolution is litigation in that country's courts.[39] It has proved difficult to persuade many of the countries of Latin America to adopt either the UNICTRAL Model Law on International Commercial Arbitration (see Chapter Eleven) or to agree to effective international enforcement of awards once those awards are rendered.

The picture is not completely bleak, however. In 1975 a number of countries including the United States gathered in Panama City, Panama to draft the Inter-American Convention on International Commercial Arbitration, a treaty that has two functions: "(1) to make agreements to arbitrate enforceable—offensively by being eligible for a judicial order to compel arbitration, and defensively by being used to avoid or postpone judicial action in respect to the dispute; and (2) to recognize and enforce arbitral awards—offensively to collect sums payable under an award, and defensively as res judicata if a party attempts to litigate the same dispute in another forum."[40] In other words, the Inter-American Convention has essentially the same scope and effect among its signatories as does the New York Convention. Currently (i.e., as of early 1992), Chile, Colombia, Costa Rica, El Salvador, Guatemala, Honduras, Mexico, Panama, Paraguay, Peru, the United States, Uruguay, and Venezuela have become contracting states under the Convention. More countries may join in the near future.

Under the Convention, parties may agree to arbitration of commercial agreements and the arbitral award is insulated from most forms of judicial interference. Party autonomy is well protected and the parties may choose either ad hoc or institutional arbitration. In addition, if the parties do not designate a procedural system for their arbitration, the Convention provides that the Inter-American Commercial Arbitration Commission's rules will apply. These rules are virtually indistinguishable from the UNCITRAL rules discussed in Chapter Eight.

There are ways to work around some of the problems in the region. First, virtually all Latin American countries recognize domestic arbitration. A

37. Abbott, *Latin America and International Arbitration Conventions: The Quandary of Non-Ratification*, 17 Harv.J.Int'l L. 131-32 (1976).

38. See, e.g., the recent reports of the Inter-American Commercial Arbitration Commission.

39. For an exceptionally hostile view see Ramirez, *Arbitraje Comercial Internacional*, 11 Revista de Law Facultad de Derecho de Mexico 477 (1961), but for a more modern view see Malamud, *El Arbitraje Comercial y el Nuevo Codigo de Procedimientos*, 4 Jurisprudencia Argentina 823 (1968).

40. Statement of Michael F. Hoellering, American Arbitration Association, before the Senate Foreign Relations Committee as quoted in AAA, *The Inter-American Convention on International Commercial Arbitration*, Lawyer's Arbitration Letter (December, 1986).

foreign company might want to agree to domestic arbitration—in lieu of litigation—even though it may be doing business in a Latin American country that refuses to join any of the multi-national recognition and enforcement conventions. Obviously, this means that the company gives up many of the possibilities of international enforcement of the award, but the award should remain enforceable within the host country.[41] Second, the promulgation of the IACA rules and the Inter-American Convention are not only useful in and of themselves, but may be an indication of growing regional interest in international commercial arbitration. Third, no one doing business in Latin America should forget that a number of countries have signed the 1958 New York Convention on Recognition and Enforcement of Foreign Arbitral Awards: Chile, Colombia, Cuba, Ecuador, Guatemala, Haiti, Mexico, Panama, Trinidad and Tobago, the United States and Uruguay. Fourth, for those limited instances in which the ICSID process is relevant, that Convention has been signed by Barbados, Costa Rica, El Salvador, Guyana, Haiti, Jamaica, Paraguay, St. Lucia, Trinidad and Tobago, and the United States. Fifth, contracting parties should consider some of those dispute resolution devices that do not require governmental intervention such as mediation/conciliation or the mini-trial.[42] Sixth, there are some imminent breakthroughs on a country-by-country basis. Brazil, for example, has entertained legislation that would enhance and promote arbitration in commercial disputes in that country after decades of intense hostility to the process. Among other things, the country has created the Brazilian Arbitration Centre and is considering the implementation of a Latin-American Arbitration Court with its headquarters in Brazil.[43] Finally, additional impetus to develop modern systems of commercial arbitration may spring from the interest in negotiating a hemispheric free trade agreement. Free trade is virtually unattainable without an effective, uniform system of commercial dispute resolution.

§ 10.6 The Middle East and Africa

The legal systems and the systems of commercial arbitration in a number of countries in the Middle East and in Africa are significantly affected by the tenets of the Islamic religion. This section will examine mainly the commercial dispute resolution system in Saudi Arabia as an example of a religiously-

---

41. For a country-by-country breakdown see INTERNATIONAL HANDBOOK ON COMMERCIAL ARBITRATION (P. Sanders, ed. 1985 & updates); for one view on Argentine views on international commercial arbitration see Naon, *Public Policy and International Commercial Arbitration: The Argentine Perspective*, 3 J.Int'l Arb. 7 (Jun. 1986). For the Brazilian perspective see, Rosenn, *Enforcement of Foreign Arbitral Awards in Brazil*, 28 Am.J.Comp.L. 498 (1980).

42. See, e.g., Fox, *Innovative Commercial Dispute Resolution Mechanisms: The Benefits for North and South America*, paper presented to the XVI Meeting of the Inter-American Bar Association, Buenos Aires, Argentina (May 13, 1987).

43. Pestalozzi, *Arbitration and Its New Prospects in Brazil*, 4 J. Int'l Arb. 131 (Sep. 1987).

influenced system. As shall be seen, this does not mean that these dispute resolution systems are unacceptable under Western standards. Indeed, the new Saudi system of commercial arbitration is quite sophisticated if one approaches it with the understanding that Saudi Arabia, like many developing countries, has been quite suspicious of Western systems of dispute resolution since those systems frequently assisted foreign countries in the unconscionable exploitation of Saudi natural resources. In reaction, the Saudis have promulgated some protective devices: for example, arbitration of commercial disputes in foreign countries arising out of contracts to be performed in Saudi Arabia is normally forbidden by the Saudi government. A 1963 decree (Decree No. 58) prohibits Saudi agencies from entering into a contract with foreign corporations if that contract contains an arbitration clause calling for arbitration outside Saudi Arabia.[44]

There are essentially five formal dispute resolution mechanisms in Saudi Arabia: (i) the Shari'a Courts which are normally limited to domestic relations, real estate and criminal matters; (ii) the Board of Grievances (*Diwan-Al-Mazalem*), which hears disputes between Saudi government agencies and private parties; (iii) the Committee for the Settlement of Commercial Disputes, which is used for resolving disputes between private parties; (iv) the Commercial Papers Committee, for disputes involving negotiable instruments and other documents of finance; and (v) the Committee for the Resolution of Labor Disputes.[45]

In 1983, to help modernize its system of commercial arbitration (a system which, quite frankly, was nearly non-existent prior to 1983), the Saudi Government issued Royal Decree M/46, a legal instrument that permits the appropriate Saudi court, described above, to supervise arbitration. In practice, this means that the courts supervise a procedure which has been described as something "between the Western concept of arbitration and the concept of conciliation in the Far East [in that] ... Saudi arbitrators [who normally must be Saudi] ... generally conceive their task to be to reach a compromise which is either brought about between the parties (settlement) or reflected in their decision.... . Also, some Ministries prefer an informal mediation by a Saudi of high reputation over a formal arbitration."[46]

Since arbitrations involving Saudi governmental entities must be conducted in Saudi Arabia under Saudi law, a number of observers have asked whether such arbitrations may be governed by rules of procedure estab-

44. See, e.g., McLaughlin, *Arbitration and Developing Countries*, 12 Int'l Law. 211 (1980), citing Setrakian, *Arbitration Under the Legal Systems of the Middle Eastern Countries*, ALI-ABA Course of Study: Construction Contracting in the Middle East (1978).

45. van den Berg, *Saudi Arabia*, in INTERNATIONAL HANDBOOK ON COMMERCIAL ARBITRATION (P. Sanders, ed., 1984) and Hamid El-Ahdab, *Arbitration in Saudi Arabia Under the New Arbitration Act, 1983 and Its Implementation Rules of 1985*, Part I in 3 J.Int'l Arb. 47 (Sept. 1986) and Part II in 3 J.Int'l Arb. 23 (Dec. 1986).

46. van den Berg, supra note 45, at 3.

lished by international bodies such as the International Chamber of Commerce or UNCITRAL. On the one hand, this may no longer be a major problem. Dr. Abdul Hamid El-Ahdab's description of the 1983 Saudi Arbitration Act and the rules promulgated in 1985 under the Act suggest that the arbitration procedures in Saudi Arabia under its new act are not terribly different—in a procedural sense—from those of the international bodies. Those rules provide for notice of the arbitration, the convening of an arbitral tribunal, the conducting of a hearing in which evidence and argument is received, the construction of a hearing record and the issuing of an award upon close of the record.[47] At the same time, there apparently have been a number of construction contract arbitrations carried out in Saudi Arabia using the UNCITRAL rules, although there is a serious question as to whether use of the UNCITRAL rules is permissible since the promulgation of the 1983 Arbitration Act.[48]

Since all arbitration in Saudi Arabia is automatically under the supervision of one of the courts enumerated above, there is normally no problem with enforcement of the award domestically. International enforcement, however, may be more of a problem. At the moment, Saudi Arabia is not a signatory of the 1958 New York Convention on the Recognition and Enforcement of Arbitral Awards, although it has ratified the ICSID Convention, the Agreement on Enforcement of Awards of the Charter of the United Nations and the Agreement with the American Institute for Guarantee of American Investments (this last is not a treaty but merely an agreement with a private association in the United States).[49]

Outside of Saudi Arabia there have been some attempts to develop modern regional approaches to international commercial dispute resolution. For example, the Asian-African Legal Consultative Committee has begun to push for more commercial arbitration in the Middle East and Africa using Cairo as a regional arbitration center.[50] In 1987 the Council of Arab Ministers of Justice meeting in Amman, Jordan, promulgated the Amman Arab Convention on Commercial Arbitration to provide uniformity among the Arab world in commercial arbitration. The Convention is based on, but not identical with, the ICSID Convention.[51] The Egyptian Civil Code, a statute that contains ingredients found in both the UNCITRAL commercial arbitration rules and the new UNCITRAL Model Law on International Commercial

---

47. El-Ahdab, supra note 45 at 24-51.

48. van den Berg, supra note 45, at 4.

49. El-Ahdab, supra note 45, at 53. For problems and questions associated with enforcing an arbitral award on behalf of a foreign private party against a private party in Oman, see Javin, *Enforcement of An Arbitration Award in Oman*, 2 J. Int'l Arb. 81 (1985).

50. See, e.g., Aboul Enein, *Arbitration under the Auspices of the Cairo Regional Centre for Commercial Arbitration*, 1 J. Int'l Arb. 23 (1984); Wall, *The Asian-African Legal Consultative Committee and International Commercial Arbitration*, 1979 Canadian Y.B. Int'l L. 324.

51. Jahil, *Amman Arab Convention on Commercial Arbitration*, 7 J. Int'l Arb. 139 (1990).

Arbitration, recognizes arbitration as a legitimate form of dispute resolution, permits arbitration under the Civil Code to take place outside Egypt; and, unlike a number of other countries in Africa and the Middle East, Egypt is a signatory of the 1958 New York Convention. Prior to the 1990-91 Gulf War the government of Kuwaiti had taken steps to develop a modern arbitration systems that should remain in effect following Kuwait's liberation from Iraqi occupation.[52]

In parts of Africa, arbitration may be a perfectly workable device for resolving commercial disputes since most of the sub-Saharan countries have arbitration statutes. If there is a gap in African practice, it is probably in the lack of institutional bodies such as Chambers of Commerce that might supervise domestic arbitration. Two Ghanian scholars suggest that one entity that might be able to fill such as role is a restructured Commission of Mediation, Conciliation and Arbitration of the Organization of African Unity (OAU).[53] Of course, that suggestion was made over ten years ago, and there seems to be absolutely no movement since then for implementing such a suggestion. The politically-charged atmosphere in which the OAU has functioned may frighten away normally conservative Western lawyers and business executives. Nonetheless, as many African countries seek to improve their international trade posture there may be a real need in the future for a regional center for commercial arbitration somewhere in Sub-Saharan Africa.

§ 10.7 The Pacific Rim

International trade between Japan and many of the countries of the Pacific Rim such as Korea, Taiwan, Hong Kong and Singapore and the Western nations is booming. But as this book has recognized throughout, increased international trading opportunities also increase the number of international commercial disputes. While no city or country on the Pacific Rim has yet developed into a major center of commercial arbitration, many governments are beginning to become aware of the advantages of resolving important commercial disputes at some location in the region and it appears that dispute resolution possibilities will grow in the future.[54]

As the largest trading nation on the Pacific Rim, Japan generates most of the discussion on dispute resolution. American lawyers became increasingly aware of the possibilities of arbitration in Japan in mid-1985 when the United States Supreme Court, in the case of *Mitsubishi v. Soler*,[55] determined

---

52. Huneidi, *Arbitration Under Kuwaiti Law*, 6 J. Int'l Arb. 75 (1989).

53. Tiewul & Tsegah, *Arbitration and the Settlement of Commercial Disputes: A Selective Survey of African Practice*, 24 Int'l & Comp. L.Q. 393 (1975).

54. See, e.g., McClelland, *A Survey of Pacific Rim Commercial Arbitration*, 40 Arb. J. 4 (March, 1985).

55. 473 U.S. 614 (1985).

that parties who sign a general arbitration clause with a choice of forum in Japan under arbitration rules promulgated by the Japan Commercial Arbitration Association may have to arbitrate even antitrust claims which may arise under U.S. law.

While one Japanese writer suggests that commercial arbitration is neither common nor popular in Japan,[56] Japan does have an established system of commercial arbitration and is a signatory of the 1958 New York Convention on the Recognition and Enforcement of Foreign Arbitral Awards. There are some possible complications, of course. The rules of the Japanese Commercial Arbitration Association require the arbitration to take place in Japan using the Japanese language unless the parties have agreed to the contrary. But at the same time, the Japanese courts normally let arbitral awards alone and an award is enforced in Japan on the same terms as a court judgment. As a major trading nation, there is normally no shortage in Japan of experienced and expert commercial arbitrators.[57] Indeed, in *Mitsubishi*, the United States Supreme Court was quite sanguine about the ability of Japanese arbitrators to deal with complicated questions of U.S. antitrust law. Apparently, many Japanese businesses are now fully amenable to writing international commercial arbitration clauses in their transnational contracts.[58] of intense research, legislation modernizing Japan's concededly archaic arbitration law was proposed. It appears that the draft legislation is based heavily on the UNCITRAL Model Arbitration Law and prospects for passage appear good.[59]

The other countries on the Pacific Rim vary in their views of international commercial arbitration. India (perhaps technically not a "Pacific Rim" country) has a modern system of commercial arbitration patterned on but not identical with the English model.[60] It appears that India has a good track record on the enforcement of foreign arbitral awards under the New York Convention.[61] Many of the other countries of the Far East are much more primitive in their approach to commercial dispute resolution; but at least one observer, Arden McClelland, believes that more and more of the countries are beginning to take a sophisticated approach to the process.[62] As he sees it, while no international arbitration center has yet emerged for the region,

56. Yamane, *Resolving Disputes in U.S.- Japan Trade: The Japanese Perspective*, 39 Arb . J. 3 (Dec. 1984)

57. Doi, *Arbitration in Japan* in 4 YEARBOOK OF COMMERCIAL ARBITRATION (P. Sanders ed. 1979).

58. Yamane, supra note 56, at 8.

59. Ogawa, *Proposed Draft of Japan's New Arbitration Law*, 7 J. Int'l Arb. 33 (Jun. 1990).

60. See Deshpande, *The India Council of Arbitration and the Practice of Arbitration in India*, 1 J. Int'l. Arb. 255 (1984); Deshpande, *International Commercial Arbitration and Domestic Courts in India*, 2 J. Int'l Arb. 45 (1985). See also, Anand, *Arbitration in the Context of Technology Transfer Agreements: The Case of India*, 7 J. Int'l Arb. 87 (Jun. 1990).

61. Nariman, *Foreign Arbitral Awards in India: Problems, Pitfalls, and Progress*, 6 J. Int'l Arb. 25 (Mar. 1989).

62. McClelland, supra note 54 at 17.

Hong Kong and Singapore seem to be good possibilities for the establishment of such a center given that they are becoming major centers of trade, that the predominant language of business in the countries is English and that there are sizeable numbers of well educated potential arbitrators. Of these two possibilities, Hong Kong may have the superior claim to becoming a regional center since it recently promulgated a modern arbitration statute patterned on the English Arbitration Act of 1979 and because it exists in close proximity to, and in 1997 will be a part of the Peoples Republic of China.[63] There may be some special problems involving the practice of arbitration in Singapore for foreign counsel. Professor Andreas Lowenfeld recently reported on a decision of the High Court of the Republic of Singapore in which counsel not admitted to the local bar were enjoined from representing clients who had chosen to arbitrate their dispute in Singapore. As Professor Lowenfeld comments: "In my experience, membership of the bar of the state where the arbitration takes place is purely coincidental. Parties choose their counsel based on long time association, or special expertise in arbitrations, or expertise in the industry involved ... or familiarity with the language or languages of the arbitration, not on the basis of the situs of the arbitration."[64] There is some question, however, whether this is an indication of a firm, long-term position by the Singapore High Court or some kind of aberrant decision that may be quickly corrected.[65]

§ 10.8 The Peoples Republic of China

Trade and commerce with China has increased so significantly over the past dozen years that many people are now quite familiar with the spirit if not the language of that old Chinese proverb: "It is better to enter a tiger's mouth than a court of law."[66] This little homily tells a great deal about Chinese attitudes toward dispute resolution. Those attitudes have been shaped by centuries of tradition and philosophy. Confrontation and the adversary process seems never to have been particularly attractive to the Chinese.[67] In developing a legal system, virtually all observers of the Chinese scene report constant tension between the concept of li—essentially an ethical construct

---

63. See Kaplan, *Arbitration in Hong Kong*, 3 J. Int'l Arb. 7 (Dec. 1986); Thomas, *Arbitration in Hong Kong*, Int'l Bus. Law. 142 (May 1986).

64. Lowenfeld, *Singapore and the Local Bar: Aberration or Ill Omen?* 5 J. Int'l Arb. 71, 73 (Sep. 1989).

65. *Id.*

66. A Chinese proverb attributed to the Analects of Confucius and first brought to the author's attention by Steven Robinson, Esq. Mr. Robinson's comments on dispute resolution in China are now contained in Robinson & Doumar, *"It is Better to Enter a Tiger's Mouth Than a Court of Law"* - *Dispute Resolution Alternatives in U.S. - China Trade*, 2 Dickinson J. Int'l L. 1 (1987). The discussion in this section relies heavily on the Robinson-Doumar article.

67. See generally J. COHEN & H. CHIU, THE PEOPLE'S REPUBLIC OF CHINA AND INTERNATIONAL LAW (1974).

that places primary emphasis on harmony among human beings and with the universe—that discourages conflict and adversarial behavior and the concept of *fa*—the idea of a formal codified legal system that finds its principles not in Confucian ethics but rather in the country's law books and government regulations.[68] It is clear that a legal system based solely on the concept of *li* could find little place for something as disruptive to harmony as litigation and conventional commercial arbitration. By contrast, *fa* may encourage some kind of formal dispute resolution mechanisms in which the rule of law, rather than the rule of ethics, is paramount. Moreover, in the case of modern China, Marxist thought further complicates matters by imposing a philosophical model developed in the West on traditional attitudes toward the legal system; and the ten year vacuum in Chinese legal and commercial education caused by the Cultural Revolution deprived China of a decade of potential progress in many of these matters.

While it is clear that the Chinese legal system has not resolved these basic tensions, China's recent interest in improving international trade to foster progress toward Deng Shao Peng's Four Modernizations seems also to have affected the country's view of international commercial dispute resolution. There is now a great deal of stability in Chinese foreign transactions although, most trade is filtered through state-controlled trading bodies. The general rule in China has been that individuals may not execute transnational contracts,[69] although even that rule is being altered as China puts more emphasis on the New Economic Zones adjacent to Hong Kong.

Most of the recent transactional stability has been contributed by two actions on the part of the Chinese government: the development of modern trading statutes, most significantly the new Joint Venture law (discussed at some length in Chapter Three, § 3.3) but also including statutes on protection of intellectual property, investment and trade; and the execution of bilateral commercial agreements such as the United States-Sino Trade Agreement in 1979.[70] The Chinese institutions primarily concerned with international commercial agreements are the commodity-based foreign trade corporations which are contained within the Ministry of Foreign Trade and Economic Relations. The Ministry also interacts with the China Council for the Promotion of International Trade (a nominally private institution) which in turn contains two formal arbitral bodies, the Foreign Economic Trade Arbitration Commission (FETAC) and the Maritime Arbitration Commission.

---

68. For a general discussion see H. KIM, FUNDAMENTAL LEGAL CONCEPTS OF CHINA AND THE WEST: A COMPARATIVE STUDY (1980). For a similar discussion in the pragmatic setting of international trade see Ellis & Shea, *Foreign Commercial Dispute Settlement in the People's Republic of China*, 10 Int'l Trade L.J. 155 (1987).

69. See, e.g., Theroux, *Technology Sales to China*, 14 J. Int'l L. & Econ. 185 (1980).

70. July 7, 1979, T.I.A.S. 9630, reported in 79 Dep't State Bull. No. 2033-34, 18 Int'l Legal Mat. 1041 (1979).

Most standard form contracts executed by the foreign trade corporations call for a two-step dispute resolution process: first the parties are
required to renegotiate the issue and failing a successful renegotiation, the
dispute is to be submitted to either FETAC or the Maritime Arbitration
Commission in Beijing. In the Chinese Joint Venture Law, the process is
actually a three step process: first the parties are required to engage in
"friendly discussion."[71] Next, the parties must engage in conciliation supervised by a Chinese arbitral body. FETAC may supervise the conciliation
under existing rules or it may use the new conciliation rules promulgated by
UNCITRAL.

If conciliation fails, the parties generally must resort to binding arbitration—a process which in the past has apparently always meant arbitration
in Beijing under the FETAC's rules but which now may call for arbitration
outside of China under some of the internationally recognized rules systems
such as the rules of the Stockholm Chamber of Commerce or the
International Chamber of Commerce or even, perhaps, ad hoc arbitration
using the UNCITRAL rules.[72] In 1988, FETAC's name was changed to "China
International Economic and Trade Arbitration Commission (CIETAC) and the
Maritime Arbitration Commission was renamed the China Maritime
Arbitration Commission (CMAC).[73] The new arbitration rules promulgated by
CIETAC and CMAC are considerably modernized, providing the form for
demands for arbitration, hearing procedures, and a fee schedule.[74]

There have not yet been a sufficient number of commercial disputes
involving China to develop firm conclusions on these various mechanisms.
One American law professor, Pat Chew, who has studied a large number of
Soviet and Chinese commercial arbitrations believes: "First, the [Chinese]
arbitrators appear to be fair toward foreign parties. Chinese arbitrators may
even show a bias in favor of non-Chinese parties. Second, the Chinese are
developing a hybrid model of arbitration that clearly incorporates a distinc-
tive Chinese approach to the resolution of disputes... . It is a process that
considers the perspective of both sides, including their respective commercial and economic positions, and reaches a result that yields the highest net
benefit in the long term for both parties. In addition, the [Chinese process of
commercial dispute resolution] encourages amicable and constructive ongo-
ing relationships between the parties, even after the dispute is resolved."[75]

---

71. Klitgaard, *People's Republic of China Joint Venture Dispute Resolution Procedures*, 1
U.C.L.A. Pac. Basin L.J. 1 (1982). There is now a short book that translates into English many of
the important Chinese legal documents. See E. LEE, COMMERCIAL DISPUTES SETTLEMENT IN
CHINA (1985).

72. Robinson & Doumar, *supra* note 66, at 18.

73. Triebel & Guojian, *International Economic, Trade and Maritime Arbitration in the People's
Republic of China: New Developments*, 6 J. Int'l Arb. 13, 14 (Jun. 1989).

74. *Id.* at 17-30.

75. Chew, *A Procedural and Substantive Analysis of the Fairness of Chinese and Soviet
Foreign Trade Arbitrations*, 21 Tex. Int'l L.J. 291 (1986).

As is characteristic of most countries, there is no trouble enforcing an arbitral award within China. Such awards are binding and have the force and effect of court judgments.[76] Moreover, in January, 1987 China became a contracting state under the New York Convention on Recognition and Enforcement of Foreign Arbitral Awards so it is now possible to obtain extraterritorial enforcement of Chinese arbitration awards in the proper circumstances. Enforcement through China's numerous bilateral treaties of friendship, commerce and navigation may also be possible. For example, the 1974 China–U.S. Trade Agreement contains express language to the effect: "both signatory countries are held responsible for the execution of arbitration rulings by concerned organs under terms provided for under the laws of the country being sought to make the ruling [e.g., the country in which enforcement is sought]."[77]

World trade with China enterered the doldrums after the 1989 incidents of violance in Tienamen Square in Beijing, but it shows some signs of reviving as the United States ponders granting most favored nation status to the Peoples Republic.

§ 10.9 The Former Soviet Union

[Note: This section has been preserved for the reader even though the Soviet Union as a political entity no longer exists. In its place is the somewhat shaky Commonwealth of Independent States. It is expected that a number of the arbitration institutions discussed below will be preserved at least in the Russian Republic for some time to come. Even so, all the language has been changed to the past tense. The reader should monitor closely future developments in this part of the world.]

International commercial arbitration in the former Soviet Union was affected by two aspects of Soviet governance. First, arbitration was well-known within the Soviet Union as a dispute resolution technique. There were essentially three types of arbitration recognized by the Soviet system: (i) state arbitration (which is very close in operation and concept to litigation in Western countries and which is frequently referred to as *arbitrazh* involves the use of expert tribunals to resolve questions that arise between and among the various economic units of the government), (ii) third-party arbitration (a device that would probably be called "court annexed" arbitration in the United States and is used for citizen disputes and permits people who would ordinarily be litigants in the regular court system to voluntarily submit their dispute to a third-party arbitrator who renders a decision), and (iii)

---

76. Klitgaard, *supra* note 71, at 31.
77. 13 Int'l Legal Mat. 872, 874 (1974).

the third form of commercial dispute resolution, foreign trade arbitration (the topic of this section).[78]

In the past all trade with the former Soviet Union was conducted through state-run organizations called Foreign Trade Organizations (FTO). The FTO's conducted business with the West under standard form contracts that called for arbitration in Moscow under the rules of the USSR's Foreign Trade Arbitration Commission (FTAC), a body within the Chamber of Commerce and Industry.[79] This take-it-or-leave-it approach probably reflects many of the Socialist countries' aversion to commercial arbitration as being too much under the control of the capitalist systems—and of the lawyers in those capitalist systems, although it is equally clear that the Socialist countries prefer international commercial arbitration to litigation in a capitalist country.[80]

In 1972 the United States and the Soviet Union signed a trade agreement that, for apparently the first time, permitted the FTOs to sign contracts containing arbitration clauses that permitted arbitration in a third country—invariably Sweden—under rules other than those of the FTAC.[81] While many of these details were worked out between the American Arbitration Association and the Soviet Union's Chamber of Commerce and Industry, the policies were relatively rigid. The FTO's were permitted to agree to one of only two alternatives: conventional arbitration in Moscow under FTAC rules or the so-called *optional* arbitration clause calling for arbitration under Stockholm under the UNCITRAL rules or the rules of the Stockholm Chamber of Commerce.

Most Western businesses elected the optional clause. The UNCITRAL rules are quite sophisticated and the FTOs apparently rarely protested the insertion of the optional clause.[82] Moreover, Stockholm contains all the support mechanisms necessary for a proper international commercial arbitration. It was not necessarily a bad or defective process. After studying hundreds of FTAC awards, Julian Lew was able to conclude:

> "[D]espite the undoubted control which the socialist States have over their arbitration tribunals, [the governments] do not interfere with the arbitrators and are particularly anxious not only to be impartial

---

78. 1 ENCYCLOPEDIA OF SOVIET LAW 53 (F.Feldbrugge ed. 1973); see also O. IOFFE & P. MAGGS, SOVIET LAW IN THEORY AND PRACTICE 306 (1983).

79. T. HOYA, EAST-WEST TRADE: COMECON LAW AND AMERICAN-SOVIET TRADE (1984). For an explanation of a parallel Soviet arbitral body see Jarvis, *The Soviet Maritime Arbitration Commission: A Practitioner's Perspective*, 21 Tex. Int'l L.J. 341 (1986).

80. See, e.g., Hanak, *The Experience of Socialist Lawyers in Arbitration Held in Non-Socialist Countries*, Int'l Bus. Law. 145 (March 1982).

81. See Holtzmann, *Dispute Resolution Procedures in East-West Trade*, 20 Int'l Law. 233 (1978); Wetter, *East Meets West in Sweden*, 20 Int'l Law. 261 (1978).

82. Note, *The Soviet Position on International Arbitration: A Wealth of Choices or Choices for the Wealthy*, 26 Va.J. Int'l L. 417 (1986).

but also to be seen to be impartial. Indeed some commentators have argued that if anything, socialist arbitration tribunals are biased in favour of a western party. To prove their impartiality the socialist tribunals generally publish their awards ... a practice which is generally opposed in the West.[83]

However, a much more detailed statistical study of FTAC awards conducted by Pat Chew is far more troubling. Having analyzed 68 arbitral awards made by FTAC, he was able to conclude: (i) generally there appeared to be no tendency on the part of FTAC to favor either the claimant or the respondent; and (ii) when the claimant was another COMECON country (included in the study were Czechoslovakia, East Germany, Hungary and Poland) FTAC arbitrations appeared to be relatively evenhanded. However, when the arbitration involved an industrial country (in Chew's study the countries were Belgium, Denmark, Finland, France, West Germany, Italy, and the United Kingdom), it was found that FTAC favored the Soviet party 81 percent of the time.[84]

Of course, these figures are only statistical developments. There was no attempt to correlate the data on the basis of the type of case, the claims made, and the more intimate aspects of the dispute; so the 81 percent figure should be taken with a large grain of salt. Another lengthy article on Soviet commercial arbitration suggested that "Soviet arbitrators are careful to avoid decisions that might be interpreted by the international arena as being politically-motivated ... [since the USSR wishes to demonstrate] to trading partners that the USSR abides by its bargains in spite of international exigencies and that a Soviet court [sic] can provide an impartial forum for settling disputes."[85] If the figure is correct, however, Western parties would be ill advised ever to opt for FTAC arbitration if they can avail themselves of the *optional* clause.

When an award is made either in the former Soviet Union or in Sweden, it is fully enforcible both domestically and on an international basis. Presumably such is now the case at least with regard to the Russian Republic since Russian has essentially succeeded to all Soviet treaty obligations. The United States, The Soviet Union and Sweden all accepted the 1958 New York Convention. While there is apparently some question as to the precise legal nature of FTAC awards since a number of commentators view them as more like court judgments than arbitral awards, there are virtually no reports of a refusal on the part of the Soviet Union to honor those awards itself.

On balance, arbitration involving the former Soviet Union seems to have been a relatively successful enterprise. Other Eastern European coun-

---

83. J. LEW, APPLICABLE LAW IN INTERNATIONAL COMMERCIAL ARBITRATION 30-31 (1978).

84. Chew, *supra* note 75, at 325-30.

85. Soviet Position, *supra* note 82, at 423, quoting Armstrong, The *Problem of Autonomy in Soviet International Contract Law*, 31 Am.J. Comp. L. 63, 77 (1983).

tries have worked out other arrangements. For example, in 1984 Hungary and the United States, working through the Hungarian Chamber of Commerce and the American Arbitration Association, signed an agreement permitting Hungarian state trading organizations and U.S. companies to sign contracts containing an arbitration clause that calls for arbitration in Vienna under the UNCITRAL rules.[86]

In the six years since these several paragraphs were written, there has been a political and economic revolution in Eastern Europe that has now moved into the former Soviet Union. As of early 1992, nothing can be guaranteed even for the immediate future. As the countries of Eastern Europe move toward a market mechanism, they also appear to be moving away from state trading companies. In Poland and Hungary, as well as Czechoslovakia, the governments now permit individual businesses to negotiate and sign international commercial agreements.[87] This means that the dispute resolution procedures adapted for the state trading companies are no longer effective. In each instance, the private companies appear to have independent authority to engage in private dispute resolution such as commercial arbitration. In the Commonwealth of Independent States the state trading companies have not yet been completely abandoned, but there appears to be a strong inclination to abolish them and permit private concerns to do their own trading—and, by definition, their own dispute resolution.   ◆

---

86. AAA, *USA-Hungarian Trade Assisted by New Arrangements for Arbitration in Vienna*, 40 Arb.J. 34 (March, 1985).

87. See, e.g., Slupinski, *Foreign Investment in the Banking Sector and Emergence of the Financial Market in Poland*, 25 Int'l Law. 127 (1991).

— 11 —
Future Trends in International Commercial Agreements
and International Commercial Dispute Resolution

§ 11.1 Introduction

The reader will not be shocked to find that the one chapter in this book that attempts to predict matters is also the shortest. Most predictions seem useful only to show how wrong they were. Recall that at the turn of the century a U.S. Commissioner of Patents resigned from office because he believed that there was nothing more the human mind could possibly invent.

This chapter is a prediction of trends, not a statement of future certainties. The chapter also contains a discussion of the United Nations (UNCITRAL) Model Law on International Commercial Arbitration, a proposal that begin as a United Nations study but that has now been adopted by an increasing number of countries and even a few of the U.S. state governments.

§ 11.2 Trends in International Commercial Agreements

The forces of free trade and the forces of protectionism remain locked in global battle. While the United States has frequently set the tone of this debate using its leverage as the world's largest trading nation, the U.S. no longer exercises the plenary economic power that it exercised after World War Two. Historically, the U.S. has never taken a consistent position on world trade; the country persistently vacillates between the promotion of global free trade and the narrowest sort of protectionism. The most dynamic major trading nation, Japan, seems bent on remaining almost unabashedly protectionist. Most other countries seem unable to form a consistent position on the topic. Thus, the fundamental world trade agreement, the General

Agreement on Tariffs and Trade (GATT), may be only a token nod in the direction of free trade while nations pursue narrower, more protectionist interests outside the GATT framework. The recent failures of the Uruguay round of GATT negotiations may be a signal that GATT's time has come and gone.

One reaction to the failures and impotence of GATT is the development of regional free trade associations, in particular the economic integration of the European Community scheduled for the end of 1992 and the ratification of the United States-Canada Free Trade Agreement. The United States, in particular, seems to be following the path of regionalism to the detriment of a genuinely global trade policy exemplified by the GATT. As this second edition goes to press, the U.S. Congress has just approved "fast-track" authority for the negotiation of a North American Free Trade Agreement. The Bush Administration has been pushing for an even larger hemispheric free trade agreement covering virtually all the nations of the Western Hemisphere. Other regions of the world, notably many of the Pacific Rim countries other than Japan, are exploring regional trade groupings—probably in reaction to the failure of GATT and to increasing regionalism elsewhere.

The activities of the World Bank and the International Monetary Fund and the continuing and astonishing debt problems faced by a large number of developing countries suggest that the world is a long way from being able to solve those nearly intractable problems which are frequently characterized as the North-South controversy. Massive financial assistance to developing countries appears to have pushed them only deeper and perhaps inextricably into debt. Thus far they have not been able to extricate themselves either through austerity programs or increased trade.

One ray of hope for increased world trade is the emergence of market economies in most of the centrally controlled economies of Eastern Europe. While the economic direction of the former Soviet Union is difficult to predict, even those republics appear to be moving away from central planning. While the Peoples Republic of China remains an enigma, that country's government seems to be loosening the controls on international trade by individual companies. Overtures made by countries such as Cuba and North Korea suggest that most non-market economies may be abolished by the turn of the century. This development can only be a boon for international trade.

As countries become more sophisticated in the ways of international business, it is clear that many of the old forms of commercial agreement, such as the much-criticized concession agreements are giving way to business arrangements over which the host country has more control. Few countries will permit the export of either their natural resources or their economic capital without significant financial benefit to their citizens. This trend clearly favors such devices as joint ventures, with majority control vested within the host country, franchises (with close regulation of termination procedures) and various types of licensing and distributorship agreements.

But the most striking development in international trade has come in the area of the sale of goods between merchants in different countries with the ratification—in January, 1987—by the United States of the United Nations Convention on Contracts for the International Sale of Goods (CISG). The U.S. ratification of the CISG, now accompanied by the ratification or acceptance by many other countries, may prove to be a watershed event in the development, after centuries of trying, of a truly *international* law of sales.[1]

The Convention should not be regarded as a panacea for world trade. We have not yet entered upon any golden age just yet. It appears that very few private contracts choose the CISG as the governing law. The trend appears to be just the opposite. In those instances when the CISG might apply, contract drafters are opting out of the Convention. Moreover, it is arguable that the *law* incident to world trade (i.e., the legal principles which govern any particular agreement) is not nearly as important to the final consummation of the deal as such things as currency exchange rates, political factors, the world economic climate and other such matters.

§ 11.3 Trends in International Commercial Dispute Resolution

International commercial arbitration will remain the preeminent mechanism for resolving international commercial disputes for the foreseeable future. Litigation is usually too expensive and time consuming; and court judgments—at least outside the European Community—have little international impact. But cost-conscious business executives may begin looking more closely at what this book calls the *less-drastic* forms of commercial dispute resolution such as mediation/conciliation and mini-trial. Granting that these devices lack finality and granting that the parties may still have to arbitrate or litigate if mediation or mini-trial fail, these less-drastic devices still make sense in a large number of instances; and far too many lawyers disregard them. It may be that business executives rather than their lawyers will have to take the lead in insisting that the attempt be made. Too many lawyers are like many surgeons: they want to cut (read "litigate") without deeper analysis when there are plenty of ways to avoid cutting.

---

1. Any mention of the CISG would now be deficient without a citation to John Honnold's important new book on the Convention, published by Kluwer Law and Taxation: J. HONNOLD, THE UNITED NATIONS CONVENTION FOR THE INTERNATIONAL SALE OF GOODS (1987).

For those disputes that must be arbitrated, there are in place a number of well-developed, efficient and effective systems of international commercial arbitration. In addition, individual countries are beginning to develop indige-nous systems of effective, efficient arbitration by adopting the new United Nations Commission on International Trade Law (UNCITRAL) Model Law on International Commercial Arbitration. See Appendix G for the text of the Model Law. The Model Law is intended to substitute modern, generally accepted arbitration principles for archaic domestic models; and it appears to be finding acceptance nearly everywhere. Indeed, a number of countries who believe they have highly sophisticated forms of commercial arbitration would do well to look closely at the Model Law as an indication of some of the best recent thinking on the issue. Moreover, we may have reached a juncture in world history where uniformity in commercial arbitration is important. In that case, the Model Law could conceivably be adopted by all trading nations. If it were, many of the issues discussed in this book in Chapters 8, 9 and 10 might be alleviated. Again, the Model Law may not issue in a new golden age of arbitration; but it is well worth reading and understanding.

The Model Law began as an attempt in the 1960s by the Council of Europe to draft a Uniform Law for Commercial Arbitration—an attempt that was impeded by what Professor Pieter Sanders (the person many call the Father of the Model Law) describes as a tendency for "each of the partici-pants in such a venture [to try] to see that the Uniform Law will deviate as little as possible from his own national law."[2] Proposing and working on a *model* (as opposed to a *uniform* law) gave the drafters "more freedom to intro-duce in the model the best solutions, which are not necessarily based on the national law of the drafters."[3]

The United Nations took some wise preliminary steps. Regarding the 1958 New York Convention on the Recognition and Enforcement of Foreign Arbitral Awards as a successful effort, the United Nations, by a 1966 resolu-tion, created UNCITRAL and directed it to study additional steps to bring some uniformity to commercial arbitration as a step toward the "progressive harmonization and unification of the law of international trade."[4] But rather than begin immediately to draft a Model Law, UNCITRAL first developed and promulgated in 1976 arbitration rules which could be used, at the option of private parties, in any number of international commercial arbitrations (see Chapter 8). UNCITRAL then recognized that many business disputes could be resolved by some process less cumbersome than arbitration and promul-gated the UNCITRAL Conciliation Rules (discussed at length in Chapter 6) in

---

2. INTERNATIONAL COUNCIL FOR COMMERCIAL ARBITRATION, UNCITRAL'S PROJECT FOR A MODEL LAW ON INTERNATIONAL COMMERCIAL ARBITRATION 23 (P. Sanders ed., 1984).
    3. Id.
    4. U.N. General Assembly Resolution No. 2205/21 (December 17, 1966), to be found in I Yearbook of UNCITRAL 1968-70 (1971).

1980 as a device which could be attempted before parties launch the comparatively-more expensive and time-consuming process of arbitration. The conciliation rules were also sparked by the general aversion of many countries, including many nations in the Far East, to the antagonistic, gut-wrenching nature of the adversary process.[5]

But even with these developments, it became apparent to the members of UNCITRAL that creating a climate of uniformity in commercial arbitration required all countries to modify their internal arbitration laws since arbitration, as discussed in Chapter 8, always needs some kind of "home"—i.e., a country of origin in which the parties can invoke the supervisory and confirmatory powers of the domestic courts. As Sir Michael Kerr puts it: "The necessary powers to give binding effect to the legal consequences of arbitration, which is the whole raison d'etre of the arbitral process, is invariably vested in the national courts by legislation.... . In the ultimate analysis the effectiveness of the private process must therefore rest upon the binding, and even coercive, powers which each State entrusts to its courts."[6] There is some commentary to the contrary—that an international commercial arbitral award is not necessarily dependent for its validity and enforceability on having a "home" in some country's domestic court system, but that position is not well accepted.[7]

Thus, adopting the Model Law has had substantial consequences for each adopting state. For example, although the Model Law on its terms is restricted to international commercial agreements, it would make little sense for a country to have one process of commercial arbitration for purely domestic disputes and a wholly different process for international disputes. Accordingly, the Model Law appears to have had an impact on the arbitration of domestic disputes in the adopting countries, as well as controlling the arbitration of international commercial disputes. Representing some of the best recent thinking on commercial arbitration generally, adoption of the Model Law may well effect all arbitration, particularly in those countries whose current system of arbitration is rudimentary or whose courts have shown a great deal of hostility to arbitration.

Still, the difficulties, realized early on, of selling the Model Law to individual nations did not discourage UNCITRAL. The UNCITRAL Working Group on the Model Law approved a final text in Vienna in June, 1985 and that text was formally adopted by UNCITRAL itself on June 21, 1985. The Act is remarkable for both its brevity and its sophistication. To begin with, there are two crucial definitions which set the Act's boundaries. The term *commer-*

---

5. Fleischauer, *UNCITRAL and International Commercial Dispute Settlement*, 38 Arb.J. 9 (Dec. 1983).

6. Kerr, *Arbitration and the Courts: The UNCITRAL Model Law*, 34 Int'l & Comp.L.Q. 1 (1985).

7. See, e.g., the discussion by Professor Park in Park, *The Lex Loci Arbitri and International Commercial Arbitration*, 32 Int'l & Comp.L.Q. 21 (1983).

cial is defined as broadly as possible to include such matters as: "any trade transaction for the supply or exchange of goods or services; distribution agreement; ... agency; factoring; leasing; construction of works; consulting; engineering; licensing; investment financing; banking; insurance; exploitation agreement or concession; joint venture ... ; carriage of goods or passengers by air, sea, rail or road."[8] The term *international* is defined as commercial agreement in which "the parties to an arbitration agreement have, at the time of the conclusion of that agreement, their places of business in different States; or [if] one of the following places is situated outside the State in which the parties have their places of business: (i) the place of arbitration ... (ii) any place where a substantial part of the obligations of the commercial relationship is to be performed ... or [where] the parties have expressly agreed that the subject-matter of the arbitration agreement relates to more than one country."[9] To insure that courts let arbitration alone, the Act expressly states: "In matters governed by this Law, no court shall intervene except where so provided in this Law."[10] As discussed above, this provision alone should have the effect of curbing judicial interference with the arbitration process. Finally, the arbitration agreement must be in writing, although the concept of a writing is defined very broadly to include such things as telex messages and recorded telephone conversations.[11]

From that foundation, the Model Law moves to language and process that are very similar to the 1976 UNCITRAL Rules of Arbitration. The Act permits the parties to agree on the number of arbitrators, but in the absence of an expressly stated number requires that there be three arbitrators. The identity and credentials of the arbitrators may be agreed upon by the parties, but a court or other authority is permitted to appoint the arbitrators if the parties cannot agree.[12] The parties may specify rules of procedure and location or such matters may be prescribed by the tribunal if the parties cannot agree or if the agreement is silent on such issues.[13]

An arbitration is commenced by a claimant sending a request for arbitration to the respondent. Either in that notice or in a separate document, the claimant states his or her statements of claim to which the respondent files a defense or counterclaim. An oral hearing may be held, the tribunal may appoint and listen to experts and the tribunal may ask the country's courts for assistance in taking evidence.[14] The tribunal must make an award in writing that contains reasons for the award. While the tribunal may sit as

---

8. Model Law, Article 1.
9. Id.
10. Id., Article 5.
11. Id., Article 7.
12. Id., Articles 10 & 11.
13. Id., Articles 19 & 20.
14. Id., Articles 21-27.

an equitable body (ex aequo et bono or as amiable compositeur) only if the parties have "expressly authorized it to do so, the tribunal may render a decision based "on the terms of the contract and shall take into account the usages of the trade applicable to the transaction."[15]

Under the Model Law, courts are expected to recognize and confirm arbitral awards in the ordinary course without changing the terms of the award. A court is authorized to set aside an award only if (i) a party was incapacitated or the underlying agreement was somehow invalid; (ii) a party was not given proper notice; (iii) the award "deals with a dispute not contemplated by or not falling within the terms of the submission to arbitration" or is somehow beyond the scope of the submission; (iv) the composition of the tribunal was not in accordance with the agreement; (v) the subject-matter of the dispute is not properly subject to arbitration; or (vi) the award conflicts with the country's public policy.[16] The grounds on which a court may refuse to recognize and enforce a foreign arbitral award are set out in the Model Act in virtually the same terms.[17]

The Model Law has generally been given rave reviews. Even the delegation to the UNCITRAL Working Group from the United States—a country that appears to be constantly suspicious of anything the United Nations does or says—commented that the Model Law in conjunction with the 1958 New York Convention and the UNCITRAL Arbitration Rules:

"provide a comprehensive framework for the arbitral resolution of disputes arising from a broad range of international commercial transactions. Basic considerations of procedural due process are generally well protected and a proper balance is struck in the relationship between arbitration and the courts. The freedom of the parties to agree to arbitral procedures that best suit their specific needs is safeguarded throughout... . The achievement of [adoption of the Model Law] will serve not only the cause of international commercial arbitration, but also as a stimulus to international trade and investment and thus the foreign policy objectives of the United States."[18]

At the same time, a few commentators and some semi-official bodies have reservations about the Model Law. In late 1989, the Mustill Committee (a British committee chaired by Lord Justice Mustill and charged with making a recommendation on British adoption of the Model Law) recommended that the Model Law *not* be adopted for England, Wales, and Northern Ireland.[19] By contrast, a similar committee investigating possible adoption in

15. Id., Article 28 - 33.

16. Id., Article 34.

17. Id., Articles 35 & 36.

18. Report of the United States Delegation set out in AMERICAN ARBITRATION ASSOCIATION, ARBITRATION AND THE LAW 1985: AAA GENERAL COUNSEL'S REPORT 151.

19. Goodman, *UNCITRAL Model Law on International and Commercial Arbitration: Divergent Approaches in England and Scotland,* 18 Int'l Bus. Law. 250 (1990).

Scotland reported favorably on the Model Law and recommended adoption.[20] The Mustill committee took the position that while English arbitration law was not perfect, it nonetheless reflected the "unique 'richness of the English jurisprudence' fully developed and tested in practice... " concluding that the English system is "essentially satisfactory."[21] By contrast, the Scottish committee worried that Scottish arbitration law was based on common law rather than statute and the inherent lack of conformity with other nations' arbitration law might hinder the use of Scotland as a site for international commercial arbitration. This rationale appears to have been incorporated by most adopting jurisdictions. It is not so much that the Model Law is perfect; or, conversely, that a nation's existing arbitration law is defective. Rather, the absence of the Model Law or something close to it may inhibit contract drafters from choosing that jurisdiction as an arbitration site.

The Model Law has now come full circle and has become the statutory law of at least six states in the United States: California,[22] Connecticut,[23] Florida,[24] Georgia,[25] Hawaii[26] and Texas.[27] However, the U.S. Congress has shown little or no interest in adopting the Model Law for the federal system. In each instance, the state legislature enacted the Model Law in an attempt to encourage the siting of international arbitrations in that state.[28] This may mark the first time in U.S. history that a promulgation of the United Nations has been transmuted into a state statute.

§ 11.4 Conclusion

There are few matters in the world as important as international trade. It is through this process that wealth is built and shared, that information is transferred and that different cultures come to appreciate each other. The global problems of population, environment, and military conflict can be alleviated by a greater attention to trade and commercial relationships. We may have truly arrived at a time when no one on the face of the earth is immune from the consequences of international trade. If this book helps only a few transactions run a bit smoother, it will have accomplished its purpose.   ◆

---

20. *Id.*
21. *Id.* at 251.
22. Calif. Civil Procedure Code §§ 1297.11 - .432.
23. 1989 Conn. Acts 89-179, approved June 1, 1989.
24. Fla. Stat. Ann. §§ 684.01 - .35.
25. Ga. Code Ann. §§ 9-9-30 to 9-9-43.
26. Haw. Rev. Stat. Ann. §§ 658D-1 to 658D-9.
27. Tex. Rev. Civil Procedure Code Ann., arts. 249-1 to 249-43.
28. For a longer discussion of these state statutes and the Model Act see Romeu-Matta, *New Developments in International Commercial Arbitration: A Comparative Survey of New State Statutes and the UNCITRAL Model Law*, 1 Am. Rev. Int'l Arb. 140 (1990).

— Appendix A —
UN Convention on Contracts for the International Sale of Goods (1980)

(Document A/CONF.97/18, Annex I)

The States Parties to this Convention,

Bearing in mind the broad objectives in the resolutions adopted by the sixth special session of the General Assembly of the United Nations on the establishment of a New International Economic Order,

Considering that the development of international trade on the basis of equality and mutual benefit is an important element in promoting friendly relations among States,

Being of the opinion that the adoption of uniform rules which govern contracts for the international sale of goods and take into account the different social, economic and legal systems would contribute to the removal of legal barriers in international trade and promote the development of international trade,

Having agreed as follows:

PART I. SPHERE OF APPLICATION AND GENERAL PROVISIONS

CHAPTER I. SPHERE OF APPLICATION

Article 1

(1) This Convention applies to contracts of sale of goods between parties whose places of business are in different States:

(*a*) when the states are Contracting States; or

(*b*) when the rules of private international law lead to the application of the law of a Contracting State.

(2) The fact that the parties have their places of business in different States is to

be disregarded whenever this fact does not appear either from the contract or from any dealings between, or from information disclosed by, the parties at any time before or at the conclusion of the contract.

(3) Neither the nationality of the parties nor the civil or commercial character of the parties or of the contract is to be taken into consideration in determining the application of this Convention.

Article 2

This Convention does not apply to sales:

(a) of goods bought for personal, family or household use, unless the seller, at any time before or at the conclusion of the contract, neither knew nor ought to have known that the goods were bought for any such use;

(b) by auction;

(c) on execution or otherwise by authority of law;

(d) of stocks, shares, investment securities, negotiable instruments or money;

(e) of ships, vessels, hovercraft or aircraft;

(f) of electricity.

Article 3

(1) Contracts for the supply of goods to be manufactured or produced are to be considered sales unless the party who orders the goods undertakes to supply a substantital part of the materials necessary for such manufacture or production.

(2) This Convention does not apply to contracts in which the preponderant part of the obligations of the party who furnishes the goods consists in the supply of labour or other services.

Article 4

This Convention governs only the formation of the contract of sale and the rights and obligations of the seller and the buyer arising from such a contract. In particular, except as otherwise expressly provided in this Convention, it is not concerned with:

(a) the validity of the contract or of any of its provisions or of any usage;

(b) the effect which the contract may have on the property in the goods sold.

Article 5

This Convention does not apply to the liability of the seller for death or personal injury caused by the goods to any person.

Article 6

The parties may exclude the application of this Convention or, subject to article 12, derogate from or vary the effect of any of its provisions.

CHAPTER II. GENERAL PROVISIONS

Article 7

(1) In the interpretation of this Convention, regard is to be had to its international character and to the need to promote uniformity in its application and the observance of good faith in international trade.

(2) Questions concerning matters governed by this Convention which are not expressly settled in it are to be settled in conformity with the general principles on which it is based or, in the absence of such principles, in conformity with the law applicable by virtue of the rules of private international law.

Article 8

(1) For the purposes of this Convention statements made by and other conduct of a party are to be interpreted according to his intent where the other party knew or could not have been unaware what that intent was.

(2) If the preceding paragraph is not applicable, statements made by and other conduct of a party are to be interpreted according to the understanding that a reasonable person of the same kind as the other party would have had in the same circumstances.

(3) In determining the intent of a party or the understanding a reasonable person would have had, due consideration is to be given to all relevant circumstances of the case including the negotiations, any practices which the parties have established between themselves, usages and any subsequent conduct of the parties.

Article 9

(1) The parties are bound by any usage to which they have agreed and by any practices which they have established between themselves.

(2) The parties are considered, unless otherwise agreed, to have impliedly made applicable to their contract or its formation a usage of which the parties knew or ought to have known and which in international trade is widely known to, and regularly observed by, parties to contracts of the type involved in the particular trade concerned.

Article 10

For the purposes of this Convention:

(a) if a party has more than one place of business, the place of business is that which has the closest relationship to the contract and its performance, having regard to the circumstances known to or contemplated by the parties at any time before or at the conclusion of the contract;

(b) if a party does not have a place of business, reference is to be made to his habitual residence.

Article 11

A contract of sale need not be concluded in or evidenced by writing and is not subject to any other requirements as to form. It may be proved by any means, including witnesses.

Article 12

Any provision of article 11, article 29 or Part II of this Convention that allows a contract of sale or its modification or termination by agreement or any offer, acceptance or other indication of intention to be made in any form other than in writing does not apply where any party has his place of business in a Contracting State which has made a declaration under article 96 of this Convention. The parties may not derogate from or vary the effect of this article.

Article 13

For the purposes of this Convention "writing" includes telegram and telex.

PART II. FORMATION OF THE CONTRACT
Article 14

(1) A proposal for concluding a contract addressed to one or more specific persons constitutes an offer if it is sufficiently definite and indicates the intention of the offeror to be bound in case of acceptance. A proposal is sufficiently definite if it indicates the goods and expressly or implicitly fixes or makes provision for determining the quantity and the price.

(2) A proposal other than one addressed to one or more specific persons is to be considered merely as an invitation to make offers, unless the contrary is clearly indicated by the person making the proposal.

Article 15

(1) An offer becomes effective when it reaches the offeree.

(2) An offer, even if it is irrevocable, may be withdrawn if the withdrawal reaches the offeree before or at the same time as the offer.

Article 16

(1) Until a contract is concluded an offer may be revoked if the revocation reaches the offeree before he has dispatched an acceptance.

(2) However, an offer cannot be revoked:

(*a*) if it indicates, whether by stating a fixed time for acceptance or otherwise, that it is irrevocable; or

(*b*) if it was reasonable for the offeree to rely on the offer as being irrevocable and the offeree has acted in reliance on the offer.

Article 17

An offer, even if it is irrevocable, is terminated when a rejection reaches the offeror.

Article 18

(1) A statement made by or other conduct of the offeree indicating assent to an offer is an acceptance. Silence or inactivity does not in itself amount to acceptance.

(2) An acceptance of an offer becomes effective at the moment the indication of assent reaches the offeror. An acceptance is not effective if the indication of assent does not reach the offeror within the time he has fixed or, if no time is fixed, within a reasonable time, due account being taken of the circumstances of the transaction, including the rapidit of the means of communication employed by the offeror. An oral offer must be accepted immediately unless the circumstances indicate otherwise.

(3) However, if, by virtue of the offer or as a result of practices which the parties have established between themselves or of usage, the offeree may indicate assent by performing an act, such as one relating to the dispatch of the goods or payment of the price, without notice to the offeror, the acceptance is effective at the moment the act is performed, provided that the act is performed within the period of time laid down in the preceding paragraph.

Article 19

(1) A reply to an offer which purports to be an acceptance but contains additions, limitations or other modifications is a rejection of the offer and constitutes a counter-offer.

(2) However, a reply to an offer which purports to be an acceptance but contains additional or different terms which do not materially alter the terms of the offer constitutes an acceptance, unless the offeror, without undue delay, objects orally to the discrepancy or dispatches a notice to that effect. If he does not so object, the terms of the contract are the terms of the offer with the modifications contained in the acceptance.

(3) Additional or different terms relating, among other things, to the price, payment, quality and quantity of the goods, place and time of delivery, extent of one party's liability to the other or the settlement of disputes are considered to alter the terms of the offer materially.

Article 20

(1) A period of time for acceptance fixed by the offeror in a telegram or a letter begins to run from the moment the telegram is handed in for dispatch or from the

date shown on the letter or, if no such date is shown, from the date shown on the envelope. A period of time for acceptance fixed by the offeror by telephone, telex or other means of instantaneous communication, begins to run from the moment that the offer reaches the offeree.

(2) Official holidays or non-business days occurring during the period for acceptance are included in calculating the period. However, if a ,notice of acceptance cannot be delivered at the address of the offeror on the last day of the period because that day falls on an official holiday or a non-business day at the place of business of the offeror, the period is extended until the first business day which follows.

Article 21

(1) A late acceptance is nevertheless effective as an acceptance if without delay the offeror orally so informs the offeree or dispatches a notice to that effect.

(2) If a letter or other writing containing a late acceptance shows that it has been sent in such circumstances that if its transmission had been normal it would have reached the offeror in due time, the late acceptance is effective as an acceptance unless, without delay, the offeror orally informs the offeree that he considers his offer as having lapsed or dispatches a notice to that effect.

Article 22

An acceptance may be withdrawn if the withdrawal reaches the offeror before or at the same time as the acceptance would have become effective.

Article 23

A contract is concluded at the moment when an acceptance of an offer becomes effective in accordance with the provisions of this Convention.

Article 24

For the purposes of this Part of the Convention, an offer, declaration of acceptance or any other indication of intention "reaches" the addressee when it is made orally to him or delivered by any other means to him personally, to his place of business or mailing address or, if he does not have a place of business or mailing address, to his habitual residence.

PART III. SALE OF GOODS

CHAPTER I. GENERAL PROVISIONS

Article 25

A breach of contract committed by one of the parties is fundamental if it results in such detriment to the other party as substantially to deprive him of what he is entitled to expect under the contract, unless the party in breach did not foresee and a reasonable person of the same kind in the same circumstances would not have foreseen such a result.

Article 26

A declaration of avoidance of the contract is effective only if made by notice to the other party.

Article 27

Unless otherwise expressly provided in this Part of the Convention, if any notice, request or other communication is given or made by a party in accordance with this Part and by means appropriate in the circumstances, a delay or error in the transmission of the communication or its failure to arrive does not deprive that party of the right to rely on the communication.

Article 28

If, in accordance with the provisions of this Convention, one party is entitled to require performance of any obligation by the other party, a court is not bound to enter a judgement for specific performance unless the court would do so under its own law in respect of similar contracts of sale not governed by this Convention.

Article 29

(1) A contract may be modified or terminated by the mere agreement of the parties.

(2) A contract in writing which contains a provision requiring any modification or termination by agreement to be in writing may not be otherwise modified or terminated by agreement. However, a party may be precluded by his conduct from asserting such a provision to the extent that the other party has relied on that conduct.

CHAPTER II. OBLIGATIONS OF THE SELLER

Article 30

The seller must deliver the goods, hand over any documents relating to them and transfer the property in the goods, as required by the contract and this Convention.

SECTION I. DELIVERY OF THE GOODS AND HANDING OVER OF DOCUMENTS

Article 31

If the seller is not bound to deliver the goods at any other particular place, his obligation to deliver consists:

(*a*) if the contract of sale involves carriage of the goods — in handing the goods over to the first carrier for transmission to the buyer;

(*b*) if, in cases not within the preceding subparagraph, the contract relates to specific goods, or unidentified goods to be drawn from a specific stock or to be manufactured or produced, and at the time of the conclusion of the contract the parties knew that the goods were at, or were to be manufactured or produced at, a particular place — in placing the goods at the buyer's disposal at that place;

(*c*) in other cases — in placing the goods at the buyer's disposal at the place where the seller had his place of business at the time of the conclusion of the contract.

Article 32

(1) If the seller, in accordance with the contract or this Convention, hands the goods over to a carrier and if the goods are not clearly identified to the contract by markings on the goods, by shipping documents or otherwise, the seller must give the buyer notice of the consignment specifying the goods.

(2) If the seller is bound to arrange for carriage of the goods, he must make such contracts as are necessary for carriage to the place fixed by means of transportation appropriate in the circumstances and according to the usual terms for such transportation.

(3) If the seller is not bound to effect insurance in respect of the carriage of the goods, he must, at the buyer's request, provide him with all available information necessary to enable him to effect such insurance.

Article 33

The seller must deliver the goods:

(*a*) if a date is fixed by or determinable from the contract, on that date;

(*b*) if a period of time is fixed by or determinable from the contract, at any time within that period unless circumstances indicate that the buyer is to choose a date; or

(c) in any other case, within a reasonable time after the conclusion of the contract.

Article 34

If the seller is bound to hand over documents relating to the goods, he must hand them over at the time and place and in the form required by the contract. If the seller has handed over documents before that time, he may, up to that time, cure any lack of conformity in the documents, if the exercise of this right does not cause the buyer unreasonable inconvenience or unreasonable expense. However, the buyer retains any right to claim damages as provided for in this Convention.

SECTION II. CONFORMITY OF THE GOODS AND THIRD PARTY CLAIMS

Article 35

(1) The seller must deliver goods which are of the quantity, quality and description required by the contract and which are contained or packaged in the manner required by the contract.

(2) Except where the parties have agreed otherwise, the goods do not conform with the contract unless they:

(a) are fit for the purposes for which goods of the same description would ordinarily be used;

(b) are fit for any particular purpose expressly or impliedly made known to the seller at the time of the conclusion of the contract, except where the circumstances show that the buyer did not rely, or that it was unreasonable for him to rely, on the seller's skill and judgement;

(c) possess the qualities of goods which the seller has held out to the buyer as a sample or model;

(d) are contained or packaged in the manner usual for such goods or, where there is no such manner, in a manner adequate to preserve and protect the goods.

(3) The seller is not liable under subparagraphs (a) to (d) of the preceding paragraph for any lack of conformity of the goods if at the time of the conclusion of the contract the buyer knew or could not have been unaware of such lack of conformity.

Article 36

(1) The seller is liable in accordance with the contract and this Convention for any lack of conformity which exists at the time when the risk passes to the buyer, even though the lack of conformity becomes apparent only after that time.

(2) The seller is also liable for any lack of conformity which occurs after the time indicated in the preceding paragraph and which is due to a breach of any of his obligations, including a breach of any guarantee that for a period of time the goods will remain fit for their ordinary purpose or for some particular purpose or will retain specified qualities or characteristics.

Article 37

If the seller has delivered goods before the date for delivery, he may, up to that date, deliver any missing part or make up any deficiency in the quantity of the goods delivered, or deliver goods in replacement of any non-conforming goods delivered or remedy any lack of conformity in the goods delivered, provided that the exercise of this right does not cause the buyer unreasonable inconvenience or unreasonable expense. However, the buyer retains any right to claim damages as provided for in this Convention.

Article 38

(1) The buyer must examine the goods, or cause them to be examined, within as short a period as is practicable in the circumstances.

(2) If the contract involves carriage of the goods, examination may be deferred until after the goods have arrived at their destination.

(3) If the goods are redirected in transit or redispatched by the buyer without a reasonable opportunity for examination by him and at the time of the conclusion of the contract the seller knew or ought to have known of the possibility of such redirection or redispatch, examination may be deferred until after the goods have arrived at the new destination.

Article 39

(1) The buyer loses the right to rely on a lack of conformity of the goods if he does not give notice to the seller specifying the nature of the lack of conformity within a reasonable time after he has discovered it or ought to have discovered it.

(2) In any event, the buyer loses the right to rely on a lack of conformity of the goods if he does not give the seller notice thereof at the latest within a period of two years from the date on which the goods were actually handed over to the buyer, unless this time-limit is inconsistent with a contractual period of guarantee.

Article 40

The seller is not entitled to rely on the provisions of articles 38 and 39 if the lack of conformity relates to facts of which he knew or could not have been unaware and which he did not disclose to the buyer.

Article 41

The seller must deliver goods which are free from any right or claim of a third party, unless the buyer agreed to take the goods subject to that right or claim. However, if such right or claim is based on industrial property or other intellectual property, the seller's obligation is governed by article 42.

Article 42

(1) The seller must deliver goods which are free from any right or claim of a third party based on industrial property or other intellectual property, of which at the time of the conclusion of the contract the seller knew or could not have been unaware, provided that the right or claim is based on industrial property on other intellectual property:

(a) under the law of the State where the goods will be resold or otherwise used, if it was contemplated by the parties at the time of the conclusion of the contract that the goods would be resold or otherwise used in that State; or

(b) in any other case, under the law of the State where the buyer has his place of business.

(2) The obligation of the seller under the preceding paragraph does not extend to cases where:

(a) at the time of the conclusion of the contract the buyer knew or could not have been unaware of the right or claim; or

(b) the right or claim results from the seller's compliance with technical drawings, designs, formulae or other such specifications furnished by the buyer.

Article 43

(1) The buyer loses the right to rely on the provisions of article 41 or article 42 if he does not give notice to the seller specifying the nature of the right or claim of the

third party within a reasonable time after he has become aware or ought to have become aware of the right or claim.

(2) The seller is not entitled to rely on the provisions of the preceding paragraph if he knew of the right or claim of the third party and the nature of it.

Article 44

Notwithstanding the provisions of paragraph (1) of article 39 and paragraph (1) of article 43, the buyer may reduce the price in accordance with article 50 or claim damages, except for loss of profit, if he has a reasonable excuse for his failure to give the required notice.

SECTION III. REMEDIES FOR BREACH OF CONTRACT BY THE SELLER

Article 45

(1) If the seller fails to perform any of his obligations under the contract or this Convention, the buyer may;

(a) exercise the rights provided in articles 46 or 52;

(b) claim damages as provided in articles 74 or 77.

(2) the buyer is not deprived of any right he may have to claim damages by exercising his right to other remedies.

(3) No period of grace may be granted to the seller by a court or arbitral tribunal when the buyer resorts to a remedy for breach of contract.

Article 46

(1) The buyer may require performance by the seller of this obligations unless the buyer has resorted to a remedy which is inconsistent with this requirement.

(2) If the goods do not conform with the contract, the buyer may require delivery of substitute goods only if the lack of conformity constitutes a fundamental breach of contract and a request for substitute goods is made either in conjunction with notice given under article 39 or within a reasonable time thereafer.

(3) If the goods do not conform with the contract, the buyer may require the seller to remedy the lack of conformity by repair, unless this is unreasonable having reard to all the circumstances. A reques for repair must be made either in conjunction with notice given under article 39 or within a reasonable time thereafter.

Article 47

(1) The buyer may fix an additional period of time of reasonable length for performance by the seller of his obligations.

(2) Unless the buyer has received notice from the seller that he will not perform within the period so fixed, the buyer may not, during that period, resort to any remedy for breach of contract. However, the buyer is not deprived thereby of any right he may have to claim damages for delay in performance.

Article 48

(1) Subject to article 49, the seller may, even after the date for delivery, remedy at his own expense any failure to perform his obligations, if he can do so without unreasonable delay and without causing the buyer unreasonable inconvenience or uncertainty of reimbursement by the seller of expenses advanced by the buyer. However, the buyer retains any right to claim damages as provided for in this Convention.

(2) If the seller requests the buyer to make known whether he will accept performance and the buyer does not comply with the request within a reasonable time, the seller may perform within the time indicated in his request. The buyer may not,

during that period of time, resort to any remedy which is inconsistent with perform-ance by the seller.

(3) A notice by the seller that he will perform within a specified period of time is assumed to include a request, under the preceding paragraph, that the buyer make known his decision.

(4) A request or notice by the seller under paragraph (2) or (3) of this article is not effective unless received by the buyer.

Article 49

(1) The buyer may declare the contract avoided:

(a) if the failure by the seller to perform any of his obligations under the contract or this Convention amounts to a fundamental breach of contract; or

(b) in case of non-delivery, if the seller does not deliver the goods within the additional period of time fixed by the buyer in accordance with paragraph (1) of article 47 or declares that he will not deliver within the period so fixed.

(2) However, in cases where the seller has delivered the goods, the buyer loses the right to declare the contract avoided unless he does so:

(a) in respect of late delivery, within a reasonable time after he has become aware that delivery has been made;

(b) in respect of any breach other than late delivery, within a reasonable time:

    (i) after he knew or ought to have known of the breach;

    (ii) after the expiration of any additional period of time fixed by the buyer in accordance with paragraph (1) of article 47, or after the seller has declared that he will not perform his obligations within such an additional period; or

    (iii) after the expiration of any additional period of time indicated by the seller in accordance with paragraph (2) of article 48, or after the buyer has declared that he will not accept performance.

Article 50

If the goods do not conform with the contract and whether or not the price has already been paid, the buyer may reduce the price in the same proportion as the value that the goods actually delivered had at the time of the delivery bears to the value that conforming goods would have had at that time. However, if the seller remedies any failure to perform his obligations in accordance with article 37 or article 48 or if the buyer refuses to accept performance by the seller in accordance with those articles, the buyer may not reduce the price.

Article 51

(1) If the seller delivers only a part of the goods or if only a part of the goods delivered is in conformity with the contract, articles 46 to 50 apply in respect of the part which is missing or which does not conform.

(2) The buyer may declare the contract avoided in its entirety only if the failure to make delivery completely or in conformity with the contract amounts to a fun-damental breach of the contract.

Article 52

(1) If the seller delivers the goods before the date fixed, the buyer may take delivery or refuse to take delivery.

(2) If the seller delivers a quantity of goods greater than that provided for in the contract, the buyer may take delivery or refuse to take delivery of the excess quantity. If the buyer takes delivery of all or part of the excess quantity, he must pay for it at the contract rate.

CHAPTER III. OBLIGATIONS OF THE BUYER
Article 53

The buyer must pay the price for the goods and take delivery of them as required by the contract and this Convention.

SECTION I. PAYMENT OF THE PRICE
Article 54

The buyer's obligation to pay the price includes taking such steps and complying with such formalities as may be required under the contract or any laws and regulations to enable payment to be made.

Article 55

Where a contract has been validly concluded but does not expressly or implicitly fix or make provision for determining the price, the parties are considered, in the absence of any indication to the contrary, to have impliedly made reference to the price generally charged at the time of the conclusion of the contract for such goods sold under comparable circumstances in the trade concerned.

Article 56

If the price is fixed according to the weight of the goods, in case of doubt it is to be determined by the net weight.

Article 57

(1) If the buyer is not bound to pay the price at any other particular place, he must pay it to the seller:

(a) at the seller's place of business; or
(b) if the payment is to be made against the handing over of the goods or of documents, at the place where the handing over takes place.

(2) The seller must bear any increase in the expenses incidental to payment which is caused by a change in his place of business subsequent to the conclusion of the contract.

Article 58

(1) If the buyer is not bound to pay the price at any other specific time, he must pay it when the seller places either the goods or documents controlling their disposition at the buyer's disposal in accordance with the contract and this Convention. The seller may make such payment a condition for handing over the goods or documents.

(2) If the contract involves carriage of the goods, the seller may dispatch the goods on terms whereby the goods, or documents controlling their disposition, will not be handed over to the buyer except against payment of the price.

(3) The buyer is not bound to pay the price until he has had an opportunity to examine the goods, unless the procedures for delivery or payment agreed upon by the parties are inconsistent with his having such an opportunity.

Article 59

The buyer must pay the price on the date fixed by or determinable from the contract and this Convention without the need for any request or compliance with any formality on the part of the seller.

SECTION II. TAKING DELIVERY
Article 60

The buyer's obligation to take delivery consists:

(a) in doing all the acts which could reasonably be expected of him in order to enable the seller to make delivery; and
(b) in taking over the goods.

SECTION III. REMEDIES FOR BREACH OF CONTRACT BY THE BUYER
Article 61

(1) If the buyer fails to perform any of his obligations under the contract or this Convention, the seller may:

(a) exercise the rights provided in articles 62 to 65;

(b) claim damages as provided in articles 74 to 77.

(2) The seller is not deprived of any right he may have to claim damages by exercising his right to other remedies.

(3) No period of grace may be granted to the buyer by a court or arbitral tribunal when the seller resorts to a remedy for breach of contract.

Article 62

The seller may require the buyer to pay the price, take delivery or perform his other obligations, unless the seller has resorted to a remedy which is inconsistent with this requirement.

Article 63

(1) The seller may fix an additional period of time of reasonable length for performance by the buyer of his obligations.

(2) Unless the seller has received notice from the buyer that he will not perform within the period so fixed, the seller may not, during that period, resort to any remedy for breach of contract. However, the seller is not deprived thereby of any right he may have to claim damages for delay in performance.

Article 64

(1) The seller may declare the contract avoided:

(a) if the failure by the buyer to perform any of his obligations under the contract or this Convention amounts to a fundamental breach of contract; or

(b) if the buyer does not, within the additional period of time fixed by the seller in accordance with paragraph (1) of article 63, perform his obligation to pay the price or take delivery of the goods, or if he declares that he will not do so within the period so fixed.

(2) However, in cases where the buyer has paid the price, the seller loses the right to declare the contract avoided unless he does so:

(a) in respect of late performance by the buyer, before the seller has become aware that performance has been rendered; or

(b) in respect of any breach other than late performance by the buyer, within a reasonable time:

    (i)   after the seller knew or ought to have known of the breach; or

    (ii) after the expiration of any additional period of time fixed by the seller in accordance with paragraph (1) of article 63, or after the buyer has declared that he will not perform his obligations with in such an additional period.

Article 65

(1) If under the contract the buyer is to specify the form, measurement or other features of the goods and he fails to make such specification either on the date agreed upon or within a reasonable time after receipt of a request from the seller, the seller may, without prejudice to any other rights he may have, make the specification himself in accordance with the requirements of the buyer that may be known to him.

(2) If the seller makes the specification himself, he must inform the buyer of the

details thereof and must fix a reasonable time within which the buyer may make a different specification. If, after receipt of such a communication, the buyer fails to do so within the time so fixed, the specification made by the seller is binding.

CHAPTER IV. PASSING OF RISK

Article 66

Loss of or damage to the goods after the risk has passed to the buyer does not discharge him from his obligation to pay the price, unless the loss or damage is due to an art or omission of the seller.

Article 67

(1) If the contract of sale involves carriage of the goods and the seller is not bound to hand them over at a particular place, the risk passes to the buyer when the goods are handed over to the first carrier for transmission to the buyer in accordance with the contract of sale. If the seller is bound to hand the goods over to a carrier at a particular place, the risk does not pass to the buyer until the goods are handed over to the carrier at that place. The fact that the seller is authorized to retain documents conrolling the disposition of the goods does not affect the passage of the risk.

(2) Nevertheless, the risk does not pass to the buyer until the goods are clearly identified to the contract, whether by markings on the goods, by shipping documents, by notice given to the buyer or otherwise.

Article 68

The risk in respect of goods sold in transit passes to the buyer from the time of the conclusion of the contract. However, if the circumstances so indicate, the risk is assumed by the buyer from the time the goods were handed over to the carrier who issued the documents embodying the contract of carriage. Nevertheless, if at the time of the conclusion of the contract of sale the seller knew or ought to have known that the goods had been lost or damaged and did not disclose this to the buyer, the loss or damage is at the risk of the seller.

Article 69

(1) In cases not within articles 67 and 68, the risk passes to the buyer when he takes over the goods or, if he does not do so in due time, from the time when the goods are placed at his disposal and he commits a breach of contract by failing to take delivery.

(2) However, if the buyer is bound to take over the goods at a place other than a place of business of the seller, the risk passes when delivery is due and the buyer is aware of the fact that the goods are placed at his disposal at that place.

(3) If the contract relates to goods not then identified, the goods are considered not to be placed at the disposal of the buyer until they are clearly identified to the contract.

Article 70

If the seller has committed a fundamental breach of contract, articles 67, 68 and 69 do not impair the remedies available to the buyer on account of the breach.

CHAPTER V. PROVISIONS COMMON TO THE OBLIGATIONS OF THE SELLER AND OF THE BUYER

SECTION I. ANTICPATORY BREACH AND INSTALMENT CONTRACTS

Article 71

(1) A party may suspend the performance of his obligations if, after the conclusion of the contract, it becomes apparent that the other party will not perform a substantial part of his obligations as a result of:

(*a*) a serious deficiency in his ability to perform or in his creditworthiness; or

(*b*) his conduct in preparing to perform or in performing the contract.

(2) If the seller has already dispatched the goods before the grounds described in the preceding paragraph become evident, he may prevent the handing over of the goods to the buyer even though the buyer holds a document which entitles him to obtain them. The present paragraph relates only to the rights in the goods as between he buyer and the seller.

(3) A party suspending performance, whether before or after dispatch of the goods, must immediately give notice of the suspension to the other party and must continue with performance if the other party provides adequate assurance of his performance.

Article 72

(1) If prior to the date for performance of the contract it is clear that one of the parties will commit a fundamental breach of contract, the other party may declare the contract avoided.

(2) If time allows, the party intending to declare the contract avoided must give reasonable notice to the other party in order to permit him to provide adequate assurance of his performance.

(3) The requirements of the preceding paragraph do not apply if the other party has declared that he will not perform his obligations.

Article 73

(1) In the case of a contract for delivery of goods by instalments, if the failure of one party to perform any of his obligations in respect of any instalment constitutes a fundamental breach of contract with respect to that instalment, the other party may declare the contract avoided with respect to that instalment.

(2) If one party's failure to perform any of his obligations in respect of any instalment gives the other party good grounds to conclude that a fundamental breach of contract will occur with respect to future instalments, he may declare the contract avoided for the future, provided that he does so within a reasonable time.

(3) A buyer who declares the contract avoided in respect of any delivery may, at the same time, declare it avoided in respect of deliveries already made or of future deliveries if, by reason of their interdependence, those deliveries could not be used for the purpose contemplated by the parties at the time of the conclusion of the contract.

SECTION II. DAMAGES
Article 74

Damages for breach of contract by one party consist of a sum equal to the loss, including loss of profit, suffered by the other party as a consequence of the breach. Such damages may not exceed the loss which the party in breach foresaw or ought to have foreseen at the time of the conclusion of the contract, in the light of the facts and matters of which he then knew or ought to have known, as a possible consequence of the breach of contract.

Article 75

If the contract is avoided and if, in a reasonable manner and within a reasonable time after avoidance, the buyer has bought goods in replacement or the seller has resold the goods, the party claiming damages may recover the difference between the contract price and the price in the substitute transaction as well as any further damages recoverable under article 74.

Article 76

(1) If the contract is avoided and there is a current price for the goods, the party claiming damages may, if he has not made a purchase or resale under article 75, recover the difference between the price fixed by the contract and the current price at the time of avoidance as well as any further damages recoverable under article 74. If, however, the party claiming damages has avoided the contract after taking over the goods, the current price at the time of such taking over shall be applied instead of the curent price at the time of avoidance.

(2) For the purposes of the preceding paragraph, the current price is the price prevailing at the place where delivery of the goods should have been made or, if there is no current price at that place, the price at such other place as serves as a reasonable substitute, making due allowance for differences in the cost of transporting the goods.

Article 77

A party who relies on a breach of contract must take such measures as are reasonable in the circumstances to mitigate the loss, including loss of profit, resulting from the breach. If he fails to take such measures, the party in breach may claim a reduction in the damages in the amount by which the loss should have been mitigated.

SECTION III. INTEREST
Article 78

If a party fails to pay the price or any other sum that is in arrears, the other party is entitled to interest on it, without prejudice to any claim for damages recoverable under article 74.

SECTION IV. EXEMPTIONS
Article 79

(1) A party is not liable for a failure to perform any of his obligations if he proved that the failure was due to an impediment beyond his control and that he could not reasonably be expected to have taken the impediment into account at the time of the conclusion of the contract or to have avoided or overcome it or its consequences.

(2) If the party's failure is due to the failure by a third person whom he has engaged to perform the whole or a part of the contract, that party is exempt from liability only if:

(a) he is exempt under the preceding paragraph; and

(b) the person whom he has so engaged would be so exempt if the provisions of that paragraph were applied to him.

(3) The exemption provided by this article has effect for the period during which the impediment exists.

(4) The party who fails to perform must give notice to the other party of the impediment and its effect on his ability to perform. If the notice is not received by the other party within a reasonable time after the party who fails to perform knew or ought to have known of the impediment, he is liable for damages resulting from such non-receipt.

(5) Nothing in this article prevents either party from exercising any right other than to claim damages under this Convention.

Article 80

A party may not rely on a failure of the other party to perform, to the extent that such failure was caused by the first party's act or omission.

SECTION V. EFFECTS OF AVOIDANCE
Article 81

(1) Avoidance of the contract releases both parties from their obligations under it, subject to any damages which may be due. Avoidance does not affect any provision of the contract for the settlement of disputes or any other provision of the contract governing the rights and obligations of the parties consequent upon the avoidance of the contract.

(2) A party who has performed the contract either wholly or in part may claim restitution from the other party of whatever the first party has supplied or paid under the contract. If both parties are bound to make restitution, they must do so concurrently.

Article 82

(1) The buyer loses the right to declare the contract avoided or to require the seller to deliver substitute goods if it is impossible for him to make restitution of the goods substantially in the condition in which he received them.

(2) The preceding paragraph does not apply:

(a) if the impossibility of making restitution of the goods or of making restitution of the goods substantially in the condition in which the buyer received them is not due to his act or omission;

(b) if the goods or part of the goods have perished or deteriorated as a result of the examination provided for in article 38; or

(c) if the goods or part of the goods have been sold in the normal course of business or have been consumed or transformed by the buyer in the course of normal use before he discovered or ought to have discovered the lack of conformity.

Article 83

A buyer who has lost the right to declare the contract avoided or to require the seller to deliver substitute goods in accordance with article 82 retains all other remedies under the contract and this Convention.

Article 84

(1) If the seller is bound to refund the price, he must also pay interest on it, from the date on which the price was paid.

(2) The buyer must account to the seller for all benefits which he has derived from the goods or part of them:

(a) if he must make restitution of the goods or part of them; or

(b) if it is impossible for him to make restitution of all or part of the goods or to make restitution of all or part of the goods substantially in the condition in which he received them, but he has nevertheless declared the contract avoided or required the seller to deliver substitute goods.

SECTION VI. PRESERVATION OF THE GOODS
Article 85

If the buyer is in delay in taking delivery of the goods or, where payment of the price and delivery of the goods are to be made concurrently, if he fails to pay the price, and the seller is either in possession of the goods or otherwise able to control their disposition, the seller must take such steps as are reasonable in the circumstances to preserve them. He is entitled to retain them until he has been reimbursed his reasonable expenses by the buyer.

Article 86

(1) If the buyer has received the goods and intends to exercise any right under the contract or this Convention to reject them, he must take such steps to preserve them as are reasonable in the circumstances. He is entitled to retain them until he has been reimbursed his reasonable expenses by the seller.

(2) If goods dispatched to the buyer have been placed at his disposal at their destination and he exercises the right to reject them, he must take possession of them on behalf of the seller, provided that this can be done without payment of the price and without unreasonable inconvenience or unreasonable expense. This provision does not apply if the seller or a person authorised to take charge of the goods on his behalf is present at the destination. If the buyer takes possession of the goods under this paragraph, his rights and obligations are governed by the preceding paragraph.

Article 87

A party who is bound to take steps to preserve the goods may deposit them in a warehouse of a third person at the expense of the other party provided that the expense incurred is not unreasonable.

Article 88

(1) A party who is bound to preserve the goods in accordance with article 85 or 86 may sell them by any appropriate means if there has been an unreasonable delay by the other party in taking possession of the goods or in taking them back or in paying the price or the cost of preservation, provided that reasonable notice of the intention to sell has been given to the other party.

(2) If the goods are subject to rapid deterioration or their preservation would involve unreasonable expense, a party who is bound to preserve the goods in accordance with article 85 or 86 must take reasonable measures to sell them. To the extent possible he must give notice to the other party of his intention to sell.

(3) A party selling the goods has the right to retain out of the proceeds of sale an amount equal to the reasonable expenses of preserving the goods and of selling them. He must account to the other party for the balance.

PART IV. FINAL PROVISIONS

Article 89

The Secretary-General of the United Nations is hereby designated as the depositary for this Convention.

Article 90

The Convention does not prevail over any international agreement which has already been or may be entered into and which contain provisions concerning the matters governed by this Convention, provided that he parties have their places of business in States parties to such agreement.

Article 91

(1) This Convention is open for signature at the concluding meeting of the United Nations Conference on Contracts for the International Sale of Goods and will remain open for signature by all States at the Headquarters of the United Nations, New York until 30 September 1981.

(2) This Convention is subject to ratification, acceptance or approval by the signatory States.

(3) This Convention is open for accession by all States which are not signatory States as from the date it is open for signature.

(4) Instruments of ratification, acceptance, approval and accession are to be deposited with the Secretary-General of the United Nations.

Article 92

(1) A Contracting State may declare at the time of signature, ratification, acceptance, approval or accession that it will not be bound by Part II of this Convention or that it will not be bound by Part III of this Convention.

(2) A Contracting State which makes a declaration in accordance with the preceding paragraph in respect of Part II or Part III of this Convention is not to be considered a Contracting State within paragraph (1) of article 1 of this Convention in respect of matters governed by the Part to which the declaration applies.

Article 93

(1) If a Contracting State has two or more territorial units in which, according to its constitution, different systems of law are applicable in relation to the matters dealt with in this Convention, it may at the time of signature, ratification, acceptance, approval or accession, declare that this Convention is to extend to all its territorial units or only to one or more of them, and may amend its declaration by submitting another declaration at any time.

(2) These declarations are to be notified to the depositary and are to state expressly the territorial units to which the Convention extends.

(3) If, by virtue of a declaration under this article, this Convention extends to one or more but not all of the territorial units of a Contracting State, and if the place of business of a party is located in that State, this place of business, for the purposes of this Convention, is considered not to be in a Contracting State, unless it is in a territorial unit to which the Convention extends.

(4) If a Contracing State makes no declaration under paragraph (1) of this article, the Convention is to extend to all territorial units of that State.

Article 94

(1) Two or more Contracting States which have the same or closely related legal rules on matters governed by this Convention may at any time declare that the Convention is not to apply to contracts of sale or to their formation where the parties have their places of business in those States. Such declarations may be made jointly or by reciprocal unilateral declarations.

(2) A Contracting State which has the same or closely related legal rules on matters governed by this Convention as one or more non-Contracting States may at any time declare that the Convention is not to apply to contracts of sale or to their formation where the parties have their places of business in those States.

(3) If a State which is the object of a declaration under the preceding paragraph subsequently becomes a Contracting State, the declaration made will, as from the date on which the Convention enters into forece in respect of the new Contracting State, have the effect of a declaration made under paragraph (1), provided that the new Contracting State joins in such declaration or makes a reciprocal unilateral declaration.

Article 95

Any State may declare at the time of the deposit of its instrument of ratification, acceptance, approval or accession that it will not be bound by subparagraph (1)(b) of article 1 of this Convention.

Article 96

A Contracting State whose legislation requires contracts of sale to be concluded in or evidenced by writing may at any time make a declaration in accordance with article 12 that any provision of article 11, article 29, or Part II of this Convention, that allows a contract of sale or its modification or termination by agreement or any offer, acceptance, or other indication or intention to be made in any form other than in writing, does not apply where any party has his place of business in that State.

Article 97

(1) Declarations made under this Convention at the time of signature are subject to confirmation upon ratification, acceptance or approval.

(2) Declaration and confirmations of declarations are to be in writing and be formally notified to the depositary.

(3) A declaration takes effect simultaneously with the entry into force of this Convention in respect of the State concerned. However, a declaration of which the depositary receives formal notification after such entry into force takes effect on the first day of the month following the expiration of six months after the date of its receipt by the depositary. Reciprocal unilateral declarations under article 94 take effect on the first day of the month following the expiration of six months after the receipt of the latest declaration by the depositary.

(4) Any State which makes a declaration under this Convention may withdraw it at any time by a formal notification in writing addressed to the depositary. Such withdrawal is to take effect on the first day of the month following the expiration of six months after the date of the receipt of the notification by the depositary.

(5) A withdrawal of a declaration made under article 94 renders inoperative, as from the date on which the withdrawal takes effect, any reciprocal declaration made by another State under that article.

Article 98

No reservations are permitted except those expressly authorized in this Convention.

Article 99

(1) This Convention enters into force, subject to the provisions of paragraph (6) of this article, on the first day of the month following the expiration of twelve months after the date of deposit of the tenth instrument of ratification, acceptance, approval or accession, including an instrument which contains a declaration made under article 92.

(2) When a State ratifies, accepts, approves or accedes to this Convention after the deposit of the tenth instrument of ratification, acceptance, approval or accession, this Convention, with the exception of the Part excluded, enters into force in respect of that State, subject to the provisions of paragraph (6) of this aticle, on the first day of the month following the expiration of twelve months after the date of the deposit of its instrument of ratification, acceptance, approval or accession.

(3) At State which ratifies, accepts, approves or accedes to this Convention and is a party to either or both the Convention relating to a Uniform Law on the Formation of Contracts for the International Sale of Goods done at The Hague on 1 July 1964 (1964 Hague Formation Convention) and the Convention relating to a Uniform Law on the International Sale of Goods done at The Hague on 1 July 1964 (1964 Hague Sales Convention) shall at the same time denounce, as the case may be, either or

both the 1964 Hague Sales Convention and the 1964 Hague Formation Convention by notifying the Govenment of the Netherlands to that effect.

(4) A State party to the 1964 Hague Sales Convention which ratifies, accepts, approves or accedes to the present Convention and declares or has declared under article 92 that it will not be bound by Part II of this Convention shall at the time of ratification, acceptance, approval or accession denounce the 1964 Hague Sales Convention by notifying the Government of the Netherlands to that effect.

(5) A State party to the 1964 Hague Formation Convention which ratifies, accepts, approves or accedes to the present Convention and declares or has declared under article 92 that it will not be bound by Part III of this Convention shall at the time of ratification, acceptance, approval or accession denounce the 1964 Hague Formation Convention by notifying the Government of the Netherlands to that effect.

(6) For the purpose of this article, ratifications, acceptances, approvals and accessions in respect of this Convention by States parties to the 1964 Hague Formation Convention or to the 1964 Hague Sales Convention shall not be effective until such denunciations as may be required on the part of those States in respect of the latter two Conventions have themselves become effective. The depositary of this Convention shall consult with the Government of the Netherlands, as the depositary of the 1964 Conventions, so as to ensure necessary co-ordination in this respect.

Article 100

(1) This Convention applies to the formation of a contract only when the proposal for concluding the contract is made on or after the date when the Convention enters into force in respect of the Contracting States referred to in subparagraph (1)(*a*) or the Contracting State referred to in subparagraph (1)(*b*) of article 1.

(2) This Convention applies only to contracts concluded on or after the date when the Convention enters into force in respect of the Contracting States referred to in supparagraph (1)(*a*) or the Contracting State referred to in subparagraph (1)(*b*) of article 1.

Article 101

(1) A Contracting State may denounce this Convention, or Part II or Part III of the Convention, by a formal notification in writing addressed to the depositary.

(2) The denunciation takes effect on the first day of the month following the expiration of twelve months after the notification is received by the depositary. Where a longer period for the denunciation to take effect is specified in the notification, the denunciation takes effect upon the expiration of such longer period after the notification is received by the depositary.

DONE at Vienna, this day of eleventh day of April, one thousand nine hundred and eighty, in a single original, of which the Arabic, Chinese, English, French, Russian and Spanish texts are equally authentic.

IN WITNESS WHEREOF the undersigned plenipotentiaries, being duly authorised by their respecitve governments, have signed this Convention.

— Appendix B —
US Uniform Commercial Code

ARTICLE 2

SALES

PART 1

SHORT TITLE, GENERAL CONSTRUCTION AND SUBJECT MATTER

§ 2 — 101. Short Title

This Article shall be known and may be cited as Uniform Commercial Code — Sales.

§ 2 — 102. Scope; Certain Security and Other Transactions Excluded From This Article

Unless the context otherwise requires, this Article applies to transactions in goods; it does not apply to any transaction which although in the form of an unconditional contract to sell or present sale is intended to operate only as a security transaction nor does this Article impair or repeal any statute regulating sales to consumers, farmers or other specified classes of buyers.

§ 2 — 103. Definitions and Index of Definitions

(1) In this Article unless the context otherwise requires

    (a) "Buyer" means a person who buys or contracts to buy goods.

    (b) "Good faith" in the case of a merchant means honesty in fact and the observance of reasonable commercial standards of fair dealing in the trade.

    (c) "Receipt" of goods means taking physical possession of them.

    (d) "Seller" means a person who sells or contracts to sell goods.

(2) Other definitions applying to this Article or to specified Parts thereof, and the sections in which they appear are:

"Acceptance". Section 2 — 606.

"Banker's credit". Section 2 — 325.

"Between merchants". Section 2 — 104

"Cancellation". Section 2 — 106(4).

"Commercial unit". Section 2 — 105.

"Confirmed credit". Section 2 — 325.

"Conforming to contract". Section 2 — 106.

"Contract for sale". Section 2 — 106.

"Cover". Section 2 — 712.

"Entrusting". Section 2 — 403.

"Financing agency". Section 2 — 104.

"Future goods". Section 2 — 105.

"Goods". Section 2 — 105.

"Identification". Section 2 — 501.

"Installment contract". Section 2 — 612.

"Letter of Credit". Section 2 — 325.

"Lot". Section 2 — 105.

"Merchant". Section 2 — 104.

"Overseas". Section 2 — 323.

"Person in position of seller". Section 2 — 707.
"Present sale". Section 2 — 106.
"Sale". Section 2 — 106.
"Sale on approval". Section 2 — 326.
"Sale or return". Section 2 — 326.
"Termination". Section 2 — 106.
(3) The following definitions in other Articles apply to this Article:
"Check". Section 3 — 104.
"Consignee". Section 7 — 102.
"Consignor". Section 7 — 102.
"Consumer goods". Section 9 — 109.
"Dishonor". Section 3 — 507.
"Draft". Section 3 — 104.
(4) In addition Article 1 contains general definitions and principles of construction and interpretation applicable throughout this Article.

§ 2 — 104. Definitions; "Merchant"; "Between Merchants"; "Financing Agency"

(1) "Merchant" means a person who deals in goods of the kind or otherwise by his occupation holds himself out as having knowledge or skill peculiar to the practices or goods involved in the transaction or to whom such knowledge or skill may be attributed by his employment of an agent or broker or other intermediary who by his occupation holds himself out as having such knowledge or skill.

(2) "Financing agency" means a bank, finance company or other person who in the ordinary course of business makes advances against goods or documents of title or who by arrangement with either the seller or the buyer intervenes in ordinary course to make or collect payment due or claimed under the contract for sale, as by purchasing or paying the seller's draft or making advances against it or by merely taking it for collection whether or not documents of title accompany the draft. "Financing agency" includes also a bank or other person who seller and buyer in respect to the goods (Section 2 — 707).

(3) "Between merchants" means in any transaction with respect to which both parties are chargeable with the knowledge or skill or merchants.

§ 2 — 105. Definitions: Transferability; "Goods"; "Future" Goods; "Lot"; "Commercial Unit"

(1) "Goods" means all things (including specially manufactured goods) which are movable at the time of identification to the contract for sale other than the money in which the price is to be paid, investment securities (Article 8) and things in action. "Goods" also includes the unborn young of animals and growing crops and other identified things attached to realty as described in the section on goods to be severed from realty (Section 2 — 107).

(2) Goods must be both existing and identified before any interest in them can pass. Goods which are not both existing and identified are "future" goods. A purported present sale of future goods or of any interest therein operates as a contract to sell.

(3) There may be a sale of a part interest in existing identified goods.

(4) An undivided share in an identified bulk of fungible goods is sufficiently identified to be sold although the quantity of the bulk is not determined. Any agreed proportion of such a bulk or any quantity thereof agreed upon by number, weight or

other measure may to the extent of the seller's interest in the bulk be sold to the buyer who then becomes an owner in common.

(5) "Lot" means a parcel or a single article which is the subject matter of a separate sale or delivery, whether or not it is sufficient to perform the contract.

(6) "Commercial unit" means such a unit of goods as by commercial usage is a single whole for purposes of sale and division of which materially impairs its character or value on the market or in use. A commercial unit may be a single article (as a machine) cr a set of articles (as a suite of furniture or an assortment of sizes) or a quantity (as a bale, gross, or carload) or any other unit treated in use or in the relevant market as a single whole.

§ 2 — 106. **Definitions: "Contract"; "Agreement"; "Contract for Sale"; "Sale"; "Present Sale"; "Conforming" to Contract; "Termination"; "Cancellation"**

(1) In this Article unless the context otherwise requires "contract" and "agreement" are limited to those relating to the present or future sale of goods. "Contract for sale" includes both a present sale of goods and a contract to sell goods at a future time. A "sale" consists in the passing of title from the seller to the buyer for a price (Section 2 — 401). A "present sale" means a sale which is accomplished by the making of the contract.

(2) Goods or conduct including any part of a performance are "conforming" or conform to the contract when they are in accordance with the obligations under the contract.

(3) "Termination" occurs when either party pursuant to a power created by agreement or law puts an end to the contract otherwise than for its breach. On "termination" all obligations which are still executory on both sides are discharged but any right based on prior breach or performance survives.

(4) "Cancellation" occurs when either party puts an end to the contract for breach by the other and its effect is the same as that of "termination" except that the cancelling party also retains any remedy for breach of the whole contract or any unperformed balance.

§ 2 — 107. **Goods to Be Severed From Realty: Recording**

(1) A contract for the sale of minerals or the like (including oil and gas) or a structure or its materials to be removed from realty is a contract for the sale of goods within this Article if they are to be severed by the seller but until severance a purported present sale thereof which is not effective as a transfer of an interest in land is effective only as a contract to sell.

(2) A contract for the sale apart from the land of growing crops or other things attached to realty and capable of severance without material harm thereto but not described in subsection (1) or of timber to be cut is a contract for the sale of goods within this Article whether the subject matter is to be severed by the buyer or by the seller even though it forms part of the realty at the time of contracting, and the parties can by identification effect a present sale before severance.

(3) The provisions of this section are subejct to any third party rights provided by the law relating to realty records, and the contract for sale may be executed and recorded as a document transferring an interest in land and shall then constitute notice to third parties of the buyer's rights under the contract for sale. As amended 1972.

PART 2
FORM, FORMATION AND ADJUSTMENT OF CONTRACT
§ 2 — 201.　Formal Requirements; Statute of Frauds

(1) Except as otherwise provided in this section a contract for the sale of goods for the price of $500 or more is not enforceable by way of action or defense unless there is some writing sufficient to indicate that a contract for sale has been made between the parties and signed by the party against whom enforcement is sought or by his authorized agent or broker. A writing is not insufficient because it omits or incorrectly states a term agreed upon but the contract is not enforceable under this paragraph beyond the quantity of goods shown in such writing.

(2) Between merchants if within a reasonable time a writing in confirmation of the contract and sufficient against the sender is received and the party receiving it has reason to know its contents, it satisfies the requirements of subsection (1) against such party unless written notice of objection to its contents is given within 10 days after it is received.

(3) A contract which does not satisfy the requirements of subsection (1) but which is valid in other respects is enforceable

- (a) if the goods are to be specially manufactured for the buyer and are not suitable for sale to others in the ordinary course of the seller's business and the seller, before notice of repudiation is received and under circumstances which reasonably indicate that the goods are for the buyer, has made either a substantial beginning of their manufacture or commitments for their procurement; or
- (b) if the party against whom enforcement is sought admits in his pleading, testimony or otherwise in court that a contract for sale was made, but the contract is not enforceable under this provision beyond the quantity of goods admitted; or
- (c) with respect to goods for which payment has been made and accepted or which have been received and accepted (Sec. 2 — 606).

§ 2 — 202.　Final Written Expression: Parol or Extrinsic Evidence

Terms with respect to which the confirmatory memoranda of the parties agree or which are otherwise set forth in a writing intended by the parties as a final expression of their agreement with respect to such terms as are included therein may not be contradicted by evidence of any prior agreement or of a contemporaneous oral agreement but may be explained or supplemented

- (a) by course of dealing or usage of trade (Section 1 — 205) or by course of performance (Section 2 — 208); and
- (b) by evidence of consistent additional terms unless the court finds the writing to have been intended also as a complete and exclusive statement of the terms of the agreement.

§ 2 — 203.　Seals Inoperative

The affixing of a seal to a writing evidencing a contract for sale or an offer to buy or sell goods deooes not constitute the writing a sealed instrument and the law with respect to sealed instruments does not apply to such a contract or offer.

§ 2 — 204.　Formation in General

(1) A contract for sale of goods may be made in any manner sufficient to show agreement, including conduct by both parties which recognizes the existence of such a contract.

(2) An agreement suffiient to constitute a contract for sale may be found even though the moment of its making is undetermined.

(3) Even though one or more terms are left open a contract for sale does not fail for indefiniteness if the parties have intended to make a contract and there is a reasonably certain basis for giving an appropriate remedy.

§ 2 — 205. **Firm Offers**

An offer by a merchant to buy or sell goods in a signed writing which by its terms gives assurance that it will be held open is not revocable, for lack of consideration, during the time stated or if no time is stated for a reasonable time, but in no event may such period of irrevocability exceed three months; but any such term of assurance on a form supplied by the offeree must be separately signed by the offeror.

§ 2 — 206. **Offer and Acceptance in Formation of Contract**

(1) Unless otherwise unambiguously indicated by the language or circumstances

   (a) an offer to make a contract shall be construed as inviting acceptance in any manner and by any medium reasonable in the circumstances;

   (b) an order or other offer to buy goods for prompt or current shipment shall be construed as inviting acceptance either by a prompt promise to ship or by the prompt or current shipment of conforming or non-conforming goods, but such a shipment of non-conforming goods does not constitute an aceeptance if the seller seasonably notifies the buyer that the shipment is offered only as an accommodation to the buyer.

(2) where the beginning of a requested performance is a reasonable mode of acceptance an offeror who is not notified of acceptance within a reasonable time may treat the offer as having lapsed before acceptance.

§ 2 — 207. **Additional Terms in Acceptance or Confirmation**

(1) A definite and seasonable expression of acceptance or a written confirmation which is sent within a reasonable time operates as an acceptance even though it states terms additional to or different from those offered or agreed upon, unless acceptance is expressly made conditional on assent to the additional or different terms.

(2) the additional terms are to be construed as proposals for addition to the contract. Between merchants such terms become part of the contract unless:

   (a) the offer expressly limits acceptance to the terms of the offer;

   (b) they materially alter it; or

   (c) notification of objection to them has already been given or is given within a reasonable time after notice of them is received.

(3) Conduct by both parties which recognizes the existence of a contract is sufficient to establish a contract for sale although the writings of the parties do not otherwise establish a contract. In such case the terms of the particular contract consist of those terms on which the writings of the parties agree, together with any supplementary terms incorporated under any other provisions of this Act.

§ 2 — 208. **Course of Performance or Practical Construction**

(1) Where the contract for sale involves repeated occasions for performance by either party with knowledge of the nature of the performance and opportunity for objection to it by the other, any course of performance accepted or acquiesced in without objection shall be relevant to determine the meaning of the agreement.

(2) The express terms of the agreement and any such course of performance, as well as any course of dealing and usage of trade, shall be construed whenever

reasonable as consistent with each other; but when such construction is unreasonable, express terms shall control course of performance and course of performance shall control both course of dealing and usage of trade (Section 1 — 205).

(3) Subject to the provisions of the next section on modification and waiver, such course of performance shall be relevant to show a waiver or modification of any term inconsistent with such course of performance.

§ 2 — 209. Modification, Rescission and Waiver

(1) An agreement modifying a contract within this Article needs no consideration to be binding.

(2) A signed agreement which excludes modification or rescission except by a signed writing cannot be otherwise modified or rescinded, but execept as between merchants such a requirement on a form supplied by the merchant must be separately signed by the other party.

(3) The requirements of the statute of frauds section of this Article (Section 2 — 201) must be satisfied if the contract as modified is within its provisions.

(4) Although an attempt at modification or rescission does not satisfy the requirements of subsection (2) or (3) it can operate as a waiver.

(5) A party who has made a waiver affecting an executory portion of the contract may retract the waiver by reasonable notification received by the other party that strict performance will be required of any term waived, unless the retraction would be unjust in view of a material change of position in reliance on the waiver.

§ 2 — 210. Delegation of Performance; Assignment of Rights

(1) A party may perform his duty through a delegate unless otherwise agreed or unless the other party has a substantial interest in having his original promisor perform or control the acts required by the contract. No delegation of performance relieves the party delegating of any duty to perform or any liability for breach.

(2) Unless otherwise agreed all rights of either seller or buyer can be assigned except where the assignment would materially change the duty of the other party, or increase materially the burden or risk imposed on him by his contract, or impair materially his change of obtaining return performance. A right to damages for breach of the whole contract or a right arising out of the assignor's due performance of his entire obligation can be assigned despite agreement otherwise.

(3) Unless the circumstances indicate the contrary a prohibition of assignment of "the contract" is to be construed as barring only the delegation to the assignee of the assignor's performance.

(4) An assignment of "the contract" or of "all my rights under the contract" or an assignment in similar general terms is an assignment of rights and unless the language or the circumstances (as in an assignment for security) indicate the contrary, it is a delegation of performance of the duties of the assignor and its acceptance by the assignee constitutes a promise by him to perform those duties. This promise is enforceable by either the assignor or the other party to the original contract.

(5) The other party may treat any assignment which delegates performance as creating reasonable grounds for insecurity and may without prejudice to his rights against the assignor demand assurances from the assignee (Section 2 — 609).

PART 3
GENERAL OBLIGATION AND CONSTRUCTION OF CONTRACT

§ 2 — 301. General Obligations of Parties

The obligation of the seller is to transfer and deliver and that of the buyer is to accept and pay in accordance with the contract.

§ 2 — 302. Unconscionable Contract or Clause

(1) If the court as a matter of law finds the contract or any clause of the contract to have been unconscionable at the time it was made the court may refuse to enforce the contract, or it may enforce the remainder of the contract without the unconscionable clause, or it may so limit the application of any unconscionable clause as to avoid any unconscionable result.

(2) When it is claimed or appears to the court that the contract or any clause thereof may be unconscionable the parties shall be afforded a reasonable opportunity to present evidence as to its commercial setting, purpose and effect to aid the court in making the determination.

2 — 303. Allocation or Division of Risks

Where this Article allocates a risk or a burden as between the parties "unless otherwise agreed", the agreement may not only shift the allocation but may also divide the risk or burden.

§ 2 — 304. Price Payable in Money, Goods, Realty, or Otherwise

(1) The price can be made payable in money or otherwise. If it is payable in whole or in part in goods each party is a seller of the goods which he is to transfer.

(2) Even though all or part of the price is payable in an interest in realty the transfer of the goods and the seller's obligations with reference to them are subject to this Article, but not the transfer of the interest in realty or the transferor's obligations in connection therewith.

§ 2 — 305. Open Price Term

(1) The parties if they so intend can conclude a contract for sale even though the price is not settled. In such a case the price is not settled. In such a case the price is a reasonable price at the time for delivery if

    (a) nothing is said as to price; or

    (b) the price is left to be agreed upon by the parties and they fail to agree; or

    (c) the price is to be fixed in terms of some agreed market or other standard as set or recorded by a third person or agency and it is not so set or recorded.

(2) A price to be fixed by the seller or by the buyer means a price for him to fix in good faith.

(3) When a price left to be fixed otherwise than by agreement of the parties fails to be fixed through fault of one party the other may at his option treat the contract as cancelled or himself fix a reasonable price.

(4) Where, however, the parties intend not to be bound unless the price be fixed or agreed and it is not fixed or agreed there is no contract. In such a case the buyer must return any goods already received or if unable so to do must pay their reasonable value at the time of delivery and the seller must return any portion of the price paid on account.

§ 2 — 306. Output, Requirements and Exclusive Dealings

(1) A term which measures the quantity by the output of the seller or the requirements of the buyer means such actual output or requirements as may occur in

good faith, except that no quantity unreasonably disproportionate to any stated estimate or in the absence of a stated estimate to any normal or otherwise comparable prior outpur or requirements may be tendered or demanded.

(2) A lawful agreement by either the seller or the buyer for exclusive dealing in the kind of goods concerned imposes unless otherwise agreed an obligation by the seller to use best efforts to supply the goods and by the buyer to use best efforts to promote their sale.

§ 2 — 307. Delivery in Single Lot or Several Lots

Unless otherwise agreed all goods called for by a contract for sale must be tendered in a single delivery and payment is due only one such tender but where the circumstances give either party the right to make or demand delivery in lots the price if it can be apportioned may be demanded for each lot.

§ 2 — 308. Absence of Specified Place for Delivery

Unless otherwise agreed

(a) the place for delivery of goods is the seller's place of business or if he has none his residence; but

(b) in a contract for sale of identified goods which to the knowledge of the parties at the time of contracting are in some other place, that place is the place for their delivery; and

(c) documents of title may be delivered through customary banking channels.

§ 2 — 309. Absence of Specific Time Provisions: Notice of Termination

(1) The time for shipment or delivery or any other action under a contract if not provided in this Article or agreed upon shall be a reasonable time.

(2) Where the contract provides for successive performances but is indefinite in duration it is valid for a reasonable time but unless otherwise agreed may be terminated at any time by either party.

(3) Termination of a contract by one party except on the happending of an agreed event requires that reasonable notification be received by the other party and an agreement dispensing with notification is invalid if its operation would be unconscionable.

§ 2 — 310. Open Time for Payment or Running of Credit; Authority to Ship Under Reservation

Unless otherwise agreed

(a) payment is due at the time and place at which the buyer is to receive the goods even though the place of shipment is the place of delivery; and

(b) if the seller is authorized to send the goods he may ship them under reservation, and may tender the documents of title, but the buyer may inspect the goods after their arrival before payment is due unless such inspection is inconsistent with the terms of the contract (Section 2 — 513); and

(c) if delivery is authorized and made by way of documents of title otherwise than by subsection (b) then payment is due at the time and place at which the buyer is to receive the documents regardless of where the goods are to be received; and

(d) where the seller is required or authorized to ship the goods on credit the credit period runs from the time of shipment but post-dating the invoice or delaying its dispatch will correspondingly delay the starting of the credit period.

§ **2 — 311.   Options and Cooperation Respecting Performance**

(1) An agreement for sale which is otherwise sufficiently definite (subsection (3) of Section 2 — 204) to be a contract is not made invalid by the fact that it leaves particulars of performance to be specified by one of the parties. Any such specification must be made in good faith and within limits set by commercial reasonableness.

(2) Unless otherwise agreed specifications relating to assortment of the goods are at the buyer's option and except as otherwsie provided in subsections (1)(c) and (3) of Section 2 — 319 specifications or arrangements relating to shipment are at the seller's option.

(3) Where such specification would materially affect the other party's performance but is not seasonably made or where one party's cooperation is necessary to the agreed performance of the other but is not seasonably forthcoming, the other party in addition to all other remedies

(a) is excused for any resulting delay in his own performance; and

(b) may also either proceed to perform in any reasonable manner or after the time for a material part of his own performance treat the failure to specify or to cooperate as a breach by failure to deliver or accept the goods.

§ **2 — 312.   Warranty of Title and Against Infringement; Buyer's Obligation Against Infringement**

(1) Subject to subsection (2) there is in a contract for sale a warranty by the seller that

(a) The title conveyed shall be good, and its transfer rightful; and

(b) the goods shall be delivered free from any security interest or other lien or encumbrance of which the buyer at the time of contracting has no knowledge.

(2) A warranty under subsection (1) will be excluded or modified only by specific language or by circumstances which give the buyer reason to know that the person selling does not claim title in himself or that he is purporting to sell only such right or title as he or a third person may have.

(3) Unless otherwise agreed a seller who is a merchant regularly dealing in goods of the kind warrants that the goods shall be delivered free of the rightful claim of any third person by way of infringement or the like but a buyer who furnishes specifications to the seller must hold the seller harmless against any such claim which arises out of compliance with the specifications.

§ **2 — 313.   Express Warranties by Affirmation, Promise, Description, Sample**

(1) Express warranties by the seller are created as follows:

(a) Any affirmation of fact or promise made by the seller to the buyer which relates to the goods and becomes part of the basis of the bargain creates an express warranty that the goods shall conform to the affirmation or promise.

(b) Any description of the goods which is made part of the basis of the bargain creates an express warranty that the goods shall conform to the description.

(c) Any sample or model which is made part of the basis of the bargain creates an express warranty that the whole of the goods shall conform to the sample or model.

(2) It is not necessary to the creation of an express warranty that the seller use formal words such as "warrant" or "guarantee" or that he have a specific intention to make a warranty, but an affirmation merely of the value of the goods or a

statement purporting to be merely the seller's opinion or commendation of the goods does not create a warranty.

§ 2 — 314. Implied Warranty; Merchantability; Usage of Trade

(1) Unless excluded or modified (Section 2 — 316), a warranty that the goods shall be merchantable is implied in a contract for their sale if the seller is a merchant with respect to goods of that kind. Under this section the serving for value of food or drink to be consumed either on the premises or elsewhere is a sale.

(2) Goods to be merchantable must be at least such as
- (a) pass without objection in the trade under the contract description; and
- (b) in the case of fungible goods, are of fair average quality within the description; and
- (c) are fit for the ordinary purposes for which such goods are used; and
- (d) run, within the variations permitted by the agreement, of even kind, quality and quantity within each unit and among all units involved; and
- (e) are adequately contained, packaged, and labeled as the agreement may require; and
- (f) conform to the promises or affirmations of fact made on the container or label if any.

(3) Unless excluded or modified (Section 2 — 316) other implied warranties may arise from course of dealing or usage of trade.

§ 2 — 315. Implied Warranty; Fitness for Particular Purpose

Where the seller at the time of contracting has reason to know any particular purpose for which the goods are required and that the buyer is relying on the seller's skill or judgment to select or furnish suitable goods, there is unless excluded or modified under the next section an implied warranty that the goods shall be fit for such purpose.

§ 2 — 316. Exclusion or Modification of Warranties

(1) Words or conduct relevant to the creation of an express warranty and words or conduct tending to negate or limit warranty shall be construed wherever reasonable as consistent with each other; but subject to the provisions of this Article on parol or extrinsic evidence (Section 2 — 202) negation or limitation is inoperative to the extent that such construction is unreasonable.

(2) Subject to subsection (3), to exclude or modify the implied warranty of merchantability or any part of it the language must mention merchantability and in case of a writing must be conspicuous, and to exclude or modify any implied warranty of fitness the ecxclusion must be by a writing and conspicuous. Language to exclude all implied warranties of fitness is sufficient if it states, for example, that "There are no warranties which extend beyond the description on the face hereof."

(3) Notwithstanding subsection (2)
- (a) unless the circumstances indicate otherwise, all implied warranties are excluded by expressions like "as is", "with all faults" or other language which in common understanding calls the buyer's attention to the exclsuion of warranties and makes plain that there is no implied warranty; and
- (b) when the buyer before entering into the contract has examined the goods or the sample or model as fully as he desired or has refused to examine the goods there is no implied warranty with regard to defects which an examination ought to in the circumstances to have revealed to him; and

(c) an implied warranty can also be excluded or modified by course of dealing or course of performance or usage of trade.

(4) Remedies for breach of warranty can be limited in accordance with the provisions of this Article on liquidation or limitation of damages and on contractual modification of remedy (Sections 2 — 718 and 2 — 719).

§ 2 — 317.   Cumulation and Conflict of Warranties Express or Implied

Warranties whether express or implied shall be construed as consistent with each other and as cumulative, but if such construction is unreasonable the intention of the parties shall determine which warranty is dominat. In ascertaining that intention the following rules apply:

(a) Exact or technical specifications displace an inconsistent sample or model or general language of description.

(b) A sample from an existing bulk displaces inconsistent general language of description.

(c) Express warranties displace inconsistent implied warranties other than an implied warranty of fitness for a particular purpose.

§ 2 — 318.   Third Party Beneficiaries of Warranties Express or Implied

Note: *If this Act is introduced in the Congress of the United States this section should be omitted. (States to select one alternative.)*

§ 2 — 319.   F.O.B. and F.A.S. Terms

(1) Unless otherwise agreed the term F.O.B. (which means "free on board") at a named place, even though used only in connection with the stated price, is a delivery term under which

(a) when the term is F.O.B. the place of shipment, the seller must at that place ship the goods in the manner provided in this Article (Section 2 — 504) and bear the expense and risk of putting them into the possession of the carrier; or

(b) when the term is F.O.B. the place of destination, the seller must at his own expense and risk transport the goods to that place and there tender delivery of them in the manner provided in this Article (Section 2 — 503);

(c) when under either (a) or (b) the term is also F.O.B. vessel, car or other vehicle, the seller must in addition at his own expense and risk load the goods on board. If the term is F.O.B. vessel the buyer must name the vessel and in an appropriate case the seller must comply with the provisions of this Article on the form of bill of lading (Section 2 — 323).

(2) Unless otherwise agreed the term F.A.S. vessel (which means "free alongside") at a named port, even though used only in connection with the stated price, is a delivery term under which the seller must

(a) at his own expense and risk deliver the goods alongside the vessel in the manner usual in that port or on a dock designated and provided by the buyer; and

(b) obtain and tender a receipt for the goods in exchange for which the carrier is under a duty to issue a bill of lading.

(3) Unless otherwise agreed in any case falling within subsection (1)(a) or (c) or subsection (2) the buyer must seasonably give any needed instructions for making deliver, including when the term is F.A.S. or F.O.B. the loading berth of the vessel and in an appropriate case its name and sailing date. The seller may treat the failure

of needed instructions as a failure of cooperation under this Article (Section 2 — 311). He may also at his option move the goods in any reasonahble manner preparatory to delivery or shipment.

(4) Under the term F.O.B. vessel or F.A.S. unless otherwise agreed the buyer must make payment against tender of the required documents and the seller may not tender nor the buyer demand delivery or the goods in a substitution for the documents.

§ 2 — 320. C.I.F. and C.&F. Terms

(1) The term C.I.F. means that the price includes in a lump sum the cost of the goods and the insurance and freight to the named destination. The term C.&F. or C.F. means that the price so includes cost and freight to the named destination.

(2) Unless otherwise agreed and even though used only in connection with the stated price and destination, the term C.I.F. destination or its equivalent requires the seller at his own expense and risk to

- (a) put the goods into the possession of a carrier at the port for shipment and obtain a negotiable bill or bills of lading covering the entire transportation to the named destination; and
- (b) load the goods and obtain a receipt from the carrier (which may be contained in the bill of lading) showing that the freight has been paid or provided for; and
- (c) obtain a policy or certificate of insurance, including any war risk insurance, of a kind and on terms then current at the port of shipment in the usual amount, in the currency of the contract, shown to cover the same goods covered by the bill of lading and providing for payment of loss to the order of the buyer or for the account of whom it may concern; but the seller may add to the price the amount of the premium for any such war risk insurance; and
- (d) prepare an invoice of the goods and procure any other documents required to effect shipment or to comply with the contract; and
- (e) forward and tender with commerical promptness all the documents in due form and with any indorsement necessary to perfect the buyer's rights.

(3) Unless otherwise agreed the term C.&F. or its equivalent has the same effect and imposes upon the seller the same obligations and risks as a C.I.F. term except the obligation as to insurance.

(4) Under the term C.I.F. or C.&F. unless otherwise agreed the buyer must make payment against tender of the required documents and the seller may not tender nor the buyer demand delivery of the goods in substitution for the documents.

§ 2 — 321. C.I.F. or C.&F.: "Net Landed Weights"; "Payment on Arrival"; Warranty of Condition on Arrival

Under a contract containing a term C.I.F. or C.&F.

(1) Where the price is based on or is to be adjusted according to "net landed weights", "delivered weights", "out turn" quantity or quality or the like, unless otherwise agreed the seller must reasonably estimate the price. The payment due on tender of the documents called for by the contract is the amount so estimated, but after final adjustment of the price a settlement must be made with commercial promptness.

(2) An agreement described in subsection (1) or any warranty of quality or

condition of the goods on arrival places upon the seller the risk of ordinary deterioration, shrinkage and the like in transportation but has no effect on the place or time of

§ 2 — 322. Delivery "Ex-Ship"

(1) Unless otherwise agreed a term for delivery of goods "ex-ship" (which means from the carrying vessel) or in equivalent language is not restricted to a particular ship and requires delivery from a ship which has reached a place at the named port of destination where goods of the kind are usually discharged.

(2) Under such a term unless otherwise agreed
   - (a) the seller must discharge all liens arising out of the carriage and furnish the buyer with a direction which puts the carrier under a duty to deliver the goods; and
   - (b) the risk of loss does not pass to the buyer until the goods leave the ship's tackle or are otherwise properly unloaded.

indentification to the contract for sale or delivery or on the passing of the risk of loss.

(3) Unless otherwise agreed where the contract provides for payment on or after arrival of the goods the seller must before payment allow such preliminary inspection as is feasible; but if the goods are lost delivery of the documents and payment are due when the goods should have arrived.

§ 2 — 323. Form of Bill of Lading Required in Overseas Shipment; "Overseas"

(1) Where the contract contemplates overseas shipment and contains a term C.I.F. or C.&F. or F.O.B. vessel, the seller unless otherwise agreed must obtain a negotiable bill of lading stating that the goods have been loaded on board or, in the case of a term C.I.F. or C.&F., received for shipment.

(2) Where in a case within subsection (1) a bill of lading has been issued in a set of parts, unless otherwise agreed if the documents are not to be sent from abroad the buyer may demand tender of the full set; otherwise only one part of the bill of lading need be tendered. Even if the agreement expressly requires a full set
   - (a) due tender of a single part is acceptable within the provisions of this Article on cure of improper delivery (subsection (1) of Section 2 — 508); and
   - (b) even though the full set is demanded, if the documents are sent from abroad the person tendering an incomplete set may nevertheless require payment upon furnishing an indemnity which the buyer in good faith deems adequate.

(3) A shipment by water or by air or a contract contemplating such shipment is "overseas" insofar as by usage of trade or agreement it is subject to the commercial, financing or shipping practices characteristic of international deep water commerce.

§ 2 — 324. "No Arrival, No Sale" Term

Under a term "no arrival, no sale" or terms of like meaning, unless otherwise agreed,
   - (a) the seller must properly ship conforming goods and if they arrive by any means he must tender them on arrival but he assumes no obligation that the goods will arrive unless he has caused the non-arrival; and
   - (b) where without fault of the seller the goods are in part lost or have so deteriorated as no longer to conform to the contract or arrive after the contract time, the buyer may proceed as if there had been casualty to identified goods (Section 2 — 613).

§ 2 — 325. "Letter of Credit" Term; "Confirmed Credit"

(1) Failure of the buyer seasonably to furnish an agreed letter of credit is a breach of the contract for sale.

(2) The delivery to seller of a proper letter of credit suspends the buyer's obligation to pay. If the letter of credit is dishonored, the seller may on seasonable notification to the buyer require payment directly from him.

(3) Unless otherwise agreed the term "letter of credit" or "banker's credit" in a contract for sale means an irrevocable credit issued by a financing agency of good repute and, where the shipment is overseas, of good international repute. The term "confirmed credit" means that the credit must also carry the direct obligation of such an agency which does business in the seller's financial market.

§ 2 — 326. Sale on Approval and Sale or Return; Consignment Sales and Rights of Creditors

(1) Unless otherwise agreed, if delivered goods may be returned by the buyer even though they conform to the contract, the transaction is

(a) a "sale on approval" if the goods are delivered primarily for use, and

(b) a "sale or return" if the goods are delivered primarily for resale.

(2) Except as provided in subsection (3), goods held on approval are not subject to the claims of the buyer's creditors until acceptance; goods held on sale or return are subject to such claims while in the buyer's possession.

(3) Where goods are delivered to a person for sale and such person maintains a place of business at which he deals in goods of the kind involved, under a name other than the name of the person making delivery, then with respect to claims of creditors of the person conducting the business the goods are deemed to be on sale or return. The provisions of this subsection are applicable even though an agreement purports to reserve title to the person making delivery until payment or resale or uses such words as "on consignment" or "on memorandum". However, this subsection is not applicable if the person making delivery

(a) complies with an applicable law providing for a consignor's interest or the like to be evidenced by a sign, or

(b) establishes that the person conducting the business is generally known by his creditors to be substantially engaged in selling the goods of others, or

(c) complies with the filing provisions of the Article on Secured Transactions (Article 9).

(4) Any "or return" term of a contract for sale is to be treated as a separate contract for sale within the statute of frauds section fof this Article (Section 2 — 201) and as contradicting the sale aspect of the contract within the provisions of the Article on parol or extrinsic evidence (Section 2 — 202).

§ 2 — 327. Special Incidents of Sale on Approval and Sale or Return

(1) Under a sale on approval unless otherwise agreed

(a) although the goods are identified to the contract the risk of loss and the title do not pass to the buyer until acceptance; and

(b) use of the goods consistent with the purpose of trial is not acceptance but failure seasonably to notify the seller of election to return the goods is acceptance, and if the goods conform to the contract acceptance of any part is acceptance of the whole; and

(c) after due notification of election to return, the return is at the seller's risk and expense but a merchant buyer must follow any reasonable instructions.

(2) Under a sale or return unless otherwise agreed

    (a) the option to return extends to the whole or any commercial unit of the goods while in substantially their original condition, but must be exercised seasonably; and

    (b) the return is at the buyer's risk and expense.

§ 2 — 328. Sale by Auction

(1) In a sale by auction if goods are put up in lots each lot is the subject of a separate sale.

(2) A sale by auction is complete when the auctioneer so announces by the fall of the hammer or in other customary manner. Where a bid is made while the hammer is falling in acceptance of a prior bid the auctioneer may in his discretion reopen the bidding or declare the goods sold under the bid on which the hammer was falling.

(3) Such a sale is with reserve unless the goods are in explicit terms put up without reserve. In an auction with reserve the auctioneer may withdraw the goods at any time until he announces completion of the sale. In an auction without reserve, after the auctioneer calls for bids on an article or lot, that article or lot cannot be withdrawn unless no bid is made within a reasonable time. In either case a bidder may retract his bid until the auctioneer's announcement of completion of the sale, but a bidder's retraction does not revive any previous bid.

(4) If the auctioneer knowingly receives a bid on the seller's behalf or the seller makes or procures such a bid, and notice has not been given that liberty for such bidding is reserved, the buyer may at his option aviod the sale or take the goods at the price of the last good faith bid prior to the completion of the sale. This subsection shall not apply to any bid at a forced sale.

Part 4
TITLE, CREDITORS AND GOOD FAITH PURCHASERS

§ 2 — 401. Passing of Title; Reservation for Security; Limited Application of This Section

Each provision of this Article with regard to the rights, obligations and remedies of the seller, the buyer, purchasers or other third parties applies irrespective of title to the goods except where the provision refers to such title. Insofar as situations are not covered by the other provisions of this Article and matters concerning title become material the following rules apply:

(1) Title to goods cannot pass under a contract for sale prior to their identification to the contract (Section 2 — 501), and unless otherwise explicitly agreed the buyer acquires by their identification a special property as limited by this Act. Any retention or reservation by the seller of the title (property) in goods shipped or delivered to the buyer is limited in effect to a reservation of a security interest. Subject to these provisions and to the provisions of the Article on Secured Transactions (Article 9), title to goods passes from the seller to the buyer in any manner and on any conditions explicitly agreed on by the parties.

(2) Unless otherwise explicitly agreed title passes to the buyer at the time and place at which the seller completes his performance with reference to the physcial delivery of the goods, despite any reservation of a security interest and even though a document of title is to be delivered at a different time or place; and in particular and despite any reservation of a security interest by the bill of lading

    (a) if the contract requires or authorizes the seller to send the goods to the buyer but does not require him to deliver them at destination, title passes to the buyer at the time and place of shipment; but

(b) if the contract requires delivery at destination, title passes on tender there.

(3) Unless otherwise explicitly agreed where delivery is to be made without moving the goods,

(a) if the seller is to deliver a document of title, title passes at the time when and the place where he delivers such documents; or

(b) if the goods are at the time of contracting already identified and no documents are to be delivered, title passes at the time and place of contracting.

(4) A rejection or other refusal by the buyer to receive or retain the goods, whether or not justified, or a justified revocation of acceptance revests title to the goods in the seller. Such revesting occurs by operation of law and is not a "sale".

§ 2 — 402. Rights of Seller's Creditors Against Sold Goods

(1) Except as provided in subsections (2) and (3), rights of unsecured creditors of the seller with respect to goods which have been identified to a contract for sale are subject to the buyer's rights to recover the goods under this Article (Sections 2 — 502 and 2 — 716).

(2) A creditor of the seller may treat a sale or an identification of goods to a contract for sale as void if as against him a retention of possession by the seller is fraudulent under any rule of law of the state where the goods are situated, except that retention of possession in good faith and current course of trade by a merchant-seller for a commercially reasonable time after a sale or identification is not fraudulent.

(3) Nothing in this Article shall be deemed to impair the rights of creditors of the seller

(a) under the provisions of the Article on Secured Transactions (Article 9);or

(b) where identification to the contract or delivery is made not in current course of trade but in satisfaction of or as security for a pre-existing claim for money, security or the like and is made under circumstances which under any rule of law of the state where the goods are situated would apart from this Article constitute the transaction a fraudulent transfer or voidable preference.

§ 2 — 403. Power to Transfer; Good Faith Purchase of Goods; "Entrusting"

(1) A purchaser of goods acquires all title which his transferor had or had power to transfer except that a purchaser of a limited interest acquires rights only to the extent of the interest purchased. A person with voidable title has power to transfer a good title to a good faith purchaser for value. When goods have been delivered under a transaction of purchase the purchaser has such power even though

(a) the transferor was deceived as to the identity of the purchaser, or

(b) the delivery was in exchange for a check which is later dishonored, or

(c) it was agreed that the transaction was to be a "cash sale", or

(d) the delivery was procured through fraud punishable as larcenous under the criminal law.

(2) Any entrusting of possession of goods to a merchant who deals in goods of that kind gives him power to transfer all rights of the entruster to a buyer in ordinary course of business.

(3) "Entrusting" includes any delivery and acquiescence in retention of possession

regardless of any condition expressed between the parties to the delivery or acquiescence and regardless of whether the procurement of the entrusting or the possessor's disposition of the goods have been such as to be larcenous under the criminal law.

(4) The rights of other purchasers of goods and of lien creditors are governed by the Articles on Secured Transactions (Article 9), Bulk Transfers (Article 6) and Documents of Title (Article7).

Part 5
PERFORMANCE

§ 2 — 501. Insurable Interest in Goods; Manner of Identification of Goods

(1) The buyer obtains a special property and an insurable interest in goods by identification of existing goods as goods to which the contract refers even though the goods so identified are non-conforming and he has an option to return or reject them. Such identification can be made at any time and in any manner explicitly agreed to by the parties. In the absence of explicit agreement identification occurs

    (a) when the contract is made if it is for the sale of goods already existing and identified;

    (b) if the contract is for the sale of future goods other than those described in paragraph (c), when goods are shipped, marked or otherwise designated by the seller as goods to which the contract refers;

    (c) when the crops are planted or otherwise become growing crops or the young are conceived if the contract is for the sale of unborn young to be born within twelve months after contracting or for the sale of crops to be harvested within twelve months or the next normal harvest season after contracting whichever is longer.

(2) The seller retains an insurable interest in goods so long as title to or any security interest in the goods remains in him and where the identification is by the seller alone he may until default or insolvency or notification to the buyer that the identification is final substitute other goods for those identified.

(3) Nothing in this section impairs any insurable interest recognized under any other statute or rule of law.

§ 2 — 502. Buyer's Right to Goods on Seller's Insolvency

(1) Subject to subsection (2) and even though the goods have not been shipped a buyer who has paid a part or all of the price of goods in which he has a special property under the provisions of the immediately preceding section may on making and keeping good a tender of any unpaid portion of their price recover them from the seller if the seller becomes insolvent within ten days after receipt of the first installment on their price.

(2) If the identification creating his special property has been made by the buyer he acquires the right to recover the goods only if they conform to the contract for sale.

§ 2 — 503. Manner of Seller's Tender of Delivery

(1) Tender of delivery requires that the seller put and hold conforming goods at the buyer's disposition and give the buyer any notification reasonably necessary to enable him to take delivery. The manner, time and place for tender are determined by the agreement and by this Article, and in particular

    (a) tender must be at a reasonable hour, and if it is of goods they must be kept available for the period reasonably necessary to enable the buyer to take possession; but

(b) unless otherwise agreed the buyer must furnish facilities reasonably suited to the receipt of the goods.

(2) Where the case is within the next section respecting shipment tender requires that the seller comply with its provisions.

(3) Where the seller is required to deliver at a particular destination tender requires that he comply with subsection (1) and also in any appropriate case tender documents as described in subsections (4) and (5) of this section.

(4) Where goods are in the possession of a bailee and are to be delivered without being moved

(a) tender requires that the seller either tender a negotiable document of title covering such goods or procure acknowledgment by the bailee of the buyer's right to possession of the goods; but

(b) tender to the buyer of a non-negotiable document of title or of a written direction to the bailee to deliver is sufficient tender unless the buyer seasonably objects, and receipt by the bailee of notification of the buyer's rights fixes those rights as against the bailee and all third persons; but risk of loss of the goods and of any failure by the bailee to honor the non-negotiable document of title or to obey the direction remains on the seller until the buyer has had a reasonable time to present the document or direction, and a refusal by the bailee to honor the document or to obey the direction defeats the tender.

(5) where the contract requires the seller to deliver documents

(a) he must tender all such documents in correct form, except as provided in this Article with respect to bills of lading in a set (subsection (2) of Section 2 — 323); and

(b) tender through customary banking channels is sufficient and dishonor of a draft accompanying the documents constitutes non-acceptance or rejection.

§ 2 — 504. Shipment by Seller

Where the seller is required or authorized to send the goods to the buyer and the contract does not require him to deliver them at a particular destination, then unless otherwise agreed he must

(a) put the goods in the possession of such a carrier and make such a contract for their transportation as may be reasonable having regard to the nature of the goods and other circumstances of the case; and

(b) obtain and promptly deliver or tender in due form any document necessary to enable the buyer to obtain possession of the goods or otherwise required by the agreement or by usage of trade; and

(c) promptly notify the buyer of the shipment.

Failure to notify the buyer under paragraph (c) or to make a proper contract under paragraph (a) is a ground for rejection only if material delay or loss ensues.

§ 2 — 505. Seller's Shipment Under Reservation

(1) Where the seller has identified goods to the contract by or before shipment:

(a) his procurement of a negotiable bill of lading to his own order or otherwise reserves in him a security interest in the goods. His procurement of the bill to the order of a financing agency or of the buyer indicates in addition only the seller's expectation of transferring that interest to the person named.

(b) a non-negotiable bill of lading to himself or his nominee reserves possession of the goods as security but except in a case of conditional delivery (subsection (2) of Section 2 — 507) a non-negotiable bill of lading naming the buyer as consignee reserves no security interest even though the seller retains possession of the bill of lading.

(2) When shipment by the seller with reservation of a security interest is in violation of the contract for sale if constitutes an improper contract for transportation within the preceding section but impairs neither the rights given to the buyer by shipment and identification of the goods to the contract nor the seller's powers as a holder of a negotiable document.

§ 2 — 506.   Rights of Financing Agency

(1) A financing agency by paying or purchasing for value a draft which relates to a shipment of goods acquires to the extent of the payment or purchase and in addition to its own rights under the draft and any document of title securing it any rights of the shipper in the goods including the right to stop delivery and the shipper's right to have the draft honored by the buyer.

(2) The right to reimbursement of a financing agency which has in good faith honored or purchased the draft under commitment to or authority from the buyer is not impaired by subsequent discovery of defects with reference to any relevant document which was apparently regular on its face.

§ 2 — 507.   Effect of Seller's Tender; Delivery of Condition

(1)   Tender of delivery is a condition to the buyer's duty to accept the goods and, unless otherwise agreed, to his duty to pay for them. Tender entitles the seller to acceptance of the goods and to payment according to the contract.

(2) Where payment is due and demanded on the delivery to the buyer of goods or documents of title, his right as against the seller to retain or dispose of them is conditional upon his making the payment due.

§ 2 — 508.   Cure by Seller of Improper Tender or Delivery; Replacement

(1) Where any tender or delivery by the seller is rejected because non-conforming and the time for performance has not yet expired, the seller may seasonably notify the buyer of his intention to cure and may then within the contract time make a conforming deliver.

(2) Where the buyer rejects a non-conforming tender which the seller had reasonable grounds to believe would be acceptable with or without money allowance the seller may if he seasonably notifies the buyer have a further reasonable time to substitute a conforming tender.

§ 2 — 509.   Risk of Loss in the Absence of Breach

(1) Where the contract requires or authorizes the seller to ship the goods by carrier

(a) if it does not require him to deliver them at a particular destination, the risk of loss passes to the buyer when the goods are duly delivered to the carrier even though the shipment is under reservation (Section 2 — 505); but

(b) if it does require him to deliver them at a particular destination and the goods are there duly tendered while in the possession of the carrier, the risk of loss passes to the buyer when the goods are there duly so tendered as to enable the buyer to take delivery.

(2) Where the goods are held by a bailee to be delivered without being moved, the risk of loss passes to the buyer

(a) on his receipt of a negotiable document of title covering the goods; or

(b) on acknowledgment by the bailee of the buyer's right to possession of the goods; or

(c) after his receipt of a non-negotiable document of title or other written direction to deliver, as provided in subsection (4)(b) of Section 2 — 503.

(3) In any case not within subsection (1) or (2), the risk of loss passes to the buyer on his receipt of the goods if the seller is a merchant; otherwise the risk passes to the buyer on tender of delivery.

(4) the provisions of this section are subject to contrary agreement of the parties and to the provisions of this Article on sale on approval (Section 2 — 327) and on effect of breach on risk of loss (Section 2 — 510).

§ 2 — 510. **Effect of Breach on Risk of Loss**

(1) Where a tender or delivery of goods so fails to conform to the contract as to give a right of rejection the risk of their loss remains on the seller until cure of acceptance.

(2) Where the buyer rightfully revokes acceptance he may to the extent of any deficiency in his effective insurance coverage treat the risk of loss as having rested on the seller from the beginning.

(3) Where the buyer as to conforming goods already identified to the contract for sale repudiates or is otherwise in breach before risk of their loss has passed to him, the seller may to the extent of any deficiency in his effective insurance coverage treat the risk of loss as resting on the buyer for a commercially reasonable time.

§ 2 — 511. **Tender of Payment by Buyer; Payment by Check**

(1) Unless otherwise agreed tender of payment is a condition to the seller's duty to tender and complete any delivery.

(2) Tender of payment is sufficient when made by any means or in any manner current in the ordinary course of business unless the seller demands payment in legal tender and gives any extension of time reasonably necessary to procure it.

(3) Subject to the provisions of this Act on the effect of an instrument on an obligation (Section 3 — 802), payment by check is conditional and is defeated as between the aprties by dishonor of the check on due presentment.

§ 2 — 512. **Payment by Buyer Before Inspection**

(1) Where the contract requires payment before inspection non-conformity of the goods does not excuse the buyer from so making payment unless

(a) the non-conformity appears without inspection; or

(b) despite tender of the required documents the circumstances would justify injunction against honor under the provisions of this Act (Section 5 — 114).

(2) Payment pursuant to subsection (1) does not constitute an acceptance of goods or impair the buyer's right to inspect or any of his remedies.

§ 2 — 513. **Buyer's Right to Inspection of Good**

(1) Unless otherwise agreed and subject to subsection (3), where goods are tendered or delivered or identified to the contract for sale, the buyer has a right before payment or acceptance to inspect them at any reasonable place and time and

in any reasonable manner. When the seller is required or authorized to send the goods to the buyer, the inspection may be after their arrival.

(2) Expenses of inspection must be borne by the buyer but may be recovered from the seller if the goods do not conform and are rejected.

(3) Unless otherwise agreed and subject to the provisions of this Article on C.I.F. contracts (subsection (3) of section 2 — 321), the buyer is not entitled to inspect the goods before payment of the price when the contract provides

   (a) for delivery "C.O.D." or on other like terms; or
   (b) for payment against documents of title, except where such payment is due only after the goods are to become available for inspection.

(4) A place or method of inspection fixed by the parties is presumed to be exclusive but unless otherwise expressly agreed it does not postpone identification or shift the place for delivery or for passing the risk of loss. If compliance becomes impossible, inspection shall be provided in this section unless the place or method fixed was clearly intended as an indispensable condition failure of which avoids the contract.

§ 2 — 514. When Documents Deliverable on Acceptance; When on Payment

Unless otherwise agreed documents against which a draft is drawn are to be delivered to the drawee on acceptance of the draft if it is payable more than three days after presentment; otherwise, only on payment.

§ 2 — 515. Preserving Evidence of Goods in Dispute

In furtherance of the adjustment of any claim or dispute

   (a) either party on reasonable notification to the other and for the purpose of ascertaining the facts and preserving evidence has the right to inspect, test and sample the goods including such of them as may be in the possession or control of the other; and
   (b) the parties may agree to a third party inspection or survey to determine the conformity or condition of the goods and may agree that the findings shall be binding upon them in any subsequent litigation or adjustment.

Part 6
BREACH, REPUDIATION AND EXCUSE

§ 2 — 601. Buyer's Rights on Improper Delivery

Subject to the provisions of this Article on breach in installment contracts (Section 2 — 612) and unless otherwise agreed under the sections on contractual limitations of remedy (Sections 2 — 718 and 2 — 719), if the goods or the tender of delivery fail in any respect to conform to the contract, the buyer may

   (a) reject the whole; or
   (b) accept the whole; or
   (c) accept any commercial unit or units and reject the rest.

§ 2 — 602. Manner and Effect of Rightful Rejection

(1) Rejection of goods must be within a reasonable time after their delivery or tender. It is ineffective unless the buyer seasonably notifies the seller.

(2) Subject to the provisions of the two following sections on rejected goods (Section 2 — 603 and 2 — 604),

   (a) after rejection any exercise of ownership by the buyer with respect to any commercial unit is wrongful as against the seller; and

(b) if the buyer has before rejection taken physical possession of goods in which he does not have a security interest under the provisions of this Article (subsection (3) of Section 2 — 711), he is under a duty after rejection to hold them with reasonable care at the seller's disposition for a time sufficient to permit the seller to remove them; but

(c) the buyer has no further obligations with regard to goods rightfully rejected.

(3) The seller's rights with respect to goods wrongfully rejected are governed by the provisions of this Article on Seller's remedies in general (Section 2 — 703).

§ 2 — 603. Merchant Buyer's Duties as to Rightfully Rejected Goods

(1) Subject to any security interest in the buyer (subsection (3) of Section 2 — 711), when the seller has no agent or place of business at the market of rejection a merchant buyer is under a duty after rejection of goods in his possession or control to follow any reasonable instruction received from the seller with respect to the goods and in the absence of such instructions to make reasonable goods and in the absence of such instructions to make reasonable efforts to sell them for the seller's account if they are perishable or threaten to decline in value speedily. Instructions are nto reasonable if on demand indemnity for expenses is not forthcoming.

(2) When the buyer sells goods under subsection (1), he is entitled to reimbursement from the seller or out of the proceeds for reasonable expenses of caring for and selling them, and if the expenses include no selling commission then to such commission as is usual in the trade or if there is none to a reasonable sum not exceeding ten per cent on the gross proceeds.

(3) In complying with this section the buyer is held only to good faith and good faith conduct hereunder is neither acceptance nor conversion nor the basis of an action for damages.

§ 2 — 604. Buyer's Options as to Salvage of Rightfully Rejected Goods

Subject to the provisions of the immediately preceding section on perishables if the seller gives no instructions within a reasonable time after notification of rejection the buyer may store the rejected goods for the seller's account or reship them to him or resell them for the seller's account with reimbursement as provided in the preceding section. Such action is not acceptance or conversion.

§ 2 — 605. Waiver of Buyer's Objections by Failure to Particularize

(1) The buyer's failure to state in connection with rejection a particular defect which is ascertainable by reasonable inspection precludes him from relying on the unstated defect to justify rejection or to establish breach

(a) where the seller could have cured it if stated seasonably; or

(b) between merchants when the seller has after rejection made a request in writing for a full and final written statement of all defects on which the buyer proposes to rely.

(2) Payment against documents made without reservation of rights precludes recovery of the payment for defects apparent on the face of the documents.

§ 2 — 606. What Constitutes Acceptance of Goods

(1) Acceptance of goods occurs when the buyer

(a) after a reasonable opportunity to inspect the goods signifies to the seller that the goods are conforming or that he will take or retain them in spite of their non-conformity; or

(b) fails to make an effective rejection (subsection (1) of Section 2 — 602), but such acceptance does not occur until the buyer has had a reasonable opportunity to inspect them; or

(c) does any act inconsistent with the seller's ownership; but if such act is wrongful as against the seller it is an acceptance only if ratified by him.

(2) Acceptance of a part of any commercial unit is acceptance of that entire unit.

§ 2 — 607. **Effect of Acceptance; Notice of Breach; Burden of Establishing Breach After Acceptance; Notice of Claim or Litigation to Person Answerable Over**

(1) The buyer must pay at the contract rate for any goods accepted.

(2) Acceptance of goods by the buyer precludes rejection of the goods accepted and if made with knowledge of a non-conformity cannot be revoked because of it unless the acceptance was on the reasonable assumption that the non-conformity would be seasonably cured but acceptance does not of itself impair any other remedy provided by this Article for non-conformity.

(3) Where a tender has been accepted

(a) the buyer must within a reasonable time after he discovers or should have discovered any breach notify the seller of breach or be barred from any remedy; and

(b) if the claim is one for infringement or the like (subsection (3) of Section 2 — 312) and the buyer is used as a result of such a breach he must so notify the seller within a reasonable time after he receives notice of the litigation or be barred from any remedy over for liability established by the litigation.

(4) The burden is on the buyer to establish any breach with respect to the goods accepted.

(5) Where the buyer is used for breach of a warranty or other obligation for which his seller is answerable over

(a) he may give his seller written notice of the litigation. If the notice states that the seller may come in and defend and that if the seller does not do so he will be bound in any action against him by his buyer by any determination of fact common to the two litigations, then unless the seller after seasonable receipt of the notice does come in and defend he is so bound.

(b) if the claim is one for infringement or the like (subsection (3) of Section 2 — 312) the original seller may demand in writing that his buyer turn over to him control of the litigation including settlement or else be barred from any remedy over and if he also agrees to bear all expense and to satisfy any adverse judgment, then unless the buyer after seasonable receipt of the demand does turn over control the buyer is so barred.

(6) the provisions of subsections (3), (4) and (5) apply to any obligation of a buyer to hold the seller harmless against infringement or the like (subsection (3) of Section 2 — 312).

§ 2 — 608. **Revocation of Acceptance in Whole or in Part**

(1) The buyer may revoke his acceptance of a lot or commercial unit whose non-conformity substantially impairs its value to him if he has accepted it

(a) on the reasonable assumption that its non-conformity would be cured and it has not been seasonably cured; or

(b) without discovery of such non-conformity if his acceptance was reasonably induced either by the difficulty of discovery before acceptance or by the seller's assurances.

(2) Revocation of acceptance must occur within a reasonable time after the buyer discovers or should have discovered the ground for it and before any substantial change in condition of the goods which is not caused by their own defects. It is not effective until the buyer notifies the seller of it.

(3) A buyer who so revokes has the same rights and duties with regard to the goods involved as if he had rejected them.

§ 2 — 609. Right to Adequate Assurance of Performance

(1) A contract for sale imposes an obligation on each party that the other's expectation of receiving due performance will not be imparied. When reasonable grounds for insecurity arise with respect to the performance of either party the other may in writing demand adequate assurance of due performance and until he receives such assurance may if commercially reasonable suspend any performance for which he has not already received the agreed return.

(2) Between merchants the reasonableness of grounds for insecurity and the adequacy of any assurance offered shall be determined according to commercial standards.

(3) Acceptance of any improper delivery or payment does not prejudice the aggrieved party's right to demand adequate assurance of future performance.

(4) After receipt of a justified demand failure to provide within a reasonable time not exceeding thirty days such assurance of due performance as is adequate under the circumstances of the particular case is a repudiation of the contract.

§ 2 — 610. Anticipatory Repudiation

When either party repudiates the contract with respect to a performance not yet due the loss of which will substantially impair the value of the contract to the other, the aggrieved party may

   (a) for a commercially reasonable time await performance by the repudiating party; or

   (b) resort to any remedy for breach (Section 2 — 703 or Section 2 — 711), even though he has notified the repudiating party that he would await the latter's performance and has urged retraction; and

   (c) in either case suspend his own performance or proceed in accordance with the provisions of this Article on the seller's right to identify goods to the contract notwithstanding breach or to salvage unfinished goods (Section 2 — 704).

§ 2 — 611. Retraction of Anticipatory Repudiation

(1) Until the repudiating party's next performance is due he can retract his repudiation unless the aggrieved party has since the repudiation cancelled or materially changed his position or otherwise indicated that he considers the repudiation final.

(2) Retraction may be by any method which clearly indicates to the aggrieved party that the repudiating party intends to perform, but must include any assurance justifiably demanded under the provisions of this Article (Section 2 — 609).

(3) Retraction reinstates the repudiating party's rights under the contract with due excuse and allowance to the aggrieved party for any delay occasioned by the repudiation.

§ 2 — 612. "Installment Contract"; Breach

(1) An "installment contract" is one which requires or authorizes the delivery of goods in separate lots to be separately accepted, even though the contract contains a clause "each delivery is a separate contract" or its equivalent.

(2) The buyer may reject any installment which is non-conforming if the non-conformity substantially impairs the value of that installment and cannot be cured or if the non-conformity is a defect in the required documents; but if the non-conformity does not fall within subsection (3) and the seller gives adequate assurance of its cure the buyer must accept that installment.

(3) Whenever non-conformity or default with respect to one or more installments substantially impairs the value of the whole contract there is a breach of the whole. But the aggrieved party reinstates the contract if he accepts a non-conforming installment without seasonably notifying of cancellation or if he brings an action with respect only to past installments or demands performance as to future installments.

§ 2 — 613. Casualty to Identified Goods

Where the contract requires for its performance goods identified when the contract is made, and the goods suffer casualty without fault of either party before the risk of loss passes to the buyer, or in a proper case under a "no arrival, no sale" term (Section 2 — 324) then

(a) if the loss is total the contract is avoided; and

(b) if the loss is partial or the goods have so deteriorated as no longer to conform to the contract the buyer may nevertheless demand inspection and at his option either treat the contract as avoided or accept the goods with due allowance from the contract price for the deterioration or the deficiency in quantity but without further right against the seller.

§ 2 — 614. Substituted Performance

(1) Where without fault of either party the agreed berthing, loading, or unloading facilities fail or an agreed type of carrier becomes unavailable or the agreed manner of delivery otherwise becomes commercially impracticable but a commercially reasonable substitute is available, such substitute performance must be tendered and accepted.

(2) If the agreed means or manner of payment fails because of domestic or foreign governmental regulation, the seller may withhold or stop delivery unless the buyer provides a means or manner of payment which is commercially a substantial equivalent. If delivery has already been taken, payment by the means or in the manner provided by the regulation discharges the buyer's obligation unless the regulation is discriminatory, oppressive or predatory.

§ 2 — 615. Excuse by Failure of Presupposed Conditions

Except so far as a seller may have assumed a greater obligation and subject to the preceding section on substituted performance:

(a) Delay in delivery or non-delivery in whole or in part by a seller who complies with paragraphs (b) and (c) is not a breach of his duty under a contract for sale if performance as agreed has been made impracticable by the occurrence of a contingency the non-occurrence of which was a basic assumption on which the contract was made or by compliance in good faith with any applicable foreign or domestic governmental regulation or order whether or not it later proves to be invalid.

(b) Where the causes mentioned in paragraph (a) affect only a part of the seller's capacity to perform, he must allocate production and deliveries among his customers but may at his option include regular customers not then under contract as well as his own requirements for further manufacture. He may so allocate in any manner which is fair and reasonable.

(c) The seller must notify the buyer seasonably that there will be delay or non-delivery and, when allocation is required under paragraph (b), of the estimated quota thus made available for the buyer.

§ 2 — 616. Procedure on Notice Claiming Excuse

(1) Where the buyer receives notification of a material or indefinite delay or an allocation justified under the preceding section he may by written notification to the seller as to any delivery concerned, and where the prospective deficiency substantially impairs the value of the whole contract under the provisions of this Article relating to breach of installment contracts (Section 2 — 612), then also as to the whole,

(a) terminate and thereby discharge any unexecuted portion of the contract; or

(b) modify the contract by agreeing to take his available quota in substitution.

(2) If after receipt of such notification from the seller the buyer fails so to modify the contract within a reasonable time not exceeding thirty days the contract lapses with respect to any deliveries affected.

(3) The provisions of this section may not be negated by agreement except in so far as the seller has assumed a greater obligation under the preceding section.

Part 7
REMEDIES

§ 2 — 701. Remedies for Breach of Collateral Contracts not Impaired

Remedies for breach of any obligation or promise collateral or ancillary to a contract for sale are not impaired by the provisions of this Article.

§ 2 — 702. Seller's Remedies on Discovery of Buyer's Insolvency

(1) Where the seller discovers the buyer to be insolvent he may refuse delivery except for cash including payment for all goods theretofore delivered under the contract, and stop delivery under this Article (Section 2 — 705).

(2) Where the seller discovers that the buyer has received goods on credit while insolvent he may reclaim the goods upon demand made within ten days after the receipt, but if misrepresentation of solvency has been made to the particular seller in writing within three months before delivery the ten day limitation does not apply. Except as provided in this subsection the seller may not base a right to reclaim goods on the buyer's fraudulent or innocent misrepresentation of solvency or of intent to pay.

(3) The seller's right to reclaim under subsection (2) is subject to the rights of a buyer in ordinary course or other good faith purchaser under this Article (Section 2 — 403). Successful reclamation of goods excludes all other remedies with respect to them. As amended 1966.

§ 2 — 703. Seller's remedies in General

Where the buyer wrongfully rejects or revokes acceptance of goods or fails to make a payment due on or before delivery or repudiates with respect to a part or the whole, then with respect to any good directly affected and, if the breach is of the whole contract (Section 2 — 612), then also with respect to the whole undelivered balance, the aggrieved seller may

(a) withhold delivery of such goods;

(b) stop delivery by any bailee as hereafter provided (Section 2 — 706);

(c) proceed under the next section respecting goods still unidentified to the contract;

(d) resell and recover damages as hereafter provided (Section 2 — 706);

(e) recover damages for non-acceptance (Section 2 — 708) or in a proper case the price (Section 2 — 709);

(f) cancel.

§ 2 — 704. Seller's Right to Identify Good to the Contract Notwithstanding Breach or to Salvage Unfinished Goods

(1) An aggrieved seller under the preceding section may

(a) identify to the contract conforming goods not already identified if at the time he learned of the breach they are in his possession or control;

(b) treat as the subject of resale goods which have demonstrably been intended for the particular contract even though those good are unfinished.

(2) where the goods are unfinished an aggrieved seller may in the exercise of reasonable commercial judgment for the purposes of avoiding loss and of effective realization either complete the manufacture and wholly identify the goods to the contract or cease manufacture and resell for scrap or salvage value or proceed in any other reasonable manner.

§ 2 — 705. Seller's Stoppage of Delivery in Transit or Otherwise

(1) The seller may stop delivery of goods in the possession of a carrier or other bailee when he discovers the buyer to be insolvent (Section 2 — 702) and may stop delivery of carload, truckload, planeload or larger shipments of express or freight when the buyer repudiates or fails to make a payment due before delivery or if for any other reason the seller has a right to withhold or reclaim the goods.

(2) As against such buyer the seller may stop delivery until

(a) receipt of the goods by the buyer; or

(b) acknowledgment to the buyer by any bailee of the goods except a carrier that the bailee holds the goods for the buyer; or

(c) such acknowledgment to the buyer by a carrier by reshipment or as warehouseman; or

(d) negotiation to the buyer of any negotiable document of title covering the goods.

(3) (a) To stop delivery the seller must so notify as to enable the bailee by reasonable diligence to prevent delivery of the goods.

(b) After such notification the bailee must hold and deliver the goods according to the directions of the seller but the seller is liable to the bailee for any ensuing charges or damages.

(c) If a negotiable document of title has been issued for goods the bailee is not obliged to obey a notification to stop until surrender of the document.

(d) A carrier who has issued a non-negotiable bill of lading is not obliged to obey a notification to stop received from a person other than the consignor.

§ 2 — 706. Seller's Resale Including Contract for Resale

(1) Under the conditions stated in Section 2 — 703 on seller's remedies, the seller may resell the goods concerned or the undelivered balance thereof. Where the resale is made in good faith and in a commercially reasonable manner the seller may recover the difference between the resale price and the contract price together with

any incidental damages allowed under the provisions of this Article (Section 2 — 710), but less expenses saved in consequence of the buyer's breach.

(2) Except as otherwise provided in subsection (3) or unless otherwise agreed resale may be at public or private sale including sale by way of one or more contracts to sell or of identification to an existing contract of the seller. Sale may be as a unit or in parcels and at any time and place and on any terms but every aspect of the sale including the method, manner, time, place and terms must be commercially reasonable. The resale must be reasonably identified as referring to the broken contract, but it is not necessary that the goods be in existence or that any or all of them have been identified to the contract before the breach.

(3) Where the resale is at private sale the seller must give the buyer reasonable notification of his intention to resell.

(4) Where the resale is at public sale

    (a) only identified goods can be sold except where there is a recognized market for a public sale of futures in goods of the kind; and

    (b) it must be made at a usual place or market for public sale if one is reasonably available and except in the case of goods which are perishable or threaten to decline in value speedily the seller must give the buyer reasonable notice of the time and place of the resale; and

    (c) if the goods are not to be within the view of those attending the sale the notification of sale must state the place where the goods are located and provide for their reasonable inspection by prospective bidders; and

    (d) the seller may buy.

(5) A purchaser who buys in good faith at a resale takes the goods free of any rights of the original buyer even though the seller fails to comply with one or more of the requirements of this section.

(6) The seller is not accountable to the buyer for any profit made on any resale. A person in the position of a seller (Section 2 — 707) or a buyer who has rightfully rejected or justifiably revoked acceptance must account for any excess over the amount of his security interest, as hereinafter defined (subsection (3) of Section 2 — 711).

§ 2 — 707.   "Person in the Position of a Seller"

(1) A "person in the position of a seller" includes as against a principal an agent who has paid or become responsible for the price of goods on behalf of his principal or anyone who otherwise holds a security interest or other right in goods similar to that of a seller.

(2) A person in the position of a seller may as provided in this Article withhold or stop delivery (Section 2 — 705) and resell (Section 2 — 706) and recover incidental damages (Section 2 — 710).

§ 2 — 708.   Seller's Damages for Non-acceptance or Repudiation

(1) Subject to subsection (2) and to the provisions of this Article with respect to proof of market price (Section 2 — 723), the measure of damages for non-acceptance or repudiation by the buyer is the difference between the market price at the time and place for tender and the unpaid contract price together with any incidental damages provided in this Article (Section 2 — 710), but less expenses saved in consequence of the buyer's breach.

(2) If the measure of damages provided in subsection (1) is inadequate to put the

seller in as good a position as performance would have done then the measure of damages is the profit (including reasonable overhead) which the seller would have made from full performance by the buyer, together with any incidental damages provided in this Article (Section 2 — 710), due allowance for costs reasonably incurred and due credit for payments or proceeds of resale.

§ 2 — 709. **Action for the Price**

(1) When the buyer fails to pay the price as it becomes due the seller may recover, together with any incidental damages under the next section, the price

(a) of goods accepted or of conforming goods lost or damaged within a commercially reasonable time after risk of their loss has passed to the buyer; and

(b) of goods identified to the contract if the seller is unable after reasonable effort to resell them at a reasonable price or the circumstances reasonably indicate that such effort will be unavailing.

(2) Where the seller sues for the price he must hold for the buyer any goods which have been identified to the contract and are still in his control except that if resale becomes possible he may resell them at any time prior to the collection of the judgment. The net proceeds of any such resale must be credited to the buyer and payment of the judgment entitles him to any goods not resold.

(3) After the buyer has wrongfully rejected or revoked acceptance of the goods or has failed to make a payment due or has repudiated (Section 2 — 610), a seller who is held not entitled to the price under this section shall nevertheless be awarded damages for non-acceptance under the preceding section.

§ 2 — 710. **Seller's Incidental Damages**

Incidental damages to an aggrieved seller include any commercially reasonable charges, expenses or commissions incurred in stopping delivery, in the transportation, care and custody of goods after the buyer's breach, in connection with return or resale of the goods or otherwise resulting from the breach.

§ 2 — 711. **Buyer's Remedies in General; Buyer's Security Interest in Rejected Goods**

(1) Where the seller fails to make delivery or repudiates or the buyer rightfully rejects or justifiably revokes acceptance then with respect to any goods involved, and with respect to the whole if the breach goes to the whole contract (Section 2 — 612), the buyer may cancel and whether or not he has done so may in addition ot recovering so much of the price as has been paid

(a) "cover" and have damages under the next section as to all the goods affected whether or not they have been identified to the contract; or

(b) recover damages for non-delivery as provided in this Article (Section 2 — 713).

(2) Where the seller fails to deliver or repudiates the buyer may also

(a) if the goods have been identified recover them as provided in this Article (Section 2 — 502); or

(b) in a proper case obtain specific performance or replevy the goods as provided in this Article (Section 2 — 716).

(3) On rightful rejection or justifiable revocation of acceptance a buyer has a security interest in goods in his possession or control for any payments made on their price and any expenses reasonably incurred in their inspection, receipt, transportation, care and custody and may hold such goods and resell them in like manner as an aggrieved seller (Section 2 — 706).

§ 2 — 712. "Cover"; Buyer's Procurement of Substitute Goods

(1) After a breach within the preceding section the buyer may "cover" by making in good faith and without unreasonable delay any reasonable purchase of or contract to purchase goods in substitution for those due from the seller.

(2) The buyer may recover from the seller as damages the difference between the cost of cover and the contract price together with any incidental or consequential damages as hereinafter defined (Section 2 — 715), but less expenses saved in consequence of the seller's breach.

(3) Failure of the buyer to effect cover within this section does not bar him from any other remedy.

§ 2 — 713. Buyer's Damages for Non-Delivery or Repudiation

(1) Subject to the provisions of this Article with respect to proof of market price (Section 2 — 723), the measure of damages for non-delivery or repudiation by the seller is the difference between the market price at the time when the buyer learned of the breach and the contract price together with any incidental and consequential damages provided in this Article (Section 2 — 715), but less expenses saved in consequence of the seller's breach.

(2) Market price is to be determined as of the place for tender or, in cases of rejection after arrival or revocation of acceptance, as of the place of arrival.

§ 2 — 714. Buyer's Damages for Breach in Regard to Accepted Goods

(1) Where the buyer has accepted goods and given notification (subsection (3) of Section 2 — 607) he may recover as damages for any non-conformity of tender the loss resulting in the ordinary course of events from the seller's breach as determined in any manner which is reasonable.

(2) The measure of damages for breach of warranty is the difference at the time and place of acceptance between the value of the goods accepted and the value they would have had if they had been as warranted, unless special circumstances show proximate damages of a different amount.

(3) In a proper case any incidental and consequential damages under the next section may also be recovered.

§ 2 — 715. Buyer's Incidental and Consequential Damages

(1) Incidental damages resulting from the seller's breach include expenses reasonably incurred in inspection, receipt, trnasportation and care and custody of goods rightfully rejected, any commercially reasonable charges, expenses or commissions in connection with effecting cover and any other resonable expense incident to the delay or other breach.

(2) Consequential damages resulting from the seller's breach include

    (a) any loss resulting from general or particular requirements and needs of which the seller at the time of contracting had reason to know and which could not reasonably be prevented by cover or otherwise; and

    (b) injury to person or property proximately resulting from any breach of warranty.

§ 2 — 716. Buyer's Right to Specific Performance or Replevin

(1) Specific performance may be decreed where the goods are unique or in other proper circumstances.

(2) The decree for specific performance may include such terms and conditions as to payment of the price, damages, or other relief as the court may deem just.

(3) The buyer has a right of replevin for goods identified to the contract if after reasonable effort he is unable to effect cover for such goods or the circumstances reasonably indicate that such effort will be unavailing or if the goods have been shipped under reservation and satisfaction of the security interest in them has been made or tendered.

§ 2 — 717.   Deduction of Damages From the Price

The buyer on notifying the seller of his intention to do so may deduct all or any part of the damages resulting from any breach of the contract from any part of the price still due under the same contract.

§ 2 — 718.   Liquidation or Limitation of Damages; Deposits

(1) Damages for breach by either party may be liquidated in the agreement but only at an amount which is reasonable in the light of the anticipated or actual harm caused by the breach, the difficulties of proof of loss, and the inconvenience or nonfeasibility of otherwise obtaining an adequate remedy. A term fixing unreasonably large liquidated damages is void as a penalty.

(2) Where the seller justifiably withholds delivery of goods because of the buyer's breach, the buyer is entitled to restitution of any amount by which the sum of his payments exceeds

    (a) the amount to which the seller is entitled by virtue of terms liquidating the seller's damages in accordance with subsection (1), or

    (b) in the absence of such terms, twenty per cent of the value of the total performance for which the buyer is obligated under the contract of $500, whichever is smaller.

(3) The buyer's right to restitution under subsection (2) is subject to offset to the extent that the seller establishes

    (a) a right to recover damages under the provisions of this Article other than subsection (1), and

    (b) the amount or value of any benefits received by the buyer directly or indirectly by reason of the contract.

(4) Where a seller has received payment in goods their reasonable value or the proceeds of their resale shall be treated as payments for the purposes of subsection (2); but if the seller has notice of the buyer's breach before reselling goods received in part performance, his resale is subject to the conditions laid down in this Article on reslae by an aggrieved seller (Section 2 — 706).

§ 2 — 719.   Contractual Modification or Limitation of Remedy

(1) Subject to the provisions of subsections (2) and (3) of this section and of the preceding section on liquidation and limitation of damages,

    (a) the agreement may provide for remedies in addition to or in substitution for those provided in this Article and may limit or alter the measure of damages recoverable under this Article, as by limiting the buyer's remedies to return of the goods and repayment of the price or to repair and replacement of nonconforming goods or parts; and

    (b) resort to a remedy as provided is optional unless the remedy is expressly agreed to be exclusive, in which case it is the sole remedy.

(2) Where circumstances cause an exclusive or limited remedy to fail of its essential purpose, remedy may be had as provided in this Act.

(3) Consequential damages may be limited or excluded unless the limitation or exclusion is unconscionable. Limitation of consequential damages for injury to the

person in the case of consumer goods is prima facie unconscionable but limitation of damages where the loss is commercial is not.

§ 2 — 720.   Effect of "Cancellation" or "Rescission" on Claims for Antecedent Breach

Unless the contrary intention clearly appears, expressions of "cancellation" or "rescission" of the contract or the like shall not be construed as a renunciation or discharge of any claim in damages for an antecedent breach.

§ 2 — 721.   Remedies for Fraud

Remedies for material misrepresentation or fraud include all remedies available under this Article for non-fraudulent breach. Neither rescission or a claim for rescission of the contract for sale nor rejection or return of the goods shall bar or be deemed inconsistent with a claim for damages or other remedy.

§ 2 — 722.   Who Can Sue Third Parties for Injury to Goods

Where a third party so deals with goods which have been identified to a contract for sale as to cause actionable injury to a party to that contract

  (a) a right of action against the third party is in either party to the contract for sale who has title to or a security interest or a special property or an insurable interest in the goods; and if the goods have been destroyed or converted a right of action is also in the party who either bore the risk of loss under the contract for sale or has since the injury assumed that risk as against the other;

  (b) if at the time of the injury the party plaintiff did not bear the risk of loss as against the other party to the contract for sale and there is no arrangement between them for disposition of the recovery, his suit or settlement is, subject to his own interest, as a fiduciary for the other party to the contract;

  (c) either party may with the consent of the other sue for the benefit of whom it may concern.

§ 2 — 723.   Proof of Market Price: Time and Place

(1) If an action based on anticipatory repudiation comes to trial before the time for performance with respect to some or all of the goods, any damages based on market price (Section 2 — 708 or Section 2 — 713) shall be determined according to the price of such goods prevailing at the time when the aggrieved party learned of the repudiation.

(2) If evidence of a price prevailing at the times or places described in this Article is not readily available the price prevailing within any reasonable time before or after the time described or at any other place which in commercial judgment or under usage of trade would serve as a reasonable substitute for the one described may be used, making any proper allowance for the cost of transporting the goods to or from such other place.

(3) Evidence of a relevant price prevailing at a time or place other than the one described in this Article offered by one party is not admissible unless and until he has given the other party such notice as the court finds sufficient to prevent unfair surprise.

§ 2 — 724.   Admissibility of Market Quotations

Whenever the prevailing price or value of any goods regularly bought and sold in any established commodity market is in issue, reports in official publications or trade journals or in newspapers or periodicals of general circulation published as the reports of such market shall be admissible in evidence. The circumstances of the preparation of such a report may be shown to affect its weight but not its admissibility.

§ 2 — 725. Statute of Limitations in Contracts for Sale

(1) An action for breach of any contract for sale must be commenced within four years after the cause of action has accrued. By the original agreement the parties may reduce the period of limitation to not less than one year but may not extend it.

(2) A cause of action accrues when the breach occurs, regardless of the aggrieved party's lack of knowledge of the breach. A breach of warranty occurs when tender of delivery is made, except that where a warranty explicitly extends to future performance of the goods and discovery of the breach must await the time of such performance the cause of action accrues when the breach is or should have been discovered.

(3) Where an action commenced within the time limited by subsection (1) is so terminated as to leave available a remedy by another action for the same breach such other action may be commenced after the expiration of the time limited and within six months after the termination of the first action unless the termination resulted from voluntary discontinuance or from dismissal for failure or neglect to prosecute.

(4) This section does not alter the law on tolling of the statute of limitations nor does it apply to causes of action which have accrued before this Act becomes effective.

— Appendix C —
International Chamber of Commerce Rules of Arbitration

NEW CONCILIATION RULES AND AMENDED ARBITRATION RULES

IN FORCE AS FROM JANUARY 1, 1988

RULES OF OPTIONAL CONCILIATION

Preamble.

Settlement is a desirable solution for business disputes of an international character.

The International Chamber of Commerce therefore sets out these Rules of Optional Conciliation in order to facilitate the amicable settlement of such disputes.

Article 1.

All business disputes of an international character may be submitted to conciliation by a sole conciliator appointed by the International Chamber of Commerce.

Article 2.

The party requesting conciliation shall apply to the Secretariat of the Court of the International Chamber of Commerce setting out succinctly the purpose of the request and accompanying it with the fee required to open the file, as set out in Appendix III hereto.

Article 3.

The Secretariat of the Court shall, as soon as possible, inform the other party of the request for conciliation. That party will be given a period of 15 days to inform the Secretariat whether it agrees or declines to participate in the attempt to conciliate.

If the other party agrees to participate in the attempt to conciliate it shall so inform the Secretariat within such period.

In the absence of any reply within such period or in the case of a negative reply the request for conciliation shall be deemed to have been declined. The Secretariat shall, as soon as possible, so inform the party which had requested conciliation.

Article 4.

Upon receipt of an agreement to attempt conciliation, the Secretary General of the Court shall appoint a conciliator as soon as possible. The conciliator shall inform the parties of his appointment and set a time-limit for the parties to present their respective arguments to him.

Article 5.

The conciliator shall conduct the conciliation process as he thinks fit, guided by the principles of impartiality, equity and justice.

With the agreement of the parties, the conciliator shall fix the place for conciliation.

The conciliator may at any time during the conciliation process request a party to submit to him such additional information as he deems necessary.

The parties may, if they so wish, be assisted by counsel of their choice.

Article 6.

The confidential nature of the conciliation process shall be respected by every person who is involved in it in whatever capacity.

Article 7.

The conciliation process shall come to an end:

(a) Upon the parties signing an agreement. The parties shall be bound by such agreement. The agreement shall remain confidential unless and to the extent that its execution or application require disclosure.

(b) Upon the production by the conciliator of a report recording that the attempt to conciliate has not been successful. Such report shall not contain reasons.

(c) Upon notification to the conciliator by one or more parties at any time during the conciliation process of an intention no longer to pursue the conciliation process.

Article 8.

Upon termination of the conciliation, the conciliator shall provide the Secretariat of the Court with the settlement agreement signed by the parties or with his report of lack of success or with a notice from one or more parties of the intention no longer to pursue the conciliation process.

Article 9.

Upon the file being opened, the Secretariat of the Court shall fix the sum required to permit the process to proceed, taking into consideration the nature and importance of the dispute. Such sum shall be paid in equal shares by the parties.

This sum shall cover the estimated fees of the conciliator, expenses of the conciliation, and the administrative expenses as set out in Appendix III hereto.

In any case where, in the course of the conciliation process, the Secretariat of the Court shall decide that the sum originally paid is insufficient to cover the likely total costs of the conciliation, the Secretariat shall require the provision of an additional amount which shall be paid in equal shares by the parties.

Upon termination of the conciliation, the Secretariat shall settle the total costs of the process and advise the parties in writing.

All the above costs shall be borne in equal shares by the parties except and insofar as a settlement agreement provides otherwise.

A party's other expenditures shall remain the responsibility of that party.

Article 10.

Unless the parties agree otherwise, a conciliator shall not act in any judicial or arbitration proceeding relating to the dispute which has been the subject of the conciliation process whether as an arbitrator, representative or counsel of a party.

The parties mutually undertake not to call the conciliator as a witness in any such proceedings, unless otherwise agreed between them.

Article 11.

The parties agree not to introduce in any judicial or

arbitration proceeding as evidence or in any manner whatsoever:

(a)   any views expressed or suggestions made by any party with regard to the possible settlement of the dispute;

(b)   any proposals put forward by the conciliator;

(c)   the fact that a party had indicated that it was ready to accept some proposal for a settlement put forward by the conciliator.

RULES OF ARBITRATION

Article 1. Court of Arbitration.

1.   The Court of Arbitration of the International Chamber of Commerce is the international arbitration body attached to the International Chamber of Commerce. Members of the Court are appointed by the Council of the International Chamber of Commerce. The function of the Court is to provide for the settlement by arbitration of business disputes of an international character in accordance with these Rules.

2.   In principle, the Court meets once a month. It draws up its own internal regulations.

3.   The Chairman of the Court of Arbitration or his deputy shall have power to take urgent decisions on behalf of the Court, provided that any such decision shall be reported to the Court at its next session.

4.   The Court may, in the manner provided for in its internal regulations, delegate to one or more groups of its members the power to take certain decisions provided that any such decision shall be reported to the Court at its next session.

5.   The Secretariat of the Court of Arbitration shall be at the Headquarters of the International Chamber of Commerce.

Article 2. The arbitral tribunal.

1.   The Court of Arbitration does not itself settle disputes. Insofar as the parties shall not have provided otherwise, it appoints, or confirms the appointments of, arbitrators in accordance with the provisions of this Article. In making or confirming such appointment. the Court shall have regard to the proposed arbitrator's nationality, residence and other relation-

ships with the countries of which the parties or the other arbitrators are nationals.

2. The disputes may be settled by a sole arbitrator or by three arbitrators. In the following Articles the word "arbitrator" denotes a single arbitrator or three arbitrators as the case may be.

3. Where the parties have agreed that the disputes shall be settled by a sole arbitrator, they may, by agreement, nominate him for confirmation by the Court. If the parties fail so to nominate a sole arbitrator within 30 days from the date when the Claimant's Request for Arbitration has been communicated to the other party, the sole arbitrator shall be appointed by the Court.

4. Where the dispute is to be referred to three arbitrators, each party shall nominate in the Request for Arbitration and the Answer thereto respectively one arbitrator for confirmation by the Court. Such person shall be independent of the party nominating him. If a party fails to nominate an arbitrator, the appointment shall be made by the Court.

The third arbitrator, who will act as chairman of the arbitral tribunal, shall be appointed by the Court, unless the parties have provided that the arbitrators nominated by them shall agree on the third arbitrator within a fixed time-limit. In such a case the Court shall confirm the appointment of such third arbitrator. Should the two arbitrators fail, within the time-limit fixed by the parties or the Court, to reach agreement on the third arbitrator, he shall be appointed by the Court.

5. Where the parties have not agreed upon the number of arbitrators, the Court shall appoint a sole arbitrator, save where it appears to the Court that the dispute is such as to warrant the appointment of three arbitrators. In such a case the parties shall each have a period of 30 days within which to nominate an arbitrator.

6. Where the Court is to appoint a sole arbitrator or the chairman of an arbitral tribunal, it shall make the appointment after having requested a proposal from a National Committee of the ICC that it considers to be appropriate. If the Court does not accept the proposal made, or if said National Committee fails to make the proposal requested within the time-limit fixed by the

Court, the Court may repeat its request or may request a proposal from another appropriate National Committee.

Where the Court considers that the circumstances so demand, it may choose the sole arbitrator or the chairman of the arbitral tribunal from a country where there is no National Committee, provided that neither of the parties objects within the time-limit fixed by the Court.

The sole arbitrator or the chairman of the arbitral tribunal shall be chosen from a country other than those of which the parties are nationals. However, in suitable circumstances and provided that neither of the parties objects within the time-limit fixed by the Court, the sole arbitrator or the chairman of the arbitral tribunal may be chosen from a country of which any of the parties is a national.

Where the Court is to appoint an arbitrator on behalf of a party which has failed to nominate one, it shall make the appointment after having requested a proposal from the National Committee of the country of which the said party is a national. If the Court does not accept the proposal made, or if said National Committee fails to make the proposal requested within the time-limit fixed by the Court, or if the country of which the said party is a national has no National Committee, the Court shall be at liberty to choose any person whom it regards as suitable, after having informed the National Committee of the country of which such person is a national, if one exists.

7. Every arbitrator appointed or confirmed by the Court must be and remain independent of the parties involved in the arbitration.

Before appointment or confirmation by the Court, a prospective arbitrator shall disclose in writing to the Secretary General of the Court any facts or circumstances which might be of such a nature as to call into question the arbitrator's independence in the eyes of the parties. Upon receipt of such information, the Secretary General of the Court shall provide it to the parties in writing and fix a time-limit for any comments from them.

An arbitrator shall immediately disclose in writing to the Secretary General of the Court and the parties any facts or circumstances of a similar nature which may arise between the arbitrator's appointment or confirmation by the Court and the notification of the final award.

8.   A challenge of an arbitrator, whether for an alleged lack of independence or otherwise, is made by the submission to the Secretary General of the Court of a written statement specifying the facts and circumstances on which the challenge is based.

For a challenge to be admissible, it must be sent by a party either within 30 days from receipt by that party of the notification of the appointment or confirmation of the arbitrator by the Court; or within 30 days from the date when the party making the challenge was informed of the facts and circumstances on which the challenge is based, if such date is subsequent to the receipt of the aforementioned notification.

9.   The Court shall decide on the admissibility, and at the same time if need be on the merits, of a challenge after the Secretary General of the Court has accorded an opportunity for the arbitrator concerned, the parties and any other members of the arbitral tribunal to comment in writing within a suitable period of time.

10.   An arbitrator shall be replaced upon his death, upon the acceptance by the Court of a challenge, or upon the acceptance by the Court of the arbitrator's resignation.

11.   An arbitrator shall also be replaced when the Court decides that he is prevented de jure or de facto from fulfilling his functions, or that he is not fulfilling his functions in accordance with the Rules or within the prescribed time-limits.

When, on the basis of information that has come to its attention, the Court considers applying the preceding subparagraph, it shall decide on the matter after the Secretary General of the Court has provided such information in writing to the arbitrator concerned, the parties and any other members of the arbitral tribunal, and accorded an opportunity to them to comment in writing within a suitable period of time.

12.   In each instance where an arbitrator is to be replaced, the procedure indicated in the preceding paragraphs 3, 4, 5 and 6 shall be followed. Once reconstituted, and after having invited the parties to comment, the arbitral tribunal shall determine if and to what extent prior proceedings shall again take place.

13.   Decisions of the Court as to the appointment, confirmation, challenge or replacement of an arbitrator shall be final.

The reasons for decisions by the Court as to the appointment, confirmation, challenge, or replacement of an arbitrator on the grounds that he is not fulfilling his functions in accordance with the Rules or within the prescribed time-limits, shall not be communicated.

Article 3. Request for Arbitration.

1.   A party wishing to have recourse to arbitration by the International Chamber of Commerce shall submit its Request for Arbitration to the Secretariat of the Court, through its National Committee or directly. In this latter case the Secretariat shall bring the Request to the notice of the National Committee concerned.

The date when the Request is received by the Secretariat of the Court shall, for all purposes, be deemed to be the date of commencement of the arbitral proceedings.

2.   The Request for Arbitration shall inter alia contain the following information:

(a)   names in full, description, and addresses of the parties,

(b)   a statement of the Claimant's case,

(c)   the relevant agreements, and in particular the agreement to arbitrate, and such documentation or information as will serve clearly to establish the circumstances of the case,

(d)   all relevant particulars concerning the number of arbitrators and their choice in accordance with the provisions of Article 2 above.

3.   The Secretariat shall send a copy of the Request and the documents annexed thereto to the Defendant for his Answer.

Article 4. Answer to the Request.

1.   The Defendant shall within 30 days from the receipt of the documents referred to in paragraph 3 of Article 3 comment on the proposals made concerning the number of arbitrators and their choice and, where appropriate, nominate an arbitrator. He shall at the same time set out his defence and supply relevant documents. In exceptional circumstances the Defendant may apply to the Secretariat for an extension of time for the filing of

his defence and his documents. The application must, however, include the Defendant's comments on the proposals made with regard to the number of arbitrators and their choice and also, where appropriate, the nomination of an arbitrator. If the Defendant fails so to do, the Secretariat shall report to the Court, which shall proceed with the arbitration in accordance with these Rules.

2.   A copy of the Answer and of the documents annexed thereto, if any, shall be communicated to the Claimant for his information.

Article 5. Counter-claim.

1.   If the Defendant wishes to make a counter-claim, he shall file the same with the Secretariat, at the same time as his Answer as provided for in Article 4.

2.   It shall be open to the Claimant to file a Reply with the Secretariat within 30 days from the date when the counter-claim was communicated to him.

Article 6. Pleadings and written statements, notifications or communications.

1.   All pleadings and written statements submitted by the parties, as well as all documents annexed thereto, shall be supplied in a number of copies sufficient to provide one copy for each party, plus one for each arbitrator, and one for the Secretariat.

2.   All notifications or communications from the Secretariat and the arbitrator shall be validly made if they are delivered against receipt or forwarded by registered post to the address or last known address of the party for whom the same are intended as notified by the party in question or by the other party as appropriate.

3.   Notification or communication shall be deemed to have been effected on the day when it was received, or should, if made in accordance with the preceding paragraph, have been received by the party itself or by its representative.

4.   Periods of time specified in the present Rules or in the Internal Rules or set by the Court pursuant to its authority under any of these Rules shall start to run on the day following the date a notification or communication is deemed to have

been effected in accordance with the preceding paragraph. When, in the country where the notification or communication is deemed to have been effected, the day next following such date is an official holiday or a non-business day, the period of time shall commence on the first following working day. Official holidays and non-working days are included in the calculation of the period of time. If the last day of the relevant period of time granted is an official holiday or a non-business day in the country where the notification or communication is deemed to have been effected, the period of time shall expire at the end of the first following working day.

Article 7. Absence of agreement to arbitrate.

Where there is no prima facie agreement between the parties to arbitrate or where there is an agreement but it does not specify the International Chamber of Commerce, and if the Defendant does not file an Answer within the period of 30 days provided by paragraph 1 of Article 4 or refuses arbitration by the International Chamber of Commerce, the Claimant shall be informed that the arbitration cannot proceed.

Article 8. Effect of the agreement to arbitrate.

1.   Where the parties have agreed to submit to arbitration by the International Chamber of Commerce, they shall be deemed thereby to have submitted ipso facto to the present Rules.

2.   If one of the parties refuses or fails to take part in the arbitration, the arbitration shall proceed notwithstanding such refusal or failure.

3.   Should one of the parties raise one or more pleas concerning the existence or validity of the agreement to arbitrate, and should the Court be satisfied of the prima facie existence of such an agreement, the Court may, without prejudice to the admissibility or merits of the plea or pleas, decide that the arbitration shall proceed. In such a case any decision as to the arbitrator's jurisdiction shall be taken by the arbitrator himself.

4.   Unless otherwise provided, the arbitrator shall not cease to have jurisdiction by reason of any claim that the contract is null and void or allegation that it is inexistent

provided that he upholds the validity of the agreement to arbitrate. He shall continue to have jurisdiction, even though the contract itself may be inexistent or null and void, to determine the respective rights of the parties and to adjudicate upon their claims and pleas.

5.   Before the file is transmitted to the arbitrator, and in exceptional circumstances even thereafter, the parties shall be at liberty to apply to any competent judicial authority for interim or conservatory measures, and they shall not by so doing be held to infringe the agreement to arbitrate or to affect the relevant powers reserved to the arbitrator.

Any such application and any measures taken by the judicial authority must be notified without delay to the Secretariat of the Court of Arbitration. The Secretariat shall inform the arbitrator thereof.

Article 9. Advance to cover costs of arbitration.

1.   The Court shall fix the amount of the advance on costs in a sum likely to cover the costs of arbitration of the claims which have been referred to it.

Where, apart from the principal claim, one or more counter-claims are submitted, the Court may fix separate advances on costs for the principal claim and the counter-claim or counter-claims.

2.   The advance on costs shall be payable in equal shares by the Claimant or Claimants and the Defendant or Defendants. However, any one party shall be free to pay the whole of the advance on costs in respect of the claim or the counter-claim should the other party fail to pay its share.

3.   The Secretariat may make the transmission of the file to the arbitrator conditional upon the payment by the parties or one of them of the whole or part of the advance on costs to the International Chamber of Commerce.

4.   When the Terms of Reference are communicated to the Court in accordance with the provisions of Article 13, the Court shall verify whether the requests for the advance on costs have been complied with.

The Terms of Reference shall only become operative and the arbitrator shall only proceed in respect of those claims for which the advance on costs has been duly paid to the International Chamber of Commerce.

Article 10. Transmission of the file to the arbitrator.

Subject to the provisions of Article 9, the Secretariat shall transmit the file to the arbitrator as soon as it has received the Defendant's Answer to the Request for Arbitration, at the latest upon the expiry of the time-limits fixed in Articles 4 and 5 above for the filing of these documents.

Article 11. Rules governing the proceedings.

The rules governing the proceedings before the arbitrator shall be those resulting from these Rules and, where these Rules are silent, any rules which the parties (or, failing them, the arbitrator) may settle, and whether or not reference is thereby made to a municipal procedural law to be applied to the arbitration.

Article 12. Place of arbitration.

The place of arbitration shall be fixed by the Court, unless agreed upon by the parties.

Article 13. Terms of Reference.

1. Before proceeding with the preparation of the case, the arbitrator shall draw up, on the basis of the documents or in the presence of the parties and in the light of their most recent submissions, a document defining his Terms of Reference. This document shall include the following particulars:

(a)   the full names and description of the parties,

(b)   the addresses of the parties to which notifications or communications arising in the course of the arbitration may validly be made,

(c)   a summary of the parties' respective claims,

(d)   definition of the issues to be determined,

(e)   the arbitrator's full name, description and address,

(f)   the place of arbitration,

(g)   particulars of the applicable procedural rules and, if such is the case, reference to the power conferred upon the arbitrator to act as amiable compositeur,

(h)   such other particulars as may be required to make the arbitral award enforceable in law, or may be regarded as helpful by the Court of Arbitration or the arbitrator.

2.   The document mentioned in paragraph 1 of this Article shall be signed by the parties and the arbitrator. Within two months of the date when the file has been transmitted to him, the arbitrator shall transmit to the Court the said document signed by himself and by the parties. The Court may, pursuant to a reasoned request from the arbitrator or if need be on its own initiative, extend this time-limit if it decides it is necessary to do so.

Should one of the parties refuse to take part in the drawing up of the said document or to sign the same, the Court, if it is satisfied that the case is one of those mentioned in paragraphs 2 and 3 of Article 8, shall take such action as is necessary for its approval. Thereafter the Court shall set a time-limit for the signature of the statement by the defaulting party and on expiry of that time-limit the arbitration shall proceed and the award shall be made.

3.   The parties shall be free to determine the law to be applied by the arbitrator to the merits of the dispute. In the absence of any indication by the parties as to the applicable law, the arbitrator shall apply the law designated as the proper law by the rule of conflict which he deems appropriate.

4.   The arbitrator shall assume the powers of an amiable compositeur if the parties are agreed to give him such powers.

5.   In all cases the arbitrator shall take account of the provisions of the contract and the relevant trade usages.

Article 14. The arbitral proceedings.

1.   The arbitrator shall proceed within as short a time as possible to establish the facts of the case by all appropriate means. After study of the written submissions of the parties and of all documents relied upon, the arbitrator shall hear the parties together in person if one of them so requests: and failing such a request he may of his own motion decide to hear them.

In addition, the arbitrator may decide to hear any other person in the presence of the parties or in their absence provided they have been duly summoned.

2.   The arbitrator may appoint one or more experts, define their Terms of Reference, receive their reports and/or hear them in person.

3. The arbitrator may decide the case on the relevant documents alone if the parties so request or agree.

Article 15.

1. At the request of one of the parties or if necessary on his own initiative, the arbitrator, giving reasonable notice, shall summon the parties to appear before him on the day and at the place appointed by him and shall so inform the Secretariat of the Court.

2. If one of the parties, although duly summoned, fails to appear, the arbitrator, if he is satisfied that the summons was duly received and the party is absent without valid excuse, shall have power to proceed with the arbitration, and such proceedings shall be deemed to have been conducted in the presence of all parties.

3. The arbitrator shall determine the language or languages of the arbitration, due regard being paid to all the relevant circumstances and in particular to the language of the contract.

4. The arbitrator shall be in full charge of the hearings, at which all the parties shall be entitled to be present. Save with the approval of the arbitrator and of the parties, persons not involved in the proceedings shall not be admitted.

5. The parties may appear in person or through duly accredited agents. In addition, they may be assisted by advisers.

Article 16.

The parties may make new claims or counter-claims before the arbitrator on condition that these remain within the limits fixed by the Terms of Reference provided for in Article 13 or that they are specified in a rider to that document, signed by the parties and communicated to the Court.

Article 17. Award by consent.

If the parties reach a settlement after the file has been transmitted to the arbitrator in accordance with Article 10, the same shall be recorded in the form of an arbitral award made by consent of the parties.

Article 18. Time-limit for award.

1. The time-limit within which the arbitrator must render

his award is fixed at six months. Once the terms of Article 9(4) have been satisfied, such time-limit shall start to run from the date of the last signature by the arbitrator or of the parties of the document mentioned in Article 13, or from the expiry of the time-limit granted to a party by virtue of Article 13(2), or from the date that the Secretary General of the Court notifies the arbitrator that the advance on costs is paid in full, if such notification occurs later.

2. The Court may, pursuant to a reasoned request from the arbitrator or if need be on its own initiative, extend this time-limit if it decides it is necessary to do so.

3. Where no such extension is granted and, if appropriate, after application of the provisions of Article 2(11), the Court shall determine the manner in which the dispute is to be resolved.

Article 19. Award by three arbitrators.

When three arbitrators have been appointed, the award is given by a majority decision. If there be no majority, the award shall be made by the Chairman of the arbitral tribunal alone.

Article 20. Decision as to costs of arbitration.

1. The arbitrator's award shall, in addition to dealing with the merits of the case, fix the costs of the arbitration and decide which of the parties shall bear the costs or in what proportions the costs shall be borne by the parties.

2. The costs of the arbitration shall include the arbitrator's fees and the administrative costs fixed by the Court in accordance with the scale annexed to the present Rules, the expenses, if any, of the arbitrator, the fees and expenses of any experts, and the normal legal costs incurred by the parties.

3. The Court may fix the arbitrator's fees at a figure higher or lower than that which would result from the application of the annexed scale if in the exceptional circumstances of the case this appears to be necessary.

Article 21. Scrutiny of award by the Court.

Before signing an award, whether partial or definitive, the arbitrator shall submit it in draft form to the Court. The Court may lay down modifications as to the form of the award and, without affecting the arbitrator's liberty of decision, may also draw his attention to points of substance. No award shall be signed until it has been approved by the Court as to its form.

Article 22. Making of award.

The arbitral award shall be deemed to be made at the place of the arbitration proceedings and on the date when it is signed by the arbitrator.

Article 23. Notification of award to parties.

1.   Once an award has been made, the Secretariat shall notify to the parties the text signed by the arbitrator; provided always that the costs of the arbitration have been fully paid to the International Chamber of Commerce by the parties or by one of them.

2.   Additional copies certified true by the Secretary General of the Court shall be made available, on request and at any time, to the parties but to no one else.

3.   By virtue of the notification made in accordance with paragraph 1 of this article, the parties waive any other form of notification or deposit on the part of the arbitrator.

Article 24. Finality and enforceability of award.

1.   The arbitral award shall be final.

2.   By submitting the dispute to arbitration by the International Chamber of Commerce, the parties shall be deemed to have undertaken to carry out the resulting award without delay and to have waived their right to any form of appeal insofar as such waiver can validly be made.

Article 25. Deposit of award.

An original of each award made in accordance with the present Rules shall be deposited with the Secretariat of the Court.

The arbitrator and the Secretariat of the Court shall assist the parties in complying with whatever further formalities may be necessary.

Article 26. General rule.

In all matters not expressly provided for in these Rules, the Court of Arbitration and the arbitrator shall act in the spirit of

these Rules and shall make every effort to make sure that the
award is enforceable at law.

Appendix 1. Statutes of the Court.

Article 1. Appointment of members.

The members of the Court of Arbitration of the International Chamber of Commerce are appointed for a term of three
years by the Council of that Chamber pursuant to Article 5.3i of
the Constitution, on the proposal of each National Committee.

Article 2. Composition.

The Court of Arbitration shall be composed of a Chairman,
of eight Vice-Chairmen, of a Secretary General and of one or
several Technical Advisers chosen by the Council of the
International Chamber of Commerce either from among the
members of the Court or apart from them, and of one member
for, and appointed by, each National Committee.

The chairmanship may be exercised by two Co-Chairmen;
in this case, they shall have equal rights, and the expression "the
Chairman", used in the Rules of Conciliation and Arbitration,
shall apply to either of them equally.

When a member of the Court does not reside in the city
where International Headquarters of the International Chamber
of Commerce is situated, the Council may appoint an alternate
member.

If the Chairman is unable to attend a session of the Court,
he shall be replaced by one of the Vice-Chairmen.

Article 3. Function and powers.

The function of the Court of Arbitration is to ensure the
application of the Rules of Conciliation and Arbitration of the
International Chamber of Commerce, and the Court has all the
necessary powers for that purpose. It is further entrusted, if
need be, with laying before the Commission on International
Arbitration any proposals for modifying the Rules of Conciliation and Arbitration of the International Chamber of Commerce
which it considers necessary.

Article 4. Deliberations and quorum.

The decisions of the Court shall be taken by a majority vote, the Chairman having a casting vote in the event of a tie. The deliberations of the Court shall be valid when at least six members are present.

The Secretary General of the International Chamber of Commerce, the Secretary General of the Court and the Technical Adviser or Advisers shall attend in an advisory capacity only.

Appendix 2. Internal Rules of the Court of Arbitration

Role of the Court of Arbitration.

1. The Court of Arbitration may accept jurisdiction over business disputes not of an international business nature, if it has jurisdiction by reason of an arbitration agreement.

Confidential character of the work of the Court of Arbitration.

2. The work of the Court of Arbitration is of a confidential character which must be respected by everyone who participates in that work in whatever capacity.

3. The sessions of the Court of Arbitration, whether plenary or those of a Committee of the Court, are open only to its members and to the Secretariat.

However, in exceptional circumstances and, if need be, after obtaining the opinion of members of the Court, the Chairman of the Court of Arbitration may invite honorary members of the Court and authorize observers to attend. Such persons must respect the confidential character of the work of the Court.

4. The documents submitted to the Court of Arbitration or drawn up by it in the course of the proceedings it conducts are communicated only to the members of the Court and to the Secretariat.

The Chairman or the Secretary General of the Court may nevertheless authorize researchers undertaking work of a scientific nature on international trade law to acquaint themselves with certain documents of general interest, with the exception of memoranda, notes, statements and documents remitted by the parties within the framework of arbitration proceedings.

Such authorization shall not be given unless the beneficiary has undertaken to respect the confidential character of the documents made available and to refrain from any publication in their respect without having previously submitted the text for approval to the Secretary General of the Court.

Participation of members of the Court of Arbitration in ICC arbitration.

5. Owing to the special responsibilities laid upon them by the ICC Rules of Arbitration, the Chairman, the Vice-Chairmen and the Secretariat of the Court of Arbitration may not personally act as arbitrators or as counsel in cases submitted to ICC arbitration.

The members of the Court of Arbitration may not be directly appointed as co-arbitrators, sole arbitrator or Chairman of an arbitral tribunal by the Court of Arbitration. They may however be proposed for such duties by one or more of the parties, subject to confirmation by the Court.

6. When the Chairman, a Vice-Chairman or a member of the Court of Arbitration is involved, in any capacity whatsoever, in proceedings pending before the Court, he must inform the Secretary General of the Court as soon as he becomes aware of such involvement.

He must refrain from participating in the discussions or in the decisions of the Court concerning the proceedings and he must be absent from the courtroom whenever the matter is considered.

He will not receive documentation or information submitted to the Court of Arbitration during the proceedings.

Relations between the members of the Court and the ICC National Committees.

7. By virtue of their capacity, the members of the Court are independent of the ICC National Committees which proposed them for nomination by the ICC Council.

Furthermore, they must regard as confidential, vis-a-vis the said National Committees, any information concerning individual disputes with which they have become acquainted in their capacity as members of the Court except when they have been requested, by the Chairman of the Court or by its Secretary

General, to communicate that information to their respective National Committees.

Committee of the Court.

8.   In accordance with the provisions of Article 1(4) of the ICC Rules of Arbitration, the Court of Arbitration hereby establishes a Committee of the Court composed as follows, and with the following powers.

9.   The Committee consists of a Chairman and two members. The Chairman of the Court of Arbitration acts as the Chairman of the Committee. He may nevertheless designate a Vice-Chairman of the Court to replace him during a session of the Committee.

The other two members of the Committee are appointed by the Court of Arbitration from among the Vice-Chairmen or the other members of the Court. At each meeting of the Court it appoints the members who are to attend the meeting of the Committee to be held before the next plenary session of the Court.

10.   The Committee meets when convened by its Chairman, in principle twice a month.

11.   (a) The Committee is empowered to take any decision within the jurisdiction of the Court of Arbitration, with the exception of decisions concerning challenges of arbitrators (Arts 2(8) and 2(9) of the ICC Rules of Arbitration), allegations that an arbitrator is not fulfilling his functions (Art 2(11) of the ICC Rules of Arbitration) and approval of draft awards other than awards made with the consent of the parties.

(b)   The decisions of the Committee are taken unanimously.

(c)   When the Committee cannot reach a decision or deems it preferable to abstain, it transfers the case to the next plenary session of the Court of Arbitration, making any suggestions it deems appropriate.

(d)   The Committee's proceedings are brought to the notice of the Court of Arbitration at its next plenary session.

Absence of an arbitration agreement.

12.   Where there is no prima facie arbitration agreement between the parties or where there is an agreement but it does

not specify the ICC, the Secretariat draws the attention of the Claimant to the provisions laid down in Article 7 of the Rules of Arbitration. The Claimant is entitled to require the decision to be taken by the Court of Arbitration.

This decision is of an administrative nature. If the Court decides that the arbitration solicited by the Claimant cannot proceed, the parties retain the right to ask the competent jurisdiction whether or not they are bound by an arbitration agreement in the light of the law applicable.

If the Court of Arbitration considers prima facie that the proceedings may take place, the arbitrator appointed has the duty to decide as to his own jurisdiction and, where such jurisdiction exists, as to the merits of the dispute.

Joinder of claims in arbitration proceedings.

13. When a party presents a Request for Arbitration in connection with a legal relationship already submitted to arbitration proceedings by the same parties and pending before the Court of Arbitration, the Court may decide to include that claim in the existing proceedings, subject to the provisions of Article 16 of the ICC Rules of Arbitration.

Advances to cover costs of arbitration.

14. When the Court of Arbitration has set separate advances on costs for a specific case in accordance with Article 9(1) (sub par 2) of the ICC Rules of Arbitration, the Secretariat requests each of the parties to pay the amount corresponding to its claims, without prejudice to the right of the parties to pay the said advances on costs in equal shares, if they deem it advisable.

15. When a request for an advance on costs has not been complied with, the Secretariat may set a time-limit, which must not be less than 30 days, on the expiry of which the relevant claim, whether principal claim or counter-claim, shall be considered as withdrawn. This does not prevent the party in question from lodging a new claim at a later date.

Should one of the parties wish to object to this measure, he must make a request, within the aforementioned period, for the matter to be decided by the Court of Arbitration.

16. If one of the parties claims a right to a set-off with regard to either a principal claim or counter-claim, such set-off

is taken into account in determining the advance to cover the costs of arbitration, in the same way as a separate claim, insofar as it may require the arbitrators to consider additional matters.

Arbitral awards: form.

17.   When it scrutinizes draft arbitral awards in accordance with Article 21 of the ICC Rules of Arbitration, the Court of Arbitration pays particular attention to the respect of the formal requirements laid down by the law applicable to the proceedings and, where relevant, by the mandatory rules of the place of arbitration, notably with regard to the reasons for awards, their signature and the admissibility of dissenting opinions.

Arbitrators' fees.

18.   In setting the arbitrators' fees on the basis of the scale attached to the ICC Rules of Arbitration, the Court of Arbitration takes into consideration the time spent, the rapidity of the proceedings and the complexity of the dispute, so as to arrive at a figure within the limits specified or, when circumstances require, higher or lower than those limits (Art 20(3) of the ICC Rules of Arbitration).

Appendix 3. Schedule of Conciliation and Arbitration Costs

1.   Costs of conciliation.

(a)   The administrative expenses for a conciliation procedure shall be fixed at one-quarter of the amount calculated in accordance with the scale of administrative expenses hereinafter set out. Where the sum in dispute in a conciliation procedure is not stated, the Secretary General of the Court of Arbitration shall fix the administrative expenses at his discretion.

(b)   The fee of the conciliator to be paid by the parties shall be fixed by the Secretary General of the Court of Arbitration. Such fee shall be reasonable in amount, taking into consideration the time spent, the complexity of the dispute and any other relevant circumstances.

2. Costs of arbitration.

(a) The advance on costs fixed by the Court of Arbitration comprises the fee(s) of the arbitrator(s), any personal expenses of the arbitrator(s) and the administrative expenses.

(b) The submission of any claim or counter-claim to the arbitrator(s) shall be made only after at least half of the advance on costs fixed by the Court has been satisfied. Terms of Reference shall only become operative and the arbitrator(s) shall only proceed in respect of those claims and counter-claims for which the totality of the advance on costs fixed by the Court has been satisfied.

(c) The Court shall fix the administrative expenses of each arbitration in accordance with the scale hereinafter set out or, where the sum in dispute is not stated, at its discretion. If exceptional circumstances so require, the Court may fix the administrative expenses at a lower figure than that which would result from application of said scale.

(d) Subject to Article 20(3) of the ICC Rules of Arbitration, the Court shall fix the fee(s) of the arbitrator(s) in accordance with the scale hereinafter set out or, where the sum in dispute is not stated, at its discretion.

(e) When a case is submitted to more than one arbitrator, the Court, at its discretion, shall have the right to increase the total fees up to a maximum of three times the fee payable to one arbitrator.

(f) When arbitration is preceded by attempted conciliation, one-half of the administrative expenses paid in respect of the said attempt shall be credited to the administrative expenses of the arbitration.

(g) Before any expertise can be commenced, the parties, or one of them, shall pay an advance on costs fixed by the arbitrator(s) sufficient to cover the expected fee and expenses of the expert as determined by the arbitrator(s).

3. Advance on administrative expenses.

(a) Each party to a dispute submitted to conciliation under the Rules of Optional Conciliation of the ICC is required to make an advance payment of US $500 on the administrative expenses.

(b) Each request to open an arbitration pursuant to the ICC Rules of Arbitration must be accompanied by an advance payment of US $2,000 on the administrative expenses.

(c) No request for conciliation or arbitration will be entertained unless accompanied by the appropriate payment. This payment is not recoverable and becomes the property of the ICC. Such payment by a party shall be credited to its portion of the administrative expenses for the conciliation or arbitration, as the case may be.

4. Appointment of arbitrators.

A registration fee of US $1,000 is payable by the requesting party in respect of each request made to the ICC to appoint an arbitrator for any arbitration not conducted under the ICC Rules of Arbitration. No request for appointment of an arbitrator will be entertained unless accompanied by said fee, which is not recoverable and becomes the property of the ICC.

Such fee shall cover any additional services rendered by the ICC regarding the appointment, such as decisions on a challenge of the arbitrator and the appointment of a substitute arbitrator.

5. Scales of administrative expenses and of arbitrator's fees.

To calculate the administrative expenses and the arbitrator's fees, the amounts calculated for each successive slice of the sum in dispute **must be added together,** except that where the sum in dispute is over US $50 million, a flat amount of US $50,500 shall constitute the entirety of the administrative expenses.

A. Administrative Expenses

Sum in Dispute	Administrative Expenses
Up to 50,000 (in U.S. dollars)	$2,000
From 50,001 to 100,000	3.00%
From 100,001 to 500,000	1.50%
From 500,001 to 1,000,000	1.00%
From 1,000,001 to 2,000,000	0.50%
From 2,000,001 to 5,000,000	0.20%
From 5,000,001 to 10,000,000	0.10%
From 10,000,001 to 50,000,000	0.05%
Over 50,000,000	50,500

B. Arbitrator's Fees

Sum in Dispute	Fees	
	Minimum	Maximum
Up to 50,000 (in U.S. dollars)	$1,000	10.00%
From 50,001 to 100,000	1.50%	6.00%
From 100,001 to 500,000	0.80%	3.00%
From 500,001 to 1,000,000	0.50%	2.00%
From 1,000,001 to 2,000,000	0.30%	1.50%
From 2,000,001 to 5,000,000	0.20%	0.60%
From 5,000,001 to 10,000,000	0.10%	0.30%
From 10,000,001 to 50,000,000	0.05%	0.15%
From 50,000,001 to 100,000,000	0.02%	0.10%
Over 100,000,000	0.01%	0.05%

For illustrative purposes only, this table indicates the resulting administrative expenses when the proper calculations have been made.

Sum in Dispute	Administrative Expenses
Up to 50,000 (in U.S. dollars)	2,000
From 50,001 to 100,000	2,000 + 3.00% of amt. over 50,000
From 100,001 to 500,000	3,500 + 1.50% of amt. over 100,000
From 500,001 to 1,000,000	9,500 + 1.00% of amt. over 500,000
From 1,000,001 to 2,000,000	14,500 + 0.50% of amt. over 1,000,000
From 2,000,001 to 5,000,000	19,500 + 0.20% of amt. over 2,000,000
From 5,000,001 to 10,000,000	25,500 + 0.10% of amt. over 5,000,000
From 10,000,001 to 50,000,000	30,500 + 0.05% of amt. over 10,000,000
From 50,000,001 to 100,000.000	50,500
Over 100,000,000	50,500

For illustrative purposes only, this table indicates the resulting range of fees when the proper calculations have been made.

Sum in Dispute	Minimum	Maximum
Up to 50,000 (in U.S. dollars)	1,000	10.00% of the sum in dispute
From 50,001 to 100,000	1,000 + 1.50% of amt. over 50,000	5,000 + 6.00% of amt. over 50,000
From 100,001 to 500,000	1,750 + 0.80% of amt. over 100,000	8,000 + 3.00% of amt. over 100,000
From 500,001 to 1,000,000	4,950 + 0.50% of amt. over 500,000	20,000 + 2.00% of amt. over 500,000
From 1,000,001 to 2,000,000	7,450 + 0.30% of amt. over 1,000,000	30,000 + 1.50% of amt. over 1,000,000
From 2,000,001 to 5,000,000	10,450 + 0.20% of amt. over 2,000,000	45,000 + 0.60% of amt. over 2,000,000
From 5,000,001 to 10,000,000	16,450 + 0.10% of amt. over 5,000,000	63,000 + 0.30% of amt. over 5,000,000
From 10,000,001 to 50,000,000	21,450 + 0.05% of amt. over 10,000,000	78,000 + 0.15% of amt. over 10,000,000
From 50,000,001 to 100,000,000	41,450 + 0.02% of amt. over 50,000,000	138,000 + 0.10% of amt. over 50,000,000
Over 100,000,000	51,450 + 0.01% of amt. over 100,000,000	188,000 + 0.05% of amt. over 100,000,000

— Appendix D —
Abitration Rules of the
American Arbitration Association

International Arbitration Rules
NEW FEES FOR CASES FILED ON OR AFTER MAY 1, 1992

Introduction

The world business community uses arbitration to resolve commercial disputes arising in the global marketplace. Supportive laws are in place. The New York Convention of 1958 has been widely adopted, providing a favorable legislative climate. Arbitration clauses are enforced. International commercial arbitration awards are recognized by national courts in most parts of the world, even more than foreign court judgments.

Arbitration institutions have been established in many countries to administer international cases. Many have entered into cooperative arrangements with the American Arbitration Association.

To encourage greater use of such services, these International Arbitration Rules have been developed. By providing for arbitration under these rules, parties can avoid the uncertainty of having to petition a local court to resolve procedural impasses.

These rules are intended to provide effective arbitration services to world business through the use of administered arbitration.

Parties can arbitrate future disputes under these rules by inserting the following clause into their contracts:

"Any controversy or claim arising out of or relating to this contract shall be determined by arbitration in accordance with the International Arbitration Rules of the American Arbitration Association."

The parties may wish to consider adding:

(a) The number of arbitrators shall be (one or three);
(b) The place of arbitration shall be (city and/or country);

(c) The language(s) of the arbitration shall be _____.

Parties are encouraged, when writing their contracts or when a dispute arises, to request a conference, in person or by telephone, with the AAA, to discuss an appropriate method for the selection of arbitrators or any other matters that might facilitate the efficient arbitration of the dispute.

Under these rules, the parties are free to adopt any mutually agreeable procedure for appointing arbitrators, or may designate arbitrators upon whom they agree. Parties can reach agreements concerning appointing arbitrators either when writing their contracts or after a dispute has arisen. This flexible procedure permits parties to utilize whatever method they consider best suits their needs. For example, parties may choose to have a sole arbitrator or a tribunal of three or more. They may agree that arbitrators shall be appointed by the AAA, or that each side shall designate one arbitrator and those two shall name a third, with the AAA making appointments if the tribunal is not promptly formed by that procedure. Parties may mutually request the AAA to submit to them a list of arbitrators from which each can delete names not accept able to it, or the parties may instruct the AAA to appoint arbitrators without the submission of lists, or may leave that matter to the sole discretion of the AAA. Parties also may agree on a variety of other methods for establishing the tribunal. In any event, if parties are unable to agree on a procedure for appointing arbitrators or on the designation of arbitrators, the AAA, after inviting consultation by the parties, will appoint the arbitrators. The rules thus provide for the fullest exercise of party autonomy, while assuring that the AAA is available to act if the parties cannot reach mutual agreement.

Parties may wish to consider the possibility of mediation or conciliation. This too can be discussed with the AAA, either when the contract is being written or after a dispute arises, and the AAA is prepared to arrange for mediation or conciliation anywhere in the world.

Further information about these rules can be secured from the American Arbitration Association at 140 West 51st Street, New York, New York 10020-1203; (212) 484-4000; telefax (212) 765-4874.

American Arbitration Association International Arbitration Rules

ARTICLE 1

1. Where parties have agreed in writing to arbitrate disputes under these International Arbitration,Rules, the arbitration shall take place in accordance,with their provisions, as in effect at the date of commencement of the arbitration, subject to whatever modifications the parties may adopt in writing.

2. These rules govern the arbitration, except that, where any such rule is in conflict with any provision of the law applicable to the arbitration from which the parties cannot derogate, that provision shall prevail.

3. These rules specify the duties and responsibilities of the administrator, the American Arbitration Association. The administrator may provide services through its own facilities or through the facilities of arbitral institutions with whom it has agreements of cooperation.

I. Commencing the Arbitration

Notice of Arbitration and Statement of Claim

ARTICLE 2

1. The party initiating arbitration ("claimant") shall give written notice of arbitration to the administrator and to the party or parties against whom a claim is being made (``respondent(s)'').

2. Arbitral proceedings shall be deemed to commence on the date on which the notice of arbitration is received by the administrator.

3.The notice of arbitration shall include the following:

(a) a demand that the dispute be referred to arbitration;

(b) the names and addresses of the parties;

(c) a reference to the arbitration clause or agreement that is invoked;

(d) a reference to any contract out of or in relation to which the dispute arises;

(e) a description of the claim and an indication of the facts supporting it;

(f) the relief or remedy sought and the amount claimed; and

(g) may include proposals as to the number of arbitrators, the place of arbitration and the language(s) of the arbitration.

Upon receipt of such notice, the administrator will communicate with all parties with respect to the arbitration, including the matters set forth in (g) above, if the parties have not already agreed on these matters, and will acknowledge the commencement of the arbitration.

Statement of Defense and Counterclaim

ARTICLE 3

1. Within forty-five days after the date of the commencement of the arbitration, a respondent shall file a statement of defense in writing with the claimant and any other parties, and with the administrator for transmittal to the tribunal when appointed.

2. At the time a respondent submits its statement of defense, a respondent may make counterclaims or assert set-offs as to any claim covered by the agreement to arbitrate, as to which the claimant shall within forty-five days file a statement of defense.

3. A respondent shall respond to the administrator, the claimant and other parties within forty-five days as to any proposals the claimant may have made as to the number of arbitrators, the place of the arbitration or the language(s) of the arbitration, except to the extent that the parties have previously agreed as to these matters.

Amendments to Claims

ARTICLE 4

During the arbitral proceedings, any party may amend or supplement its claim, counterclaim or defense, unless the tribunal considers it inappropriate to allow such amendment because of the party's delay in making it or of prejudice to the other parties or any other circumstances. A claim or counterclaim may not be amended if the amendment would fall outside the scope of the agreement to arbitrate.

II. The Tribunal

Number of Arbitrators

ARTICLE 5

If the parties have not agreed on the number of arbitrators, one arbitrator shall be appointed unless the administrator determines in its discretion that three arbitrators are appropriate because of the large size, complexity or other circumstances of the case.

Appointment of Arbitrators

ARTICLE 6

1. The parties may mutually agree upon any procedure for appointing arbitrators and shall inform the administrator as to such procedure.

2. The parties may mutually designate arbitrators, with or without the assistance of the administrator. When such designations are made, the parties shall notify the administrator so that notice of the appointment can be communicated to the arbitrators, together with a copy of these rules.

3. If within sixty days after the commencement of the arbitration, all of the parties have not mutually agreed on a procedure for appointing the arbitrator(s) or have not mutually agreed on the designation of the arbitrator(s), the administrator shall, at the written request of any party, appoint the arbitrator(s) and designate the presiding arbitrator. If all of the parties have mutually agreed upon a procedure for appointing the arbitrator(s), but all appointments have not been made within the time limits provided in that procedure, the administrator shall, at the written request of any party, perform all functions provided for in that procedure.

4. In making such appointments, the administrator, after inviting consultation with the parties, shall endeavor to select suitable arbitrators. At the request of any party or on its own initiative, the administrator may appoint nationals of a country other than that of any of the parties.

Challenge of Arbitrators

ARTICLE 7

Unless the parties agree otherwise, arbitrators acting under these rules shall be impartial and independent. Prior to accepting appointment, a prospective arbitrator shall disclose to the administrator any circumstance likely to give rise to justifiable doubts as to the arbitrator's impartiality or independence. Once appointed, an arbitrator shall disclose any additional such information to the parties and to the administrator. Upon receipt of such information from an arbitrator or a party, the administrator shall communicate it to the parties and to the arbitrator.

ARTICLE 8

1. A party may challenge any arbitrator whenever circumstances exist that give rise to justifiable doubts as to the arbitrator's impartiality or independence. A party wishing to challenge an arbitrator shall send notice of the challenge to the administrator within fifteen days after being notified of the appointment of the arbitrator, or within fifteen days after the circumstances giving rise to the challenge became known to that party.

2. The challenge shall state in writing the reasons for the challenge.

3. Upon receipt of such a challenge, the administrator shall notify the other parties of the

challenge. When an arbitrator has been challenged by one party, the other parties may agree to the acceptance of the challenge and, if there is agreement, the arbitrator shall withdraw. The challenged arbitrator may also withdraw from office in the absence of such agreement. In neither case does this imply acceptance of the validity of the grounds for the challenge.

ARTICLE 9

If the other party or parties do not agree to the challenge or the challenged arbitrator does not withdraw, the decision on the challenge shall be made by the administrator in its sole discretion.

Replacement of an Arbitrator

ARTICLE 10

If an arbitrator withdraws after a challenge, or the administrator sustains the challenge, or the administrator determines that there are sufficient reasons to accept the resignation of an arbitrator, or an arbitrator dies, a substitute arbitrator shall be appointed pursuant to the provisions of Article 6, unless the parties otherwise agree.

ARTICLE 11

1. If an arbitrator on a three-person tribunal fails to participate in the arbitration, the two other arbitrators shall have the power in their sole discretion to continue the arbitration and to make any decision, ruling or award, notwithstanding the failure of the third arbitrator to participate. In determining whether to continue the arbitration or to render any decision, ruling or award without the participation of an arbitrator, the two other arbitrators shall take into account the stage of the arbitration, the reason, if any, expressed by the third arbitrator for such nonparticipation, and such other matters as they consider appropriate in the circumstances of the case. In the event that the two other arbitrators determine not to continue the arbitration without the participation of the third arbitrator, the administrator on proof satisfactory to it shall declare the office vacant, and a substitute arbitrator shall be appointed pursuant to the provisions of Article 6, unless the parties otherwise agree.

2. If a substitute arbitrator is appointed, the tribunal shall determine at its sole discretion whether all or part of any prior hearings shall be repeated.

III. General Conditions

Representation

ARTICLE 12

Any party may be represented in the arbitration. The names, addresses and telephone numbers of representatives shall be communicated in writing to the other parties and to the administrator. Once the tribunal has been established, the parties or their representatives may communicate in writing directly with the tribunal.

Place of Arbitration

ARTICLE 13

1. If the parties disagree as to the place of arbitration, the place of arbitration may initially be determined by the administrator, subject to the power of the tribunal to determine finally

the place of arbitration within sixty days after its constitution. All such determinations shall be made having regard for the contentions of the parties and the circumstances of the arbitration.

2.The tribunal may hold conferences or hear witnesses or inspect property or documents at anyplace it deems appropriate. The parties shall be given sufficient written notice to enable them to be present at any such proceedings.

Language
ARTICLE 14

If the parties have not agreed otherwise, the language(s) of the arbitration shall be that of the documents containing the arbitration agreement, subject to the power of the tribunal to determine otherwise based upon the contentions of the parties and the circumstances of the arbitration. The tribunal may order that any documents delivered in another language shall be accompanied by a translation into such language or languages.

Pleas as to Jurisdiction
ARTICLE 15

1. The tribunal shall have the power to rule on its own jurisdiction, including any objections with respect to the existence or validity of the arbitration agreement.

2. The tribunal shall have the power to determine the existence or validity of a contract of which an arbitration clause forms a part. Such an arbitration clause shall be treated as an agreement independent of the other terms of the contract.

3. Objections to the arbitrability of a claim must be raised no later than forty-five days after the commencement of the arbitration and, in respect to a counterclaim, no later than forty-five days after filing the counterclaim.

Conduct of the Arbitration
ARTICLE 16

1. Subject to these rules, the tribunal may conduct the arbitration in whatever manner it considers appropriate, provided that the parties are treated with equality and that each party has the right to be heard and is given a fair opportunity to present its case.

2. Documents or information supplied to the tribunal by one party shall at the same time be communicated by that party to the other party or parties.

Further Written Statements
ARTICLE 17

The tribunal may decide whether any written statements, in addition to statements of claims and counterclaims and statements of defense, shall be required from the parties or may be presented by them, and shall fix the periods of time for submit ting such statements.

Periods of Time
ARTICLE 18

The periods of time fixed by the tribunal for the communication of written statements should not exceed forty-five days. However, the tribunal may extend such time limits if it considers such an ex tension justified.

Notices
ARTICLE 19

1. Unless otherwise agreed by the parties or ordered by the tribunal, all notices, statements and written communications may be served on a party by air mail or air courier addressed to the party or its representative at the last known address or by personal service. Facsimile transmission, telex, telegram, or other written forms of electronic communication may be used to give any such notices, statements or written communications.

2. For the purpose of calculating a period of time under these rules, such period shall begin to run on the day following the day when a notice, statement or written communication is received. If the last day of such period is an official holiday at the place received, the period is extended until the first business day which follows. Official holidays occurring during the running of the period of time are included in calculating the period.

Evidence
ARTICLE 20

1. Each party shall have the burden of proving the facts relied on to support its claim or defense.

2. The tribunal may order a party to deliver to the tribunal and to the other parties a summary of the documents and other evidence which that party intends to present in support of its claim, counterclaim or defense.

3. At any time during the proceedings, the tribunal may order parties to produce other documents, exhibits or other evidence it deems necessary or appropriate.

Hearings
ARTICLE 21

1. The tribunal shall give the parties at least thirty days' advance notice of the date, time and place of the initial oral hearing. The tribunal shall give reasonable notice of subsequent hearings.

2. At least fifteen days before the hearings, each party shall give the tribunal and the other parties the names and addresses of any witnesses it intends to present, the subject of their testimony and the languages in which such witnesses will give their testimony.

3. At the request of the tribunal or pursuant to mutual agreement of the parties, the administrator shall make arrangements for the interpretation of oral testimony or for a record of the hearing.

4. Hearings are private unless the parties agree otherwise or the law provides to the contrary. The tribunal may require any witness or witnesses to retire during the testimony of other witnesses. The tribunal may determine the manner in which witnesses are examined.

5. Evidence of witnesses may also be presented in the form of written statements signed by them.

6. The admissibility, relevance, materiality and weight of the evidence offered by any party shall be determined by the tribunal.

Interim Measures of Protection

ARTICLE 22

1. At the request of any party, the tribunal may take whatever interim measures it deems necessary in respect of the subject-matter of the dispute, including measures for the conservation of the goods which are the subject-matter in dispute, such as ordering their deposit with a third person or the sale of perishable goods.

2. Such interim measures may be taken in the form of an interim award and the tribunal may require security for the costs of such measures.

3. A request for interim measures addressed by a party to a judicial authority shall not be deemed incompatible with the agreement to arbitrate or a waiver of the right to arbitrate.

Experts

ARTICLE 23

1. The tribunal may appoint one or more independent experts to report to it, in writing, on specific issues designated by the tribunal and communicated to the parties.

2. The parties shall provide such an expert with any relevant information or produce for inspection any relevant documents or goods that the expert may require. Any dispute between a party and the expert as to the relevance of the requested information or goods shall be referred to the tribunal for decision.

3. Upon receipt of an expert's report, the tribunal shall send a copy of the report to all parties, who shall be given an opportunity to express, in writing, their opinion on the report. A party may examine any document on which the expert has relied in such a report.

4. At the request of any party, the parties shall be given an opportunity to question the expert at a hearing. At this hearing, parties may present expert witnesses to testify on the points at issue.

ARTICLE 24

1. If a party fails to file a statement of defense within the time established by the tribunal without showing sufficient cause for such failure, as determined by the tribunal, the tribunal may proceed with the arbitration.

2. If a party, duly notified under these rules, fails to appear at a hearing without showing sufficient cause for such failure, as determined by the tribunal, the tribunal may proceed with the arbitration.

3. If a party, duly invited to produce evidence, fails to do so within the time established by the tribunal without showing sufficient cause for such failure, as determined by the tribunal, the tribunal may make the award on the evidence before it.

Closure of Hearing

ARTICLE 25

1. After asking the parties if they have any further testimony or evidentiary submissions and upon receiving negative replies or if satisfied that the record is complete, the tribunal may declare the hearings closed.

2. If it considers it appropriate, on its own motion or upon application of a party, the tribunal may reopen the hearings at any time before the award is made.

Waiver of Rules

ARTICLE 26

A party who knows that any provision of the rules or requirement under the rules has not been complied with, but proceeds with the arbitration without promptly stating an objection in writing thereto, shall be deemed to have waived the right to object.

Awards, Decisions and Rulings

ARTICLE 27

1. When there is more than one arbitrator, any award, decision or ruling of the arbitral tribunal shall be made by a majority of the arbitrators.

2. When the parties or the tribunal so authorize, decisions or rulings on questions of procedure may be made by the presiding arbitrator, subject to revision by the tribunal.

Form and Effect of the Award

ARTICLE 28

1. Awards shall be made in writing, promptly by the tribunal, and shall be final and binding on the parties. The parties undertake to carry out any such award without delay.

2. The tribunal shall state the reasons upon which the award is based, unless the parties have agreed that no reasons need be given.

3. An award signed by a majority of the arbitrators shall be sufficient. Where there are three arbitrators and one of them fails to sign, the award shall be accompanied by a statement of whether the third arbitrator was given the opportunity to sign.

4. The award shall contain the date and the place where the award was made, which shall be the place designated pursuant to Article 13.

5. An award may be made public only with the consent of all parties or as required by law.

6. Copies of the award shall be communicated to the parties by the administrator.

7. If the arbitration law of the country where the award is made requires the award to be filed or registered, the tribunal shall comply with such requirement.

8. In addition to making a final award, the tribunal may make interim, interlocutory, or partial orders and awards.

Applicable Laws

ARTICLE 29

1. The tribunal shall apply the substantive law or laws designated by the parties as applicable to the dispute. Failing such a designation by the parties, the tribunal shall apply such law or laws as it determines to be appropriate.

2. In arbitrations involving the application of contracts, the tribunal shall decide in accordance with the terms of the contract and shall take into account usages of the trade applicable to the contract.

3. The tribunal shall not decide as *amiable compositeur* or *ex aequo et bono* unless the parties have authorized it to do so.

Settlement or Other Reasons for Termination
ARTICLE 30

1. If the parties settle the dispute before an award is made, the tribunal shall terminate the arbitration and, if requested by all parties, may record the settlement in the form of an award on agreed terms. The tribunal is not obliged to give reasons for such an award.

2. If the continuation of the proceedings becomes unnecessary or impossible for any other reason, the tribunal shall inform the parties of its intention to terminate the proceedings. The tribunal shall thereafter issue an order terminating the arbitration, unless a party raises justifiable grounds for objection.

Interpretation or Correction of the Award
ARTICLE 31

1. Within thirty days after the receipt of an award, any party, with notice to the other parties, may request the tribunal to interpret the award or correct any clerical, typographical or computation errors or make an additional award as to claims presented but omitted from the award.

2. If the tribunal considers such a request justified, after considering the contentions of the parties, it shall comply with such a request within thirty days after the request.

Costs
ARTICLE 32

The tribunal shall fix the costs of arbitration in its award. The tribunal may apportion such costs among the parties if it determines that such apportionment is reasonable, taking into account the circumstances of the case. Such costs may include:

(a) the fees and expenses of the arbitrators;

(b) the costs of assistance required by the tribunal, including its experts;

(c) the fees and expenses of the administrator;

(d) the reasonable costs for legal representation of a successful party.

Compensation of Arbitrators
ARTICLE 33

Arbitrators shall be compensated based upon their amount of service, taking into account the size and complexity of the case. An appropriate daily or hourly rate, based on such considerations, shall be arranged by the administrator with the parties and the arbitrators prior to the commencement of the arbitration. If the parties fail to agree on the terms of compensation, an appropriate rate shall be established by the administrator and communicated in writing to the parties.

Deposit of Costs
ARTICLE 34

1. When claims are filed, the administrator may request the filing party to deposit appropriate amounts, as an advance for the costs referred to in Article 32, paragraphs (a), (b) and (c).

2. During the course of the arbitral proceedings, the tribunal may request supplementary deposits from the parties.

3. If the deposits requested are not paid in full within thirty days after the receipt of the request, the administrator shall so inform the parties, in order that one or the other of them may make the required payment. If such payments are not made, the tribunal may order the suspension or termination of the proceedings.

4. After the award has been made, the administrator shall render an accounting to the parties of the deposits received and return any unexpended balance to the parties.

Confidentiality
ARTICLE 35

Confidential information disclosed during the proceedings by the parties or by witnesses shall not be divulged by an arbitrator or by the administrator. Unless otherwise agreed by the parties, or required by applicable law, the members of the tribunal and the administrator shall keep confidential all matters relating to the arbitration or the award.

Exclusion of Liability
ARTICLE 36

The members of the tribunal and the administrator shall not be liable to any party for any act or omission in connection with any arbitration conducted under these rules, except that they may be liable to a party for the consequences of conscious and deliberate wrongdoing.

Interpretation of Rules
ARTICLE 37

The tribunal shall interpret and apply these rules insofar as they relate to its powers and duties. All other rules shall be interpreted and applied by the administrator.

Administrative Fees

The AAA's administrative charges are based on filing and service fees. Arbitrator compensation, if any, is not included. Unless the parties agree otherwise, arbitrator compensation and administrative fees are subject to allocation by the arbitrator in the award.

Filing Fees

A nonrefundable filing fee is payable in full by a filing party when a claim, counterclaim, or additional claim is filed, as provided below.

Amount of Claim	Filing Fee
Up to $25,000	$300
Above $25,000 to $50,000	$500
Above $50,000 to $250,000	$1,000
Above $250,000 to $500,000	$2,000
Above $500,000 to $5,000,000	$3,000
Above $5,000,000	$4,000

When no amount can be stated at the time of filing, the filing fee is $1,000, subject to adjustment when the claim or counterclaim is disclosed.

When a claim or counterclaim is not for a monetary amount, an appropriate filing fee will be determined by the AAA.

Hearing Fees

For each day of hearing held before a single arbitrator, an administrative fee of $100 is payable by each party.

For each day of hearing held before a multiarbitrator panel, an administrative fee of $150 is payable by each party.

Postponement Fees

A fee of $100 is payable by a party causing a postponement of any hearing scheduled before a single arbitrator.

A fee of $150 is payable by a party causing a postponement of any hearing scheduled before a multiarbitrator panel.

Processing Fees

No processing fee is payable until 180 days after a case is initiated.

On single-arbitrator cases, a processing fee of $150 per party is payable 180 days after the case is initiated, and every 90 days thereafter, until the case is withdrawn or settled or the hearings are closed by the arbitrator.

On multiarbitrator cases, a processing fee of $200 per party is payable 180 days after the case is initiated, and every 90 days thereafter, until the case is withdrawn or settled or the hearings are closed by the arbitrators.

Suspension for Nonpayment

If arbitrator compensation or administrative charges have not been paid in full, the AAA may so inform the parties in order that one of them may make the required payment. If such payments are not made, the arbitrator may order the suspension or termination of the proceedings. If no arbitrator has yet been appointed, the AAA may suspend the proceedings in such a situation.

Hearing Room Rental

Rooms for hearings are available on a rental basis. Check with our local office for availability and rates.

Commercial Arbitration Rules

REVISED RULES AND FEES FOR CASES FILED ON OR AFTER MAY 1, 1992

Introduction

Each year, many millions of business transactions take place. Occasionally, disagreements develop over these business transactions. Many of these disputes are resolved by arbitration, the voluntary submission of a dispute to a disinterested person or persons for final and binding determination. Arbitration has proven to be an effective way to resolve these disputes privately, promptly, and economically.

The American Arbitration Association (AAA) is a public-service, not-for-profit organization offering a broad range of dispute resolution services to business executives, attorneys, individuals, trade associations, unions, management, consumers, families, communities, and all levels of government. Services are available through AAA headquarters in New York City and through offices located in major cities throughout the United States. Hearings may be held at locations convenient for the parties and are not limited to cities with AAA offices. In addition, the AAA serves as a center for education and training, issues specialized publications, and conducts research on all forms of out-of-court dispute settlement.

The parties can provide for arbitration of future disputes by inserting the following clause into their contracts:

Standard Arbitration Clause

Any controversy or claim arising out of or relating to this contract, or the breach thereof, shall be settled by arbitration in accordance with the Commercial Arbitration Rules of the American Arbitration Association, and judgment upon the award rendered by the arbitrator(s) may be entered in any court having jurisdiction thereof.

Arbitration of existing disputes may be accomplished by use of the following:

We, the undersigned parties, hereby agree to submit to arbitration under the Commercial Arbitration Rules of the American Arbitration Association the following controversy: (cite briefly). We further agree that the above controversy be submitted to (one)(three) arbitrator(s). We further agree that we will faithfully observe this agreement and the rules, and that we will abide by and perform any award rendered by the arbitrator(s) and that a judgment of the court having jurisdiction may be entered upon the award.

The services of the AAA are generally concluded with the transmittal of the award.

Although there is voluntary compliance with the majority of awards, judgment on the award can be entered in a court having appropriate jurisdiction if necessary.

Administrative Fees

The AAA's administrative fees are based on service charges. There is a filing fee based on the amount of the claim or counterclaim, ranging from $300 on claims below $25,000 to a maximum of $4,000 for claims in excess of $5 million. In addition, there are service charges for hearings held and postponements and a processing fee for prolonged cases. This fee information, which is contained on pages 21 and 22 of this pamphlet, allows the parties to exercise control over their administrative fees. The fees cover AAA administrative services; they do not cover arbitrator compensation or expenses, if any, reporting services, or any postaward charges incurred by the parties in enforcing the award.

Mediation

The parties may wish to submit their dispute to mediation prior to arbitration. In mediation, the neutral mediator assists the parties in reaching a settlement, but does not have the authority to make a binding decision or award. Mediation is administered by the AAA in accordance with its Comercial Mediation Rules. There is no additional administrative fee where parties to a pending arbitration attempt to mediate their dispute under the AAA's auspices.

If the parties want to adopt mediation as a part of their contractual dispute settlement procedure, they can insert the following mediation clause into their contract in conjunction with a standard arbitration provision:

> If a dispute arises out of or relates to this contract, or the breach thereof, and if said dispute cannot be settled through negotiation, the parties agree first to try in good faith to settle the dispute by mediation under the Commercial Mediation Rules of the American Arbitration Association, before resorting to arbitration, litigation, or some other dispute resolution procedure.

If the parties want to use a mediator to resolve an existing dispute, they can enter into the following submission:

> The parties hereby submit the following dispute to mediation under the Commercial Mediation Rules of the American Arbitration Association. (The clause may also provide for the qualifications of the mediator(s), method of payment, locale of meetings, and any other item of concern to the parties.)

Commercial Arbitration Rules

1. Agreement of Parties

The parties shall be deemed to have made these rules a part of their arbitration agreement whenever they have provided for arbitration by the American Arbitration Association (here-inafter AAA) or under its Commercial Arbitration Rules. These rules and any amendment of them shall apply in the form obtaining at the time the demand for arbitration or submission agreement is received by the AAA. The parties, by written agreement, may vary the procedures set forth in these rules.

2. Name of Tribunal

Any tribunal constituted by the parties for the settlement of their dispute under these rules shall be called the Commercial Arbitration Tribunal.

3. Administrator and Delegation of Duties

When parties agree to arbitrate under these rules, or when they provide for arbitration by the AAA and an arbitration is initiated under these rules, they thereby authorize the AAA to administer the arbitration. The authority and duties of the AAA are prescribed in the agreement of the parties and in these rules, and may be carried out through such of the AAA's representatives as it may direct.

4. National Panel of Arbitrators

The AAA shall establish and maintain a National Panel of Commercial Arbitrators and shall appoint arbitrators as provided in these rules.

5. Regional Offices

The AAA may, in its discretion, assign the administration of an arbitration to any of its regional offices.

6. Initiation under an Arbitration Provision in a Contract

Arbitration under an arbitration provision in a contract shall be initiated in the following manner:

(a) The initiating party (hereinafter claimant) shall, within the time period, if any, specified in the contract(s), give written notice to the other party (hereinafter respondent) of its intention to arbitrate (demand), which notice shall contain a statement setting forth the nature of the dispute, the amount involved, if any, the remedy sought, and the hearing locale requested, and

(b) shall file at any regional office of the AAA three copies of the notice and three copies of the arbitration provisions of the contract, together with the appropriate filing fee as provided in the schedule on page 21.

The AAA shall give notice of such filing to the respondent or respondents. A respondent may file an answering statement in duplicate with the AAA within ten days after notice from the AAA, in which event the respondent shall at the same time send a copy of the answering statement to the claimant. If a counterclaim is asserted, it shall contain a statement setting forth the nature of the counterclaim, the amount involved, if any, and the remedy sought. If a counterclaim is made, the appropriate fee provided in the schedule on page 21 shall be forwarded to the AAA with the answering statement. If no answering statement is filed within the stated time, it will be treated as a denial of the claim. Failure to file an answering statement shall not operate to delay the arbitration.

7. Initiation under a Submission

Parties to any existing dispute may commence an arbitration under these rules by filing at any regional office of the AAA three copies of a written submission to arbitrate under these rules, signed by the parties. It shall contain a statement of the matter in dispute, the amount involved, if any, the remedy sought, and the hearing locale requested, together with the appropriate filing fee as provided in the schedule on page 21.

8. Changes of Claim

After filing of a claim, if either party desires to make any new or different claim or counterclaim, it shall be made in writing and filed with the AAA, and a copy shall be mailed to the other party, who shall have a period of ten days from the date of such mailing within which to file an answer with the AAA. After the arbitrator is appointed, however, no new or different claim may be submitted except with the arbitrator's consent.

9. Applicable Procedures

Unless the AAA in its discretion determines otherwise, the Expedited Procedures shall be applied in any case where no disclosed claim or counterclaim $50,000, exclusive of interest and arbitration costs. Parties may also agree to using the Expedited Procedures in cases involving claims in excess of $50,000. The Expedited Procedures shall be applied as described in Sections 53 through 57 of these rules, in addition to any other portion of these rules that is not in conflict with the Expedited Procedures.

All other cases shall be administered in accordance with Sections 1 through 52 of these rules.

10. Administrative Conference, Preliminary Hearing, and Mediation Conference

At the request of any party or at the discretion of the AAA, an administrative conference with the AAA and the parties and/or their representatives will be scheduled in appropriate cases to expedite the arbitration proceedings. There is no administrative fee for this service.

In large or complex cases, at the request of any party or at the discretion of the arbitrator or the AAA, a preliminary hearing with the parties and/ or their representatives and the arbitrator may be scheduled by the arbitrator to specify the issues to be resolved, to stipulate to uncontested facts, and to consider any other matters that will expedite the arbitration proceedings. Consistent with the expedited nature of arbitration, the arbitrator may, at the preliminary hearing, establish (i) the extent of and schedule for the production of relevant documents and other information, (ii) the identification of any witnesses to be called, and (iii) a schedule for further hearings to resolve the dispute. There is no administrative fee for the first preliminary hearing. With the consent of the parties, the AAA at any stage of the proceeding may arrange a mediation conference under the Commercial Mediation Rules, in order to facilitate settlement. The mediator shall not be an arbitrator appointed to the case. Where the parties to a pending arbitration agree to mediate under the AAA's rules, no additional administrative fee is required to initiate the mediation.

11. Fixing of Locale

The parties may mutually agree on the locale where the arbitration is to be held. If any party requests that the hearing be held in a specific locale and the other party files no objection thereto within ten days after notice of the request has been sent to it by the AAA, the locale shall be the one requested. If a party objects to the locale requested by the other party, the AAA shall have the power to determine the locale and its decision shall be final and binding.

12. Qualifications of an Arbitrator

Any neutral arbitrator appointed pursuant to Section 13, 14, 15, or 54, or selected by mutual choice of the parties or their appointees, shall be subject to disqualification for the reasons specified in Section 19. If the parties specifically so agree in writing, the arbitrator shall not be subject to disqualification for those reasons.

Unless the parties agree otherwise, an arbitrator selected unilaterally by one party is a party-appointed arbitrator and is not subject to disqualification pursuant to Section 19.

The term "arbitrator" in these rules refers to the arbitration panel, whether composed of one or more arbitrators and whether the arbitrators are neutral or party appointed.

13. Appointment from Panel

If the parties have not appointed an arbitrator and have not provided any other method of appointment, the arbitrator shall be appointed in the following manner: immediately after the filing of the demand or submission, the AAA shall send simultaneously to each party to the dispute an identical list of names of persons chosen from the panel.

Each party to the dispute shall have ten days from the transmittal date in which to strike any names objected to, number the remaining names in order of preference, and return the list to the AAA. If a party does not return the list within the time specified, all persons named therein shall be deemed acceptable. From among the persons who have been approved on both lists, and in accordance with the designated order of mutual preference, the AAA shall invite the acceptance of an arbitrator to serve. If the parties fail to agree on any of the persons named, or if acceptable arbitrators are unable to act, or if for any other reason the appointment cannot be made from the submitted lists, the AAA shall have the power to make the appointment from among other members of the panel without the submission of additional lists.

14. Direct Appointment by a Party

If the agreement of the parties names an arbitrator or specifies a method of appointing an arbitrator, that designation or method shall be followed. The notice of appointment, with the name and address of the arbitrator, shall be filed with the AAA by the appointing party. Upon the request of any appointing party, the AAA shall submit a list of members of the panel from which the party may, if it so desires, make the appointment.

If the agreement specifies a period of time within which an arbitrator shall be appointed and any party fails to make the appointment within that period, the AAA shall make the appointment.

If no period of time is specified in the agreement, the AAA shall notify the party to make the appointment. If within ten days thereafter an arbitrator has not been appointed by a party, the AAA shall make the appointment.

15. Appointment of Neutral Arbitrator by Party-Appointed Arbitrators or Parties

If the parties have selected party-appointed arbitrators, or if such arbitrators have been appointed as provided in Section 14, and the parties have authorized them to appoint a neutral arbitrator within a specified time and no appointment is made within that time or any agreed extension, the AAA may appoint a neutral arbitrator, who shall act as chairperson.

If no period of time is specified for appointment of the neutral arbitrator and the party-appointed arbitrators or the parties do not make the appointment within ten days from the date of the appointment of the last party-appointed arbitrator, the AAA may appoint the neutral arbitrator, who shall act as chairperson.

If the parties have agreed that their party-appointed arbitrators shall appoint the neutral arbitrator from the panel, the AAA shall furnish to the party-appointed arbitrators, in the manner provided in Section 13, a list selected from the panel, and the appointment of the neutral arbitrator shall be made as provided in that section.

16. Nationality of Arbitrator in International Arbitration

Where the parties are nationals or residents of different countries, any neutral arbitrator shall, upon the request of either party, be appointed from among the nationals of a country other than that of any of the parties. The request must be made prior to the time set for the appointment of the arbitrator as agreed by the parties or set by these rules.

17. Number of Arbitrators

If the arbitration agreement does not specify the number of arbitrators, the dispute shall be heard and determined by one arbitrator, unless the AAA, in its discretion, directs that a greater number of arbitrators be appointed.

18. Notice to Arbitrator of Appointment

Notice of the appointment of the neutral arbitrator, whether appointed mutually by the parties or by the AAA, shall be sent to the arbitrator by the AAA, together with a copy of these rules, and the signed acceptance of the arbitrator shall be filed with the AAA prior to the opening of the first hearing.

19. Disclosure and Challenge Procedure

Any person appointed as neutral arbitrator shall disclose to the AAA any circumstance likely to affect impartiality, including any bias or any financial or personal interest in the result of the arbitration or any past or present relationship with the parties or their representatives. Upon receipt of such information from the arbitrator or another source, the AAA shall communicate the information to the parties and, if it deems it appropriate to do so, to the arbitrator and others. Upon objection of a party to the continued service of a neutral arbitrator, the AAA shall determine whether the arbitrator should be disqualified and shall inform the parties of its decision, which shall be conclusive.

20. Vacancies

If for any reason an arbitrator is unable to perform the duties of the office, the AAA may, on proof satisfactory to it, declare the office vacant. Vacancies shall be filled in accordance with the applicable provisions of these rules.

In the event of a vacancy in a panel of neutral arbitrators after the hearings have commenced, the remaining arbitrator or arbitrators may continue with the hearing and determination of the controversy, unless the parties agree otherwise.

21. Date, Time, and Place of Hearing

The arbitrator shall set the date, time, and place for each hearing. The AAA shall send a notice of hearing to the parties at least ten days in advance of the hearing date, unless otherwise agreed by the parties.

22. Representation

Any party may be represented by counsel or other authorized representative. A party intending to be so represented shall notify the other party and the AAA of the name and address of the representative at least three days prior to the date set for the hearing at which that person is first to appear. When such a representative initiates an arbitration or responds for a party, notice is deemed to have been given.

23. Stenographic Record

Any party desiring a stenographic record shall make arrangements directly with a stenographer and shall notify the other parties of these arrangements in advance of the hearing. The requesting party or parties shall pay the cost of the record. If the transcript is agreed by the parties to be, or determined by the arbitrator to be, the official record of the proceeding, it must be made available to the arbitrator and to the other parties for inspection, at a date, time, and place determined by the arbitrator.

24. Interpreters

Any party wishing an interpreter shall make all arrangements directly with the interpreter and shall assume the costs of the service.

25. Attendance at Hearings

The arbitrator shall maintain the privacy of the hearings unless the law provides to the contrary. Any person having a direct interest in the arbitration is entitled to attend hearings. The arbitrator shall otherwise have the power to require the exclusion of any witness, other than a party or other essential person, during the testimony of any other witness. It shall be discretionary with the arbitrator to determine the propriety of the attendance of any other person.

26. Postponements

The arbitrator for good cause shown may postpone any hearing upon the request of a party or upon the arbitrator's own initiative, and shall also grant such postponement when all of the parties agree.

27. Oaths

Before proceeding with the first hearing, each arbitrator may take an oath of office and, if required by law, shall do so. The arbitrator may require witnesses to testify under oath administered by any duly qualified person and, if it is required by law or requested by any party, shall do so.

28. Majority Decision

All decisions of the arbitrators must be by a majority. The award must also be made by a majority unless the concurrence of all is expressly required by the arbitration agreement or by law.

29. Order of Proceedings and Communication with Arbitrator

A hearing shall be opened by the filing of the oath of the arbitrator, where required; by the recording of the date, time, and place of the hearing, and the presence of the arbitrator, the parties, and their representatives, if any; and by the receipt by the arbitrator of the statement of the claim and the answering statement, if any.

The arbitrator may, at the beginning of the hearing, ask for statements clarifying the issues involved. In some cases, part or all of the above will have been accomplished at the preliminary hearing conducted by the arbitrator pursuant to Section 10.

The complaining party shall then present evidence to support its claim. The defending party shall then present evidence supporting its defense. Witnesses for each party shall submit to questions or other examination. The arbitrator has the discretion to vary this procedure but shall afford a full and equal opportunity to all parties for the presentation of any material and relevant evidence.

Exhibits, when offered by either party, may be received in evidence by the arbitrator.

The names and addresses of all witnesses and a description of the exhibits in the order received shall be made a part of the record.

There shall be no direct communication between the parties and a neutral arbitrator other than at oral hearing, unless the parties and the arbitrator agree otherwise. Any other oral or written communication from the parties to the neutral arbitrator shall be directed to the AAA for transmittal to the arbitrator.

30. Arbitration in the Absence of a Party or Representative

Unless the law provides to the contrary, the arbitration may proceed in the absence of any party or representative who, after due notice, fails to be present or fails to obtain a postponement. An award shall not be made solely on the default of a party. The arbitrator shall require the party who is present to submit such evidence as the arbitrator may require for the making of an award.

31. Evidence

The parties may offer such evidence as is relevant and material to the dispute and shall produce such evidence as the arbitrator may deem necessary to an understanding and determination of the dispute. An arbitrator or other person authorized by law to subpoena witnesses or documents may do so upon the request of any party or independently.

The arbitrator shall be the judge of the relevance and materiality of the evidence offered, and conformity to legal rules of evidence shall not be necessary. All evidence shall be taken in the presence of all of the arbitrators and all of the parties, except where any of the parties is absent in default or has waived the right to be present.

32. Evidence by Affidavit and Posthearing Filing of Documents or Other Evidence

The arbitrator may receive and consider the evidence of witnesses by affidavit, but shall give it only such weight as the arbitrator deems it entitled to after consideration of any objection made to its admission.

If the parties agree or the arbitrator directs that documents or other evidence be submitted to the arbitrator after the hearing, the documents or other evidence shall be filed with the AAA for transmission to the arbitrator. All parties shall be afforded an opportunity to examine such documents or other evidence.

33. Inspection or Investigation

An arbitrator finding it necessary to make an inspection or investigation in connection with the arbitration shall direct the AAA to so advise the parties. The arbitrator shall set the date and time and the AAA shall notify the parties. Any party who so desires may be present at such an inspection or investigation. In the event that one or all parties are not present at the inspection or investigation, the arbitrator shall make a verbal or written report to the parties and afford them an opportunity to comment.

34. Interim Measures

The arbitrator may issue such orders for interim relief as may be deemed necessary to safeguard the property that is the subject matter of the arbitration, without prejudice to the rights of the parties or to the final determination of the dispute.

35. Closing of Hearing

The arbitrator shall specifically inquire of all parties whether they have any further proofs to offer or witnesses to be heard. Upon receiving negative replies or if satisfied that the record is complete, the arbitrator shall declare the hearing closed.

If briefs are to be filed, the hearing shall be declared closed as of the final date set by the arbitrator for the receipt of briefs. If documents are to be filed as provided in Section 32 and the date set for their receipt is later than that set for the receipt of briefs, the later date shall be the date of closing the hearing. The time limit within which the arbitrator is required to make the award shall commence to run, in the absence of other agreements by the parties, upon the closing of the hearing.

36. Reopening of Hearing

The hearing may be reopened on the arbitrator's initiative, or upon application of a party, at any time before the award is made. If reopening the hearing would prevent the making of the award within the specific time agreed on by the parties in the contract(s) out of which the controversy has arisen, the matter may not be reopened unless the parties agree on an extension of time. When no specific date is fixed in the contract, the arbitrator may reopen the hearing and shall have thirty days from the closing of the reopened hearing within which to make an award.

37. Waiver of Oral Hearing

The parties may provide, by written agreement, for the waiver of oral hearings in any case. If the parties are unable to agree as to the procedure, the AAA shall specify a fair and equitable procedure.

38. Waiver of Rules

Any party who proceeds with the arbitration after knowledge that any provision or requirement of these rules has not been complied with and who fails to state an objection in writing shall be deemed to have waived the right to object.

39. Extensions of Time

The parties may modify any period of time by mutual agreement. The AAA or the arbitrator may for good cause extend any period of time established by these rules, except the time for making the award. The AAA shall notify the parties of any extension.

40. Serving of Notice

Each party shall be deemed to have consented that any papers, notices, or process necessary or proper for the initiation or continuation of an arbitration under these rules; for any court action in connection therewith; or for the entry of judgment on any award made under these rules may be served on a party by mail addressed to the party or its representative at the last known address or by personal service, in or outside the state where the arbitration is to be held, provided that reasonable opportunity to be heard with regard thereto has been granted to the party.

The AAA and the parties may also use facsimile transmission, telex, telegram, or other written forms of electronic communication to give the notices required by these rules.

41. Time of Award

The award shall be made promptly by the arbitrator and, unless otherwise agreed by the parties or specified by law, no later than thirty days from the date of closing the hearing, or, if oral hearings have been waived, from the date of the AAA's transmittal of the final statements and proofs to the arbitrator.

42. Form of Award

The award shall be in writing and shall be signed by a majority of the arbitrators. It shall be executed in the manner required by law.

43. Scope of Award

The arbitrator may grant any remedy or relief that the arbitrator deems just and equitable and within the scope of the agreement of the parties, including, but not limited to, specific performance of a contract. The arbitrator shall, in the award, assess arbitration fees, expenses, and compensation as provided in Sections 48, 49, and 50 in favor of any party and, in the event that any administrative fees or expenses are due the AAA, in favor of the AAA.

44. Award upon Settlement

If the parties settle their dispute during the course of the arbitration, the arbitrator may set forth the terms of the agreed settlement in an award. Such an award is referred to as a consent award.

45. Delivery of Award to Parties

Parties shall accept as legal delivery of the award the placing of the award or a true copy thereof in the mail addressed to a party or its representative at the last known address, personal service of the award, or the filing of the award in any other manner that is permitted by law.

46. Release of Documents for Judicial Proceedings

The AAA shall, upon the written request of a party, furnish to the party, at its expense, certified copies of any papers in the AAA's possession that may be required in judicial proceedings relating to the arbitration.

47. Applications to Court and Exclusion of Liability

(a) No judicial proceeding by a party relating to the subject matter of the arbitration shall be deemed a waiver of the party's right to arbitrate.

(b) Neither the AAA nor any arbitrator in a proceeding under these rules is a necessary party in judicial proceedings relating to the arbitration.

(c) Parties to these rules shall be deemed to have consented that judgment upon the arbitration award may be entered in any federal or state court having jurisdiction thereof.

(d) Neither the AAA nor any arbitrator shall be liable to any party for any act or omission in connection with any arbitration conducted under these rules.

48. Administrative Fees

As a not-for-profit organization, the AAA shall prescribe filing and other administrative fees to compensate it for the cost of providing administrative services. The fees in effect when the demand for arbitration or submission agreement is received shall be applicable.

The filing fee shall be advanced by the initiating party or parties, subject to final apportionment by the arbitrator in the award.

The AAA may, in the event of extreme hardship on the part of any party, defer or reduce the administrative fees.

49. Expenses

The expenses of witnesses for either side shall be paid by the party producing such witnesses. All other expenses of the arbitration, including required travel and other expenses of the arbitrator, AAA representatives, and any witness and the cost of any proof produced at the direct request of the arbitrator, shall be borne equally by the parties, unless they agree otherwise or unless the arbitrator in the award assesses such expenses or any part thereof against any specified party or parties.

50. Neutral Arbitrator's Compensation

Unless the parties agree otherwise, members of the National Panel of Commercial Arbitrators appointed as neutrals will serve without compensation for the first day of service.

Thereafter, compensation shall be based on the amount of service involved and the number of hearings. An appropriate daily rate and other arrangements will be discussed by the administrator with the parties and the arbitrator. If the parties fail to agree to the terms of compensation, an appropriate rate shall be established by the AAA and communicated in writing to the parties.

Any arrangement for the compensation of a neutral arbitrator shall be made through the AAA and not directly between the parties and the arbitrator.

51. Deposits

The AAA may require the parties to deposit in advance of any hearings such sums of money as it deems necessary to cover the expense of the arbitration, including the arbitrator's fee, if any, and shall render an accounting to the parties and return any unexpended balance at the conclusion of the case.

52. Interpretation and Application of Rules

The arbitrator shall interpret and apply these rules insofar as they relate to the arbitrator's powers and duties. When there is more than one arbitrator and a difference arises among them concerning the meaning or application of these rules, it shall be decided by a majority vote. If that is not possible, either an arbitrator or a party may refer the question to the AAA for final decision. All other rules shall be interpreted and applied by the AAA.

Expedited Procedures

53. Notice by Telephone

The parties shall accept all notices from the AAA by telephone. Such notices by the AAA shall subsequently be confirmed in writing to the parties. Should there be a failure to confirm in writing any notice hereunder, the proceeding shall nonetheless be valid if notice has, in fact, been given by telephone.

54. Appointment and Qualifications of Arbitrator

The AAA shall submit simultaneously to each party an identical list of five proposed arbitrators drawn from the National Panel of Commercial Arbitrators, from which one arbitrator shall be appointed.

Each party may strike two names from the list on a peremptory basis. The list is returnable to the AAA within seven days from the date of the AAA's mailing to the parties.

If for any reason the appointment of an arbitrator cannot be made from the list, the AAA may make the appointment from among other members of the panel without the submission of additional lists.

The parties will be given notice by telephone by the AAA of the appointment of the arbitrator, who shall be subject to disqualification for the reasons specified in Section 19. Within seven days, the parties shall notify the AAA, by telephone, of any objection to the arbitrator appointed. Any objection by a party to the arbitrator shall be confirmed in writing to the AAA with a copy to the other party or parties.

55. Date, Time, and Place of Hearing

The arbitrator shall set the date, time, and place of the hearing. The AAA will notify the parties by telephone, at least seven days in advance of the hearing date. A formal notice of hearing will also be sent by the AAA to the parties.

56. The Hearing

Generally, the hearing shall be completed within one day, unless the dispute is resolved by submission of documents under Section 37. The arbitrator, for good cause shown, may schedule an additional hearing to be held within seven days.

57. Time of Award

Unless otherwise agreed by the parties, the award shall be rendered not later than fourteen days from the date of the closing of the hearing.

Administrative Fees

The AAA's administrative charges are based on filing and service fees. Arbitrator compensation, if any, is not included. Unless the parties agree otherwise, arbitrator compensation and administrative fees are subject to allocation by the arbitrator in the award.

Filing Fees

A nonrefundable filing fee is payable in full by a filing party when a claim, counterclaim, or additional claim is filed, as provided below:

Amount of Claim	Filing Fee
Up to $25,000	$300
Above $25,000 to $50,000	$500
Above $50,000 to $250,000	$1,000
Above $250,000 to $500,000	$2,000
Above $500,000 to $5,000,000	$3,000
Above $5,000,000	$4,000

When no amount can be stated at the time of filing, the filing fee is $1,000, subject to adjustment when the claim or counterclaim is disclosed.

When a claim or counterclaim is not for a monetary amount, an appropriate filing fee will be determined by the AAA.

Hearing Fees

For each day of hearing held before a single arbitrator, an administrative fee of $100 is payable by each party.

For each day of hearing held before a multiarbitrator panel, an administrative fee of $150 is payable by each party.

Postponement Fees

A fee of $100 is payable by a party causing a postponement of any hearing scheduled before a single arbitrator.

A fee of $150 is payable by a party causing a postponement of any hearing scheduled before a multiarbitrator panel.

Processing Fees

No processing fee is payable until 180 days after a case is initiated.

On single-arbitrator cases, a processing fee of $150 per party is payable 180 days after the case is initiated, and every 90 days thereafter, until the case is withdrawn or settled or the hearings are closed by the arbitrator.

On multiarbitrator cases, a processing fee of $200 per party is payable 180 days after the case is initiated, and every 90 days thereafter, until the case is withdrawn or settled or the hearings are closed by the arbitrators.

Suspension for Nonpayment

If arbitrator compensation or administrative charges have not been paid in full, the AAA may so inform the parties in order that one of them may make the required payment. If such payments are not made, the arbitrator may order the suspension or termination of the proceedings. If no arbitrator has yet been appointed, the AAA may suspend the proceedings in such a situation.

Hearing Room

Rental Rooms for hearings are available on a rental basis. Check with our local office for availability and rates.

— Appendix E —
The Arbitration Rules of the UN Commission for International Trade Law (UNCITRAL)

Section I. Introductory Rules

Scope of application
Article 1

1. Where the parties to a contract have agreed in writing that disputes in relation to that contract shall be referred to arbitration under the UNCITRAL Arbitration Rules, then such disputes shall be settled in accordance with these Rules subject to such modification as the parties may agree in writing.

2. These Rules shall govern the arbitration except that where any of these Rules is in conflict with a provision of the law applicable to the arbitration from which the parties cannot derogate, that provision shall prevail.

Notice, calculation of periods of time
Article 2

1. For the purposes of these Rules, any notice, including a notification, communication or proposal, is deemed to have been received if it is physically delivered to the addressee or if it is delivered at his habitual residence, place of business or mailing address, or, if none of these can be found after making reasonable inquiry, then at the addressee's last known residence or place of business. Notice shall be deemed to have been received on the day it is so delivered.

2. For the purposes of calculating a period of time under these Rules, such period shall begin to run on the day following the day when a notice, notification, communication or proposal is received. If the last day of such period is an official holiday or a non-business day at the residence or place of business of the addressee, the period is extended until the first business day which follows. Official holidays or non-business days occurring during the running of the period of time are included in calculating the period.

Notice of arbitration
Article 3

1. The party initiating recourse to arbitration (hereinafter called the "claimant") shall give to

the other party (hereinafter called the "respondent") a notice of arbitration.

2. Arbitral proceedings shall be deemed to commence on the date on which the notice of arbitration is received by the respondent.

3. The notice of arbitration shall include the following:

    (a) A demand that the dispute be referred to arbitration;

    (b) The names and addresses of the parties;

    (c) A reference to the arbitration clause or the separate arbitration agreement that is invoked;

    (d) A reference to the contract out of or in relation to which the dispute arises;

    (e) The general nature of the claim and an indication of the amount involved, if any;

    (f) The relief or remedy sought;

    (g) A proposal as to the number of arbitrators (i.e. one or three), if the parties have not previously agreed thereon.

4. The notice of arbitration may also include:

    (a) The proposals for the appointments of a sole arbitrator and an appointing authority referred to in Article 6, paragraph 1;

    (b) The notification of the appointment of an arbitrator referred to in Article 7;

    (c) The statement of claim referred to in Article 18.

Representation and assistance
Article 4

The parties may be represented or assisted by persons of their choice. The names and addresses of such persons must be communicated in writing to the other party; such communication must specify whether the appointment is being made for purposes of representation or assistance.

Section II. Composition of the Arbitral Tribunal

Number of arbitrators
Article 5

If the parties have not previously agreed on the number of arbitrators (i.e. one or three), and if within 15 days after the receipt by the respondent of the notice of arbitration the parties have not agreed that there shall be only one arbitrator, three arbitrators shall be appointed.

Appointment of arbitrators (Articles 6 to 8)
Article 6

1. If a sole arbitrator is to be appointed, either party may propose to the other:

    (a) The names of one or more persons, one of whom would serve as the sole arbitrator; and

    (b) If no appointing authority has been agreed upon by the parties, the name or names of one or more institutions or persons, one of whom would serve as appointing authority.

2. If within 30 days after receipt by a party of a proposal made in accordance with paragraph 1 the parties have not reached agreement on the choice of a sole arbitrator, the sole arbitrator shall be appointed by the appointing authority agreed upon by the parties. If no appointing authority has been agreed upon by the parties, or if the appointing authority agreed upon refuses to act or fails to appoint the arbitrator within 60 days of the receipt of a party's request therefore, either party may request the Secretary-General of the Permanent Court of Arbitration at The Hague to designate an appointing authority.

3. The appointing authority shall, at the request of one of the parties appoint the sole arbitrator as promptly as possible. In making the appointment the appointing authority shall use the following list-procedure, unless both parties agree that the list-procedure should not be used or unless the appointing authority determines in its discretion that the use of the list-procedure is not appropriate for the case:

(a) At the request of one of the parties the appointing authority shall communicate to both parties an identical list containing at least three names;

(b) Within 15 days after the receipt of this list, each party may return the list to the appointing authority after having deleted the name or names to which he objects and numbered the remaining names on the list in the order of his preference;

(c) After the expiration of the above period of time the appointing authority shall appoint the sole arbitrator from among the names approved on the lists returned to it and in accordance with the order of preference indicated by the parties;

(d) If for any reason the appointment cannot be made according to this procedure, the appointing authority may exercise its discretion in appointing the sole arbitrator.

4. In making the appointment, the appointing authority shall have regard to such considerations as are likely to secure the appointment of an independent and impartial arbitrator and shall take into account as well the advisability of appointing an arbitrator of a nationality other than the nationalities of the parties.

Article 7

1. If three arbitrators are to be appointed, each party shall appoint one arbitrator. The two arbitrators thus appointed shall choose the third arbitrator who will act as the presiding arbitrator of the tribunal.

2. If within 30 days after the receipt of a party's notification of the appointment of an arbitrator the other party has not notified the first party of the arbitrator he has appointed:

(a) The first party may request the appointing authority previously designated by the parties to appoint the second arbitrator; or

(b) If no such authority has been previously designated by the parties, or if the appointing authority previously designated refuses to act or fails to appoint the arbitrator within 30 days after receipt of a party's request therefor, the first party may request the Secretary-General of the Permanent Court of Arbitration at The Hague to designate the appointing authority. The first party may then request the appointing authority so designated to appoint the second arbitrator. In either case, the appointing authority may exercise its discretion in appointing the arbitrator.

3. If within 30 days after the appointment of the second arbitrator the two arbitrators have not agreed on the choice of the presiding arbitrator, the presiding arbitrator shall be appointed by an appointing authority in the same way as a sole arbitrator would be appointed under Article 6.

Article 8

1. When an appointing authority is requested to appoint an arbitrator pursuant to Article 6 or Article 7, the party which makes the request shall send to the appointing authority a copy of the notice of arbitration, a copy of the contract out of or in relation to which the dispute has arisen and a copy of arbitration agreement if it is not contained in the contract. The appointing authority may require from either party such information as it deems necessary to fulfil its function.

2. Where the names of one or more persons are proposed for appointment as arbitrators, their full names, addresses and nationalities shall be indicated, together with a description of their qualifications.

Challenge of arbitrators (Articles 9 to 12)
Article 9

A prospective arbitrator shall disclose to those who approach him in connection with his possible appointment any circumstances likely to give rise to justifiable doubts as to his impartiality or independence. An arbitrator, once appointed or chosen, shall disclose such circumstances to the parties unless they have already been informed by him of these circumstances.

Article 10

1. Any arbitrator may be challenged if circumstances exist that give rise to justifiable doubts as to the arbitrator's impartiality or independence.

2. A party may challenge the arbitrator appointed by him only for reasons of which he becomes aware after the appointment has been made.

Article 11

1. A party who intends to challenge an arbitrator shall send notice of his challenge within 15 days after the appointment of the challenged arbitrator has been notified to the challenging party or within 15 days after the circumstances mentioned in Articles 9 and 10 became known to that party.

2. The challenge shall be notified to the other party, to the arbitrator who is challenged and to the other members of the arbitral tribunal. The notification shall be in writing and shall state the reasons for the challenge.

3. When an arbitrator has been challenged by one party the other party may agree to the chal-

lenge. The arbitrator may also, after the challenge, withdraw from his office. In neither case does this imply acceptance of the validity of the grounds for the challenge. In both cases the procedure provided in Article 6 or 7 shall be used in full for the appointment of the substitute arbitrator, even if during the process of appointing the challenged arbitrator a party had failed to exercise his right to appoint or to participate in the appointment.

Article 12

1. If the other party does not agree to the challenge and the challenged arbitrator does not withdraw, the decision on the challenge will be made:

    (a) When the initial appointment was made by an appointing authority, by that authority;

    (b) When the initial appointment was not made by an appointing authority, but an appointing authority has been previously designated, by that authority;

    (c) In all other cases, by the appointing authority to be designated in accordance with the procedure for designating an appointing authority as provided for in Article 6.

2. If the appointing authority sustains the challenge, a substitute arbitrator shall be appointed or chosen pursuant to the procedure applicable to the appointment or choice of an arbitrator as provided in Articles 6 to 9 except that, when this procedure would call for the designation of an appointing authority, the appointment of the arbitrator shall be made by the appointing authority which decided on the challenge.

Replacement of an arbitrator
Article 13

1. In the event of the death or resignation of an arbitrator during the course of the arbitral proceedings, a substitute arbitrator shall be appointed or chosen pursuant to the procedure provided for in Articles 6 to 9 that was applicable to the appointment or choice of the arbitrator being replaced.

2. In the event that an arbitrator fails to act or in the event of the de jure or de facto impossibility of his performing his functions, the procedure in respect of the challenge and replacement of an arbitrator as provided in the preceding articles shall apply.

Repetition of hearings in the event of the replacement of an arbitrator
Article 14

If under Articles 11 to 13 the sole or presiding arbitrator is replaced, any hearings held previously shall be repeated; if any other arbitrator is replaced, such prior hearings may be repeated at the discretion of the arbitral tribunal.

Section III: Arbitral Proceedings

General provisions

Article 15

1. Subject to these Rules, the arbitral tribunal may conduct the arbitration in such manner as it considers appropriate, provided that the parties are treated with equality and that at any stage of the proceedings each party is given a full opportunity of presenting his case.

2. If either party so requests at any stage of the proceedings, the arbitral tribunal shall hold hearings for the presentation of evidence by witnesses, including expert witnesses, or for oral argument. In the absence of such a request, the arbitral tribunal shall decide whether to hold such hearings or whether the proceedings shall be conducted on the basis of documents and other materials.

3. All documents or information supplied to the arbitral tribunal by one party shall at the same time be communicated by that party to the other party.

Place of arbitration

Article 16

1. Unless the parties have agreed upon the place where the arbitration is to be held, such place shall be determined by the arbitral tribunal, having regard to the circumstances of the arbitration.

2. The arbitral tribunal may determine the locale of the arbitration within the country agreed upon by the parties. It may hear witnesses and hold meetings for consultation among its members at any place it deems appropriate having regard to the circumstances of the arbitration.

3. The arbitral tribunal may meet at anyplace it deems appropriate for the inspection of goods, other property or documents. The parties shall be given sufficient notice to enable them to be present at such inspection.

4. The award shall be made at the place of arbitration.

Language

Article 17

1. Subject to an agreement by the parties, the arbitral tribunal shall, promptly after its appointment, determine the language or languages to be used in the proceedings. This determination shall apply to the statement of claim, the statement of defence, and any further written statements and, if oral hearings take place, to the language or languages to be used in such hearings.

2. The arbitral tribunal may order that any documents annexed to the statement of claim or statement of defence, and any supplementary documents or exhibits submitted in the course of the proceedings, delivered in their original language, shall be accompanied by a translation into the language or languages agreed upon by the parties or determined by the arbitral tribunal.

Statement of claim
Article 18

1. Unless the statement of claim was contained in the notice of arbitration, within a period of time to be determined by the arbitral tribunal, the claimant shall communicate his statement of claim in writing to the respondent and to each of the arbitrators. A copy of the contract, and of the arbitration agreement if not contained in the contract, shall be annexed thereto.

2. The statement of claim shall include the following particulars:
   (a) The names and addresses of the parties;
   (b) A statement of the facts supporting the claim;
   (c) The points at issue;
   (d) The relief or remedy sought.

The claimant may annex to his statement of claim all documents he deems relevant or may add a reference to the documents or other evidence he will submit.

Statement of defence
Article 19

1. Within a period of time to be determined by the arbitral tribunal, the respondent shall communicate his statement of defence in writing to the claimant and to each of the arbitrators.

2. The statement of defence shall reply to the particulars (b), (c) and (d) of the statement of claim (Article 16, para. 2). The respondent may annex to his statement the documents on which he relies for his defence or may add a reference to the documents or other evidence he will submit.

3. In his statement of defence, or at a later stage in the arbitral proceedings if the arbitral tribunal decides that the delay was justified under the circumstances, the respondent may make a counterclaim arising out of the same contract or rely on a claim arising out of the same contract for the purpose of a set-off.

4. The provisions of Article 18, paragraph 2, shall apply to a counterclaim and a claim relied on for the purpose of a set-off.

Amendments to the claim or defence
Article 20

During the course of the arbitral proceedings either party may amend or supplement his claim of defence unless the arbitral tribunal considers it inappropriate to allow such amendment having regard to the delay in making it or prejudice to the other party or any other circumstances. However, a claim may not be amended in such a manner that the amended claim falls outside the scope of the arbitration clause or separate arbitration agreement.

Pleas as to the jurisdiction of the arbitral tribunal
Article 21

1. The arbitral tribunal shall have the power to rule on objections that it has no jurisdiction,

including any objections with respect to the existence or validity of the arbitration clause or of the separate arbitration agreement.

2. The arbitral tribunal shall have the power to determine the existence or the validity of the contract of which an arbitration clause forms a part. For the purposes of Article 21, an arbitration clause which forms part of a contract and which provides for arbitration under these Rules shall be treated as an agreement independent of the other terms of the contract. A decision by the arbitral tribunal that the contract is null and void shall not entail ipso jure the invalidity of the arbitration clause.

3. A plea that the arbitral tribunal does not have jurisdiction shall be raised not later than in the statement of defence or, with respect to a counterclaim, in the reply to the counterclaim.

4. In general, the arbitral tribunal should rule on a plea concerning its jurisdiction as a preliminary question. However, the arbitral tribunal may proceed with the arbitration and rule on such a plea in their final award.

Further written statements
Article 22

The arbitral tribunal shall decide which further written statements, in addition to the statement of claim and the statement of defence, shall be required from the parties or may be presented by them and shall fix the periods of time for communicating such statements.

Periods of time
Article 23

The periods of time fixed by the arbitral tribunal for the communication of written statements (including the statement of claim and statement of defence) should not exceed 45 days. However, the arbitral tribunal may extend the time-limits if it concludes that an extension is justified.

Evidence and hearings (Articles 24 and 25)
Article 24

1. Each party shall have the burden of proving the facts relied on to support his claim or defence.

2. The arbitral tribunal may, if it considers it appropriate, require a party to deliver to the tribunal and to the other party, within such a period of time as the arbitral tribunal shall decide, a summary of the documents and other evidence which that party intends to present in support of the facts in issue set out in his statement of claim or statement of defence.

3. At any time during the arbitral proceedings the arbitral tribunal may require the parties to produce documents, exhibits or other evidence within such period of time as the tribunal shall determine.

Article 25

1. In the event of an oral hearing, the arbitral tribunal shall give the parties adequate advance notice of the date, time and place thereof.

2. If witnesses are to be heard, at least 15 days before the hearing each party shall communicate to the arbitral tribunal and to the other party the names and addresses of the witnesses he intends to present, the subject upon and the languages in which such witnesses will give their testimony.

3. The arbitral tribunal shall make arrangements for the translation of oral statements made at a hearing and for a record of the hearing if either is deemed necessary by the tribunal under the circumstances of the case, or if the parties have agreed thereto and have communicated such agreement to the tribunal at least 15 days before the hearing.

4. Hearings shall be held in camera unless the parties agree otherwise. The arbitral tribunal may require the retirement of any witness or witnesses during the testimony of other witnesses. The arbitral tribunal is free to determine the manner in which witnesses are examined.

5. Evidence of witnesses may also be presented in the form of written statements signed by them.

6. The arbitral tribunal shall determine the admissibility, relevance, materiality and weight of the evidence offered.

Interim measures of protection
Article 26

1. At the request of either party, the arbitral tribunal may take any interim measures it deems necessary in respect of the subject-matter of the dispute, including measures for the conservation of the goods forming the subject matter in dispute, such as ordering their deposit with a third person or the sale of perishable goods.

2. Such interim measures may be established in the form of an interim award. The arbitral tribunal shall be entitled to require security for the costs of such measures.

3. A request for interim measures addressed by any party to a judicial authority shall not be deemed incompatible with the agreement to arbitrate, or as a waiver of that agreement.

Experts
Article 27

1. The arbitral tribunal may appoint one or more experts to report to it, in writing, on specific issues to be determined by the tribunal. A copy of the expert's terms of reference, established by the arbitral tribunal, shall be communicated to the parties.

2. The parties shall give the expert any relevant information or produce for his inspection any relevant documents or goods that he may require of them. Any dispute between a party and such expert as to the relevance of the required information or production shall be referred to the arbitral tribunal for decision.

3. Upon receipt of the expert's report, the arbitral tribunal shall communicate a copy of the report to the parties who shall be given the opportunity to express, in writing, their opinion on the report. A party shall be entitled to examine any document on which the expert has relied in his report.

4. At the request of either party the expert, after delivery of the report, may be heard at a hearing where the parties shall have the opportunity to be present and to interrogate the expert. At this hearing either party may present expert witnesses in order to testify on the points at issue. The provisions of Article 25 shall be applicable to such proceedings.

Default
Article 28

1. If, within the period of time fixed by the arbitral tribunal, the claimant has failed to communicate his claim without showing sufficient cause for such failure, the arbitral tribunal shall issue an order for the termination of the arbitral proceedings. If, within the period of time fixed by the arbitral tribunal, the respondent has failed to communicate his statement of defence without showing sufficient cause for such failure, the arbitral tribunal shall order that the proceedings continue.

2. If one of the parties, duly notified under these Rules, fails to appear at a hearing, without showing sufficient cause for such failure, the arbitral tribunal may proceed with the arbitration.

3. If one of the parties, duly invited to produce documentary evidence, fails to do so within the established period of time, without showing sufficient cause for such failure, the arbitral tribunal may make the award on the evidence before it.

Closure of hearings
Article 29

1. The arbitral tribunal may inquire of the parties if they have any further proof to offer or witnesses to be heard or submissions to make and, if there are none, it may declare the hearings closed.

2. The arbitral tribunal may, if it considers it necessary owing to exceptional circumstances, decide, on its own motion or upon application of a party, to reopen the hearings at any time before the award is made.

Waiver of Rules
Article 30

A party who knows that any provision of, or requirement under, these Rules has not been complied with and yet proceeds with the arbitration without promptly stating his objection to such non-compliance, shall be deemed to have waived his right to object.

Section IV. The Award

Decisions
Article 31

1. When there are three arbitrators, any award or other decision of the arbitral tribunal shall be made by a majority of the arbitrators.

2. In the case of questions of procedure, when there is no majority or when the arbitral tribunal so authorizes, the presiding arbitrator may decide on his own, subject to revision, if any, by the arbitral tribunal.

Form and effect of the award
Article 32

1. In addition to making a final award, the arbitral tribunal shall be entitled to make interim, interlocutory, or partial awards.

2. The award shall be made in writing and shall be final and binding on the parties. The parties undertake to carry out the award without delay.

3. The arbitral tribunal shall state the reasons upon which the award is based, unless the parties have agreed that no reasons are to be given.

4. An award shall be signed by the arbitrator and it shall contain the date on which and the place where the award was made. Where there are three arbitrators and one of them fails to sign, the award shall state the reason for the absence of the signature.

5. The award may be made public only with the consent of both parties.

6. Copies of the award signed by the arbitrators shall be communicated to the parties by the arbitral tribunal.

7. If the arbitration law of the country where the award is made requires that the award be filed or registered by the arbitral tribunal, the tribunal shall comply with this requirement within the period of time required by law.

Applicable law, amiable compositeur
Article 33

1. The arbitral tribunal shall apply the law designated by the parties as applicable to the substance of the dispute. Failing such designation by the parties, the arbitral tribunal shall apply the law determined by the conflict of laws rules which it considers applicable.

2. The arbitral tribunal shall decide as amiable compositeur or ex aequo et bono only if the parties have expressly authorized the arbitral tribunal to do so and if the law applicable to the arbitral procedure permits such arbitration.

3. In all cases, the arbitral tribunal shall decide in accordance with the terms of the contract and shall take into account the usages of the trade applicable to the transaction.

Settlement or other grounds for termination
Article 34

1. If, before the award is made, the parties agree on a settlement of the dispute, the arbitral tribunal shall either issue an order for the termination of the arbitral proceedings or, if requested by both parties and accepted by the tribunal, record the settlement in the form of an arbitral award on agreed terms. The arbitral tribunal is not obliged to give reasons for such an award.

2. If, before the award is made, the continuation of the arbitral proceedings becomes unnecessary or impossible for any reason not mentioned in paragraph 1, the arbitral tribunal shall inform the parties of its intention to issue an order for the termination of the proceedings. The arbitral tribunal shall have the power to issue such an order unless a party raises justifiable grounds for objection.

3. Copies of the order for termination of the arbitral proceedings or of the arbitral award on agreed terms, signed by the arbitrators, shall be communicated by the arbitral tribunal to the parties. Where an arbitral award on agreed terms is made, the provisions of Article 32, paragraphs 2 and 4 to 7, shall apply.

Interpretation of the award
Article 35

1. Within 30 days after the receipt of the award, either party, with notice to the other party, may request that the arbitral tribunal give an interpretation of the award.

2. The interpretation shall be given in writing within 45 days after the receipt of the request. The interpretation shall form part of the award and the provisions of Article 32, paragraphs 2 to 7, shall apply.

Correction of the award
Article 36

1. Within 30 days after the receipt of the award, either party, with notice to the other party, may request the arbitral tribunal to correct in the award any errors in computation, any clerical or typographical errors, or any errors of similar nature. The arbitral tribunal may within 30 days after the communication of the award make such corrections on its own initiative.

2. Such corrections shall be in writing, and the provisions of Article 32, paragraphs 2 to 7, shall apply.

Additional award
Article 37

1. Within 30 days after the receipt of the award, either party, with notice to the other party, may request the arbitral tribunal to make an additional award as to claims presented in the arbitral proceedings but omitted from the award.

2. If the arbitral tribunal considers the request for an additional award to be justified and considers that the omission can be rectified without any further hearings or evidence, it shall

complete its award within 60 days after the receipt of the request.

3. When an additional award is made, the provisions of Article 32, paragraphs 2 to 7, shall apply.

Costs (Articles 38 to 40)
Article 38

The arbitral tribunal shall fix the costs of arbitration in its award. The term "costs" includes only:

(a) The fees of the arbitral tribunal to be stated separately as to each arbitrator and to be fixed by the tribunal itself in accordance with Article 39;

(b) The travel and other expenses incurred by the arbitrators;

(c) The costs of expert advice and of other assistance required by the arbitral tribunal;

(d) The travel and other expenses of witnesses to the extent such expenses are approved by the arbitral tribunal;

(e) The costs for legal representation and assistance of the successful party if such costs were claimed during the arbitral proceedings, and only to the extent that the arbitral tribunal determines that the amount of such costs is reasonable;

(f) Any fees and expenses of the appointing authority as well as the expenses of the Secretary-General of the Permanent Court of Arbitration at The Hague.

Article 39

1. The fees of the arbitral tribunal shall be reasonable in amount, taking into account the amount in dispute, the complexity of the subject matter, the time spent by the arbitrators and any other relevant circumstances of the case.

2. If an appointing authority has been agreed upon by the parties or designated by the Secretary-General of the Permanent Court of Arbitration at The Hague, and if that authority has issued a schedule of fees for arbitrators in international cases which it administers, the arbitral tribunal in fixing its fees shall take that schedule of fees into account to the extent that it considers appropriate in the circumstances of the case.

3. If such appointing authority has not issued a schedule of fees for arbitrators in international cases, any party may at any time request the appointing authority to furnish a statement setting forth the basis for establishing fees which is customarily followed in international cases in which the authority appoints arbitrators. If the appointing authority consents to provide such a statement, the arbitral tribunal in fixing its fees shall take such information into account to the extent that it considers appropriate in the circumstances of the case.

4. In cases referred to in paragraphs 2 and 3, when a party so requests and the appointing authority consents to perform the function, the arbitral tribunal shall fix its fees only after consultation with the appointing authority, which may make any comment it deems appropriate to the arbitral tribunal concerning the fees.

Article 40

1. Except as provided in paragraph 2, the costs of arbitration shall in principle be borne by the unsuccessful party. However, the arbitral tribunal may apportion each of such costs between the parties if it determines that apportionment is reasonable, taking into account the circumstances of the case.

2. With respect to the costs of legal representation and assistance referred to in Article 38, paragraph (e), the arbitral tribunal, taking into account the circumstances of the case, shall be free to determine which party shall bear such costs or may apportion such costs between the parties if it determines that apportionment is reasonable.

3. When the arbitral tribunal issues an order for the termination of the arbitral proceedings or makes an award on agreed terms it shall fix the costs of arbitration referred to in Article 38 and Article 39, paragraph 1, in the text of that order or award.

4. No additional fees may be charged by an arbitral tribunal for interpretation or correction or completion of its award under Articles 35 to 37.

Deposit of costs
Article 41

1. The arbitral tribunal, on its establishment, may request each party to deposit an equal amount as an advance for the costs referred to in Article 38, paragraphs (a), (b) and (c).

2. During the course of the arbitral proceedings the arbitral tribunal may request supplementary deposits from the parties.

3. If an appointing authority has been agreed upon by the parties or designated by the Secretary-General of the Permanent Court of Arbitration at The Hague, and when a party so requests and the appointing authority consents to perform the function, the arbitral tribunal shall fix the amounts of any deposits or supplementary deposits only after consultation with the appointing authority which may make any comments to the arbitral tribunal which it deems appropriate concerning the amount of such deposits and supplementary deposits.

4. If the required deposits are not paid in full within 30 days after the receipt of the request, the arbitral tribunal shall so inform the parties in order that one or another of them may make the required payment. If such payment is not made, the arbitral tribunal may order the suspension or termination of the arbitral proceedings.

5. After the award has been made, the arbitral tribunal shall render an accounting to the parties of the deposits received and return any unexpended balance to the parties.   ◆

— Appendix F —
Convention on the Recognition and Enforcement of Foreign Arbitral Awards

NEW YORK, JUNE 10, 1958

Article I

1. This Convention shall apply to the recognition and enforcement of arbitral awards made in the territory of a State other than the State where the recognition and enforcement of such awards are sought, and arising out of differences between persons, whether physical or legal. It shall also apply to arbitral awards not considered as domestic awards in the State where their recognition and enforcement are sought.

2. The term 'arbitral awards' shall include not only awards made by arbitrators appointed for each case but also those made by permanent arbitral bodies to which the parties have submitted.

3. When signing, ratifying or acceding to this Convention, or notifying extension under article X hereof, any State may on the basis of reciprocity declare that it will apply the Convention to the recognition and enforcement of awards made only in the territory of another Contracting State. It may also declare that it will apply the Convention only to differences arising out of legal relationships, whether contractual or not, which are considered as commercial under the national law of the State making such declaration.

Article II

1. Each Contracting State shall recognize an agreement in writing under which the parties undertake to submit to arbitration all or any differences which have arisen or which may arise between them in respect of a defined legal relationship, whether contractual or not, concerning a subject matter capable of settlement by arbitration.

2. The term 'agreement in writing' shall include an arbitral clause in a contract or an arbitration agreement, signed by the parties or contained in an exchange of letters or telegrams.

3. The court of a Contracting State, when seized of an action in a matter in respect of which the parties have made an agreement within the meaning of this article, shall, at the request of one of the parties, refer the parties to arbitration, unless it finds that the said agreement is null and void, inoperative or incapable of being performed.

Article III

Each Contracting State shall recognize arbitral awards as binding and enforce them in accordance with the rules of procedure of the territory where the award is relied upon, under the conditions laid down in the following articles. There shall not be imposed substantially more onerous conditions or higher fees or charges on the recognition or enforcement of arbitral awards to which this Convention applies than are imposed on the recognition or enforcement of domestic arbitral awards.'

Article IV

1. To obtain the recognition and enforcement mentioned in the preceding article, the party applying for recognition and enforcement shall, at the time of the application, supply:

(a) The duly authenticated original award or a duly certified copy thereof;

(b) The original agreement referred to in article II or a duly certified copy thereof.

2. If the said award or agreement is not made in an official language of the country in which the award is relied upon, the party applying for recognition and enforcement of the award shall produce a translation of these documents into such language. The translation shall be certified by an official or sworn translator or by a diplomatic or consular agent.

Article V

1. Recognition and enforcement of the award may be refused, at the request of the party against whom it is invoked, only if that party furnishes to the competent authority where the recognition and enforcement is sought, proof that:

(a) The parties to the agreement referred to in article II were, under the law applicable to them, under some incapacity, or the said agreement is not valid under the law to which the parties have subjected it or, failing any indication thereon, under the law of the country where the award was made; or

(b) The party against whom the award is invoked was not given proper notice of the appointment of the arbitrator or of the arbitration proceedings or was otherwise unable to present his case; or

(c) The award deals with a difference not contemplated by or not falling within the terms of the submission to arbitration, or it contains decisions on matters beyond the scope of the submission to arbitration, provided that, if the decisions on matters submitted to arbitration can be separated from those not so submitted, that part of the award which contains decisions on matters submitted to arbitration may be recognized and enforced; or

(d) The composition of the arbitral authority or the arbitral procedure was not in accordance with the agreement of the parties, or, failing such agreement, was not in accordance with the law of the country where the arbitration took place; or

(e) The award has not yet become binding on the parties, or has been set aside or suspended by a competent authority of the country in which, or under the law of which, that award was made.

2. Recognition and enforcement of an arbitral award may also be refused if the competent authority in the country where recognition and enforcement is sought finds that:

(a) The subject matter of the difference is not capable of settlement by arbitration under the law of that country; or

(b) The recognition or enforcement of the award would be contrary to the public policy of that country.

Article VI

If an application for the setting aside or suspension of the award has been made to a competent authority referred to in article V (1)(e), the authority before which the award is sought to be relied upon may, if it considers it proper, adjourn the decision on the enforcement of the award and may also, on the application of the party claiming enforcement of the award, order the other party to give suitable security.

Article VII

1. The provisions of the present Convention shall not affect the validity of multi-lateral or bilateral agreements concerning the recognition and enforcement of arbit-ral awards entered into by the Contracting States nor deprive any interested party of any right he may have to avail himself of an arbitral award in the manner and to the extent allowed by the law or the treaties of the country where such award is sought to be relied upon.

2. The Geneva Protocol on Arbitration Clauses of 1923 and the Geneva Conven-tion on the Execution of Foreign Arbitral Awards of 1927 shall cease to have effect between Contracting States on their becoming bound and to the extent that they become bound, by this Convention.

Article VIII

1. This Convention shall be open until 31 December 1958 for signature on behalf of any Member of the United Nations and also on behalf of any other State which is or hereafter becomes a member of any specialized agency of the United Nations, or which is or hereafter becomes a member of any specialized agency of the United Nations, or which is or hereafter becomes a party to the Statute of the International Court of Justice, or any other State to which an invitation has been addressed by the General Assembly of the United Nations.

2. This Convention shall be ratified and the instrument of ratification shall be deposited with the Secretary-General of the United Nations.

Article IX

1. This Convention shall be open for accession to all States referred to in article VIII.

2. Accession shall be effected by the deposit of an instrument of accession with the Secretary-General of the United Nations.

Article X

1. Any State may, at the time of signature, ratification or accession, declare that this Convention shall extend to all or any of the territories for the international relations of which it is responsible. Such a declaration shall take effect when the Convention enters into force for the State concerned.

2. At any time thereafter any such extension shall be made by notification addres-

sed to the Secretary-General of the United Nations and shall take effect as from the ninetieth day after the day of receipt by the Secretary-General of the United Nations of this notification, or as from the date of entry into force of the Convention for the State concerned, whichever is the later.

3. With respect to those territories to which this Convention is not extended at the time of signature, ratification or accession, each State concerned shall consider the possibility of taking the necessary steps in order to extend the application of this Convention to such territories, subject, where necessary for constitutional reasons, to the consent of the Governments of such territories.

Article XI

In the case of a federal or non-unitary State, the following provisions shall apply:

(a) With respect to those articles of this Convention that come within the legislative jurisdiction of the federal authority, the obligations of the federal Government shall to this extent be the same as those of Contracting States which are not federal States;

(b) With respect to those articles of this Convention that come within the legislative jurisdiction of constituent states or provinces which are not, under the constitutional system of the federation, bound to take legislative action, the federal Government shall bring such articles with a favourable recommendation to the notice of the appropriate authorities of constituent states or provinces at the earlies possible moment;

(c) A federal State Party to this Convention shall, at the request of any other Contracting State transmitted through the Secretary-General of the United Nations, supply a statement of the law and practice of the federation and its constituent units in regard to any particular provision of this Convention, showing the extent to which effect has been given to that provision by legislative or other action.

Article XII

1. This Convention shall come into force on the ninetieth day following the date of deposit of the third instrument of ratification or accession.

2. For each State ratifying or acceding to this Convention after the deposit of the third instrument of ratification or accession, this Convention shall enter into force on the ninetieth day after deposit by such State of its instrument of ratification or accession.

Article XIII

1. Any Contracting State may denounce this Convention by a written notification to the Secretary-General of the United Nations. Denunciation shall take effect one year after the date of receipt of the notification by the Secretary-General.

2. Any State which has made a declaration or notification under article X may, at any time thereafter, by notification to the Secretary-General of the United Nations, declare that this Convention shall cease to extend to the territory concerned one year after the date of the receipt of the notification by the Secretary-General.

3. This Convention shall continue to be applicable to arbitral awards in respect of which recognition or enforcement proceedings have been instituted before the denunciation takes effect.

Article XIV

A Contracting State shall not be entitled to avail itself of the present Convention against other Contracting States except to the extent that it is itself bound to apply the Convention.

Article XV

The Secretary-General of the United Nations shall notify the States contemplated in article VIII of the following:

(a) Signatures and ratifications in accordance with article VIII;

(b) Accessions in accordance with article IX;

(c) Declarations and notifications under articles I, X and XI;

(d) The date upon which this Convention enters into force in accordance with article XII;

(e) Denunciations and notifications in accordance with article XIII.

Article XVI

1. This Convention, of which the Chinese, English, French, Russian and Spanish texts shall be equally authentic, shall be deposited in the archives of the United Nations.

2. The Secretary-General of the United Nations shall transmit a certified copy of this Convention to the State contemplated in article VIII.

— Appendix G —
UNCITRAL Model Law on International Commercial Arbitration

(*As adopted by the United Nations Commission on International Trade Law on June 21, 1985*)

CHAPTER I. GENERAL PROVISIONS

Article 1. Scope of Application*

(1) This Law applies to internatioal commerical** arbitration, subject to any agreement in force between this State and any other State or States.

(2) The provisions of this Law, except articles 8, 9, 35 and 36, apply only if the place of arbitration is in the territory of this State.

(3) An arbitration is international if:

(a) the parties to an arbitration agreement have, at the time of the conclusion of that agreement, their places of business in different States; or

(b) one of the following places is situated outside the State in which the parties have their places of business:

(i) the place of arbitration if determined in, or pursuant to, the arbitration agreement;

(ii) any place where a substantial part of the obligations of the commercial relationship is to be performed or the place with which the subject-matter of the dispute is most closely connected; or

(c) the parties have expressly agreed that the subject-matter of the arbitration agreement relates to more than one country.

(4) For the purposes of paragraph (3) of this article:

(a) if a party has more than one place of business, the place of business is that which has the closest relationship to the arbitration agreement;

(b) if a party does not have a place of business, reference is to be made to his habitual residence.

(5) This Law shall not affect any other law of this State by virtue of which certain

disputes may not be submitted to arbitration or may be submitted to arbitration only according to provisions other than those of this Law.

Article 2. Definitions and Rules of Interpretation

For the purposes of this Law:

(a) "arbitration" means any arbitration whether or not administratered by a permanent arbitral institution;

(b) "arbitral tribunal" means a sole arbitrator or a panel of arbitrators;

(c) "court" means a body or organ of the judicial system of a State;

(d) where a provision of this Law, except article 28, leaves the parties free to determine a certain issue, such freedom includes the right of the parties to authorize a third party, including an institution, to make that determination;

(e) where a provision of this Law refers to the fact that the parties have agreed or that they may agree or in any other way refers to an agreement of the parties, such agreement includes any arbitration rules referred to in that agreement;

(f) where a provision of this Law, other than in articles 25 (a) and 32 (2) (a), refers to a claim, it also applies to a counter-claim, and where it refers to a defence, it also applies to a defence to such counter-claim.

Article 3. Receipt of Written Communications

(1) Unless otherwise agreed by the parties:

(a) any written communication is deemed to have been received if it is delivered to the addressee personally or if it is delivered at his place of business, habitual residence or mailing address; if none of these can be found after making a reasonable inquiry, a written communication is deemed to have been received if it is sent to the addressee's last-known place of business, habitual residence or mailing address by registered letter or any other means which provides a record of the attempt to deliver it;

(b) the communication is deemed to have been received on the day it is so delivered.

(2) The provisions of this article do not apply to communications in court proceedings.

Article 4. Waiver of Right to Object

A party who knows that any provision of this Law from which the parties may derogate or any requirement under the arbitration agreement has not been complied with and yet proceeds with the arbitration without stating his objection to such non-compliance without undue delay or, if a time-limit is provided therefor, within such period of time, shall be deemed to have waived his right to object.

Article 5. Extent of Court Intervention

In matters governed by this Law, no court shall intervene except where so provided in this Law.

Article 6. Court of Other Authority for Certain Functions of Arbitration Assistance and Supervision

The functions referred to in articles 11 (3), 11 (4), 13 (3), 14, 16 (3) and 34 (2) shall be performed by ... [Each State enacting this model law specifies the court, courts or, where referred to therein, other authority competent to perform these functions.]

CHAPTER II. ARBITRATION AGREEMENT
Article 7. Definition and From of Arbitration Agreement

(1) "Arbitration agreement" is an agreement by the parties to submit to arbitration all or certain disputes which have arisen or which may arise between them in respect of a defined legal relationship, whether contractual or not. An arbitration agreement may be in the form of an arbitration clause in a contract or in the form of a separate agreement.

(2) The arbitration agreement shall be in writing. An agreement is in writing if it is contained in a document signed by the parties or in an exchange of letters, telex, telegrams or other means of telecommunication which provide a record of the agreement, or in an exchange of statements of claim and defence in which the existence of an agreement is alleged by one party and not denied by another. The reference in a contract to a document containing an arbitration clause constitutes an arbitration agreement provided that the contract is in writing and the reference is such as to make that clause part of the contract.

Article 8. Arbitration Agreement and Substantive Claim Before Court

(1) A court before which an action is brought in a matter which is the subject of an arbitration agreement shall, if a party so requests not later than when submitting his first statement on the substance of the dispute, refer the parties to arbitration unless it finds that the agreement is null and void, inoperative or incapable of being performed.

(2) Where an action referred to in paragraph (1) of this article has been brought, arbitral proceedings may nevertheless be commenced or continued, and an award may be made, while the issue is pending before the court.

Article 9. Arbitration Agreement and Interim Measures by Court

It is not incompatible with an arbitration agreement for a party to request, before of during arbitral proceedings, from a court an interim measure of protection and for a court to grant such measure.

CHAPTER III. COMPOSITION OF ARBITRAL TRIBUNAL
Article 10. Number of Arbitrators

(1) The parties are free to determine the number of arbitrators.

(2) Failing such determination, the number of arbitrators shall be three.

Article 11. Appointment of Arbitrators

(1) No person shall be precluded by reason of his nationality from acting as an arbitrator, unless otherwise agreed by the parties.

(2) The parties are free to agree on a procedure of appointing the arbitrator or arbitrators, subject to the provisions of paragraphs (4) and (5) of this article.

(3) Failing such agreement,

  (a) in an arbitration with three arbitrators, each party shall appoint one arbitrator, and the two arbitrators thus appointed shall appoint the third arbitrator; if a party fails to appoint the arbitrator within thirty days of receipt of a request to do so from the other party, or if the two arbitrators fail to agree on the third arbitrator within thirty days of their appointment, the appointment shall be made, upon request of a party, by the court, or other authority specified in article 6;

  (b) in an arbitration with a sole arbitrator, if the parties are unable to agree on the arbitrator, he shall be appointed, upon request of a party, by the court or other authority specified in article 6.

(4) Where, under an appointment procedure agreed upon by the parties,

(a) a party fails to act as required under such procedure, or

(b) the parties, or two arbitrators, are unable to reach an agreement expected of them under such procedure, or

(c) a third party, including an institution, fails to perform any function entrusted to it under such procedure,

any party may request the court or other authority specified in article 6 to take the necessary measure, unless the agreement on the appointment procedure provides other means for securing the appointment.

(5) A decision on a matter entrusted by paragraph (3) or (4) of this article to the court or other authority specified in article 6 shall subject to no appeal. The court or other authority, in appointing an arbitrator, shall have due regard to any qualifications required of the arbitrator by the agreement of the parties and to such considerations as are likely to secure the appointment of an independent and impartial arbitrator and, in the case of a sole or third arbitrator, shall take into account as well the advisability of appinting an arbitrator of a nationality other than those of the parties.

Article 12. Grounds for Challenge

(1) When a person is approached in connection with his possible appointment as an arbitrator, he shall disclose any circumstances likely to give rise to justi-fiable doubts as to his impartiality or independence. An arbitrator, from the time of his appointment and throughout the arbitral proceedings, shall without delay disclose any such circumstances to the parties unless they have already been informed of them by him.

(2) An arbitrator may be challenged only if circumstances exist that give rise to justificable doubts as to his impartiality or independence, or if he does not possess qualifications agreed to by the parties. A party may challenge an arbitrator appointed by him, or in whose appointment he has participated, only for reasons of which he becomes aware after the appointment has been made.

Article 13. Challenge Procedure

(1) The parties are free to agree on a procedure for challenging an arbitrator, subject to the provisions of paragraph (3) of this article.

(2) Failing such agreement, a party who intends to challenge an arbitrator shall, within fifteen days after becoming aware of the constitution of the arbitral tribunal or after becoming aware of the constitution of the arbitral tribunal or after becoming aware of any circumstance referred to in article 12 (2), send a written statement of the reasons for the challenge to the arbitral tribunal. Unless the challenged arbitrator withdraws from his office or the other party agrees to the challenge, the arbitral tribunal shall decide on the challenge.

(3) If a challenge under any procedure agree upon by the parties or under the procedure of paragraph (2) of this article is not successful, the challenging party may request, within thirty days after having received notice of the decision rejecting the challenge, the court or other authority specified in article 6 to decide on the challenge, which decision shall be subject to no appeal;

which such a request is pending, the arbitral tribunal, including the challenged arbitrator, may continue the arbitral proceedings and make an award.

Article 14. Failure or Impossibility to Act

(1) If an arbitrator becomes *de jure* or *de facto* unable to perform his functions or for other reasons fails to act without undue delay, his mandate terminates if he withdraws from his office or if the parties agree on the termination. Otherwise, if a controversy remains concerning any of these grounds, any party may request the court or other authority specified in article 6 to decide on the termination of the mandate, which decision shall be subject to no appeal.

(2) If, under this article or article 13 (2), an arbitrator withdraws from his office or a party agrees to the termination of the mandate of an arbitrator, this does not imply acceptance of the validity of any ground referred to in this article or article 12 (2).

Article 15. Appointment of Substitute Arbitrator

Where the mandate of an arbitrator terminates under article 13 or 14 or because of his withdrawal from office for any other reason or because of the revocation of his mandate by agreement of the parties or in any other case of termination of his mandate, a substitute arbitrator shall be appointed according to the rules that were applicable to the appointment of the arbitrator being replacd.

CHAPTER IV. JURISDICTION OF ARBITRAL TRIBUNAL

Article 16. Competence of Arbitral Tribunal to Rule on Its Jurisdiction

(1) The arbitral tribunal may rule on its own jurisdiction, including any objections with respect to the existence or validity of the arbitration agreement. For that purpose, an arbitration clause which forms part of a contract shall be treated as an agreement indepdent of the other terms of the contract. A decision by the arbitral tribunal that the contract is null and void shall not entail *ipso jure* the invalidity of the arbitration clause.

(2) A plea that the arbitral tribunal does not have jurisdiction shall be raised not later than the submission of the statement of defence. A party is not precluded from raising such a plea by the fact that he has appointed, or participated in the appointment of, an arbitrator. A plea that the arbitral tribunal is exceedig the scope of its authority shall be raised as soon as the matter alleged to be beyond the scope of its authority is raised during the arbitral proceedings. The arbitral tribunal may, in eithr case, admit a later plea if it considers the delay justified.

(3) The arbitral tribunal may rule on a plea referred to in paragraph (2) of this article either as a preliminary question or in an award on the merits. If the arbitral tribunal rules as a preliminary question that it has jurisdiction, any party may request, within thirty days after having received notice of that ruling, the court specified in article 6 to decide the matter, which decision shall be subject to no appeal; while such a request is pending, the arbitral tribunal may continue the arbitral proceedings and make an award.

Article 17. Power of Arbitral Tribunal to Order Interim Measures

Unless otherwise agreed by the parties, the arbitral tribunal may, at the request of a party, order any party to take such interim measure of protection as the arbitral tribunal may consider necessary in respect of the subject-matter of the dispute. The arbitral tribunal may require any party to provide appropriate security in connection with such measure.

CHAPTER V. CONDUCT OF ARBITRAL PROCEEDINGS

Articler 18. Equal Treatment of Parties

The parties shall be treated with equality and each party shall be given a full opportunity of presenting his case.

Article 19. Determination of Rules of Procedure

(1) Subject to the provisions of this Law, the parties are free to agree on the procedure to be followed by the arbitral tribunal in conducting the proceedings.

(2) Failing such agreement, the arbitral tribunal may, subject to the provisions of this Law, conduct the arbitration in such manner as it considers appropriate. The power conferred upon the arbitral tribunal includes the power to determine the admissibility, relevance, materiality and weight of any evidence.

Article 20. Place of Arbitration

(1) The parties are free to agree on the place of arbitration. Failing such agreement, the place of arbitration shall be determined by the arbitral tribunal having regard to the circumstances of the case, including the convenience of the parties.

(2) Notwithstanding the provisions of paragraph (1) of this article, the arbitral tribunal may, unless otherwise agreed by the parties, meet at any place it considers appropriate for consultation among its members, for hearing witnesses, experts or the parties, or for inspection of goods, other property of documents.

Article 21. Commencement of Arbitral Proceedings

Unless otherwise agreed by the parties, the arbitral proceedings in respect of a particular dispute commence on the date on which a request for that dispute to be referred to arbitration is received by the respondent.

Article 22. Language

(1) The parties are free to agree on the language or languages to be used in the arbitral proceedings. Failing such agreement, the arbitral tribunal shall determine the language or languages to be used in the proceedings. This agreement or determination, unless otherwise specified therein, shall apply to any written statement by a party, any hearing and any award, decision or other communication by the arbitral tribunal.

(2) The arbitral tribunal may order that any documentary evidence shall be accompanied by a translation into the language or languages agreed upon by the parties or determined by the arbitral tribunal.

Article 23. Statements of Claim and Defence

(1) Within the period of time agreed by the parties or determined by the arbitral tribunal, and claimant shall state the facts supporting his claim, the points at issue and the relief or remedy sought, and the respondent shall state his defence in respect of these particulars, unless the parties have otherwise agreed as to the required elements of such statements. The parties may submit with their statements all documents they consider to be relevant or may add a reference to the documents or other evidence they will submit.

(2) Unless otherwise agreed by the parties, either party may amend or supplement his claim or defence during the course of the arbitral proceedings, unless the arbitral tribunal considers it inappropriate to allow such amendment having regard to the delay in making it.

Article 24. Hearings and Written Proceedings

(1) Subject to any contrary agreement by the parties, the arbitral tribunal shall decide whether to hold oral hearings for the presentation of evidence or for oral argument, or whether the proceedings shall be conductd on the basis of documents and other materials. However, unless the parties have agreed that no hearings shall be held, the arbitral tribunal shall hold such hearings at an appropriate stage of the proceedings, if so requested by a party.

(2) The parties shall be given sufficient advance notice of any hearing and of any meeting of the arbitral tribunal for the purposes of inspection of goods, other property or documents.

(3) All statements, documents or other information supplied to the arbitral tribunal by one party shall be communicated to the other party. Also any expert report or evidentiary document on which the arbitral tribunal any expert report or evidentiary document on which the arbitral tribunal may rely in making its decision shall be communicated to the parties.

Article 25. Default of a Party

Unless otherwise agreed by the parties, if, without showing sufficient cause,

(a) the claimant fails to communicate his statement of claim in accordance with article 23 (1), the arbitral tribunal shall terminate the proceedings;

(b) the respondent fails to communicate his statement of defence in accordance with article 23 (1), the arbitral tribunal shall continue the proceedings without treating such failure in itself as an admission of the claimant's allegations;

(c) any party fails to appear at a hearing or to produce documentary evidence, the arbitral tribunal may continue the proceedings and make the award on the evidence before it.

Article 26. Expert Appointed by Arbitral Tribunal

(1) Unless otherwise agreed by the parties, the arbitral tribunal

(a) may appoint one or more experts to report to it on specific issues to be determined by the arbitral tribunal;

(b) may require a party to give the expert any relevant information or to produce, or to prodive access to, any relevant documents, goods or other property for his inspection.

(2) Unless otherwise agreed by the parties, if a party so requests or if the arbitral tribunal considers it necessary, the expert shall, after delivery of his written or oral report, participate in a hearing where the parties have the opportunity to put questions to him and to present expert witnesses in order to testify on the points at issue.

Article 27. Court Assistance in Taking Evidence

The arbitral tribunal or a party with the approval of the arbitral tribunal may request from a competent court of this State assistance in taking evidence. The court may execute the request within its competence and according to its rules on taking evidence.

CHAPTER VI. MAKING OF AWARD AND TERMINATION OF PROCEEDINGS
Article 28. Rules Applicable to Substance of Dispute

(1) The arbitral tirbunal shall decide the dispute in accordance with such rules of law as are chosen by the parties as applicable to the substance of the dispute. Any designation of the law or legal system of a given State shall be construed, unless otherwise expressed, as directly referring to the substantive law of that State and not to its conflict of laws rules.

(2) Failing any designation by the parties, the arbitral tribunal shall apply the law determined by the conflict of laws rules which it considers applicable.

(3) The arbitral tribunal shall decide *ex aequo et bono* or as *amiable compositeur* only if the parties have expressly authorized it to do so.

(4) In all cases, the arbitral tribunal shall decide in accordance with the terms of the contract and shall take into account the usages of the trade applicable to the transaction.

Article 29. Decision-Making by Panel of Arbitrators

In arbitral proceedings with more than one arbitrator, any decision of the arbitral tribunal shall be made, unless otherwise agreed by the parties, by a majority of all its members. However, questions of procedure may be decided by a presiding arbitrator, if so authorized by the parties or all members of the arbitral tribunal.

Article 30. Settlement

(1) If, during arbitral proceedings, the parties settle the dispute, the aribtral tribunal shall terminate the proceedings and, if requested by the parties and not objected to by the arbitral tribunal, record the settlement in the form of an arbitral award on agreed terms.

(2) An award on agreed terms shall be made in accordance with the provisions of article 31 and shall state that it is an award. Such an award has the same status and effect as any other award on the merits of the case.

Article 31. Form and Contents of Award

(1) The award shall be made in writing and shall be signed by the arbitrator or arbitrators. In arbitral proceedings with more than one arbitrator, the signatures of the majority of all members of the arbitral tribunal shall suffice, provided that the reason for any omitted signature is stated.

(2) The award shall state the reasons upon which it is based unless the parties have agreed that no reasons are to be given or the award is an award on agreed terms under article 30.

(3) The award shall state its date and the place of arbitration as determined in accordance with article 20 (1). The award shall be deemed to have been made at that place.

(4) After the award is made, a copy signed by the arbitrators in accordance with paragraphy (1) of this article shall be delivered to each party.

Article 32. Termination of Proceedings

(1) The arbitral proceedings are terminated by the final award or by an order of the arbitral tribunal in accordance with pargraph (2) of his article.

(2) The arbitral tribunal shall issue an order for the termination of the arbitral proceedings when:

  (a) the claimant withdraws his claim, unless the repsondent objects thereto and the arbitral tribunal recognizes a legitimate interest on his part in obtaining a final settlement of the dispute;

(b) the parties agree on the termination of the proceedings;

(c) the arbitral tribunal finds that the continuation of the proceedings has for any other reason become unnecessary or impossible.

(3) The mandate of the arbitral tribunal terminates with the termination of the arbitral proceedings, subject to the provisions of articles 33 and 34 (4).

Article 33. Correction and Interpretation of Award; Additional Award

(1) Within thirty days of receipt of the award, unless another period of time has been agreed upon by the parties:

(a) a party, with notice to the other party, may request the arbitral tribunal to correct in the award any errors in computation, any clerical or typographical errors or any errors of similar nature;

(b) if so agreed by the parties, a party, with notice to the other party, may request the arbitral tribunal to give an interpretation of a specific point or part of the award.

If the arbitral tribunal considers the request to be justified, it shall make the correction or give the interpretation within thirty days of receipt of the request. The interpretation shall form part of the award.

(2) The arbitral tribunal may correct any error of the type referred to in paragraph (1) (a) of this article on its own initiative within thirty days of the date of the award.

(3) Unless otherwise agreed by the parties, a party, with notice to the other party, may request, within thirty days of receipt of the award, the arbitral tribunal to make an additional award as to claims presented in the arbitral proceedings but omitted from the award. If the arbitral tribunal considers the request to be justified, it shall make the additional award within sixty days.

(4) The arbitral tribunal may extend, if necessary, the period of time within which it shall make a correction, interpretation or an additional award under paragraph (1) or (3) of this article.

(5) The provisions of article 31 shall apply to a correction or interpretation of the award or to an additional award.

CHAPTER VII. RECOURSE AGAINST AWARD

Article 34. Application for Setting Aside as Exclusive Resource Against Arbitral Award

(1) Recourse to a court against an arbitral award may be made only by an application for setting aside in accordance with paragraphs (2) and (3) of this article.

(2) An arbitral award may be set aside by the court specified in article 6 only if:

(a) the party making the application furnishes proof that:

(i) a party to the arbitration agreement referred to in article 7 was under some incapacity; or the said agreement is not valid under the law to which the parties have subjected it or, failing any indication thereon, under the law of this State; or

(ii) the party making the application was not given proper notice of the appointment of an arbitrator or of the arbitral proceedings or was otherwise unable to present his case; or

(iii) the award deals with a dispute not contemplated by or not falling within the terms of the submission to arbitration, or contains decisions on matters beyond the scope of the submission to arbitration, provide that, if the decisions on matters submitted to arbitration can be separatd from those not so submitted, only that part of the award which contains decisions on the matters not submitted to arbitration may be set aside; or

(iv) the composition of the arbitral tribunal or the arbitral procedure was not in accordance with the agreement of the parties, unless such agreement was in conflict with a provision of this Law from which the parties cannot derogate, or, failing such agreement, was not in accordance with this Law, or

(b) the court finds that:

(i) the subject-matter of the dispute is not capable of settlement by arbitration under the law of this State; or

(ii) the award is in conflict with the public policy of this State.

(3) An application for setting aside may not be made after three months have elapsed from the date on which the party making that application had received the award or, if a request had been made under article 33, from the date on which that request had been disposed of by the arbitral tribunal.

(4) The court, when asked to set aside an award, may, where appropriate and so requested by a party, suspend the setting aside proceedings for a period of time determined by it in order to give the arbitral tribunal an opportunity to resume the arbitral proceedings or to take such other action as in the arbitral tribunal's opinion will eliminate the grounds for setting aside.

CHAPTER VIII. RECOGNITION AND ENFORCEMENT OF AWARDS
Article 35. Recognition and Enforcement

(1) An arbitral award, irrespective of the country in which it was made, shall be recognized as binging and, upon application in writing to the competent court, shall be enforced subject to the provisions of this article and of article 36.

(2) The party relying on an award or applying for its enforcement shall supply the duly authenticated original award or a duly certified copy thereof, and the original arbitration agreement referred to in article 7 or a duly certified copy thereof. If the award or agreement is not made in an official language of this State, the party shall supply a duly certified translation thereof into such language. * * *

Article 36. Grounds for Refusing Recognition or Enforcement

(1) Recognition or enforcement of an arbitral award, irrespective of the country in which it was made, may be refused only:

(a) at the request of the party against whom it is invoked, if that party furnishes to the competent court where recognition or enforcement is sought proof that:

(i) a party to the arbitration agreement referred to in article 7 was under some incapacity; or the said agreement is not valid under the law to which the parties have subjected it or, failing any indication thereon, under the law of the country where the award was made; or

(ii) the party against whom the award is invoked was not given proper notice of the appointment of an arbitrator or of the arbitral proceedings or was otherwise unable to present his case; or

(iii) the award deals with a dispute not contemplated by or not falling within the terms of the submission to arbitration, or it contains dicisions on matters beyond the scope of the submission to arbitration, provided that, if the decisions on matters submitted to arbitration can be separated from those not so submitted, that part of the award which contains decisions on matters submitted to arbitration may be recognized and enforced; or

(iv) the composition of the arbitral tribunal or the arbitral procedure was not in accordance with the agreement of the parties or, failing such agreement, was not in accordance with the law of the country where the arbitration took place; or

(v) the award has not yet become binding on the parties or has been set aside or suspended by a court of the country in which, or under the law of which, that award was made; or

(b) if the court finds that:

(i) the subject-matter of the dispute is not capable of settlement by arbitration under the law of this States; or

(ii) the recognition or enforcement of the award would be contrary to the public policy of this State.

(2) if an application for setting aside or suspension of an award has been made to a court referred to in paragraph (1) (a) (v) of this article, the court where recognition or enforcement is sought may, if it considers it proper, adjourn its decision and may also, on the application of the party claiming recognition or enforcement of the award, order the other party to provide appropriate security.

Article headings are for reference purposes only and are not to be used for purposes of interpretation. The term "commercial" should be given a wide interpretation so as to cover matters arising from all relationships of a commerical nature, whether contractual or not. Relationships of a commerical nature include, but are not limited to, the following transactions: any trade transaction for the supply or exchange of goods or services; distribution agreement; commercial representation or agency; factoring; leasing; construction of works; consulting; engineering; licensing; investment; financing; banking; insurance; exploitation agreement or concession; joint venture and other forms of industrial or business co-operation; carriage of goods or passengers by air, sea, rail or road.

*** The conditions set forth in this paragraph are intended to set maximum standards. It would, thus, not be contrary to the harmonization to be achieved by the model law if a State retained even less onerous conditions.

Bibliography

ARTICLES:

AAA, *Handling the Complex Commercial Case*, 46 ARB. J. 6 (1991)

AAA, *USA-Hungarian Trade Assisted by New Arrangements for Arbitration in Vienna*, 40 Arb.J. 34 (March, 1985)

Abbott, *Latin America and International Arbitration Conventions: The Quandary of Non-Ratification*, 17 Harv.J.Int'l L. 131-32 (1976)

Aboul Enein, *Arbitration under the Auspices of the Cairo Regional Centre for Commercial Arbitration*, 1 J. Int'l Arb. 23 (1984)

Aksen, *American Arbitration Accession Arrives in the Age of Aquarius: United States Implements United Nations Convention on the Recognition and Enforcement of Foreign Arbitral Awards*, 3 S.W.L.Rev. 1 (1971)

Anand, *Arbitration in the Context of Technology Transfer Agreements: The Case of India*, 7 J. Int'l Arb. 87 (Jun. 1990)

Arkin, *International Ad Hoc Arbitration: A Practical Alternative*, 15 Int'l Bus. Law. 5 (1987)

Armstrong, *Letters of Credit in East-West Trade: Soviet Reception of Capitalist Custom*, 18 Vand.J.Transnat'l L. 329 (1984)

Armstrong, The *Problem of Autonomy in Soviet International Contract Law*, 31 Am.J. Comp. L. 63 (1983)

Asante, *The Concept of the Good Corporate Citizen in International Business*, 4 ICSID Review/Foreign Investment L.J. 1 (1989)

Baade, *International Civil and Commercial Litigation: A Tentative Checklist*, 1973 Tex.Int'l L.J. 5

Baker & Rushkoff, *The 1988 Justice Department International Guidelines: Searching for Legal Standards and Reassurance*, 23 Cornell Int'l L.J. 405 (1990)

Bangemann, *Fortress Europe: The Myth*, 9 Northwestern J. Int'l L. & Bus. 480 (1989)

Barry, *Application of the Public Policy Exception to the Enforcement of Foreign Arbitral Awards Under the New York Convention: A Modest Proposal*, 51 Temple L.Q. 832 (1978)

Barton, *The Economic Basis of Damages for Breach of Contract*, 1 J.Legal Stud. 277 (1972)

Baxter, *International Conflict of Laws and International Business*, 34 Int'l & Comp. L.Q. 538 (1985)

Belland, *The Iran-United States Claims Tribunal: Some Reflections on Trying a Claim*, 1 J.Int'l Arb. 237 (1984)

Bellet & Mezger, *L'arbitrage international dans le nouveau code de procedure civile*, 70 Revue Critique de Droit International Prive 611 (1981)

Benjamin, *Penalties, Liquidated Damage and Penal Clauses*, 9 Int'l & Comp. L.Q. 600 (1960)

Berman & Bustin, *The Soviet System of Foreign Trade*, 7 L. & Pol'y in Int'l Bus. 987 (1975)

Berman & Kaufman, *The Law of International Commercial Transactions (Lex Mercatoria)*, 19 Harv. Int'l L.J. 221 (1978)

Birmingham, *Breach of Contract, Damage Measures, and Economic Efficiency*, 24 Rutgers L. Rev. 273 (1970)

Bond, *A Comment on an Appraisal*, 1 Am. Rev. Int'l Arb. 108 (1990)

Born, *Reflections on Judicial Jurisdiction in International Cases*, 17 Ga.J.Int'l & Comp.L. 1 (1987)

Brace, *Joint Ventures in the People's Republic of China (Non-Corporate Form)*, 1985 Int'l Bus. Law. 434

Branson, Commentary on Ethics for International Arbitrators, 3 Arb. Int'l 72 (1987)

Branson & Tupman, Selecting an Arbitral Forum: A Guide to Cost-Effective International Arbitration, 24 Va. J. Int'l L. 917 (1984)

Bretz, Current Developments on DISCs, 19 N.C.J.Int'l L. & Com'l Reg. 385 (1984)

Broderick & Calmann, Introduction to a New Europe: A Primer for 1992, 20 Int'l Bus. Law. 9 (Jan.1992)

Brown, The Impact of European Community Antitrust Law on United States Companies, 13 Hastings Int'l & Comp. L.Rev. 383 (1990)

Brown, Commercial Arbitration and the European Economic Community, 2 J.Int'l Arb. 21 (1985)

Brunsvold, Negotiating Techniques for Warranty and Enforcement Clauses in International Licensing Agreements, Vand.J.Transnat'l L. 281 (1981)

Burkard, Termination Compensation to Distributors Under German Law, 7 Int'l Law. 185 (1973)

Byington, Planning and Drafting of International Licensing Agreements, 6 N.C.J. Int'l L. & Com. Reg. 193 (1984)

Carbonneau, The Elaboration of a French Court Doctrine on International Commercial Arbitration: A Study in Liberal Civilian Judicial Creativity, 55 Tul.L.Rev. 1 (1980)

Carbonneau, Mitsubishi: The Folly of Quixotic Internationalism, 2 Arb. Int'l 116 (1986)

Carl, Suing Foreign Governments in American Courts: The United States Foreign Sovereign Immunities Act in Practice, 33 Southwestern L. J. 1009 (1979)

Chew, A Procedural and Substantive Analysis of the Fairness of Chinese and Soviet Foreign Trade Arbitrations, 21 Tex. Int'l L.J. 291 (1986)

Christenson & Gambrel, Constitutionality of Binational Panel Review in Canada-U.S. Free Trade Agreement, 23 Int'l Law. 401 (1989)

Cigoj, International Sales: Formation of Contracts, 23 Netherlands Int'l L. Rev. 257 (1976)

Cinelli, The Impact of 1992 on United States Export Control Laws, 13 Hastings Int'l & Comp. L. Rev. 395 (1990)

Conant, The Act of State Doctrine and Its Exceptions, 12 Vand. J. Transnat'l L. 259 (1979)

Coulson, The Decisionmaking Process in Arbitration, 45 Arb. J. 37 (Sep.1990)

Cowen & Da Costa, The Contractual Forum: A Comparative Study, 43 Can.B.Rev. 453 (1965)

Craig, Uses and Abuses of Appeal from Awards, 4 Arb. Int'l 174 (1988)

Cremades & Plehn, The New Lex Mercatoria and the Harmonization of the Laws of International Commercial Transactions, 2 Boston U. Int'l L.J. 317 (1984)

Dawson, Judicial Revision of Frustrated Contracts: Germany, 63 B.U.L.Rev. 1039 (1983)

Delaume,. The European Convention on the Law Applicable to Contractual Obligations: Why a Convention?, 22 Va.J.Int'l L. 107 (1981)

Delaume, The State Immunity Act of the United Kingdom, 73 Am.J.Int'l L. 185 (1979)

Delaume, International Arbitration Under French Law: The Decree of May 12, 1981, 37 Arb. J. 38 (1982)

Delaume, ICSID Arbitration in Practice, 2 Int'l Tax & Business Law. 58 (1984)

Delaume, ICSID Arbitration: Practical Considerations, 1 J.Int'l Arb. 101 (1984)

Deshpande, The India Council of Arbitration and the Practice of Arbitration in India, 1 J. Int'l. Arb. 255 (1984)

Deshpande, International Commercial Arbitration and Domestic Courts in India, 2 J. Int'l Arb. 45 (1985)

Dessomenet, Transfer of Technology Under UNCTAD and EEC Draft Codifications, 12 J.Int'l L.& Econ. 1 (1979)

Dobson & Gaudenzi, Agency and Distributorship Laws in Italy, 20 Int'l Law. 997 (1986)

Dore, Peaceful Settlement of International Trade Disputes: Analysis of the Scope of Application of the UNCITRAL Conciliation Rules, 21 Colum. J. Int'l L. 339 (1983)

Elliott, Writing Arbitral Awards in Plain Language, 46 Arb.J. 53 (Dec.1991)

Ellis & Shea, Foreign Commercial Dispute Settlement in the People's Republic of China, 10 Int'l Trade L.J. 155 (1987)

Fleischauer, UNCITRAL and International Commercial Dispute Settlement, 38 Arb.J. 9 (Dec. 1983)

Fouchard, L'arbitrage en France Apres le decret du 12 Mai 1981, 109 J.de Droit International 394 (1982)

Fox, Mitsubishi v. Soler and Its Impact on International Commercial Arbitration, 19 J.World Trade L. 579 (1985)

Frankel, The Search for Truth: An Umpireal View, 123 U.Pa.L.Rev. 1031 (1975)

Frilet, Price and Terms of Payment in Large International Turnkey Contracts, 18 Int'l Bus. Law. 362 (Sep.1990)

Fugate, The New Justice Department Antitrust Enforcement Guidelines for International Operations—A Reflection of Reagan and, Perhaps, Bush Administration Antitrust Policy, 29 Va.J. Int'l L. 295 (1989)

Fuller, Mediation—Its Forms and Functions, 44 S.Calif.L.Rev. 305 (1971)

Garro, Enforcement of Arbitration Agreements and Jurisdiction of Arbitral Tribunals in Latin America, 1 J. Int'l Arb. 293 (1984)

Garvey & Heffelfinger, Towards Federalizing U.S. International Commercial Arbitration Law, 25 Int'l Law. 209 (1991)

Gilmore, In Memoriam: Karl Llewellyn,71 Yale L.J. 813 (1962)

Goebel, The Uneasy Fate of Franchising Under EEC Antitrust Laws, 10 Eur.L.Rev. 87 (1985)

Goldberg, Considerations for the Elimination of International Double Taxation: Toward a Developing Country Model, 15 L. & Pol'y in Int'l Bus. 833 (1983)

Goldsmith, How to Draft Terms of Reference, 3 Arb. Int'l 298 (1987)

Goodman, UNCITRAL Model Law on International and Commercial Arbitration: Divergent Approaches in England and Scotland, 18 Int'l Bus. Law. 250 (1990)

Grabow, Negotiating and Drafting Contracts in International Barter and Countertrade Transactions, 9 N.C.J. Int'l L. & Com. Reg. 255 (1984)

Green, Settling Large Case Litigation: An Alternative Approach, 11 Loyola of Los Angeles L.Rev. 493 (1978)

Griffin & Bravin, Beyond Aerospatiale: A Commentary on Foreign Discovery Provisions, 25 Int'l Law. 331 (1991)

Griffin et al, U.S. Department of Commerce Takes Further Steps to Ease Export License Requirements, 18 Int'l Bus. Law. 42 (Jan.1990)

Gruson, Forum Selection Clauses in International and Interstate Commercial Agreements, 1982 U.Ill.L.Rev. 133

Guyot, Countertrade Contracts in International Business, 20 Int'l Law. 921 (1986)

Hacking, Where We Are Now: Trends and Developments Since the Arbitration Act (1979), 1 J.Int'l Arb. 9 (1985)

Hamid El-Ahdab, Arbitration in Saudi Arabia Under the New Arbitration Act, 1983 and Its Implementation Rules of 1985, Part I in 3 J.Int'l Arb. 47 (Sept. 1986) and Part II in 3 J.Int'l Arb. 23 (Dec. 1986)

Hanak, The Experience of Socialist Lawyers in Arbitration Held in Non-Socialist Countries, Int'l Bus. Law. 145 (March 1982)

Haney, The Trial of A Contract Dispute in China, 22 Int'l Law. 475 (1988)

Hawkland, Uniform Commercial "Code" Methodology, 1962 U.Ill.L.F. 291

Herber, The Rules of the Convention Relating to the Buyer's Remedies in Cases of Breach of Contract, 7 Digest of Commercial Laws 104 (1980)

Herzog, The Common Market Convention—An Interim Update, 17 Va.J.Int'l L. 417 (1977)

Hochuli, Role of the Engineer Under FIDIC Standard Contracts, 19 Int'l Bus. Law. 542 (Dec.1991)

Holtzmann, Dispute Resolution Procedures in East-West Trade, 20 Int'l Law. 233 (1978)

Horlick, A Manual of United States Trade Laws, 13 Int'l Bus. Law. 249 (1985)

Horlick, A Practical Guide to Service of United States Process Abroad, 14 Int'l Law. 637 (1980)

Hoya & Stein, Drafting Contracts in U.S.-Soviet Trade, 7 L & Pol'y in Int'l Bus. 1057 (1975)

Huie & Hogan, The New European Community Merger Control Regulation and the Short-Term Horizon of United States Firms, 6 Am U. J. Int'l L. & Pol'y 325 (1991)

Huneidi, Arbitration Under Kuwaiti Law, 6 J. Int'l Arb. 75 (1989)

Hurst, Drafting Contracts in an Inflationary Era, 28 U.Fla.L.Rev. 884 (1976)

Hushon, Joint Ventures Between Multinationals: Government Regulatory Aspects, 9 N.C.J.Int'l L. & Com.Reg. 207 (1984)

Jacobson, International Sales of Goods, 3 Int'l & Comp. L.Q. 659 (1954)

Jahil, Amman Arab Convention on Commercial Arbitration, 7 J. Int'l Arb. 139 (1990)

Jarvin, London as a Place for International Arbitration, 1 J.Int'l Arb. 59 (1985)

Jarvis, The Soviet Maritime Arbitration Commission: A Practitioner's Perspective, 21 Tex. Int'l L.J. 341 (1986)

Jaslow, Practical Considerations in Drafting a Joint Venture Agreement with China, 31 J.Am.Comp.L. 209 (1983)

Javin, Enforcement of An Arbitration Award in Oman, 2 J. Int'l Arb. 81 (1985)

Jones, Punitive Damages in Arbitration in the USA, 14 Int'l Bus. Law. 188 (June, 1986)

Jones, Practical Aspects of Commercial Agency and Distribution Agreements in the European Community, 6 Int'l Law. 107 (1972)

Jones, Act of State in English Law, 22 Va J. Int'l L. 433 (1982)

Jones, Punitive Damages as an Arbitration Remedy, 4 J. Int'l Arb. 35 (1987)

Jones, The Iran-United States Claims Tribunal: Private Rights and State Responsibility, 24 Va.J.Int'l L. 259 (1984)

Kakbadse, Trade in Services and the Uruguay Round, 19 Ga. J. Int'l & Comp. L. 384 (1989)

Kaplan, von Mehren & Schaefer, Phases of German Civil Procedure, 71 Harv.L.Rev. 1193 (1958)

Kaplan, Arbitration in Hong Kong, 3 J. Int'l Arb. 7 (Dec. 1986)

Kazanjian & Craig, The Canada-United States Free Trade Agreement, 16 Int'l Bus. Law. 112 (March, 1988)

Kerr, Arbitration and the Courts: The UNCITRAL Model Law, 34 Int'l & Comp.L.Q. 1 (1985)

King, Legal Aspects of Appointment and Termination of Foreign Distributors and Representatives, 17 Case W.Res. J. Int'l L. 91 (1985)

Klitgaard, People's Republic of China Joint Venture Dispute Resolution Procedures, 1 U.C.L.A. Pac. Basin L.J. 1 (1982)

Kohler, Practical Experience of the Brussels Jurisdiction and Judgments Convention in the Six Original Contracting States, 34 Int'l & Comp. L.Q. 563 (1985)

Korah, Group Exemptions for Exclusive Distribution and Purchasing in the EEC, 21 Common Market L.Rev. 53 (1984)

Kripke, The Principles Underlying the Drafting of the Uniform Commercial Code, 1962 U.Ill.L.F. 311

Lacey, Technology and Industrial Property Licensing in Latin America, 6 Int'l Law. 388 (1972)

Lacy, Brown, & Rubin, Technology Transfer Laws Governing Federally Funded Research and Developments, 19 Pepperdine L.Rev. 1 (1992).

Lalive, L'immunite de juridiction des Etats et des Organizations Internationales, 3 Recueil des Cours 285 (Hague Academy of Int'l Law, 1953)

Lazar, Services and the GATT: US Motives and a Blueprint for Negotiations, 22 J. World Trade L. 135 (1989)

Lilly, Jurisdiction Over Domestic and Alien Defendants, 69 Va.L.Rev. 85 (1983)

Lochner, Countertrade and International Barter, 19 Int'l Law. 725 (1985)

Lowe, Choice of Law Clauses in International Contracts: A Practical Approach, 12 Harv. Int'l L. J. 1 (1971)

Lowenfeld, Some Reflections on Transnational Discovery, 8 J.Comp.Bus.& Cap.Mkt. L. 419 (1986)

Lowenfeld, The Mitsubishi Case: Another View, 2 Arb. Int'l 178 (1986)

Lowenfeld, The Iran-U.S. Claims Tribunal: An Interim Appraisal, 38 Arb.J. 14 (1983)

Lowenfeld, Singapore and the Local Bar: Aberration or Ill Omen? 5 J. Int'l Arb. 71, 73 (Sep. 1989)

MacKellar, To Consolidate or Not to Consolidate: A Study of Federal Court Decisions, 44 Arb. J. 15 (Dec. 1989)

Malamud, El Arbitraje Comercial y el Nuevo Codigo de Procedimientos, 4 Jurisprudencia Argentina 823 (1968)

Marasinghe, A Reassessment of Sovereign Immunity, 9 Ottowa L. Rev. (1977)

Marcantonio, Unifying the Law of Impossibility, 8 Hastings Int'l & Comp. L.Rev. 41 (1984)

Marriott, Arbitrating International Commercial Disputes in the United Kingdom, 44 Arb. J. 3 (Sep. 1989)

Matsuo, Jurisdiction in Transnational Cases in Japan, 23 Int'l Law. 6 (1989)

McClelland, A Survey of Pacific Rim Commercial Arbitration, 40 Arb. J. 4 (March, 1985)

McCormack, The Commercial Activity Exception to Foreign Sovereign Immunity, 16 L. & Pol'y Int'l Bus. 477 (1984)

McLaughlin, Arbitration and Developing Countries, 12 Int'l Law. 211 (1980)

McVey, Countertrade: Commercial Practices, Legal Issues and Policy Dilemmas, 16 L.& Pol'y Int'l Bus. 1 (1984).

Meessen, Europe en Route to 1992: The Completion of the Internal Market and Its Impact on Non-Europeans, 23 Int'l Law. 359 (1989)

Menkel-Meadow, Toward Another View of Legal Negotiation: The Structure of Problem-Solving, 31 U.C.L.A. L.Rev. 754 (1984)

Menkel-Meadow, Legal Negotiation: A Study of Strategies in Search of a Theory, 1983 Am.Bar.Fdn.Res. J. 905

Miller, The Adversary System: Dinosaur or Phoenix, 69 Minn.L.Rev. 1 (1984)

Millett, The New European Court of First Instance, 38 Int'l & Comp. L.Q. 811 (1989)

Molot & Jewett, The State Immunity Act of Canada, 20 Can. Y.B. Int'l L. 79 (1982)

Morgan, Discovery in Arbitration, 3 J.Int'l Arb. 9 (1986)

Mullinex, The New Federal Express: Mail Service of Process Under Amended Rule 4, 4 Rev. of Litigation 299 (1985)

Naon, Public Policy and International Commercial Arbitration: The Argentine Perspective, 3 J.Int'l Arb. 7 (Jun. 1986)

Nariman, Foreign Arbitral Awards in India: Problems, Pitfalls, and Progress, 6 J. Int'l Arb. 25 (Mar. 1989)

Nicholas, Force Majeure and Frustration, 27 Am.J.Comp.L. 231 (1979)

Noonan, Technology Licensing: Common Market Competition Implications, 19 N.C.J. Int'l L. & Com'l Reg. 439 (1984)

Norberg, United States Implements Inter-American Convention on Commercial Arbitration, 45 Arb. J. 23 (1990)

Note, Some Aspects of Frustrated Performance of Contracts Under Middle Eastern Law, 33 Int'l & Comp. L.Q. 1046 (1984)

Note, Return to Europe: Integrating Eastern European Economies into the European Market Through Alliance with the European Community, 31 Harv. Int'l L.J. 660 (1990)

Note, Incoterms and the British Export Trade, 1965 J.Bus.L. 114

Note, Federalism, Due Process and Minimum Contacts, 80 Colum.L.Rev. 1341 (1980)

Note, An Argument Against the Availability of Punitive Damages in Commercial Arbitration, 62 ST. John's L. Rev. 270 (1988)

Note, The Public Policy Defense to Recognition and Enforcement of Foreign Arbitral Awards, 7 Calif.W.Int'l L.J. 228 (1977)

Note, Enforcing International Commercial Arbitration Agreements and Awards Not Subject to the New York Convention, 23 Va.J.Int'l L. 75 (1982)

Note, The Soviet Position on International Arbitration: A Wealth of Choices or Choices for the Wealthy, 26 Va.J. Int'l L. 417 (1986)

Note, The United Nations Convention on Contracts for the International Sale of Goods: Contract Formation and the Battle of the Forms, 21 Colum.J.Transnat'l L. 529 (1983)

O'Kane, Obtaining Evidence Abroad, 17 Vand.J.Transnat'l L. 69 (1984)

O'Neill, Has Switzerland Solved Its Problems as a Site for Arbitration? 45 Arb. J. 16 (1990)

Ogawa, Proposed Draft of Japan's New Arbitration Law, 7 J. Int'l Arb. 33 (Jun. 1990)

Osakwe, The Public Interest and the Role of the Prosecutor in Soviet Civil Litigation, 18 Tex.Int'l L.J. 37 (1983)

Park, The Lex Loci Arbitri and International Commercial Arbitration, 32 Int'l & Comp.L.Q. 21 (1983)

Parmalee, International Service of Process: A Guide to Serving Process Abroad under the Hague Convention, 39 Okla L. Rev. 287 (1986)

Paulsson, Arbitration Unbound: An Award Detached from the Law of the Country of Origin, 30 Int'l & Comp.L.Q. 358 (1981)

Paulsson, A Better Mousetrap: 1990 ICC Rules for a Pre-arbitral Referee Procedure, 18 Int'l Bus. Law. 214 (1990)

Perlman & Nelson, New Approaches to the Resolution of International Commercial Disputes, 17 Int'l Law. 215 (1983)

Pestalozzi, Arbitration and Its New Prospects in Brazil, 4 J. Int'l Arb. 131 (Sep. 1987)

Pestalozzi, Arbitration and Its New Prospects in Brazil, 4 J. Int'l Arb. 131 (Sep. 1987)

Policy Dilemmas, 16 Law & Policy Int'l Bus. 1 (1984)

Puelinckx, Frustration, Hardship, Force Majeure, Imprevision, Wegfall der Geschaftsgrundlage, Unmoglichkeit, Changed Circumstances: A Comparative Study in English, French, German and Japanese Law, 1 J.Int'l Arb. 47 (1986)

Ramirez, Arbitraje Comercial Internacional, 11 Revista de Law Facultad de Derecho de Mexico 477 (1961)

Rand, Hornick & Friedland, ICSID's Emerging Jurisprudence: The Scope of ICSID's Jurisdiction, 19 Int'l L. & Politics 33 (1986)

Rapsomanikis, Frustration of Contract in International Trade Law and Comparative Law, 18 Duq.L.Rev. 551 (1980)

Rhodes & Sloan, The Pitfalls of International Commercial Arbitration, 17 Vand. J. Transnat'l L. 19 (1984)

Robinson & Doumar, "It is Better to Enter a Tiger's Mouth Than a Court of Law" - Dispute Resolution Alternatives in U.S. - China Trade, 2 Dickinson J. Int'l L. 1 (1987)

Roffe, Transfer of Technology: UNCTAD's Draft International Code of Conduct, 19 Int'l Law. 689 (1985)

Romeu-Matta, New Developments in International Commercial Arbitration: A Comparative Survey of New State Statutes and the UNCITRAL Model Law, 1 Am. Rev. Int'l Arb. 140 (1990)

Rosenbloom, Tax Treaty Abuse Policies and Issues, 15 L. & Pol'y in Int'l Bus. 763 (1983)

Rosenn, Enforcement of Foreign Arbitral Awards in Brazil, 28 Am.J.Comp.L. 498 (1980)

Samuel, The 1979 Arbitration Act—Judicial Review of Arbitration Awards on the Merits in England, 1 J.Int'l Arb. 53 (1985)

Sanders, Procedures and Practices Under the UNCITRAL Rules, 27 Am.J.Comp.L. 453 (1979)

Sanders, A Twenty Years' Review of the Convention on the Recognition and Enforcement of Foreign Arbitral Awards, 18 Int'l Law. 269 (1978)

Schmidthoff, Arbitration and EEC Law, Common Market L. Rev. 143 (1987)

Schmitthoff, Countertrade, J.Bus.L. 115 (Mar.1985)

Schmitz & Van Hamme, Franchising in Europe—The First Practical EEC Guidelines, 22 Int'l Law. 717 (1988)

Selby & Stewart, Practical Aspects of Arbitrating Claims Before the Iran-United States Claims Tribunal, 18 Int'l Law. 211 (1984)

Selby & Stewart, Practical Aspects of Arbitrating Claims Before the Iran-United States Claims Tribunal, 18 Int'l Law. 211 (1984)

Selected Bibliography on Europe 1992, 11 Mich.J.Int'l L. 526 (1990)

Semkow, Syndicating and Rescheduling International Financial Transactions, 18 Int'l Law. 869 (1984)

Sinclair, The European Convention on State Immunity, 22 Int'l & Comp. L.Q. 254 (1973)

Slupinski, Foreign Investment in the Banking Sector and Emergence of the Financial Market in Poland, 25 Int'l Law. 127 (1991)

Smit, Frustration of Contract: A Comparative Attempt at Consolidation, 58 Colum.L.Rev. 287 (1958)

Smit, Elements of International Arbitration in the United States, 1 Am.Rev.Int'l Arb. 64 (1990)

Smith & Dzienkowski, A Fifty Year Perspective on World Petroleum Arrangements, 24 Tex. Int'l L. J. 13 (1989)

Speidel, Excusable Non-Performance in Sales Contracts: Some Thoughts About Risk Management, 32 S.C.L.Rev. 241 (1980)

Sperling, Termination Under Dutch Law of Agency Agreements, 18 Int'l Bus. Law. 462 (Nov.1990)

Stein & Wolman, International Commercial Arbitration in the 1980s: A Comparison of the Major Arbitral Systems and Rules, 38 Bus.Law. 1685 (1983)

Stewart & Sherman, Developments at the Iran-United States Claims Tribunal: 1981-1983, 24 Va.J.Int'l L. 1 (1983)

Stone, A Primer on Codification, 29 Tul.L.Rev. 303 (1955)

Storme, Belgium: A Paradise for International Commercial Arbitration, 1986 Int'l Law. 294

Street, U.S. Exports Banned for Domestic Use, but Exported to Third World Countries, 6 Int'l Trade L.J. 95 (1981)

Stulberg, The Theory and Practice of Mediation: A Reply to Professor Susskind, 6 Vt.L.Rev. 85 (1981)

Sullivan, Punitive Damages in the Law of Contract: The Reality and the Illusion of Legal Change, 61 Minn.L.Rev. 207 (1977)

Surrey, Fishburne & Chaudhri, Joint Ventures in China: The First Water Stop, 21 Tex.J.Int'l L. 221 (1986)

Sutherland, The World Bank Convention on the Settlement of Investment Disputes, 28 Int'l & Comp.L.Q. 367 (1979)

Symposium, Franchising in Europe, 1987, 16 Int'l Bus. Law. 117 (Mar.1988)

Symposium, Restructuring of Sovereign Debt, 23 Colum. J. Transnat'l L. 1 (1984)

Symposium, 1992: Doing Business in the European Internal Market, 9 Northwestern J. Int'l L. & Bus. 463 (1989)

Symposium, A Guide to International Civil Practice, 17 Vand.J.Transnat'l L. 1 (1984)

Symposium, Transnational Litigation, 18 Int'l Law. 522 (1984)

Symposium, The Influence of Modern American Conflicts Theories on European Law, 30 Am J.Comp. L. 1 (1982)

Symposium, International Sales of Goods Convention, 18 Int'l Law. 3 (1984)

Symposium on Barter and Countertrade, 17 Int'l Bus. Law. 360-72 (1989)

Symposium on the Transfer of Technology in the International Marketplace, 7 B.C. Int'l & Comp. L. Rev. 235 (1984).

Tanikawa, Risk of Loss in Japanese Sales Transactions, 42 Wash.L.Rev. 463 (1967)

Theroux, Technology Sales to China, 14 J. Int'l L. & Econ. 185 (1980)

Thilmany, Fonctions et Revisibilite des Clauses Penale en Droit Compare, 1980 Revue Internationale de Droit Compare 17

Thomas, Arbitration in Hong Kong, Int'l Bus. Law. 142 (May 1986)

Tiewul & Tsegah, Arbitration and the Settlement of Commercial Disputes: A Selective Survey of African Practice, 24 Int'l & Comp. L.Q. 393 (1975)

Toepke, EEC Law of Competition: Distribution Agreements and Their Notification, 19 Int'l Law. 117 (1985)

Trakman, The Evolution of the Law Merchant: Our Commercial Heritage, 12 J.Mar.L. & Com. 1 (1980)

Triebel & Guojian, International Economic, Trade and Maritime Arbitration in the People's Republic of China: New Developments, 6 J. Int'l Arb. 13 (Jun. 1989)

Tuomi, The Canada-U.S. Free Trade Agreement: implications for the Bilateral Trade Balance, 13 Maryland J. Int'l L. & Trade 105 (1988)

Tupman, Discovery and Evidence in U.S. Arbitration: The Prevailing Views, 44 Arb J. 27 (Mar.1989)

Unkovic, Negotiating and Preparing an International Licensing Agreement, 25 Prac.Law. 77 (1979)

Van Bael, A Practitioner's Guide to Due Process in EEC Antitrust and Antidumping Proceedings, 18 Int'l Law. 841 (1984)

van Empel, Franchising and Strict Liability in the EEC, 18 Int'l Bus. Law. 169 (Apr.1990)

Verdera y Tuells, International Commercial Arbitration and the Spanish Court of Arbitration, 3 J.Int'l Arb. 47 (Mar. 1986)

Vergne, The "Battle of the Forms" under the 1980 United Nations Convention on Contracts for the International Sale of Goods, 33 Am.J.Comp.L. 233 (1985)

Vock, The Evolution of the Legal Relationship Between International Petroleum Mining Companies and Host Countries, 1983 Int'l Bus. Law. 244

von Mehren, Transnational Litigation in American Courts: An Overview of Problems and Issues, 3 Dick.J.Int'l L. 43 (1984)

von Mehren, Recognition and Enforcement of Foreign Judgments, 167 Recueil des Cours 13 (1980)

von Mehren, International Commercial Arbitration: The Contribution of the French Jurisprudence, 46 La. L. Rev. 1045 (1986)

Wall, The Asian-African Legal Consultative Committee and International Commercial Arbitration, 1979 Canadian Y.B. Int'l L. 324

Weintraub, How to Choose the Law and How Not To: The EEC Convention, 17 Tex. Int'l L.J. 155 (1982)

Wesley, The Procedural Malaise of Foreign Investment Disputes in Latin America: From Local Tribunals to Factfinding, 7 Law & Pol'y in Int'l Bus. 813, 818 (1975)

Wetter, The Present Status of the International Court of Arbitration of the ICC: An Appraisal, 1 Am Rev. Int'l Arb. 91 (1990)

Wetter, A Multi-Party Arbitration Scheme for International Joint Ventures, 3 Arb. Int'l 2 (1987)

Wetter, East Meets West in Sweden, 20 Int'l Law. 261 (1978)

White, The Pros and Cons of Getting to Yes, 34 J.Leg.Educ. 115 (1984)

White, Machiavelli and the Bar: Ethical Limitations on Lying in Negotiation, 1980 Am.B.Fdn.Res.J. 926, 927

Wieacker, The Importance of Roman Law for Western Civilization and Western Legal Thought, 4 B.C. Int'l & Comp. L.Rev. 257 (1981)

Winship, Formation of International Sales Contracts Under the 1980 Vienna Convention, 17 Int'l Law. 1 (1983)

Woods, Franchising in Hong Kong, 1985 Int'l Bus. Law. 440

Wright, California's International Commercial Arbitration Act, 17 Int'l Bus. Law. 45 (1989)

Yamane, Resolving Disputes in U.S.- Japan Trade: The Japanese Perspective, 39
Arb. J. 3 (Dec. 1984)

Zaphiriou, Choice of Forum and Choice of Law Clauses in International
Commercial Agreements, 3 Int'l Trade L.J. 311 (1978)

BOOKS:

ADAPTATION AND RENEGOTIATION OF CONTRACTS IN INTERNATION-
AL TRADE AND FINANCE (N. Horn, ed.1985)

ANTITRUST, TECHNOLOGY TRANSFER AND JOINT VENTURES IN
INTERNATIONAL TRADE (B. Hawk ed. 1983)

ATWOOD, J., & K. BREWSTER, ANTITRUST AND AMERICAN BUSINESS
ABROAD (2d ed., 1981)

AUERBACH, J., JUSTICE WITHOUT LAW? RESOLVING DISPUTES WITH-
OUT LAWYERS (1983)

BARTELS, M., CONTRACTUAL ADAPTATION AND CONFLICT RESOLU-
TION (KLUWER, 1985)

BELLOW, G., & B. MOULTON, NEGOTIATION (1979)

BEREDJICK, N. & T. WALDE (eds.), PETROLEUM INVESTMENT POLICIES
IN DEVELOPING COUNTRIES (1988)

BISCHEL, L., FUNDAMENTALS OF INTERNATIONAL TAXATION (1985)

BLAIR, J., THE CONTROL OF OIL (1976)

BOK, S., LYING (1979)

BORN, G., & D. WESTIN, INTERNATIONAL CIVIL LITIGATION IN UNITED
STATES COURTS (1988)

BROWNLIE, I.A., PRINCIPLES OF PUBLIC INTERNATIONAL LAW (3d ed.
1979)

CASSE, P., & S. DEOL, MANAGING INTERCULTURAL NEGOTIATIONS:
GUIDELINES FOR TRAINERS AND NEGOTIATORS (1985)

COHEN, J., & H. CHIU, THE PEOPLE'S REPUBLIC OF CHINA AND INTER-
NATIONAL LAW (1974)

COULSON, N., COMMERCIAL LAW IN THE GULF STATES: THE ISLAMIC
LEGAL TRADITION (1984)

CRAIG, W., W. PARK AND J. PAULSSON, INTERNATIONAL CHAMBER OF
COMMERCE ARBITRATION (1984)

CURTIN, P., CROSS-CULTURAL TRADE IN WORLD HISTORY (1984)

DAVID, R., ARBITRATION IN INTERNATIONAL TRADE (1985)

DAVID, R., & J. BRIERLEY, MAJOR LEGAL SYSTEMS IN THE WORLD
    TODAY (3d ed. 1985)

DELAUME, G., TRANSNATIONAL CONTRACTS (1983)

DICKERSON, F.R., THE FUNDAMENTALS OF LEGAL DRAFTING (1965)

DICKERSON, F.R., MATERIALS ON LEGAL DRAFTING (1981)

DOBKIN, J., INTERNATIONAL TECHNOLOGY JOINT VENTURES IN THE
    COUNTRIES OF THE PACIFIC RIM (1988)

DOMKE ON COMMERCIAL ARBITRATION: THE LAW AND PRACTICE OF
    COMMERCIAL ARBITRATION (G. WILNER, ed., 1984)

ECKSTROM, L., LICENSING IN FOREIGN AND DOMESTIC OPERATIONS
    (1983)

EDDY, J., & P. WINSHIP, COMMERCIAL TRANSACTIONS: TEXT, CASES &
    PROBLEMS (1985)

EDWARDS, H., & J. WHITE, THE LAWYER AS NEGOTIATOR (1977)

EMERGING STANDARDS OF INTERNATIONAL TRADE AND INVEST-
    MENT: MULTINATIONAL CODES AND CORPORATE CONDUCT (S.
    Rubin & G. Hufbauer, eds. 1984)

FARNSWORTH, E.A., CONTRACTS (1982)

FELSENFELD, C., & A. SIEGEL, WRITING CONTRACTS IN PLAIN ENGLISH
    (1981)

FIDIC, CONDITIONS OF CONTRACT (INTERNATIONAL) FOR WORKS OF
    CIVIL ENGINEERING CONSTRUCTION (3d ed. 1977)

FISHER, R., & W. URY, GETTING TO YES: NEGOTIATING AGREEMENT
    WITHOUT GIVING IN (1981)

FISHER, R., & W. URY, GETTING TOGETHER (1988)

FISHER, R., & W. URY, INTERNATIONAL MEDIATION: A WORKING
    GUIDE (1978)

FOLBERG, J., & A. TAYLOR, MEDIATION (1984)

FOX, W., FEDERAL REGULATION OF ENERGY (1983)

FRIEDENTHAL, J., M. KANE & A. MILLER, CIVIL PROCEDURE (1985)

FRIEDMANN, W.G., THE CHANGING STRUCTURE OF INTERNATIONAL
    LAW (1964)

FURTADO, C., ECONOMIC DEVELOPMENT OF LATIN AMERICA (1976)

GLENDON, M., M. GORDON & C. OSAKWE, COMPARATIVE LEGAL TRA-
    DITIONS (1985)

GOFFMAN, E., STRATEGIC INTERACTION (1969)

GOING INTERNATIONAL: INTERNATIONAL TRADE FOR THE NON-SPE-
CIALIST (P. Vishny, ed., 1992)

GOLDBERG, G., A LAWYER'S GUIDE TO COMMERCIAL ARBITRATION
(2d ed. 1983)

HARTLEY, T., THE FOUNDATIONS OF EUROPEAN COMMUNITY LAW (2d
ed. 1988)

HAZARD, J., W. BUTLER & P. MAGGS, THE SOVIET LEGAL SYSTEM (3d
ed. 1977)

HONNOLD, J., THE UNITED NATIONS CONVENTION FOR THE INTERNA-
TIONAL SALE OF GOODS (1987)

HOYA, T., EAST-WEST TRADE: COMECON LAW AND AMERICAN-SOVI-
ET TRADE (1984)

INTERNATIONAL COUNCIL FOR COMMERCIAL ARBITRATION, UNCI-
TRAL'S PROJECT FOR A MODEL LAW ON INTERNATIONAL COM-
MERCIAL ARBITRATION (P. Sanders ed., 1984)

INTERNATIONAL ENCYCLOPEDIA OF COMPARATIVE LAW (1983)

INTERNATIONAL HANDBOOK ON COMMERCIAL ARBITRATION (P.
SANDERS ed., 1984)

INTERNATIONAL NEGOTIATION: ART & SCIENCE (D. BENDAHMANE &
J. MCDONALD eds. 1983)

IOFFE, O., & P. MAGGS, SOVIET LAW IN THEORY AND PRACTICE 306
(1983)

ISENBERGH, J., INTERNATIONAL TAXATION: U.S. TAXATION OF FOR-
EIGN TAXPAYERS AND FOREIGN INCOME (1990)

JOHNSON, J. & J. SCHACHTER, THE FREE TRADE AGREEMENT: A COM-
PREHENSIVE GUIDE (1988)

JOHNSON, T., INTERNATIONAL DISTRIBUTOR AND AGENCY AGREE-
MENTS (1967)

KAPOOR, A., PLANNING FOR INTERNATIONAL BUSINESS NEGOTIA-
TION (1985)

KAYE, H., P. PLAIA, M. HERTZBERG, INTERNATIONAL TRADE PRACTICE
(1981)

KIM, H., FUNDAMENTAL LEGAL CONCEPTS OF CHINA AND THE WEST:
A COMPARATIVE STUDY (1980)

THE KNOW HOW CONTRACT IN GERMANY, JAPAN AND THE UNITED
STATES (1984)

KONIGSBERG, A., INTERNATIONAL FRANCHISING (1991)

LAZAR, R., TRANSNATIONAL ECONOMIC AND MONETARY LAW (1981)
LEE, E., COMMERCIAL DISPUTES SETTLEMENT IN CHINA (1985)
LEGAL PROBLEMS OF CODES OF CONDUCT FOR MULTINATIONAL
   ENTERPRISES (Horn ed., Kluwer, 1980)
LEW, J., THE APPLICABLE LAW IN INTERNATIONAL COMMERCIAL
   ARBITRATION (1978)
LOWENFELD, A., INTERNATIONAL PRIVATE TRADE (2d ed. 1981)

MAYERS, H., & B BRUNSVOLD, DRAFTING PATENT LICENSE AGREE-
   MENTS (2d ed. 1984)
MERRYMAN, J. & D. CLARK, COMPARATIVE LAW: WESTERN EURO-
   PEAN AND LATIN AMERICAN SYSTEMS (1978)
MOORE, W., FEDERAL PRACTICE (1988)
MUSTILL, M., & S. BOYD, THE LAW AND PRACTICE OF COMMERCIAL
   ARBITRATION IN ENGLAND (2d ed., 1988)

NIBOYET, E., TRAITE DE DROIT INTERNATIONAL PRIVE FRANCAIS
   (1948)
NIERENBERG, R., FUNDAMENTALS OF NEGOTIATING (1973)

PETERSON, C., AND C. MCCARTHY, ARBITRATION STRATEGY AND
   TECHNIQUE (1986)
POSNER, R., ECONOMIC ANALYSIS OF THE LAW (2d ed. 1977)
POSTLEWAITE, P., & M. COLLINS, INTERNATIONAL INDIVIDUAL TAXA-
   TION (1982)
POSTLEWAITE, P., INTERNATIONAL CORPORATE TAXATION (1980)

RAIFFA, H., THE ART AND SCIENCE OF NEGOTIATION (1982)
REITHMANN, C., INTERNATIONALES VERTRAGSRECHT (2d ed. 1972)
RODMAN, R., COMMERCIAL ARBITRATION WITH FORMS (1984)

SALACUSE, J.W., MAKING GLOBAL DEALS: NEGOTIATING IN THE
   INTERNATIONAL MARKETPLACE (1991)
SPERBER, P., ATTORNEY'S PRACTICE GUIDE TO NEGOTIATIONS (1985)
STEINER, H., & D. VAGTS, TRANSNATIONAL LEGAL PROBLEMS (3d ED.
   1986)

STEIN, P., LEGAL INSTITUTIONS: THE DEVELOPMENT OF DISPUTE SETTLEMENT (1984)

SMITH, D., & B. WELLS, NEGOTIATING THIRD WORLD MINERALS AGREEMENTS (1975)

THE SOURCES OF THE LAW OF INTERNATIONAL TRADE 88 (C. SCHMITTHOFF, ED. 1964).

THE TRANSNATIONAL LAW OF INTERNATIONAL COMMERCIAL TRANSACTIONS (N.HORN & C.M. SCHMITTHOFF EDS. 1982)

UNCITRAL, LEGAL GUIDE ON DRAWING UP INTERNATIONAL CONTRACTS FOR THE CONSTRUCTION OF INDUSTRIAL WORKS (1988)

UNCITRAL, PRELIMINARY STUDY OF LEGAL ISSUES IN INTERNATIONAL COUNTERTRADE (1988)

VAGTS, D., TRANSNATIONAL BUSINESS PROBLEMS (1986).

VERZARIU, P., COUNTERTRADE, BARTER & OFFSETS (1985)

VON MEHREN, A.T., THE CIVIL LAW SYSTEM (1958)

WELT, L.G.B., TRADE WITHOUT MONEY: BARTER & COUNTERTRADE (1984)

WETTER, J.G., THE INTERNATIONAL ARBITRAL PROCESS: PUBLIC AND PRIVATE (1979)

WHITE, J., & R. SUMMERS, UNIFORM COMMERCIAL CODE (1972)

WILLIAMS, G., LEGAL NEGOTIATION AND SETTLEMENT (1983)

WILLISTON ON CONTRACTS (3D ED. 1957)

WOOD, P., LAW AND PRACTICE OF INTERNATIONAL FINANCE (1984)

WRIGHT, C. & A. MILLER, FEDERAL PRACTICE AND PROCEDURE

Index